A History of
Early Medieval Europe

FROM 476 TO 911

MARGARET DEANESLY D. LITT. M.A.

Professor Emeritus of History
in the University of London

LONDON: METHUEN & CO LTD
11 New Fetter Lane, E.C.4

First published June 7, 1956
Second edition 1960
Reprinted, with minor corrections, 1963
Reprinted, with bibliographical
additions 1969
SBN 416 43500 9
2.3

First published as a University Paperback 1969
SBN 416 29970 9
1.1

Printed in Great Britain
by John Dickens & Co. Ltd., Northampton

Distributed in the U.S.A. by Barnes & Noble Inc.

PREFACE

IN dealing with so large a subject as the history of early medieval Europe, and in a relatively small volume, the temptation to give most space to what most interests oneself is very strong. I can only say in apology that I share my interests with the present generation of history students: or that they have, more probably, inspired them in me. I have tried, in fact, while dealing with the political backbone, the succession of events, in early medieval Europe, to indicate also the ancestry of her culture and institutions. This is, indeed, not quite a simple matter, for though undoubtedly our richest inheritance comes from our Greco-Roman and Germanic forbears, we had culturally a lot of incidental ancestors as well. It was the nomads settled in the Crimea who taught us to use safety-pins, and the Syrian merchants to eat black [French] plums at Christmas.

With regard to the brief chronological treatment of the history of the different European countries, I have probably overloaded the story with proper names, but this is intended to guide students using the chroniclers and the larger monographs. I have used the forms of proper names given in the *Cambridge Medieval History*, while preferring (if there is a difference) those of *The Shorter Cambridge Medieval History*. I have used the modern forms of place-names (if such exist), and, where possible, those of *The Oxford Atlas*, O.U.P., 1951.

As customary in this series, the history of Britain is omitted, except for casual references in allusion or for comparison.

The bibliographical notes again are highly selective. It is to be hoped that in addition to the maps provided, recourse will be had to R. L. Poole's *Historical Atlas of Modern Europe*, the maps in the *Cambridge Medieval History*, or Muir's *Historical Atlas: medieval and modern*, ed. G. Goodall and R. F. Treharne, 8th ed. 1952.

To those who have kindly helped me I owe great thanks, in particular to Professor Joan Hussey for Byzantine illumination in general and for reading and correcting the Byzantine chapters. For me, Professor Hussey lit the Byzantine candles. I owe thanks to the late Professor R. R. Betts with regard to the Slavs and for reading chapter xxv: to Professor B. Lewis with regard to Islam and reading chapter xi: and to Dr Florence Harmer with regard to the Scandinavians and for reading the relevant part of chapter xxiv. I am most grateful also to Professors M. Cary and F. Wormald, for help over a number of years.

MARGARET DEANESLY

196 CLARENCE GATE GARDENS
LONDON, N.W.1

PREFACE TO THE SECOND EDITION

I should like to thank the reviewers of the first edition of this book, and those who wrote letters about it, pointing out slips and errors and making many suggestions. The errors I hope I have corrected in this edition. The suggestions I have tried to use, short of rewriting large portions of the book or much increasing its length.

The suggestion that the first edition of the book has a strong west-European bias I have tried to deal with, short of serious alteration of spacing. In this matter I have to thank Mr. W. Jardine Grisbrooke, whose learning and attractions are east European than west European, for much help; I also owe him many thanks for general help in proof reading.

MARGARET DEANESLY

196 CLARENCE GATE GARDENS
LONDON, N.W.1

PREFACE TO THE 1963 REPRINT

SINCE 1960, published studies in Byzantine and Carolingian history have illuminated without greatly changing older views. In the history of western monasticism, however, a factor so important for the transmission of secular learning and Christian ideals in early medieval Europe, certain doubts have been resolved. The precedence of the old *Regula Magistri* to the Benedictine rule has been accepted, and the nature of the 'mixed rule' in Benedict's and pope Gregory's day illuminated. The names of Vanderhofen, Hallinger and Porcel are outstanding in these studies; their works appear in the bibliographical note on p. 184.

MARGARET DEANESLY

196 CLARENCE GATE GARDENS
LONDON, N.W.1

PREFACE TO THE 1969 REPRINT

SINCE the publication of *Early Medieval Europe*, historical interest, and writing, has largely followed Toynbee's view of the importance of "civilisations" or "cultures" in the history of mankind. The ten volumes of his *A Study of History* were published by the Oxford University Press between 1933 and 1954, and their impact is not yet exhausted. Among the most important studies of the *haut moyen age*, the period largely covered in *Early Medieval Europe*, have been those about "societies", their rise, their interactions and their decline. They cover: the transition from the Roman Empire to early Germanic Europe; the transition from the Hellenistic Greek world, left after the conquests of Alexander, to the Byzantine empire at Constantinople, which involved the adoption of the first Christianity, the Greek Christianity of the east Mediterranean; and, finally, the build-up of the Germanic, Carolingian, empire and its decline. Such studies have included investigation of the Latin Christian foundations of Charlemagne's empire, and its adoption of the Roman imperial title with the concept of universal rule, as against the "hegemonial" implications of *imperator* in Britain and Spain. Some of these studies have been mentioned in addition to the bibliographical notes at the ends of chapters.

MARGARET DEANESLY

196 CLARENCE GATE GARDENS
LONDON, N.W.I

x

CONTENTS

xi

MAPS

FRONTISPIECE

Triumph of a Byzantine Emperor. Barberini ivory: Early
6th century.

(*By courtesy of the Warburg Institute: photo, Giraudon, Paris*)

CHAPTER I

THE ROMAN HERITAGE IN 476

THE year 410 had brought to all Europe a sound of a falling palace and a collapsing judgment seat: the Roman empire, it seemed, had fallen, and the underpinning of civilization with it. All men knew it. But no such general appreciation of great events accompanied the year 476: no European uneasiness, no Christian misgivings. Yet, on looking back, it seems that, if the year 410 be taken as a point of collapse and destruction, for no Visigothic kingdom arose in Italy after 410 to crown Alaric's conquest of Rome, the year 476 may be taken as significant of a beginning of a Germanic kingship of Italy, the mother land of the Roman empire.

What happened in the year 476? Odovacar, a barbarian general and the real ruler of Italy, deposed the young emperor of the west, Romulus Augustulus, the son of Odovacar's predecessor, Orestes, and took the government openly into his own hands. He sent envoys, claiming to speak for the Roman senate, to the emperor Zeno at Constantinople, to tell him that the army of the west had slain Orestes, its *magister militum* and patrician, and deposed Romulus: they laid at Zeno's feet Romulus' diadem and purple robe and (here was the novelty) did not ask for them back for anyone else. It would suffice, they said, that they, for the west, should do homage to Zeno: one emperor should suffice for the empire. Let Zeno confer upon the senatorial candidate for the rule of Italy, upon Flavius Odovacar, the title of patrician, and the position would be regularized. Zeno, only emperor himself since 474, and in no strong position, demurred but finally complied. Odovacar, a leader of the Germanic *Scyrrii, Rugii*, etc., from the lower Vistula, became patrician of Italy: but he was less versed in Roman practice and tradition than the barbarian ministers who before him had governed Italy under the nominal rule of an emperor, and he conceived of himself, as did his contemporaries, rather as a Germanic king than a Roman magistrate. He issued grants in the name, not of Odovacar Patricius, but of Odovacar Rex: and for the first time, barbarian troops were quartered permanently on the Italian countryside. The barbarians had begun to rule the heart of the empire: their kingdoms had already been set up in the outlying provinces. The future in the west of Europe lay with them, as for

many centuries at Constantinople it still lay with the old, unbroken
rule of Rome.

Odovacar ruled Italy and Noricum for seventeen years from his
citadel in marsh-girt Ravenna, and five other barbarian kings in the
year when he slew Orestes shared the rule of western Europe between them. Euric the Visigoth ruled a people settled between the
Loire and the straits of Gibraltar: Gaiseric and his Vandals ruled
north Africa: Gundobad and his Burgundians were settled in the
valleys of the Rhone and the Saône: Frankish princes, one of them
the father of Clovis, held the mouths of the Meuse, Moselle and
Rhine: the Suevi had a small kingdom in Portugal and north Spain.
In Britain there was as yet no single Germanic kingdom: but in 477
Ælla landed in Sussex, and by 490, through capturing Pevensey
and turning the Roman fortified line of defence, he was saluted as
overking or bretwalda of the invading Saxons. There was now,
therefore, no large area in western Europe where a Roman magistrate ruled: Syagrius the patrician, indeed, defended himself and
his provincials at Soissons till 485, and in Brittany, Wales and
Strathclyde the provincials, relapsing in fact to a primitive tribal
life, still cherished the religion and the memory of Rome, and the
name of Constantine for a ruler. As a whole, however, if a political observer could have flown above Europe in a plane from the
Adriatic to the Bay of Biscay and from the Rhine mouth to Tripolitania, he would have seen the fair-haired, moustached, short
tunicked or trousered Germanic invaders settled among and ruling
the many races of dark-eyed Roman provincials.

All these Germanic invaders had braved the difficulties of migration and conquest for the same object: to possess themselves of
homes in warmer, richer, more fertile lands than the trans-Rhenane
and the trans-Danubian forest and plains whence they had come in
the latter stages of their wanderings. To possess, moreover, lands
rich because planted with cities and traversed by traders. The
Roman empire where they coveted rule was, to them, unimagin-
ably rich, because fertile and long civilized. But when they had
fought their way in and fought their way through a great part of
western Europe, and when their tribal leader, sprung from the
sacred royal family of the tribe and raised on the shield in approbation by the nobles and freemen, had carved himself out a new
kingdom: the invaders found themselves with another heritage
than the cornlands and vineyards and riches of the Roman world.
They inherited the Roman past.

They lived among provincials in most cases more numerous than
themselves and in some cases much more numerous: and these

provincials, now their fellow subjects, had their own institutions, laws and religion. The conquerors might take their villas, or their lands; but the conquerors, or their leaders, had a suspicion that their conquered subjects could do some things better than they themselves could: they could not, of course, fight as well, but they could write. Notaries were useful enough in government, and most Germanic kings used them. And build: most of the Germanic peoples had used timber for the king's hall and any other structure; but, settled in a land of marble and stone buildings, they admired and copied the stone buildings they found. Their attitude to the Roman heritage differed from tribe to tribe and depended partly on the extent of their previous intercourse with Roman civilization, and partly on the education and statesmanship of their kings: Alaric the Visigoth admired and Gaiseric the Vandal despised the Roman heritage; but, in any case, it was there, for them to use. 'We admire the titles bestowed by the emperors more than our own,' said one barbarian king, writing to an emperor. Most of them did, in fact, solicit recognition and a Roman title from the emperor at Constantinople: and while some admired the Roman heritage more than others, all built their new kingdoms on a Roman substructure. A Germanic society settled down upon Roman foundations, till, curiously enough, a particularly successful Germanic king, surrounded by a band of scholar ministers, and with a pope at hand to serve his own purposes by taking the initiative, assumed or acquiesced in the assumption of the old Roman title of emperor. On Christmas Day in the year 800 the wheel had come full circle.

To consider then the Roman heritage, as it offered itself to Odovacar's 'Rugians' or 'Scyrrians', *hospitati* on the provincials of north Italy: or to the Franks in Gaul, equally devout to the celebration of the Lord's passion and the preservation of the Germanic blood feud; or to the Anglo-Saxons in Britain who had little enough of *Romanitas*: in what did the Roman heritage consist? It consisted of a society, in the modern cant phrase, a way of life, with a government that had been in the past amazingly successful in combining central rule with preservation of local social and legal custom; an agriculture that fed or paid for feeding the populations of the towns; an urban population, with a developed commerce and currency: an art of building and a learning inspired by the Greek east, and a law that was peculiarly Roman. It included also, in the year 476, the Christian religion, with the majority of its bishops and sees in the eastern empire, but its magistral chair for the west in the old capital of Rome.

In dealing even shortly with the Roman heritage, it is of some importance to remember that the Germanic settlers could not be immediately well informed about it, because they did not, for the most part, use the instrument of writing. They had their own culture, and it was an unwritten, oral culture; their tribal history was handed down in the songs of bards, acclaiming the king and his ancestors at court banquets: their Germanic law was unwritten and preserved in the memories of councillors. Few of them could write, though their princes, ruling bands of federates in the Balkans or on the Rhine, used notaries who could. Wulfila indeed translated at least portions of the Old and New Testaments into Gothic, and there was enough writing skill to ensure that copies were made, certain of which have survived. But in the main, the Germanic tribes had an oral culture, and it was not from books, but from provincial scholars and ministers that Germanic kings learned of the law and achievement of Rome. They knew of the *autokrator* at Constantinople; they wondered at the Roman arts of peace; but they knew little Roman history. They knew the titles of certain great officers who upheld the empire; they knew the standards of the legions and the *vexilla* of the cohorts; they knew the diadem of golden laurel leaves and the purple belt with its gold ornaments of the Roman magistrate; but naturally little of the origin of the office he held.

The Roman empire had been founded by Augustus, who ruled from 27 B.C. to A.D. 14, and had, with considerable skill and the experience of Julius Caesar behind him, converted the old Roman republic into an empire. In appearance the republic was preserved and power shared between Augustus and the senate.

To describe for a moment the political side of the Roman heritage: its scheme of government. The old republican officers, the two yearly consuls, the pro-consuls, the *duces* of the legions, the tribunes of the cohorts and the lesser civil and military officers, remained. They were to remain for 400 years of empire and their titles were to persist in the new courts of the barbarian kings; but Augustus himself in fact controlled the Roman civil service and the Roman army. He had his own imperial treasury or fisc, and appointed the governors of all border provinces. The senate's position was honourable and its powers, under him, still considerable; but they soon shrank. The emperor's household came to govern the empire, and the emperor alone provided for and controlled the army.

Local government in the provinces of the empire was carried on by the emperor's deputy; taxes were raised by the province;

imperial villas or corn lands in each province belonged to the fisc and contributed to the revenue. The boundaries of the empire were defended by the legions, and within them the *pax Romana* made up to peasant and townsman for a time for the levies of the tax collector. These boundaries enclosed an empire focussed on the Mediterranean, for though Spain, Gaul and (since A.D. 43) Britain were within the empire, there was no Atlantic outlook to other islands or land mass. The Roman empire from Augustus' time included western Europe to the line of the Rhine and the Danube; the upper waters of these rivers rise near together by lake Constance, and the re-entrant angle formed by their upper waters in the eastward slant of this frontier was abolished by the *limes* joining its extremities, constructed by the Flavian emperors. It was the only part of this northern frontier which needed walled defence; elsewhere the rivers themselves supplied a *limes* which was in use rather a line of customs posts than a contested barrier. The emperor Hadrian, after Claudius had added Britain to the empire, visited it and surveyed its northern defences, and drew the *limes* of Hadrian's Wall across northern Britain.

To the north, then, the frontiers of the empire were natural; in the east they included the Black Sea, the mountains of Armenia, and the sandy deserts east of Palestine and Arabia. To the south the Saharan desert and its tribes hemmed in the narrow but fertile strip of Roman Africa, and to the west the Atlantic bounded the Roman empire and the known world. Within these frontiers the Augustan empire numbered twenty-seven provinces.

For some 200 years from Augustus the system worked well: but two inherent difficulties were even then apparent and were to threaten collapse later. The first was the succession difficulty and the second that of securing continuous statesmanship in a one-man government. The empire was not, theoretically, hereditary, but elective; and though Augustus and his successors tried to avoid disputed successions by adopting a candidate and making him a Caesar, with the prospect of succession, this system only worked as long as there was a respected imperial family to draw upon, the Caesars, the Claudians, the Flavians. Even in the early period there was the possibility that an emperor might be assassinated and the succession seized. The second difficulty in the Augustan scheme of government, where so much depended on the man at the top, was to secure hard-working, well-balanced and able emperors; while the system supplied a Hadrian and a Marcus Aurelius, it also supplied a Caligula and a Nero. Moreover, though Roman government, Roman law, the Roman civil service were good articles of their kind, they were expensive: by the time of the Antonine emperors, A.D. 138–180, taxes had already become crushing.

After working fairly well for nearly 200 years, the Roman scheme of government nearly broke down over the succession difficulty. The Roman army from the time of the Antonines had to withstand continuous pressure on the Rhine–Danube frontier, as well as defend Armenia and Syria from the Persians; it was vital to security, and it was now composed, not of Italians or even Roman citizens, but of the barbarian nations willing to enlist. Support of the army came, in the third century, to condition a candidate's chances of election to the imperial throne: the third century, that of the 'barrack emperors', saw many disputed successions and short-lived emperors. Collapse seemed possible; but a great constructive reform carried out by the emperors Diocletian and Constantine (284–337) prolonged the régime.

The empire, as the barbarians found it at the beginning of the fifth century, was governed on the lines laid down by these two emperors. The frequent periods of anarchy in the empire, due to civil war over the succession, and the impossibility of a one-man government's coping with attacks on distant frontiers, were both remedied by Diocletian's scheme, at a further cost in the expense of the government. Diocletian planned that the empire should have two *Augusti* and two Caesars, each heir to the position of the Augustus who had adopted him. From A.D. 288 there were two such Augusti and two Caesars: Diocletian being the predominant partner. The succession scheme, however, did not work out exactly as planned: and in 306 the young Constantine, son of a general then defending Britain, had himself proclaimed emperor. After eighteen years' struggle and civil war, he succeeded in making himself sole emperor, and the founder of a dynasty much stronger than that of any recent imperial family. He preserved, however, and completed the reorganization begun by Diocletian, and this is of importance because the Roman empire which the barbarian nations found was working, or collapsing, roughly according to this scheme.

The defence of the northern and eastern frontiers had proved easier with the defence organized and led from four palaces: Diocletian himself had remained usually at Nicomedia; and though Constantine had united the empire under his sole rule, at Constantinople, the earlier system of divided control prepared the way for an empire divided into east and west.

Local government had been completely separated from military command and much subdivided, so as to minimize possible danger from pretenders. The empire was divided now into four praetorian prefectures: the Gauls (including Britain); Italy, with Africa and Pannonia; Illyricum (the Balkans); and the East. These four prefectures, under their 'illustrious' prefects, were divided into thirteen dioceses (a purely secular term in origin) under imperial vicars, who ranked as *spectabiles*: under the vicars, various governors of various ranks but all *clarissimi* ruled the 116 new provinces. Provinces were much smaller than under the Augustan scheme; Britain had two provinces in the first century, but five after this reform. The system of official ranks and titles was retained by the more intelligent Germanic rulers; the early Merovingians used *illustres* plentifully, and Cassiodorus compiled for the Ostrogoths a collection of diplomas, or letters of appointment, to be sent to recipients of the various titles.

Finally, it should be noted about this matter of Roman government, as the barbarians found it, that the empire did not remain undivided, as under Constantine: and that the later emperors reigned but did not rule. Constantine had moved his capital, and his Latin-speaking court, to Byzantium, and the main fund of *Romanitas* remained from this time rather in the east than the west. But not completely. Constantine died in 337, and the empire was divided between his three sons; a single emperor followed, Constantius II (351–361), and then two others, Julian and Jovian, till 364. The rule of Valentinian and Valens followed, Valentinian ruling the west and Valens the east. The able Valentinian died in 375: when Valens was killed in battle in 378, he was succeeded by Theodosius the great, ruling the east only at first, but east and west from 383 till his death in 395. From that year the empire was permanently ruled by two emperors, in east and west; the first were Theodosius' two sons, Arcadius and Honorius. This division of power in the empire conditioned the barbarian settlements in the west. The Balkans were nearer the Gothic home in south Russia, and on the Danube, and Byzantium would have been a rich prize to the Goths; but after two emperors, Decius and Valens, had both been defeated and killed in trying to defend the Balkans by arms, the later emperors of Constantinople, Zeno in particular, resorted to the policy of letting the west go to save the east. On intimation of danger to Illyricum, they were willing to deflect the barbarians to Italy and the west. Honorius ruled the latter unfortunately till 423, acquiescing in the loss of Britain, but encouraging the provincials to go on defending themselves there from their encircling raiders: his minister Stilicho did much to regularize, though he could not prevent, the Frankish settlements in north Gaul;

Valentinian III had a long reign, 423 till 455, and there followed nine western emperors, the real power resting usually in the hands of some barbarian general. The last of them was Orestes, murdered in 476. It was natural enough that Odovacar and his followers should find no particular attraction in the title of emperor, since for about seventy years the Roman officer in the west who opposed or dealt with them had been a barbarian minister or *magister militum* rather than the emperor himself.

The Roman army underwent great changes in the period of Diocletian and Constantine. In the earlier period, and from Republican days, it had been, though composed of legions of infantry, an army of manœuvre, a shock force. The Roman legions, with their standard the eagles, and their subdivision the cohort, officered by the tribune and with the light-air dragon, suspended from a lance, as its own standard, had marched where directed and been a match for such mounted forces as barbarians might bring against them. Such enemies (like the Roman cavalry *auxilia*) could not deliver a charge to break the legions, because they rode bareback, without saddle or stirrups and with their horses unshod. Such a band of horsemen usually contented themselves with hurling spears, when near enough, and if an embattled force stood firm against them they turned and rode off.

In the course of the third century, however, in that home of the horse-borne nomad, the grasslands of central Asia, Persia and the Ukraine (Sarmatia), great discoveries arose to change the course of military history. Horses there were now shod with iron, and ridden with saddles and stirrups. The horseman, firmly supported now in the saddle, and armed with spurs, could begin to wear defensive armour: to use a leather jerkin strengthened with iron rings or scales, a head-piece, and, for weapons, a sword or long lance. The charge of such horsemen could break a line of Roman legionaries.

Though the Romans met such forces on the eastern frontier, it was the Germanic tribes, long in touch with eastern Europe, who first took to imitating their manner of fighting on horseback. The Goths, pushing out the Sarmatians in the Ukraine, adopted their skilled horsemanship. Pressure from the Huns spread the practice among Vandals, Gepids and the Alemans. The Roman army, forced, as M. Ferdinand Lot says, to adopt the same method of fighting or disappear, adopted it, but at first with small success. The astonishing defeats of the emperors Decius, Valerian and Valens show that the Roman armies practised a new tactic clumsily and unsuccessfully; in the past, when dealing with armed horsemen like the Persians, they had tried to meet the difficulty by increasing their auxiliary cavalry. The desperate need of heavy cavalry in the Roman army in the fourth and fifth centuries accounts partly for the ever-increasing numbers of barbarians enrolled: they had more experience of this manner of fighting, for which the peasant *coloni* of the landowners were quite unqualified.

The legionary army of Augustus had become, in the three inter-vening centuries not a shock force, but a stationary frontier guard: *limitanei:* and it had shrunk in numbers. The number of legions at its highest, under Septimius Severus, had risen to 33; if each legion had numbered the traditional 6,000 men, this would have meant a force of some 198,000 legionaries. Such a force was, however, im-possible to recruit in peace time from the towns, or even from the young peasants, who could, moreover, ill be spared; and thus the legionary forces were, while retaining the name of legions, reduced in strength to mere cohorts. For the striking force, the army of manœuvre, which was now plainly needed in addition to the fron-tier legions, three armies were raised, for Italy, for Gaul and for the east, and raised as cavalry forces, as *comitatenses*, or companions of the emperor. They were more highly paid than the old legions, and as *palatini*, or palace troops, had a higher status. They might be led, even, by barbarian officers of the highest rank, for such men were versed in the new tactics, and could scarcely become danger-ous by aspiring to the imperial diadem. In the early fourth cen-tury, public opinion could scarcely have conceived of a barbarian emperor. Britain, it is true, in the course of the fourth century, supplied an unusual number of military pretenders, for there it was possible to persuade legionary troops to follow to the continent a general who raised their status and their pay from *limitanei* to *comitatenses*; but neither Maximus nor Constantine III attained permanent success.

It should be noticed, however, that though Diocletian's reform of the army succeeded in some cases in holding the invading bar-barian in the fourth century, it broke down in the fifth: perhaps because the barbarian invaders were now more numerous: but also, possibly from the crushing expense of maintaining it. The Roman cavalry army seems, in fact, to have dwindled to very small propor-tions. Possibly, also, the barbarians had more direct access to that supply of horse power, the Ukraine. It has been computed that the generals of the emperor Constantius II had at their disposal against the invading Franks and Alemans, no more than 35,000 men for the defence of Gaul, Rhaetia and Italy: a very small force. The evidence of the *Notitia Dignitatum*, dealing with a period fifty years later, gives the regiments of infantry and cavalry available to hold back the migrating barbarians at figures obviously inadequate. In 409 the emperor Honorius, blockaded in Ravenna, prepared to sail for Constantinople: he was saved by the arrival from the east of as small a force as 4,000 men: six *numeri*. Stilicho failed to prevent the passage of the Rhine by a horde of barbarians in 406 by leaving Gaul and Britain denuded of troops; the army of the Rhine was gone, and Gaul was ravaged. The pretenders themselves, Constantine III from Britain (407), Jovinus from Gaul (413), led no Roman armies, but only locally raised levies. When Aëtius prepared to resist Attila and his Huns in 451, he brought a force from Italy, but the Roman army of Gaul had disappeared: he could only summon to the contest contingents of Visigoths and barbarians settled in Gaul. Twenty years before the Roman empire fell in the west in 476, the Roman army as organized in the past, *limitanei, comitatenses, numeri,* or barbarian levies (*arithmos* in Greek) had disappeared; barbarian generals as *magistri militum* commanded the only armies at the emperor's disposal, and they were contingents of federate barbarians.

The society which the Germanic invaders overthrew had been an urban society with a relatively high level of civilization and trade: they replaced it by a society of peasant farmers living under their tribal kings and nobles. The extent to which foreign trade declined and the century when it began to do so is still in dispute: but there is no dispute that some 'recession' in the progress of civilization took place. In course of time, Herr Dopsch says earlier and M. Pirenne said later, a mainly food and services economy replaced a money economy. But the barbarians of the fifth century found a civilization in which the two most characteristic organizations, the towns and the villas, had already largely decayed.

The Roman empire which the barbarians found had in the second century, perhaps its prime (when the largest number of men enjoyed the greatest comfort in life), presented, in M. Rostovtzeff's words, 'the appearance of a vast federation of city states'. The Roman towns, apart from those of ancient foundation in Italy and the east, were laid out by the Roman army surveyor, the *gromaticus*, on the same lines as an army camp; that is, with streets parallel or at right angles, and the centre of the town a rectangular open space, surrounded by the chief civic buildings. They were, for the first two centuries, unwalled, and stone built; the houses were inward looking, as in Italy where shade was a prerequisite; and either adjoined each other closely, with their two wings going back from the street and enclosing a small open court, or as corridor houses along the street; on the outskirts of the town the houses stood in their own grounds. The towns had a good, scientific drainage system, an abundant water supply brought sometimes even to the upper storeys of the houses by means of skilfully built aqueducts, covered porticoes lining the streets, to protect pedestrians from sun and rain; markets with a good water supply: beautiful baths, splendid temples with sacred groves, and, outside the city, cemeteries where beautiful funerary monuments bordered the public roads. The public buildings of the city would include *curiae*, meeting-places for the local senate or *ordo*, offices for the magistrates, a basilica for the judge and the meetings of business men and traders, theatres, *stadia*, circuses, in some cities public libraries, and in many the *scolae* where the rhetors lectured to their classes. When the Ostrogoths reached Italy and the Burgundians the Rhone valley, the rhetors were still lecturing and receiving a salary from the state. That soon ceased. But the stone-built towns, the marble monuments, of the Romans remained after their settlement and must, more than anything else, have passed on to the new populations the traditions of Roman *imperium*.

Though the splendour of the cities was due to the munificence of the wealthier citizens, or, in the newer provinces of the empire, to forced labour exacted by the chief of the tribe from his tribesmen at the prodding of the central government, the day-to-day expenses of the cities were met by various local charges and taxes: customs duties, charges for holding land in the city, for the right to exercise a trade, to use markets and shops, etc. The city revenue went, not in salaries to its magistrates, for these were unpaid, but in the small salaries of minor officials or the maintenance of *servi publici*: to the maintenance of public buildings, the upkeep of roads, the securing of an abundance of foodstuffs, the upkeep of temples, and even the payment of teachers for the education and physical training of the young. The construction and maintenance of local roads fell upon the cities, since they were needed for the transport of food supplies. The *curator annonae*, a municipal officer, was charged with the maintenance of the corn supply. Wealth was more evenly distributed in the second century than earlier, and the bourgeois aristocracy of the cities was able to undertake civic office and bear the municipal liturgies. To the existence of this rich, bourgeois class large, expensive tombs all over the empire bear witness, including even the remote Danubian provinces.

The commerce of the Roman empire certainly, about the year 200, was the main source of its wealth: especially foreign and inter-provincial trade. 'The richest cities of the empire, the cities in which the most opulent men of the Roman world resided were those that had the most developed commerce and lay near the sea or great trade routes or were centres for a lively river traffic.' Sea and river transport was much cheaper than land transport. Trade was decentralized, Italy and her towns no longer taking the lead; Gaul was now what Italy had once been, the greatest industrial land of the west. She supplied other provinces, and even Italy herself, with her red-glazed pottery, glass, woollen cloaks and bronze safety-pins.

All this commerce rested partly on coined money, and partly on the credit transactions of banks and private money-lenders. An astonishing amount of currency was demanded, even in peace time, and was in fact supplied by the mines of Europe and Asia and the mints that existed everywhere throughout the empire. Whereas earlier states had relied on silver for currency, and to some extent on gold, the Roman empire, while using both these metals, added to them the use of copper; it may indeed, in one sense, be said to have rested on the basis of the copper coin. Not only were the legionaries paid in coin, but their officers, and the civil servants. The Latin language had a word for a 200 *sestercii*-a-year-man, a *ducenarius*: and so forth. Aulus Plautius conquered Britain in A.D. 43 at a very moderate money salary.

Out in the countryside, the tribal chieftains and the heads of the civil service lived in the villas, great landed estates focussed in the owner's colonnaded, inward-looking house, or simply in the farm buildings of the bailiff or *conductor*, who worked the corn lands for his master or for the emperor. Even in a distant province like Britain, the stone-built house of the villa, with its baths, chapel, apsidal chambers, and elaborately designed mosaic floors, was no rarity. At Low Ham, near Taunton, the mosaic pavement has a spirited design with ships and sailors with peaked Phrygian caps: and the ground plan of the villa on the East Cliff at Folkestone is a complex of chambers and small courts. In Italy, Gaul and the east, such country houses of the Roman aristocracy and official class were even more numerous.

With the third century, however, the prosperity of the towns had declined, with the indirect result that Roman wealth and culture withdrew for a time to the villas, before they too were wrecked by marauding bands, civil war, or the coming of invaders. The cause of the decline in Roman prosperity after the second century has been much discussed (see *infra*, p. 116); the violence of the third century interrupted communications, perhaps already lessening the profitable trade with Asia; and the heaviness of taxation after the age of Diocletian and Constantine wrecked in particular the prosperity of the towns. With the fall in prosperity, population too tended to fall. The new cavalry army was expensive to maintain, as were the two, three or four imperial headquarters, and the multiplied provincial staff. 'The state was constantly draining the capital which was the life-blood of the empire.' While the imperial efforts to get more money too often in the third century involved confiscation and violence, in the fourth, systematic taxation was apparently more just, but not less harmful. The *curiales* of the towns were personally responsible for the collection of imperial taxes, and deficits in the ever-increasing sums demanded had to be provided out of their own pockets; even a bad harvest, temporarily ruining the countryside, was no excuse: the *curiales* were themselves ruined in making good the amounts demanded. Membership of the curial class was hereditary, and when the burden in the fourth century was so crushing, its members sought escape in any way possible, either by seeking to join some humble *collegium* or trade-gild, or becoming the *coloni* of some landholder, or leaving their estates and obligations to flee (contrary to the law) to some other part of the empire. The landowner too was responsible for the payment of the land and corn tax from his estate, and from the time of Constantine the free peasant was forbidden to move from the land which, as *colonus*, he cultivated for his lord or patron; such movement would have diminished the yield of the estate to the tax collector. The tax was first levied by Constantine in 314, and the assessment of each fiscal unit was surveyed every fifteen years—every indiction. For ordinary purposes of dating, the first, second, etc. year of the indiction became as important as the dating by the year of the two consuls at Rome. The *coloni* could not be taken from the estates to receive military training, because, in the fourth century the Roman army was an expensive, professional army, and their labours had to pay for it. But when the army failed them, the untrained *coloni* themselves were no match for even small bands of mounted and armed invaders. M. Lot has pointed out the smallness of the force that Theoderic the Ostrogoth brought with him to the conquest of Italy; at one moment of difficulty in the summer of 489–490 he was forced to shut himself up inside Ticenum (Pavia) 'with all his people', and Ticenum was then a very small town; but small as were the bands the invaders brought against the *coloni* and the citizens, they were enough.

The invaders found then, the Roman heritage of towns and commerce already decayed; they might not, as farmers, wish to live in the towns themselves; but they wondered at the majesty of Roman

buildings. It was no Burgundian, surveying the ruins of Aix in
Provence, no Ostrogoth wondering at an Italian town, but a reflec-
tive Anglo-Saxon, surveying a ruined Roman city who wrote:

> Wondrously wrought and fair its wall of stone,
> Shattered by Fate! The castles rend asunder,
> The work of giants moldereth away . . .
> The mighty men that built it,
> Departed hence, undone by death, are held
> Fast in the earth's embrace . . .
> There stood the courts of stone. Hotly within
> The stream flowed with its mighty surge. The wall
> Surrounded all with its bright bosom: there
> The baths stood, hot within its heart.[1]

Again, the Christian faith and its practice had come to seem, to
the barbarians, part of the Roman heritage. Ostrogoths, Visigoths
and Vandals had, indeed, their own form of the faith, deriving,
through their apostle, Wulfila, from the teaching of Arius that
Christ was not 'of one substance with the Father', but a creature.
It is perhaps no accident that while Arianism had been rejected at
the council of Nicaea in 325, and the decision upheld at the council
of Chalcedon in 451, a form of faith that did not commend itself
to the profound Greek minds of Christian theologians because it
equated the position of Christ with that of the heroic semi-divine
figures of classical and barbarian antiquity, was for that very reason
more acceptable to the barbarians themselves; the missionary
whose labours produced the widest conversions, through the
spreading of the Goths through Europe, was this Arian teacher,
Wulfila. But apart from the difference in their theology, the worship and practices of these Arian Christians must have seemed very
different to the invaders themselves from the ordered worship of
the Christian basilicas of Italy, Spain or Africa. Presumably the
Germanic tribes taught by Wulfila used a vernacular liturgy: the
Goths at least may be presumed to have done so, for one manuscript of the Gothic Bible he made for them, the codex Argenteus,
is an altar book for the reading of the gospels at mass, and at so
early a date the reading of the gospel in the vernacular in the
middle of a Latin (or Greek) mass was not yet practised: a Gothic
gospel implies a Gothic mass. Western Europe, however, used the
Latin rite, and that in itself would seem to have created a practical
religious barrier more obvious to the simple Goth than the difference of belief about the person of Christ. In any case, the religious
gulf was not bridged for three or four generations.

[1] Cook and Tinker: *Translations from Old English Poetry*, p. 56.

In the case of Franks and Anglo-Saxons, who settled as pagans, Christianity seemed even more clearly a part of the Roman heritage. Clovis finally accepted Christianity, as he had already adopted the notaries and *formulae* of the Roman king of Soissons. The Anglo-Saxons, delaying to be converted a hundred years and more after the invasion, seem no less to have accepted Christianity as part of the Roman heritage. Æthelbert was baptized in one old Canterbury church, and gave others to Augustine to establish therein his *cathedra* and *familia*; Edwin was baptized, not in his ancestral headquarters near the Malton gap, but in the newly conquered Roman city of York; Italian and Frankish missionaries baptized in Roman centres like Caratacum and Dorchester, when they could, as well as in the rivers and streams.

Finally, one most valuable part of the Roman heritage: Roman learning and Roman law, less easily perceptible and understandable to the first generation of Germanic barbarians, may be left for later discussion (see chaps. IX, XIII). The use of papyrus, sheets of writing material made by laying the pith of reeds from the Nile across one another on a frame, and damping and pressing them, had provided the Roman empire with a cheap writing material for her commerce, letters, official mandates, and literature; only valuable and solemn books, such as copies of the gospels and the *codex iuris Romani* were normally written upon the much more expensive vellum or parchment. The barbarian kings, taking over the Roman medium of local government, took over the scribes of the Roman law courts and imperial palaces, the notaries: and they had their letters and edicts issued in the notarial manner and writing, on papyrus. Enlightened kings, like Theoderic or Alaric, used notable scholars at their court: but that was as far as the assimilation of Roman learning could at first go.

BIBLIOGRAPHICAL NOTE

For this and subsequent chapters the standard reference books are the *Cambridge Medieval History*, vols. i to iv, the last of which, on Byzantine history, will shortly be replaced by a new volume: and the *Shorter Cambridge Medieval History*, vol. i, 1952, with excellent illustrations. *Les destinées de l'empire en occident de 395 à 888*, by F. Lot, C. Pfister and F. L. Ganshof, is valuable and published in 1928, later than the *Camb. Med. Hist.*: it is tome i in the *Histoire du moyen age* of Glotz' *Histoire Générale*. Two shorter but useful general histories are C. Dawson's *The Making of Europe*, 1939, and H. St L. B. Moss, *Birth of the Middle Ages*, 1935. These books should be used throughout all the chapters for the political history of the period and much else, but will not be referred to again in the bibliographical notes to the chapters. For this chapter, F. Lot's

Fin du monde antique et le début du moyen âge is classical [trans. P. and M. Leon, *End of the Ancient World and the Beginning of the Middle Ages,* 1931]: the last ed. of 1951 embodies revisions and corrections. See also *Camb. Anc. Hist.,* vol. xii: S. Dill, *Roman Society in the Last Century of the Roman Empire,* 1898: E. S. Duckett, *Gateway to the Middle Ages,* 1938, and *Latin Writers of the Fifth Century,* 1930: M. P. Charlesworth, *Trade Routes and Commerce of the Roman Empire,* 1926 ed., and 'Virtues of a Roman Emperor', in *Proc. Brit. Acad.,* 1937: O. Brogan, *Roman Gaul,* 1953: C. E. Stevens, *Sidonius Apollinaris and his Age,* 1933. See also L. Bréhier, *L'art en occident du Vᵉ siècle au XIᵉ siècle,* 1938, the first 2 tomes in G. Huisman's *Histoire Générale de l'art,* and the note on general reference books at the end of chapter xxix. See also, H. Dannenbauer, *Die Enstehung Europas von der Spätantike zum Mittelalter,* Bund I. Stuttgart, 1959; R. Folz, *L'Idée d'Empire en Occident du Vᵉ au XIVᵉ siècle,* Paris, 1953; E. Barker, G. Clark and P. Vaucher, *The European Inheritance,* Oxford, 1954; A. H. M. Jones, *The Later Roman Empire,* Oxford, 1964.

CHAPTER II

THE BARBARIAN MOVEMENTS AND SETTLEMENTS

WHEN Augustus drew the northern *limes* of the empire at the Rhine and the Danube, he was not trying to delimit an ethnic frontier. He had regard rather to strategical considerations and communications: to the needs of military defence and of trade. The great rivers were in themselves defences: and they were also water roads, uniting the old native trade routes and the military roads of the army surveyors, many of which led up to the *limes*. A region cannot be defended if its roads are, as it were, the spokes of a wheel, with no means of travelling from the end of one radius to another, except that of travelling back to some junction between the spokes: some kind of road must be made to connect the ends of the spokes. This is very clearly shown when, in Britain, between A.D. 47 and 51, it was found necessary to make a new military road, the Fosseway, between Exeter and Lincoln, to connect the ends of the three military roads pushed out from London by Aulus Plautius. The Fosseway was only temporarily a frontier, for the three roads of the spokes that had been driven out of London soon passed beyond the Fosseway; but the great *limes* of the Rhine and the Danube, at once a water road and a defence needing no maintenance, was the Roman frontier for 400 years and more.

Augustus saw no need for any ethnic frontier. His empire indeed was singularly successful in dealing with racial differences within its boundaries. The bulk of its inhabitants spoke one of the speech varieties of the European half of the Indo-European speech family: Latin, Greek, Celtic, Gaelic, German, Slav. The provincials of north Africa, akin to the desert tribes of the Sahara, were an exception and not of Indo-European provenance; and on the Danube and the eastern frontier some Mongol and some Arab subjects acknowledged Roman rule. But there was no colour bar, no colour question in the empire, partly because Rome ruled no great number of subjects of colour much darker than her own Mediterranean races; and partly because the Roman administrators dealt with newly conquered additions to the empire on a basis of 'culture', in the archaeologist's sense, rather than that of race. When the basis of Roman citizenship was gradually extended, it was without regard to race.

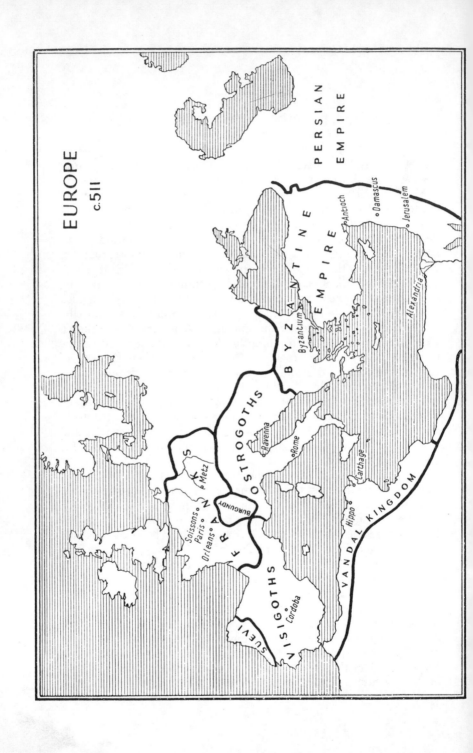

EUROPE c.511

PERSIAN EMPIRE

BYZANTINE EMPIRE

Damascus
Antioch
Jerusalem
Byzantium
Alexandria

OSTROGOTHS
Ravenna
Rome

FRANKS
Metz
BURGUNDY
Soissons
Paris
Orleans

VISIGOTHS
Cordoba
SUEVI

VANDAL KINGDOM
Hippo
Carthage

About the barbarians outside the Rhine–Danube frontier (for no great tribal immigration came from any other): they fall into two groups and two cultures, those of the Germanic peoples and the Tartars or Mongols,[1] the nomads who came originally from the high grass pastures, the steppes, of Asia. While the Germanic migrations led to the setting up of new national kingdoms in western Europe, those of the Mongol tribes led to no important permanent settlement within the empire at this date. The nomads were, however, of great importance, as producing continuous pressure on the Goths and other Germanic tribes, as introducing them to the warlike possibilities of the horse, as producing the great Hunnish raid of 451, and, at a rather later stage, after 476, as leading to the settlement of certain nomad tribes of non-Indo-European speech, in the Balkans.

The European peoples, the parents of those who in early European history appear as the Goths, Vandals, Norsemen, Swedes, Danes, Russians, Germans, Franks, Anglo-Saxons, Lombards, etc., spoke a language deriving from the Indo-European speech family. The European branch of this primitive language, that is, had the same parent forms for the most commonly used words in Sanskrit, Persian and various 'Indian' tongues: so that in Persian and Sanskrit, Greek and Latin, Old Irish, English and Russian, and their various derivatives, words like father, mother, brother, sister, bread, etc., go back to a common root; the Greek word for house and the Latin word for village had a common root: Burnham Beeches in Buckinghamshire recalls the Bukovina in Roumania. To this speech family the tongues of the Germanic races belonged, and they were akin to the languages of the empire, Latin and Greek: but quite alien from that of the northern nomads, which would seem to have been akin to Chinese.

The European peoples, again, were at a different stage of civilization from the nomads; they practised a primitive agriculture, using a plough, and possessing sheep and oxen. The nomads, and the Huns among them, belonged essentially to the belt of grass pasture in central Asia and the Ukraine, and lived upon and by means of their horses and flocks; the word nomad comes from the verb for 'to feed', and the need to feed his cattle (or, indeed, his reindeer or his horses) determined the whole character of nomad life. There was no geographical barrier between the nomads and the Slav and Gothic tribes of central Europe, for between the Caspian and the Volga the gently swelling hills of the Arals constituted no natural

[1] See G. Vernadsky, *Kievan Russia* (1948): vol. ii in G. Vernadsky and M. Karpovich, *History of Russia*.

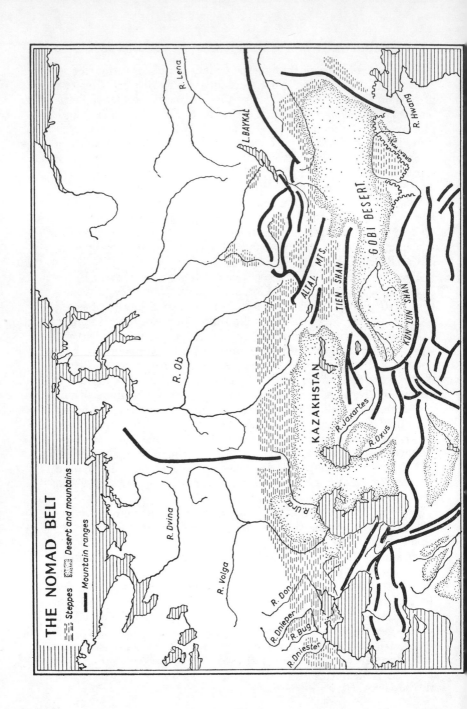

THE NOMAD BELT

≡≡ Steppes   ▒ Desert and mountains

— Mountain ranges

R. Lena

L. BAYKAL

ALTAI MTS.

TIEN SHAN

GOBI DESERT

GREAT WALL

KUN-LUN-SHAN

R. Hwang

R. Ob

KAZAKHSTAN

R. Jaxartes

R. Oxus

R. Ural

R. Dvina

R. Volga

R. Don

R. Dnieper

R. Bug

R. Dniester

obstacle: famine among the nomads of the Eurasian steppes led to pressure on their Germanic neighbours. There was also, back into prehistoric times, a trade route up the Russian rivers from the Black Sea, across the narrow stretch that unites them with the upper waters of rivers flowing into the Baltic, and down those same rivers: and where merchants pass, migratory bands and tribes can, on occasion, pass too. Tatar influence thus passed northward from the Black Sea, and the Finno-Ugrian tribes of the eastern end of the Baltic were akin in origin to the Mongols of the steppes rather than the Indo-European Germans. The high cheek-bone and Mongol droop to the outer fold of the eyelid derive from Tatar ancestry.

While the Germanic tribes had been pressing against the Roman frontier long before the fourth century, without occasioning the breaking of that frontier, the scale and the success of their attacks in the fourth and fifth centuries seem to have been due to pressure from the nomads. The term 'nomad', though excluding settled peoples, itself includes those of a range of development, between tribes for whom survival depended on movement too quick for flocks of sheep or goats, and those who could lead such flocks from pasture to pasture. There must, that is, have been development between the cultures of the nomads of the Asian steppes and those of the Ukraine.

In prehistoric, geological times, the Mediterranean sea had joined the Black Sea, the Caspian and the Aral, prolonging itself into a great Mediterranean sea of central Asia. In historic times, however, the most eastern part of this sea had long dried into a dry, salt sea bed, the zone of the deserts stretching from the Caspian sea to the Khin-gan mountains, the land of the steppes. Here the soil is too salt for cultivation: such moisture as falls evaporates, and no rivers reach the sea. Only with much irrigation are the most favourable parts of this old sea bed cultivable: the rest is a parched land, marked in spring by a bright, brief crop of luxuriant grass and the steppe flowers. In such land, from prehistoric times almost to our own day, only a primitive nomad people could have, and has lived, for life has depended on moving the tribe from the well-watered northern summer pastures to the Aral–Caspian basin where there is grass in winter. The country was too poor for a primitive agriculture. The nomads had acquired a special technique of living, taming animals and using them for food and transport: and the swiftest means of transport, making possible the greatest range of pasture, was found to be the horse. The Eurasian steppes were the land of the horse, and the only human life that could survive was life in the saddle. Only such crafts could develop as were consistent with such a life; only such kindly practices as regard for the young, the weak and the old, as were compatible with it, and these were necessarily few. On the other hand, the urgent need for mobility, for passing ever from the dried up to the fresher pasture as the sun drew to midsummer and back again, made the nomad races terrible as raiders to any settled or semi-pastoral people.

The need for swift movement, again, conditioned the whole apparatus of nomad life. Their dwellings were normally tents, and only for a great chieftain winter quarters even wooden structures. Their clothes were close-fitting and meant to preserve them from the extremes of heat and cold; all their possessions had need to be portable: weapons, clothes, horse gear.

The language of this great reservoir of Aral-Altaic or Tatar people of the steppes was certainly not Indo-European, though they bordered on Indo-European peoples both in Europe and Asia. In Asia they contended with the Persians and the tribes of the Himalayas and northern India, looting their metal work and textiles and borrowing their art-forms, as they did to a lesser extent those of the Mongols of China; in Europe they lived on the steppe belt that extended from the Volga to the Carpathians and the Danube, and struggled and contended with the autochthonous Cimmerians of south Russia, the Greeks and the Goths. Pressure from these nomads affected the migrations of the Germanic peoples in the early middle ages, and were to disturb eastern Europe throughout the middle ages. In two respects, however, the nomads were to have particular importance for the history of medieval Europe: their establishment of the brief Hunnish empire in the fifth century, and their contacts with the Slav peoples of medieval Russia. For their own settlements in Russia, their raids, and the Asian influences which they brought to bear on the Slav peoples throughout the middle ages, see chapter XXV.

Of one band of these northern nomads, the Huns, we know nothing for certain earlier than the description of Ammianus Marcellinus (+ 390), who wrote of them:

> The nation of the Huns, scarcely known to ancient documents, dwelt beyond the Maeotic marshes beside the frozen ocean, and surpassed every extreme of ferocity.

Jordanes, who summarized and preserved the gist of Cassiodorus' lost *History of the Goths*, and who admired both the Goths and east Romans, speaks of the Huns with a loathing which suggests not merely national animosity, for the Huns had defeated his Gothic ancestors, but racial antipathy: the Huns were

a stunted, foul and puny tribe, scarcely human and having no language save one which bore but slight resemblance to human speech:
. . . they were fond of hunting and had no skill in any other art. They made their foes flee in horror because their swarthy aspect was fearful, and they had, if I may call it so, a sort of shapeless lump, not a head, with pin-holes rather than eyes. Their hardihood is evident in their wild appearance, and they are beings who are cruel to their children on the very day they are born. For they cut the cheeks of the males with a sword, so that before they receive the nourishment of milk they must learn to endure wounds. Hence they grow old beardless. They are short in stature, quick in bodily movement, alert horsemen, broad shouldered, ready in the use of bow and arrow . . . Though they live in the form of men, they have the cruelty of wild beasts.⌋

But long before the year 370, when the Huns, with their subject nomads, the Alans, overthrew the great Ostrogothic kingdom to the north of the Black Sea, and set the east Germanic tribes awandering, they had made the crucial discoveries: the shoeing of the horse, and the use of saddle and stirrups. Whereas the earlier nomads, like the barbarian *auxilia* used by the Romans, had ridden bareback, carrying only a light spear,[1] the nomad horsemen, drawing upon the metal supplies of Asia as loot, had learned to travel great distances on their metal shod horses, to wear body armour, to carry a heavy sword, and to shoot on horseback with a metal bow. Their horsemanship was so expert that they normally held council and ate on horseback, and their enemies doubted if they could walk upon the ground. Their numbers were much smaller than early Roman writers, eastern or western, have suggested: but their effectiveness as shock troops suggests that of tank troops in the recent war. Though the Roman army had been remodelled to cope with them, the Goths could do nothing against them: nor could any other of the Germanic barbarians, till subjection or proximity had taught them a similar skill in making war. The Gothic kingdom of Ermanaric went down before them: in 376 fugitive Goths were permitted to settle south of the Danube, and in 378 they defeated and killed the emperor Valens at Adrianople, not, apparently, unhelped by the Huns: for not all the tribes of the nomads as yet acknowledged a single ruler. Nor did all the Huns appear exclusively later as the enemies of Romans, Goths or Persians: the new barbarians were divided among themselves and willing to ally themselves as mercenaries, and even to fight as mercenaries against each other. Those whom they served, and those

[1] F. Lot: *L'art militaire et les armées au moyen âge*, tom. i, p. 20.

whom they subjected, began to learn from them to fight as heavy cavalry; as, for instance, the Franks of central Germany. Even the Anglo-Saxon invaders of Britain, arriving as they did by sea, had as their leaders two Jutish warriors, named or nicknamed, Hengest and Horsa. Hengest is a 'horse' word with varying meanings: Horsa explains itself: and the names could scarcely have been given except in a tribe using and venerating the horse as an engine of war.

The Huns received very large tributes in gold and silver at times from the eastern emperor, at times from Aëtius or the ministers of the western emperor, who thus hoped to avoid or postpone attack. Some recent students of Hun society believe the Huns did not work the precious metals themselves, the difficulty of carrying about raw material and tools being too great: but what they lacked in their own crafts, they provided for themselves by loot, carpets from Persia, and the metal work of the Sarmatians, the Goths of the Crimea, and the Greeks. Both men and women wore much jewellery, brooches, torques and armlets, and they used the Greek (or Chinese) mirrors of polished metal. They helped to spread the nomad animal ornament among the Germanic races: the most frequently used reindeer with its horned hind as well as stag, and the frequently used bird of prey: from this creature came the beak-head ornaments, and such widely used forms as the bird of prey and the Daniel-in-the-lions'-den ornaments on the Sutton Hoo purse. One of the envoys of the Byzantine court to Attila, Priscus, describes the riches he found there: he came through 'tented houses' to the inner courts wherein were 'wooden houses put together elegantly of carved wood, some having beams of gilded wood'. Here were pavements covered with woollen tapestries and here lived Attila's wife.

In war, the nomads used powerful bows, shooting from the saddle: their equipment included also bow cases, sheath-knives, swords (and whetstones for sharpening them), javelins, shields and armour; on all these, and on their jewellery, the stylized animal ornament ranged from the sharply modelled reindeer to animals with Persian or Celtic hip and shoulder curls, and Persian and Chinese griffins and dragons. They used 'dragons' indeed for signalling between the bands of horsemen that rode the steppes: that is, they used dragon kites as standards. While in Europe the flying of kites (called after the forked-tail bird of that name) has been no more than a pastime, in Asia (China, Japan, Korea, Malaya, etc.) kite-flying was used in signalling and even in religious ceremonial. The Chinese concept of the dragon, as representing the animal world (part bird, part beast, part fish), was seen in concrete form in the flying kite, a creature with a mouth of metal through which the wind could stream, and a kite-tail, or body of cloth or paper. Europe got its concept of the dragon from the kite-flying Mongols, and even the Roman army, in the fourth century, adopted the light *draco* as the standard of the cohort.

The existence of this horde of steppe nomads threatened Asiatic civilizations at various times as well as European: and if the nomads detached Avars, Magyars, Bulgars and finally Turks in warfare with Europe, they attacked Asia as well. The Chinese, under the Han dynasty, drove certain nomads, the Hsiung Nu, out from China in the first century B.C., building walls and fortresses to keep them out; but the Han dynasty ended in 320, and rule in China was divided in the period of 'the Three Kingdoms' (320–589). The Hsiung Nu again pushed north-west into China and seized land north of the Yangtze, while the Chinese sought to push them back from the south. Though the Mongol dynasty did not prevail in China till 1280, there was ceaseless border warfare.

The west Germanic peoples first appear in written history as settled round the western extremity of the Baltic, in Sweden, Jutland, Sleswig-Holstein and the southern shores of the Baltic: this was, indeed, the home alike of the Goths, Scandinavians and the west Germanic peoples according to their own sagas and folk tales. Some of the west Germans moved south of the Baltic to the Rhine mouth in very early times. Caesar speaks of the Germans of the lower Rhine and Tacitus, writing his *Germania* in the year A.D. 98, describes them in the same region and along the south of the Baltic as a people just ceasing to be migratory hunters and reaching the agricultural stage. They had flocks and herds, ploughed a field for grain for a year or two and then left it fallow for a time to recover. The simplicity and loyalty of their tribal customs Tacitus compared very favourably with the political and social life of Rome: but here he is suspected of political bias. The pressure of these fair-haired, grey-eyed people on the Rhine frontier had, indeed, begun before his time and was continually more persistent. The legions of the Rhine could, however, in Tacitus' day, as yet resist them: their camps had become the rich trading towns or Cologne and Trier, and the capitalist Roman traders planted the vineyards on the Rhine to supply them with wine, rather than transport it from Italy. A flourishing trade was done across the Rhine frontier. In 258, however, a band of Alemans crossed the Rhine and succeeded in occupying Rhaetia; and another branch of the same race, the

Franks, attempting to conquer Gaul, were repulsed, but left settled bands there. The great home land of the Franks, on the right bank of the Rhine, was by this time the area later to be known as Franconia, the central duchy of medieval Germany, centring in the basin of the Main and the city of Frankfurt.

Meanwhile, while the west Germanic peoples were first moving southwards to the Rhine, the east Germanic peoples, including pre-eminently the Goths, had also moved southwards. They had come from Gothland, south Sweden, carrying from the cradle of their race the name Goths or Grentungi, as long ago as *c.* 500 to 300 B.C. They had now moved from the south shore of the Baltic and passed south-east of the Pripet marshes. By about A.D. 250 they had contact with the nomads of the steppes, and had founded a great, loosely compacted empire on the northern shore of the Black Sea, the river Dniester running through it. They had the Finns as their neighbours to the north-west, and to the east the Alans, a nomad tribe from Persia. They had also heard of the rich and civilized empire of the Romans south of them in the Balkans, and by A.D. 250 they moved south against them.

They were astonishingly successful, for they had apparently already learned from the nomads to fight as heavy cavalry. They killed the emperor Decius in a battle in the Dobrudja in 251, and pressed in 260 into the Balkans, unchecked by the emperor Valerian. They were not yet eager, apparently, to migrate in large bodies to the Balkans; in their extensive empire the Ostrogoths (or shining Goths) were settled round about Kerch, in the Crimea, and to the west of them, divided from them by the river Dniester, the Visigoths had an ample territory. By about 350 the whole of this loosely compacted empire was ruled by Ermanaric: a villain in saga, but strong and energetic; the Huns destroyed his kingdom in 376 and drove him in his old age to suicide. Athanaric, the *judex* of the Visigoths, also resisted the Huns in vain: his people in alarm poured south to the Danube and in 376 were allowed to settle: then, dissatisfied with the east Roman terms, or their keeping, and perhaps aided by a section of the Huns themselves, they defeated and killed the emperor Valens in 378, at Adrianople.

The Goths had won the battle of Adrianople by a charge of heavy cavalry, riding down the Roman infantry and the newly formed cavalry regiments. But against the Huns, their masters and teachers in the art of cavalry fighting, they could do nothing. The Ostrogoths north of the Black Sea pass out of history for a century, part remaining east of the Dniester in captivity to the Huns, part escaping and passing west of the Dniester. The work of the Christian missionary Wulfila, their 'priest and primate' as Jordanes called him, was mainly done before the separation of Ostrogoths and Visigoths: he died in 388.

The first great chapter in the history of the Visigoths was finished by the time Odovacar was made patrician in 476. Disturbed in their settlements south of the Danube by the raids of the Huns, whom the emperor Theodosius (378–395) could not stop from making settlements of their own in the northern Balkans, they pressed farther to the south. At the death of Theodosius, the Visigoths 'deprived of the customary gifts (of the eastern emperor), appointed Alaric to be king over them . . . for he was of famous stock, second only to that of the Amals, for he came from the family of the Balthi, who, because of their daring valour had long ago received among their race the name of Balthi, that is, "the Bold" '. Jordanes then relates how in the year 400 Alaric raised an army and entered Italy: he crossed the bridge over the river Candidianus at the third milestone from Ravenna.

The Visigothic conquest of north Italy occupied the years 400 to 410; for many summers, before 410, they came over the head of the Adriatic; and, when they had established themselves in north Italy, it took Alaric three summer sieges to take Rome, and his success was at least partly due to the death of Stilicho, executed by the order of Honorius in 408. There was no one to replace him: and when Alaric besieged Rome for the third summer in 410, he took it. The houses of the Roman nobles were plundered and burned, but no general massacre followed; Alaric, though an Arian, spared the churches and ancient monuments; for the Visigoths, regarding themselves as federates, if rebels, came against Rome as desiring a place in the Roman sun rather than as wishing to destroy her. But none the less the shock of the city's fall and the loss of prestige were very great: no such disaster had befallen Rome since the Gauls had sacked the city early in her history.

But though Alaric had Rome at his feet as a splendid prize, his people were peasants and desired grain-yielding lands rather than the olive groves, vineyards and restricted cornfields of Italy. Jordanes speaks of them before their entrance to Italy as 'not even knowing that vineyards existed anywhere: most of them drank milk'. Alaric noted how the grain ships that fed Rome came from Sicily and north Africa, of which the Vandals had not yet possessed themselves. He planned to cross to Africa and set about collecting transport: but his ships were wrecked in a storm and he himself died towards the end of 410. No lordly tomb in the Roman manner, no barrow in whose heart he might sit in his chair surrounded by his treasures, was possible for this conqueror whose people were leaving him in a hostile land: so they buried him in a river bed, his sepulchre unknown. Athaulf, his brother-in-law, succeeded him as king and as leader in the migration from Italy.

Athaulf's attitude to the Romans was one of intelligent admiration. He desired pre-eminence for the Goths, but he had no wish to replace Honorius as emperor of the west himself: he seems to have doubted whether his Goths could run so complex a concern as the Roman empire. He desired, however, that his people, as federates, should restore the vigour of the empire: he looked upon himself as a *restitutor orbis Romani*, though his brother-in-law's decision to vacate Italy held. Transport to Africa having failed, he desired to settle in the Roman province of the Rhone valley, or indeed to possess himself of all Gaul, the most Romanized part of the empire outside Italy. He led his Goths therefore from the toe of Italy, where he himself had been awaiting transport at Alaric's death, up through the narrow plains that lie between the Apennines and the western coast of the peninsula, through Turin, along the Mediterranean coast road to the Rhone mouth and Arles on the Rhone; then along the coast road to Barcelona, and, apparently misliking the aridity of the hills and valleys of Spain, he turned north again and recrossed the Pyrenees, this time at their northern end. By 412 he was in Toulouse, the future Visigothic capital.

Possibly Athaulf's vacation of Italy was purchased by the honourable marriage allowed him by the emperors. The fifth-century emperors, as those of Byzantium later, saw no objection to intermarriage of the royal house with barbarian leaders or nobles, provided they were of sufficient status and had some claims to civilized manners. The two sons of Theodosius, Arcadius and Honorius, had a step-sister, Galla Placidia, a very beautiful and able woman, who was to have an extraordinary influence on her generation: Athaulf captured her in Rome and carried her off into Gaul. At Narbonne he married her, without imperial permission or any imperial recognition of his own status. Difficulties over this action and the cutting of his communications by a Roman fleet seem to have occasioned his move into Spain; at Barcelona Galla Placidia bore him a son, who soon died. When Athaulf died in 415, he ruled part of Spain and two-thirds of Gaul; he had stood for the Gothic admiration for things Roman, but there was a conservative minority among the Goths who did not share his admiration. His death gave the anti-Roman minority their chance: their leader, the

Visigothic prince Sigeric, seized power, killed all Athaulf's children by an earlier marriage and ill-treated Galla Placidia, but he was murdered after a week's power by another noble, Wallia.

Galla Placidia was the subject of an agreement between Wallia and Rome in 415. She was to be sent back to Italy and corn supplies were to be sent to the Visigoths; in return, Wallia was recognized as federate ruler of Aquitaine (all modern France south of the Loire), and the Visigoths were to clear the Alans and Sueves from Gaul and Spain. The Roman provincials, in return for this benefit, had to suffer the Visigoths to be *hospitati* upon them: installed as patrons of their estates, receiving a third of their produce.

Galla Placidia's career was, however, only begun. She married the patrician Constantius, who became co-emperor with Honorius in 421, and when Honorius died in 423, she became for twenty-five years the real ruler of the west, during the reign of her negligible son, Valentinian III. The court lived in Ravenna, fairly safe from barbarian surprise or capture and their communications with Byzantium by sea safeguarded by the Byzantine fleet. Already the builders of Constantinople had adopted the domed roof from Mesopotamia for Christian buildings (see chap. XIII), and Galla Placidia's mausoleum in Ravenna, cruciform in plan and barrel vaulted, has a domed roof over the intersection of the arms and nave. This small church, its domed roof of blue and green studded with gold stars, and its mosaic of the Good Shepherd, adds to the charm of its proportions a splendour of colour which has survived the centuries. Galla Placidia lived less than a century after Constantine, but her mausoleum is eastern in form and colouring, as no doubt were the dress and manners of the court at Ravenna. Her career is an instance of the awkward mingling of the ruling classes of Roman and barbarian, and an example of Byzantine willingness to let a woman share in imperial rule. She died at Rome in 450.

Meanwhile, the Visigoths were founding a kingdom that included most of Gaul and Spain. Wallia ruled from the autumn of 415, his chief work for the preservation of Roman life being the clearing of the Alans from Spain, and the shutting of their friends, the Germanic Sueves, into the province of Galicia, the north-west corner of Spain. His successors prevented the Vandals from settling in any numbers in Gaul or Spain: Gaiseric, their leader, sailed for Africa in 429. The Visigoths also took the main share in repelling Attila at the battle of the Catalaunian fields in 451. By 476 they had possessed themselves of all Spain except Galicia, and when Romulus Augustulus was deposed, their king Euric was stronger than any other ruler in western Europe. His realm included the

Pyrenees, and his power was focussed in southern Gaul: Toulouse
was then, and usually, the Visigothic capital.

Another Germanic kingdom had also been formed in Gaul by
the Burgundians, a people who had moved southwards from the
Baltic towards the Rhine frontier before the Augustan period. Tall
and blond, they were reputed by the provincials to have stentorian
voices and enormous appetites; Jordanes says they were 'mild in
character, harsh in voice: and greased their hair with rancid butter'.
By 286 they were pressing against Mainz, where the emperor
Maximian organized a campaign against them. In the great westward expansion of the Huns in 405–6, they were driven across the
Rhine. In 413 some were allowed to settle as federates, south of the
Franks round Worms, Mainz and Speyer. But in 437 Aëtius, desiring to save Gaul, induced the Huns to attack and put an end to this
first Burgundian kingdom of Worms: the story survived as the historical basis of the epic of the Nibelungs. The survivors of the
catastrophe were, however, allowed to migrate south and settle in
443 in the basin of the upper Rhone; the district of Savoy became
the medieval Burgundy. In the disturbed period before Odovacar's
seizure of power, their king Gundobad held the commanding position in Roman politics left vacant by the death of his uncle, Ricimer the patrician, in 472. They were, as a people, Arians: but their
Catholic princess Clotilde was later to influence the fate of the
Franks by her marriage to Clovis, conqueror of Gaul.

These Franks flowed over the Rhine frontier when it had been
successively broken by the Vandals in 406, the Sueves in 409,
and the Burgundians. They had not, like the east Germanic or
Gothic tribes, long been subject to the influence of the east
Romans before they broke the frontier; they had in the past traded
with the legions of the Rhine, and even crossed the Rhine as early
as *c.* 350: but they were still heathen, had kings (or representatives
of the *cyn*, the royal *cyn*), and warrior nobles who formed their
comitatus, and who were grey-eyed, clean shaven, yellow haired,
and wore close-fitting tunics.

But if the Franks had had no commerce with the Greeks, they
had been influenced by another culture than that of their Roman
neighbours of the Rhine; they were in contact with the Huns, and
were expert horsemen. The Franks who pressed against the Rhine,
according to Gregory of Tours, when the British pretender to
empire, Maximus, was holding out in Aquileia, were only the
western fringes of a confederation of Germanic tribes whose homeland was the later duchy of Franconia. The basin of the Main,

flowing westward into the Rhine, was the focus of the land of the Franks when for twenty years Attila ruled an empire stretching from the Caspian to the Rhine; and before his time Franks and Huns were neighbours in central Europe.

After the penetration of the Rhine, the Franks settled within it in two bands, the Salian Franks (temporarily) in modern Belgium and Holland, and particularly between the rivers Moselle (Sala) and Scheldt. They became federates, and supplied Roman soldiery: the *Notitia Dignitatum* in its lists of legions, cohorts and *numeri*, speaks of the *Salii seniores* and the *Salii juniores*. The other band of Franks, the Ripuarians, strove to settle on the banks of the Rhine, around Cologne and Trier, and with such success that the administrative capital of Roman Gaul, long Trier, after the breaking of the frontier in 406 had to be moved to Arles. In 410 Honorius, hard pressed elsewhere, made a treaty with the Franks, both Salian and Ripuarian, and recognized their settlements.

They were still thus settled when Odovacar became patrician in 476: their next great forward movement, their great advance across north Gaul under Clovis, began ten years later in 486. As to their fate between 410 and 486: they were gathering strength, especially the Salian Franks, but they were to some extent controlled by the imperial ministers, Aëtius and Ricimer and king Gundobad, and advance westward was blocked by a representative of the Roman 'king' of Soissons. Tides of barbarians swirled across Gaul and across Britain, with intervals of Roman recovery, temporary only; what Ambrose Aurelianus and Arthur did obscurely in Britain, Aegidius and Syagrius did at Soissons and in its surrounding territory. Conditions among the Roman provincials in Gaul were disturbed, but not so disturbed, either in Gaul or Britain, but that bishop Germanus of Auxerre (in Aegidius' 'Roman kingdom' of Soissons) could visit Britain in 429 and (?) 447, to secure the province from the Pelagian heresy. Germanus had been a fine soldier before his consecration as bishop: finding the Britons harried by the Picts, he was well qualified to lead them in the campaign where they gained the Alleluia victory, in 429: when the moneyers wished to put a suitable image of him on the coins of his mint, they selected for the verso the die of an emperor on horseback, merely drawing a symbolic halo round his head. Gaul seemed in a turmoil, with the passage of barbarians through her, and their settlements and negotiations within: but not in such a turmoil but that Germanus could visit Galla Placidia and the emperor Valentinian at Ravenna in 448, to negotiate about the terms of settlement of the barbarians in Gaul. He died at Ravenna that year, and his followers brought his body back to Auxerre for burial; everywhere his body rested on the journey they set up *signa crucis*. It is an example of Byzantine influence working through Ravenna: Helena had discovered the Lord's cross in the Holy Land, and churches were already built cruciform in the east and in Ravenna: but it was a hundred years before Justin I should send a relic of the holy cross to Poitiers, and the Irish begin to mark the place of burial with the Lord's cross, set up on a tall, slender pyramid of stone.

Meanwhile, and before Odovacar took Ravenna in 476, other branches of the Germanic tribes, close in custom, language and race to the Franks, began the invasion of Britain. These were the Angles, Saxons and Jutes, from the region round the bay of Heligoland, and the Rhine mouth, and from the hinterlands of these coasts. Hengest and Horsa were invited by the Vortigerna, a Welsh overking of Britain, to come as his *foederati* to defend Britain from the Picts, and possibly himself from other rivals for leadership. They came in three ships in 449, received land in Kent, were dissatisfied with their reward, and fought against the Vortigerna and the Romano-British provincials, establishing their headquarters in Canterbury. Other bands followed, and though the Celtic warleader Arthur held up the Saxon advance for a generation between 516 and 537, they were in possession of most of 'England' by the end of the sixth century.

BIBLIOGRAPHICAL NOTE

For the barbarian settlements in Europe, see F. Lot, *Les Invasions Germaniques*, 1945 ed., and *Les Invasions Barbares et le peuplement de l'Europe*, 2 vols., 1937; L. Halphen, *Les Barbares*, 1926: J. M. Wallace-Hadrill, *The Barbarian West, 400–1000*, 1952, particularly useful for the Franks and Lombards: F. Vercauteren, 'Étude sur les civitates de la Belgique seconde', in Acad. royale de Belgique, Classe des lettres, Mémoires, sér. 2, vol. 33, 1934, an illuminating essay on the transformation of Roman institutions under barbarian attack in this province: for the Germanic invaders, P. Grierson, 'Election and inheritance in early Germanic kingship', *Camb. Hist. Journ.*, vol. vii, 1941. For the nomad invaders, R. Grousset, *L'empire des steppes*, 1939, E. A. Thompson, *A History of Attila and the Huns*, 1948, and *The Historical Work of Ammianus Marcellinus*, 1947: E. H. Minns, 'Art of the northern nomads', *Proc. Brit. Acad.*, 1942: for the effect on the Roman army of the shoeing, saddling, etc. of their horses by the nomads, F. Lot, *L'art militaire et les armées au moyen âge*, tom. 1, 1946. See also, L. Musset, *Les Invasions : Les vagues Germaniques*, Paris, 1965; H. Trevor-Roper, *The Rise of Christian Europe*, London, 1965.

CHAPTER III

THE OSTROGOTHS IN ITALY

THE undisturbed rule of Odovacar and his Rugians (Scyrrians) in Italy lasted only thirteen years, 476 to 489, but it laid foundations for that of the Ostrogoths: the shock of having a class of barbarian federates superimposed on their landowning class fell upon the Roman provincials under Odovacar, and was merely continued by Theoderic. For our knowledge of both régimes we owe much to Cassiodorus, and should owe more had not the text of his twelve books of the *History of the Goths* perished, except for a meagre digest preserved in Jordanes' *Getica*.

Flavius Magnus Aurelius Cassiodorus Senator (477–570) belonged to one of those families who had held high civil office both under the later emperors and the Germanic conquerors; his grandfather had been the friend of Aëtius and notary to Valentinian III, his father filled high office under Odovacar and Theoderic, governed Sicily as *consularis*, administered his native provinces of Lucania and Bruttii as *corrector*, and from 503 to 507 held the splendid post of praetorian prefect. Cassiodorus himself was scholar-minister to Theoderic. He became *quaestor sacri palatii* (for court titles at Ravenna followed those of Byzantium) soon after 500, then patrician, *consul ordinarius* in 514 and finally *magister officiorum*, which office he held in 526 when Theoderic died. He resigned it when he became praetorian prefect in 533–4, and pronounced the public eulogy on Theodohad when he succeeded Athalaric in 534. He held office again under Witigis: and when the Goths were overcome by the Greeks, Cassiodorus retired to his family estates at Squillace and there founded a monastery of scholar-monks. He lived to be a very old man, dying in his ninety-third year. He had sought to preserve the old Roman amenities in the new Germanic Italy, the old Latin written instrument among barbarians who gave oral orders; he undertook the formidable task of summarizing the old Latin and Greek liberal arts; he was the patron of the monastic life, newly brought to Italy from the east; and he seems to have been at heart something of a naturalist. On some occasions at least he added to the substance of a letter dealing with some administrative matter, a brief discourse on the habits of the nautilus or some other creature, excusing himself on the ground that he had a good large sheet of clean papyrus before him. It is very hard that Cassiodorus' twelve books of Gothic history should have been lost; he tells us in his 'book of various letters' (*Variae*) that he did write them, and it would have been of great interest to see how he dealt with the Gothic history that must have been largely transmitted orally; as it is, he tells us that he rejected the oral tradition that the Goths had actually fought in (? raided) Britain, been reduced to servitude, and ransomed at a price.

In fact, the lives of Cassiodorus and his family show the old senatorial class striving to make the best of Germanic rule in Italy and save the Roman culture and tradition. Odovacar had, in fact, ruled Italy by the grudging consent of the east Roman emperor Zeno, though he himself imposed taxes, appointed officials, concerned himself with the election of bishops and made war and peace. His constitutional position was ambiguous, as was inevitable in the case of a barbarian 'king' ruling in Italy. Jordanes describes him as already 'king of the Torcilingi' when he invaded Italy at the head of the Scyrrii, Heruli and other allies of various races: he was king, that is, of a tribe, for regional kingship was as yet unknown. In Italy, he was, strictly, patrician; but his official scribes spoke of his royal, not his patrician, magnificence. He ruled Italy and Noricum, the Balkan province across the head of the Adriatic.

Meanwhile, the collapse of Attila's empire after his abortive raid of 451 had freed the Ostrogoths from subjection; the Huns had been ruled by *primates* before Attila had attained a personal tyranny over them, and after he had suffocated in his drunken sleep beside his bride, his sons divided up the subject peoples like family property, hoping to retain the Hunnish supremacy. But, from central Europe to the steppes, the subject peoples revolted, a decisive battle being fought in Pannonia in 455, and the Hunnish empire fell apart. It was not possible for the war-leaders of the Huns in the dozen years or so after Attila's death to build up an empire again on the steppes: other warlike nomads were too strong there; the Avars, now heard of for the first time, were themselves pressing westward towards the empire. The remnants of the Huns became mere raiders on the borders of the empire.

The Ostrogoths, some of whom had been allowed to settle in Hungary by Theodosius, had been even there dominated by the Huns, and fought for Attila as his subject allies at the Catalaunian Fields; but they took a prominent part in the revolt of his subjects after his death, and freed themselves. In 471 Theo-

deric (a Germanization of the Greek Theodoric: like Theuderich
and Dietrich) became one of the Ostrogothic chieftains; he had
been sent as a hostage in his eighth year to Byzantium and when
brought to the emperor Leo, being a very goodly child, he won
the imperial favour. He must have learned something of *Romanitas*
in his ten years spent at the eastern court: he never learned to
write, but that, after all, was the business of a notary, not a Gothic
chieftain. It sufficed Theoderic to trace *legi* on his official acts
later through a golden stencil.

He was sent back to his father Theodemer by the emperor Leo
at the age of eighteen with gifts, perhaps in the hope of restraining
the plundering raids of the now free Goths: but Theoderic and
his father still raided and plundered the cities of Thessaly: 'peace
was distasteful to men for whom war had long furnished the
necessities of life'. They led an army to Salonika, and the Roman
general gained a truce with them by handing over certain cities.
Soon after, Theodemer died, and the emperor Zeno hoped to
avert further Ostrogothic encroachment by playing off Theoderic
against Theoderic Strabo, another Ostrogothic noble who led a
band of federates in the Roman army.

In 478 Theoderic was invited to visit Zeno, received with
honour, given the title of consul, and honoured by the setting up
of his equestrian statue before the palace; but the young chieftain,
living in honour and winning the ascendancy over the rival Theoderic, was uneasy at rumours that his Goths in Illyricum were not
yet content. He made a suggestion to which Zeno was not unwilling to listen, for it would remove the Goths from the Balkans.
He asked permission to conquer 'the western country . . . long
ago governed by the rule of your ancestors and that city which was
the head and mistress of the world. Wherefore is it now shaken by
the tyranny of the Torcilingi and the Rugii? Send me there with
my race.'

Zeno had no desire to uphold Odovacar: and apparently no
scruple at exposing Italy to civil war between rival barbarian
hosts: he let Theoderic go, with letters commending him to the
senate and the Roman people: he gave him the rank of *magister
militum* and patrician. In 488 Theoderic set out for the head of the
Adriatic 'with the whole tribe of the Goths'. He defeated Odovacar on the Adda in 490; the senate accepted him; for two years he
dealt with such of the north Italian towns as continued to support
Odovacar, and for three he besieged him in the strongly fortified
city of Ravenna. He could not attack the city from the sea, for he
had no fleet; he could not find and take the long narrow causeway,

among the reeds and water lilies, by which alone the city could be approached from the land. He came to terms with Odovacar, promising to divide the rule of Italy with him, but intending treachery; ten days later he invited him to a feast, and himself slew his guest with a single sweeping blow of the sword. 'Thou didst thus to my friends,' said Theoderic, relapsing from his Arian Christianity to the duty of vengeance according to the Germanic blood feud.

Theoderic's position in Italy was a dual one, but more clearly defined than that of Odovacar. His Gothic warriors had hailed him as king: he was king of the Goths in Italy, not, of course, of the Romans in Italy, or of Italy as a territory. His Gothic nobles, *saiones*, like the Anglo-Saxon *gesiths*, served at his court, did his errands, and acted as his bodyguard in battle; they seem to have been the Gothic equivalent of the Roman *agentes in rebus*. Among his Gothic subjects, the old Germanic customary law held, modified in respects involving Christian practice (like the duty of the blood feud) by Theoderic's written edicts. With regard to the maintenance of his followers, these stepped into the shoes of Odovacar's federates, taking the third of the produce of the landed estate on which they were *hospitati*; their numbers, even although the whole tribe followed Theoderic, must have been small compared to those of the Roman provincials, with whom, by Roman law as it stood, they were not allowed to intermarry. The army and its officers remained purely Gothic, as was to be expected, since the *raison d'être* of the Gothic federates in Italy was their military defence of the Roman lands.

Theoderic was, at first, in a strong position with regard to the Roman provincials. He was a Roman citizen, adding Flavius to his own name to signify a kind of semi-adoption into the *gens Flavia*. He wrote to the emperor as son and servant; *ego qui sum servus vester et filius*: and spoke in one letter of his kingdom as 'an imitation of yours, a copy of your unique empire'. He added that, if his Goths lagged behind the emperor's subjects, yet they far outstripped other races: 'affection is added to the venerable name of Rome'.

In other respects he, or his notaries and officials, were careful not to infringe the imperial rights. His gold coins, struck at Ravenna, Rome and Milan, bore the emperor's name, not his own; on the reverse there was sometimes Theoderic's monogram. He made no *leges*, such as those of the emperor, only issuing *edicta* as occasions arose. He used the old respectful address to the senate: *Patres Conscripti*. Strategic reasons and long usage may have dictated his keeping his court at Ravenna, not at Rome: but the decision was acceptable to a distant emperor, the senate and the Catholics. He went there once only on a visit, in the year 500, gave a feast and returned. But though claiming no imperial rights over the city, he took care, as a Roman magistrate, to provision it; Sicily was included in his dominion and the Sicilian cornlands were still at his disposal, though the Vandals had taken Africa, Sardinia and Corsica. In addition, he repaired the Roman aqueducts and paid the salaries of the rhetors as of old; the sons of Roman provincials could still prepare for the civil service by attendance at their schools.

Theoderic's maintenance of the whole fabric of Roman civil life for the provincials was perhaps occasioned by his knowledge of and veneration for *civilitas*, for the Roman life he had known at Constantinople; but would seem to have been, in any case, inevitable. In view of the small numbers of the Goths, it was not possible to reduce provincials who had lived under the complex and subtle Roman law, with centuries of development behind it, with lawyers and law courts and legal *formulae* and a fairly plentiful supply of papyrus for writing, both commercial and legal— to reduce such people to living under Germanic tribal law, with its equally subtle but much more primitive wergelds, tariffs for injuries, and system of personal status and protection. Theoderic's local government was therefore carried out by the old Roman officials, headed, as of old, by counts of his appointment: the Roman civil service, the Roman law courts remained. Theoderic's *comes gothorum* tried cases between two Goths or between Goths and Romans, protected Romans from abuse by the Gothic *domini*, and inquired into administrative abuses.

Throughout the whole of Italy, and even in his court of Ravenna, the headquarters of his government, Theoderic followed the precedent of the late imperial offices and titles. The officers of the *Notitia Dignitatum*, compiled by some clerk of the imperial bureaux in the first half of the fifth century, appear again as the recipients of royal commissions in the *formulae* written by Cassiodorus in the sixth and seventh books of his *Variae*. Certain Byzantine titles appearing in the *formulae* were either used by the Roman government in the period intervening between the compilation of the *Notitia* and the beginning of Theoderic's rule, or borrowed in his time from Byzantium. The list of the forty-seven *formulae* supplies in itself a terse and accurate description of Theoderic's machine of government.

Selecting from it, and from Cassiodorus' eloquently chatty summing-up in each *formula* of the duties and honourable nature of the office, it appears that the consul of the year was expected, not to govern, but to supply state entertainment on a grand scale: 'we have the labours,' Theoderic's commission runs, 'you the joys of your office . . . Wear your *tunica palmata*, go forth from your home in your golden sandals, mount your curule chair with its many steps to show the magnificence of your office: we rule and take counsel, but you as consul give your name to the year. . . . Spare not then your private fortune.'

While the consulship was honorary and expensive, and the patriciate an honourable status entailing no definite duties, the post of praetorian prefect was the summit of office, entailing the active rule of Italy under Theoderic. 'It is a kind of priesthood', the *formula* states, 'to fulfil worthily the high office of praetorian prefect.' Of the four praetorian prefectures in the scheme of Diocletian, those of Illyricum and Africa had lapsed, and that of the Gauls was filled by Theoderic only when he seized Provence after the death of Alaric II. Beneath the praetorian prefect, the prefect of the city ruled Rome and a region a hundred miles beyond; he had as subordinate the vicar of the city, who had a court of his own and wore the military *chlamys*.

At Ravenna itself, the *magister officiorum* headed the administration. He controlled the minor court officials, the soldiers of the royal household, the reception of foreign embassies and the conduct of foreign affairs, the *cursus publicus*, and the buying of the food supply. Under him worked the counts (*comitiaci*), the old *agentes in rebus* under a newer name: they supervised provincial officials and various government departments. The count of the sacred largesses was also *primicerius* of the notaries, who were divided (as in the *Notitia*) into four bureaux or *scrinia* (*memoriae, dispositionum, epistolarum*, and *libellarum*); he not only controlled the royal disbursements, but those who brought goods to Italian shores, and merchants 'who supply the necessities of life . . . For let whatever in garments, whatever in bronze, whatever in silver, whatever in gems human ambition holds precious be subject to your orders, and let those who come from the extreme ends of the earth flock to your judgment seat.' The *comes privatarum* and the *comes patrimonii* accounted for and administered the royal demesnes and the private property of the sovereign; the *comes primi ordinis*, though not *illustris* himself, headed the next rank, the *spectabiles*, and was summoned to the royal council or consistory; the count of Syracuse and the count of Naples had local rule. The count of the port of Rome had, as the *formula* informs him, a delightful post: for he could watch the approach of a multitude of ships and the sail-studded ocean bringing the pilgrim peoples: safe himself, how many fine spectacles of sweet things he would see! He must arrange for this traffic, and if offerings and gifts were made to him, he must receive them in moderation. *Formulae* are also provided for the appointment of the count of the Goths, a count of a province, and of certain cities; and also for the 'count of the physicians', *comes archiatrorum*, who had the right of entry to the royal palace, and even to enjoin fasts upon the sovereign in the name of health.

Among the *illustres*, the fifteen or so greatest men in the kingdom, the *quaestor* at Ravenna, always an eloquent lawyer, 'spoke with the voice of the sovereign', and must defend both the sovereign and the various departments with his eloquence; he must advise the king when lawsuits were brought before him, as well as acting, as it were, as public relations officer and attorney general.

The backbone of the Ostrogothic administration, as well as that of the contemporary Germanic rulers, the emperor at Constantinople, the pope at Rome, the patriarch at Constantinople, and all great churches, was the notariat. The official scribes of the old Roman law courts, versed in legal *formulae* and able to authenticate a document by their individual professional signature, formed the four *scrinia* at Ravenna, and the Cassiodoran *formula* emphasized the secrecy needed for their work, though they were not yet technically called secretaries. 'All that we do is public, but many things must not be known till they are ready for publication . . . where many eyes are looking, there is it more necessary for many things to be unknown.' Notaries must be like those chests where archives are stored: when the settlement of any point is needed, then they speak; otherwise, they maintain complete silence, like wise men who know nothing (*quasi nesciant scientes*). Though the office of referendary was used at Theoderic's court, and though the *formula* used suggests that the holder would need to have had notarial training, the referendary does not appear to have exercised any headship of a *scrinium*, or to have authenticated documents, as among the Franks; the *formula* enjoins that he shall question litigants and petitioners before the sovereign, and set forth to him the questions at issue, that justice may be done: or even bring accusations of treason, as the referendary Cyprian in the case of Albinus (see p. 43).

It would be, probably, unfair to Theoderic to represent his tolerance of Catholic bishops and practice in Italy as merely a policy of continuing and authorizing the *status quo*, for his famous observation that religious belief cannot be compelled breathes

Byzantine intellectual tolerance, and must be accepted as a genuine personal judgment. 'We cannot order a religion,' Cassiodorus makes him say, 'because no one is forced to believe against his will.' But again, it would hardly have been possible to compel the Roman provincials to attend a Greek or Gothic mass, or to supply Gothic priests for them. The difference between Arian and Catholic at the council of Nicaea had been argued by the acute minds of Greek theologians, realizing the implications of doctrinal definitions; the difference between the newly settled Gothic Arians and the provincial Catholics must have been one of practice. The Goths had bishops and priests: but it is difficult to see how, in the passage of the Gothic people from south Russia through the Balkans, they can have been territorial officers, or been able to acquire much learning. The missionary Christianity of Wulfila must have developed in isolation among a warlike and barely settled people, and the only Christian contacts the Goths would have made must have been with the Greeks. To leave the provincials with their own churches and clergy must have been as natural as to leave them with their own law courts; and, till suspicions of Catholic loyalty to the régime arose at the end of his life, Theoderic did so. The grave and orderly antiphonal singing practised by St Ambrose's clergy in Milan remained undisturbed; the grave, simple and very lengthy rendering of canticles and 'the Ambrosian hymn' suffered no eclipse under Theoderic.

In some respects, particularly that of foreign affairs, Theoderic's position resembled much more that of a Stilicho or a Ricimer, with a general competence in west European affairs, than that of a barbarian king in the west like Clovis or Alaric II. Theoderic regarded himself as the emperor's representative, and in some sense the western emperor's successor in Italy, a position that gave him as it were a protectorate over the other Germanic kings. These formed, till the conversion of Clovis to Catholic Christianity, a ring of Arian sovereigns round Italy; the accession of the Franks to Catholicism added religious difference to political rivalry. After the battle of the 'campus Vogladensis' in 507, when the Franks defeated the Visigoths, Theoderic expended much effort to avert the danger that the Franks might reach the Mediterranean, keep the Visigoths under political dominance, and upset his own political primacy in western Europe.

He took specific measures to prevent this, notably in maintaining the corridor along the French Mediterranean coast to secure Italian communication with Toulouse; in appointing the Ostrogoth count Theudis, as regent, to rule Visigothic Spain from Narbonne in the name of Theoderic's young grandson; and in supporting the enemies of the Franks. He welcomed the refugee Alemans after their defeat by the Franks; and, on the Frankish borders, he protected the Thuringians and the Heruli as their suzerain.

Theoderic buttressed his policy of suzerainty by a system of alliance by marriage. In 493, when, as Jordanes says, he 'laid aside the garb of a private citizen and assumed a royal mantle', he sent an embassy to Clovis, king of the Franks, probably in 495, and 'asked for his sister, Audofleda, in marriage, which was granted. But the Franks, none the less, continued to fight the Goths and each other'. Audofleda was apparently a pagan before her marriage: she was baptized by an Arian bishop on becoming Theoderic's queen; she had no son, but her daughter, Amalasuntha, was trained by Roman tutors in the lore of Roman literature and *civilitas*. Again, Theoderic married his sister Amalafrida to Thrasamund, king of the Vandals, one daughter to the Burgundian prince Sigismund and another to the Visigothic king, Alaric II. Strengthened by such dynastic alliances, Italy had, under Theoderic, a kind of hegemony of the west for the first quarter of the sixth century.

Described by the pen of an official panegyrist, such as Cassiodorus, or by the other historical source for Theoderic's reign, the Anonymus Valesii, the Ostrogothic rule in Italy, mild, tolerant and respectful of tradition, deserved permanence. That it nevertheless lasted only some sixty years may be attributed perhaps to four causes: the division between Arian and Catholic, the permanent threat of reconquest by the constitutionally supreme emperor at Constantinople, the ambition and ability of Justinian, and, above all, the fact that Theoderic had no male heir, or male relative of great ability.

In 515 he tried to obviate his lack of a son by summoning from Spain a young Visigothic prince, Eutharic, and marrying him to Amalasuntha. In 519 this prince consort held the consulship in the same year as the emperor Justin, a great honour: and magnificent games and combats were celebrated at Rome and Ravenna. A son and a daughter were born of this marriage, but Eutharic soon died, leaving his wife with no protector but her father. In 526 Theoderic presented his nine-year-old grandson, Athalaric, to the Gothic nobles, and proclaimed him their future king: but both the internal and external peace of his kingdom was already threatened.

In the first place, the emperor who had succeeded Anastasius in 518 was Justin, an illiterate Illyrian soldier who had risen through his own ability to high office, but a firm Catholic: the senatorial and Catholic class in Italy could now look to an outside protector in difficulty. This was the more dangerous to Theoderic as Justin succeeded in healing the schism which for thirty-five years divided the sees of Rome and Constantinople. Visigothic Arianism, again, was less tolerant than Ostrogothic, and the Visigothic Eutharic is suspected of having influenced Theoderic's policy in the direction of harshness to the Catholics in Italy. So far, the Catholic churches, even in Ravenna, had been left to the Catholic bishops, though Theoderic built a great church, now St Apollinare Nuovo, which served both as his palatine chapel, and as the Arian cathedral, and some other churches for the Arians. For a reason unknown to us, suspicions of treason of some sort, Theoderic late in his reign ordered the Catholic church of St Stephen in the suburbs of Verona to be destroyed.

Good relations between the king and his Roman subjects were further worsened by difficulties over the Jews, to whom all the Arian sovereigns were more tolerant than the Catholic. At Rome, Milan and Ravenna mob violence injured the Jews, and at Rome even destroyed a Jewish synagogue. Theoderic then imposed a tax on all the Christian citizens of Ravenna, to pay for the damage, addressing his order to Eutharic and the bishop, and arousing much resentment. Even the Roman senate were now wavering in their loyalty, and Theoderic in alarm forbade any Roman provincial to wear arms, or even small knives.

Cassiodorus in these years was Theoderic's *magister officiorum* at Ravenna: the senators at Rome found no leader of their discontent in him. But there were other Roman nobles of equally high birth willing to take a risk, notably two of the *gens Anicia*, Symmachus and Boethius. Symmachus' ancestor of the same name had taken the lead in the defence of a dying paganism, requesting the emperor not to remove the Altar of Victory from the senate house; the present Symmachus had been prefect of the city under Theoderic and was now patrician and chief of the senate (*caput senatus*); he was old, rich, venerated and generous. Boethius had been educated by him, had married his daughter, and rivalled or even excelled Cassiodorus as philosopher, orator and exponent of the liberal arts. Theoderic had consulted him about the making of a water-clock and sundial, to be presents to the king of Burgundy, and showed the esteem in which he held him by raising both his sons to the consulship. Up to 523, that is, both Symmachus and Boethius had joined with Cassiodorus and the senatorial party in general in trying to make the Gothic régime work.

The year 523 is the watershed of Theoderic's reign. The referendary (see p. 39) Cyprian, who had lately made an embassy to Constantinople, accused the patrician Albinus of having treasonable correspondence with the Byzantine emperor, and in the debate that followed, Boethius declared the charge false: 'Whatever Albinus did, I and the whole senate of Rome did the same. The charge is false.' Cyprian then included Boethius and other noble Romans in the charge, curiously described as 'desiring the safety of the senate', adding to that against Boethius an additional charge of 'sacrilege and necromancy'. Mathematics and astronomy, the crown of the liberal arts and Boethius' special field of study, were already, it would seem, regarded as perilously akin to magic. Boethius and Albinus were imprisoned at Pavia, and Boethius was condemned after a hurried and unjust trial in the Roman senate: fear of Theoderic's wrath eclipsed loyalty to their own order. For some months Boethius languished in prison, enduring with the calm of a good Stoic the reversal of his fortunes and the prospect of death; in those months he wrote the *Consolation of Philosophy* that was to be one of the fundamental books of the Christian middle ages; and in 524, in prison, he met his reputedly barbarous end.

Theoderic's danger was now real: Justin in Constantinople took their churches from the Arians and gave them to the Catholics, and forcibly converted certain Arians; and Theoderic's own subjects looked to him as able to displace Theoderic, as once an emperor had displaced Odovacar. Theoderic hastily summoned pope John I to come to Ravenna and ordered him to go to Constantinople and tell Justin that 'he must in no wise attempt to win over those whom he calls heretics to the Catholic religion': a difficult embassy. The pope, taking with him the bishop of Ravenna, three senators and other bishops and nobles, set out in 525, and was received with veneration by the populace of Constantinople, and with the formal gestures of adoration by Justin himself, whom he crowned with great magnificence. The interview between pope and emperor was private, and followed by some lessening of the persecution of the Arians and restoration of some of their churches: but to the restoration of the converted Arians to their original belief Justin would not agree.

The moderate success achieved by the embassy, and the news of the rapprochement between the pope and Justin, was treated by Theoderic as a dangerous reverse. He threw the whole embassy into prison, and there pope John died, on 25 May 526; Symmachus also, as a probable sympathizer, was imprisoned in Ravenna and put to death. At this dangerous juncture, the young Athalaric was presented as Theoderic's successor; and on 26 August, after a three days' illness, Theoderic died. All the Catholic churches of Italy were to have been given up to the Arians on 30 August 526.

The Gothic wars which followed his death destroyed not only the Ostrogoths as a nation, but that old Roman traditional culture which the senatorial party, and pre-eminently Cassiodorus, had striven to preserve. The second half of the sixth century saw the dying out of the senatorial class in Italy, and the traditions that it stood for: in so far as these did not pass over into the keeping of the bishop of Rome and other Catholic bishops. The late Roman magistrate had been accompanied ceremonially by torchbearers, and to the Christian bishop in the age of Constantine his subjects could show no less respect; the Christian bishop also had his torchbearer. But when the Christian bishop from that time throughout the middle ages was accompanied by his acolyte or acolytes with lights, it was no accident, but a symbol: for here walked, not only the shepherd of souls, but the Roman magistrate.

The occasion of the Gothic wars, when the East Roman empire recovered the metropolitan lands of Italy, was closely connected with the succession difficulty. The young Athalaric became king, with his mother Amalasuntha for regent, and with Cassiodorus, as master of offices, apparently holding the helm. When, six years later, in 533, king Athalaric presented Cassiodorus to the senate for the praetorian prefectship, with a panegyric address apparently written by Cassiodorus himself, he said of him:

> In the early days of our reign what labour he gave to the settling of our affairs! He alone was sufficient for all. The duty of making public harangues, our private counsels, required him; he laboured that the empire might have rest. We found him *magister officiorum*; but he discharged the duties of *quaestor*, and willingly bestowed on us, the heir, the experience which he had gained in the counsels of our grandfather . . . he helped the beginning of our reign both with his arms and with his pen. For when the care of our shores occupied our royal meditation, he suddenly emerged from the seclusion of his study, boldly, like his ancestors, assumed the office of general, and triumphed . . . For he maintained the Gothic warriors at his own charges, so that there should be no robbery of the provincials on the one hand, nor too heavy burden on the exchequer on the other . . . Then, when the time for victualling the ships was over . . . he shone as an adminis-

trator rather than a warrior, healing, without injury to the litigants, the various suits which arose out of the sudden cessation of contracts.

Amalasuntha, learned lady as she was and reader of Vergil and Sophocles, was no statesman: she first ordered the murder of three Gothic nobles whom she suspected, and then, to strengthen her position on the death of Athalaric, took as partner in the government of her kingdom her cousin Theodohad, the nearest male heir of Theoderic. But she had reckoned without the Germanic blood-feud: Theodohad, in vengeance for the three murdered nobles, imprisoned her, and allowed their kinsmen to murder her in her bath.

Amalasuntha had, before her death, been negotiating with the Greek emperor Justinian to surrender Italy to him and herself take refuge with him at Byzantium; he had even sent the ex-consul Peter to arrange the transfer of power. The news of Amalasuntha's murder greeted Peter on his arrival: in the emperor's name he proclaimed a war of vengeance. Rome and south Italy appeared more likely to the Greeks to approve this change of masters than north Italy: and while Cassiodorus carried on the Gothic government, as master of offices, for Theodohad at Ravenna, Justinian in 536 sent count Belisarius to Naples, which he captured. His forces then threatened Rome, and in the north the Goths deposed Theodohad and elected Witigis, who married Theoderic's granddaughter Matsuentha. Of this change Cassiodorus approved, continuing to hold office.

In 537 Belisarius took Rome and held it through a notable siege, from March 537 to March 538. He took Ravenna in 540, imprisoning Witigis and appointing Fidelis praetorian prefect with the emperor's consent; Cassiodorus was allowed to retire from public life. The war seemed to have ended with a Greek victory.

But the spirit of Gothic resistance was not dead, and in 542 and 543 it flared up into revolt under Totila, who in 546 even captured Rome. Meanwhile the leaders of the old senatorial party, now anti-Gothic, had fled for refuge to Sicily; they included Liberius, who had testified to Justinian of the wrongs done to Amalasuntha, pope Vigilius, and Cassiodorus; when Totila appeared in Sicily, they fled for refuge to Constantinople. In 550 Justinian appointed Germanus general for a fresh reconquest of Italy, to march by the northern route used by Theoderic himself against Ravenna. Germanus married Matsuentha, the widow of Witigis, but died at the end of 550. It was left to the eunuch Narses, already seventy-four years old, to reconquer Italy; only four Italian cities, including Ravenna, and most of Sicily, were

holding out in the imperial cause, and the Gothic army under
Totila rode at large in the countryside. Narses entered Ravenna,
and rode out, down the old Via Flaminia towards Rome. South-
west of Ancona, where the old Roman road crosses the Apennines, he met and defeated the Gothic army; Totila himself was
killed.

Italy was restored to the Roman empire; but word was brought
back to the Germanic barbarians by certain Lombard federates
fighting as part of Narses' army in Italy: and sixteen years later,
in 568, the Lombards were to win back what the Ostrogoths had
lost.

In describing the life of Ostrogothic Italy, the evidence about
the Roman provincials and their institutions is more plentiful
than that for the arts and customs of the Goths, which is, in fact,
limited to the grave-finds of a few cemeteries, a few splendid pieces
of Ostrogothic jewellery (as, for instance, those of the Cesena
treasure), and the casual allusions in sixth-century writers. The
treasure found at Cesena, some twenty miles south of Ravenna,
where the imperial tradition was strong, but subject to barbarian
pressure, may be regarded as the product of Ostrogothic Italy
just before the death of Theoderic in 526. These splendid pieces
of barbarian gold jewellery, inlaid with garnet cloisonné, include
an elaborate earring and hairpin, pendants, sheaths for small
knives in filigree, and two breast ornaments in cloisonné. On
these the Latin cross is inlaid with garnets and flanked by fishes,
commonly used as a Christian symbol, the Greek word 'fish'
(ichthus) being formed of the initial letters of 'Jesus Christ, Son of
God, Saviour'. But the number of Ostrogothic finds thus clearly to
be distinguished from Lombard ones is small; moreover the Ostrogoths, being Christians, did not bury with so many grave-goods as
the pagan Anglo-Saxons or Scandinavians. Nils Åberg says of their
art that under Theoderic 'a popular Gothic style, with its roots in
south Russia, and points of contact with the Germanic world on the
other side of the Alps, came to stand side by side with a Gothic
court art which was no longer Germanic, but Roman and Byzantine: on the one hand, the grave-finds of Gothic brooches, buckles
and garnet work, and, on the other, Theoderic's palace buildings
and churches, mosaics, and works in marble, ivory diptychs and
magnificent manuscripts. The contrast between the barbarian and
the Roman was too great for the gulf to be bridged over, or for
the two worlds to merge.'

When Theoderic built, he built in the East Roman manner:

great basilican, colonnaded churches, with mosaic friezes, and a domed roof over the apse, also splendid with mosaics. One basilica richly adorned with mosaics, he had dedicated to Christ the Saviour; when Ravenna passed to the Byzantines, they rededicated it to St Martin, the apostle of Gaul, and it was known as the church of St Martin, *in coelo aureo* from its golden ceiling. The mosaics above the arcade of the nave, probably dealing with subjects connected with Theoderic, Justinian had destroyed and replaced, on the one side by a procession of virgin martyrs, starting from a representation of Classis, the port of Ravenna, and ending before the Virgin Mother and her Child, enthroned in glory; on the other, by a procession of male martyrs starting from Theoderic's *palatium* at Ravenna, each martyr offering his crown of suffering to the martyred Christ. The Arian baptistery, a small octagonal building, has a mosaic of the baptism of Christ, with an old river god standing in the water beside St John the Baptist: the early Christian exorcisms, still used in the ritual for the blessing of holy water, were at this early period clearly needed, before the use of water for baptism from a stream regarded as sacred to some nymph or river god.

The patron saint of Ravenna was its first bishop St Apollinaris, a Syrian who had actually preached and been buried in Classis, where the early bishops of the see continued to be buried. In accordance with Roman civil law, he had been buried, not in any building, but in a cemetery; when Justinian's bishop replaced the small oratory in the cemetery by a fine basilica (549), he was reburied in the narthex. The apsidal mosaic of the church of St Apollinaris-in-Classe is a most lovely and mysterious representation of St Apollinaris, his hands raised in prayer or exhortation, in a pastoral scene of sheep, birds, lilies and bushes; above, in the summit of the dome, the mosaic shows the Transfiguration. Christ himself, transfigured, is represented by a jewelled cross, and the three apostles on the mount, only figuratively, by three sheep; Moses and Elias, however, beside the mount, are draped figures.

The palace of Theoderic has perished, but, as known to us from the mosaic and from inscriptions, must have been surrounded by *porticus*, adorned with mosaics, and divided into banqueting halls and *triclinia*. It was surmounted by a magnificent tower: on the pediment beneath the roof, a mosaic depicted Theoderic in armour, between draped women representing the cities of Rome and Ravenna. For his own tomb, he built a round marble tower in the manner of the tomb of Hadrian, but with a domed roof of marble in a single block. The tower remains, but no trace of the actual sepulture.

The Gothic language of Theoderic's people would seem to have died out with the fall of the kingdom, and though Germanic heroic poetry preserved the great name of Theoderic of Verona (Dietrich of Bern), no single version of early medieval date has come down to us. His widespread fame among the Germanic peoples is however attested by the various forms of the heroic poem and by allusions to his name by medieval writers. Ermanaric, his ancestor, Attila, and Gundahar of Burgundy are other Germanic chiefs of history who share this old poetic honour with Theoderic; and such poetry would seem to have been the instrument accounting for heroic name-giving in distant Germanic tribes. Theoderic (Theuderich) is thus found among Visigothic and Frankish princes; as is Eormanric (Ermanaric) among the more distant Oiscingas of Kent.

Though all the efforts of Cassiodorus and the senatorial party failed to give Ostrogothic rule in Italy permanence, yet they did by their efforts forge two instruments all-important in the founding of the new Europe: the carrying over of the old learning into the new age, and the practice of the monastic life. As to Greco-Roman architecture, in a land so thick with ancient monuments and in close touch with new Rome, that preserved itself by normal process of development: the new influence of the day was eastern, not Gothic: but Greco-Roman learning owed much to the conscious effort of Cassiodorus and his friends.

Towards the end of his political career, with Narses' reconquest of Italy in sight, Cassiodorus turned to another means of preserving *Romanitas*. A century earlier, Jerome and Rufinus had begun to translate the basic books for Christian scholars from Greek into Latin, but there was still much to be done, and in Italy even the text of the Vulgate (as it was called in the late middle ages and after) was not established. Cassiodorus had, apparently, edited the *Variae* in 537, and he wrote his treatise *De anima* immediately before his retirement. After his flight to Sicily from Ravenna, he sailed for Constantinople, there meeting at least two scholars who had attended courses at the Jewish theological school at Nisibis, and an earlier project for establishing a great school of theology and letters took shape in his mind. He returned to his paternal estate at Squillace, and prepared to found his school there, in the form of a monastic community. He had earlier made an aquarium, fish ponds hewn out of the rock, at Squillace, and here too, comparing the monastic enclosure with the walls of the rock pool, he founded his Vivarium for monks on a beautiful site.

The city of Squillace, which is so placed as to look down upon the Hadriatic Gulf [he had earlier written], hangs upon the hills like a cluster of grapes: not that it may pride itself upon their difficult ascent, but that it may voluptuously gaze on verdant plains and the blue black of the sea. . . . It enjoys a translucent air, but withal so temperate that its winters are sunny and its summers cool, and life passes there without sorrow, since hostile seasons are feared by none.

Squillace has also an abundant share of the delicacies of the sea, possessing near it those gates of Neptune which we ourselves constructed. At the foot of the Moscian Mount we hollowed out the bowels of the rock, and tastefully introduced therein the eddying waves of Nereus. Here a troop of fishes, sporting in free captivity, refreshes all minds with delight and charms all eyes with admiration.

Sometime, then, after his return from Constantinople, *c.* 548, Cassiodorus founded Vivarium. The monastic life had already passed to Italy from the east; Liberius the patrician had founded a monastery at Alatri in Campania before 534; Venantius the patrician another on his property at Fondi, in Samnium; and Belisarius himself a convent at Orta, on the Via Flaminia. Benedict of Nursia had died at about the time of Cassiodorus' foundation, *c.* 548; both these great founders desired to practise the 'vita monachica' of the desert fathers, both had (slightly variant) forms of the old *Regula Magistri* to guide them, neither can be proved to have borrowed from the practice of the other.

Cassiodorus was a great scholar and a rich man: there were more scribes, more learning and more MSS. at Vivarium than at Monte Cassino. Yet both houses were aiming at the Egyptian ideal! Cassiodorus indeed provided in his rule for the hermit life of such of his monks as should wish to lead it, up in the 'sweet recesses of Monte Castellum', above the main monastery of Vivarium; while Benedict made no such provision for those who wished to 'fight the lonely battle of the desert'. Cassiodorus' intention however was to provide a school of sound learning: his reference once to his own 'conversion', and the reference of pope Vigilius to him as 'religiosus vir', may mean that he actually became a monk of his own foundation, or merely that he withdrew from the world and lived in retirement. In any case, he gave himself up to study, with the express purpose of establishing a text of the scriptures, providing Latin versions of the Greek theologians and a synopsis of the liberal arts for his monks.

3

His first work, proper to one entering on the life of 'conversion' and presumably reciting the hours of the divine office, was a commentary on the psalms. He seems to have surrounded himself with a small but capable band of scholars and translators, and describes his aim in his *Institutiones divinarum et humanarum litterarum*, an encyclopedia of theological literature and the liberal arts, intended for his monks.

> Perceiving that the schools were swarming with students because of their great longing for secular letters . . . I was, I confess, extremely sorry that the divine scriptures had no public teachers . . . I strove with the most holy Agapetus, bishop of the city of Rome [535–536], to collect subscriptions and to have Christian rather than secular schools receive professors in the city of Rome, just as the custom is said to have existed for a long time at Alexandria, and is said to be even now cultivated by the Hebrews in Nisibis, a city of the Syrians . . . But although my ardent desire could in no way have been fulfilled because of the struggles that seethed and raged excessively in the Italian realm, inasmuch as a peaceful affair has no place in anxious times, I was driven by divine charity to this device, namely, in the place of a teacher to prepare for you, under the Lord's guidance, these introductory books.[1]

Cassiodorus then gave the list of the contents of the *Institutiones*: in the first book the text of the whole Bible, with patristic commentaries and homilies: and, in his second book, treatises on the liberal studies, grammar, rhetoric, logic, mathematics, 'which embraces four sciences, arithmetic, geometry, music and astronomy'. For the purposes of his theological works, he also made many collations of texts of the scriptures, and assembled a text of Jerome's version, in a 'codex grandior littera clariore conscriptus'. This revised text he divided into nine volumes, dividing the books of the Bible into chapters, and using punctuation (the method proper to exponents of the liberal arts) only in those portions of the scriptures not translated by Jerome; where usage had established Jerome's own method of writing the text in uneven lines, according to the sense, without punctuation, Cassiodorus adopted the received method. The text from Cassiodorus' 'codex grandior' appears to have been used in the famous codex Amiatinus, written at Jarrow in the eighth century; the frontispiece to this codex represents the prophet Ezekiel correcting the scriptures, seated before a press (*armarium*) containing Cassiodorus' nine volumes: there is a link then between Vivarium and Jarrow.

[1] Jones, L. W.: *Introduction to Divine and Human Readings*, p. 67.

Cassiodorus' greatest work for the preservation of *Romanitas* was probably this heavy task of textual collation and translation of the whole field of knowledge known to him as a great rhetor and biblical scholar; he added to it a translation of the *Antiquities* of Josephus; an ecclesiastical history obtained by combining the histories of Theodoret, Sozomen and Socrates, called the *Historia Tripartita*; a treatise *De Orthographia*, and the *Historia Gothorum*.

Cassiodorus' work for the preservation of learning was only rivalled by that of the other great Italian rhetor, Boethius. The latter planned to translate into Latin the whole works of Plato and Aristotle, reconciling their philosophies; but he did not live to accomplish his work. Nevertheless, his treatises on Aristotle introduced him to western learning, and his treatises on Greek logic and music surpassed those of Cassiodorus; his exposition of the other liberal arts was more slight.

Meanwhile, the father of western monachism had founded in Ostrogothic Italy his three houses of Subiaco, Monte Cassino and Terracina. He is not mentioned in any contemporary writing, for, though he was born of substantial parentage in Umbrian Nursia, he fled from the world to the desert too soon to attain any eminence in the civil service: for which, indeed, he seems only to have been preparing himself. His contemporaries mentioned casually that this senator and that had founded a monastery: none of them mentioned Benedict of Nursia. It was left for pope Gregory the Great (590–604), himself a monk and in some sense a spiritual son of Benedict, to relate in book II of his *Dialogues* what he had learned from monks of Monte Cassino driven by the Lombard ravages to take refuge in Rome.

'There was a man of venerable life,' he begins, 'by grace and by name Benedict.' He must have been born *c.* 480, and sent as a youth to the *scholae publicae* in Rome; 'but', says Gregory, 'he drew back: he sought the habit of holy conversation: despising the study of letters, he left Rome *scienter nescius et sapienter indoctus*.' He went up into the foothills of the Appenines, forty miles from Rome, to where the cliff of Subiaco overhung the lake; there he was given the monastic habit by a certain monk Romanus, and began to live in the 'holy cave', the cradle of Benedictinism, the hermit life. The rumour of his holiness and austerity spread, and certain monks asked him to be their abbot, and then, regretting it, tried to poison him. But round him, as once round Anthony in the desert, disciples gradually collected, and he built for them twelve small monasteries, each containing twelve monks, retaining himself the general guidance of the group of cells. Religious men from Rome began to come to him, and Roman nobles confided to him their sons, among whom were two later famous in the history of his monks, Placidus and Maurus.

The jealousy of a neighbouring priest, however, drove Benedict to take a few disciples, make his journey southwards, and found his greatest monastery on Monte Cassino, on a spur of the Apennines round which winds the road from Rome to Naples. Here, *c.* 520, he hewed down two old pagan statues, made the enclosures of his monastery, perhaps the limits of the old Roman camp itself, and built within it two oratories and the cells for his monks; a cell for the porter and guests and one for the novices; a refectory and kitchen, and cells for dormitories where his monks might sleep together, each group under their *decanus* or dean, as their numbers increased.

There Benedict settled the *horarium* of his monks' day, modifying it according to the season, and as experience suggested: a monastic time-table is the necessary preliminary to any rule. This time-table varied between the summer and winter seasons, for the Roman day itself, twelve hours between sunrise and sunset, varied in length according to the season, and while the long summer day was divided for the monk by the siesta taken by all peasants and field workers, the winter's day was not; the long winter's night provided more hours of sleep. The monks' day was divided between prayer, reading (*meditatio*) and manual work in the garden or fields. The divine office (to which, Benedict said, nothing whatever was to be preferred) included a long night office (called indifferently Matins, Nocturns, or Vigils), and seven day hours: Lauds, Prime, Terce, Sext, None, Vespers and Compline. Exact punctuality at office was to be secured by a simple means: Let the monks, said Benedict, at the first sound of the signal for office, drop from his hands the tools of his work or whatever they held, and proceed quickly, though with due decorum, to chapel. 'Seven times a day', as the psalmist said, 'have I praised thee; and at night I will give thanks to thee': there is the archetype of the *opus Dei*.

Benedict wrote a rule for his monks: and the comparison made by Dom Chapman with the canons of certain eastern councils, and with the text of Justinian's *Digest* and *Novels*, suggests strongly that he did it after a thorough study of canonical regulations on the subject (for instance) of episcopal elections, to which he assimilated his own chapter on the election of the abbot. The Scythian monk Dionysius Exiguus, working at Rome for the pope, had compiled a great collection of eastern and western canons, translating the Greek ones; the last papal decretals he included were those of Anastasius II (d. 498). It is true that Dionysius spent the last part of his life at Vivarium and not at Monte Cassino; but in this age of the transmission of Greek learning to the west, it would not be astonishing that Benedict, with his Roman regard for law, should have acquainted himself with the 'sacred canons'. Resemblances and borrowings apart, the hypothesis that Benedict should have studied the sacred canons, as well as the rule of Basil, Cassian and other monastic *monumenta*, would explain the extraordinary reverence with which Benedict regarded his own rule. He calls it *'magistra regula'*, *'sancta regula'*, and again and again enjoins that nothing is to be done contrary to the rule. This rule, in later centuries, was to be to the west something akin to what the Basilian rule was to the east.

Benedict died some time between 543 and 548, in any case after he had been visited by the Gothic king Totila in 543 or 544; he had already a reputation for holiness, attested by miracles, and there is nothing to show whether Totila came from awe and curiosity, or because, as Benedict said, 'a monastery is never without guests'. He would have found at least one Gothic monk within the monastery, of whom the *Dialogues* relates that he dropped his iron tool into the pond, and Benedict pulled it out for him again, restoring it with the words to become classical in the Benedictine life: *Labora, et nolite tristari*.

BIBLIOGRAPHICAL NOTE

For primary sources on Ostrogothic history, see C. C. Mierow, *The Gothic History of Jordanes:* English version, 1915: and, for Ostrogothic administration, Cassiodorus' *Variae*, ed. Mommsen, in *M.G.H.*, Auctores antiquissimi, vol. xii, 1894. For his transmission of Latin learning, L. W. Jones's *Introduction to Divine and Human Learning, by Cassiodorus Senator*, Columbia Univ. Press, 1946: for the Latin text of this work R. A. B. Mynors, *Cassiodori Senatoris Institutiones*, 1937: for Cassiodorus' monastery, 'Les Institutions de Cassiodore et sa fondation de Vivarium', in *Rev. Bened.*, lxiii (1941), pp. 59–88. See also E. R. Curtius, *European Literature and the Latin Middle Ages*, and P. Courcelles, *Les Lettres Grecques en Occident*, 1943. For Ostrogothic and Lombard jewellery, a parallel to Anglo-Saxon grave-finds, see N. Åberg, *Die Goten und Langobarden in Italien*, 1923, and 'The Cesena treasure', in *Brit. Mus. Quarterly*, viii (1933–4), plate xiii; for Ostrogothic art and architecture, E. Will's 'Saint Apollinaire de Ravenne', in *Publications de l'université de Strasbourg*, fasc. 74, 1936, and the finely illustrated *Sacred Fortress. Byzantine Art and Statecraft in Ravenna*, O. von Simson, Chicago Univ. Press. See also bibliog. to chapter x.

CHAPTER IV

THE FRANKS

OF all the provinces of the western empire, Gaul was the most completely Romanized and the most industrialized. The problem of its defence towards the end of the fourth century was urgent; barbarians from beyond the Rhine had long been pressing against the frontier, against Mainz, Cologne and Trier, long the administrative capital of Gaul; but only a cavalry army could cope with the barbarian raiders, and the army of Gaul had shrunk to very small proportions. The emperor and his minister could only rely on federate troops. The Franks and Alemans, who were to possess themselves of northern Gaul in the fifth century, were now Roman federates: Stilicho used them to repel Alaric's invasion of Italy in 401. Generals of these federate troops themselves pretended to the empire of the west, and their efforts witness to a certain desire of the Gallo-Roman aristocracy, the senatorial class, to see the Italian rule of the west transferred to Gaul. Maximus, the 'tyrant' from Britain, and then Arbogast the Frank, both failed to secure a supremacy; Theodosius established himself as sole and effective Roman emperor. Constantine III, Constans, Jovinus, made their attempt at the rule of the west, and met a tragic fate; but the Gallo-Roman aristocracy of the central plateau and south Gaul looked favourably on the success of Avitus, one of their most distinguished representatives, when he was made an emperor by the support of the Visigoth, Theoderic II. But though all attempts at establishing a 'Gallic empire' failed of permanence, Roman nationality and traditions were defended longer in Gaul than in Italy itself.

The Franks were finally to attain a Gallic hegemony, but they were not the first to break the eastern frontiers of Gaul. The Vandals, Alans and Sueves in 406 faced Mainz from across the right bank of the Rhine, and, on the last day of the year, succeeded in crossing it. No resistance met them on the other side; Mainz and even Trier were captured, Amiens, Thérouanne and Tournai were sacked and burnt. Alemans and Burgundians, behind the Vandals, occupied the right bank of the river, the Burgundians in Worms, Speyer and Mainz, the Alemans in Alsace. Vandals, Alans and Sueves passed into Gaul and were thrust out by the Visigoths. Gaul was threatened by Attila in 451, but the danger passed.

Meanwhile, the fair-haired, grey-eyed Franks, not easily distinguishable from their Anglo-Saxon neighbours except by their weapons, passed from the valley of the Main, the heart of the later central German duchy of Franconia, to the valleys of the Moselle and the Rhine. The Salian Franks had been allowed to settle in Toxandria (northern Belgium) in 358; in the fifth century they became semi-independent, and their Germanic tongue replaced the Latin of the provincials. The Salian Franks were not a single tribe, but a group of tribes, as were the Ripuarian Franks, settled in the fourth century on the right bank of the Rhine, and only gradually able, in the disorders of the fifth century, to penetrate the left bank. About 470 the Ripuarians had established themselves in a compact territory including Aix-la-Chapelle and Bonn, and had penetrated towards, without being able to take, Metz. Other Frankish tribes, notably the Hessian Franks, remained in Franconia.

The society of these Frankish settlers, whose structure would appear [1] to approximate to that of the so-called code of Clovis (? 507–511), hinged upon the tribe, headed by some long-haired king or sub-king: and the family. The tribal territory was the *pagus*, subdivided into hundreds (cantons) headed by the *centenarius*. The patriarchal families of the tribe supported the king, and were now responsible for the payment of wergeld, if one of their members failed to pay it. The older social effort to prevent murder, the Germanic blood feud, was already partly superseded by the system of securing peace by the payment of a sum of money according to status: but the instinct to revert to the older system was still immensely strong and dangerous.

Like the Anglo-Saxons, the Frankish men wore moustaches, fastened their tunics or cloaks with brooches whose design mingled the animal ornament of south Russia with motifs borrowed from late Roman art. They buckled their tunics with a leather belt fastened with an ornamented buckle. Since the Franks were early converted, their cemeteries do not contain the treasure of barbaric ornament which the pagan Anglo-Saxons buried with their dead; but even a Christian corpse among the Franks was buried with his tunic, belt and buckle, and such buckles have been found in some numbers.

The most valuable historical source for early Frankish history is

---

[1] No MS. of the *Lex Salica* earlier than late eighth or early ninth century survives: for the question of its redaction to writing and date, see Mr Wallace-Hadrill's 'Archbishop Hincmar and Lex Salica' in *Revue d'Histoire du Droit*, xx, 1952.

entitled the *Ecclesiastical History of Georgius Florentius*, otherwise
Gregory, bishop of Tours, in ten books. The drop in the level of
learning between Gregory's works (for he wrote other treatises, all
however with a bearing on church history or practice) and those of
Cassiodorus' encyclopedic volumes, is great. Cassiodorus, however,
was a Roman scholar, outstanding even in the Italy of his day,
while Gregory was a bishop of central Gaul, who frequently
lamented his own *rusticitas*, whose main work was the protection
of the liberties of his church and its rights of sanctuary, and whose
opportunities for either learning or writing were far more limited
than those of Cassiodorus. He set out, moreover, to write an ecclesiastical history, like Eusebius before him and Bede after him,
and his history is perhaps most valuable for the light it throws,
by allusion and direct narrative, on the succession and acts of the
Gallo-Roman bishops who preceded him, and who were his contemporaries; and also on the church buildings, and ecclesiastical
practices of his day. But this history, generally known as the *History of the Franks*, is, beyond that, a general secular history, beginning with the period between Adam and Eve and the passion
of St Martin of Tours in book I: dealing with the Vandals, the
Huns and the history of the early Franks and Clovis in book II:
Frankish history from Clovis to the death of his grandson Theudebert (547) in book III, and, in greater detail thereafter, with the
history of Gregory's near contemporaries down to the death of
king Sigebert in 575; books VII to X were added by Gregory in
the form of a diary to his main history: they cover the period from
584 to 591.

Gregory himself belonged to a Gallo-Roman senatorial family,
which was also an episcopal one on both his father's and his
mother's side. He had a great grandfather, St Gregory, bishop of
Langres, and an episcopal grandfather; St Nizier of Lyons was his
great-uncle; Gallus of Tours, his uncle and his predecessor in the
see of Tours, was his cousin. In those days of slow passage through
the seven clerical orders and late ordination to the priesthood, and
also of the sudden promotion of lay nobles and civil servants to the
episcopate, many bishops had families in early life; they were required to leave their wives and families in their paternal villas, and
live with their clergy in the *secretarium* or church house, when they
were consecrated bishop. Gregory, however, as was becoming
usual was sent for training as a young household lector, at the age
of eight, to his uncle Avitus, bishop of Clermont; the rhetors'
schools had perished, and Gregory's education was received entirely in the bishop's household. This education was founded on

the reading of the psalter, New Testament and the lives of saints and ascetics, but included a little Vergil and Sallust. The reputation for *rusticitas* which has become associated with Gregory's name derives partly from his own self-depreciation and partly from his decision to write in the fluid Latin of his day, with its cases failing and changing, so as to be understood of his own clergy. His mother Armentaria consoled him for not possessing the literary culture of a Fortunatus by pointing out that if he wrote in everyday language, he would be understood by everybody.

Gregory was consecrated bishop of Tours in 573, when central France was again joined to the Austrasian kingdom under Sigebert (see p. 266), and he became inevitably involved in the bitter struggle between the followers of the queens Brunhilde and Fredegund (see p. 267). His courage and constancy, and more than a little of the *prudentia* of the Roman magistrate, brought him safely through the dangers involved in defending the rights of St Martin and his church against Merovingian kings and queens. A Frankish bishop's relation to his king was one of peculiar responsibility and even independence; he was not frankly appointed by the king, as even the counts, domestics and other civil servants were, though the Merovingian kings early sought to grasp that share in a bishop's election originally exercised by the *laos* or *plebs* of his diocese and, in the east, by the Byzantine emperor; he was mysteriously protected by the patron saint of his see; he stood for *Romanitas*; and, moreover, like an Old Testament prophet, for the mysterious wishes and preferences of the Christian God. The Merovingian king could not disregard the bishop, and normally worked with him; though he occasionally had him murdered. This connexion with government and affairs of state brought a bishop much work, and frequent journeys within Gaul, as was clearly the case in Gregory's own life. That he should have written as much as he did is somewhat remarkable, especially in view of his close supervision and firm rule of the clergy, monks and nuns of his own diocese: he died in 594.

Beside the ten books of the *Historia Francorum*, Gregory wrote what he calls 'seven books of miracles', including the *De Gloria Martyrum*, four books of the miracles of St Martin, and the *De gloria confessorum*, saints mainly connected with the city of Tours and Clermont. He also wrote a *Vitae Patrum*, twenty lives of Gallic bishops, abbots and hermits, a commentary on the psalter (now lost), a life of St Andrew translated from the Greek, and a history of the Seven Sleepers of Ephesus, translated from the Syriac: it was not impossible, even in central Gaul, to obtain help in translation from Greek or Syrian refugees or traders. He also composed a manual to enable the clergy to determine the hours of the different night offices from the position of the stars, calling it *De cursibus ecclesiasticis*. The duty of calling for night office must have been a serious one, in all monasteries and bishop's *familiae*; St Benedict, in his rule, has to give instructions that when calling has been late, the office must be somewhat curtailed, and Gregory would seem to have been as impressed as St Benedict with the duty of the regular recitation of the office.

The conquest and union of Gaul under the Franks was to be accomplished by Clovis (Chlodovech), king of the Salian Franks. His grandfather, Merovech, brought a contingent of Franks to fight for Aëtius against the Huns in 451; when he died in 456, his son Childeric I maintained good relations for a time with the Romans, then led a raid across the territory of Syagrius and captured Angers on the Loire. He had by-passed Soissons, where Syagrius maintained an isolated Roman rule as 'rex Romanorum', and Reims, the city of Syagrius' archbishop: the valley of the Seine and the central plain of Gaul were still Roman, though small bands of Saxon pirates were settling round the mouth of the Somme, and the Romano-Britons from Cornwall and the southwest were taking refuge in large numbers in Brittany, the monk historian Gildas among them later.

In 481 Childeric died, leaving his fifteen-year-old son, Clovis, to do what Maximus and Avitus had failed in doing, give Gaul a limited hegemony of the west, a great conquering reign: with the chief Salian leader Ragnachar he advanced from the region of Tournai and Cambrai against Syagrius, taking Soissons; he had taken Rouen, Reims and Paris by 486. Paris indeed had long been besieged by the Franks, according to the life of St Geneviève:

> At the time therefore that the siege of Paris had been maintained by the Franks for ten years, as they say, the territory of this city was so afflicted with hunger that some are known to have starved. Geneviève therefore set out from Arcis-sur-Aube by boat to buy corn.

Geneviève's help did not, in the end, save Paris from Clovis: it was too valuable a city and port. After taking it he next fought against and killed Ragnachar and other Salian kings: defeated the Ripuarians and defeated the Alemans after a dangerous conflict *c.* 496. From Orleans and Paris he commanded the valleys of the Loire and the Seine, and the heart of his kingdom lay between Paris, Soissons, Reims, Cambrai and Cologne; but his rule actually

extended south to the Mediterranean corridor maintained by Theoderic between Italy and Visigothic Spain, and south-east to Burgundy at the head waters of the Rhone; in the east it included the
valleys of the Rhine and the Main.

The Franks had, before the invasion, been longer in contact
with *Romanitas* than any other west Germanic tribe, and the conversion of Clovis to Catholic Christianity began a further process
of Romanization at the hands of the Catholic bishop. Clovis had
about 493 married the Burgundian princess Clotilde, niece of king
Gundobad who had killed her father Chilperic; she now desired
the conversion of her pagan husband. From the point of view of
securing the allegiance of the conquered provincials and recognition by the East Roman emperor, Clovis's conversion was clearly
desirable. Gregory of Tours' narrative of the baptism is not necessarily chronologically reliable, for he apparently had no written
record to go by, but it would seem to have taken place some years
after 493 and at Reims: Soissons, the heart of Clovis's conquered
territory, was in the see of Reims, and an act intended to win over
the Roman provincials may well have taken place there. Gregory
does not state the place of baptism, but he describes it as administered by Remigius, the bishop of Reims. To Gregory, the baptism
of Clovis was as epoch-making as the conversion of Constantine,
for it led to the conversion of a whole people. The queen Clotilde,
he says, approached Remigius, entreating him to instil into the
ears of the king the words of salvation, and Remigius accordingly
exhorted him to believe in God, the maker of all, and burn his
idols. After hesitating on the ground that his people would not
desert the old gods, Clovis inquired of them, received a favourable
answer, and yielded. Remigius, filled with joy, prepared for the
royal baptism: the open space before the basilica was hung with
coloured cloths: the low building of the atrium before the narthex
was draped in white, the large font within the baptistery had its
waters solemnly blessed, according to the ritual, with oil and balsam, the candles shone and diffused the odour of hot wax, and the
'whole temple of the baptistery' was filled with so heavenly a frag-
rance that the onlookers thought themselves in paradise. The new
Constantine moved towards the font, to wash away the old stains
of sin; and Remigius, beginning the rite, adjured him in the words
of Christian rhetoric (for he was a great rhetor): 'Bow thy neck in
meekness, O Sicambrian: adore what thou hast burned and burn
what thou hast adored.' It was much that Clovis had become Constantine: but the imperious violence of the Germanic chieftain was
not so quickly wiped out, either from the king or his descendants.

Three traditions, however, instead of two, were now free to form the future Frankish kingdom: Germanic tribal law, *Romanitas*, and the tradition of mercy and equality in the sight of God proper to Catholic Christianity.

Stronger after his conversion, because 'a great number of the inhabitants of Gaul now desired to have the Franks for masters', Clovis prepared for his crowning struggle with the Visigoths of Toulouse. They were his strongest neighbours and his possible rivals for the possession of Gaul, which might, it would seem, have been united from the Romanized south as probably as from the more barbaric north. With barbarian simplicity, however, Clovis sought and found support for his war from his Catholic subjects and bishops: 'I take it very ill', Gregory of Tours reports him as saying, 'that these Arians should hold a part of Gaul: with God's help, let us go and conquer them and their territories.' In the year 507 he summoned his army and made his way to Poitiers, where Alaric II was lodged; when an officer of his army, passing through the rural part of the see of Tours, transgressed his order by seizing a poor man's stock of hay, he had him killed with the sword: 'Where shall be our hope of victory,' he cried, 'if we offend blessed Martin?' Then the king sent a messenger to the holy basilica, to see if perchance auspices of victory might be obtained from that holy house: giving him gifts to offer to the saint, he prayed: 'If thou, O Lord, art my helper and hast decreed that thou wilt deliver into my hands this unbelieving people: deign graciously to reveal this at the entrance of the basilica of St Martin.' And when his young messengers were entering the holy basilica at his orders, the leader of the choir unexpectedly intoned this antiphon: 'Thou hast girded me, O Lord, with strength unto battle and trodden mine enemies down before me.' This good omen they reported to the king, and further encouraged by the sight of a mysterious light shining from the basilica of St Hilary at Poitiers, Clovis met the Visigoths in the 'campus Vogladensis', at the tenth milestone from Poitiers, and won the victory. The Goths fled, Alaric was slain, his son Amalaric fled to Spain, and Clovis returned to Tours, offering many gifts to St Martin. Toulouse, the Visigothic capital, had fallen to the Franks, and Septimania to the Burgundians.

It was at this juncture that Clovis received at Tours a complimentary embassy from the eastern emperor, Anastasius. They bore to this new Catholic conqueror of Arian Visigoths the consular robe and insignia: the purple tunic, only less long than that of the emperor, and apparently the laurel wreath. He became a *consularis* and 'wore the purple', as Gildas relates of the ancestors of Ambrose

Aurelian, and other British magnates who had certainly never been one of the two consuls of the year. But to Clovis the robe of the Roman magistrate was useful as a recognition of his rule. He received the written diploma of the consulship, and was invested with the purple in the basilica of St Martin; then, mounting his horse, he rode from the basilica to that of St Gatien, the cathedral, scattering gold and silver coins to the crowd with his own hand; but whether as Germanic ring-giver, bestowing the fruits of his victory on his followers, or as exercising the traditional liberality of the consul, no one can tell.

Clovis's realm, which he ruled henceforth from Paris, saw a more effective fusion of the Roman and Germanic cultures than the Ostrogoths had been able to achieve in Italy. The Franks would seem to have been more numerous in proportion to the Gallo-Roman population than the Ostrogoths, at least in north Gaul, and to have become less of a separate caste. Clovis and his notaries and domestics at Soissons took over the villas and lands of the Roman fisc, and his nobles would seem similarly to have been provided for by expropriation, and, no doubt, by marriage with Gallo-Roman heiresses. The Franks moved as a tribe across northern France; in the centre and south, Frankish rule was maintained by an official Frankish class. But nowhere was the movement of population large enough to displace the Latin language, except in the parts of Toxandria where the Franks had originally settled. In the towns, even those we hear of as burned and plundered in the course of the fifth-century wars, the street plan remained the same, and development was continuous.

Further signs of Clovis's intention to preserve *Romanitas* were his issue of a similar Roman currency, his retention of Syagrius' staff of notaries, and his maintenance of Roman law for the provincials, and in some sense for all his subjects. Roman coined money was still needed, certainly for trade, and possibly for the payment of his quasi-Roman secretariat and court officers, a class long tenacious of their right to be paid in cash rather than in kind. Clovis minted no gold coins of his own: and contented himself with adding an initial and final C to the name of Anastasius on the legend of his coins.

The machine of government, or its relics, preserved by Syagrius at Soissons, passed over to the service of the Frankish king; records were kept on the papyrus sheets used by Roman scribes in the past, and, though no originals have come down to us from the time of Clovis, or indeed for nearly 150 years after, later redactions of letters, privileges and grants of this early period supply the titles of the officers of the early Merovingian kings; as do the pages of Gregory of Tours, etc. As in the court of the emperors of the west, Clovis was served solely by laymen: his Frankish chieftains at first supplied his *comites*, both those retained at court, and those who ruled some *pagus* or *civitas*; the count of the palace judged suits arising among them. His steward or butler was described by the Vulgate word *pincerna*, and he had a *comes stabuli*, the forerunner of the later marshal. In the second half of the sixth century, under Byzantine influence, *duces* appear in some numbers as leaders of armies; domestics and *agentes in rebus* controlled the royal demesne and the levy of 'tribute' (see p. 68). Almost from the first, trusted Roman provincials appear among the officers of the early Merovingian court.

In the old Roman *civitates* and the smaller *castella*, justice was done by the count or *grafio* (a word connected apparently with the Germanic *gerefa* or steward rather than with the Byzantine *graphiarius*, a variant of notary). In the *civitas* the bishop might be called on to sit with the count as co-judge, but not by normal routine. He judged the *clerici*, those in the special service of the church, in a court of his own.

The civilizing influence of Roman law and administration reached the Franks mainly by their use of notaries, at court, in the count's court, in the bishop's secretariat, and in the household of the Merovingian princes and princesses. They were the old, trained scribes of the Roman law courts; they wrote on their sheets of ridged papyrus in the difficult cursive hand; they knew the answers to legal problems. They could draw up a will, or a marriage contract, or write a commission to office in due form. They could make valid instruments for the setting free of a slave (some war captive, probably), the grant of a 'privilege' to a monastery, by which it was freed from the customary payments to the king, or the grant of some 'immunity', by which a church or monastery was relieved from passing on the tributes or tax due from its lands or market to the king's fisc. Land, according to Roman law, could be sold, bequeathed, or bestowed upon some church or royal servant, by the instruments of the notaries; if it was bestowed for life only, as by a bishop to one of his senior clergy, that was a *beneficium*. Finally, the notaries wrote the king's letters using the appropriate official titles of the recipient, *illustris* and the rest, and authenticating them by signature: there was no need of witnesses. At the head of the royal notariat was the referendary, a Frankish noble trained in the technical business of writing, and, as the king's issuing officer, responsible for the royal edicts and letters; to judge from a lively story in Gregory's pages, the forgery of a referendary's signature was not unknown.

It was, no doubt, mainly through the notary's knowledge of legal *formulae* and processes that Roman law survived among the Franks, as it did among the Ostrogoths and Visigoths: but certain Roman law books also survived. The code of Theodosius II was, in effect, in the sixth century, 'Roman law', as was the epitome of Roman law drawn up for the Visigoths, and known as the *Breviarium Alarici*. When Justinian's *Institutes*, *Code*, and *Digest* were issued, they were apparently at first known among the Franks, but the knowledge died out with the sixth century.

It was not possible, however, to expect the Frankish conquerors to forgo their Germanic customary law; and it was also necessary, as later under king Æthelbert of Kent, to assign a status to the Christian bishop and clergy in the Frankish tariff of wergelds and payments for injury. Clovis therefore may have recognized some written summary of the old, customary 'Salic law' some time between 507 and 511, dealing, subject by subject, with varieties of offences, and the penalty by which composition was to be made for them. In the *Lex Salica* as it has come down to us, undoubtedly with additions and emendations since Clovis's day, the laws are rendered into Latin, so that the *grafio* may enforce them, but the society thus protected is primitive and Germanic. The first penalties stated are those for non-attendance at the *mallus*, once a folk-moot and now the assembly presided over by the *grafio* or *comes*; then come penalties for offences against the flocks, herds and farm animals; possibly, this points to the seniority of such offences in a semi-nomadic people to offences against the crops, i.e. letting the farm animals get in among them: which offences are dealt with later in the code. The code thus deals with the theft of pigs (and many varieties of this offence), of calves, oxen, cows, bulls, sheep, goats, dogs, birds and bees; of stolen slaves (*servi*), of attacks on another's villa, of arson, of the various kinds of wounding, of the killing of children, women (free and unfree), of reaping another's harvest, of stealing eel nets and eels from the river; of hunting, hedges, and homicide. And finally, of the killing of a *grafio* and the compensation; and of alods and inheritance. The scribe who wrote the laws employed some very strange Latin words: for he was dealing with what must have been, to him, a foreign peasant society and its customs.

Besides these Salic laws, a similar tariff of compensations and wergelds for the Alemans has come down to us, and another for the Bavarians; as one is traditionally headed *Pactus Alemannorum*, its

original may have been thought to date from Clovis's conquest of
these people. The same terms for freeman (*baro*), and somewhat
the same social grades, of freemen, laets and slaves (*servi, ancillae*),
occur in all; and in all, compensation for injury to bishop and priest
is included.

The fitting together of Franks and Romans into one society is
shown by the wergelds of the different social classes of each: the
wergeld of the corresponding Gallo-Roman class was half that of
the Frankish class. This does not in itself signify solely a social
degradation of the Gallo-Romans, the upper classes of whom seem
to have held much the same social position as in Roman Gaul: it
was also a measure of police protection. The conquerors, living in
most regions as a minority among the Gallo-Romans, whom they
must in many cases have dispossessed of their villas and *praedia*,
were likely subjects for private murder; the Jutes when they conquered the provincials of Kent, the Saxons when they conquered
the west Welsh of Somerset, the Danes when they were confirmed
in the Danelaw, all subjected the conquered population to a lower
tariff of wergelds. To murder a Frank cost much more than to
murder a Gallo-Roman, and these were days of violence. Princes
of the Merovingian house murdered their relations and ordered
offenders to be hastily cut down with the sword; violent and hastily
ordained clerics pursued their archdeacons with axes through
woods, hoping to murder them; violent and hastily ordained
bishops might even order the murder of a cleric whose land they
coveted. The attribution of a high wergeld to the Franks was less
of a burden than the weakness of the whole system of composition
by money payments, as against the older system of blood feud.

Frankish society had, it appears, other classes than that of the
free warrior and the noble; the *laeti* were an intermediate class between free men and slaves, with a higher wer, however, than the
coloni of the *villae*. The high honour attributed to the skilled metal
worker or goldsmith in the northern heroic poetry, where the king
rewards his goldsmith with grants of land 'which he gladly re-
ceives', is reflected in the wergeld higher than that of the normal
freeman allotted to the Frankish goldsmith. The craftsman who
made the sword of Childeric I, with its cloisonné hilt (it was buried
with Childeric in 481 in his tomb and there discovered) must have
had a high wergeld; as must the goldsmith who made the beautiful
chalice and rectangular paten discovered at Gourdon, with their
filigree ornament, cloisonné of flat garnet, and the Latin cross
(dated from accompanying coins as earlier than 527).

St Eligius, indeed, who was born in 590 of Roman parents at

Limoges and trained as a goldsmith under Abbo, master of the Frankish mint there, so impressed Lothar II with the honesty with which he used a supply of gold and gems given him to make a throne in making two thrones, that he made him his councillor; he was one of the chief ministers at court under Lothar's successor, Dagobert: and he became a great builder of churches, founder of monasteries, the friend of the great bishop of Rouen, Dado, and finally, bishop of Noyon-Tournai himself (640-660). The craft of the goldsmith had been as sure a road to promotion as the notariat of the Frankish court, by which Dado rose; and considering the artistic merit of the goldsmith work used by Eligius and his fellows, there is no wonder that the Franks rated the goldsmiths highly.

The period of Merovingian rule between the death of Clovis in 511, and the accession to power of Charles Martel in 719, saw France usually divided between princes of the Merovingian line, and only united at two points. France was divided between the rule of Clovis's four sons at his death in 511, and reunited only when violence or natural death had removed three of them, leaving the youngest, Lothar I, to rule alone from 558 to 561. History then repeated itself. Lothar's four sons ruled separate kingdoms till the youngest of them alone was left to rule all France from 613 to 629: he too was named Lothar, Lothar II, and he was followed by the last great Merovingian, Dagobert, who also ruled all France. After him, the kings of Austrasia, Neustria or Burgundy were shadow kings, unable to dispute the claim of their mayors of the palace to exercise the real power.

The reigns of Clovis's four sons really belong to the era of the conquest of Gaul, and form one social period with that of Clovis himself, for his sons maintained their father's aggressive policy towards their neighbours, and the kingdom of the Franks was pushed to its widest extension under them. By Germanic custom, the lands of a king passed to his sons like a family estate: as Gregory put it: 'When Clovis the king was dead, his four sons, Theoderic, Chlodomer, Childebert and Chlotacharius (Lothar), received his kingdom and divided it equally.' The unity of the kingdom was still preserved, however, in the title *regnum Francorum*, and the four capitals of the four sons, Reims or Metz, Orleans, Paris and Soissons were all near the centre of the *regnum Francorum* and strategically well placed for combined action.

Theoderic (Theuderich, Thierry), as the eldest son, received the old homeland of the Franks, the basins of the Rhine and the Main; this was the most Germanic part of Clovis's realm, and the future

kingdom of the east Franks, Austrasia. It included the old lands of
the Ripuarians, with their capital at Cologne; but the court, moving from place to place in ox wagons, was usually at Reims or Metz.
To this inheritance, Theoderic added a share of the southern kingdom conquered from the Visigoths, stretching from Clermont to
Albi; Gregory describes him as a 'handsome and useful' young
man. Chlodomer's kingdom included the valleys of the Loire and
Garonne and was ruled from Orleans: Childebert ruled the Seine
valley from Paris, and (nominally) Armorica; Lothar, from Soissons, held the old Toxandria, the countries of the Scheldt and the
Rhine mouth. All these brothers, says Gregory, were so strong and
vigorous that Amalaric, king of Spain, sought their sister in marriage, and she was sent off to him 'with a great mass of ornaments'.

In this period of fresh conquests, the kingdom of Burgundy fell.
It had lost its chance of access to the sea by Theoderic the Ostrogoth's determination to secure communications with Spain, and
the acceptance of the Catholic as against the Arian faith by king
Sigismund availed neither to secure strong Gothic alliance, nor the
good will of the Franks. The kingdom of Burgundy in Clovis's day
had been the scene of the labours of the scholars Avitus of Vienne
and Caesarius of Arles; the state schools of the rhetors continued
in the Rhone valley longer than elsewhere in Europe, and individual rhetors taught there for fees later still. But the Franks meant
to conquer Burgundy: in 532 the kings Childebert and Chlodomer
attacked it, conquered Sigismund and threw him, his wife and
children down a well. Next year, king Gundobad of Burgundy
attacked and slew Chlodomer of Orleans; whereupon Childebert
and Lothar cut the throats of Chlodomer's two children and took
possession of his kingdom. But the kingdom of Burgundy soon
perished.

The Frankish attacks on the Visigoths were less successful;
though Chlodomer's raid on their province of Narbonne in 531
drove Amalaric back to Barcelona and led to his death.

The real gain in the period of Clovis's successors was on the
eastern frontier. Theoderic died in 533, but was succeeded by a
young and able son, Theudebert, who built churches, gave alms to
the poor, led his army well, but otherwise behaved with barbarian
violence and treachery. His ambitions extended themselves to Italy,
to Germany, and even to Constantinople. When Justinian was preparing to reconquer Gothic Italy from Witigis, he sent Theudebert
and Childebert large sums to secure their services as federates
against the Goths; they took the money, led an army to Italy, and
then joined Witigis on his promise to cede them Provence and

Rhaetia. In 539, when East Romans and Goths were fighting desperately, Theudebert led an army into north Italy, in his own interest plundering the cities from the gulf of Genoa to the head of the Adriatic; he kept no great territorial gains, but with the looted gold he, first of the Frankish kings, minted gold coins in his own name: the inscription ran *Dominus Theudebertus Augustus*. Though the words imply a sense that there was now a vacancy of power in Italy, and a barbarian disregard of Justinian, and though one chronicler credits Theudebert with the intention to march next on Constantinople, no such grandiose scheme of conquest materialized.

The real contribution of Theudebert to Frankish power, and even to a certain diffusion of *Romanitas*, was his conquest of south Germany. His father Theoderic had in 531 conquered Thuringia, north east of the valley of the Main: he had conquered, that is, all north Germany up to the coastal regions of the Frisians and the Saxons, the land of tribes in flux from the inroads of fresh Scandinavian invaders, and, in any case, filled with primitive Germanic fighters; Saxony was not conquered by the Franks till the days of Charlemagne. After his Italian expeditions, between 541 and 545, Theudebert set himself to conquer the old province of Noricum, once part of the Ostrogothic kingdom. The remnants of Theoderic's subjects here appear to have combined with such Rugians, Scyrrians, *Turcilingi* and *Heruli* as had remained outside Italy, under a duke of the 'Bavarians', and this new duchy Theudebert conquered, and made tributary. His conquests prepared the way for the later Carolingian empire: and a certain difference in character in medieval and modern times between north and south Germany (thus early conquered) may look back to an early contact with Frankish *Romanitas*.

Theudebert died in 548, and the reign of his young son, Theudebald, was marked only by a great disaster to the Ripuarian kingdom, when an army sent to plunder Italy in the last stages of the Gothic wars was defeated by Narses in Apulia, and perished of want and the plague. In 555 Theudebald died without heirs and his council elected his great-uncle, Lothar of Soissons, as king; as violent and treacherous a prince as any of the Merovingian house. He was now seventy years old: but he renewed the Frankish efforts to conquer the Saxons, meeting, however, only with disaster. In 558 his brother, Childebert of Paris, died: and Lothar became king of all the dominions of Clovis, in addition to Burgundy, Thuringia, Provence and Bavaria. When his son, Chramm, raised a rebellion against him with the aid of the Bretons in Armorica, he defeated the rebels, bound Chramm to the wooden settle in a poor woman's cottage, and, shutting his wife and children in with him, had the cottage closed and fired. They needed no burial; but Lothar himself soon after died of fever, in the fifty-first year of his reign, at his villa of Compiègne; and his four sons buried him in state in the new basilica at Soissons that he had recently built for St Médard. Gregory of Tours relates all this without comment: had not Lothar offered great gifts with tears of devotion to St Martin of Tours? In dealing with the barbarian kings, Gregory was always a realist and hoped for the best: 'but', he observes after recording Lothar's death, 'he died exactly a year to the day after the killing of Chramm'.

In the accommodation of the Gallo-Roman population to Frankish rule, the Merovingian bishop played a part of great importance. Not only was he often directly concerned in the domestic feuds of the house of Clovis, in efforts to minimize royal injustice by asserting his church's right to give sanctuary, and in attempts to avoid the assessment of his people to tribute, all matters liable to lead to violent outbursts and sudden dangers; but he shared occasionally in the administration of justice in the *civitas* (see p. 298). The area of his see was, as in late Roman days, the same as that of the chief administrative town of the province, and, in north Gaul, the same as the Frankish *pagus*. In central and south Gaul, count and bishop administered a curious *ad hoc* law, mainly Roman; in northern Gaul, with a larger Frankish population, the count's court, the *mallus* (see p. 63) must have been, in effect, a slightly Romanized folk-moot. In dealing with suits and pleas between his own clergy, the bishop, sitting as in a tribunal, leaned even more heavily on Roman law; the procedure in episcopal courts never adopted the Germanic custom of hearing plaintiff, witnesses and defendants all in court together, but maintained the procedure of the old Roman courts. Compurgation, however, the practice by which a clerk purged himself by bringing oath-helpers, was taken over by the church courts from the practice of the Germanic tribes.

Within his own see (called as yet more often *parochia* than diocese), the bishop was the absolute ruler of his clergy. He received them as boys and trained them as his household lectors; he alone could ordain them; he alone could, of right, preach and say mass in his own basilica (*ecclesia cathedralis*); he baptized catechumens, at Easter and Whitsuntide, and he absolved penitents. All the property of the see was at his disposal, and though he was bound to maintain the clergy he had ordained, he did this for the most part by maintaining them as the clergy of his basilica, partly with food grants, partly with money stipends. To the senior clergy of his basilica, the archdeacon who headed the (small) order of deacons in his church, and the archpriest, who headed the presbyters or who ruled a mother church out in the *rus*, he might grant a *beneficium*, a piece of land or a vineyard, returnable at death. Only a few rural parishes had as yet financial independence and their own landed endowment, and these were usually served by a small group of clergy. Outside the city, the countryside depended on the priests or clerks who served the private oratories or chapels of the *villae*, the bishop's and other, and the preaching of travelling missionaries and clerics. Gregory of Tours often speaks of the bishop as himself making a tour of his *rus*, his *territorium*, his dioceses (or rural parishes), and of the *villae* belonging to his church.

As to the church buildings of early Merovingian Gaul, very little has survived, for most of the churches were of wood, sometimes rude, wattled shelters, sometimes of smoothed wooden planks, well fitted together. In the cities, however, stone churches were gradually built, though only a few survive, even in part, e.g. the baptistery of St John at Poitiers, and the crypt at Jouarre, both of which belong to the second half of the seventh century.

As all over the Roman empire, the churches were built on different plans, from the open-ended trefoil chapel of the old cemeteries, built over the grave of some martyr (as in the very ancient church whose foundations still exist at La Gayole, Var, and the crypt of St Lawrence of Grenoble), to the colonnaded basilica with its apsidal east end, narthex, *porticus*, row of lateral cells for the *secretarium*, and separate baptistery, referred to in various places by Gregory of Tours. In all these churches, rounded arches and beautifully carved marble capitals followed the classical tradition in Roman architecture. Intermediate in size between these types, and owing something to Byzantine as well as Roman influence, quatrefoil churches with four small apses, square churches under a central dome, and round churches, were all built in France; the church of Saint-Germain l'Auxerrois at Paris was round, and the separate baptisteries often round or octagonal. Barbarian art appears to have added only one feature to the construction of Merovingian basilicas: the *turris* or tower built over the junction of nave and transepts in a church cruciform in plan. The detail of Merovingian carving is all classical: the acanthus leaf, the vine, the palmette, the naturalistic scene, as that of the horseman and trees on the seventh-century sarcophagus from the cemetery of Saint-Sernin of Toulouse; animal ornament and the stylized human

figure did not intrude themselves in the marbles of the early
Merovingian period.

But if the Franks left the Gallo-Roman bishops to build and
adorn the churches they endowed, their own ornaments and that
of their vases, lamps, weapons and shields followed their own Germanic patterns and used their own technique. Though classical
motifs like the scroll or the *guilloche*, or the Latin cross, might
be borrowed, the characteristic ornament of the north Frankish
brooches and buckles is the animal-headed, interlaced plait work,
such as occurs in the grave-finds of old Franconia and of the upper
Rhine (Salin. style II); in southern Gaul the earlier art-forms of the
Visigoths, or Roman influence, prevented the spread of this twist-
ing, writhing Germanic animal, with its jaws sometimes open,
sometimes biting the plait-work of its own body or limbs. This
animal style came ultimately from south Russia, but it developed
its characteristic Germanic form in central Europe: and it occurs
on the buckles, brooches, strapmounts of the widely extended
Merovingian kingdom, from Rouen to Bavaria. Another barbarian
feature, the beautiful flat-garnet cloisonné was used, not only for
brooches, but for larger objects dedicated to the service of the
church: as in the extant fragments of the cross of St Eligius, and
the chalice preserved at the abbey of Chelles, also attributed to
'St Eloi'. In the seventh century the nunnery (double monastery?)
of Chelles was one to which the Kentish and East Anglian kings
and nobles sent their daughters for training in the monastic life, or
to become nuns there permanently; intercourse across Channel
must have been fairly frequent.

The monastic life had reached Gaul as well as Italy and Africa,
before the Merovingian period, and it spread within it. St Eloi, for
instance, founded several monasteries and nunneries, like the
Ostrogothic senators in Italy, and the more so when he became a
bishop; he was a special patron of the Celtic form of monastic life,
planted by Columbanus in Gaul. In the introduction of the monastic life to Gaul, however, three names stand out, those of St
Martin of Tours, St Honoratus of Lérins and St Caesarius of
Arles. These men and their followers laid the foundations of the
monasticism of early Merovingian Gaul, the loosely-organized,
primitive monasticism of the Mediterranean basin and Ireland.
This monasticism drew its inspiration from Egypt and largely from
that picture of the Nitrian cells at the turn of the fifth century contained in the *Collations* of John Cassian. It was a monasticism of
ascesis and withdrawal: the caves in the rock side where Martin's

followers lived recall the 'holy cave' of Subiaco: but the groups of solitaries under a leader came to lead a more or less close community life, and by practising the Christian virtue of compassion and the old Greco-Roman devotion to letters, to spread civilization in a barbarian society. Radegunde, bathing the sick at Poitiers, and Caesarius, poring over his Latin and Greek papyri at Arles, both had a contribution to make to the new Frankish society.

The early fourth century saw Martin, the young Roman soldier from Pannonia, start to lead the solitary life with only such knowledge of the Egyptian ascetics as reached Gaul and the Mediterranean basin generally. He had already been trained in the *familia* of the great bishop, Hilary of Poitiers, when he began to lead the solitary life at Ligugé; a crowd of disciples gathered round him, and a *laura*, a group of cells, grew up in this Gallic Thebaid. He was elected by popular acclamation to the episcopate of Tours in 372, and combined the work of a bishop with the monastic life, founding the monastery of Marmoutier a short distance from Tours. When he died at Candes, in the diocese, his body was taken to Tours, and buried in the cemetery in a stone sarcophagus, above which later bishops built first a simple *oratorium* and then, in 470, the famous basilica served by monks. Martin became a great wonder worker, and the patron of the Frankish kings, who cherished the half of his famous cloak which he had kept when, as a catechumen, he gave the other half to Christ; later, the right to this precious relic was to give a later French dynasty the title of Capetians (from *capa*, cloak).

Honoratus of Lerins (*c.* 350–429), another admirer of the Egyptian fathers, founded a famous monastery on the wild island of Lerins, at the mouth of the Rhone: it became a house of learning and a nursery of missionaries and bishops. In 426, at a time when the Rhone valley was disturbed by Visigothic Arianism, and the heresy of the Manichees that came over the water from Africa and the east Mediterranean, Honoratus was summoned to become archbishop of Arles. He succeeded in strengthening the faith of the Catholic provincials as bishop, while maintaining the direction of his own monastery at Lérins. Whether he gave a rule to his monastery is not certainly known, for none has been preserved, but the daily routine and practice of a monastery precede a rule, and it was the monastic practice of Lérins that Patrick would appear to have taken with him to Ireland. John Cassian visited Lérins and dedicated to Honoratus some of his *Collations*; Honoratus died in 429.

Caesarius of Arles, unlike the two first great monks, lived when the Franks had already conquered Gaul (*c.* 470–543). His episcopate of Arles (502–543) covered the period when the kingdom of Burgundy, long threatened by the Franks, finally fell; Caesarius was involved in the political struggles of the kings of Burgundy, the Visigoths and the Ostrogoths, and between the Arianism of the Burgundian and Gothic kings and the Catholicism of the senatorial class in Gaul. He had been trained in the monastic life of Lérins when young, and then as clerk at Arles in the household of bishop Æonus, by whom he was made deacon and priest. He succeeded Æonus in 503 as metropolitan of Arles and ruled the province for forty years. Arles had been the old Roman capital of Gaul, after the evacuation from Trier, and it had great strategic importance in maintaining communications between the Visigoths at Toulouse and the Ostrogoths at Ravenna; Caesarius was accused by Alaric II of treason, on the charge that he wished to deliver the city to the Burgundians. In 506, however, Alaric relented, allowed Caesarius to summon a council of bishops to Agde, and there to publish the *Breviarium Alarici*, for the benefit of the provincials of Gaul. In 507, however, the Frankish victory brought peril to Arles and Caesarius; the city was besieged, but the Ostrogoths took it and deported Caesarius, as suspected of favouring the Burgundians and the Franks. In 513, Theoderic summoned him to Ravenna, but treated him with respect and even distinction. He was able to visit Rome and pope Symmachus, who gave him the pallium and, in 514, made him vicar of the apostolic see in Gaul. He returned to live through the conquest of Burgundy and Arles by the Franks, Childebert and Chlodomer, and the annexation of the kingdom by Childebert and Lothar; but in spite of wars and royal assassinations, he was able to hold councils of bishops at Arles in 524, Carpentras, 527, Vaison, 526 and Marseilles, 533. These councils regulated the growing life of the church by canons: and Caesarius' concern for the earlier foundations of canon law found expression in his drawing up a résumé of earlier canons known as the *Statuta Ecclesiae Antiqua*. His access to the archives and the notaries of the old Gallic seat of administration, and to those of his own metropolitan see, made this piece of ecclesiastical research the easier; and Greek was, in the Rhone delta, still a spoken language.

Caesarius, still accounted a monk while he lived as bishop, and certainly acquainted with the monastic practice of Lérins and the rule of St Augustine, may have added to this knowledge acquaintance with the legislation affecting the church in Justinian's new *Code* of 529; as a notable canonist, this might be expected. In the two rules which he composed, for monks and nuns, the influence

EARLY MEROVINGIAN KINGS

CLOVIS I, 481–511

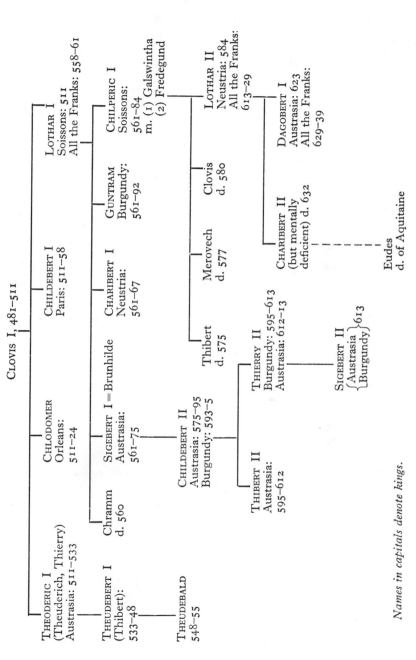

Names in capitals denote kings.

of Cassian and St Augustine is certainly evident. His sister, St Caesaria, was abbess of a nunnery at Arles, and for her he composed a rule founded on the rule of St Augustine, and having certain resemblances, on the other hand, to those of St Benedict and Cassiodorus. Pope Hormisdas wrote to him confirming the exemption of 'this choir, not of clerks nor of monks but of maidens, that you have instituted', from the authority of the local bishop. The rule laid down that the furnishing of the convent must be simple, and that there should be no pictured coverings (*tapetas*) to the beds: the nuns should occupy themselves with spinning and domestic work: but also with the copying of 'the divine books'. It became the rule of St Radegunde's nunnery at Poitiers; before the last quarter of the seventh century the Benedictine rule had not met with any wide acceptance in Gaul.

BIBLIOGRAPHICAL NOTE

The primary source for this period is Gregory of Tours' history of the Franks, for which see O. M. Dalton's translated text, preface and notes: for the Latin text, the new ed. in *M.G.H.* of Gregory's *Libri Historiarum*, 3 vols., 1951, the third volume with an important preface by B. Krusch and W. Levison; see also J. M. Wallace-Hadrill, *The Barbarian West 400–1000* (1952), and on the work of Gregory of Tours in *Trans. R. Hist. Soc.*, 5th Series, vol. i, pp.25–45. See also S. R. Dill, *Roman Society in Gaul in the Merovingian Age*, 1926, and the important E. Salin's *Civilisation Mèrovingienne d'aprés les sépultures, les textes et le laboratoire*, which contains much of interest in addition to the archaeological matter: also N. Åberg, *The Merovingian Empire*, Stockholm, 1947: W. Levison, *Aus Rheinischer und Fränkischer Frühzeit* 1948: R. Lantier and J. Hubert, *Les origines de l'art français*, 1947; E. Mâle, *La fin du paganisme en Gaule*, 1950: O. Chadwick, *John Cassian*, 1950, for a study of primitive monasticism in Gaul: H. G. J. Beck, *The Pastoral Care of Souls in South-east France during the Sixth Century*, 1950 (Analecta Gregoriana, vol. li, Series facultatis hist. ecclesiasticae). See also, J. M. Wallace-Hadrill, *The Long-Haired Kings and other studies*, London, 1962. For the survival of slavery in southern France and Spain, see C. Verlinden, *L'esclavage dans l'Europe médiévale*, Bruges, 1955.

CHAPTER V

THE VANDALS

THE greatest period of Vandal rule in Africa occurred just before 476, for Gaiseric, the conqueror of the north African provinces, died in the year following. Nevertheless, the Vandal conquest, and the Vandal loss, of Africa, cannot be passed over in the study of the new, Germanic Europe, if only because it was a more important factor in economic change than almost any other Germanic settlement. Europe passed from the mainly money economy of the Roman empire to the mainly food and service economy of the new kingdoms; some distinguished historians hold that the dominance of the Mediterranean by the Vandal fleet was, more than any other single factor, responsible for this change (see chap. VII).

The Roman diocese of Africa included the coastal strip south of the gulf of the Great Syrtes westward nearly to the promontory opposite the modern Gibraltar (Tingis): the province of Tingitana formed part of the prefecture of the Gauls. All this north African coast had more rainfall and was more fertile than in modern times, especially the provinces inland from Carthage and Hippo Regius (Bona); the diocese was one of the most thoroughly Romanized and richest in the Roman empire. Carthage had a fine temple to Mercury, and was known in the sixth century as the Mercurian city, and her headland as the Mercurian promontory; the episcopate of St Cyprian of Carthage (248–258) had rendered her church famous. The diocese of Africa was Latin speaking and, with the islands of Corsica, Sardinia and Sicily, part of the praetorian prefecture of Italy; it was the southern part of an empire bounded by the Saharan deserts and their tribes, and not by the coast of the Mediterranean. The eastern trade could be borne by Byzantine or Syrian fleets to Italy, Gaul and Spain because the Mediterranean was a Roman lake, and safer. That safety was lost with the Vandal conquest; and the Latin Christianity that had produced some of the earliest councils and canons, and a figure like St Augustine of Hippo, was lost too.

The Asdingian and Silingian Vandals had crossed the Pyrenees into Spain, with the Sueves and Alans, in 409; they had to fight with the Visigothic king Wallia for their settlements in 416, and the Silingian Vandals appear to have been nearly wiped out. From

418 the Vandals were led, as were the Alans, by the Asdingian king. They were hard pressed for a time, but in 421–422 defeated a Roman army and possessed themselves of the Mediterranean coast of Spain. They took New Carthage (Cartagena), and presumably, with it, certain ships in the harbour, as they did later when attacking Roman ports: they began to build up a fleet, not accidentally, but because the coastal districts which they conquered were already served by ships bringing eastern goods to Spain, and even passing through the straits of Gibraltar and outside the Atlantic promontories to Britain. The Vandals were good horsemen, who had once been associated with the nomadic Huns: but the plunder of the ships and the sea ports turned their mind to sea piracy. They had more ships built and started out to plunder the Balearics and the African province of Mauretania.

In 428 the Vandal king, Gunderic, died, and was succeeded by Gaiseric, and in May, probably, of that year, he led the Vandal fleet across the straits to Africa; it has been suggested that count Boniface, ruler of the diocese of Africa and now in disgrace at the court of Ravenna, invited the Vandals over as federates and supplied some of the ships. He was, in any case, in difficulties with the Moors. By 430, however, he was fighting in defence of his province: the Vandals could take the open countryside, but the walled towns of Hippo, Cirta and Carthage held out. Augustine, bishop of Hippo, died during the siege of his city. In 435 Valentinian III was forced to allow the Vandals to settle as federates in six African provinces; Carthage and its small but rich adjacent province, the emperor kept. By 439, however, Gaiseric was able to take Carthage and make it his capital, and in 440 a fresh peace was made, the Vandals now holding all north Africa from Tingitana to the boundary between the provinces of Byzacium and Tripoli (the modern Mareth Line).

For the rest of Gaiseric's life, the Vandals were extremely dangerous to the western emperor. The Vandal fleet ruled the Mediterranean, raided the islands of Sicily, Sardinia and Corsica, and cut off all supplies from Italy. When, in 455, Valentinian murdered Aëtius and was himself murdered by Aëtius' followers, Gaiseric led his fleet to Ostia, the port of Rome, met pope Leo and agreed not to sack the city, but spent eleven days in completely stripping it of its wealth. He carried off the widowed empress Eudoxia and her two daughters, 'and a great mass of gold and silver and the furnishing of the imperial household'. He took away too, half the roof of the temple of Capitoline Jove, for it was roofed with the best bronze. Of the ships at Ostia, he sank one that bore the imperial *simulacra* and the rest he had taken away to Carthage. He had Eudoxia married to his eldest son, Huneric, and carried off all three ladies as valuable hostages to Africa: the next year a Vandal fleet raided Sicily and the bordering coast of south Italy.

Both in east and west, the emperors desired to reckon with the Vandals: but their other barbarian enemies were nearer and seemed more dangerous. In 458 and 460 the emperor Majorian made expeditions preparatory to a reconquest of Africa from Spain, without success. The Vandals were now plundering, not only the Mediterranean islands and Italy, but Illyricum, Greece and the east Mediterranean as well; even Alexandria, key port of the eastern trade, was threatened. The emperor Leo sent a Byzantine fleet to Cape Bon to attack the pirates in their stronghold, but had no success. When Gaiseric died in 477, he had obtained a peace treaty with the eastern empire, and could pass on his kingdom to his eldest son, with directions for the future succession of a single king to all his dominions, instead of the partition of the realm among sons, according to the usual Germanic practice. His rules for the passage of the crown to the eldest male heir of sufficient age also met with acceptance, and showed statesmanship.

The kingdom which Gaiseric set up on his capture of Carthage, and whose years he reckoned from the day of the city's capture, 19 October 439, lasted for ninety-five years, till the surrender of king Gelimer to Belisarius in 534. It was the rule of a sub-tropical province by a race of Germanic raiders who had learned little of *Romanitas* since they left their homes in the horse-plains of Hungary, and fought their way through Gaul and Spain to Africa. Their brooches, buckles and other jewellery were barbaric, and the Vandal grave-finds of Africa are of coarser workmanship than the Ostrogothic or Merovingian jewellery. Two sets of ornaments from graves near Bona include from the woman's grave a fine bead necklace, and earrings and buckle with cloisonné set with garnet and red and green glass; and from the man's, two large disc brooches for holding drapery at the shoulder, the large, coarse cloisons set with blue and green enamel, turquoise, and amber; and two smaller disc brooches with garnet cloisonné, and two buckles, one with a man fighting a horse or some creature, engraved on a gold ground. Since the Vandals were professional plunderers, it is hard to say that their own goldsmiths made a particular ornament, as in the case of the buckle last described: but the Vandal cloisonné jewellery, with its blue, red and green

insets had its ancestry in south Russian art, like that of the other
Germanic peoples.

The Vandals from 439 settled down to rule the province from
Carthage; their status was recognized by the western emperor in a
treaty of 442. The estates on which they settled were all in the good
land in the neighbourhood of Carthage. The historian, Procopius
of Caesaria, who was later to accompany Belisarius' expedition
to Carthage, and who was well informed about Vandal affairs,
states that there was no formal thirding of the land of the provincials, but simply expropriation. 'If any citizen of Africa were
noble and rich, he (Gaiseric) gave them with all their *latifundia*
and household staff, yes, and with their own persons, as slaves
(*servi* or *coloni*) to his sons, Huneric and Genzoni. Some lands he
allowed the Africans to redeem at a price, but the greater part, and
the best lands, he divided among his Vandals.' Whence, he explains,
the origin of the phrase: *sortes Vandalorum*. 'Thus every kind of
calamity befel the African.'

Military reasons, as well as agricultural, had dictated the con-
centration of the Vandals in Zeugitana, around Carthage; the
Catholic clergy whose church happened to fall within the *sortes
Vandalorum*, were driven from their churches, as were the bishops
of Carthage and Hippo Regius. Elsewhere, in the other provinces,
the landowning classes and the townsmen remained undisturbed,
as did the Catholic clergy at first. But all the provincials, from
Tingitana to Byzacium, had suffered in the conquest, and were
now a subject people, their land held only at the pleasure of the
Vandal king. The walls of all the towns were destroyed by Gaiseric,
except those of the Vandal strongholds, the Castle Septa at the
Straits of Gibraltar, Hippo Regius and Carthage; a measure that
made easier the encroachments of the desert tribes, the Moors
(Mauri), against whom the Roman provincial governors had for
long struggled. It was to make easier also the final reconquest by
Belisarius.

The Vandal monarchy under Gaiseric and his successors seems
to have been more absolute than that of the other Germanic kings,
and, except for its rule of hereditary succession within the old
sacred family of the Asdings, something more akin to 'tyranny'.
No council of Vandal nobles had, for instance, the weight in his
counsels that the Frankish nobles could exercise; Gaiseric's ability
to set aside the Germanic practice of partitioning the royal inheritance among sons is further evidence of his power. The cause
of such royal independence is probably the fact that the Vandal
power was not based on the land, or on the achievements of a class

of warriors fighting normally on land. Whereas the Franks, settled
in Gaul, came to depend, after the first era of loot and conquest,
on the produce of their estates and such rights of tolls and customs
from merchants as were granted them by the sovereign, or usurped
from him: the Vandal power rested on the products of a perpetual
stream of piracy. Just as the Byzantine empire never developed a
feudal society, but obtained its revenue from the profits of a great
sea trade, so the Vandals, both king and nobles, relied on that
earlier form of sea trade, piracy and raiding. The Vandals had
acquired a large number of the Greek ships, and built more; if they
had not acquired the Byzantine trading monopoly of the Mediterranean, because direct looting was as yet more profitable, they
had completely disrupted Mediterranean trade. The Vandal king
found his richest followers, a race of sea pirates, a less dangerous
rival than a class of landed, fighting nobles.

The Vandal army fought, of course, on its ships, as well as in
raids on a hostile countryside; sailors manned the ships, but for
hundreds of years were not its fighting crew. There was some
effort to organize the Vandal army in the West Roman or East
Roman manner, none the less. Procopius tells us that Gaiseric
set over his Vandal and Alan cohorts eighty '*duces*' called *chiliarchs*,
because they were tribunes of 1,000 men (the tribune was the
Roman officer who commanded a cohort, a subdivision of the
legion). Under these officers, with their Byzantine names, Gaiseric
might reckon to have some 80,000 warriors under his *signa* (the
old standards of the legions). Only the Moors, some of whom he
enlisted and sent yearly to raid Sicily and Italy, fought in their
own regiments: among the Vandals and Alans, and such Heruls,
Sueves and Goths as had accompanied them, or enlisted, no
distinction was made. According to Procopius, very little strategic
planning was done by Gaiseric before the fleet started on its raid:
'Sometimes when he went aboard in the port of Carthage, the
steersman of the ship would ask him, what people they were
about to attack? and men remembered that he would answer:
Let us go against the people with whom God is wroth,' i.e. not
normally against the Arians.

From the first, the Vandals' relations with the Catholics of
Africa were bad, though they deteriorated as time went on: it is
probable that the significance of the name 'Vandal' owed as much
to reaction against fierce religious persecution as to hatred of a
race of pirates. There was no senatorial class, no order of Catholic
bishops, trying to make the régime work, as in Italy and Gaul:
the one had been expropriated, the other persecuted. Religious

hatred also weakened the Vandals in their efforts to keep the desert tribes out of the province. In the reign of Thrasamund, Procopius tells us, there was very great injury to the Vandals from the *Mauri*.

When the Vandals advanced against the Moors in Tripoli, Cabaon was the Moorish general. He divided his camp into two enclosures, each surrounded by a *vallum*; within one walled camp were the men, within the other, the women. He sent out scouts, and ordered them, whenever they saw the Vandals dishonour a Christian temple, to wait till they were gone, and then to approach the church respectfully and say: Though they had not the same notion of God as the Christians, yet it behoved them to protect that worship which the Vandals treated with contempt; for the Vandals stabled their horses in Christian churches, and left no shameful injury undone. They buffeted the bishops, beat them on the back, and set them to the vilest services. Then the watchers of Cabaon would come swiftly, and clean out the church, carrying out all filth, and relighting the hanging lamps. They would kneel before the bishop and embrace him with all reverence, and give silver to the mendicants sitting round the church. Then they followed the Vandals: and the Vandals were never without these Moorish watchers when they robbed and plundered the churches.

Church life in Africa before the Vandal invasion was established early, and there are still some remains there of early basilicas, and small round or square churches in the Syrian manner, notably the basilicas of Tebessa, Orleansville (324), Tiposa, in Algeria; and in Tunisia, Birmali and le Kef. There are no remains, however, of a specifically 'Arian' church, nor would such, as far as we know, have been distinguished in its plan or architecture from the Catholic churches, with their low altar on the chord of the apse, their *secretarium* or series of chambers for the bishop and his clergy, and their separate baptisteries.

On the death of Gaiseric, his son Huneric, husband of the imperial princess Eudoxia, succeeded him, and at a moment of difficulty (25 January 477). The Moorish hill tribes had revolted, and, in spite of his efforts, succeeded in renouncing the Vandal supremacy; he had, moreover, a quarrel on his hands with the eastern emperor about Eudoxia's fortune, and he even contemplated allowing the see of Carthage to be filled again by its Catholic bishop (481). He soon perceived, however, that no real danger threatened from East Rome, and began to revenge himself on those whom he feared in his own family, and on the Catholics. 'No man', says Procopius, 'oppressed the Christians so cruelly, so unjustly, as Huneric'; he tortured and even burned them alive. By an edict of 484, he ordered that all the edicts made by the Roman emperors against heresy should be set in force against the Catholics, unless they became Arians; he deported the Catholic bishops to Sardinia, forbade Catholic priests to hold churches, build new ones, administer the sacraments, or even reside in any town or village. All the Catholic churches and their property were transferred to the Arians, the Catholic laity at court were deprived of their offices, graduated money fines according to rank were imposed on all Catholics, and the Arian clergy were commissioned to put in force these intolerant measures. The emperor and the pope remonstrated, but to no purpose.

Huneric was succeeded by two more moderate rulers, brothers: Gunthamund, 484–496, and Thrasamund, 496–523. The first persecuted, but less fiercely: most of the Catholic churches were reopened in 487, though some bishops were still retained in Sardinia. This milder policy was perhaps due to Gunthamund's frequent wars with the Moors. Thrasamund, in his long reign, is the only Vandal king to win praise from his Greek or Latin contemporaries: they represent him as dignified in speech, and of great prudence and magnanimity. His reign coincides with the great Ostrogothic reign of Theoderic, when the Arian Germanic kings seemed to have attained some security of rule in the west. Thrasamund, desiring Theoderic's alliance, asked for his sister, Amalafrida, in marriage, and Theoderic sent her with a magnificent train of 1,000 fighting nobles as escort. But while the Vandal position in the Mediterranean seemed secure, the Moors slew great numbers of Vandals on their flanks, and inflicted at least one severe defeat. When he led a force of Vandals against the Moors of the interior, they fought a defensive battle, though sending out scouts to bring word of his movements. Their camp, surrounded by a *vallum*, with the women and children at the centre, surrounded by a ring of warriors with shields, was traversed by a lane to allow freedom of movement to a large force of camels, who were also posted in groups at the circumference to meet attack from any direction from the Vandal horsemen. But the Vandals hesitated to attack, for their mobile raids had not trained them to take a defended position. They were no mounted archers, like the Huns, and some of the Byzantine forces: nor were they trained spearthrowers; they were not used to fighting on foot. When they charged, they used the stabbing spear and sword, but at this battle their horses, terrified of the camels, refused to charge and force the position. In the end, the Vandals fled and the Moors killed many in pursuit.

The next king, Hilderic, son of Huneric and Eudoxia, reigned

4

from 523 to 531: but his double ancestry betrayed him. He had lived long at Constantinople, and proved a sovereign more Roman than Vandal in policy. He favoured his mother's Catholicism rather than his father's Arianism, and it was said of him that *nullo modo unquam Christianos vexavit*. He was unpopular among his subjects as elderly, Catholic and timid. He had promised Thrasamund not to restore the churches to the Catholics, but on his accession he at once did so, and recalled their bishops. Beyond that, he had Amalafrida, the great Arian princess, imprisoned and put to death: and Theoderic still lived. In 531 he was dethroned and imprisoned by his cousin Gelimer.

The eastern empire had a reckoning to make with the Vandals, who had long harried the Balkans and the east Mediterranean, and it was now ruled by perhaps the greatest of the East Roman emperors, Justinian, 527–565. His vigorous predecessor, Justin, had been a Catholic, and turned the eyes of the oppressed Catholic subjects of Arian kings to the east; to religious orthodoxy Justinian now added a vigorous foreign policy, and the ability to choose good military leaders to put in force his aim to revive the Roman *imperium* in the Mediterranean. Even apart from his desire to revive *Romanitas*, however, the Vandal sea-power was a real menace to the sea-power at Constantinople, at whose expense it had been mainly founded. When Justinian heard of the deposition and imprisonment of Hilderic, in whose veins ran the blood of the great Theodosius, he was prevented by difficulties on the Persian frontier and insecurity at home from dealing peremptorily with Gelimer; he negotiated, and suggested that Hilderic, an old man, might be left with nominal rule, while Gelimer governed the kingdom in his name. To this, however, Gelimer returned an arrogant refusal.

Then, in 532, Justinian's hands were strengthened. The very dangerous *Nika* riots were suppressed, and he was able to make a 'perpetual peace' with the Persian ruler, Chosroes I. In the seventh year of Justinian's reign, Procopius the historian tells us, on 22 June 533, count Belisarius was sent with some 15,000 fighting troops (apart from the sailors) to reconquer Africa. He himself accompanied the expedition; he was already, by the beginning of Justinian's reign, counsellor and secretary to Belisarius, illustrious in rank, and notable as a man of letters at the cultivated and learned Byzantine court. His relationship to Belisarius made possible the spirited and independent account in his *Books about the Wars*, of the Persian, the Vandal, and the Gothic War; he accompanied the Byzantine forces on all of them.

Although grave doubts had been expressed as to the desirability of the expedition to Carthage on the grounds of expense and the exhaustion of the army after the Persian campaigns, certain factors encouraged Justinian's hopes of success. His own Greek merchants clamoured for the attempt; and the Vandal bishops assured him the provincials would support Belisarius. A rising did, indeed, break out in Tripolitania against the Vandals, and in Sardinia their officer, Godas, a Goth by race, wavered in his loyalty, particularly in view of the Goths' own difficulties under Amalasuntha. King Gelimer was driven to send a force under his brother, Tzazo, to suppress disloyalty in Sardinia. Moreover, the greatest difficulty in the reconquest of Africa was transport, and here the Byzantine empire was operating on its own element, and much better placed to put a force ashore near Carthage than any emperor of the west had been. Belisarius' force, then, embarked in 500 transports, 10,000 of them infantry and some 5,000 cavalry; the horses, according to Procopius, being partly picked up *en route*, for they had been pastured in Thrace.

Procopius relates that Belisarius with his wife Antonia and 'the writer of this history, himself', embarked in the *Navis Praetoria*—the headquarters of the legion, the *Praetorium*, transferred aboard ship—and sailed from Byzantium at the summer solstice. They crossed the Aegean, and had difficulties with naval stores and water shortage; only in Belisarius' own ship did the water stay fresh. That was because Antonia was skilled in the art of preserving water; she had glass *amphorae* filled with water and stored in a small chamber down in the vessel's hold, where the sun's rays could not strike. She had the *amphorae* packed in sand: and the water remained fresh; which throws light, incidentally, on the question of how so large a quantity of glass ware was transported for trading purposes, in late imperial times, by sea.

In the hopes of receiving fresh stores promised by Amalasuntha, the fleet landed in Sicily, at some distance from Syracuse; there Procopius went off alone to obtain news of the Vandal dispositions, hearing with joy that a large Vandal force was occupied in Sardinia. Belisarius then sailed, and at length the south wind bore him to Caput-Vada, five days' journey from Carthage. Belisarius held a council on the *Navis Praetoria* on the problem of attacking Carthage, and in the third month from their start from Byzantium, they landed and built themselves a *vallum* round their camp, surrounding it with a fence of stakes, and all in a single day. They had encamped where there was a spring, wonder enough in that dry land, sufficient for man and beast. That night they slept in camp, leaving fifteen archers on each ship as a guard; and the next day they advanced, Belisarius warning his troops not to spoil the crops or pluck the fruit of the provincials: for the Africans, he said, are descendants of Romans, and hate the Vandals. 'We are about to sweep away your tyrant,' Belisarius told the provincials themselves. And that same day, the procurator of the *cursus publicus* handed over to him his 'public horses'.

Then Belisarius drew up his line and marched: and on 13 September 533, he met and defeated Gelimer *ad Decimum* (at the tenth milestone from Carthage to the south), the king himself retreating westward into Numidia. It was a great victory, obtained with unexpected ease; and that evening Belisarius and Antonia came to Carthage, finding all quiet. There seemed nothing to stop their entry, for the Carthaginians had unlocked the gates and lit the hanging lamps: all that night the city was open and lit up, and the Vandals left within lay as suppliants in the churches. But Belisarius, fearing an ambush, did not enter.

Next day, the ships arrived at Mandraccium, the port of Carthage, and the Carthaginians, pulling away the chains that guarded the harbour, offered them entrance. The day following Belisarius entered the city, ordering his troops not to harm the Africans, who bore the Vandal yoke unwillingly. He entered Gelimer's *palatium* and sat upon his throne.

Then, says Procopius, Belisarius ordered *prandium* to be prepared in the place where Gelimer used to feast the Vandal princes: and this place the Romans called the Delphic chamber—a Greek, and not a Latin name, and indeed a very old name. For in that part of the Roman *palatium* where the imperial guests feasted, there used to stand a bronze tripod, on which the emperor's cup bearers (*pincernae*) used to place the cups. Now the tripod, which was first used at Delphi, the Romans called Delphic; and hence the Byzantine custom has arisen that, in the royal apartments, the supper room is called the Delphic chamber. 'And so Belisarius feasted, with the nobles of his army: the feast had been prepared for Gelimer, but it fell to us to feast on their dishes; and the servants of Gelimer bore the dishes and served the cups.'

And so the old prophecy which the children of Carthage had long cried in their games without understanding, was fulfilled:

> G fugabit B
> ac rursus B fugabit G

> [Gaiseric fugabit Bonifacium,
> ac rursus Belisarius fugabit Gelimer.

As to the Arians, Procopius continues, they all recanted: the bishops purified the churches, they hung up the votive offerings, long hidden away: the beautifully ornamented hanging bowls, the sacred vessels, furniture and hangings: all these they prepared for their proper use. The Arian priests fled, and the Catholics re-entered the temple of Cyprian, lit the lamps, and performed the sacred rites.

All this is very good reporting by Procopius of a great occasion: but the sequel was not so happy. Gelimer had taken refuge with those Moors who remained faithful to him at *Bulla Regia*, in Numidia; he had recalled his brother Tzazo with his army from Sardinia, and he cut the aqueduct that supplied Carthage with water and blockaded the city. Belisarius was driven to march out and fight him; he defeated Gelimer at Tricameron, twenty-six miles to the west of Carthage, and Tzazo was killed in battle. The king himself again took refuge with the Moors, at Pappua; and Belisarius seized the Vandal treasure at Hippo and sent his lieutenants to seize Sardinia, Corsica and the Balearics. He even took the Castle at Septa (the modern Ceuta), far away to the west; and Gelimer submitted and gave himself up.

Justinian, then believing the Vandals crushed, recalled Belisarius and assigned him a triumph, in which Gelimer walked; he himself assumed the titles of Vandalicus and Africanus. He ordered the restoration of Roman government in the conquered province; but the Moors rose in a rebellion which necessitated the recall of Belisarius from Sicily. A Vandal resistance movement coupled with the continued threat from the desert tribes prolonged the war for fifteen years after Belisarius had first set out from Constantinople; but the impoverished province was in 548 restored to the Roman peace.

The fall of the Vandals, and the disappearance of their culture from Africa, may be traced to three causes. In the first place, the Vandals were numerically insufficient to maintain either; their numbers may have doubled or trebled between 429 and 533, but they were still only a small minority. Again, although, living as they did in the midst of the Romano-Africans of the provinces of Proconsularis and Byzacene, they adopted the Roman administration and, to some extent, the Latin language, they still remained separated from the provincials by religious difference and a legacy of resentment. Dracontius, poet and rhetor, and almost the only one produced by the régime, tells us that the children of both races frequented his school, and in course of time, co-operation might have been achieved; but the time was lacking. Then again, effective Vandal rule only existed in the region round Carthage and Hippo; Tripolitania, Numidia, Mauretania were actually held by Moorish princes owing only a nominal allegiance. Expansion, to the Vandals, meant sea piracy, not a gradual, piecemeal extension of their rule by settlement east and west along the coast.

If it is asked: what share had the diocese of Africa in transmitting the Roman heritage, the answer must be, that it had a very considerable share, but the transmission mainly took place just before the Vandals came. It is true that the Vandals used notaries, counts, prefects, and the old *conductores*, the stewards of the Roman *latifundia* and villas in Africa; some Vandal princes, Thrasamund especially, had buildings erected in the Roman manner. Justinian restored the old Roman government of the province and the Catholic clergy, and in this land of old Roman basilicas, baths and circuses, there might have been continuity. But what the Vandal wars and religious strife had left, was overrun and overthrown by the Arab invasion of the seventh century.

Yet there are two great Africans whose names cannot be left out in the history of the new Germanic society in Europe; those of Martianus Capella, and, above all, Augustine of Hippo, both rhetors, the one the first great encyclopedist of the liberal arts, the other philosopher, theologian, bishop, and the fountain head of a particular stream of theology, a particular philosophy of history, and a particular form of the monastic life.

The subjects that the Roman rhetors had long taught in their school, the disciplines they had taken over from the Greeks, had been discussed in various treatises during the Roman empire, and even earlier, but there had been no attempt at a comprehensive treatise on the whole range of the 'arts' before the fifth century. But now, with Roman society falling apart, and uncertainty prevailing how long any central government could maintain and pay a civil service, of which the rhetors were a branch: the desire came to more than one scholar to codify the learning of the day: to provide teachers possibly without salary, school or library, with the apparatus of teaching, a conspectus of the liberal arts. The great encyclopedists all belong to the fifth and sixth centuries, though Isidore of Seville lived till 636.

Martianus Capella composed his treatise, the *De Nuptiis philologiae et Mercurii*, at some time between the taking of Rome by Alaric in 410, and the conquest of Africa by Gaiseric in 429. He was a native of Madaura, south of Hippo Regius, and learned his rhetoric there and at Carthage, where he taught, and practised in the law courts (the *formulae* of the civil law were largely taught as a branch of rhetoric). His treatise is in the line of Varro's *Disciplinae*, and from him he borrowed the judgment that medicine and law should not be reckoned among the liberal arts: they were concerned only with earthly things, i.e. they were applied as against pure sciences, to use modern phraseology. Both Cicero before him and Augustine, his younger contemporary, discussed the same problem, Cicero being willing to place them among the liberal arts, with certain qualifications, and Augustine disallowing them; in fact, through the middle ages, neither was included in the arts course. Both remained postgraduate subjects of study, only certain universities providing faculties of medicine and law. It was probably Martianus Capella's treatise which fixed in the early medieval mind the number of the arts as seven; though this was supported by the much-quoted text from the book of Wisdom: *Wisdom hath builded herself an house, she hath hewn out seven pillars.*

While, however, Martianus Capella followed certain traditional lines in discussing the content of learning, he cast his treatise in the form of the old *Satyra*, a romance in a medley of prose and verse, modelling himself upon Apuleius. The work shows no evidence that its author was Christian, and deals allegorically with the old pagan gods; indeed, in his use of allegory, Martianus Capella looked forward to the middle ages, rather than back to the classical. In his curious plot, Mercury (to whom there was a fine temple in Carthage) desires to wed: but Wisdom, Divination and the Soul refused the alliance. Then Apollo recommends him to wed Philology, a charming maiden, though human; the gods consent. Philology is made divine, the virtues, the muses and the graces prepare her for the wedding. Then seven young maidens, Grammar, Dialectic, Rhetoric, Geometry, Arithmetic, Astronomy and Music are offered her, in Apollo's name, to be her bridesmaids: and the romance suddenly becomes a text-book, for each maiden delivers a long discourse covering her own field of knowledge, Music finally conducting the Bride to the marriage chamber. The discourses were not original, but consisted of one or more long extracts from earlier works on the subject.

But though Martianus' work has no literary merit, it had wide influence as a manual in the schools. At the end of the fifth century the African Fulgentius composed a work modelled on it, the text was known in Rome in the mid sixth century, and Gregory of Tours mentions that it was used in the schools of Gaul.

Aurelius Augustinus, St Augustine of Hippo (354–430), was a far greater figure than Martianus Capella. He was born at Tagaste, in east Numidia, the son of Patricius and Monica, who were both Africans of Roman descent. Augustine, however, seems to have been acquainted with the Punic language, and, when a bishop, insisted on having priests who could speak it. In 366 he went to learn grammar (Latin literature) to Madaura, and in 371 to Carthage to study rhetoric. After some years he crossed to Italy, hoping to obtain a post as rhetor in Rome, and finally obtained one at Milan, where he was much influenced by Ambrose the bishop; at Easter, in 387, he was baptized by Ambrose. He had already, in Africa, been a Manichee and then rejected Manichaeism; at Milan, he was attracted by Neoplatonism, and also first heard of the ascetic and solitary life led by Anthony in the desert. He decided to return to Africa and lead a communal and retired life with certain of his friends who had a similar attraction; on the way, his mother Monica died, and he describes their last evening together in the famous chapter of his *Confessions* beginning: If to any, the tumult of the flesh were hushed . . . But though he intended a life of *ascesis* (withdrawal) he had not done with learning: he wrote six books *De Musica* and published them when he returned to Africa.

Augustine then founded in 388 at Tagaste, in his own villa garden, a lay community which was to lead to a form of monasticism as important for the new Europe as that founded by St Benedict. It was not, however, to remain a lay community, for in 391 Augustine and his friend Possidius visited the basilica at Hippo Regius, where the aged bishop was publicly exhorting his people to find him a good candidate for the priesthood; the crowd pressed Augustine forward and clamoured for his ordination, and in this tumultuary fashion he was ordained. He continued to direct his community as Pater, or Praepositus, as well as to debate with the Donatists and other heretical teachers: when Augustine used the word Pater in his rule, it may be that he was simply translating the Syriac, Abba, instead of lifting it into the language of Latin monasticism, as was usual later. In 395 Augustine was consecrated bishop in anticipation of the aged Valerius' death, a practice common at the time but restricted by the canons later, and in 396, by Valerius' death, he became bishop of Hippo. He remained bishop till he died during the siege of Hippo in 430.

Possidius, his friend and biographer, tells us that when Augustine was made bishop, he established a monastery within the borders of the church grounds (at Hippo), and set himself to live with the servants of God according to the manner and rule instituted by the holy apostles. There is no reference here to *ascesis*, or Anthony, or the Egyptian desert: the essential in the community was to possess nothing of one's own, for as the verse in *Acts* says: 'No man said that he had anything of his own, but they had all things in common': this was the true *vita apostolica*, the community life. 'His clergy lived with him always', Possidius relates. 'They shared his house and his table; food and clothing were bought at the common expense.' Possidius is quite clear that Augustine required all his clergy (of the cathedral basilica) to live with him thus in common, even refusing to ordain those who would not agree to his condition: and he conceived of himself as having the right to require this, because this had been the life of the holy apostles. There were to be many doctors in the church later to argue, like Augustine, that all clergy ought to live in common; other bishops sometimes lived in common with all their clergy (for the rural parish was not yet developed): and all clergy for two hundred years were to live in common with the boy clerks of their *familia*, for there was nowhere else that they could be educated; but the church in her councils never accepted Augustine's contention that the clerk, *qua* clerk, might be forced to live with his bishop without a stipend. The councils continued to allow the clergy to receive stipends from their bishop and to hold individual property. But meanwhile at Hippo, as respect for the learning and holiness of Augustine's clergy grew, other churches began to demand from him the clergy he had trained. 'There were a dozen men, holy and venerated either for their austerity or their learning, whom Augustine gave at their request to divers churches, some of whom even were ranked among the most considerable. And, trained as they had been in the manner of life of the saints, these men founded like monasteries themselves.'

Augustine had written a rule (*regula*, the Latin translation of the Greek κανών) for his community while he was still its Pater: he continued to use it as bishop: the stress which he laid on obedience to the Pater received an added sanction when he became priest and bishop. The history of this rule has recently been made clear by Père Mandonnet [1]: it contained in Augustine's day, the working time-table of the community, with directions for the office and the two meals a day (the *Disciplina*); then a commentary on the rule, stressing the duties and practices of the common life. Moreover, a rule for sisters (*Regula Sororum*), an adaptation of Augustine's rule for men, was sent by him to his sister, herself the head of a community of women. (This is known as Letter 211, and called by Père Mandonnet the *Transcript*.) Augustine's rule had a curious history: the Vandal invasions wiped it out from Africa;

---

[1] P. Mandonnet: *Saint Dominique*, ii, pp. 103–62 (1937).

but it was known in the masculine form to Caesarius of Arles, and
to later founders of monasteries; but the office prescribed soon
became old-fashioned (the day hours ended with vespers, as in
the contemporary Greek east, and not with compline, the office
Benedict of Nursia ordered to be said in the twilight, immediately
before the monks' retirement to bed); and the provision of only
two meals a day, possible in north Africa, was very difficult in
colder climates. Hence, those bishops who desired to live communally with their clergy could not use Augustine's rule un-
modified; it was not till the beginning of the twelfth century that
the difficulty was solved by cutting off the *Disciplina*, and adopting
the vaguer exhortations of the commentary only as the Augustinian
rule.

It was then found so pliant and suitable for various kinds of
communities, that orders as different as the Praemonstratensian
canons, the Templars, and the Dominicans, had it as their basic
rule. And beyond these famous orders, numberless small communities, nunneries, hospitals of different kinds, and communities
of canons had the commentary, the Rule of St Austin, as their
rule. It was of extreme importance in medieval civilization, for
canons' houses sometimes had schools, and what we should call
the 'social work' of the middle ages, the nursing of the sick, the
care of infants (as at St Leonard's, York), the care for the old,
provision for guests, pilgrims and occasional grammar scholars,
was carried out by the hospitals. As St Benedict is reckoned the
father of western monasticism, St Augustine can be reckoned the
father of the strict, canonical life for the clergy, and a variety of
religious communities dedicated to the service of God and particular forms of good work.

Leaving aside Augustine's theological works and doctrine of
grace, themselves of historical importance for the future of Europe,
something must be said of his treatise, the *De Civitate Dei*, which
helped to form the 'climate of opinion' of European thought
throughout the middle ages. It may be noted that no great book is
an index to the climate of opinion of the years in which it is
written: that expression has been used by modern philosophers of
the mass of beliefs accepted by ordinary folk, and therefore only
referred to casually, by allusion: for no assertion or explanation is
needed. A great book dealing with human thought and conditions
is nearly always a protest against the climate of opinion, though it
may itself form the climate of opinion in future generations.

The twenty-two books of the *De Civitate Dei* were written
between 410, when Alaric sacked Rome and proposed to go on

and sack Africa, and 426, in the intervals of an episcopal life never leisured. The thought in it is disconnected: each book was published as a separate treatise between 413 and 426, and the contentions in the treatise are not always logically worked out, or always even quite consistent. Augustine wrote it, because the climate of opinion of his day saw the fall of Rome as a sign of divine displeasure. To the 'pagans' it was clearly a sign that the old gods, the true gods, were angry: and Europe was very far from Christian, though the emperors had accepted Christianity. Julian the Apostate had died only forty years before Augustine began his book; the country people still tried to safeguard their flocks and herds by the old rites and customs; and even the Christians were daunted at an apparent failure of divine protection. It was part of the climate of opinion, in a sense, for both pagan and Christian, that the old gods of Rome, or the *Providentia* of the emperor, or *Christus Victor*, in his struggle with the powers of darkness, would protect the mother city of the empire: and no such protection had been forthcoming.

Augustine therefore struggles to prove two main contentions: that the old gods and the old religions had no concern with right and wrong, with 'justice', with moral values, nor any teaching to guide men to attain a future life; a successful pagan empire without justice had nothing to commend it: without justice, what were kingdoms but great robberies (*remota iustitia, quid sunt regna nisi magna latrocinia*)? Righteousness (the *iustitia* of the Vulgate) was what mattered, not, in itself, success. Then further, Augustine set forth a philosophy of history: God had been long preparing the kingdom of his son, the whole world as Christian, and as one. He had trained and guarded his own people till Christ appeared among them; and he had prepared the one world state, the city of Rome which had become an empire. In the fulness of time the *civitas terrena* had fallen: but the *civitas Dei*, for which it had been a preparation, remained.

The thesis which Augustine had, somewhat confusedly, set forth, that the Roman empire having providentially prepared the world for Christianity, had perished because its mission was accomplished, was set forth more firmly and clearly in the sermons of pope Leo the Great (d. 461). 'God, who is good, and just, and omnipotent,' he said, 'has willed that all mortal men in common should come to the knowledge of his abundant goodness; and that this unspeakable grace should be spread throughout the whole world, divine providence prepared the Roman realm. For it was most fitting to the divine disposition that many kingdoms should be joined together in one empire, in order that a general preaching should reach an accessible people, whom the rule of one city should retain.'

BIBLIOGRAPHICAL NOTE

Procopius, *De bello Vandalico* (part of his *History of the Wars*) is a primary source and not only authoritative but lively reading. Procopius would have made a very good journalist: for an English translation of all Procopius' works, in 7 vols., see H. B. Dewing (Loeb ed.), 1914. See also L. Schmidt, *Geschichte der Wandalen*, 2nd ed., trans. by H. E. del Medico as *Histoire des Vandales*, Paris, 1954; W. H. C. Frend, *The Donatist Church*, 1952; C. N. Cochrane, *Christianity and Classical Culture*, 1940; C. A. Julien, *Histoire de l'Afrique du Nord*, 1931. There is an enormous literature about St Augustine: see H. I. Marrou, *St Augustin et la fin de la culture antique*, 1938, and for an English version of his *De civitate dei*, the Everyman trans. of J. Healey, 1945; see also *A monument to St. Augustine*, ed. Sheed and Ward. For the text of Martianus Capella's *De Nuptiis philologiae et Mercurii*, see A. Dick's ed., 1925. See also, M. Courtois, *Victor de Vita et son oeuvre*, Algiers, 1954; C. Courtois, *Les Vandales et l'Afrique*, Paris, 1955.

CHAPTER VI

THE VISIGOTHS

THE Visigothic kingdom of Spain preceded and outlasted the two other Germanic kingdoms of the Mediterranean basin, the Ostrogothic and the Vandal; it lasted from 466 to 711. It started when a Germanic chieftain aspired to be something less than an emperor of the west, but to rule, at any rate, the praetorian prefecture of the Gauls, in which the Pyrenees had been no *limes*, nor any barrier to the coast road carrying the Roman trade from Marseilles to Narbonne and on to Tarragona. In days when both Gaul and Spain looked towards the Mediterranean, this road was a more important means of communication than that running from the Cantabrian hills and the Asturias, round the western end of the Pyrenees, to the Garonne; but such a road there was as well. Only Alaric's death had saved Italy from a Visigothic settlement: but it seemed to the victorious Visigoths, intending not to destroy the empire but to revive it, that they might well rule the Gauls. Even after their defeat at the 'campus Vogladensis' and restriction to Septimania, the Mediterranean coastal province, Visigothic kings, it seems, did not forget their earlier claims.

The cause of their failure to reassert themselves after 507, to push back again, at least to the Loire, is probably their being cut off from any further accession of Germanic population: other barbarian races had pressed in behind them, blocking the way. The strength of their enemies the Franks lay in Austrasia, where the Germanic population was thickest, and where such population could increase by infiltration from central Germany; there was no such possibility for the Visigoths.

Yet though the Visigoths lost Aquitania, which they held only for some forty-five years, it was they and not the Franks who stamped the character of their barbarian art upon this region; there is a change in Merovingian barbarian ornament, as between the north and the south of Gaul, that corresponds to the boundaries between Franks and Goths before 507. It is true that this region was richer in Roman buildings than the north, and also had more access to Byzantine inspiration and trade in the sixth and seventh centuries; but the rarity of Germanic animal ornament south of the Loire, like the distinction in medieval France between the *langue d'oui* and the *langue d'oc*, points to some survival of

93

Visigothic population in Aquitaine after 511. The Visigoths in Septimania and Spain were the weaker because they had lost the headquarters of their original settlement.

Visigothic society falls in with Ostrogothic, Lombard and Vandal society, as against that of the Franks and the Anglo-Saxons, as belonging to a Mediterranean world. Visigothic Spain was a land of Roman temples, villas and basilicas, not all destroyed, and it drew its inspiration in government and art from East Rome. In the sixth and seventh centuries Byzantium was to the Mediterranean world the arbiter of taste and the lamp of learning, and though Italy and Spain slipped again from the political government of the eastern empire after Justinian, Byzantium was still the centre of civilization. The crowns that the late Visigothic kings hung in votive offerings before the altars are decorated with Germanic cloisonné, but their inspiration goes back to the mosaics of the crowned emperors and the crowns held ready for offering, in such mosaics as that of the procession of martyrs in St Apollinare-within-the-walls at Ravenna. The great Visigothic treasure found at Guarrazar near Toledo was probably the precious ornaments and vessels of some church, hastily buried before the Muslim invasion: it included two gold votive crowns hung by chains from a point, offered by king Swinthila (621–631) and king Recesvinth (649–672): and also a pendant gold cross, inset with precious stone and enriched with pendant pearls, and ornament in the Lombard manner; all very Byzantine in conception and detail.

The structure, too, of the radiate brooches of the Visigothic ladies, with the pins projecting beyond the semi-circular head-plate of the safety-pin brooch of south Russia, is Germanic; but the number and elaboration of the radiating pin heads, the fineness of the metal work, the naturalistic ornament—all these look to Byzantium. A well-dressed Visigothic lady had brooches and rings as good as any in Byzantium, and very similar; a well-dressed Frankish lady from Paris would have had ornaments that seemed to her Greek sister interesting but a little outlandish.

Two other points of comparison between the Visigothic and other Germanic kingdoms call for mention. With regard to the succession problem, the passing on of authority without a break for civil war, that same problem which the later Roman empire had found so intractable but which East Rome managed with conspicuous success: the Germanic kingdoms treated the matter with some variety. All had behind them the tradition of a semi-divine royal house, and also of elective monarchy, where a council of nobles passed over heirs who were children or incapable.

Among the Franks, the need to satisfy sons who already in their father's lifetime had some share of regional government, often led to partition, but the primitive reverence for the royal house of the Merovings prevented any noble outside it from seizing the throne for 250 years. The ambitions and rivalries of the nobles fought themselves out in the following up of royal blood feuds, and, at length, in the struggle for success as mayors of the palace. Among the Vandals, the succession law was unwontedly strong, under Byzantine influence. Among the Visigoths, the royal house of the Balts became extinct with Amalaric; nobles outside it were elected, and in the final collapse before the Moors, the struggle of rival candidates for the throne played a fatal part.

The other point of comparison concerns subject populations. The Franks in Gaul had a Celtic, Gallo-Roman population to deal with, and one, except in Brittany, well Romanized; but in Brittany, the Celtic population remained only restively subservient to the king of Paris and the archbishop of Tours. Not much force of arms was, however, needed to preserve the Frankish supremacy in the Merovingian period. Among the Ostrogoths of north Italy, there was no large, separate population group to be disaffected. The Vandals were planted among Moorish tribes and surrounded by them; the Arab conquest was in one sense a reconquest by the desert.

The Visigoths, however, had particular population difficulties; they brought with them the Sueves, settled them in Galicia (Portugal) and claimed overlordship over them; but the Sueves had a king of their own, and were frequently at war with the Goths. The autochthonous Wascones or Basques, speaking a dialect possibly not even Indo-European and certainly not Celtic, inhabited the north-eastern corner of Spain and spread down the valley of the Ebro, and the upper waters of the Douro and the Tagus; they were a compact and alien population, little Romanized; much Visigothic effort was expended in pushing them back to the north, and finally driving them back beyond the Pyrenees. Again, the perpetual difficulties of Visigothic kings with the Jews of the southern ports, and their policy of alternate tolerance and, latterly, persecution, probably reflects difficulties other than religious. The Visigoths had ports, access to the Mediterranean and, between the Vandal and Arab dominance of Mediterranean trade, apparently a chance to develop a class of sea-traders, always a source of royal revenue. The worst period of persecution of the Jews came when the Visigothic kings seem to have desired to get trading riches into their own hands and those of their nobles.

To turn to the political history of the Visigoths between the reigns of Euric and Roderick (466 to 711). The Visigoths had reached Gaul under Athaulf and made Toulouse their capital by 412; but the Romans still held north Gaul, and, when Euric murdered his brother, Theoderic II, and became king in 466, Syagrius still maintained an isolated Roman rule at Soissons. Euric's policy differed from his murdered brother's, in that he was the leader of the Visigothic party who stood for an independent Visigothic state and no subservience to Roman tradition and alliance. In 469 he launched an attack clearly meant to give him the rule both of Gaul and Spain: but the central plateau of France, the plateau of the Auvergne with Clermont as its chief city, held out firmly against him. He defeated a Roman fleet under Basiliscus; he succeeded in 470 in taking Bourges, to the north of the Auvergne; but it took him years to get the Auvergne itself. Ecdicius and the bishop of Clermont, Sidonius Apollinaris, defended the city against him in a series of sieges. Auvergne was only ceded to him, in 475, by Julius Nepos, emperor of the west, when a section of the Ostrogoths threatened to invade north Italy, and Nepos needed Visigothic support. To save Italy, he ceded the Gauls: for by this treaty Euric was left in possession of his conquest in Spain and southern Gaul up to the Rhone, and of central Gaul up to the Loire.

In 476 Euric even led his Visigoths into north Italy against Odovacar. Though he could not dispute Odovacar's claim to replace Romulus Augustulus, he had enough success to make the emperor Zeno yield him by treaty, at Odovacar's expense, the territory between the Rhone and the Alps, south of the Durance.

Euric won no more victories, though the military renown of the Visigoths was such, that provincials from Gothic Italy, and envoys from various Germanic tribes and even from the Persians, came to Toulouse to ask his alliance and military help. He published a code of Roman law for the provincials; he allowed the old Roman provinces of the Gauls to remain, though the title of the old proconsular governors was soon changed to *dux*; he retained the *civitas* as the old administrative centre under its *comes*; and he retained the old Roman assessment to taxation, and the Roman fisc as his treasury. One of his laws refers to the earlier 'thirding' of the land by the Visigoths by which, apparently, a third of the produce could be claimed by the new *possessor* from the former owner and the cultivators; it shows that boundary disputes had been caused between the provincials and those *hospitati* upon them. Those who removed boundaries were subjected to penalties, and it was ordered that these *sortes Gothicae* and *tertiae Romanorum* which had not been revoked for fifty years might not be called in question. Other Eurician laws dealt with theft, slaves and marriage, and laid down that arms supplied to the *saiones* for service should not be reclaimed.

Like all the Germanic kings (except Clovis, and the Anglo-Saxon kings) Euric was an Arian, identifying Arianism with Germanic independence, and Catholicism with the international universalism of the Roman empire. It was not theology alone that divided Goth and provincial in Spain or Africa: it was the issue of German sovereignty. The emperor at Byzantium was 'sanctus' and his palatium 'sacrum': he protected, but also dominated, the Christian church; to accept his version of the Christian religion was to lack full Germanic sovereignty. Euric and his early successors were not violent persecutors of the Catholics, though Euric banished Sidonius Apollinaris from Clermont, and one or two other bishops; but their Arianism alienated the Catholic clergy.

Euric died at Arles in 484, and was succeeded by his son Alaric II, no warrior and no match for his rival Clovis in energy. When Syagrius fled to him for refuge after the battle of Soissons in 486, Alaric gave him up, thus allowing Clovis to become the heir to the Roman kingdom of Soissons. But more dangerous to Alaric than this loss was Clovis's conversion to Catholicism, which took him out of the ring of friendly Germanic kings, and made his rule acceptable to the Gallic provincials. Alaric's attitude to his Catholic bishops became more tolerant, and he allowed them to meet in council at Agde in 506, before which he had published from Toulouse the famous *Breviarium Alarici* for the benefit of the Roman provincials. This short code, composed of certain imperial edicts and the verdicts of jurists, obtained a wide popularity in the west: but it left unchanged the Roman law forbidding intermarriage between Goth and provincial.

In 507 Clovis launched his attack against the Visigoths, an attack prepared for by negotiation with the emperor Anastasius. The Burgundians, his allies, invaded the Auvergne, and he himself crossed the Loire at Amboise and followed the Roman road to Poitiers. The Auvergnats fought for the Visigoths, but the Visigothic king Alaric lost the battle of the 'campus Vogladensis', and his own life. Franks and Burgundians joined forces, and took and burned the capital city of Toulouse: the famous Visigothic treasure, including that taken by Alaric I from Rome in 410, passed to the Franks. Clovis took Angoulême, Saintes, Bordeaux, and, finally, Tours, and his eldest son, Theoderic, ravaged the Visigothic countryside.

Alaric's five-year-old son, Amalaric, was saved from the battle, and, after a short interval when Alaric's bastard but full-grown son Gesalech was king, Amalaric reigned under the protection of Theoderic's Ostrogothic defender, count Theudis. The possibility of an Ostrogothic regency had rested on the chance of defending Arles, strategic for communications: but Theoderic's generals defeated the Frankish prince Theoderic at the battle of Arles in 511 and cleared the corridor to Narbonne, now the Visigothic capital. After the great Theoderic's death in 526, Amalaric's reign was unfortunate: he married Clovis's daughter, named, like her mother, Chlotilde, and then desired her to become an Arian; she refused and he maltreated her. In 531, her brother, king Childebert of Paris, raided Septimania, the Gallic province remaining to the Visigoths, took Narbonne and a Visigothic treasure and delivered his sister; Amalaric fled by sea to Barcelona, and was there killed by his own followers.

In 531 count Theudis became king, since the royal race of the Balts was extinct, and ruled for twenty years, which is in itself evidence of the kinship still felt by the two branches of the Gothic race: for he could look for no support from Ostrogothic Italy, now in eclipse. His reign marks the transfer of the centre of Visigothic power to Spain; he had earlier ruled from Narbonne, but his capital was now moved to Barcelona. The Frankish kings Childebert and Lothar in 541 pursued him even into Spain: but though they besieged Saragossa, they could not take it. For his part, Theudis in 543 seized the castle of Septa (Ceuta) from the empire; but he could not keep it. He died at Seville in 548 and had a short-lived successor, Theudegesil, who was assassinated.

The next king, Agila (548–554), made a notable change in Visigothic policy, by giving up the old conception of Visigothic rule of 'the Gauls' and concentrating on Spain. So far, the kings had resided at Toulouse, Narbonne or Barcelona, leaving the provincials of Spain under only nominal rule; Agila now moved his capital to Merida on the Guadiana and set about subduing the provincials of the old province of Baetica (Andalusia). But a Catholic revolt followed: he was defeated at Cordova and his son killed.

Agila's persecution of the Catholics as well as attempt to subjugate the semi-independent Andalusian nobles, inspired a rival, the Visigothic noble Athanagild, to seek military help from Justinian. The Gothic wars in Italy were not going well for the

Byzantines: but in 550 Justinian was able to spare a fleet and a very small army, and send them from Sicily to Spain under the patrician Liberius, a very indifferent commander. But the help seems to have been enough: Athanagild defeated Agila at Seville in 554, and when Agila died at Merida that year, Athanagild became king (554–567).

Though Athanagild was the strongest Visigothic king of the sixth century, his reign saw the setting up of a Byzantine province in Spain, the price of Justinian's help. The province of Baetica, and part of Cartaginiensis, together with the ports of Malaga and Cartagena and the cities of Cordoba and Seville, returned to Roman rule; a *magister militum Spaniae* was appointed to defend them for the Greeks. Athanagild, pushed out from the south, moved his capital to Toledo, at the heart of central Spain, and this choice of a capital made possible the real penetration of the peninsula by the Visigoths. He may have accepted in some way the suzerainty of the emperor himself, for his coins bear the imperial image; but he maintained a brilliant court at Toledo, fought the Basques with success, pushing them northwards into Navarre, and prevented the Franks from making further gains in Septimania. It was Athanagild's daughters, Brunhilde and Galswintha, whom the Frankish kings Sigebert of Austrasia and Chilperic of Paris sought in marriage, and who were to involve the Franks in the blood feud between Brunhilde and Fredegund. The future lay with the Frankish kings: but, at the time, the Frankish conquerors and new-comers found honour in these marriage alliances with the senior conquerors of Gaul and with the more cultivated court of Toledo.

The struggle between a pro-Byzantine and a pro-Gothic party among the Visigoths was, however, to continue, finding expression in almost alternate reigns. The pro-Byzantine Athanagild was succeeded in 568 by his two brothers Leova and Leovigild (Liuvigild), both of whom favoured Gothic self-sufficiency and independence. Leova died in 572: and Leovigild's reign may be reckoned from 568 to 586.

Leovigild desired to rule the whole peninsula, and rule it with Byzantine prestige. He increased the splendour and ceremonial of his court, and struck gold coins in his own name. He had four practical tasks: to push out the Greeks from south Spain; to push the Basques back into the north; to assert his authority over the Sueves of Galicia, and to strengthen his own authority in central Spain over the provincials, to which the opposition of the Catholic bishops was an obstacle. He was not as yet in a position to deal with the Greeks, though they were gradually limited more and more to the coast itself and the ports: in 571 and 572, he took Medina Sidonia (then Assidonia) and Cordoba from the Greeks.

For the next five years he was occupied in dealing with risings of the subject races, and of his own nobles: he fought campaigns over the whole Spanish peninsula. The Sueves of Galicia, under their king Mir (Theodomir), allied with the Cantabrians of the hill country south of the Bay of Biscay: in 569 Leovigild had taken Leon and Zamora from them, but border warfare continued. There were revolts in Cordoba and Toledo assisted by his own nobles, and danger from the Franks in Septimania. In 573 Leovigild gave one of his sons Septimania to rule, and gave another the 'duchy' of Toledo. The rebellious Gothic nobles met with very harsh treatment, and their confiscated estates enriched the fisc.

Leovigild's policy was essentially warlike, and aimed at subjecting the whole peninsula to his rule; but it was complicated by the religious difficulty, and that in his own family, as well as among his subjects. No strong Germanic king had as yet renounced his royal Arianism to accept the emperor's Catholicism; but in Africa and Italy the old religion of the conquerors had lost the day. Leovigild's policy to the Catholics was therefore not consistent; he persecuted dangerous Catholic bishops, but later in his reign was driven to find some accommodation with the Catholics.

His two sons, Hermenegild and Recared, had been born of his own marriage with a Byzantine lady, and he married the eldest, Hermenegild, to Ingundis, the daughter of the Spanish princess Brunhilde and king Sigebert. There was again trouble over this lady's religion, when Athanagild's widow urged Ingundis to become Arian, and she refused. To avoid domestic disputes, which he was apparently unwilling to settle by royal decree, Leovigild sent off Hermenegild and his wife to live in Seville. But there Hermenegild came under the influence of the most striking Catholic figure in Spain, bishop Leander of Seville, a cultivated ecclesiastic and a notable musician. Hermenegild decided to become Catholic (579) and the population of Andalusia heard the news with joy; but Leovigild was still set on uniting his subjects under the Arian form of Christianity, and wrote forbidding him to take such a step. The king of the Sueves had, meanwhile, taken just this step: and Hermenegild entered into negotiations both with him and the emperor. It looked as if Leovigild would have against him his eldest son, the Sueves, the emperor, the Basques and the Roman provincials.

Arianism and the old king, however, made a last fighting effort to avoid surrender. He desired to make it possible for the Catholic bishops to accept Arianism; he therefore summoned them to a plenary council at Toledo (580). He offered them his grace and favour if they would accept his faith by a laying-on of hands, without a second baptism, which had been exacted before: they might thus turn from what he called the 'Roman religion' to the Catholic faith, by which he meant, Arianism. It was a formula of compromise, and some bishops accepted the way out; but most refused, and on them the king launched a fierce persecution. Some bishops and nobles were even put to death, and the Catholic clergy lost their status and privileges.

Leovigild then led successful campaigns against the Sueves and the Basques, winning victories over both, and founding the city of Vitoria to hold down the Basques. Between 581 and 583 he won victories over both the Sueves and the Greeks, and forced Hermenegild to withdraw his forces to the line of the Guadalquivir and Seville. After a two years' siege, Seville was taken by Leovigild, and Hermenegild was sent from the city that favoured him to Tarragona; there he was repeatedly commanded to abjure, and, on his refusal, slain (585). That year, too, Leovigild made yet another expedition against the Sueves, whose king, Mir, had died in 583; he took Porto and Braga and annexed the kingdom of the Sueves to the Visigothic state. Only against the Franks was he less successful: for they were not willing to accept his vigorous and violent Gothic policy without protest. Hermenegild, they claimed, had died a martyr; the princess Ingundis had died a refugee in Byzantine Africa: Childebert II, Ingundis' brother, and king Guntram of Burgundy planned revenge. They sent a Frankish fleet to encourage the Sueves to revolt, and the Burgundians invaded Septimania. But the fleet was captured, and the Burgundians driven out by Recared, the king's second son, though without disaster. Leovigild died in May, 586: he had made an outstanding effort at uniting his subjects by military victory, some show of compromise to get the Arian faith accepted, and personal violence to all who opposed him. His son Recared, who had fought in his campaigns and in whose name he had founded a new city (Recopolis) in Alcaria, was to take the other road to union.

The chief event of Recared's reign (586–601) was the conversion of the Visigothic nation to Catholicism. Bishop Leander, of noble Roman family from Cartagena, had been involved in royal displeasure over the conversion of Hermenegild, and sailed for refuge to Constantinople; there he had met the *apocrysarius*, or envoy, Gregory, afterwards to be Gregory I. Both were Latin speakers in a Greek world and both were monks; the two became and remained friends. Leander remained at Constantinople from 579 to 586; the news of Recared's accession made him return at once to Spain. Bishop Masona of Merida also returned from exile.

Ten months after Recared's accession the cathedral at Toledo was consecrated with the Catholic rite, on Sunday, 13 April 587. Persecution of the Catholics was remitted, many Arian bishops were converted, and Recared had himself consecrated king with the holy oils by the *katholikos* of Toledo, a Byzantine proceeding in which, perhaps, Leander's influence can be traced.

The formal profession of the Catholic faith by the king and the Visigothic nation followed at the III council of Toledo, 589. This assembly of sixty-two bishops and five metropolitans was presided over by the king and attended by the queen and many nobles. After formal debate, the council explicitly renounced Arius and his teaching, the names of the Arian bishops who accepted Catholicism being explicitly recorded, and accepted the definitions of the councils of Nicaea, Constantinople, Ephesus and Chalcedon; indeed, in their anxiety to safeguard the dignity of the Son, they inserted into the creed a novel formula (*filioque*) concerning his relation to the Holy Ghost; an action the consequences of which were centuries later to prove destructive of the unity of Christendom. The king proposed that the Greek custom should be adopted, by which the whole congregation recited the creed aloud at mass, and this was accepted. The strong Byzantine influence under which this council was held was further shown by the fusion of secular and religious personnel at the council, the secular and religious subjects dealt with, and the royal presidency. The council of Toledo, thus constituted of bishops, royalty, and lay nobles, became the most characteristic part of the Visigothic constitution, and was summoned on many occasions; the canons of the council of Toledo became the civil law of the state.

The fifteen years of Recared's reign are recorded by Gregory of Tours and Isidore of Seville, Leander's brother, as fortunate for the kingdom: the military exploits of his father had procured peace, and the subject population were now content; though the pro-Arian, Gothic party were not reconciled. Four years after his conversion, Recared wrote to pope Gregory, informing him that he had embraced the Catholic faith, and sending him a gold chalice adorned with gems; apparently he also requested him to negotiate with the emperor Maurice about the old treaties concerning the Greek cities in Spain. Gregory, for his part, wrote congratulating Recared on having brought so many souls with him to the faith, and sent him a 'small key' which had lain upon the body of St Peter, made from fragments of the chains of his imprisonment. He also wrote on the matter of the negotiations with Maurice: some time ago Recared has sent him a message, by means of a young man going to Naples, asking him to request the emperor to have search made in his chancery (*cartophylacium*), for the *pacta* made between the prince Justinian (of pious memory) and lawful authority in Spain; and asking that the emperor would have collected from these *pacta* the points which Recared ought to observe. This, Gregory says, he has not done, for two good reasons: one, because the chancery of Justinian has been injured by fire, so that of the papyri of those times almost nothing remains; and the second, because it would be better to seek evidence about these points in his own records, and send it to Gregory to set forth to the emperor. In any case, the letter of Gregory shows that the remnant of Byzantine power still lingered in Spain.

Recared died in 601, but he was unhappy in his heirs. Leova II, his son, who continued his Catholic policy, lived only till 603, and was dethroned and killed in a rising of the pro-Gothic party led by count Witteric. The latter was elected king in 603, tried to restore Arianism, and was assassinated after a seven years' attempt to try to reverse his predecessor's policy. A noble, Gundemar, was in 610 elected king by the Catholics and reigned two years; he fought the Basques, and broke with the Greeks. In 612 he was succeeded by another Catholic noble, Sisebut, according to Isidore of Seville a lettered prince, but as good a general as Leovigild. He fought the Basques, now pushed north of the Pyrenees but anxious to return, and he fought a Byzantine general so successfully that the emperor Heraclius sued for peace; in the treaty that followed, the Byzantines gave up the Mediterranean coast, and were left with only a diminished province in the west, between Gibraltar and the Algarves.

Sisebut's Catholic policy, or his desire to control the seaports lost by the Byzantines and the merchants who used them, led him to a fierce persecution of the Jews; such Mediterranean trade as existed appears to have been in the hands of Jews, Syrians and Byzantines, and the term 'Jew' is often used in contemporary writing as equivalent to 'merchant'. Since imperial times they had lived in Spain in some numbers. By the Roman law of Alaric II's *Breviarium* the Jews could not marry Christians, hold Christian slaves, or fill public office; but they were free to practise

their religion and observe the Jewish law; they had their own law
courts. Their numbers had increased, for in practice mixed
marriages were made, and wealthy Jews both held office and had
Christian slaves. The III council of Toledo began a policy of
greater severity against them, ordering the children of mixed
marriages to be baptized, and Sisebut went further: he ordered all
Jews to be baptized, under pain of banishment and the confiscation
of their goods. Most of the Jews complied; but the fisc was enriched
by the wealth of some thousands who preferred to flee to Gaul.

Sisebut died in 621, and was succeeded by his son, Recared II,
who reigned only a few months. The throne was seized from him
by duke Swinthila, one of Sisebut's successful generals; he renewed the policy of military expeditions against the king's more
reluctant subjects, took the remaining district of the Algarves from
the Greeks, and firmly drove back the Basques beyond the
Pyrenees. All Spain was now ruled in his name; and to secure
the rule of his family, he associated with him in the government
his wife Theodora, his son Ricimer, and his brother, in the
Byzantine manner. This, however, roused the opposition of the
nobles, who desired to keep the monarchy elective in their own
interest; Sisenand, the governor of Septimania, was able in 631
to ally with the Franks, drive Swinthila from the throne, and make
himself king. The IV council of Toledo, c. 631, condemned Swinthila to lose the crown, debarred his family from the succession,
and formally proclaimed the monarchy elective at the hands of the
nobles and the bishops; it also repeated the canons against the
Jews and ordered their children to be taken from them and brought
up in the Catholic faith. As the nominee and agent of the council
of Toledo, Sisenand ruled in peace till 636. The same policy was
pursued by the kings next elected by the council, Chintila and his
son Tulga; but opposition was gathering. There was now no
question of returning to a vigorous pro-Arian, anti-Byzantine
policy as of old, for Arianism had died out and the Greeks had
gone; but the lay nobles of the council of Toledo now objected
to clerical preponderance and desired a more nationalist policy.

In 642 the lay nobles of the council were strong enough to
declare Chindaswinth elected king, and to drive Tulga off to the
cloister. Chindaswinth only maintained himself by a vigorous and
violent policy that looked back to Leovigild: he and his son
Receswinth killed or banished or reduced to slavery some 500 of
the nobles who opposed his régime; their families fled, as did
certain of the clergy. When Chindaswinth summoned the VII
council of Toledo in 646, it was sufficiently overawed to pass a

canon excommunicating and confiscating the property of rebels and emigrants, including churchmen who had fled the country. But after this violent beginning, Chindaswinth had a peaceful reign, marked by expeditions against the Basques but by no rebellions; he gave great gifts to churches, and his son succeeded him in 653.

The reign of Receswinth (653–672) was less pitiless, though still harsh, to the Jews, of whom, in spite of all previous repressive measures, there still seems to have been a large number in Spain. The VIII council of Toledo, held in 653, shows that many still observed the rites of their own religion in Spain: when the council refused to take further measures against the unconverted, the king himself, by edict, ordered all apostates from the Christian faith to be stoned or burned alive, or at least, to be liable to this penalty. This measure no doubt had fiscal implications; but the long series of laws against the Jews suggests that the ports of Spain had a population similar to those of the east Mediterranean, and that when this population was no longer protected by Byzantine sovereignty, the Visigoths wished to displace it.

One important step towards the unification of the Visigothic and Roman population was taken by Receswinth in 654, in the issuing of a new legal code, the *Liber Judiciorum* or *Forum Judicum*. Whereas the law of Alaric II had forbidden intermarriage, the new code removed the interdict, which had apparently in practice been disregarded from the time of Leovigild. The *Forum Judicum* was a real legal digest, divided according to subjects into 12 books, 54 titles and 595 articles; it incorporated the judgments of Visigothic kings for two centuries and was meant to be a systematic code, covering all branches of law. Following the precedent of Justinian's legal reform, supplementary *Novels* were also issued in the years following 654. The work shows clerical inspiration, but was the first Germanic code to attempt a real fusion of Roman and Germanic law; Latin was made the sole language for the court. This code, and some supplementary laws of Receswinth, deal with conditions in a warm countryside, and also with offences in a land with some trade and some money circulating. Various forms of damage to fruit trees are dealt with, boundary questions, and disputes involving streams, as well as penalties for dangerous dogs and wandering pigs. This code maintained its authority for hundreds of years, and, as the *Fuero juezgo*, was quoted as a moral authority even by the Musulmans later.

The next king, Wamba, was elected by the nobles at Valladolid, where Receswinth had died, in September 672. He fought the

Basques successfully, then heard that duke Paul in Septimania had betrayed him and called in the Franks to help him to secure the crown. Wamba, however, fought his way from Barcelona to Narbonne, Agde and Nîmes, where Paul was holding him. He held a triumphal procession at Toledo in 673, the defeated Paul walking in it, his head shaved.

Meanwhile, however, when the problem of internal unity, apart from succession disputes, seemed in the way of being solved, the Arab danger was beginning to show over the horizon. The Arabs had taken Tangier, and an Arab fleet even appeared to raid the Spanish coast, though it was defeated by a Visigothic squadron. The Visigoths, however, were now long settled and less willing to regard fighting as a normal occupation; Wamba attempted to recruit his army by disallowing certain exemptions of the clergy from military service, and even requiring landowners to arm a tenth of their serfs. Such measures proved unpopular and ineffective, and his attempt to pull up the standard of clerical discipline and abolish strange, semi-pagan corruptions of church rites (e.g. the use of milk instead of wine at the mass) added to his unpopularity. In 680, when he was ill and believed to be dying, his son Erwig tricked his attendants into clothing him in the penitent's habit for death, and when he recovered, was strong enough to get the council of Toledo to declare this a valid act of abdication and take an oath to him, Flavius Ervigius, as king.

For the next thirty years the growing Arab danger remained unrealized and unshielded. In 687 Erwig was succeeded by a relation of Wamba, Egica, who persecuted the family of his predecessor, and the Jews. The plots of the nobles, and of the archbishop of Toledo, disturbed the reign: in 694, at the XVII council of Toledo, it was complained that the Jews were inviting 'people from overseas' into Spain to protect them: the reference may have been to Greeks or, more probably, Arabs. Egica's son, Witiza, reigned from 700 to 709 or 710, but the records of his reign are lost. Again there was a disputed succession; the 'senate', i.e. the council of nobles and bishops, chose Roderick, duke of Baetica; but Roderick's opponents, Achilla, the son of Witiza, and his followers summoned to their help the Muslims from Africa: two considerable minorities in Spain now looked to foreign deliverance from Visigothic rule.

In 711, the final catastrophe came with a suddenness surprising to the attackers and the attacked. No order to conquer Spain was given by the caliph, and even though Tarik, the leader of the Muslims, was the lieutenant of Musa, the governor of Mauretania, it is very doubtful if Musa regarded the expedition as more than a raid. The fact that the invaders were summoned seems evidenced by the fact that the partisans of Achilla fought with the Muslims, and it would seem that the Visigoths themselves and king Roderick at first regarded the war as a party struggle. Tarik had brought a fairly large force of Muslim troops, and he took Gibraltar and the neighbouring cities with no great difficulty; Roderick was away in the north, fighting the Franks and the Basques. On hearing the news of Tarik's success, he collected a large army and marched to meet him, and on 19 July 711, the two armies met on the shores of lake Janda, between Medina Sidonia and the town of Jerez de la Frontera, in the province of Cadiz. Part of the Visigothic army, unrecognized partisans of Achilla, deserted to the Muslims; bishop Oppas was among them, and Sisebert, a relation of Witiza. Alternate rule by different families of nobles seems to have destroyed the Visigothic state, and as yet there was no popular resistance to the Muslims. They took Seville, Cordoba, and finally Toledo: the Visigothic capital city was to become their own. The campaign was not yet fought out, however: king Roderick rallied his army and advanced to threaten Tarik in Toledo. The governor Musa was asked to bring reinforcements, and he brought a large army and took Merida and other strongholds, in 712; the Jews in the town welcomed the Arab victors.

So far, the Muslims appear to have been regarded as the allies of Achilla's party; now, however, with Arab conquest possible, Musa began to act as the vicegerent of the caliph, conquering the country for Islam. He now had to deal with a popular, though not well armed or well led, resistance: and he needed to deal with Roderick, now holding out in the wild, mountainous country on the borders of Galicia. There he pursued him, and at Segoyuela, in the province of Salamanca, in September 713, he fought Roderick and defeated him; in all probability, Roderick was killed in battle. Musa marched to Toledo, proclaimed the caliph (of Damascus) as sovereign, restored his estates and residence at Toledo to Achilla, and gave the archbishopric of Toledo to Oppas. Intermarriage of some of Achilla's supporters with the Muslims followed, and helped to establish the Muslim régime in Cordoba.

In assessing the causes of the Visigothic collapse the relatively small numbers of the Germanic ruling caste must have counted, as in all the new kingdoms except that of the Franks; but a more important cause was the failure to make Germanic kingship prevail over the nobles. The church, standing for peace and order on

the Byzantine model, was usually ready to support a king who
wished to secure the succession to his sons; but the nobles wished
to keep the monarchy elective in their own interest. The council
of Toledo usually made the decision in particular cases.

This characteristic feature of the Visigothic constitution, the
council of Toledo, needs to be understood in a Byzantine context,
rather than as an Anglo-Saxon witan (which did include such
bishops as the king summoned as well as the nobles), or as a
normal church synod in the Latin west. The king alone summoned
the council of Toledo and he alone appointed and could dis-
possess the bishops who attended it; the lay element consisted
of the palace officials, all men of 'magnificent and noble rank'.
On ecclesiastical matters, the bishops (with, later, the vicars and
abbots who attended) alone debated and passed canonical decrees;
on secular matters, it would seem, the lay lords exercised their
function of giving counsel to the king; but all decrees of the council
were equally binding.

It is notable that when the Visigoths accepted Catholicism at
the third council of Toledo in 589, under the influence of Leander,
the archbishop of Toledo (as also the archbishop of Merida) was
termed *katholikos*. In Persia, outside the Roman empire, the church
of Seleukia-Ctesiphon was a great missionary church, a patriarchate in all but name, and in 410 the bishop of Seleukia-Ctesiphon
had formally adopted this title of *katholikos*. The term was used
to imply autocephalous primacy, the metropolitan in question
having, among other privileges, the right of consecrating all bishops
dependent upon him, whatever their rank. The term was sometimes used much later of certain patriarchs and metropolitans in
the Greek east; wherever it was used, in addition to its canonical
implications, it carried the connotation of primacy within a
national church, of the ecclesiastical leadership in a society with
a highly developed consciousness of the intimate inter-relation
between 'church' and 'state'. To the sixth- and seventh-century
Visigoth, thinking of kingship and the church in Byzantine terms,
there was nothing strange in the fusion of secular and sacred legislation and jurisdiction in the council of Toledo.

There is no Visigothic historian of the same stature as Cassiodorus and Gregory of Tours; although Gregory, and Cassiodorus'
epitomist, Jordanes, refer to Visigothic history, it is not, to
them, the subject of primary interest. The figure who dominates
the history of learning in Visigothic Spain is Isidore of Seville,
and here again, though interested in the early history of his

country as in everything else, it is with this limitation: Isidore was not primarily a historian. The family of Isidore of Seville, flourishing at the time of Recared's conversion to Catholicism, and the figure of Martin of Braga, the canonist of the Sueves, stand out in the late sixth century as agents of the transmission of the Roman and Christian heritage.

Leander, Isidore, Fulgentius and Florentina were the children of Severianus, a noble of Roman birth in the province of Carthage; Severianus however died and the family moved to Seville. The three sons all became bishops, Leander of Seville from 579 to c. 600, Isidore from c. 600 to 636, and Fulgentius of Astigi, in the province of Seville, from c. 600 to c. 633. The sister Florentina became an abbess, and Leander wrote for her a rule, *De Institutione Virginum*. Leander, in addition to his intervention in politics in the reigns of Leovigild and Recared, appears to have cherished ecclesiastical learning in his household school at Seville, and particularly the study of Greek music. His brother Isidore wrote of him in his *De Viris Illustribus*, that he 'was by profession a monk, and as monk made bishop of the province of Baetica in the Spanish church. He was of eloquent speech and an industrious preacher and writer against the Arians, and laboured at the ecclesiastical offices; he wrote prayers for the whole psalter . . . and in the sacrifice (the mass) also, with lauds and psalms he composed much that was sweet sounding (*multa dulci sono*).'

So little is known of Isidore's career, beyond his attendance at, or presiding over certain church councils, that it may be inferred that he intervened little in politics. He devoted himself to learning and won a great reputation even in his own day. His pupil Braulio, bishop of Saragossa, wrote of him that:

God raised him up in recent times after the many reverses of Spain (I suppose to revive the works of the ancients that we might not grow continually duller from boorish rusticity), and set him as a kind of support. And with good right do we apply to him the words of the philosopher (Cicero): While we were strangers in our own city and, so to speak, strangers who had lost our way, your books brought us home, as it were, so that we could at last recognize who and where we were. You have discussed the antiquity of our fatherland, the orderly arrangement of chronology, the laws of sacrifices and of priests, the discipline of the home and the state, the situation of regions and places, the names, kinds, functions and causes of all things human and divine.

Braulio, in his introduction to the works of Isidore, proceeds to give a list of these works, with comments, and they included a

Prœmia, a *De Ortu et Obitu Patrum*, a book on the *Officia* (addressed to his brother Fulgentius), a *Synonyma*, the *De Natura Rerum*, the *De numeris* (not on arithmetic but the mystical properties of numbers), the *De Nominibus Legis et Evangeliorum*, the *De Haeresibus*, the *Sententiae* (a treatise on Christian doctrine and morals owing much to the *Moralia* of Gregory the Great), the *Chronica*, the *Contra Judaeos*, the *De Viribus Illustribus*, the *De Origine Gothorum et Regno Suevorum et etiam Vandalorum Historia*, the *Quaestiones*, and the *Etymologies*, 'a vast book', says Braulio, 'which he left unfinished, and which I have divided into twenty books, since he wrote it at my request. There is an exceeding elegance in his treatment of the different arts in this work, in which he has gathered well nigh everything that ought to be known.'

Turning to Isidorus' historical work first: Isidore lived when dating by the years of the consuls had necessarily dropped out of use in the west, and when general knowledge of Dionysius Exiguus' dating by the era of the Incarnation was still long ahead; he had therefore to depend on such chronological apparatus as the comparative tables of Eusebius, latinized by Jerome, and the like. He apparently made for himself his own tables of this kind, commonly known as *Chronica*, making his short tractate run, in a single book, from the creation of the world to the times of the emperor Heraclius and king Sisebut (*c.* 616). His *Chronica* thus is a piece of apparatus rather than a history. His history of the Goths and Vandals begins unfortunately by stating that the Goths, a people of undoubted antiquity, 'are suspected of deriving their origin from Magog, son of Japhet, from the similarity of the last syllable', though some scholars call them *Geticae*. Towards the end of the history, however, having apparently read another source, he connects the origin of the Goths more reasonably with the Scythians. The book is short, though valuable when it deals with Isidore's own day; it reaches Alaric's sack of Rome very swiftly, deals briefly with each Visigothic king till Leovigild, of whom he has more to say. Leovigild was a very fierce Arian, forcing even bishops to apostatize by accepting re-baptism; he filled the fisc with his confiscations and had to build a special *aerarium* for the spoils of the persecuted nobles; whereas all Gothic kings before him had worn a common dress with their nobles and sat among them in council as one of themselves, he for the first time wore the (Byzantine) ceremonial robes and sat upon a throne. He has similarly much to say of the mildness, liberality and kindness of Recared.

Isidore's influence on the learning of medieval Europe was

exerted through his twenty books of *Etymologies*, and that, apparently, for two reasons. Though it is a far less learned work than those of Cassiodorus and Boethius, it covers a much wider field, and it is systematically arranged by subjects, with a very brief exposition of each subject, amounting sometimes only to a single line (e.g. under *De Habitaculis*: *Habitatio* ab *habendo* voc ta, ut habitare casas; *Cella* dicta, quod nos occultet et *celet*, etc.). In days when books had no indexes, or tables of contents, it was easy to consult a treatise which dealt thus with subjects and categories of objects; if you wished to look up *aratrum*, you would expect to find it in book XX, under the heading *De instrumentis domesticis et rusticis*. You would learn very little about *aratrum* when found, except that it had a share, a *vomer*, so called because it made the earth to vomit, and that the *dentale* was the front part of the *aratrum*, in which the share ended as in a *dens*.

Isidore in his *Etymologies* follows the method and subject matter of a succession of Roman encyclopedists, Varro, Verrius Flaccus, the elder Pliny, Suetonius, Pompeius Festus, Nonius Marcellus, and others. Whereas Cassiodorus and Boethius had limited themselves to the exposition of the liberal arts, Isidore, though he treats of the liberal arts, goes much farther afield. He used, apparently, only Latin authorities, but his Latin authors had dealt with subjects of natural history, medicine, biology, etc., first studied with a Greek curiosity and desire of knowledge for its own sake, and not for its use in the formation of character, even of free men. The great merit of Isidore's work for the transmission of the classical heritage to the middle ages was that he took it for granted men wanted to know, not only the whole field of knowledge necessary for bishops and clerics, not only about abstract subjects like the various branches of mathematics, but about medicine and buildings and animals, worms and fishes and dragons, rocks and precious metals, weights and measures and the proper names of trees, cucumbers and why they are sometimes bitter, and the whole business of how, in Isidore's day, things got done. It is true that the information was in snippets, epitomes of what earlier writers had said, and it is true that the information was often at fault and frequently so grotesque as to be absurd: Isidore used no critical faculty on his miscellaneous sources and he frequently guessed and guessed wrong: but he kept alive interest in a wider field of knowledge than the liberal arts. This can be seen from the contents of his twenty books, covering grammar, rhetoric, logic, arithmetic, geometry, music, astronomy, medicine, law, chronology, theology, human anatomy and physiology, zoology, cosmography and physical geography, architecture and surveying, mineralogy, agriculture and military science.

The one leading principle in the *Etymologies*, which contributed not a little to its fund of errors, and yet was vital to the arrangement and succinctness that made the work so usable, was Isidore's belief that the road to knowledge lay through the origins of words. By supplying their etymology he hoped to explain the thing they stood for; he did not, for instance, write a treatise on architecture, but devoted a chapter to buildings, and in it explained the origins of different parts of buildings. He frequently got his etymologies wrong: *Fanum*, for instance, is not derived from the *fauns* for whom men built temples, as he says; but that was incidental to Isidore's almost complete ignorance of philology, at that day no hindrance to his popularity.

Isidore's work sprang from Visigothic Andalusia: that of Martin of Braga, his slightly earlier contemporary, from the remote kingdom of the Sueves. Here, while it was still part of the Roman province, and while Christianity was still very young, the Priscillianist heresy had disputed the day with orthodoxy. The Priscillianists held the 'heresy of *ascesis*', a reverence for east Mediterranean monastic practice that belittled the apostolic work of priests, combined with the claim to add certain apocryphal sentences and interpretations to the text of scripture. On this church of Galicia and the Cantabrian hills, the focus of Priscillianist teaching long after its official condemnation, the Sueves imposed their Arianism, and the three religious forms, the old Priscillianist still active in the north-east of the kingdom, orthodoxy, and the Arianism of the court, struggled with the old gods and goddesses of the countryside.

The conversion of the king and kingdom to Catholicism was accomplished in 560 by Martin, bishop of Braga (Bracara). He was, like his namesake, St Martin, a Pannonian; he had taken the monastic habit in Palestine, and come as a missionary *ad portum Galiciae*; he was soon made abbot of Dumio (near Braga) and bishop of Braga. Gregory of Tours calls him one of the most learned men of his day. He converted king Mir to Catholicism in 560, and in 563 the Sueves by synod accepted the faith; in 579 Martin presided as archbishop of Braga, the capital of the Sueves.

Martin's most important work was the small collection of canons, about bishops, clerks and laity, which he drew up for the use of his own church (see p. 72). He wrote also, for king Mir, a *Formula Vitae Honestis*, echoing the teaching of Seneca, and stressing the four cardinal virtues of prudence, magnanimity, temperance and justice. He translated from the Greek for his monks the *Ægyptiorum patrum sententiae et verba seniorum*, and he wrote for his brother bishop Polemius a long sermon *De Correctione Rusticorum*.

This tract is of considerable interest, not only as indicating a Suevish bishop's difficulties with his rustic *pagani*, but as affording a picture of the tenacity with which the Latin cults, of the Olympic deities and of the countryside, still kept their hold of western Europe at the end of the sixth century. There is, apparently, no reference in the tractate to the Germanic gods of the invaders, or their cults; unless a charge that rustics pour on heathen altars the blood, not only of beasts, but of men, hints at some dark Germanic or Celtic rite. For the most part, the practices blamed are clearly connected with classical paganism, or eastern incantations, and involve no blood shedding. Martin begins by explaining to his 'beloved sons', that God created all things, including certain spiritual beings, one of whom fell and lost his glory and became 'a dark and horrible devil'. Some of the angels followed him, and they became 'demons'. Such demons showed themselves to men under various forms, demanding that sacrifice should be offered to them on high mountains or in leafy woods: they took the names Jove, Juno, Minerva, Venus, Mars, Mercury, Saturn and the rest. Mercury, the inventor of thefts and deceits, is worshipped by men greedy for gold, and in passing a cross road, they cast a stone in sacrifice upon the heap there raised. And ignorant rustic people worship these gods with sacrifices, and also those of the fallen spirits who preside over the sea, or rivers, or streams, or woods: in the springs, they are called nymphs, and in the woods *lamiae*. It is shocking that the very days of the week are named after these demons: *dies Martis*, *dies Mercurii*, etc., and yet these demons never made a day at all: God made the light and the dark and the day and the week.

Martin then attacks the superstitious practices of his 'beloved children'. They keep the Kalends, believing falsely that it is the beginning of the year: a miserable man thinks that he will pass the whole year according to the beginning, and that therefore he must leap and rejoice on New Year's Day; and he reckons that he will be very unlucky if he doesn't, secretly or openly. And even more unbecoming is it to Christian men, and very stupid, to keep the festival of 'moth and mice' (the days when Tellus and Ceres were venerated to keep the crops and household stuff from harmful creatures). Yet Christians think that if, at this season, moth

5

and mice are not venerated by putting outside cask or coffer or bread or cloth, they will not spare what they find within!

Martin then recalls to them the solemnities of their baptism. 'When you were given a name at the font, perhaps John or Peter or some other name, you were, you remember, questioned by the *sacerdos*: "How will you be called?" Then you answered, if you could answer, or indeed, he who was your sponsor, he who lifted you up from the font said, perhaps: "He is called John." And the *sacerdos* questioned you: "John! Do you renounce the devil and his angels, his worship and his idols, his thefts and deceits, his fornication and drunkenness, and all his works: do you renounce them?" And you answered: "I renounce them."

'You have made a pact with God, beloved, and you break it if you return to the worship of devils. For what else than the worship of devils is the cult of trees, of springs, of burning candles at a cross road? What are divinations and auguries and keeping the Vulcanalia and the Kalends and adorning tables and decking with laurels? What are taking omens from footsteps and putting fruit and wine on the hearth and bread in the spring? Women who weave call upon Minerva, and invoke Venus at weddings and when they go out on the public way: and what else is this but to worship devils? And to make incantations with herbs and utter the names of demons: what else is this but the worship of the devil?'

Finally, Martin deplores the slackness of his country parishioners in keeping Sunday, a day when the pagans so zealously worship Jove. 'You ought to keep Sunday: and if you go out on that day, it should be for some holy purpose, to visit holy places, or visit a brother or a friend, or console the sick or those in trouble or bear help in some good cause. That is how a Christian man should keep Sunday.'

Martin's discourse has a ring as of a Victorian vicar preaching in an English village church: but it is an authentic voice from sixth-century Visigothic Spain. In the end, the pagan Olympians were driven from the countryside to the constellations of the night sky; but the witches, the herb magic, the bee charms—it took long before they left the countryside; if they have.

BIBLIOGRAPHICAL NOTE

For the political history, in addition to the standard general works, see H. M. Leclercq, *L'Espagne chrétienne*; F. Dahn, *Die könige der Germanen*, tom. v, 1861–1911; A. K. Ziegler, *Church and State in Visigothic Spain*; R. Menendez Pidal, *Historia de Espana*, vol. 3, 1935; W. Reinhart,

Mission Historica de los Visigodos, Segovia, 1954. For administrative history, see P. Goubert, 'L'administration de l'Espagne byzantine', in *Études Byzantines*, tom. 3: also *Études Byzantines*, tom. 2 (1944). For Visigothic art and archaeology, N. Åberg, *Die Franken und Westgothen in der volkerwanderungszeit*, Uppsala, 1922. For Visigothic learning, W. M. Lindsay, *Isidori Etymologiae*, and E. Bréhaut, *An Encyclopaedist of the Dark Ages: Isidore of Seville*, 1912 (Columbia Univ. Studies, vol. 48), and C. P. Caspari, *Martin von Bracara's schrift: De correctione rusticorum*, 1883, and for a new edition of his works, C. W. Barlow, *Martini Episcopi Bracarensis opera omnia*, Yale, 1950. See also, H. Livermore, *History of Spain*, London, 1958; R. M. Pidal, *El Imperio Hispanico y los Cinio Reinos*, Madrid, 1950; E. P. Colbert, in Cath. Univ. of America, Studies in Med. Hist. XVII, *The Martyrs of Cordoba (850–859)*, Washington D.C., 1962.

CHAPTER VII

ECONOMIC CHANGE

SINCE Edward Gibbon finished the *Decline and Fall of the Roman Empire* in 1787, much water has flowed under the bridges and every country in Europe has experienced an industrial revolution; the twentieth century, indeed, has seen the rise of technology and the technological state. All of which has reacted on historical writing and focussed interest on the economic side of the transition from the Roman empire to the Europe of the new barbarian kingdoms, a subject much newer than the political history of the fifth, sixth and seventh centuries. To the study of the old historical sources, chronicles, histories, saints' lives, letters, cartularies, etc., have been added a more intensive study of record material (such as the Egyptian and Merovingian papyri), and two new historical disciplines: the scientific study of archaeology and the history of art. Working thus largely upon archaeological material, and the papyrus records, M. Rostovtzeff made a distinguished contribution to the social and economic history of the Roman empire, and others followed him. The new interest in economic history and the new methods of historical study have, in fact, somewhat modified the story of the decline and fall of the Roman empire, as Gibbon saw it, and the last thirty years have seen a notable outburst of historical work on the transition and the actual point at which it occurred, in which German, French, English and Slav scholars, and Byzantines in general, have joined with the utmost zest and all the resources of scholarship.

The traditional view of the transition was that it occurred, with some sharpness, in the fifth century: that a single political society, an urban society, using coined money as a medium of exchange and enjoying large-scale commerce, was overthrown and succeeded by a natural economy under Germanic rulers. The barbarism of their social institutions was suggested by the violence of these kings: a rural society was held to have replaced civilized Roman institutions and to have been in the main Germanic. This statement over-simplifies the picture drawn by the nineteenth-century historians; but it is broadly true to say that they held that the change of society, the change of economic structure, came with the barbarian invasions of the fifth century.

The two main challenges to the accepted theory have been those of Professor Alfons Dopsch, and the late Professor Henri Pirenne. Professor Dopsch, a close student of archaeology as well as of social history, emphasized the continuity of Roman institutions in the new Europe, which, in fact, he hardly allowed to have been a new Europe at all. Archaeology had shown the continuity of habitation of the Roman towns on the continent, and he emphasized also the continuity of the imperial demesnes, the demesnes of the fisc, with those of the new Germanic kings and the continuity of the villa with the medieval manor. He first set forth his concept of a gradual evolution of the new Europe out of the old in his *Wirtschaftliche und soziale Grundlagen*, published at Vienna in 1918–1920.

Pirenne's thesis, on the other hand, claimed (as of old) that there had been a catastrophic change between the old Europe and the new, but set it at a different point. Pirenne argued that large-scale trade, carried by the Mediterranean between eastern and western Europe, survived the *bouleversement* of the fifth century, and made the régime of the Merovingians substantially the same as that of the empire it had, in the west, replaced: 'the Merovingian epoch is only the prolongation of antiquity and not the beginning of a new age'. It was the invasion of Islam, he held, which cut the Mediterranean basin in two, separated west and east, extinguished the great sea trade of the Merovingians, threw the land of the Franks back upon itself, substituted for a gold-using Mediterranean economy one with a much reduced medium of exchange, and made the rural demesne, the rural estate, an autonomous self-sufficing cell. 'Then only did the true middle age begin.' What contemporary economists were calling the 'economic recession' from the Roman world, with its money economy, to the food and services economy of early medieval Europe, Pirenne placed in the second half of the seventh century; he sought to establish the continuity of Mediterranean commerce between Byzantium, Smyrna, Sidon, Alexandria and Leptis Magna, with Ostia, Carthage and Marseilles alike in the imperial and Merovingian periods. He denied, in fact, any economic recession on the part of Merovingian Gaul. Syrian merchants, he claimed, travelled as before from the east to Gaul with their eastern wares: 'the foundations in the fifth century of barbarian kingdoms in Italy, Spain, Africa and Gaul not only did not interrupt, but does not seem to have even sensibly changed, their relations with these countries'. This thesis Pirenne set forth in an article in the *Revue Belge* in 1922, in his *Contrast économique, Mérovingien et Carolingien*, 1923, his *Villes du moyen âge*, 1927, and in his *Mahomet et Charlemagne*. This book, containing his final and perfected views on the early Germanic kingdoms, the conquest of the Mediterranean kingdom by Islam, and the cessation of trade with the east under the Carolingians, he left finished just before his death, in 1935, and it was published in 1937.

The work of Herr Dopsch and Henri Pirenne inspired much later work by their pupils and other savants; almost no writer on the period could, indeed, afford to neglect it. Madame E. Patzelf, a pupil of Professor Dopsch, contended with Pirenne's views in *Die Frankische Kultur und der Islam*, 1932; and among those who, accepting Pirenne's views in general, elaborated some point of them or criticized them in some detail, may be mentioned Professor F. L. Ganshof, F. Vercauteren, H. Laurent, F. Lot, G. J. Brantianu (who adopted the reign of Heraclius († 641) as the terminus of Byzantine antiquity), G. Ostrogorsky, P. Lambrecht and F. Olivier-Martin, who accepted Pirenne's views of the persistence of Roman legal institutions in his *Précis d'Histoire du Droit Français*, 1932. The late Professor Eileen Power assessed the contemporary, and probably the final views of historians in the matter in the *Economic History Review* of 1940; she accepted the 'economic recession' in Europe after the Arab conquests, but regarded it as having started earlier: economic stability had received many hard knocks previously. Professor Norman Baynes, similarly, has been a little unwilling to accept the uninterrupted relations of Gaul with the east Mediterranean under the Merovingians: he has held the Vandal fleet responsible for partly, if not wholly, interrupting such relations.

It should be noticed that economic historians so far used the phrases 'money economy' and 'food and services economy' as self-explanatory, and the transition from one to the other as the root cause of much social change. It is now usual to admit the use of some coined money even in very early societies usually described as having a 'natural economy' or a 'food and services economy'. This is stressed by Professor M. M. Postan in an article in the *Economic History Review*, vol xiv (1944); he also points out that movement towards or away from a money economy was less continuous and less general than has been imagined, and that the barbarian nations in many cases preferred to put their supply of the precious metals into plate and ornaments. These considerations do not, however, invalidate the use of the phrases, providing the limitations are recognized. There would seem to have been a far greater number of transactions by means of coined money or credit in the Greco-Roman empire than among the early Anglo-Saxons or the Carolingian Franks.

Turning from those who have written about this economic change to the economic phenomena themselves: the whole evidence for the transition, sudden or gradual, cannot be discussed here, but some obvious signs may be mentioned. First, those for the existence of a money economy and large-scale commerce in the Roman empire and even the late Roman empire; secondly, for the continuity of large-scale commerce and a money economy in the Merovingian age; and thirdly, that for the disappearance of trade and a money economy after the Arab conquests, and in the succeeding Carolingian period.

The money economy in the Roman empire rested on the maintenance of good and plentiful currency, and on the reputation of the Roman merchant for good, honest dealing. The state mints existed all over the empire and turned out a bronze, a silver, and above all, a gold currency: since Julius Caesar had established the *solidus aureus* as the imperial unit of exchange, with silver tied to it in a definite proportion, Roman merchants had been able to trade even with Asia. For the first 200 years of the empire there was, it appears, a favourable balance of trade with the east, so that the gold and silver supplies of Europe were increased by those of the other continent. Asia, in antiquity, would appear to have been much richer in the precious metals than Europe: metal urns or vases were used in India where a Frankish or Anglo-Saxon peasant would have used pottery, and sheets of metal laid over wooden frames could even be used for roofing; as, for instance, in the double- or single-curved roofs of towers and minarets. In Europe, the use of even lead for roofing was late and expensive: Edward the Confessor's church at Westminster was roofed with curly earthenware tiles, such as are still seen on old English barns. The gold and silver ornaments of the great in Persia and India witness to an ampler supply of the precious metals than that of Roman or medieval Europe. It would seem, then, that even a small favourable balance of trade, in the days of *la haute empire* (the first and second century), would bring in a considerable accession of the precious metals to Europe. Most historians believe that the change in the fourth and fifth centuries to an unfavourable balance of trade with the east was a sign of, or even a cause of, the fiscal embarrassment of the Roman state.

Rome had, however, in *la haute empire*, very considerable resources of the precious metals in Europe. The state, in the person of the emperor, owned all mines, sometimes working them directly, sometimes letting them out to individual merchants to work, or to gilds (*collegia*) of merchants. The western part of the empire was, in the first and second centuries, richer than the eastern half: Spain was much the richest province of the empire in all minerals, including lead, iron, copper, silver and gold; the richest mines lay around Carthago Nova, in Baetica, and in Galicia and the Asturias. These Spanish mines were scientifically managed by the Romans, the engineering and draining was good, and the shafts ran deep into the mountains. Galicia produced some 20,000 pounds of the precious metals annually; and the Ebro valley and the Cantabrian highlands were great industrial centres, where Spanish swords, breastplates and armour were made for the Roman army and for commerce. Much tin and a little silver was mined in Britain, some silver in Aquitania, and copper and silver in the Balkans, especially in Dalmatia. The gold once mined in Asia Minor and the silver in Greece had long since been exhausted. There is evidence, however, that increased care was given to the mines in the eastern part of the empire in the third and fourth century: a *comes metallorum* was appointed for Illyricum, and a *praepositus metallorum* for the Levant.

The evidence for a massive use of currency in the period is varied and convincing. The Roman legionary was paid in coin, and even the higher officers and the civil servants received their stipend in coin: e.g. a *ducenarius*. The Roman state was a great user of coins and precious metals. The large coin finds found buried all along the frontier regions were probably the sums sent for the pay of the army and the civil service, hastily buried in disturbed times, particularly round the turn of the fifth century. Other evidence of the relative plenty of gold is that of the very large gold medallions, presented by the emperors as a mark of honour: medals about five inches in diameter which could be worn on the breast or melted down for their considerable intrinsic value. The very number of the Roman mints argue a large output of coins and their situation, near great mercantile towns like Pavia, or Trier, or Antioch, show that a large currency was needed for trade, as well as paying the army.

The very large sums in gold that eastern emperors could afford to pay to the Huns and other barbarians are also a sign that the imperial gold supply was not yet exhausted at the end of the fourth and the first half of the fifth century. The Hun Uldis defeated the German Gainas and his followers in 401, and was rewarded by alliance with the emperor Theodosius and the promise of an annual tribute, or retaining fee. Aëtius' military success was partly due to his ability to hire, or get rid of, the Huns by money 'gifts'; when he induced some 60,000 of them to return home in 425, the sum must have been large. Priscus of Panium, a reliable authority, states that the emperor in 430 agreed by treaty to give Rua the Hun a tribute of 350 lb. of gold per annum; in 435, this tribute was doubled. In 443 a treaty was signed with the Huns by which 6,000 lb. of gold was to be paid in a lump sum against arrears of tribute, and the annual payment was to be, in future, 2,100 lb. of gold. (That these payments were very large is shown by the fact that in the late Roman empire the gold pound was worth 72 *solidi aurei*, coins of roughly the same weight and size as the English sovereign; the Byzantine empire at the period was run mainly on a coinage of gold and bronze.) These imperial payments did not cover the whole of the drain of gold and silver to the barbarians, for individual ransom money paid for prisoners must have amounted to a large sum. Uldis had had so many prisoners that he sold them off at one gold *solidus* per head; but by 443 the price had risen, and Roman prisoners fetched 12 *solidi* per head, while important individuals paid as much as 500 *solidi*. All this was in addition to the enormous amount of gold ornaments and silver plate looted by barbarians in east and west.

The revenue, the immense revenue, of the Roman state was also collected partly in coin. The revenue from the demesnes of the fisc was transported to the capital in coin; the varied tolls (*telonia*) were also collected in coin. In *la haute empire* the tax for provisioning the army, the *annona militaris* was assessed in kind (on wheat, wood, wine, etc.), but might be paid in cash by the *adaeratio*. The receipts of Egyptian tax collectors in the period of Diocletian and Constantine show that the *annona militaris* was still levied, and the tax paid in money: one Aurelios Isidoros paid items like 800 and 400 (silver) drachmas several times, in the period just before Constantine's reform of taxation. After that reform, other local officials paid 4,000 drachmas, 3,600 drachmas, 800 drachmas, and many items as large, as well as smaller transport charges for getting taxes paid in kind to the troops. After the Constantinian reform, it is true, the wheat for the *annona civica*, for the feeding of Rome and Constantinople, was for the time paid in kind; but the large payments in drachmas later suggest that the Egyptian taxpayer might commute the render for a money payment, plus the transport charges. Egypt was a rich province: most of the eastern trade came through Alexandria: and it may

be that in other provinces the money collected in taxes amounted
to less: there are unfortunately few papyrus tax receipts extant
for the rest of the empire; but such evidence as does exist points
to a large supply of currency in all the provinces. It is clear that
in the difficulties of the second half of the fourth century the
government, particularly in the reign of Julian the Apostate, made
a resolute effort to maintain a system of payments *in natura*, and
that this effort failed. The army and the civil service were averse
to it: they insisted on the principle of the *adaeratio*, and by their
insistence prevented a recession to a natural economy. The partial
recession of the early fourth century had showed itself in government transactions and requisitions, but had never been adopted in
commerce.

But all this massive use of currency in the empire, down to the
end of the fourth century, was not the only medium of exchange:
credit transactions were widely used all over the empire, and
bankers were numerous. M. Rostovtzeff has demonstrated this
from the papyrus records of Egypt (mainly), and it should be
noted that only in the warm, dry air of Egypt have papyri survived
on any large scale. Papyrus is very friable material, rots in the damp,
and is easily destroyed by fire; the day-to-day records of merchants
were needed for practical purposes for some few years, but were
never intended as permanent memorials: no special care was taken
to preserve them. Yet papyrus was the writing material used all
over the empire for every purpose, except the writing of such
solemn and valuable volumes as the works of Vergil, and, later,
the Christian scriptures and the *Digest*, which might be written on
expensive parchment. That all this immense volume of papyrus
receipts, the rolls or registers of the municipal *curiae*, and the
accounts of bankers, has, in the main, perished does not, however,
render less valuable such papyrus records as have survived: and
they attest certain conclusions. In the west, inscriptions recording
the votive offering of some banker, and even carvings in relief
of the banker and his table, accord with the Egyptian evidence.
On part of a funerary monument at Trier, a banker and his two
assistants, all in Roman dress, and clean shaven, receive payments
from bearded Celtic peasants: they are depositing coins in a wide
shallow basket, already well filled.

Credit and credit operations were certainly fully developed in
the cities of the empire, as is shown by Roman commercial law
and legal treatises. The Egyptian papyri attesting the different
forms of contract, and the existence at Alexandria of an institution
that served both as a land register and a record office for storing

statistics about the fortunes of all residents in the district, both illustrate a highly developed economic life. The important grain supply of Egypt, her unique papyrus industry, her cotton and linen industries, all demanded accounts and book-keeping and the Egyptian merchants, writing the rapid cursive hand on their own papyrus, dealt with their correspondence, bills and account rolls themselves.

The growth of trade, and the number of rich landowners living in the cities, made necessary large amounts of currency, and credit transactions to supplement it; private ventures in local and foreign trade, and money-lending, were profitable both to rich men and to the professional banker. Such men transacted complicated business, accepted money on deposit, paid interest on some of the deposits, and effected payments by mere transfer from one account to another. Transfers of money from one city to another were sometimes carried out through the medium of the local banks, and customers were accommodated with loans for the payment of taxes. The Roman fisc was the greatest of all bankers and did very profitable business. The banking system had come to the west from Greece and the Greek east, and such evidence as we have shows that the banks of Rome, Italy and the provinces had much the same range of business as the banks of Egypt. In short, credit operations everywhere supplemented the metal currency.

Large-scale trade with Asia was carried out by individual Roman merchants, though some imperial care was given to fostering it: as when, in the time of Claudius and Nero, Roman stations were established at Adana and Socotra, in the Indian Ocean. The greatest sea trade with the east, in *la haute empire* and later, was not merely a luxury trade: it passed chiefly through Alexandria, a sea-borne trade carried on by Alexandrian merchants with the merchants of Arabia and India. Cotton, and perhaps silk, were imported by way of the Red Sea, and worked up in the factories of Alexandria: in exchange, the Alexandrian merchants exported glass, metal ware, linen, corn and timber. Roman gold and silver coins have been found in India; but these may have been carried thence over the caravan routes, where no other method of payment was possible; and their number decreased in the second century, showing the development of a favourable balance of trade. There was certainly a large-scale trade with the east in bulky goods through Alexandria.

While bulky goods necessarily followed this sea route to India (for uncertain relations with the kingdom of Parthia had rendered

uncertain the route by caravan to Palmyra and thence by the
Persian Gulf), luxury goods of light weight reached the east
Mediterranean by caravan route. Of such goods, the spices of
India and the east were in constant demand, not only as a flavour-
ing and as medicine, but for the curing and pickling of winter
supplies of meat, and, in the later empire, for incense for the
Easter ceremonies of the churches and the Easter and Whitsun
baptisms. The embroidered vestments and silks of Persia and all
the varieties of precious stones reached the west by caravan, as
did the carpets, woollen fabrics, and red-dyed silks of Armenia.
Furs and leather goods, and even arms and goldsmiths' work,
found their way to the west, as did the famous dried, black plums
of Damascus. The caravan routes went along the coast of Syria,
from Gaza, Tyre and Antioch to Edessa, between the upper
waters of the Tigris and Euphrates, and then on through the hill
country of Armenia with its green, fertile valleys, to Trebizond on
the Black Sea, to Ctesiphon, the summer palace of the kings of
Parthia, and eastward through the mountains to Tashkurghan,
where the Oxus rises in the northern ranges of the Hindu Kush.
Here, three civilizations, three cultures met: those of the Greco-
Roman world, of India and of China.

While the eastern trade was profitable to the empire, the main
large-scale Roman trade was inter-provincial, and a trade conducted along the frontiers of the empire with the tribes beyond.
The Roman legionaries themselves traded with the frontier tribes,
and swarming commercial suburbs, *cannabae*, grew up outside
the frontier camps and walled towns. Barbarian movements,
however, disturbed frontier and inter-provincial trades before
the foundations of the barbarian kingdoms; towns were looted and
burned, industries were wrecked and the mechanism of commerce
dislocated.

Examination of archaeological finds has shown this very clearly
in the case of Gaul. The second half of the third century was a
period of barbarian irruptions and fiscal devaluation: prices between 256 and 280 rose some 1,000 per cent: trade was interrupted
and towns reduced the area within their boundary walls. The
collegia disappeared, flourishing villas were abandoned, and barbarian chiefs carried off to Germany the riches of Gaul. Gallic
industry, moreover, collapsed: the bronze workers and the potters,
who had exported their wares to the farthest parts of the empire,
could no longer export profitably. It is certain that after the great
invasion of 276 the potteries of the Argonne no longer made
Samian ware (*terra sigillata*). Precise research has made it equally

certain that the bronze exports of Gaul which had found their way
en masse to the Danubian provinces no longer did so.

But after this half century of collapse, in the beginning of the
fourth century, certain branches of Gallic industry saw a remarkable
renaissance. From *c.* 350 (but not earlier) the potters of the Argonne
again began to turn out *terra sigillata,* clearly to be distinguished,
however, in form and decoration from the earlier make. This
pottery renaissance lasted till the barbarian inroads of 406–407,
a disaster that put a lamentable end to the kilns that had again
been exporting their products to Switzerland, Bavaria, Austria,
Hungary, Holland and Britain. Even more important was the fate
of the Gallic glass industry. In the fourth century it had attained
a very large production and diffusion: glass ware became cheap
and began even to take the place of pottery: from Strasbourg to
Cologne, along the length of the Rhine, in Belgica Secunda
(Normandy) and even on the Atlantic coast, glass was used in
profusion, until the industry suffered the same interruption as that
of pottery. It recovered, however, with the fourth century. After
the fearful economic dislocation of the third century, Gaul did
not experience continuous economic recession: there was a remarkable recovery in town life, and a period of economic revival.

This period of recovery in northern Gaul coincided with a
movement of the centre of gravity in Gaul from the south to the
north. The third century had found the towns of the Midi much
larger, more Romanized and more prosperous than those of the
north. Then came the danger to the northern frontier, the disasters
of the mid third century, the period of Septimius Severus when
everything was subordinated to the needs of military defence,
and when immense payments by the Roman state were made to
the armies defending the Rhine and its hinterland, the basin of
the Moselle. Trade moved to the north, with the Roman merchant
who supplied the army and the civil governors of north Gaul.
The towns of the Midi declined, as inscriptions show, between
250 and 300, and the glass industry of the Rhone valley, originally
introduced from Carthage, passed to the north and never recovered the leadership. Examples of the splendid glass of fourth-
century Cambrai have been found in Pannonia, Scandinavia,
Russia and even in Asia.

The swing of the political pendulum from Provence to the
north followed the creation of the Gauls into an independent
praetorian prefectship in 368, with the fixing of the prefect's
residence, not in the Rhone valley, but at Trier. The army disposed in Belgica Secunda and along the Rhine had to be fed,

clothed, armed and paid, and much economic activity followed. All the traffic of the Rhine met that from Brittany, Britain and the Seine valley at Trier, and met also that coming north from the Rhone valley. There was a rich, Romanized bourgeoisie at Trier: from 368 Trier was the official residence of the western emperor: Jews and Syrians in some numbers brought their wares to Trier, ivory, textiles, incense, precious stones, papyrus, fruits and oil. The city had, for the period, a very large area and circuit walls, and the remains of several dozen pagan temples found near-by attest a rich bourgeoisie. St Jerome visited Trier and called it a second Rome. When the Franks settled in the modern Belgium and north Gaul, they were settling in a province ravaged by earlier barbarian raids in the fourth and fifth century but in one that had once been the economic and political focus of Gaul.

In examining the problem of how far a breach of social continuity, a change from a money to a natural economy, occurred in the Merovingian period, Pirenne devoted himself mainly to demonstrating the continuity of the trade between the east and west Mediterranean; though he also dealt with the less disputed survival of Roman money, weights and measures, institutions, the area of the acceptance of Roman Law, and the continuity of the Latin language and learning. The survival of a money economy was closely connected with that of foreign trade, for the supply of precious metals in Europe was insufficient to maintain the necessary currency for two hundred years, apart from outside supplies of gold obtained by commerce or other means. On the question of the gold supply in Merovingian and Carolingian times, the distinguished historian, the late Professor Marc Bloch, shed much light (see p. 133).

As to the Mediterranean trade, it is accepted that the Byzantine empire did succeed in protecting the commerce and sea ways of its own coasts. Till the Arab conquests of the seventh century, Syria and Egypt were its provinces, and the east Mediterranean a Greek lake; it was possible to ship cargoes in safety from Naples, Otranto and Aquileia to Byzantium. Pirenne collected evidence that it was also possible to sail from Byzantium to Marseilles and Narbonne, and that, in fact, the west Mediterranean trade continued also uninterrupted. He stressed the focussing of the economic life of the new kingdoms on the Mediterranean, and contended that the Syrians, often mentioned in the writings of Gregory of Tours and in early saints' lives, carried the papyrus, oil, embroidered tunics from Persia, purses from Phoenicia, spices, precious stones and ivories as before to Gaul: the ports of the Tyrrhenian Sea were as open to eastern commerce as before. Gregory of Tours mentions the colony at Orleans of Syrians and Jews who acclaimed Lothar I in their own tongues going out to greet him with their standards and *vexilla*. An early life of St Geneviève speaks of St Simon Stylites as hearing the report of her holiness from merchants *euntes ac redeuntes* between Egypt and Gaul. A rich Syrian at Bordeaux possessed a house with an oratory well furnished with relics of eastern saints; and Gregory of Tours mentions others. Caesarius of Arles composed hymns in Greek as well as Latin for the use of the Christians of the Rhone valley.

Apart from such references to Syrians and spices, mainly from Gregory of Tours, Pirenne's argument rested on the evidence he collected for the wide diffusion of eastern goods in Gaul, and a use of coined money as great (he argued) as in imperial times. He established that the Merovingian kings maintained a storehouse of the fisc (*cellerarium fisci*) at Marseilles and at Fos near the Moselle: a parallel to the Great Wardrobe of the Tower in later English history. The Byzantine emperors in the sixth century maintained such a royal store house; both the Greek and the Frankish *celleraria* go back, in fact, to a Roman model.

For the nature of the goods stored at the *cellerarium* of the fisc at Fos, and available for supply at the royal command, Pirenne commented on two interesting Merovingian texts. One is a *trattoria* for the *formulae* of Marculf (see p. 313), that is, a direction to the king's *agentes in rebus* to supply the 'apostolic man' and the 'illustris' whom the king is sending on a legation to such and such a place with the following food and commodities. The high rank of the envoys should be noted: *illustris* would be the title of a count or duke, and, though 'apostolic' may mean no more than bishop, it probably implies a metropolitan or bishop of importance. Every day of their journey coming from and going to the king, they are to be supplied with suitable transport, and so much white bread, wine, beer, lard, flesh, pigs and piglets, lambs and pheasants, hens and eggs, fodder for their horses and —these presumably from the fisc—cinnamon, pepper, spices, mastic, pistacchio, almonds, etc. The different spices are carefully specified by name, and must have come from the east. The other list is that of a yearly allowance of commodities to be supplied from the fisc at Fos to the abbey of Corbie, by grant of Lothar III (657–673), confirmed later. It comprises 10,000 lb. of oil (which must have been transported from Provence, Spain or Africa), 20 lb. of rice, 10 'skins of Cordova', 50 rolls of papyrus, 50 lb. of dates, 100 lb. of figs, and a carefully specified variety of spices. While in the *trattoria* of Marculf the eastern goods are all light in weight, the Corbie list mentions goods of considerable bulk, such as the oil, dates and figs. Papyrus is light, and the dates need only have come from Africa. The two lists certainly establish a certain continuance of the eastern trade, but not much more than a luxury trade, plus that in papyrus, which would be needed for all letters, books and account keeping. Of all these commodities, papyrus, which certainly came from Egypt, and in some bulk, is perhaps the most important as evidence of a surviving trans-Mediterranean commerce in the Merovingian period.

Another indication of the survival of Mediterranean trade is the prosperity of Marseilles and the towns of the Midi in the sixth century: the pendulum of economic prosperity had swung back from the north of Gaul to the south; commercially, Gaul was the hinterland of the port of Marseilles. While the political future lay with the kings of Paris and Metz, and even while Clovis I, Lothar I and Lothar II were overlords of all Gaul, spending power clearly predominated in the south. While the Frankish kings in the north fought their enemies on their eastern frontier, no great accession of treasure would have come from their conquest; the Visigoths and Burgundians, on the other hand, lived in a land of now prosperous towns, an old, cultivated countryside, and some surviving commerce. The acceptance of the economic pre-eminence of the south particularly in the early Merovingian period, however, does not imply the existence of a purely 'natural' economy in north Gaul. M. Vercauteren, in his notable *Étude sur les civitates de la Belgica Secunda*, traced by coin finds and written sources the trade route from Marseilles up the Rhone valley and along those of the Saône, Yonne and Seine to Paris, and between the tributaries of the Seine to Troyes, Soissons, Reims and north Gaul. At Reims coins were regularly struck from the beginning of the sixth century. The existence of ships bringing oil and wine from Bordeaux to north Gaul is also attested. But the scale of commerce was clearly greater in the towns of the south and was supported by at least a partial survival of eastern trade.

The question whether the Merovingian and other barbarian kings disposed of a large money revenue, comparable to that received by tax officials in the late Roman empire, is difficult to decide from the very sparse survival of papyrus records; though the evidence marshalled by Pirenne from other written sources, the *History of the Franks*, saints' lives and the like, illuminated a

field hitherto considered dark. Before referring to Marc Bloch's
direct examination of the gold supply, the points dealt with by
Pirenne should be noted.

He contended that the Merovingian kings, besides being great
landed proprietors, enjoying the resources of the lands of the fisc,
and of mines, disposed of a formidable treasure in coined money.
The kings paid their functionaries in coined money (the direct
evidence for this is slight); they could assign very large sums from
their treasury, as when the abbey of Saint-Denis obtained a yearly
grant of 200 gold *solidi*, or when Desiderius, bishop of Verdun,
obtained from king Theoderic 7,000 gold *solidi* for the relief of his
distressed citizens (the king had been, however, in possession of
the exiled bishop's land and treasure and had done him many
injuries). Other considerable offerings of treasure are recorded;
as also is the frequent increase of the kings' own treasures by the
confiscation of their subjects' ornaments, money and lands: 'they
killed to get wealth'. They did not simply hoard wealth in their
treasury, but by using it kept it in circulation. Apart from purchasing eastern goods for their courts, making grants and offerings
to churches, and presumably meeting the expenses of their frequent
frontier and fratricidal wars, they used their gold on occasion to
buy off frontier tribes (as the Avars in 596) and normally for the
bribery of envoys and their principals. The Visigothic pretender
Sisenand offered king Dagobert 200,000 gold *solidi* to have his
alliance and Leovigild promised the emperor's lieutenant 30,000
to have his help. These are large sums, if they were actually paid;
the lesser ones for the routine bribery of envoys would seem to
have been normally paid. All these gold *solidi*, however, appear to
have been money of account.

The evidence for Pirenne's contention that the Goths and
Vandals, *hospitati* on the countryside, received their 'third' of the
revenue of the estate in money is almost completely lacking as is
that for the assertion that the great domanial estates in Gaul all
produced a money revenue: the papyri that would have determined
this have not survived. Gregory the Great in Italy paid his higher
clergy a money stipend, but he also made them food allowances
from the patrimony, and analogy suggests that already the estates
of the landed proprietors were valuable mainly as feeding the
family and servants of the proprietor, though some of the produce
may probably also have been sold.

The question of the tax revenue of the Merovingians is of great
interest: Pirenne contended that the *tonlieu* (toll, *telonia*) was paid
exclusively in silver. It was the direct descendant of the various

imperial customs and taxes (the *portaticum* or harbour dues, the
rotaticum or transport tax, etc.) and was levied directly for the
profit of the king. The collectors of the tax were frequently Jews,
and the tax was let out to farm; injustice must sometimes have been
done, for some royal efforts were made to curb it. In 614 Lothar II
intervened to order that tolls should remain as they had ever
been; Theoderic the Great also wrote to his agents in Spain,
giving directions about the collection of the customary tolls. The
Merovingian kings occasionally relaxed the toll for the benefit of
an abbey, but never granted it away till the period of the collapse
of their power. Pirenne held that the product of money taxes to
the Merovingian kings was very great: partly as an inference from
the fact that they could dispose of such large sums.

It is certainly true that all the barbarian kings minted money,
and possible that some of them mined small quantities of precious
metal: but whether the volume of currency they could maintain
was as great as that handled by the officials of the later empire
remained in considerable doubt. As to minting, the laws of
Receswinth state penalties for those, of whatever status, who
forge money or clip coins or adulterate the gold given them by
another to make *ornamenta*, etc.; the detailed regulations suggest
a good supply of the precious metals and the possibility that the
Spanish mines were not yet exhausted. Gaul, however, had never
produced the precious metals to anything like the same extent,
and any wastage of the Merovingian currency due to payments for
foreign goods must, as Pirenne emphasized, have been made good
by payments for exports, or the direct buying of gold. He instanced
the sale of wheat as bringing gold to Gaul, and also that of a very
large number of slaves from the slave market at Marseilles, and
elsewhere; a quite exceptionally large trade in war captives (many
of them carried off from Britain) was done in the sixth century.
Both trades would have helped to give Gaul a favourable balance
of trade.

Some gold also entered Gaul by way of purchase and as subsidy
or diplomatic present from the emperor or the barbarian kings.
The buying of gold is evidenced by a form of the tariff of customary charges made by the canons of Tournai in the twelfth
century. Their church had been rebuilt by king Chilperic († 584)
who had also granted them an immunity, i.e. the right to collect
the royal toll at Tournai: though the tariff as written belongs to
the twelfth century, it contains very old material. 'If a man slave
or a woman slave or an ounce of gold is sold', one item runs,
'let the seller pay 4*d*. [a *triens*] and the buyer 4*d*.' Gregory of Tours

also speaks of king Chilperic's envoys bringing back supplies of gold from Constantinople, some of which they saved from shipwreck at Agde. The emperor Maurice, says Gregory, sent Chilperic gold coins, or ingots, of a pound's weight: from this Byzantine gold Chilperic had a very fine gold bowl made of 50 lb. weight 'for the honour of his kingdom'. Whether this gold was directly bought, or was sent in return for some kind of invisible diplomatic export, is not clear from Gregory's account.

Pirenne also emphasized, in support of his argument for large-scale trade in Merovingian Gaul, that usury was still lawful there, as by Roman law. When the above-mentioned bishop of Verdun tried to get a loan from king Theoderic, he offered to repay him 'with legitimate usury'. This, however, it should be noted, was not for a mercantile venture but to relieve the starving population of his city. The collectors of the royal tolls sometimes, Pirenne showed, lent money to important personages: though at least on one occasion they got murdered when they asked for repayment. 'Legitimate usury', a *triens* in the *solidus* or 33 per cent, was, it seems, occasionally practised: though the evidence that credit transactions occurred in Mediterranean Gaul to anything like the scale of the later empire is lacking.

The evidence as to the origin of the 'decentralized' currency of Merovingian Gaul, which Pirenne himself accepted, points rather to a shortage of currency than anything else. In Merovingian Gaul, as in the other barbarian kingdoms, gold continued the official unit of exchange, though both gold and silver coins were minted, following their Roman prototypes so closely that Pirenne styled them 'pseudo-imperial'. The coin designs followed the changes introduced into Byzantine money: e.g. the cross replaced the old symbol of the emperor's victory, a draped female figure. It was clearly necessary for foreign trade to maintain the old Roman uniformity of coinage, and the emperor's name appeared on the coins of the Germanic kings. But whereas late Roman Gaul had been supplied with a gold, silver and bronze currency from four state mints, Arles, Lyons, Marseilles and Trier, the Franks struck coins, not only in the palace and in various cities but (as Pirenne put it) 'by an infinity of moneyers'. The kings' names do not appear upon these coins, but instead the name of the *vicus, castrum* or villa where they were struck, and the name of some lay official or bishop. It used to be held that the lay official's name was the name of the moneyer who struck the coin, and that these numerous local mints, in places of such small importance that they cannot always be identified, were merely the workshops of individual craftsmen, who had escaped from the imperial mints when Roman Gaul was overrun.

This theory was difficult to maintain, however, since about a hundred years' gap intervened between the break-down of the imperial mints, and the appearance of those small local mints whose coins bear neither an emperor's nor a French king's name. (Clovis's coins, with the emperor Anastasius' name between two C's, would doubtless have been struck by Roman trained moneyers: Reims had actually been an official imperial mint for a short time in the fourth century, and Roman goldsmiths would have been available to him.) M. Ferdinand Lot, however, and Pirenne following him, accepted an origin for the 'decentralized' Merovingian mints connected with the imposition of the *tonlieu*: they regarded the personal name on the coins as that of the collector of the tax, of some royal steward, or of the steward of some abbey which was authorized by its 'immunity' to collect the *tonlieu* for its own benefit. It was convenient, that is, for the royal collector, or the steward of a demesne, to receive 'payments in kind, foreign money or ancient money or metals by weight', and to render his account to the fisc, or to his own abbey, in the coins he had caused to be minted on the spot. The coins bore his signature as guarantee of their origin and value, and the place of minting as a sign to recall where the tax was collected.

Bishops, similarly, minted their own coins less as the usurpation of a regalian right than in the effort to mobilize their resources; if minting was a process of account on the demesnes of the fisc, it is likely that it would also be used for the collection of revenue from episcopal lands, and particularly for payments of one kind or another to the king, or for incense and oil. Episcopal lands within the *civitas* were from the beginning the subject of a grant of immunity, and for those outside in the *territorium* immunity was gradually sought and acquired: favours granted by the king were often preceded by gifts to him, and coined money was useful. Nevertheless, it is very difficult to believe that the adoption of this system of local minting, even as part of an accounting system, meant anything but that currency was in short supply. The Theodosian code had provided for the coining into ingots of money paid in taxation: a precaution against pilfering in transport and a method of assessing by weight the worth of local currencies. The Merovingian system, however, could only have been adopted when a uniform royal currency, even within the separate Frankish kingdoms, was lacking; it also suggests a fairly frequent payment in plate.

Payment for the Merovingian *descriptiones* would appear to have been in kind, or to have involved 'mobilization of resources' and minting. From Gregory of Tours' references, these *descriptiones* appear to have been occasional and heavy, though in one or two passages he implies the normal levy of something like a land or property tax, at less high rates. King Chilperic, he says, commanded that new and heavy *descriptiones* should be made in all his kingdom, by means of which many left their cities and their private possessions, thinking it better to be refugees than to put themselves in such peril. For it was appointed that the owner of a private estate should pay one amphora of wine for each arpent of vineyard; and many other charges were laid on other land and on that worked by serfs, which could not be paid. For taxation as heavy as this, the normal supply of currency could scarcely have sufficed.

This shortage of Merovingian currency is supported also by the conclusions of Marc Bloch. First, he showed that the Constantinian gold *solidus*, weighing 4 gr. 48 of fine metal, was no longer coined in the west; the Byzantine empire maintained it under the new name of *nomisma* and *huperperon* (*hyperpère*), and though the value of this coin fluctuated, it diminished only in a slow downward movement; perhaps in consequence of the need to equalize the value of the new coins with old, worn gold coins. As late as 1200, however, the *hyperpère* equalled in weight of fine metal about three-quarters that of its Roman ancestor; the gold *solidus* had practically been maintained. The currencies of the barbarian kings, on the other hand, were poor in gold, and in bad reputation. Among the Franks, the gold *solidus* dropped out, and fractions of it the half *solidus* and the *triens* were minted: the *triens* became the normal gold coin of the barbarian kingdoms. Among the Anglo-Saxons an even weaker, silver gilt coinage, that of the *sceattas*, was all that could be struck till the reign of Offa.

This weakness of the gold currency of the barbarians, and the comparative scarcity of silver, must have been increased by the disuse of the Roman copper coinage. The latter was, in the fourth century, only a money of account: bronze coins were still minted in the fourth century, but their nominal worth bore no relation to the value of the metal contained. But neither the barbarian kings, nor the decentralized mints of the Merovingians, had the authority to maintain a money of account, valuable as it must have been in local trading; its function had to be taken over by a weak silver currency, increasing the general shortage.

The continuity, however, of a culture, a society, in the Mediterranean basin from late Roman times to the Arab conquests is not

evidenced solely by economic continuity: continuity of royal and
local administration by notaries has long been accepted (see
pp. 299, 399), as has the influence of a survival of Roman law
(see p. 105). 'By the continuity of the form of her administration,
as by her cultural prestige,' wrote Pirenne, 'Rome survived her
fall.' It is, however, his distinctive contribution to have recognized
the survival of the trans-Mediterranean trade with the east, of a
partial money economy among the Franks, and the arrival of
papyrus from Egypt with all its social implications. If his assertion
of a scarcely disturbed or diminished money economy in the west
has not met with acceptance, his vision of a mainly Roman
Mediterranean society, ruled by Germanic dynasties, but speaking
a popular Latin, using Roman legal forms, obeying officers with
the old Latin titles and wearing east Roman *ornamenta*, maintaining
the villas of the fisc and of private owners, obeying in the countryside the count of the old *civitas* and in the towns the successors of
the old senatorial *ordo*: this vision has illuminated the history of
the sixth and seventh centuries, and will live.

The Arab conquests of the seventh century brought a further
economic recession to western Europe. Syria fell under Arab
dominion in 634–636; Egypt between 640 and 642, Africa between
643 and 708, and Spain in 711. All these countries were drawn into
the orbit of Islam and Mediterranean unity was broken. The sea
became 'an uncrossable ditch' between the western and eastern
parts of the Roman world. Arab mastery of the Tyrrhenian Sea
was so complete that no Christian vessel dared to cross it. If any
vessels made their way safely between Marseilles and the Levant,
they were very few.

The Byzantine empire, thanks to its war fleet, succeeded in
sheltering its own coasts from the Muslim pirates: her merchant
ships could pass safely to the Black Sea, the Aegean, Greece, south
Italy and the Adriatic: Constantinople had communications with
Venice, Taranto, Amalfi and Naples: but not with Marseilles or
Narbonne. The Spanish ports were in Muslim hands, and the
Tyrrhenian Sea was dead to large-scale commerce. Pilgrims for
the east from Gaul or Britain for the most part took the land
route to Naples and sailed from there.

There are two striking pieces of evidence for the economic
results of the Arab conquests on the west, and on the Carolingian
empire when it arose: the disappearance of a gold currency, and
of an east-west Mediterranean commerce.

In the matter of currency, a monetary schism in the Carolingian period divided Europe: the Arabs and the Byzantines used a gold standard, and the Carolingian empire and England a silver standard and this of necessity. The Byzantine empire after the Arab conquests of its provinces was no longer synonymous with 'the east': the gold-using area included its shrunken territories, and those of the Arabs; the Levant, Egypt, Maghreb (Morocco), south Italy as partly Greek and partly Arab, Sicily as first Greek and then Arab, and the greater part of Spain. The Arabs had inherited a double tradition of a gold currency, that of the Byzantines and that of Sassanid Persia, and they continued to issue gold coins of the same weight, though eventually with Arabic inscriptions, as those of the countries they conquered. They had the eastern trade, and it gave them supplies of gold. The map of Europe was divided between the gold monetary area of the Greeks and Arabs, and the silver monetary area of the Carolingian empire and England. To the gold area in this map was added for a short period at the end of the tenth century Varangian Russia; otherwise it held good till the middle of the twelfth century.

In the west, an exclusively silver coinage was used by the Carolingian Franks; Professor Grierson has shown that there was more gold in Spain and England than used to be believed,[1] though in England it was used for ornaments that could be melted down at need rather than in the normal minting of gold coins. Charlemagne and Louis the Pious issued certain gold coins once more, but only rarely and for quite exceptional needs. Among the Anglo-Saxons the amount of gold used in the coinage was unimportant compared to that needed for such ornaments as those found in the seventh-century cenotaph at Sutton Hoo. Even the gold coinage of Offa was soon discontinued. When, on the continent, new mints were opened for countries that had never earlier had their own currency (Germany east of the Rhine, Bohemia, Poland and the Scandinavian states), they minted only silver. The silver *denier* (*denarius*) of Carolingian Gaul spread all over western Europe: the scarcity of metal is shown by its lightness, and it became successively lighter and lighter till the thirteenth century.

Money, in the Carolingian empire, meant silver, and the only coin was the silver penny. The *solidus* survived as a money of account only, and it was now reckoned as a silver *solidus*: twelve deniers, for the most part, went to the *solidus* (the *sous*). Though for accounting purposes, payment might normally be reckoned in

[1] Explained in a paper entitled *The Myth of the Mancus*, given to the Anglo-American Congress, London, 14 July 1951.

silver *solidi* (shillings), for the purpose of a natural economy a payment could be used of *solidi* 'in grain'. Though this silver coinage of the Carolingian empire was scanty and poor, the resources of the Franks enabled them to support it: the silver mines of the central plateau were used throughout the middle ages.

The history of the later imperial and early medieval gold currency hinged on the fact that Europe was poor in gold: new gold could only be obtained by conquest or in commercial exchange with countries that produced it, and from the eighth to the twelfth century little of the latter was possible. The eastern trade came to Byzantines and Arabs, or passed up the Russian rivers to the Scandinavians. Nevertheless, some gold circulated in western Europe, though to a limited extent and without an official currency. Gold ornaments were a resource at need, and were apparently often melted down; gold circulated in the form of ingots, dust and rings. Payments reckoned in gold appear later in Domesday Book, and the payment of an ounce of gold (by weight) occurs in various records and chronicles.

In the eighth and ninth centuries two gold coins circulated in the central and western Mediterranean, and were at least known to the Franks: the Byzantine and Arabic forms of the old *solidus aureus*. The Greek *hyperpère* is met with in the *Chanson de Roland* as the *besanz*, and elsewhere in Carolingian sources; the *dinar* struck by the Arab caliphs and then by the Syrian amirs and the Umayyad caliphs of Cordoba was also widely known in western Europe. *Dinars* have been found among the silver coins of the Carolingian Franks, and one of between 724 and 743 occurred in a find at Eastbourne.

The assessment of the relative volume of Arabic or Byzantine gold coins in western Europe depends upon the meaning of the term 'mancus'. It used to be believed that the mancus was the Arab *dinar*, or a western or English imitation of the *dinar*, or the weight in gold of the *dinar* used as a unit of account, as in England. Professor Grierson and other numismatists have now shown that the mancus was not an Arabic coin or the term derived from an Arabic word: the mancus, in the second half of the eighth century, was an Italian-minted Byzantine coin, a lighter or less fine version of the *solidus aureus*, in fact, a *solidus mancus*. It circulated in Rome, south Italy and Catalonia and the term occurs in the records of the famous Lombard abbey of Farfa. In Bavaria it was accounted worth 30 silver *deniers* and, with variations, this valuation held good throughout the west. Istria paid its contribution to the

Carolingian fisc in mancuses. Towards the end of the ninth century the term mancus disappears from Latin texts of the Mediterranean regions and was replaced by marabotius, used especially of Almoravid coins: but this coin was still actually the old *solidus*, though now in an Arabic rather than Italian-Byzantine form.

The mancus figures regularly in Anglo-Saxon wills, charters, etc., of the period, but as a money of account. Professor Grierson has shown that there is no reason to believe that the mancuses minted by Offa for an annual offering to the pope were *dinars*, but in all probability copies of the south Italian mancus then circulating in Rome, of which returning pilgrims would have knowledge. Numismatists reject as quite insufficient the evidence that the single *dinar* found in Italy with some English associations was actually one of Offa's mancuses. Moreover, the trading connexions between England and Spain were apparently almost non-existent: and the word used of Offa's coin was actually mancus and not *dinar*.

As to the other sign of economic recession in the Carolingian period, the diminution of an east-west Mediterranean trade, the most striking phenomenon was the sudden disuse of papyrus in the west between *c.* 670 and 680, most clearly shown in the documents issued from the Merovingian writing office in those years. It is usually held that papyrus had become unobtainable and parchment was therefore used to replace it: though it has been recently suggested that the change was due to desire for a less friable material for use with a seal. But authentification by seal alone was not immediately adopted by the Merovingians on the change-over to parchment, though the more solid material, once adopted, certainly hastened the use of the seal. It has also been asserted that vellum was now cheaper than papyrus, which may well have been if papyrus was almost unobtainable: though in the days of the unhindered supply of papyrus, as under the Roman empire, papyrus would have been a much cheaper writing material than vellum. The place of papyrus was, in any case, soon after 670 taken in legal and administrative business, correspondence and for books, by parchment. Cheap writing material for the merchants was unobtainable; but as bulky eastern goods could no longer come by sea from Egypt or the Levant, and large-scale commerce dwindled, there was the less occasion for business letters and accounts. Italy could still obtain papyrus, after the tenth century from Sicily, where the Arabs introduced it, or from the merchants of Amalfi, Naples or Venice, who continued to traffic with the Muslims of Egypt, contrary to all the prohibitions of the church.

It is of interest that the notaries of the papal *scrinium* continued to use papyrus, and the old cursive hand appropriate to it, long after the chanceries of western Europe, and particularly those of the Carolingian emperors, had adopted parchment. Parchment was a much more lasting material, with a smooth surface, and the new script evolved for it became universally recognized and understood in Europe, while ability to read the cursive hand died out. Yet the Roman curia went on issuing papyrus documents (sometimes accompanying them with a readable parchment copy in the new script) till the eleventh century. The Roman curia was always a notably conservative body: the old Roman *prudentia* seems usually to have prevented the adoption of administrative or liturgical practices originating in western Europe for about 200 years: but its use of papyrus seems to have been due to something more than notarial conservatism. The curia desired to follow Byzantine practice. The manufacture of papyrus in fifth- and sixth-century Egypt was an imperial monopoly, and for the prevention of forgery notaries were compelled to use only the *basilike charte*. Imperial Byzantine documents of the greatest importance were written on such papyrus with purple ink and sealed with golden seals bearing the emperor's effigy; documents of lesser importance, or those issued by the imperial family, were written with silver ink and sealed with a leaden seal. The pope at Rome and his curia, following Byzantine law, seem to have conformed their practice with that of Constantinople, using the leaden bulla of documents of the second class. When the Arabs conquered Egypt and possessed themselves of the papyrus industry, they did not at once prohibit the export of papyrus; they did so during the course of their quarrel with Justinian II, but some supplies seem always to have reached Italy, though not western Europe.

Spices also, and the embroidered silken ceremonial cloths of the east, became rare luxury imports in the west in the eighth century. Importers were generally Jews, who brought a few sacks of pepper or spices from Muslim Spain or the Byzantine ports of Italy: kings or the church might get occasional supplies of spices or incense, but the regular commerce in spices from Marseilles dropped suddenly. The question whether Syrian traders completely ceased to visit the Carolingian empire after the Arab conquest of the Mediterranean has been much disputed by savants; there was undoubtedly a rush of refugee Syrian Christians to Europe in the seventh century, when the eastern provinces were overrun, and the manuscripts, textiles and ornaments they brought had a notable effect on art. Byzantine and even Syrian and Armenian influence was strong in western Europe at the end of the seventh century through their refugee Syrians; but, as Pirenne argued, a few refugee Syrian bishops and their icons might well influence art-forms without affording any evidence for east-west Mediterranean trade. Some Syrians became popes, like Sergius I (687–701) and Constantine I (708–719), and the Greek monk Theodore became archbishop of Canterbury (668–693): but while East Roman forms influenced religion and art, east Roman trade with the west dwindled.

With the dwindling of large-scale commerce, the Carolingian empire reached the last stage of 'recession': a domanial economy focussed on the large estate, a natural economy tempered by the use of a small currency, replaced the Merovingian régime, where at least more money and merchants had been in circulation. The Carolingian empire was shut in on the east by the Avars, on the north by the Scandinavians, who traded with the Arabs down the Russian rivers, and by Arab dominance of the west Mediterranean: it has been called a closed economy, without outlets, with an insufficient supply of the precious metals to maintain a good currency. The gold coinage had disappeared and land became the only source of wealth. The Carolingian emperors and kings were forced to pay their servants, especially the counts, in land, and hence arose the extension of the system of the grants of *beneficia*, to laymen as well as to churchmen; the *cellararium fisci* ceased to be provisioned with eastern goods, and abbeys which had had privileges exempting them from paying customs on goods bought in the markets of Marseilles and Fos ceased to claim them, for the goods desired were not there. A Carolingian *trattoria* assigned quantities of home-grown food to envoys, but no longer spices and rolls of papyrus.

The question whether, in this domanial economy, any produce of the estate was grown for sale in the Carolingian period, has been answered in the affirmative by M. Ganshof; and the question, whether any Syrian merchants at all reached Gaul was answered by the instancing of the Syrian *Cappi* mentioned in the capitulary of Quierzy, by the American historian, J. W. Thomson; Professor Dopsch also and his pupils have claimed that the Arab influence on the cutting off of trade has been over-emphasized. Other scholars too have denied the complete cutting of Frankish intercourse with Sicily in the ninth and tenth centuries. But if eastern commodities reached the west, it must have been in small quantity, and trade done in corn, wine or external goods in the towns between the Seine and the Rhine was done by means of a relatively small, silver currency. No peasant paid a money rent for his land; he paid by services on his lord's demesne, he held his small farm freely, or he commended it and himself to the patronage of some lord; the king's officials held their land by reason of service, not, till the ninth century, military. There was no longer a royal land tax, collected in money, and though the customary tolls were paid partly in coin, they went, by this time, largely to the immunists, not to the king or emperor. All this recession towards a natural economy, the parent of ninth-century feudalism, hinged upon shortage of currency and absence of sufficient large-scale commerce. It was a purely economic phenomenon: and not, till the latter half of the ninth century, connected with the need of military defence.

The change which the barbarian invasions brought to European agriculture was less marked than that caused to town life and commerce; but it had its part in the gradual extension of arable at the expense of brushwood and forest, which is the main historical feature of European agriculture in the middle ages. Agriculture round the Mediterranean basin was already old and the cultivable land had long been laid out for vineyards or in the small rectangular (or irregular) fields by the *aratrum*. But in the hinterland of the Mediterranean, in north Spain, north Gaul, the Rhine lands, central Europe and the Balkans there was still much uncleared forest and heath land, and here the making of assarts (clearings, *défrichements*) went on gradually in the early middle ages, and was rapidly extended in the thirteenth century. In the Merovingian and Carolingian period, when wars and disturbances threw land out of cultivation only too often, clearing often meant only the removal of brushwood and copses which had grown up on land once cultivated. The clearing of the great forests was very heavy work not at first attempted in the days of the Germanic settlements; moreover, where Germanic influence was strong, there may have been reluctance to meddle with the territory of the gods who dwelt in the deep woods.

Only two points can be here briefly mentioned: the effect of the Germanic settlements on the lands the Germans conquered: and the connexion between the layout of the countryside and the kind of plough used.[1]

---

[1] These points, and others, are dealt with very fully in vol. i of the *Camb. Econ. Hist.*, ed. Clapham, J. H., and Power, E., 1941.

Three zones of agrarian settlement can be distinguished in Europe after the barbarian settlements. The first was that where, by the system of *hospitalitas*, the conquerors drew a share of the Roman landlord's revenue or produce from his estates, or even replaced him altogether. To the *coloni* or *servi* who worked the villa or the demesne, this could have made little difference, for only enough to support life, and that meagrely, was allowed him already. Nor was there any reason to introduce new methods of cultivation or new instruments: the villas were worked as before, nor is there reason to think that in this first zone the conquerors settled in the *vici* and tilled the land themselves. This zone comprised the Mediterranean lands: Spain and south Gaul, under the Visigoths and later the Franks; the Rhone country of the Burgundians, and Ostrogothic and Lombard Italy. Here no traditions of Germanic agriculture or village life appear to have affected the countryside.

The second zone was that settled in some numbers by the Franks, Alemans and Bavarians: in Gaul, that is to say, to the Loire, the Rhine mouth, Lorraine, Switzerland and Bavaria. Here the Germans were more numerous from the beginning, and here they received gradual reinforcements. The Salic Law and the laws of the Alemans and Bavarians provide for a land settled in small villages; in Salian Gaul three or four conquering Franks seem to have possessed themselves of some villa and worked it themselves with their followers, or with the *coloni* and serfs of the dispossessed landowner. Germanic place-names with a personal name and *-ingen* or *heim* point to ownership by a Frankish noble and his people: these place-names occur in the Rhineland. The place-name element *thun* (= Anglo-Saxon *tun*) in Normandy may point to an original Frankish population; but south of the Loire Frankish ownership did not imply Frankish settlers.

The third zone of German settlement was that of land outside the Rhine and Danube frontiers, where Roman traditions and Roman agriculture had never existed. It includes the Frankish territory on the right bank of the Rhine, and the lands of the Frisians, Saxons, Danes and Scandinavians. Here villages of freemen might be found and a sharing out of strips in the common fields by decision in the folk-moot; but here too were villages where some noble, or freeman of higher status than other freemen, had great, compact estates. There were grades of freemen among the Franks, athelings or *edelingen* (nobles) among the Saxons, and everywhere *laeti*, or the half-free conquered villagers, and slaves: and social status was accompanied by difference of holding, or absence of holding. Probably, as in Anglo-Saxon England, the lordless village of free *ceorls* (Charlton, Carlton) was the exception.

The countryside in western Europe has been laid out by two types of plough, the *aratrum* and the *carruca*, and, speaking broadly, the *aratrum* was the plough used in the Roman empire in the fifth century and long before, and the *carruca* was the plough used by the Germanic invaders. The *aratrum* was a light plough, ox-drawn, the handles supported only by the hands of the plough-man, and the share driving a light furrow on the surface of the field; to let sufficient air into the soil, it was necessary to cross the fur-rows with others running in the other direction. For such a field a small, rectangular plot was best, for it would not be possible to cross-plough a long, narrow one. The small fields of hilly country could be dealt with by the *aratrum*, if indeed they were not so sloping that they must be cultivated by hoe, mattock or *caschrom*. The coulter, or knife fastened before the share, to cut the skin of grass or weeds and make the passage of the share easier, was actually invented by the Romans for use with the *aratrum*, but most of these light, primitive ploughs would have been with-out it.

The word plough is itself Germanic, and was used of the wheeled plough, the *carruca* (connected with *currus* and *charrue*). It was a heavy plough and drawn by anything up to eight oxen; the weight of the plough now rested on the wheels: it is first mentioned by Pliny († A.D. 79) as used in Rhaetia, and appears to have been used by the Germanic tribes who practised extensive agriculture. A heavy wheeled plough would be much more effective in bringing new land into tillage than the lighter *aratrum*, and this apparently explains its extensive use by tribes on the borders of the empire, or in its less cultivated regions, for the Celts also used the wheeled plough. The furrow driven by the *carruca* was deeper than that drawn by the *aratrum* and it was hence unnecessary to cross plough; a day's work by the *carruca* with its team of oxen would result in a long, narrow strip, an *ager*, or acre strip. These would be disposed, according to the lie of the land, in parallel strips, or in bunches of strips lying in different directions, and the whole would form a great open field (*champagne*, *campania*, champion farming): the open field itself would be fenced, but there would be no division between the strips. A peasant's holding would consist of strips in different parts of the field, and the lord's demesne in this arable field would similarly consist of these unfenced strips.

To preserve the fertility of the soil, both in the small, hedged fields of the light plough, and the large open fields laid out by the *carruca*, the land was left fallow in either a two-year or a three-year course. In the Mediterranean basin the older, two-year course long prevailed, for the soils were light and better crops were thus obtained; but among the Franks the three-course system, where introduced, was capable of yielding a larger produce. The next important development in the technique of ploughing, the use of a mould-board to turn the sod, did not occur till later than the Carolingian period.

BIBLIOGRAPHICAL NOTE

Full bibliographies, listing the works of economic historians of east and west Europe about these early centuries, are now readily accessible in the two published volumes of the *Cambridge Economic History*: vol. i, ed. J. H. Clapham and Eileen Power, *The Agrarian Life of the Middle Ages*, 1941, and vol. ii, ed. M. Postan and E. E. Rich, *Trade and Industry in the Middle Ages*, 1952. In view of the length of these bibliographies, it may be as well to mention specially: M. Rostovtzeff, *Social and Economic History of the Roman Empire*, 1926: T. Frank, *Economic Survey of Ancient Rome*, 5 vols., 1933: A. Dopsch, *Wirtschaftliche und soziale grundlagen*, 1918, trans. M. G. Beard and N. Marshall, *Social and Economic Foundations*, 1937: H. Pirenne, *Mahomet et Charlemagne*, 1937 ed., and, for criticism of Dopsch and Pirenne's theories, H. Laurent, 'Les travaux de M. Henri Pirenne sur la fin du monde antique', in *Byzantion*, vii (1932), pp. 495–509: E. E. Power, 'A Problem of Transition', in *Econ. Hist. Rev.*, vol. x (1940), p. 60: G. C. Boyce in *Byzantion*, xv (1940–1), p. 449, and R. S. Lopez, 'Mohammed and Charlemagne: a Revision', in *Speculum*, xx (1945), p. 16. See also R. Latouche, *Les origines de l'économie occidentale*, *IV*ᵉ–*XI*ᵉ *siécle*, 1956: A. E. R. Boak, 'Early Byzantine Tax Receipts from Egypt', in *Byzantion*, xvii (1944–5), p. 16: M. Bloch's valuable 'Le problème d'or au moyen âge', in *Annales d'hist. écon. et soc.*, v (1933), p. 1: M. Lombard's 'L'or Musulman du VIIᵉ au XIᵉ siècle', in *Annales: Economies: Sociétés: Civilisations*, no. 2 (1947): E. Sabbe, 'L'importation des tissus orientaux', *Revue Belge de philol. et d'hist.*, 1935. For a general warning about misuse of the phrase 'rise of a money economy', see Prof. Postan in *Econ. Hist. Rev.*, vol. xxiv, p. 126, and for western numismatics at the period, P. le Gentilhomme, *Mélanges de numismatique Mérovingienne*, 1940, and C. H. V. Sutherland, *Anglo-Saxon Gold Coinage in the light of the Crondall Hoard*, Oxford, 1948. See also, for criticism of Pirenne's theory of the great importance of Mediterranean trade, R. Latouche (trans. E. Miller), *Les Origines de l'économie occidentale* (*IV*ᵉ–*XI*ᵉ *siècle*), Paris, 1956; and A. R. Lewis, *Naval Power and Trade in the Mediterranean, 500–1100*, London, 1951. For a study of price-history, L. Fébure, *Pour une histoire à part entière*, Paris, 1962.

CHAPTER VIII

THE FORMATION OF THE EASTERN EMPIRE

TO an Englishman today, studying for a moment the foundations of modern Europe, it seems natural to study first the history of the west and the settlements of the invaders. To a Roman citizen of even moderate culture in the fifth century, it would probably have seemed rather that the future of Europe and civilization depended on Constantinople and its fate. Civilization was focussed in the east, not the west: New Rome (and this was the official title of the city) was really Rome herself, planted there by Constantine in the year 330. The Rome of Constantine, it is true, was not the Rome of Augustus: the Roman empire was already, in fact, a Greco-Roman empire long before Constantine; but the fate of the Latin tradition and much else seemed to depend on the survival of 'New Rome'. Byzantium, the royal city, 'city of lights' as a later pope was to call Paris, was, to all who knew, at once the fortress and the capital of Europe: the rest, barbarian fringe. Byzantine history, at least till the Crusades, is not a strand of history adjacent to that of Europe, possibly omissible; it is, in a sense, the central strand of European history.

A great English Byzantinist [1] would set the beginning of the Byzantine empire at the very foundation of the city by Constantine, rather than at its reorganization in the eighth century by the emperor Leo III, after the losses to the Arabs. This was the beginning. All living states grow and change, in answer to the requirements of their environment, and Byzantium became progressively more Hellenistic, more Asiatic even, in the course of her history: but the project for which she was founded remained her aim through the centuries and gave her development continuity. She was never, at any point, 'orientalized'.

Three factors then determined her development, all present in the original concept of Constantine. First, New Rome was to be a Greco-Roman city, using the Latin language for law and administration. Secondly, she was to be Christian: for Constantine had triumphed by the marvellous interposition of the Christian god,

[1] Norman H. Baynes: see his introduction to *Byzantium: an Introduction to East Roman civilization.*

144

and his new empire had a divine mission. Thirdly, by setting his new city in the Greek east, he faced the increased absorption of Hellenistic culture by his subjects and especially his capital. Alexander had carried the Greek life into Asia and the succession states of his empire had produced a civilization where Greek culture was cross-fertilized by native arts and learning: Greco-Persian, Greco-Syrian, Greco-Egyptian, Greco-Armenian, Greco-Indian arts and life formed a culture called, shortly, 'Hellenistic'. Rome herself had long sat at the feet of the Greeks as regards learning and the arts, and Mark Antony had anticipated later developments by working for a Roman empire centred in the east Mediterranean rather than Rome: Alexandria might have been an imperial capital early in our era. The Orontes had already poured itself into the Tiber; there was no essential hostility in the fourth century between the Latin mind and Hellenistic culture, or (since the fathers Clement of Alexandria and Origen had set forth the implications of the Christian faith in terms intelligible to Greek scholars and philosophers) between Christianity and Hellenism: Constantine saw no 'cultural' danger to either *Romanitas* or Christianity in moving his capital farther to the learned, the civilized, the rich, the warm, the fruitful east, which, after all, was to him the centre.

Probably his more immediate aim was to secure the strategic site of Constantinople, always one of the greatest assets of the Byzantine empire. The old city of Byzantium lay on the narrow sea that joined the Pontic and the Mediterranean worlds, and on the great east-west land route that joined the valley of the Danube with that of the Euphrates. The corn of south Russia could be brought by sea to the city, and the overland trade from China, India, Persia came through Armenia and Asia Minor to Byzantium as to a great emporium. The capital was sited also to be a 'defence in depth' to the north-eastern and eastern frontiers of the empire: to those of the Danube, of Armenia and of Syria. On this site, with its harbour within the Golden Horn, Constantine built his New Rome, with its imperial palace, its churches, its hippodrome, its baths: here he encouraged the heads of Roman families to build themselves ancestral villas and to settle.

The Latin tradition, moreover, though set in a city bound to become more and more assimilated to its Greek background, did not disappear. Certain evidence has been quoted to show the success of eastern influence: the use of prostration (*proskynesis*) before the sovereign: mutilation as a punishment: some forms of ascetic contemplation: the use, in church music, of Syrian rhythms familiar to the early Christians: and the use of the bow by cavalry,

6

as in Persian warfare. But there is stronger evidence that the Byzantine empire remained Roman; it was never basically orientalized. It retained the Roman tradition in law and government, the Hellenistic tradition in language, literature and philosophy, and a Christian tradition thought out and refashioned under Greek influence. In those important political issues of Monophysitism (see p. 156) and Iconoclasm (see p. 409), it was a Greco-Roman policy and not an oriental policy that won the day.

The setting up of a Christian empire by Constantine was deliberate, though it was not of course possible to accomplish the conversion of all his subjects in his own day. The Christian purpose of the Byzantine empire was, however, never abandoned; the Byzantines were convinced that their empire was willed by God, and that they were protected by him, and by the emperor, his anointed. They fought the divine battles and could expect supernatural aid. Their empire as a state realized the divine purpose for human society, and this entailed at least four obligations: the defence of the Christian faith, by the emperor himself, as the supreme vicegerent and champion of God: the defence of the empire as the Christian society, by imperial armies fighting under the *signum* of the Christian monogram: the strong conservatism and traditionalism of East Rome: and a compassion (*philanthropia*) for the humble and the poor both from the individual and the state which exceeded the 'welfare institutions' of the pagan empire.

The Byzantine empire was not merely conceived of as itself a Christian society, but as a great missionary force. Conversion from paganism befitted its subjects, and was in the end enforced by the state; and conversion was owed, as a duty, by the empire to the tribes beyond the frontiers. As Professor Norman Baynes has, in a brilliant essay, defined the thought-world of east Rome, untying the knots of pagan and Christian philosophy, so Professor André Grabar has demonstrated the Byzantine concept of the emperor's relation to the pagan border tribes, outside the Greek *oikoumenē*, by means of the imperial iconography. Whereas the pagan emperors had been represented in sculpture as trampling the barbarians beneath their horses' feet (all will remember the small, wretched Romano-Briton beneath the horseman's feet on the slab at Hexham, a very common motif): from Constantine's time the representation gradually changes. The emperor's majesty is still vindicated by his stature, greater than that of the barbarians: he is still, as before, sometimes shown seated with his foot upon the little barbarian's head: [1] but the small barbarian is now no longer a

[1] See frontispiece.

squalid savage, but a child to be instructed, portrayed with delicacy and even affection. Rather later, the traditional representation of the emperor, resting his foot on the little barbarian's head, is felt to be unfitting to a Christian, and the emperor now holds out the cross to a row of little barbarians, without the posture of abject submission. Later still, the barbarian nations are shown as beautiful (though small) women, presumably already converted, and gratefully offering a diadem to the emperor.

All the Byzantine emperors then, from Constantine onwards, faced the same task, had the same function, and could rely on the same elements of strength. They knew themselves to have the divine protection. They exercised a unique autocracy; they appointed all officials, and Roman law ran within their whole empire and extended into all spheres of the citizen's life. They had, moreover, and never lost, their right to lead their armies in the field, as to direct all departments of civil life: even the decisions of the church needed their approval. They were supreme legislators and judges. They were able to maintain a gold currency acceptable everywhere, by a system of taxation efficient though burdensome: their revenue, huge for the day, was sufficient to maintain a small, mobile, highly trained professional army, and, occasionally, fleet. Their civil service was efficient, if often corrupt: it functioned even in times of palace revolution or under weak emperors. Finally, the morale of the Byzantine citizens was supported by the Byzantine church. Within an empire of various races and nationalities, the Christian religion was a unifying force: the Byzantine citizen, asked to what nation or state he belonged, preferred to describe himself as *Romaios*, implying citizenship of the Christian empire: implying too, the service of *Christus Victor*, as the Byzantine church saw him. The Byzantine emperors had as a source of strength the faith that promised themselves and their subjects a share in Christ's resurrection: 'the banishing of that ancient terror which beset the life of man: that it is which has won and kept the allegiance of the masses'.

The power of the Byzantine emperors rested not only on tradition, culture and orthodoxy, but on the economic strength of their empire. Population was for those days, very large: it has been reckoned that Constantinople never numbered less than 500,000 souls and at many periods more. There were many towns where commerce and industry promoted a large population, and the Christian tradition of marriage stopped the voluntary restriction of births previously obtaining in Greece and Italy. Monastic celibacy, on the other hand, somewhat restricted population. Moreover, the emperors gave asylum to refugees, distributed land to soldiers, freed slaves to populate deserted regions, and pursued a useful policy of home colonization.

International trade was a great source of Byzantine wealth, and made possible the maintenance of a gold coinage everywhere acceptable: the gold *solidus*, the *nomisma* or bezant was a truly international coin (see p. 136). The empire had a great number of ports, some the outlets of inland territories, like Salonika for the Balkans and Trebizond for Persia, some with industries of their own, like Alexandria. Textiles from the east, gold and silversmiths' ware, wine and dried fruits came to these ports, as did furs, slaves, honey and wax of south Russia. Nor did this trade consist of luxury goods alone: the large population could not have existed without the transport of great quantities of bulky goods, corn, wine, timber, etc.

Industries flourished in the towns, producing some articles for the masses, and many articles of luxury, important as exports. Great silver dishes from the east, engraved chrism spoons, penetrated to London and an east Anglian king's court in the seventh century, and not without profit to Byzantium. The ceremonies of the Byzantine court itself, and those of hundreds of churches and monasteries, required ceremonial garments, heavy gold brocades, altar plate adorned with cloisonné enamel, reliquaries, ivories, glassware, bronzes. All these articles of beautiful design and fine workmanship were produced by the gilds: all Byzantine industry was organized on the gild system. But whereas in medieval Europe the gilds themselves settled prices, wages and rules of labour, in Byzantium the state fixed profits, terms of admission and all regulations: the prefect of Constantinople could inspect all workshops.

The state also concerned itself with agriculture and particularly, though more at some periods than others, with the maintenance of peasant holdings. At all times in the history of Byzantine agriculture there were great estates and peasant holdings: the balance between them swung now to one side now to another in response to political and military needs. Briefly, it was always advantageous to the emperor to protect the small farmer, because the latter could less easily safeguard himself from the tax collector than the great landowner; and in times of acute military need, as after the Arab successes, it was vital to have a free peasantry, liable to military service, from which to recruit the army. The *coloni* of a Roman villa had never made good soldiers. On the other hand, large-scale farming produced more, the Byzantine merchant liked to invest his profits in land, and political disgrace, accompanied by confiscation, tended to increase the imperial demesne: there were always factors tending to increase the large estates at the expense of the small farmer. In the early days of the Byzantine empire, land was mainly concentrated in the hands of great landowners: in the days of the iconoclast emperors it was divided between their estates and small holdings, and there was later a reversion to the systems of large estates. But between the days of Justinian I and the Palaeologi small holdings never completely disappeared. The great landmark in their history is the reorganization of the army in the early seventh century, the lands of the border provinces of the empire being allotted to peasants who held on the obligation of hereditary and military service (see p. 214). The provinces of the empire were then regrouped in 'themes'; but in the days of Justinian I the old provincial administration of Diocletian and Constantine still obtained, though Justinian took some steps towards grouping the small provinces in larger units. In the pre-Heraclian period large estates were the rule, though the *limitanei* or frontier troops had small, military holdings.

In this period then, before the loss of Egypt and her grain supply to the Arabs, Byzantine farmers grew corn (though not as extensively as after the loss of Egypt) and had extensive vineyards: they grew also fruits, herbs, cotton and mulberries (the Peloponnese got its name, Morea, from these mulberry trees). Bee-keeping flourished, and the farmer had too cattle, sheep, pigs and horses. Racehorses were needed: and numbers of horses for the army, where the cavalry was the superior arm. From the forests on the edge of cultivation came the timber needed for houses and ships and, indeed, all the scaffolding and beams needed for the *castella* and the great domed buildings of Justinian's age.

A very large imperial revenue was raised, as in the late Roman empire, from the large imperial demesne, from various forms of land tax and levies in kind, and, very largely, from customs and charges on traders. The state property included not only agricultural estates, kept largely by confiscations, but imperial factories where silk was woven and the army needs supplied: the emperor moreover owned many caravanserais and bazaars and charged merchants for their use. With his huge revenue the emperor had to pay for fortifications, city walls and frontier defence: the small but expensive army and, sometimes, navy: mercenary soldiers and the heavy presents needed in diplomacy: the whole burden of official salaries, partly in cash, partly in kind: largesses to the army, the church, and the populace: the maintenance of costly palaces and palace servants: great sums of money, and landed endowment for churches, monasteries and 'welfare institutions' (hospitals for the poor, the aged, the sick, etc.): and great sums for the splendid 'games and circuses' of the capital. So great needs strained even the great revenue of the Byzantine emperors, but they never adopted the resource, so commonly used at the time, of debasing the currency. The Byzantine empire was set in what was then a rich and fertile part of the earth: but it could never have maintained its position on the profits of agriculture alone: the imperial management of the currency is evidence both that the supply of precious metals was relatively adequate, and that the importance of mercantile sources to the revenue was realized.

As to the machinery by which the Byzantine empire functioned, its civil administration had grown out of the service of the later Roman empire, as described in the eastern part of the *Notitia Dignitatum*. The emperor was the supreme Roman magistrate, though his office had acquired a Christian significance and his autocracy an eastern character in imitation of the Persian monarchy. His title up to 629, however, remained Imperator Augustus, rendered in Greek, *Autokrator Augustos*: the Greek word for king, *basileus*, was not officially used till Heraclius had conquered the Persians who used it. As the Roman emperor had been *pontifex maximus*, with a supremacy over all pagan religions, the emperors from Constantine onwards took over, as it were, the guardianship of the Christian religion. Just as in imperial iconography motifs representing qualities or powers of the pagan emperor were not dropped when the empire became Christian, but Christianized: as, the winged victory on the globe to a cross, and the two legionary standards held by a standing emperor to two tall crosses (*signa crucis*): so the sacredness of the pagan emperor was preserved in the Christian régime. It was no original part of the Christian conviction that kingship was itself sacred, but the church teaching that 'the powers that be are ordained of God', found the sacred character of its imperial protector no stumbling block. The coronation rite was only added to the ceremonies of an imperial succession after the reign of Leo I (d. 474); and the rite of anointing not till the ninth century; but it was always the patriarch who conferred the diadem, and so necessary was the patriarch's part, that in a disputed succession a rival claimant would obtain the creation of his own patriarch canonically or uncanonically to crown him.

The central staff of the emperor resided at Constantinople: the *magister officiorum*, who headed not only the imperial *scrinia* or chanceries, but the arms factories, the post, and the palace body-guard: he was Head of all Departments. He had under him *agentes in rebus*, holding high civil and military posts. The *quaestor sacri palatii* presided over the council, the *consistorium*, and was supreme minister of justice; he drafted edicts and answered petitions. Finance was managed by the *comes sacrarum largitionum* and the *comes rerum privatarum*, the first officer administering the treasury once called the *fiscus*, which collected revenue, all tribute paid in money, taxes on trade and industry and various other cash sources. The *comes rerum privatarum* administered the imperial demesne and the privy purse, though this was later the duty of an official with a treasury of his own, the *sacellarius*. Following old Roman usage, officials, military and civil, were graded in dignity and honorific address: *illustres, spectabiles* and *clarissimi*. The original title of official companion of the emperor, *comes*, was also graded in three classes. High office both in the army and civil service was open to all, and promotion was normally by seniority. The officials of the age of Justinian were organized on much the same lines as those of the *Notitia Dignitatum* in the fifth century: major change came in the days of Heraclius, though from those of Justinian there was a tendency to split up the large departments, and bring the heads of all the departments into immediate dependence on the emperor.

Local government, depending on the division of the empire into provinces, rested in Justinian's day on the system inaugurated by Diocletian and Constantine. The western prefectures of the system had been lost: but the east, the Byzantine empire of the sixth century, consisted of two prefectures: Oriens, with five dioceses (comprising the Asiatic provinces, Egypt and Thrace): and Illyricum, with two dioceses, including the rest of the Balkans. The two praetorian prefects had not only supreme legal and administrative power, but collected the *annona* or land tax, with which to pay salaries and feed the army. Under the prefect, the imperial vicars governed the dioceses, and under the praetorian prefect of the east, the prefect of the city, residing in Constantinople, supervised the food supplies, the gilds and the administration of the capital. The dioceses had been subdivided by Constantine into small provinces, where city and military office was held separately. This division of powers was first set aside by Justinian in regions of acute military danger: exarchs, combining civil and military authority, were appointed for Africa after the conquest of the Vandals, and for Italy, invaded by the Lombards.

Succession in the East Roman empire was theoretically elective, and in practice much influenced by relationship to the preceding emperor. The use of adoption, a custom long familiar in Roman law, made possible the existence of imperial dynasties in a system nominally elective. The succession was normally peaceful, though sometimes disturbed, or occasioned, by palace revolutions. The dynasty of Constantine I, despite the enormous prestige of its founder and the possibility of adoption, had ended with Julian (d. 363): the dynasty of Theodosius had lasted from 379 to 457 and seen the division, for administrative purposes, of the Roman empire, Arcadius taking the eastern portion in 395. The dynasty of Leo I lasted from 457 to 518, and profited by the long peace on the eastern frontier with the Sassanid princes of Persia; but could not prevent in 476 the setting up of barbarian rule in Rome.

BIBLIOGRAPHICAL NOTE
[to chapters viii, ix, xii and xxi]

J. B. Bury's *History of the Later Roman Empire, A.D. 395–565*, is useful, though superseded by C. Diehl and C. Marcais' *Le monde oriental de 395 à 1081*, ed. 1944. See also N. H. Baynes's short and sound *The Byzantine Empire*, 1925: G. Ostrogorsky, *History of the Byzantine State*, tr. J. M. Hussey, 1956: L. Bréhier, *Vie et mort de Byzance*, 1947: E. Stein's *Histoire du Bas-Empire* (to death of Justinian), 1949: and A. A. Vasiliev, *History of the Byzantine Empire*, ed. 1953. An illuminating and well illustrated account of the Byzantine empire by a group of Byzantinists, under the editorship of N. H. Baynes and H. St L. B. Moss, is entitled *Byzantium*, 1948; for other of N. H. Baynes's writings, see especially 'Eusebius and the Christian Empire' in *Mélangès Bidez*, Brussels, 1934: *The Hellenistic Civilization and East Rome*, 1945, and *The Thought World of East Rome*, 1947. See also A. H. M. Jones, *Constantine and the Conversion of Europe*, 1948: P. N. Ure, *Justinian and his Age*, 1951: N. Iorga, *Relations entre l'Orient et l'Occident au Moyen Age*, 1928; for archaeological and artistic evidence of the concept of the Christian emperor at Byzantium, A. Grabar, *L'empereur dans l'art Byzantin*, 1936: for a description of Byzantine cities and fortifications, Procopius' *The Buildings*, in the Loeb ed.: for Byzantine art, O. M. Dalton, *Byzantine Art and Archaeology*, 1911: C. Diehl, *Manuel d'art byzantin*, 2 vols., ed. 1925–6: L. Bréhier, *L'art Byzantin*, 1930: D. Talbot Rice, *Byzantine Art*, 1935: A. Grabar, *L'art Byzantin*, 1938. For light on Greco-Roman officials and their relation to their successors in medieval Europe, see the Theodosian Code, *passim*, and specially Book vi in *Theodosiani libri xvi*, ed. Mommsen and Meyer, 1905, or in C. Pharr, for trans., *The Theodosian Code and the Sirmondian Constitutions*, Princeton Univ. Press, 1952, or in G. Haenel, *Corpus iuris antejustiniani*, vol. I, 1841. See also as a monument in Byzantine history, the new ed. of the *Camb. Med. Hist.*, vol. IV, which was published in 1923 under the title 'The East Roman Empire'. The new ed., edited by J. M. Hussey, is in two parts: Part i, 'Byzantium and its neighbours',

Cambridge, 1966; and Part ii, 'Government, Church and Civilisation', 1967. The whole vol. is entitled 'The Byzantine Empire', and this empire treated as claiming universal rule, in succession to the Roman emperors of the past. The story is told from the accession of the first Christian emperor, Constantine. There is a very full bibliography, running to 330 pages, and a full index. Chapter XXX, 'The place of Byzantium in the medieval world', and its bibliography, is of special interest for this book.

For an examination of the two conflicting theories of government in the middle ages, that power 'ascends' from the people, and that it 'descends' from God, see W. Ullmann, *Principles of Government and Politics in the middle ages*, London, 1961. Byzantium, with its gathered Hellenistic knowledge, and its Christian emperor, had sources for the support of both theories. See also P. V. Sellers, *The Council of Chalcedon : a Historical and Doctrinal Survey*, London, 1953; A. A. Vasiliev, *Justin the First, an Introduction to the Epoch of Justinian the Great*, Cambridge, Mass., 1950; G. Downey, *Constantinople in the age of Justinian*, Oklahoma, 1960; N. H. Baynes, *The Emperor Heraclius and the Military Theme System*, E.H.R., 1952, p. 380; N. Zernov, *Eastern Christendom*, London, 1961; N. H. Baynes, *Byzantine Studies and other Essays*, London, 1955.

CHAPTER IX

EAST ROMAN IMPERIAL POLICY FROM ZENO TO JUSTINIAN (474-565)

THROUGHOUT the reigns of these emperors, and indeed till the Arab victories of the seventh century, the rulers of Byzantium faced a dual frontier problem, and with both of them the imperial attitude on the Christological controversy was intimately connected. In Constantine's day the Latin tradition in the capital had perhaps outweighed the Greek, but in the sixth century an imperial reconquest of the west seemed to some provincials subjugation by an eastern, alien power. Yet in the struggle to keep the eastern provinces from outside attack and internal revolt, imperial policy was not free to conciliate the beliefs of oriental Christians because it had to maintain the dogmas accepted by east and west at Nicaea and Chalcedon.

The reign of Zeno (474-491) began with conspiracy and an inglorious withdrawal by Zeno from the throne: he regained his throne in 476. The date was epochal not through events in Constantinople, but for the loss of the empire in Rome. The reign saw the settlement of Theoderic and his followers in Italy (see p. 36), and left the Isaurian tribes used by Leo I as mercenaries against the Goths still discontented. On Zeno's death his brother Longinus sought with their help to make himself emperor, but the influence of Zeno's widow secured the succession of the elderly civil servant, Anastasius I (491-518). Concerned with the defence of the frontiers and the capital, he rebuilt fortresses, reorganized the *limitanei*, and raised in defence of Constantinople the famous Long Wall across the peninsula on which the city was built. His desire to secure the loyalty of the eastern provinces led him, however, as it did later emperors, to follow a policy of religious comprehension that only succeeded in disturbing his whole empire.

Zeno's effort to conciliate the eastern provinces was the first in a series of imperial interventions in the definition of Christian dogma, matters of great importance in the history of the Christian church and no less in the political history of the East Roman empire. This preoccupation of many Byzantine emperors arose not only from their quasi-apostolic guardianship of the Christian faith, but, in the fifth and sixth centuries, from the political need to satisfy and retain the eastern provinces of the empire. Armenia, the land of east-west mountain valleys south of the Black Sea, valleys stretching from the upper waters of the Halys in Asia Minor across the head waters of the Tigris and Euphrates to those of the Kura and Araxes, was a land of transit, the border province between Rome and the Sassanids. She had been early converted from Antioch and her missionaries had gone out to Seleukia-Ctesiphon and India; she occupied a position of balance between orthodox Christianity and that of the Persians, orthodox at first and later Nestorian. She was a land of mountains and deep, green, fertile valleys: of long winters and short summers that were yet long enough to ripen her vineyards and plum orchards. Her craftsmen made and dyed the rich textiles of the east, her merchants travelled with them throughout the empire, her peasants of the mountainsides made excellent mercenaries. It was necessary for an emperor to have an eye and ear to Armenia, and Armenia had many Monophysites and Nestorians.

Syria also was a border province, with a camel-borne eastern trade passing from Mesopotamia to Damascus and the ports of Palestine: Syrians as traders penetrated the empire as far west as did Jews and Greeks: but they had not the same importance as mercenaries as the Armenians. Egypt again, with its great sea port and university of Alexandria, and its hinterland of the Nile valley and Abyssinia, was all important to the royal revenue, and still supplied much food to the capital and stores to the army. Armenia, Syria, Egypt, all converted in the earliest days to Christianity, all sources of revenue and the two northern ones of great military importance: all, especially Egypt, the scene of lively native cultural movements and the more difficult to hold within the Greco-Roman tradition: the desire to hold these provinces was a great argument to conciliation in matters of the faith.

The story of the Christological controversies forms part of the political history of Byzantium. Their importance to an empire whose founder was quasi-apostolos (as it were, as sacredly bound to safeguard the *paradosis*, the Christian faith, as the bishops themselves) should not be minimized: the obligation in the end was stronger than the political expediency. Constantine had summoned the council of Nicaea in 325 to preserve religious unity in view of controversy over the nature of Christ: the teaching of Arius, presbyter of Alexandria, that Christ was a creature: that 'there was a time when he was not', that he was by no means of the same nature (*homoousion*) as the Father, was condemned, and anathematized. The religious unity of the Greco-Roman world was preserved: in the west, it was the barbarians who preserved Arianism: but even in the east there were conservatives who disliked the definition of dogma by any word non-scriptural (like *homoousion*). Rivalry, moreover, between the patriarchates as great schools of theology, with an authority implicit in their apostolic foundation, contributed to the rivalry between the Christological doctrines they held: there was rivalry between Antioch and Alexandria in the time of Constantine. The claim of Constantinople from Theodosius' reign to rank as a patriarchate contributed to the firmness with which she upheld her own Christological teaching.

The followers of Nestorius, patriarch of Constantinople and theologian of the school of Antioch, stressed the human nature of Christ at the expense of his godhead: he taught that the Virgin was the mother of Christ, but not the mother of God (*theotokos*): the divinity had come to dwell in the humanity of Christ 'as in a temple'. There were those who protested that this teaching divided the Christ, and Cyril, patriarch of Alexandria, a far older theological school than Constantinople and of apostolic foundation, led the protests. All the Greeks and Copts of Egypt supported him. At the council of Ephesus, 431, Cyril and his teaching were accepted. His followers, however, went beyond the moderate position he had taken up at the council, and the monk Eutyches openly preached a single nature in Christ, and that divine. Pope Leo I at Rome protested against this 'Monophysitism', and at the council of Chalcedon, in 451, the teaching that Christ was perfect God and perfect man (that he existed in two natures, indivisibly united, but not 'confused' as Cyril of Alexandria had taught) was accepted. The teaching of pope Leo's *Tome* had been substantially accepted: and henceforth to the orthodox, in east and west alike, acceptance of the definitions of Chalcedon was the touchstone of orthodoxy. At the same time, in the eastern provinces, the council was by many held accursed as dividing the person of Christ: the northern provinces largely followed Nestorius in stressing the single human nature: Egypt was solidly behind the Monophysite position that Christ was divine, and his humanity 'phantasmal' only. But all the eastern provinces disliked Chalcedon.

To return to the emperor Zeno: he desired to conciliate the east and in 484 he published a reunion edict or *Henotikon*, agreed by the patriarchs of Constantinople and Alexandria. The *Henotikon* repeated the older creeds, anathematizing those who taught otherwise, 'whether at Chalcedon or elsewhere': this led to a breach between Constantinople and Rome between 484 and 518.

Anastasius, who ruled from Zeno's death in 491 till 518, was hard pressed by the northern barbarians: he was himself a Monophysite and he replaced the orthodox patriarch of Antioch, Flavian, by Sergius, more sympathetic to Monophysitism. Orthodox risings then took place throughout the empire and even in Constantinople, in 513: the empire was not willing to accept the Monophysite solution.

The senate, therefore, on his death, diverted the succession from any of his nephews, and elected a firmly Chalcedonian candidate, Justin I (518–527). This elderly and childless Macedonian was illiterate, of peasant stock, and owed his advancement to a career in the army and the palace guard. Peace and reconciliation with Rome followed. He had adopted and now brought forward as his heir a younger Macedonian peasant, of Latin stock, Justinian. He had prepared for the glories of the next reign by giving him an excellent education, literary, theological and administrative: his pupil had a remarkable mind, and a remarkable appreciation of the Roman inheritance.

Procopius, whose accounts of the African and Italian wars of Justinian are a primary historical record, might have been expected to give valuable information on the state of the empire at the time. In one respect, he gives most valuable information: in his *De Aedificiis* he lists and describes the countless buildings repaired or built by Justinian's orders: numberless *castella* from Singidunum (Belgrade) on the middle Danube, to Erzerum and Trebizond in Armenia and Palmyra, on the borders of the Syrian desert. Vandal Africa, when reconquered, was studded with Roman fortresses. The scheme of imperial defence is set forth in the *De Aedificiis* in detail, and the detail is confirmed by the ruins of such fortresses as, planted in land soon desert, still remain.

But in another respect, the evidence of Procopius on Justinian, his court and his policy is difficult to assess: for the complimentary picture in the *History* contrasts with the bitter and often scandalous account given in the *Secret History* (*Anecdota*) usually attributed to him. The latter would appear to have been written in discredited and disappointed old age, after Belisarius his patron had twice fallen from favour and been dispossessed. Procopius' account of Theodora, her early courtesan life, and her vices, may be discounted; while the account of the impoverishment of the reconquered territories, contrasting with the relative ease of the reconquest itself, can be partly accounted for by the discontents usually following wars, even successful ones. The evidence of economic history does not confirm the impression that the empire was financially ruined by Justinian's wars.

Justinian then had to face, in 527, the turbulence of his capital,

the resistance of the eastern provinces to Justin's orthodox measures, and danger on the eastern frontier from the Persians. With
a mind of brilliant quality and an untiring store of energy, he preferred to rule from his palace, working tirelessly and keeping his
hand on all the threads of government. His own life was simple,
laborious and almost ascetic: but he maintained the imperial prestige by the magnificence of the ceremonies by which life at the
Byzantine court was marked, and by the careful performance of
all parts of an emperor's duty. He protected the faith even though
he would have liked to make the decisions of Chalcedon supportable
to the east: he was a very notable theologian. He had had for his
tutor Leontius of Byzantium, the remarkable theologian who was
the first Greek to use Aristotelian methods in theology, and the
writings of Leontius and Justinian are held to have laid the foundation of orthodox teaching about the hypostatic union; they
underlay the more developed teaching of John of Damascus (d.
756). But beyond his duty (as he conceived it) to protect and even
define the faith, the frontiers must, he held, everywhere be protected: beyond that, the old frontiers of the *imperium Romanum*
must if possible be regained: justice and order must be maintained,
partly for the sake of the collection of that revenue which should
make a great reconquest possible: churches must be built and the
heathen converted: Constantinople must have a great church
worthy of her: monasteries and hospitals (*xenodochia*) must perform the imperial duty of praise to God and compassion to the poor.

The long reign of Justinian, thirty-eight years, falls into three
periods. From 527 to 533 Justinian's policy was occupied mainly
with preparation: above all, with the preparation for better and
more orderly government to follow a reformation and reissue of
Roman law. From 533 to 540 followed the period of action and
military success; and from 540 to 565 the period of reaction,
reverses, and above all of financial difficulty.

The greatest achievement of the preparatory period was the sim-
plification, codification and reissue of existent Roman law, chiefly
through the agency of Tribonian the praetorian prefect, a man of
bold and creative mind. The Theodosian Code of 438 had left the
pre-Constantinian edicts unaffected, had published an authoritative selection of the edicts between Constantine and 438, and had
left the confused mass of the *responsa prudentum* undealt with.
Roman law remained, in many cases, self-contradictory and uncertain, and the volume of legal opinion to be consulted immense and
difficult of access. Justinian and Tribonian desired a *ius novum*. In
February 528 a commission was appointed and in fourteen months

it defined this *ius novum*, retaining certain edicts or constitutions as valid, and issuing them as the *Codex Constitutionum* on 7 April 529; all other imperial edicts were thereby repealed. To cut the knot of the difficulty of interpretation, all commentaries were forbidden, a decision impossible long to maintain. The *Code* was in Latin, and that there were difficulties of interpretation is shown by the issue of a second edition in 534, the sole edition in which the *Code* survived.

Meanwhile, certain legal points still remained determinable only by the *ius vetus*. In December 530 a commission was set up, presided over by Tribonian, to procure and read all the authorized jurists, those who had the *ius respondendi* on doubtful points presented to them by the Roman magistrate. These expert opinions contained the flower of Roman law: the commission was ordered to divide their results into fifty books, subdividing each into titles, following the arrangement of the Perpetual Edict of Hadrian. This order had been followed in the *Code*, and though unscientific to modern minds, was in fact the order familiar to lawyers of the day. The commission worked for four years, and presented their treatise to Justinian, who issued it as an imperial statute on 16 December 534. For this Latin *Digest* a Greek translation was almost at once issued, the *Pandects*. As with the *Code*, all appeal to other forms of the *ius vetus* became at once invalid.

Two legal problems remained. All legal manuals or textbooks had become automatically out of date, and therefore a new one, the *Institutes*, a manual for law students, was published on 21 November 532. Before Tribonian's death in 545, certain constitutions (*Novellae constitutiones post Codicem*) were also issued, most of them in Greek, some in both Latin and Greek, affording a useful check on the contemporary equivalence of many terms (e.g. *kanon* and *regula*). These four imperial edicts, the *Code*, *Digest*, *Institutes* and *Novels* constitute the *corpus iuris civilis*, the body of Roman law, the foundation law of medieval Europe and a large part of the modern world.

Meanwhile, the harshness and unpopularity of Justinian's other minister, the praetorian prefect, John of Cappadocia, had provoked risings in the capital, rendered dangerous by the faction fights of the Circus. In 532 a dangerous riot broke out in the emperor's presence in the Hippodrome, but troops under Belisarius and Narses restored the situation, massacring the rebels. Justinian had turned his most dangerous corner. He set about rebuilding the basilica of Santa Sophia with unrivalled splendour, and was able to witness its solemn consecration on the 26 December 537.

The great accomplishments of Justinian's middle period included the reconquest of Africa, part of Spain, and Italy, mentioned above (pp. 84, 99, 46). It was a reconquest that overstrained the resources of the empire, making the demands of the tax collector almost unendurable: but it seemed fitting to a sovereign who valued the Roman inheritance to restore to the empire lands once hers: it seemed fitting to the champion of orthodoxy to reclaim them for the true form of the Christian faith, and it seemed admirable to the East Roman strategist and merchant to make the Mediterranean again a Byzantine lake. The reconquest of Justinian should not be seen as an isolated adventure; the eastern empire, being the Roman empire, never renounced the lands it had lost in the west: it never negotiated with a barbarian king as with an equal, as it did with the Sassanids of Persia and, in a sense, reconquest was always its permanent, long-distance policy. Other emperors than Justinian hoped for it.

The great military effort of the reign was accompanied by the great castle-building described in the *De Aedificiis*, and by a rebuilding of towns destroyed by the enemy. Antioch, for instance, was sacked by the Persians in 540, and Procopius in the *De Aedificiis* describes how Justinian rebuilt and made it stronger than it had been formerly. The city wall was redrawn, making the circuit much shorter but strategically better planned: the river Orontes, which used to flow in a winding course before the walls he caused to change its bed, cutting an artificial channel bringing it much nearer to the city walls. The description is of interest to town planners in these days:

> Since everything was everywhere reduced to ashes and levelled to the ground, and since many heaps of ruins were all that remained of the burned city, it became impossible for the people of Antioch to recognize the site of any person's house, when first they carried out the débris, and to clear out the remains of the burned houses; and since there were no longer any public *stoas* [porticoes] or colonnaded courts, nor any market place remaining anywhere, and since the side streets no longer marked off the main thoroughfares of the city, they could not undertake the construction of any house. But the emperor without delay transported the débris as far as possible from the city, and thus freed the air and the ground from all encumbrances; then he first of all covered the foundations of the city everywhere with stones large enough to load a wagon. Next he marked it off with colonnades and market places, and defining all the blocks of houses by means of streets, and setting up channels and fountains and sewers, which are the adornment of the city, he constructed in it theatres and baths, ornamenting it with all the other public buildings by means of which

the prosperity of a city is wont to be shown. He also, by bringing in a number of artisans and craftsmen, made it easy and less troublesome for the inhabitants to build their own homes.

In short, according to Procopius' panegyric, Justinian made Antioch more splendid than formerly, and built there two great churches, to the Mother of God and to St Michael.

For the great church of Santa Sophia (the Holy Wisdom: Christ) we are not dependent only on descriptions, for Justinian's church has survived the Muslim conquest of Constantinople, and, though it has never been restored to Christian service, the whitewash with which Islam covered every representation of the human figure is being progressively removed. Before the building, Justinian issued a circular to all the provincial governors, bidding them send to the capital the most beautiful marbles, and such rich spoils of ancient monuments as could be built into the new church. For architects, he used the skill of Anthemius of Tralles and Isidore of Miletus, both from Asia Minor and versed in the construction of the dome (see p. 69). They built the great church of brick, almost square in plan, and on one side approached by a great atrium. The narthex or porch opens into the church by nine doors, and within, the broad nave is crowned by a great dome supported to the east and west by semi-domes. The church is, in short, a domed basilica, but the dome, semi-domes, piers and windows are so complex and balanced that an effect of great lightness is attained, as if the roof were hanging in the air. The brick structure moreover is so covered with sheets of marble, so studded with splendid ornament, so enriched with mosaics where the design shone out from a dark blue or silver background, that the colour of Santa Sophia has as astonishing an effect as the structural triumph. Dante, in the *Paradiso*, placed Justinian in the heaven of Mercury for his royal justice and his royal law: but the Byzantine citizen, less appreciative of the working of Justinian's law, believed that God had certainly received him into Paradise for this sole reason: that he had built Santa Sophia.

The third period of Justinian's reign began in 540 with Belisarius' reduction of Ravenna, but also with a dispute with the Persians about Armenia and a great raid by Chosroes, king of Persia, on northern Syria. Chosroes marched up the Euphrates, left the Byzantine fortresses of Dara and Edessa on his flank, and marched on Antioch. His attack had been expected in Mesopotamia, and the defence of Antioch, seat of the praetorian prefect of the east, was hastily improvised and ineffective. Chosroes took the city, burnt it, and led away most of the inhabitants to captivity in Persia. It was an astonishing success.

Justinian now had to fight a war upon two fronts, with the new resistance of the Goths under Totila and with a great attack by Chosroes on the eastern provinces. Taxation became extortionate and unjust in collection: John of Cappadocia was a harsh and unscrupulous finance minister, and though he quarrelled with the empress and fell from power in 541, his successors were equally rapacious. To add to Byzantine miseries, the rat-borne, ship-borne bubonic plague came in 542 from its reserves in northern India, up the Euphrates valley, across Syria and Asia Minor, to Constantinople. The city and empire was ravaged by one of the worst epidemics in history; taxpayers and tax collectors alike were swept away, and Justinian was one of the very few who, having contracted the plague, recovered.

The danger to the eastern provinces in this period of strain was great. In 541 Belisarius had arrived to lead the defence in Mesopotamia, and Chosroes had then crossed the Armenian mountain ranges, arrived at the Black Sea, and taken the fortress of Petra. When a truce was concluded in 545, the Persians kept their conquests in northern Armenia, and were paid 2,000 lb. of gold to evacuate the rest. The truce was to last five years (545–550).

Meanwhile, the Ostrogothic war dragged on: Belisarius fell into disgrace, was readmitted to favour and given command in Italy. He recovered Rome, but could not clear the peninsula with his small forces. In 548 he was recalled and given command of the palace guard: but no younger general was more fortunate in defeating the Goths. It was not till 552 when Justinian by an unlikely choice gave the elderly eunuch Narses the command, that the end came: he defeated Totila in 553 and the remnant of the Goths submitted and were allowed to leave Italy by the northern passes. But the desolation of Italy was great and a vacuum had been created. Nor was peace yet secured on the eastern frontier: war had begun again in 549 over the Persian conquests in Colchis, and after six years' fighting in that region, the Persians renounced their supremacy there to Rome, and Roman possession of the old Armenian frontier was safeguarded.

In the Balkans too there was no security. Justinian had sought to protect Illyricum by building a triple line of defence from the right bank of the Danube to Thrace, by completing the Long Walls of Anastasius to protect the approaches to the capital, by fortifying some 400 towns and villages, and by using against each other the tribes on the left bank of the Danube. He used the Lombards against the Gepids, different bands of Huns against each other, and the Avars against the Slavs. But his fortresses were too weakly held to withstand the immense barbarian pressure: plundering bands penetrated the defences and surged down towards Greece and almost up to the walls of Constantinople: in 558 a horde of Huns even penetrated the Long Walls. The aged Belisarius, with very small forces, repelled them.

It is against this background of danger in Armenia, and, before the death of Theodora in 548, of the firm Monophysitism of his wife, that Justinian's effort to soften down the decisions of Chalcedon should be seen. Theology in the sixth century was no merely academic matter. Justinian's religious policy had been orthodox, though he had allowed Theodora openly to shelter Monophysites at Constantinople. He knew that the council of Chalcedon was widely disliked by the Christians of Syria and Armenia. In 543, therefore, acting on his own initiative, and without summoning a council, he issued an edict known as the Three Chapters, intended to conciliate the Monophysites, in which he attacked the views of three deceased Nestorians, Theodore of Mopsuestia, Theodoret of Cyr, and Ibas of Edessa. He succeeded only in exasperating everybody; the Monophysites saw at once that the edict merely added to the decisions of Chalcedon, and in no way altered them; the Nestorians of Syria were naturally furious; and in the west and in Africa, the Latin bishops, whose minds were not equal to the theological subtlety of the issues involved, thought that it was an attack on Chalcedon. Justinian summoned to Constantinople the recalcitrant pope Vigilius, who at first refused to subscribe the edict, then issued a Judicatum of his own condemning the writings in dispute and then, having at once been excommunicated by the African bishops, and deserted at the very altar by his own deacons, withdrew it. Justinian, unable to force Vigilius to change his mind yet again, despite the violent methods of persuasion used, summoned a council, which met in 553, and, despite the extraordinary circumstances attending it, has been reckoned in east and west alike as the Fifth Oecumenical Council. It agreed with Justinian, after some persuasion, in condemning the three chapters in dispute; six months later pope Vigilius accepted its verdict. He died on the way back to Rome. The new pope, Pelagius, began his pontificate in very bad odour: the Latin bishops, many of whom as yet refused to accept the judgment of the council, had lost much of their customary veneration for the papacy as the result of the vacillations of Vigilius, and Pelagius, who adhered to the council, could find only two bishops willing to consecrate him; the great metropolitans of Milan and Aquileia broke communion with him, in Tuscany his name was struck out of the service-books, and the bishops of Gaul, headed by king Childeric, demanded a confession of faith from him, as a reassurance of his orthodoxy. The fact that the Latin bishops were thoroughly confused as to the theological issues at stake is perhaps less interesting than the very independent attitude they displayed towards the Roman see.

As for Justinian, whose attempt at conciliation had caused nothing but strife, when he died at an advanced age in 565, having lately taken up an obscure Egyptian heresy, no man mourned him, despite all his achievements. Evagrius, indeed, the orthodox ecclesiastical historian, wrote of him, as with historical certainty, that he had departed to the lowest region of hell, as he deserved.

Justinian's religious activity had three other important aspects: it was directed against the intellectual paganism of his empire, against the popular paganism of country folk within the empire, and towards the conversion of the heathen outside by means of missions. The university of Athens favoured Neo-Platonism, and Justinian suppressed the school of law there and the faculty of philosophy. The pagan philosopher Damascius went with his disciples to Chosroes in Persia, and translated the Dialogues of Plato for his new hearers. Justinian declared the Jews heretics, and took measures against the rural paganism of Anatolia, Syria and the Nile valley: he ordered that all pagans should be instructed in the Christian religion and be baptized, and that those who took part in pagan rites should be put to death. The sanctuary of Isis at Phile, that of Jupiter Ammon south of Cyrenaica and the great temple of Baalbek in Syria still had their worshippers: the first two Justinian closed. He sent out bands of missionaries, often monks, from Mesopotamia: some were Monophysite, such as John of Amida, a stylite from the Tigris valley, grave and learned, who founded a monastery in a ruined temple near Tralles, and preached to the pagans of Asia Minor with great success, but the missions of Justinian's reign spread orthodoxy as well as the forms of the faith dissident from Chalcedon.

CHAPTER X

THE CHURCH FROM THE FIFTH TO THE EIGHTH CENTURY

THE structure of the Christian church in these centuries hinged, as has been said above (pp. 68–69), on territorial responsibility and jurisdiction: the bishop had a paternal jurisdiction over his see, he was grouped with other bishops in a province under the metropolitan, and the metropolitans looked for guidance in emergency to some see, patriarchate or archbishopric, which had, in most cases, converted that region by its missionaries. The patriarchates, that is, had all been great missionary sees in the early days of Christianity: and, as was natural in such cases, they had all been cities of world-wide importance. Jerusalem was an exception: but it had been the first centre of Christian expansion: Antioch was the capital of the middle east when St Paul started on his missionary journeys: Alexandria was the great port of the eastern trade: Rome was the capital of the west. It is accepted that, in the late Roman empire and that of the new barbarian kingdoms, Christian organization followed secular: the bishop had his see in a *civitas* and ruled the secular province (or the *territorium* in the west) administered by the *civitas*. Metropolitan jurisdiction also followed secular; and if the secular authority divided a province, erecting two cities to the rank of provincial capitals, the church also provided two bishops and two sees. But all this acceptance of geographical delimitation as a thing indifferent, involved indeed by the need to supply spiritual care for large population groups, does not in the least explain the Christian conception of the church. The historian will not expect to understand this without regard to the climate of opinion of the day: to the beliefs held by all Christians, and so generally that, in the various crises and disputes of Christian history, all conceded them as a common standing ground.

When the church came up out of the catacombs and was made a legal religion by the edict of Milan in 313, the great disputes over the definition of the Christian faith still lay ahead: but certain institutions and a certain conception of the church, were already taken for granted. The church was the body of Christ, in whom he still lived and worked, and co-extensive with the whole body of Christians, excluding heretics, who were not accepted as Christians at all. The church, in the language of theologians, had four marks: she was one, holy, catholic and apostolic. All Christians, whether in Persia or Armenia (for there were already Christian missionaries there), the Greek east or the Latin west, had the same faith, sacraments and church order: they were ruled by bishops; they were one, though in the difficult communications of the first three centuries, a local church might have little knowledge of distant churches. Contact was rather by travellers and missionaries and the letters they brought than by a diffused rule of the church, even by the patriarchates. In emergency, however, unity was maintained by synods or councils of bishops: after Constantine's day, by the great universal or oecumenical councils.

All thus confessed one church, and all similarly confessed her holy: the disciplinary canons of councils struggled to put in practice a moral ideal. It is still, in fact, part of the climate of opinion of the day that the church should be holy.

The other two marks of the church are today, however, less generally understood. The church was Catholic, as holding the faith 'once for all delivered to the saints', as well as held in the famous phrase of Vincent of Lérins 'always, everywhere, by all men'.

And she was 'apostolic', as holding the faith delivered to the apostles, and handed on by their successors. This fourth 'mark' of the church is of great historical importance for the understanding of her structure.

The first teachers of the faith, as all held, were the apostles, who had been taught by the Lord himself in Galilee, and who knew his mind and were his friends. The Christian faith was the apostolic teaching, passed on, in the main, verbally. The Christian scriptures were not written when the apostles set out from Jerusalem to teach in the year A.D. 33, and though by the end of the first century the books of the New Testament had been written, so had other Christian writings and there was as yet no canon of scripture, no 'Bible'. (The first written evidence of a Christian canon of scripture, of the setting of certain books within the 'Bible' and the leaving of others outside, is that of the list in the Muratorian fragment, which certainly dates from the lifetime of the learned anti-pope, Hippolytus, d. A.D. 230, and may have been his work). For over 200 years, that is, there was no Bible as final authority about the Christian faith, and for much later than that, written scriptures were so costly and rare, that the plain man in process of being converted to Christianity could certainly not have studied them. He lived in a world, for five or six centuries at least, where knowledge was passed on orally: if he desired to be secure that the faith he was being taught was, in fact, that taught by the Lord in Galilee, his only guarantee was security about his teacher. Many strange religions penetrated the west from the east in these early centuries, and they were all passed on orally. Men lived in a world of oral information, not of books. The Greco-Roman merchant might scribble his accounts on his papyrus: the greatest Christian teachers wrote letters to the churches they had founded and left, and they were treasured and read later, by the church to whom they had been sent: but the general means of Christian instruction was not that of the written word. The common man did not read the Christian books, and this was not strange because he did not read any books. Books were scarce and precious. Even the rhetors, lecturing in the public *scolae*, taught orally, commenting on texts which they dictated orally to their scholars. The sign of the *magisterium*, the office of teacher, was the chair on which he sat to teach, his scholars standing in a circle round him, and not the representation of some learned tome. The Roman empire was a great user of the written word for contracts and legal business: but even the Roman empire could only teach orally.

Hence it came about that the Christian faith was passed on orally, by the apostles and first Christian missionaries, to those who succeeded them in the care of the local churches, and the safeguarding of this handed-on faith, this *paradosis*, was the chief charge and duty of these Christian shepherds. The Greek *paradosis* (the Latin 'tradition') was the faith itself, not any mere outlying region of the faith, and for the first two centuries there could be no appeal from the *paradosis* to a canon of scripture: each great church used certain scriptural books, but they were guaranteed as in accordance with the faith by the local *paradosis*, and not *vice versa*. The third century saw a certain conflict between views as to the canonical scriptures held by the great churches, and out of this conflict finally emerged the recognized canon; but for 300 years the faith had been safeguarded by the *paradosis*. This *paradosis* was from the founder of the church to the 'supervisor', *episcopos*, bishop who had succeeded him, and who had transmitted it in turn. Hence the importance of the office of bishop. In the days of persecution the bishop held no office of secular importance; he was, it is true, the great minister of the sacraments in his see, for as yet only he baptized (after long instructions by himself or his presbyters), only he ordained his own clergy, and he was the normal celebrant of the liturgy, but his chief charge was the defence of the faith committed to him, and that to the point of martyrdom.

Hence it followed that each church guarded carefully the memory of its succession of bishops from the founder of the see, in which doctrinal orthodoxy was as important as sacramental validity. Irenaeus, bishop of Lyons (†c. 190), when he wrote his *Adversus haereses* against the Gnostics, appealed to the original teaching of the apostles, as handed on in the *paradoses* of the churches of Jerusalem, Rome, Ephesus, etc., continuing:

> Yet because it would be a very lengthy proceeding in a book such as this to set out the series of succession belonging to all the churches, we are proposing to show that the existing faith of that most noble, ancient and well-known church, founded and established at Rome by the two most famous apostles, Peter and Paul, the faith I say which it still holds, and which comes down to our time by means of a series of succession of bishops, is actually identical with the *paradosis* given by the apostles, that is, the faith *proclaimed to all mankind*.

The connexion of the bishop's office with the *paradosis* appears in very early patristic writings; the Letter of Clement of Rome, of *c*. A.D. 95, speaks of the apostles as 'taught the gospel for our sakes at the feet of the Lord Jesus Christ . . . Having therefore received his instructions . . . they went forth with full conviction from the holy spirit and preached that the kingdom of God was soon to come. And so, as they preached in the country and in the town, they appointed the first fruits of their work to be *episcopoi* and deacons among them that should believe . . . No less did the apostles know that through our Lord Jesus Christ that there would be strife over the dignity of a bishop's office. For this very reason they appointed the aforesaid bishops and deacons and ordained that at their death their ministry should pass into the hands of other tried men.' Polycarp, martyr and bishop of Smyrna, Irenaeus wrote, had been taught by the apostles and 'conversed much with them who had seen our Lord . . . and these things he taught ever which he had learned from the apostles, which moreover the church handed down and which alone are true. He was a true witness of the apostolic *paradosis*.' The monarchical rule of the bishop in his see throughout the middle ages followed from this conception: as did the reverence to be paid to sees of apostolic foundation. A special *magisterium* attached to the see of Antioch, where Peter taught, to Alexandria where Mark, the disciple of Peter taught, and to Rome, where Peter and Paul, princes of the apostles, taught and were martyred.

Apostolic foundation did not in itself render a Christian see a patriarchate, or secure its survival. St John, as Irenaeus wrote, handed on at Ephesus the *paradosis* published by himself: but Ephesus could not send out missions on the scale to render itself a great mother see and patriarchate. The importance of Jerusalem waned, though the city remained a patriarchate. Antioch and Alexandria were great theology schools and centres of missions, the one to Syria, Armenia, Persia and even India, the other up the Nile valley, along the coast of north Africa, and to Ethiopia. Two other great churches not of apostolic foundation merited by their secular importance and zeal in the sending out of missions to be erected into patriarchates (if this could be without apostolic foundation): Constantinople and Seleukia-Ctesiphon.

The claim of the church of Constantinople to apostolic foundation was but tenuous: but from the time of its building in 336–339 and Constantine's removal of his capital thither, it was in fact New Rome, the seat of government, and a great missionary church. Constantine's conversion had meant the conversion of the Roman empire, and so great an apostolate, to the Greek theologians, merited for him the title of 'equal to an apostle', Isapostolos. New Rome was, in fact, Old Rome carried to the Golden Horn, and she carried with her, as it were, the grace of apostolic foundation. To this, however, the holder of St Peter's see at Old Rome would never agree; though personally the pope was the emperor's subject, yet it was the pope who held Peter's chair, and in him alone Peter spoke. The council of Chalcedon, 451, in its 28th canon (following the 3rd canon of Constantinople, 381), declared Constantinople as New Rome equal in primacy and privilege to Old Rome: declared it, in fact, a patriarchate. The sees of Antioch and Alexandria subscribed the canon: but pope Leo the Great refused to accept it. Though unity was still preserved after Chalcedon, relations between the two primatial sees of east and west were uneasy. The chief cause of this uneasiness was, it is true, political. Old Rome and New Rome were, in a sense, rivals within the Roman empire, and their interests often interlocked, more especially in the provinces of Illyricum, which included the whole of Greece and Crete, and were claimed by the popes as part of the Roman patriarchate.

Christianity took its rise in a province near the *limes* of the Roman empire, and could, in fact, easily pass that *limes* and expand outside the empire to the east and south. From the Syriac church of Edessa, on the upper waters of the Euphrates, it spread into Persia (Iran), an autonomous state outside the empire, but federate and also Syriac speaking. The Iranian plateau, commanding the cross roads between west and east, and also the roads to the Caspian, to Mongolia, and to India, was a position of great strategic

importance to a missionary church. Christianity spread along the
Tigris and into all parts of the Persian empire without hindrance
from its kings, and their Parthian successors after A.D. 226 offered
asylum to Christians fleeing from persecution in the Roman empire.
Under the Sassanid kings Christianity was usually treated with
tolerance, though it never became the official religion of the kingdom, as it was in the Roman empire after the time of Constantine.
The bishop of Seleukia-Ctesiphon, the royal residence, began early
to claim a certain ascendancy over the other Persian sees; and a
certain parallelism appears between the conversion of the barbarians within the Roman empire by the sees of Old and New
Rome, and that of the heathen, including the Mazdaites, in the
Persian empire and the east generally, by Seleukia-Ctesiphon.

The faith and the organization of the Persian church in no way
differed from that of Christians within the Roman empire: bishops,
metropolitans and, from 410, a quasi-patriarch ruled territorial sees
and provinces. There was a certain consciousness of unity with the
Christians 'of the west', i.e. within the Roman empire, and remem-
brance of the origin of the Persian church from Edessa. When in
410, at the famous synod which met at Seleukia-Ctesiphon, the
primate of Persia adopted the title of *katholikos*, the canons of the
council of Nicaea were formally accepted, and ecclesiastical appeal
could still be made to the patriarchs of 'the west'. In 424, however,
the autocephalous (recognizing the authority of no mother church,
but only of the canons of oecumenical councils) position of the
church of Seleukia-Ctesiphon was further emphasized: 'Easterners
shall not complain of their own patriarch to the western patriarchs:
any case that cannot be settled by him shall await the tribunal of
Christ.' Seleukia-Ctesiphon became, in fact, a patriarchate of the
sees its first missionaries had converted: as the patriarch of Constantinople similarly came to preside over the bishops of Bulgaria,
Roumania and Serbia.

All these eastern patriarchates cherished their right of independence, their *autocephalia*, and none were averse from the use of the
vernacular of their converts for the scriptures and the mass; the
churches of Armenia and Ethiopia were in a way to becoming
similar, quasi-national churches. Where Greek or Persian missionaries converted pagans in a countryside not using Greek or Persian,
no effort was made to teach them to use these tongues for Christian
rites. The contrast in this respect with the missionaries of the Latin
west arose, as it were, by accident, because the western missionaries
found the pagan provincials using Latin generally, and even in
their pagan cults. There was no case for using a language other

than Latin. But this difference of liturgical language among the Greeks, Persians and their missionary sees, and the uniform use of Latin in the west, made for a subsequent division between Rome and Constantinople, rather than between the sees originally within the Roman empire and those outside.

Some space has thus been given to a description of the patriarchates, their origin and their concept of church order, because it represents the state and extent of the church at the mid-fifth century, when the church meant much more than the Latin west, and also because it explains the weakness of these distant, autocephalous churches under Muslim attack. Before Chalcedon, these churches were orthodox: but when this council condemned the Nestorian and Monophysite heresies, their leaders left the immediate rule of Constantinople for Antioch, Alexandria and (as imperial suppression became more searching) for yet more distant sees. The Syriac and Persian churches became largely Nestorian, and the Egyptian and Ethiopian churches Monophysite, before they were overrun by Islam.

Against this background, this regard for the faith as guaranteed by the *paradosis* of a great church to be apostolic, the rise of the Roman see to the effective rule of the whole western church, and its claim to primacy over the whole church, can be seen as a matter of Christian thought and acceptance, and not merely a result of historical circumstance. The climate of opinion accepted the Roman primacy in the west, as in the east the climate of opinion accepted the *autocephalia* of the great churches, within the limits of an orthodox holding of the apostolic faith.

To mention first, the theory of the Roman primacy, and then the circumstances contributing to the rise of papal power in the west:

The Roman claim to primacy in the church rested upon the apostolic foundation of the Roman see by the two greatest of the apostles, Peter and Paul; and upon the Petrine declaration of our Lord to Peter: *Tu es Petrus, et super hanc petram aedificabo ecclesiam meam.* The above-mentioned letter of Clement (p. 168) appears to imply the apostolic foundation of the church at Rome, and was itself a letter of reprimand to the church at Corinth, implying at least a paternal supervision of that church. Ignatius of Antioch, writing *c.* 110–117, allowed to the Roman church a primacy of good work, a 'presidency of love', and spoke of her as 'she who hath the presidency in the region of the Romans'. Irenaeus, writing *c.* 185, spoke of her as 'the most great and ancient and universally known church, founded and established at Rome by the two most glorious apostles, Peter and Paul', and, elsewhere, of all Christians resorting to this church as to the most eminent of the great sees where the apostolic tradition was duly conserved; he was careful to give a list of bishops succeeding each other in the apostolic see. Cyprian also, bishop of Carthage (d. 258), wrote to the pope and clergy of Rome, as having a pre-eminence in matters of the faith, although he was careful to emphasize, both in word and deed, that this authority was not above, and separate from, that of the whole episcopate.

But above all, the work and writings of the statesman pope, Leo the Great (440–461), crystallized Latin theological thought about the primacy of Peter in the Petrine see. His words, addressed as sermons to great concourses gathered in St Peter's basilica usually on the feast of the apostles, June 29, or some other great festivity, were echoed by later popes throughout the middle ages:

> This gathering lacks not, I trust, the benevolent kindness and faithful love of Peter the apostle, nor does he leave unregarded your devotion, whose reverence has gathered you together. For he indeed rejoices in your love and welcomes in those who share in the honour bestowed on him the observance of that which the Lord commanded, and proves the ordered charity of the whole church, which embraces Peter in Peter's see, and in the love of so great a shepherd grows not weary of the person of so unworthy a successor . . . In this manner, beloved, is today's festival celebrated with a reasonable service, when in my humble self he is indeed honoured in whom abides the care of all the shepherds and of the flocks committed to them . . . This devotion is shown in the first place to him whom they know to be the head of this see and primate of all bishops . . . Peter ceases not to be head of his see, in that he has obtained unfailing fellowship with the eternal priest; that stability which he, being made a rock, has received from Christ the rock, he conveys to his successors; and when aught of stability is shown, there without doubt is seen the strength of the shepherd.

Within the context of a church whose bishops were successors of the apostles, the primacy of Peter among them followed from the text of the gospels. In the world of space and time and historical development, however, certain steps can be traced to the rise of papal power in the west, between the year A.D. 64 when, tradition-ally, Peter was crucified on the Vatican mount, and Paul beheaded on the road to Ostia (both in the Neronian persecutions), and the rule of Odovacar in Italy. Perhaps the first was the papacy of Victor I, c. 189–198, when the Greek-speaking church of Rome adopted Latin; the old Roman creed and half the inscriptions in the catacombs had been in Greek: early bishops of Rome had written in Greek. But now Victor wrote (minor) theological tracts in Latin, and his pontificate saw a general Latinizing of the Roman see, though the language of the mass at Rome continued Greek till the beginning of the fourth century. Nevertheless, a foreign religious sect in Rome now itself became Roman. The second landmark was the transfer of the seat of empire to New Rome under Constantine, which permanently removed the bishop of Rome from the overshadowing influence of the emperor. Moreover, the drift of Greeks Romewards towards the imperial court now changed to a drift eastwards to Constantinople, and Rome remained the bulwark of the Latin tradition. The work of Augustine, bishop of Hippo, may be taken as the third landmark (see p. 90), and that of pope Leo I, 440-461, as the fourth. The prestige of the Roman see grew, as Leo faced the barbarian invaders, Attila and Gaiseric, and as he protested against the decree of the council of Chalcedon equating the prestige and privilege of Constantinople with those of Rome. Moreover, he defended the papal jurisdiction in Illyricum, and asserted the papal primacy more effectively than any of his predecessors.

In view of the weight attached by Christians to the office of bishop and patriarch, the method of choice of these officers and its history is of importance. Even in the Letter of Clement of Rome reference is made to 'strife over the dignity of a bishop's office'. But·what had been merely the affair of a local religious sect before the edict of Milan assumed political importance when Christianity became the state religion: a new factor appears to influence what had been a local choice, the wishes of emperor, barbarian king or local magistrate or chieftain. A bishop's election, and still more, a papal election was sometimes complicated, more often simplified, by this overriding consideration. But before dealing with this subject of episcopal elections, something must be said briefly of the great popes between the days of Odovacar and Charlemagne.

Leo I had preached a lofty conception of the primacy of the Petrine see in the days of the failing empire of the west; Gelasius I, in a short but notable papacy (492-496), wrote of the relation of the secular and spiritual powers in Christendom in a manner to win acceptance down to the eleventh century or Hildebrandine reform. Gelasius was an African who had, however, long been a member of the Roman clergy, and become a theologian of some importance: he had written against the Monophysites and the Pelagians, and as pope, to secure the due training of the clergy, he wrote insisting on the observances of the 'interstices', or due intervals between the reception of the minor orders. He was pope while Theoderic was conquering north Italy from Odovacar, a time of violence, and his

pontificate was unmarked by any concessions. In a letter to the
emperor Anastasius I he wrote of the divine appointment of two
powers to rule the world:

> There are two, O august emperor, who share between them in chief
> the rule of the world: the sacred authority of the popes and the royal
> power. And of these two, the burden of the *sacerdotes* is the heavier,
> for they must render account for kings as for themselves in the day of
> judgment.

The word *sacerdos* at the time, as an offerer of holy things, is
usually translated 'priest'; but now and later was used above all of
'bishop', who alone, as yet, offered the holy mysteries. The priestly
episcopal power, particularly in the see of Peter, is set over against
the power of the emperor, recognized in the Greek east as also
religious in character (see p. 146).

In the period following, the question of a Greek preponderance
in the affairs of the church underlay the troubles of the successive
pontificates. Anastasius II (496–498) showed himself entirely complaisant to the emperor Anastasius, whose orthodoxy was suspect;
when he died, the party supporting the Latin tradition at Rome was
ranged against the followers of Anastasius II. While the majority
of the clergy elected the deacon (and therefore the right-hand man)
of Gelasius, Symmachus, in the Lateran basilica, the Byzantinist
section of the clergy and the majority of the senate acclaimed the
archpriest Lawrence, who stood for a conciliatory policy to the
emperor. King Theoderic, hearing of the disturbance, came to
Rome and declared pope Symmachus (498–514) validly elected.
Troubles continued, however, throughout his pontificate, over one
of which, the question of the dating of Easter, Theoderic sided
against Symmachus.

This question of the dating of Easter, which was to cause difficulties between the Celtic and Roman Christians later, hinged
upon the mathematical difficulty of determining a calendar, when
it was only known that a solar year consisted of 365 days and a
fraction still undetermined. The church had laid down that Easter
day should fall upon the Sunday after the first full moon after the
vernal equinox. In the east, the mathematicians of Alexandria made
their calculations based upon a vernal equinox on 21 March; but
at Rome the staunch upholders of the Latin tradition remained
faithful to the calendar of Julius Caesar, which set the equinox at
25 March. Moreover, at Rome tradition disallowed the celebration
of Easter before 25 March or after 21 April, a ruling unobserved
in Alexandria. Again, to calculate the month (the lunar months) the

Alexandrians were now using the cycle of Meton, a cycle of nine-teen years, while the Romans used an older and less satisfactory cycle of eighty-four years. Thus Rome, calculating for the west, might arrive at an Easter date a week or even a month different from that of Alexandria, which calculated for the Greek east. In 501 Symmachus solemnized Easter, according to the Roman tra-dition, on 25 March, while the other Christian churches left it till 22 April. Theoderic commanded Symmachus' presence at Ravenna, and, when he did not obey, sent an episcopal legate to Rome to review the old difficulties which had arisen again between Symmachus and Lawrence, certain charges against Symmachus, and this Easter question. The bishop, arriving at Rome, quashed the election claims of both Symmachus and Lawrence, and celebrated Easter all over again on 22 April. Schism nevertheless followed between the clergy supporting the two popes, accom-panied by rioting and massacre and polemical writing: when Symmachus died in 514, he had not been reconciled with the Greek church.

Out of the polemical writing of the schism, however, emerged an important historical record, the *Liber Pontificalis*, or history of the popes. This series of papal biographies stretched from St Peter to (eventually) Pius II (d. 1464). Duchesne has shown that the author of the first series of biographies was a contemporary of Anasta-sius II and Symmachus, writing probably in the pontificate of Symmachus' successor, Felix III (d. 530). For the *Liber Pontificalis* the fourth century *Liberian Catalogue* of Roman bishops was a primary authority: and to write the 'series of successions' of Roman bishops meant, to write in some sense the history of the see. Many of the biographies before Anastasius II, as Duchesne showed, are full of historical errors, but from Anastasius II onwards the infor-mation about the popes is historically valuable; after this first part of the *Liber Pontificalis*, a single compilation, the histories of the popes seem to have been added unsystematically down to the ninth century. The compiler of the first part, though following the tra-ditional form of the biographies, appears to have sympathized with Symmachus as against Lawrence: he regards him as validly elected; he recounts in detail his good works, his ransoming of prisoners, and the additions he made to the Roman churches, particularly to St Peter's, which was for many years his cathedral. On the other hand, the adherents of Lawrence appear to have compiled a variant version of the *Liber Pontificalis* with evident partiality; and some years later, a partisan of Symmachus composed a *Liber Pontificalis* in vulgar Latin, full of fanciful traditions and apocryphal detail, a manifest piece of propaganda. Both sides in the Symmacho-Laurentian schism desired to get their candidate accepted in the line of the Roman popes, and the schism was thus a valuable stimulus to the keeping of a record.

Another polemical document belonging to the second half of the fifth century, and arising from the tension between Rome and Byzantium over Zeno's *Henotikon* (484) rather than that between Rome and Theoderic, was the historical romance (W. Levison) known as the *Actus beati Silvestri*. The basis of the imperial claim to rule the church and even define dogma was the isapostolic position of Constantine, in virtue of his conversion of the Roman empire: the *Actus beati Silvestri* was written to challenge the isapostolic claim, by showing that it was pope Silvester, represented as the ideal Latin bishop, who had accomplished the baptism of Constantine, healing him also of his leprosy. Constantine had been, in fact, baptized in 337, a few days before his death, by Eusebius, bishop of Nicomedia; but this new life of Silvester represented Silvester as hastening at Constantine's request *ad montem Seraptim* (or *Syraptim*), healing him of his leprosy, and supervising his catechumenate and immersion. As part of his catechumenate Silvester bade Constantine retire to his *cubiculum*, lay aside his royal garments and give himself to prayer and penitence: the significance of this laying aside of the royal insignia was to be emphasized and reinterpreted later in the great eighth-century forgery, the *Donation of Constantine*. Meanwhile, the Latin text of the *Actus* won widespread authority in the west from its acceptance as a source in the *Liber Pontificalis*, and was later translated into Greek and Syriac. This unscrupulous fiction was to be of the greatest importance in the development of the papal claim, not only to spiritual but also to temporal supremacy, though in the document itself it is the spiritual implications of the baptism by Silvester rather than Constantine's cession of the imperial insignia at the pope's request that was emphasized.

Another class of records important in the history of the early middle ages, and like the *Liber Pontificalis* of ecclesiastical origin, were the liturgical calendars. They were built up gradually by all great churches and monasteries, for the practical purpose of securing that each saint had his due commemoration as the year went round on his *dies natalicia* (birthday into heaven, day of martyrdom or death). Not only does this establish some dates in an obscure period, but by custom the lessons of the second nocturn of the saint's night office, said before his mass, gave examples of the good deeds, holiness and some events of his life, or of his martyrdom.

Such short lives, or accounts of death, must have been recited in the office and became the germ of the later saints' lives, passages from which came to supplant them later in the office itself.

Meanwhile, from the issue of the emperor Zeno's *Henotikon* or reunion edict in 482, a schism had endured between the sees of Rome and Constantinople. The condemnation by the council of Chalcedon of both the Nestorians who emphasized our Lord's human nature at the expense of his divine, and the Monophysites, who did exactly the opposite, had been acceptable to the west, for it embodied the theology of pope Leo I's Tome; but had not been held decisive by either of the condemned sects in the east. Zeno, in his desire for peace, issued a terse and nearly orthodox theological pronouncement in the *Henotikon*: but it quietly dropped the decision of Chalcedon and Leo's Tome. Pope Hormisdas entered into negotiations with Anastasius about the schism of 515, but they failed: the schism ended with the accession of the orthodox Justin in 518 and a papal embassy to Constantinople in that year, after which the names of the upholders of the *Henotikon*, Zeno, Anastasius and certain bishops, were erased from the diptychs. Pope Hormisdas lived till 523, and was called on to deal with another effort to reinterpret or go behind the decisions of Chalcedon: certain Scythian monks at Rome adopted a formula directed against the surviving sympathizers with Nestorianism, but Hormisdas declared that the decisions of Chalcedon sufficed. The Scythians found a sympathizer in the learned computist and canonist, Dionysius Exiguus, also resident at Rome during their visit; but not to the point of his following them when Hormisdas requested them to leave Rome.

The difficulties of pope John I (523–526) with Theoderic have been related (p. 43), and those of pope Vigilius with Justinian belong rather to the general history of his reign (see p. 163), as do imperial efforts to conciliate the Monophysites to those of his successors.

The papacy of Gregory I (590–604) was clearly one of decisive importance for the Roman see and for the history of Italy itself: through Gregory's influence the Lombard invaders obtained an unwilling recognition of their conquests from the emperor, and the harried Italian provincials obtained peace. In many respects, Gregory's action influenced secular history as well as religious, but possibly we should be less well aware of the fact had not Gregory been a great letter writer and keeper of orderly records. His letters open a window on the sixth century, and were either much more

7

numerous than those of earlier popes or (probably) were more carefully preserved. It was possible to compile an extensive register
later from the loose papyrus sheets. As a specimen letter not of the
greatest importance, but showing the detailed instructions Gregory
was in the habit of giving his agents, his letter to a bishop about
the payment of his clergy, may be quoted:

> First, that you should without delay offer [*praebere*] a whole fourth
> of the rents of your church to the clergy, according to the merit or
> office or labour of each, as you shall see fit to give to each one. And
> from the offerings of the faithful also you shall not delay to give a
> fourth part, in money [*solidi*] or in food [*cellario*], according to early
> custom, the remainder of all moveables remaining however at your
> own disposal. But real estate (immoveables) shall be added to the
> revenues of the church, that as these grow in value, the fourth part
> of your clergy shall, with God's grace, be increased.

Gregory lived at a time when all the Mediterranean world looked
to the Greek east: his name, meaning 'watchful', would fifty years
earlier have been Vigilius. Yet he was as much a guardian of the
Latin tradition against an eastern preponderance as Leo I or Symmachus or Vigilius. He lived also in times of extreme difficulty.
The Arian Lombards were still at the stage of piecemeal conquest
when he became pope: war was ever at the gate: men fought and
starved. Rome had been ravaged by the Gothic wars and was not
yet rebuilt. The very accession of Gregory in 590 was due to the
pestilence that ravaged Italy and carried off his predecessor Pelagius II (578–590). It fell to Gregory to direct the military defence
of central Italy, care for the plague-stricken and feed the hungry
at Rome, as well as guide the church, and that through a great part
of his pontificate.

He was prepared for his task by a great inheritance and a triple
training. He was a Roman citizen, brought up in a Rome owing
obedience to the exarch at Ravenna (see p. 180), to the praetorian
prefect and the civil hierarchy. He was a Catholic Christian, the
son of a regionary notary: for the popes used the old, lay notaries,
and had divided the city into seven regions for the registration of
martyrdoms in their region and the transaction of ecclesiastical
business; Gregory's father, Gordianus, must have been one of the
seven. His family must have been in touch with the papal curia and
devout: his sisters became dedicated virgins, living in their own
house.

In the Roman literary inheritance too, he must have had some
share, though the public rhetoric schools in Rome appear to have
broken down in the Gothic wars; Gregory was trained, however,

for the civil service, the secular militia, and he had enough classics and rhetoric to read Augustine and the Fathers, and to become a doctor of the church. The encyclopedias of Boethius and Cassiodorus were accessible to him, as well as patristic commentaries on the scriptures and theological treatises, and the works on canon law of Dionysius Exiguus: but Gregory himself wrote as a shepherd of souls, passing on to others the reflections of a well-informed mind. His *Dialogues*, the *Moralia* and, above all, the *Regula Pastoralis* were read throughout the middle ages. What his works lacked in originality they made up for in moral earnestness. The thought of the starving: the familiar sight of prisoners of war, yoked together as beasts and led off to the slave market at Marseilles were ever with him, as well as the imminence of final judgment. Day by day, he wrote, all things are driven onwards, and we are brought nearer to the trial we shall have to endure before the eternal, the terrible judge. Life was like a voyage; whatever the passengers did, all the time the ship was bearing him onwards to the final goal: 'every day, every moment, we draw nearer the end': and the end was a reckoning.

Beyond his inheritance, Gregory's work as pope rested upon three kinds of training. He entered the civil service and went up its ladder till he was praetorian prefect, with jurisdiction a hundred Roman miles round the city: Roman administrative experience lay behind his achievement as bishop of Rome, as it had lain behind that of Ambrose at Milan. Then, at the summit of his career, he threw all his chances away to embrace the life of monastic ascesis and contemplation: he renounced his possessions, selling them and giving to the poor and founding six monasteries on his Sicilian patrimony. He turned his paternal villa at the *Clivus Scauri* into a seventh, dedicating it to St Andrew, and becoming a simple monk there himself under the abbot Valentius; the practice of the house is inferred to have been Benedictine from Gregory's insertion of a long account of St Benedict in his *Moralia*. Gregory thus shared the training in the monastic life of complete self-devotion which was to have such effect in Europe. Thirdly, he was taken from the monastery by pope Pelagius and initiated into the work of a great clerical household: he was ordained one of the seven Roman deacons who already shared in the notarial work of the papal curia, and were specially charged with the relief of the poor. For several years, however, Gregory served as Pelagius' *apocrysarius* (secretary) or foreign envoy at Constantinople, meeting Leander of Seville, and the emperor Maurice. After his return, in a year of calamity when the Tiber overflowed and plague decimated the city, Gregory was elected pope by direct acclamation of the people. The emperor's consent was awaited for some weeks, and when it was received, Gregory was consecrated on 3 September 590.

He was pope for fourteen years, living at the Vatican with a few monks to help him to preserve the monastic intention of a life now full of activity. His Lombard policy finally prevailed over the emperor's. The Lombards under Alboin had taken Milan in 569: but though they besieged Pavia in 572, the king was murdered and various *duces* were left to try to occupy Italy piecemeal; in 572 the Lombards took Ravenna. The emperors Justin II and Maurice were not uninterested in the loss of Italy, but they had heavy commitments on the Danube frontier and in the east (see p. 214). Maurice (d. 602) never renounced Justinian's reconquest of the Mediterranean basin, for which the loss of Italy was a disaster: but his troops were insufficient for all fronts. He created an exarch to be a real vice-emperor for Italy, to reside at Ravenna and head both the civil and military government, but he had only weak forces to give him. Smaragdus, exarch 585–589, and Romanus, 589–596, nevertheless retook some cities from the Lombards and bought off certain Lombard chiefs; but Romanus' attempt to buy Frankish help resulted only in abortive expeditions. Conditions for the provincials in this war-ridden Italy were deplorable: but to the emperor at Constantinople the game seemed by no means lost.

To the city of Rome, the Lombards in the north were less of a danger than Ariulf, duke of Spoleto, a Lombard possession in the Apennines blocking the Via Flaminia from Rome to Ravenna. In the summer of 592 Ariulf suddenly attacked Rome and it was left to Gregory to direct the defence of the city, as he had earlier by letter directed the defence of central Italy. The duke of Benevento this year also attacked Naples, threatening to hem in the Campagna and Rome itself: and in the north the exarch Romanus gave no help. When king Agilulf appeared at Rome, Gregory signed a peace treaty with him, promising the payment of a tribute in return for peace; an action in direct opposition to the policy of Maurice and Romanus, who desired no respite in the Lombard war. In the end, Gregory's policy prevailed: Romanus was recalled, a new exarch, Callinicus, sent to replace him, and he signed a peace treaty with the Lombards in 598 (renewed in 603).

The feeding of the poor also preoccupied Gregory. The free corn from Egypt had long ceased, and yet it was both a traditional obligation of the Roman magistrate and the Christian bishop that the poor should be fed. The normal division of a bishop's revenue included a portion, a fourth or a third, for the poor; and Gregory, like all good bishops, maintained his guesthouse (*xenodochium*) for the poor and travellers, and fed the poor from his own table. Beyond that, to serve the exceptional needs of the time, he used the food rents from the papal patrimony and his own, to feed the poor. Some of the food rents had, according to the imperial systems, been commuted for money payments, but supplies of corn, oil, vegetables, eggs, bacon and wine were still laboriously brought to Rome and distributed. Arrangements for transport were a great business, and Gregory closely supervised it, writing detailed letters of instruction to the *conductores* who managed the Sicilian farms. On the first day of every month distributions in kind were made to the poor from the 'monasteries' of the seven Roman deaconries: the deacon and some clerks in minor orders, that is, lived communally and gave out the food.

Gregory's correspondence has been mentioned; he wrote to kings, queens and the distant emperor: to Recared the Visigoth and Leander, and to Theodelinda the Lombard queen: to bishops, about the chaotic finances of their sees, and about the scandal they caused by ploughing up their neighbour's landmark, about the transfer of clergy to serve some desolated parish. His correspondence with the bishop of Ravenna and the patriarch of Constantinople had special interest.

The relations of the bishop of Ravenna with the popes were necessarily difficult. The exarch, or the Lombard king holding court at Ravenna, required the exaltation of the bishop: but historically Gregory had grounds for resisting this desire. Italy in the mid-fourth century had been divided between two ecclesiastical jurisdictions: suburbicarian Italy, depending on the pope, included all Italy south of the Apennines and the Italian islands; Italy north of the Apennines depended on the metropolitan of Milan, the only area excluded being the old bishopric or patriarchate of Aquileia, regarded as metropolitan at the end of the fourth century. The bishop of Ravenna was a simple bishop in the suburbicarian province of the pope, but in 431 Valentinian III had made the see metropolitan by adding to it certain sees subtracted from the jurisdiction of Milan. Yet though now a metropolitan as regards these sees, the archbishop of Ravenna continued to depend entirely on the pope, whose consent had to be sought for his election, and who alone could consecrate him, and at Rome. He had a dual character, remaining a simple bishop of the primatial see of Rome, though metropolitan as regards that part of his province that had been subtracted from Milan. Under the Byzantine exarchs and the Lombard kings, he desired perhaps naturally to rank with the metropolitans of Milan and Aquileia, and even with the auto-cephalous patriarchates of the east; during the reign of archbishop Maurus (648–671) the see of Ravenna practically enjoyed such *autocephalia*.

The issue between Gregory and the archbishop turned upon the latter's wearing of the *pallium* not merely at the solemnity of the mass, but at other times, and even in the streets. Archbishop John of Ravenna was reprimanded for this practice through the notary Castorius, and a sharp correspondence followed, the archbishop defending his action as a privilege of his church. When he died in 595, Gregory obtained the appointment of a monk from his own monastery of St Andrew, carefully outlining for him the manner in which it was allowed to him to wear the *pallium*; but the exarch's influence was dominant in Ravenna, and Gregory had occasion to complain that, in the matter of obtaining Romanus' assent to a peace treaty, he suspected the archbishop had 'gone to sleep'.

In Gregory's relations with the patriarch of Constantinople, the use of the title 'oecumenical bishop' was the chief source of diffi-culty, involving an oblique disrespect for the Petrine see, by the patriarch of Constantinople who used it. Justinian in his legislation had freely accorded a primacy of honour, a paternal authority and a principal guardianship of the faith to the see of Peter: but when his political needs led to a theological clash with papal views, he had always subtly distinguished between the person of the pope and the authority of the apostolic see. In 588, however, the patri-arch John the Faster assumed with prominence a title used earlier of Constantinople and other patriarchates but never by a patriarch of himself: pope Pelagius had protested to the emperor. Gregory, through his envoy, did likewise, and was told to let the matter rest. He then wrote to the patriarch himself, explaining that 'oecu-menical' could only mean 'sole' bishop, a proud and sinful title: but the patriarch continued its use. Gregory was willing to accord a share in the apostolic primacy to Antioch and Alexandria, where Peter and Peter's disciple had taught, but not to Constantinople: much less the use of oecumenical as an exclusive title. In effect, he could not compel its disuse, and within a hundred years all the patriarchs, including the popes themselves were found using it.

Finally, Gregory's zeal for the faith, and for missions, extended the limits of his own patriarchate. He saw the conversion of Visi-gothic Spain, and rejoiced at the orthodox baptism of the child of Agilulf and Theodelinda in 602. This completed the return to orthodoxy of the old patriarchate of the west, for the Franks were already orthodox. But when Gregory despatched Augustine and a band of thirty monks to convert the bretwalda of the Anglo-Saxons, he brought a new area under papal jurisdiction. The action was bold, for though Gregory must have known of the Catholicism of the Frankish princess married as long ago as 560 to the young prince of Kent, Æthelbert, paganism was very strong among the Anglo-Saxons. All depended on whether Augustine and the queen could win over the bretwalda; once that was done, in 597, the missionaries made a safe lodgment in Kent. Gregory wrote to Augustine, giving him instructions for the eventual setting up of metropolitans and their provinces: at Canterbury (and, or, London) and York. Since the rulers of London (East Anglia) and York (Northumbria) were as yet unconverted, it may be suspected that Gregory was aware that bishops from London and York had attended the council of Arles in 314. Not only was 'the church of the English' added to the Roman patriarchate, but, as a consequence, the later English missionary, Boniface, added to the patriarchate regions beyond the Rhine that had never formed part of the old empire.

In the beginning of the seventh century the church in the west was entering on her most constructive work for the new Europe under Germanic rule, while the eastern church was about to suffer the incursions of Islam. The western church had provided a system for training clergy and bishops by which clerks, receiving the tonsure of episcopal adoption at an early age, passed some years in each of the grades of doorkeeper, exorcist, lector, acolyte, subdeacon, deacon, priest. The bishop's control over and responsibility for all his clergy was already safeguarded in the canons. The west had adopted from Egypt the monastic life, and spread it from Lérins in the fifth century, from Ireland and Monte Cassino in the sixth; the Benedictine life was to spread still further through the work of Gregory the Great, and to be one of the formative influences of the new society growing up.

Another ecclesiastical institution, the use of election or free choice by clergy or monks of their spiritual ruler, had already been formalized in both eastern and western churches: it had its origin in the Greco-Roman world and became part of lex Romana, familiar to notaries and the higher clergy. It was a process of reasoned selection in which all those who made the choice had the right to express their opinion: they had a vox, a voice, a vote. It differed from the Germanic method of making a choice, a decision, for there the deciding body, some folk-moot or witan, was conceived of as an entity whose single will had to be elicited. The Greco-Roman procedure, however, not the Germanic, was finally adopted for the summoning of popular assemblies to counsel the king or hear his will. Medieval ecclesiastical elections (see pp. 296, 240) were to be of great importance in the development of secular government and of corresponding interest.

BIBLIOGRAPHICAL NOTE

For a short church history, see M. Deanesly's *History of the Medieval Church*, 1969; for the early patriarchates, F. Dvornik, *National Churches and the Church Universal*, 1944: for apostolic tradition, the papacy, and the episcopate, T. G. Jalland, *The Church and the Papacy*, 1944; H. E. Symonds, *The Church Universal and the See of Rome*, 1939; C. Mirbt, *Quellen zur Geschichte des Papsttums*, 1911 (most of the authorities quoted are in Latin); for the *Liber Pontificalis*, see T. Mommsen, *Gesta Pontificum Romanorum*, vol. i, 1897; for a short but clear exposition, *Western Canon Law*, by R. C. Mortimer; for patristic (and Carolingian) study of the scriptures, B. Smalley's *Study of the Bible in the Middle Ages*, ed. 1952; for early medieval canonization, E. W. Kemp's *Canonization and Authority in the Western Church*, 1948. The best text of the Benedictine rule is that edited by d. Cuthbert Butler, *Sancti Benedicti Regula Monasteriorum*, 1935; for another text in Latin and English see d. O. Hunter Blair's *Rule of St. Benedict*, 1934. In view both of the importance of the Benedictine life for monasticism and for the transmission of Greco-Roman learning, see also d. C. Butler's *Benedictine Monachism*, 1924, and d. J. Chapman's *Saint Benedict and the Sixth Century*, 1929. See also T. Jalland, *Pope Leo the Great*, 1941, and for a long study of Gregory the Great, with many quotations from his letters, see F. H. Dudden, *Gregory the Great*, 2 vols., 1905. For the Greek and Latin texts of the canons of councils, see G. D. Mansi, *Sanctorum Conciliorum . . . collectio*, 1758–98, etc.; for a French collection, H. Leclercq and C. J. Hefele, *Histoire des Conciles*, 1907, etc. For an abridged collection in English, with the council names arranged alphabetically, see E. H. Landon, *Manual of Councils*, 2 vols., 1909. See also H. Wheeler Robinson (editor), *The Bible in its Ancient and English Versions*, new ed. 1954. See also T. Klauser, *The Western Liturgy and its History*, 1952.

For the history of western monachism, see H. Vanderhofen, F. Masai and P. B. Corbett, *La Règle du Maître*, 1953 (Scriptorium, iii), K. Hallinger, *Papst Gregor der Grosse und der hl. Benedikt*, 1957 (Studia Anselmiana, Fasc. xlii); O. Porcel, *San Gregorio magno y el monacato : cuestiones controvertidas*, 1960; reviews in *Collect. Ord. Cistere. Ref.*, 1962 and 1963; G. Ferrari, *Early Roman Monasteries*, 1957. See also, B. Blumenkranz, *Juifs et Chrétiens dans le monde occidentale, 430–1096*, Paris, 1960; for ecumenical councils, Jédin, *Conciliorum Decumenicorum Decreta*, Freiburg-Rome, 1962; for canon law from its beginnings, H. E. Feine, *Kirchliche Rechtsgeschicte*, Bund I. Weimar, 1950; G. W. Greenaway, *Saint Boniface*, London, 1955; for papers on his twelfth hundred anniversary, *Gedenkgabe*, Fulda, 1954; T. Schieffer, *Winfrid-Bonifatius und die christliche Grundlegund Europas*, Freiburg, 1954; H. Reinhardt, *Der St. Gallenklosterplan*, St. Gall, 1952.

CHAPTER XI

ISLAM: ORIGINS AND CONQUESTS

THE impact of Islam on medieval Europe cannot be ignored, though, strictly speaking, Islam was an eastern and not a European civilization, empire and religion. The medieval world scene knew three power blocs, not nation states, but civilizations held together by common religions and traditions. 'Throughout the middle ages, a man is a Christian or a Muslim first, a native of his own home district and subject of the local lord next, and only last a Frenchman, an Egyptian or a German' (Grünebaum). The three power blocs were: the kingdoms of the Germanic races in western Europe, with Latin as their common tongue, and a religion looking to the patriarch of the west; the Greco-Roman empire centred at Constantinople, using Greek as a common and a legal language, though the various eastern patriarchates allowed the use of vernacular liturgies; and Islam, which was in origin an Arab religion, an Arab state and, even when non-Arab races had come to outnumber the Arabs, continued to use Arabic as a common, liturgical, legal and literary tongue. Territorially, Islam a hundred years after Muhammad's death, when her first conquests had been achieved, held only the southern fringe of Europe: Spain, Sicily, and some of the Mediterranean islands; but she held north Africa and the east Mediterranean: and remembering how largely early medieval Europe was still a Mediterranean civilization, as the Roman empire had once been, it was of the gravest consequence that Islam shared the Mediterranean with Europe, which she thus girdled and contained. Economic development in western Europe was restricted, the territories of the eastern empire diminished and her activities deflected; and slowly, gradually, the learning and the art of the Latin west and the Greek east were infiltrated and influenced by those of Islam. The history of Islam may seem to lie outside that of Europe, but the character of the great, warm, southern civilization: warlike, religious, learned, sensuous, needs appreciation for the understanding of medieval Europe. To such appreciation, the beautiful illustrations in N. A. Faris's *The Arab Heritage* may be a first clue.

As to the relations of these three power blocs: it has been pointed out that, while Latin and Greek Christianity claimed legitimate

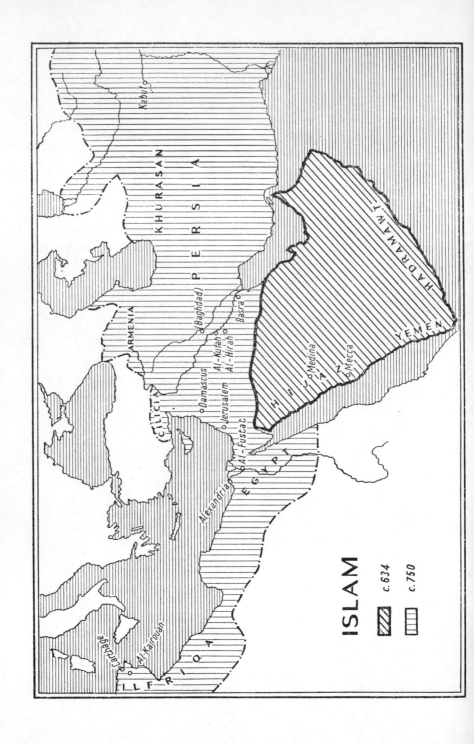

ISLAM

c. 634

c. 750

succession to imperial Rome, Islam had no claim by origin to share in the Roman tradition. But she took possession of provinces once part of the Byzantine or Latin empire, and hence appropriated Greco-Roman traditions of finance, learning and architecture. With only tribal organization and an oral literature at her origin, Islam took over the Roman, Persian and biblical backgrounds as her own and, perhaps most important of all, she took over the administration and cultural heritage of Hellenism. She learned administrative and imperial practices from the Byzantines and the Sassanids; her science, philosophy, art and architecture were deeply influenced by Hellenism. 'It was only the transfer of this heritage to the terms and conceits of the Arabic language and its harmonization with koranic requirements that gradually made the Muslims forget that process of borrowing of which in the beginning they had been perfectly aware.' Islam was a succession state of Alexander's Greco-Persian empire, and in one sense a succession state of the Greco-Roman empire as well, so that the thought of Islam, as well as her art and architecture, had something in common with those of the other two power blocs.

Furthermore, Islam was important to Europe as a transmitter and carrier of culture, using the word of social usage as well as learning. Arabic was her original and became her classical language. It was, before the days of Muhammad, one of the Semitic languages spoken only by the nomads and sedentarized nomads of the Arabian peninsula; but between the death of Muhammad in 632 and the halting of the Muslim advance by the Franks in 732, the Arab conquerors spread their language and religion over Egypt, north Africa and Spain in the west, and over Syria, Armenia and Persia in the east. In a century when (as Arnold Toynbee has shown) the means of communication, the links that held civilization together, were the camel, the horse, and the boat that passed over rivers and canals as well as the open sea, Islam held that region of central Asia that joined China and India to Persia, and Persia to Syria, north Africa and Spain. Islam, that is, was really a 'junction culture', in the days before the fifteenth century, when no ship had as yet linked Europe, Asia and Africa together by passing round the Cape of Good Hope. When that happened, horse and camel were to some extent displaced, and a different linkage of empires and cultures arose; but from the eighth century till the fifteenth the great land mass of the three continents was held in a certain unity of trade and culture by Islamic merchants, scholars and caravans. The Arabs were great carriers. The old civilizations of India and China had contact with Arab-conquered Persia: with the

Arab-conquered Byzantine provinces of Armenia, Syria, Egypt and north Africa: and with Arab-conquered Spain.

If Arabic and the Indian learning (notably mathematics) did not spread faster than they did to Italy and the countries bordering the Mediterranean (and they spread notably slowly), it was not only that Arabic is a difficult language to learn, but because the three great power masses, the Muslim caliphates, the Byzantine empire and the Latin civilization of the west, were not much interested in each other. Distance, difference of language, relative economic self-sufficiency, difference of religion and everyday habits made for isolation, and a certain antagonism. Moreover, in theory each civilization was supreme, with a divine mandate to world supremacy. The three great cultures turned, as it were, their backs on each other and faced outwards. Expansion also was outwards: Latin Christianity expanded towards the Celts and the Scandinavians; Greek Christianity pressed northwards up the Balkans, to the middle Danube and to south Russia; Islam expanded towards the Berbers of the Sahara, the nomads of central Asia, and the tribes of north-west India. The Christian world before the Crusades devoted little enough attention to Islam, but it received less. The Byzantine empire, having suffered more at the hands of Islam than the Latin west, was more apprehensive and conscious of Islam than western Europe: and also more apprehensive and conscious of Islam than Islam was of her.

With Islam, political domination was co-extensive with religion. Till 745 the three caliphates were still one, as the dar-el-Islam, the part of the world already conquered for the religion of Allah, and his prophet, Muhammad: the rest of the world was the dar-el-harb, the house of war, the part as yet to be conquered. The known world consisted of the three continents, Europe, Africa to the south of the Sahara and Madagascar, and Asia; and, in this great, triple, land mass, Islam held the areas of communication: the Mediterranean, with its southern, eastern, and some of its northern shores: Syria and Armenia: and the central Asian steppes and plateau that led to China and India. In the realm of world strategy, she acquired a dominating position, and acquired it by conquest and the sword.

The question of the origins of Islam, and the cause of her swift rise to power, have long engaged historians. That a single Arab prophet and his followers should win, before his death, an ascendency in the Hijaz and Mecca its capital was not surprising; but that these same followers should, within a generation, defeat the Byzantine and Persian emperors and spread Arab rule from Sind to Tunis, was very surprising. It has long been recognized that the

mutual exhaustion of the Persian and Byzantine empires gave the
followers of Muhammad their opportunity; it has more recently
been realized that the untutored Arabs founded a civilization because they absorbed the culture of their newly conquered Greek
and Persian provinces, that the ruler of Islam was, as it were, the
ghost sitting robed and crowned on the throne of Alexander; more
recently still, the origins of Islam in Arabia, and her debt to
Judaism and Christianity, have been intensively studied.

The pre-Islamic background in Arabia itself has been studied
from epigraphic evidence and the scanty, literary references of
Hebrew, Latin and Greek writers. The Arabs themselves had only
poetic literature till Muhammad composed the Qur'an. Arabia is
a large, barren peninsula, perhaps once more fertile: her *wadi's*
were once dried river beds, but long before Muhammad's birth.
Her population was Semitic, and in his day still mainly nomad,
though sedentarized round certain oases and wells. Two very old
civilizations had existed, one in the south and one in the north of
the peninsula, as ruins (not yet scientifically investigated) still
testify. The south Arabian civilization, with its four kingdoms, the
Sabaeans ('the kings of Arabia and Saba shall bring gifts'), the
Minaeans, the Hadramautians and the Qatabanians, had a language
different from classical Arabic and similar to Ethiopian, of which
it is the parent. Their script was related to the Phoenician; their
people were traders, producing and conveying frankincense and
spices up through western Arabia and along the Red Sea to Egypt,
and through Gaza to the Mediterranean. While these south
Arabian kingdoms flourished, northern Arabia was poor, a country
of half-starved nomads, ever streaming out against the cultivated
land on their borders, in Syria and Mesopotamia.

The conquest of Alexander, on the other hand, had important
repercussions in the north of Arabia as against the south: a civilization arose, less old than the southern, and stemming from Mesopotamia. Sedentarized Bedouins here used an Aramaic tongue for
inscriptions, and Arabic for their everyday language. The first
north Arabian state of which any detailed information is available,
that of the Nabataeans, built such cities as Petra (the 'rose red city,
half as old as time'), Basra (Bosra), and even an early Damascus.
They captured south Arabian trade, and the southerly kingdoms
declined; but not before the south Arabians had crossed into Africa
and founded the kingdom of Ethiopia (Abyssinia), at the beginning
of our era. But all this while the great central fund of central
Arabians remained nomad.

When in 63 B.C. Pompey led an army to Syria, the Nabataeans

as Rome's allies appeared for the first time in world history. They succeeded temporarily in fusing Greek and oriental elements with their own population, and might have antedated Islam as a junction state between Europe and Asia; but they were never more than caravan states and lacked Islam's religious fervour and her genius for fighting. Above all, they faced the Roman empire at the peak of its power, remaining only a pawn in Roman politics. Trajan in A.D. 106 turned the Nabataean kingdom into *provincia Arabica*. Three cities throve in the Nabataean decline: Edessa, which introduced Christianity into northern Mesopotamia and Ctesiphon: Dara on the Euphrates, which controlled the Indian trade coming up the Persian Gulf: and Palmyra, an emporium on the caravan route from the Euphrates to the Syrian coast.

A curious 'dark age in Arabia' succeeded these early civilizations in the north and the south: the Bedouin influence, the nomad life, spread as the standard of life fell. The desert extended itself over land once cultivated, and in both south and north Arabia a transition from urban to rural life comparable to that known by Europe in the fifth century followed. The influence of Rome and Sassanid Persia seems to have blocked the old eastern trade and Arabia was much more isolated than she had been earlier. The kingdoms had perished with the cities, though in the south a Himyarite kingdom preserved its power between the fourth and sixth centuries A.D., between two conquests from Abyssinia. In this dark age, of which there are very few literary records, Judaism found many proselytes in south Arabia, and Christianity, both Nestorian and Monophysite, penetrated from the north.

In this dark and hungry period also, waves of Arabian migration from south to north set up two new states: that of the Ghassanids, who ruled the inland territory beyond the Jordan, Damascus and Antioch, and al-Hirah on the Euphrates and the western shores of the Persian Gulf; the Ghassanids looked to Byzantium and the Lakhmids to the Sassanids for protection and tutelage. The population of both states, semi-sedentarized Bedouins, had embraced Christianity, but while the Ghassanids were Monophysite, the Lakhmids were Nestorian. The road of Islam up the 'fertile crescent' of the east Mediterranean was prepared in local political and religious rivalry. It was prepared also by the nomadism which had become again the dominant feature of Arabian life. The gleam of civilization in north and south had almost faded, and the Arabs, using their Arabic tongue, reverting to Semitic nomadism and to their old local cults, and largely hunger-driven, were ready to react to Muhammad's preaching. Drawing his inspiration from the north, not the south, his efforts arrested this decline to nomadism, for he assailed the tribal organization, and preached a way of life foreign to that of the Bedouin. The Islamization of Arabia changed the nomadic pattern of life.

In two respects, however, the fifth and sixth centuries laid foundations for Muhammad's work: the fusion of the tribal dialects into a single Arabic language, and the practice of tribal government under an elected sheikh. While in the Arabian peninsula 'the only exception to the nomadic way of life was the oasis' (B. Lewis), the oasis of Kinda succeeded in uniting the central and northern Arabian tribes into a petty kingdom. Through Kinda fine poetry, a common poetic language and some orally transmitted learning passed generally among the Bedouin tribes. Moreover, the tribal nomadism of the Arabs was to condition the secular organization of Islam in the generations immediately succeeding Muhammad. Each tribe was headed by an elected *sayyid* or *sheikh*, who acted as arbitrator within the tribe and was advised by a council of elders called the *majlis*, the representatives of clans within the tribe. Tribal life was regulated by ancestral custom, the *Sunna*, and violence was limited by the primitive obligation of the blood feud, or obligation on the family of a murdered man to pursue and kill the murderer. The election of the sheikh and the obligation to observe the *Sunna* were to be of political importance to Islam.

Against such a background, but himself a member of the sedentarized tribe of the Quraish, the guardians of the Kaʿba or building housing the Black Stone of Mecca, Muhammad was born, in 570 or 571. His father died before his birth, and he was brought up by his grandfather and his paternal uncle, abu-Talib. There are no sources for his life other than Arabic, and the earliest Arabic life of the Prophet was composed in 767, 135 years after his death. There were Christians and Jews in Arabia during Muhammad's youth, and from them he may have learned orally about their beliefs; the evidence that he made a journey with abu-Talib into Syria at the age of twelve is now disputed, and it is unlikely that he then first came into contact with Christian teaching. When twenty-five years old, he married Khadijah, the widow of a well-to-do merchant, and fifteen years older than himself. While she lived, he would have no other wife, and he found in her a supporter of his prophetic desires to speak to his people. He now had leisure to pray and meditate, withdrawing often to a little cave outside Mecca called Hira. It was here that he received the call to prophesy, and the words of this and later revelations are recorded in the *surahs* of the Qur'an.

Since the religion taught by Muhammad was to be the foundation and driving force of Islam, his own religious background and
borrowings are of interest. In what was later called the Jahiliyah
(the time of ignorance before Muhammad's mission), religion was
to the Arabs an affair of the clan, each of which had its local cult.
A diffused animism, with local gods, goddesses and fetiches, prevailed. At Mecca, veneration for the goddesses Manat, al-Lat,
al-'Uzza, and the god al-Lah ('who is greater than they'), was connected with veneration for the famous Black Stone, the Ka'ba.
Allah was, in fact, the most notable of the gods of the Arab pan-
theon and the god of Mecca, which, with its spring, marked an
important stage for caravans on the route to Basra. There, in the
simple, roofless, gateless enclosure, the Quraish guarded the Ka'ba,
an object of pilgrimage in the grape harvest and the scene of a
popular fair. There was no cultivation at Mecca: Arab riches came
entirely from trade, and Arab religion, itself very primitive, was
now contrasted through the caravan trade with the Zoroastrianism
of Persia, the sectarian Christianity of Syria, Egypt and Abyssinia,
and with the teaching of a strong Jewish colony at Yathrib. Christianity and Judaism were monotheist, in contrast to the local animism, and, of the two, Judaism had apparently the stronger influence
on Muhammad. Besides the influence which Judaism and Christianity had already attained in some of the tribes, an Arabic source
states that the Quraish had already received some knowledge from
a sect of Christianized Gnostics, the Zandaqa. Muhammad was
deeply stirred at the concept of the unity of God; he did not at first
identify the one God, the merciful, the compassionate, with the
Meccan al-Lah. For a time he directed that the posture of praying
among his followers should be towards Jerusalem, the central
shrine of Judaism and Christianity: later, he ordered that it should
be transferred towards Mecca, as the shrine of Allah.

As to the sources of Jewish and Christian influence: the Christians of the north have been already mentioned, and there were
Christians also in Yemen (southern Arabia) and Abyssinia. In 523
the Abyssinians had taken the Christians of Yemen under their
protection. But from the second century there was a stronger and
more renowned Jewish community at Yemen, in contact with
Jewish centres in Syria and Babylon. The Jewish community had
formerly been predominant also in Yathrib, the scene of Muhammad's first triumphs, and to become al-Madinah (Medina), the
city of the Prophet. Yathrib seemed, indeed, on the way to becoming a kind of Jewish commonwealth, with the Synagogue for its
state church. It had been an old colony from Palestine and had

rabbis of great distinction: Muhammad's biographer, ibn-Ishaq, compiled a list of them, commending their mastery of the Torah. Later, the first two caliphs frequented the Jewish 'house of learning' at Medina, in order to understand the better the Prophet's teaching.

The contact between Mecca and Medina had, even before Muhammad's day, given rise to a certain Jewish-Christian monotheism embraced by some Arabs, and even some of the Quraish. They professed 'the religion of Abraham', an embracing monotheism: and regarded the setting up of the Black Stone as the work of Abraham, connecting the city cult with the universal monotheism they professed. Mecca, that is, as the capital of a great commercial empire and the site of a local Arab cult, was marked out to be the holy city of Islam. Its cult was of sufficient importance in the year of Muhammad's birth for the Abyssinian viceroy of Yemen to send a great expedition to Mecca, expressly to destroy the Ka'ba, as the central shrine of Arabic paganism. It failed; but there were plenty of Jewish and Christian influences abroad in Mecca, and when forty years later Muhammad sought to bring the common people of Mecca to a belief in one God, he had no great difficulty in converting them: the ground was prepared. It was from the leading families of the Quraish, with their tribal and functional interest in the shrine, that he met with opposition.

The two older religions made another contribution to Islam of the first importance: the art of writing and literacy, the all-important agent of Muhammad's success. There was no written Arabic literature before Muhammad; some inscriptions even in the north and south were in older tongues (though a few were in Arabic) and in more recent times in Aramaic. The considerable Arab literature of pre-Islamic days (poetry, folk lore, proverbs, etc.) was all handed down orally, and was only committed to writing later by the piety of Muslim scholars. The writing down of Muhammad's revelations in the Qur'an was of the first importance for culture as well as religion. It was the first Arabic book. The need to study the Qur'an became the foundation of Arabic scholarship.

Muhammad himself could not write: but he had, later, a secretary who could, in the Medinese scribe, Zayd-ibn-Thabit; there were very few able to write in Arabic at the time. It has been suggested that the art of writing Arabic came from the Christian scholars of al-Hirah and was introduced by them into the Hijaz. We hear of a Meccan Christian who wrote the Gospel, in Hebrew letters, and it has been suggested that Arabic translations of the Gospel were written in Hebrew characters. Hebrew characters were also used in writing Aramaic texts. Muhammad knew also of the scrolls and folios in which the Jews treasured their sacred literature. The writing of Arabic was in his time still fluid and imprecise: but the Aramaic and Hebrew, and above all, Syriac characters were chiefly used in the evolution of an Arabic script.

There was no deliberate hostility to the two older monotheisms in Muhammad's day, and Islam was at first meant to be a synthesis of those who, professing them, were willing to accept Allah as the one God and Muhammad as his prophet. Although in Muslim theory the Qur'an is literally the word of God, Muhammad had, in fact, no scruple in borrowing from either of the older religions; but he borrowed most from Judaism. To him, both Jews and Christians, but the Jews especially, were the people of a Book, the Jews of the Torah (the Pentateuch) and the Christians of the Evangel (the Gospel). The writing down of the Qur'an was a deliberate emulation of the two older religions, and Islam became, like them, the religion of a Book. The creation of the Qur'an (written down by others) was perhaps Muhammad's most considerable achievement: it equated the Muslims with Christians and Jews, and it brought literacy to the Arabs. Arabic was a literary vehicle sensitive to many shades of meaning and able to express, not only the thoughts of an Arab merchant and his paraphrases of biblical stories and rabbinical teaching, but also abstract ideas and mathematical concepts. The study of the Qur'an, and therefore of Arabic, was known to be acceptable to God. 'We have made (the Qur'an) easy in thy tongue,' said God to Muhammad, 'that thou mayest thereby give good tidings to those who show piety.' Arabic became to Islam the idiom of piety, science and the People of Paradise.

Many expressions in the Qur'an came ultimately from the Jewish and Christian scriptures, either as already in use in Mecca in Muhammad's day, or as borrowed by him: expressions such as 'Day of Judgment', 'Hellfire', 'Shaytan' (Satan). They were widely used in Syriac and western Aramaic, and the immediate sources of Muhammad's knowledge of them are not easy to distinguish.

Muhammad, or later Islamic theologians, regarded the corpus of his revelations as the embodiment of a book already existing in the mind of God, the earthly image of a heavenly Qur'an. With this thought of a 'heavenly book' in mind, Muhammad often spoke of God as 'writing' in the sense of establishing a decree or issuing an ordinance. All authority, in Muhammad's mind, is connected with the heavenly book. So Moses had been given the Book and Salvation: so Jesus acted and suffered that a word of scripture 'might be fulfilled'. The revelation to Moses was primary, to Jesus secondary

as confirming that of Moses, and to himself, final. He makes God
say of Moses 'We gave Moses the Book ... we gave Jesus the
Evidences.' The Rabbis taught that disregard of the Book and the
Evidences was sin: and Muhammad taught it of the Qur'an.

As to his own position in the history of revelation, and his use of
the terms Islam and Muslim: Muhammad felt the analogy between
his own position and that of Abraham, who passed from primitive
religious belief to monotheism. He speaks of such uninstructed
monotheists as Hanifs:

> Who is more beautiful in religion than one who surrenders himself
> to God in sincerity and follows the confession of Abraham as a
> heathen? . . . Abraham was not a Jew, nor was he a Christian; rather,
> he was a heathen [*hanifan*] surrendering himself to God (*musliman*)
> and not one of the idolators. (J. Obermann.)

Islam is surrender to God, and the Muslim he who surrenders. All
is written in the heavenly book, and he who so surrenders follows
willingly his predestined path; but whether he follows it willingly
or not, his fate is predestined. Next to Muhammad's incommunic-
able experience in the cave on Hira, the theory of revelation as it
had come to him through Judaism was the chief factor in shaping
his career; each chapter, *surah*, in the Book was the record of a
revelation, a sign, a command, greatly though the *surahs* differ in
character and moral worth.

Four other points may be mentioned in connexion with the
Qur'an.

First, Muhammad claimed to be the Messenger of God to all
men; scholars differ as to whether Muhammad conceived of his
own commission as extending beyond Arabia, or indeed to the
whole human race. He failed, however, to win over the people of
the Torah and the Evangel. He did win over his own people, and
in time an ever-increasing number of other races and communities accepted Islam: predominantly those at the same stage of
civilization as his own Arabs.

Secondly: there is a great contrast between the long history of
revelation among the Jews, and even the Christians, and the single
writing down of the whole canon of Muhammad's revelations: even
though this was supplemented by *hadith*, the traditions of the
Prophet, written down later.

Thirdly: scholars agree that, though a considerable amount of
biblical matter is embedded in the Qur'an, Muhammad can have
had no first-hand acquaintance with the scriptures. He can have
used no text or translations. He had acquired his whole store of

scriptural knowledge orally, and probably from the exposition of non-canonical literature, especially the rabbinical Agada. He had clearly visited the synagogues. He had heard expounded the 'non-canonical periphery of scripture', the Targum and the Midrash; and heard also expositions of apocryphal and homiletic Christian writings.

Fourthly: Muhammad taught about man's future destiny a doctrine of reward and punishment at the last day, the final reckoning. The heavenly book should be opened, and each man placed on the Right Hand or Left Hand of God. In the early *surah's* (those concerned with moral precepts rather than the administrative orders given as revelations in Muhammad's later career), a Muslim is qualified to sit on the Right Hand mainly by the practice of prayer and almsgiving. He shall, we are told, set the bondman free, feed the hungry in the day of famine, endure and have compassion, pray and be mindful of the Name of God, and give to the beggar and the outcast.

To return to Muhammad's career and the political history of Islam.

Muhammad's first preaching as the messenger of Allah met with small response, though Khadijah his wife, his cousin Ali and their kinsman abu-Bakr were early converted. The Quraish found his teaching heretical and opposed to their economic interests, and as the number of converts increased, resorted to persecution. In 615 certain Meccan families among his followers emigrated to Abyssinia where the Christian negus protected them. Persecution became hotter, but 'Umar, the later caliph, became a believer; Khadijah and abu-Talib died; in later tradition (not in the Qur'an) Muhammad now announced his own mysterious nocturnal journey to Jerusalem, a parallel to Christ's temptation before his ministry; Muhammad, however, was said to have travelled on a winged horse with a woman's face and a peacock's tail, and was borne up to the seventh heaven. In 620 the men of Yathrib invited him to settle with them; and believing his cause hopeless in Mecca, Muhammad and his followers in 622 made the *hijra* (hegira: the flight) and slipped quietly into Medina. Here he found himself an honoured chief, the chief magistrate of a community, and in 624 he and 300 Muslims raided a caravan of 1,000 Meccans at Badr, and won the first military victory of Islam. Further minor engagements of Medinese and Meccans followed. Within Medina, agreement between the Meccan immigrants, the Medinese and the Jews was confirmed by Muhammad by proclamation. Over this new community, the Umma, he alone had jurisdiction. Though each tribe retained its old customs and privileges, only the Umma could make peace and war.

During his residence at Medina, 622–632, the Prophet broke with Judaism and Christianity, appointed Friday instead of Saturday as a sabbath for his followers, ordered the call to be made from the minaret, instituted the fast of Ramadan, and authorized the pilgrimage to Mecca and the kissing of the Black Stone. Islam was nationalized as an Arab religion. In January 630, he was strong enough to enter Mecca and smash the many idols of the sanctuary, none protesting. The territory round the Ka'ba was declared sacred and forbidden to non-Muslims. Three months after his own pilgrimage to Mecca in 632, Muhammad died.

The problem of succession to the Prophet was not easy. He had had, apparently, nine wives, but his son Ibrahim had died. The community of Muhammad's followers (for 'every Muslim', the Prophet said, 'is brother unto every other Muslim') found themselves a theocracy, with no priesthood except the leader in prayer at the mosque, the *imam*, acting as commander of the faithful. Abu-Bakr, the Prophet's father-in-law, by a kind of *coup d'état*, became his caliph or successor, though not without the opposition of certain tribes. Islam had, in any case, no precedent for hereditary succession, but only of the tribal election of a new sheikh. Abu-Bakr was of the tribe of the Quraish, and acceptable to the Medinese, but the more distant tribes who had accepted Muhammad's rule by treaty or contract, regarded themselves as freed from their contract by his death, and entitled to elect themselves new sheikhs. They did not formally reject Islam, though Islamic tradition termed their movement for independence the *Ridda*, or apostasy. Within the short rule of abu-Bakr (632–634), these more distant tribes were forced to acknowledge the new caliph, at the point of the sword. The wars of the *Ridda*, traditionally represented as a war of reconversion, led to wars of conquest far outside the boundaries of Arabia. The real beginning of the Arab conquests was the victory of Khalid, abu-Bakr's chief general, at 'Agraba in 633, in the eastern Najd (central Arabia). This was a battle in the *Ridda* war.

The strategy of the Islamic wars of conquest was the strategy of the desert, with which the Arabs were familiar and their opponents not. 'They could use it as a means of communication for supplies and reinforcements, as a safe retreat in times of emergency' (Bernard Lewis). When they conquered a new province, they established a base on the edge of the desert, like al-Kufa and Basra in Iraq, or Qairawan in Tunisia. The conquests had an inconspicuous beginning when Khalid sent small raiding forces into Palestine and Syria, withdrawing to the desert with their plunder. In response to these raids on Byzantine provinces, the emperor Heraclius mobilized an army: but Khalid moved swiftly from Iraq (the region of the lower Euphrates), and looted Damascus without Byzantine opposition in the spring of 634. His followers dispersed in Palestine and threatened the safety of Jerusalem, the scene of Heraclius' earlier triumph. Heraclius therefore prepared a larger army, which was defeated by a far smaller force of Arabs at the battle of the Yarmuk river, in July 636. Khalid followed up his victory by conquering the whole province of Syria, which gave him access both to Persia and Egypt: to Iraq he already had access. He held a position of great strategic importance.

The conquest of Iraq was actually initiated by the adjacent Arab tribes, who realized they were bound to be involved in wars between Persia and Islam. The sheikh al-Muthanna, the ally of Khalid, in 635 won a victory on the Euphrates: 'Umar had now succeeded abu-Bakr as caliph, but Islam was still governed by Medina: and of Medina, and even of Islam, al-Muthanna knew little. 'Umar sent one of the companies of the Prophet to bring reinforcements against the Persians and to take over the command. The Persian leader Rustam was out-generalled at Qadisiya, near al-Hirah, in 637, and Persia was won by the Arabs, both the highly civilized Iraq, at the head of the Persian Gulf, and, later, the wilder, hill-country of Iran, which stretched from the lower Euphrates across to the Indus.

The Arab victory at Qadisiya was followed the same summer by their triumphal entry into Ctesiphon. The greatest royal city in Asia, the luxuries, comfort and art of a high civilization, lay at their disposal, though, according to Arabic chroniclers, they scarcely knew camphor from salt or gold from silver. The Arab general, Sa'd, built a fine mosque in Ctesiphon; but the caliph ordered the capital to be moved to al-Kufa, as nearer to al-Hirah and less dangerously distant from Mecca. Al-Kufa and Basra became the garrison cities of Iraq and the east.

Byzantine Armenia was raided in 640 by 'Iyad: but the country was difficult, and not subdued till 652. This new province too was to be placed under al-Kufa, and although 'Umar urged a Meccan simplicity of life on the Arab rulers, the sophistication of Persia was too attractive, and a royal palace was built there like the old palace at Ctesiphon. Al-Kufa and Basra remained the great desert cities of eastern Islam, till the Abbasid Mansur built his famous capital at Baghdad. From Basra in the reign of the caliph Mu'awiya the conquest of eastern Khurasan was completed (663–671); the

Islamic forces crossed the Oxus and raided Bukhara in distant Turkestan.

The conquest of Egypt was made by planned campaigning rather than, as in the case of Syria, Persia and Armenia, by casual raids. But even here, the caliph 'Umar gave only a limited authorization, and the victory was due to the Arab leader 'Amr, who had traded with Egypt in the days of the Jahiliyah, knew the country, and was eager to eclipse the exploits of Khalid. He had already conquered Palestine west of the Jordan: he took the old coast road through Pelusium at the mouth of the Nile, and he defeated Heraclius' general Theodorus, with a much larger force, in the strong castle of Babylon (just south of Cairo); a seven months' siege ended victoriously in 641. Alexandria, that great city, still rested untaken on the westward extremity of the Delta: it was defended by a strong garrison and the Byzantine navy: the Arabs were unused to the catapults hurling stones from the walls, and they looked on Alexandria and retreated. But there was division in Constantinople on Heraclius' death in 641, and Cyrus, patriarch of Alexandria and imperial vicegerent of Egypt, concluded a treaty with 'Amr at Babylon, by which Egypt became tributary to the Arabs as the price of the evacuation of the country by 'Amr's army. 'Umar received the news, and thanksgivings were said in the Prophet's mosque at Medina. The site of 'Amr's camp outside Babylon became the new Arab capital of Egypt, called al-Fustat (Old Cairo), and it remained the capital till the Fatimid caliphs built their new capital, Cairo, in 969. From al-Fustat the ancient canal leading through Heliopolis to al-Qulzum on the Red Sea was cleared by 'Amr, and a direct waterway was opened to the Arab cities on the Red Sea. On the whole, the old Byzantine system of administration was retained. The easiness of the conquest of the Delta is explained by the willingness of the Coptic peasants, as Monophysites, to receive the enemies of Heraclius, under whom they had suffered religious persecution and financial oppression. As in Syria and other conquered regions, new converts began to throng to Islam. So clearly had their conquerors identified Islam with the Arabs, that at first they could only enter the faith by becoming *mawali* or clients of one or other of the Arab tribes. They thus became entitled to exemption from most of the taxes imposed upon the conquered, and to most of the material benefits of Islam. They did not, in fact, always obtain the exemptions to which they were entitled.

The Byzantines had not, however, relinquished hope of regaining Egypt, especially as Arab tax collectors roused some resentment.

The emperor Constans II sent an expedition which retook
Alexandria in 645, and 'Amr, who had been recalled by the caliph,
was sent back to defend Egypt. In 646 he retook Alexandria, de-
molished her walls and secured her for Islam. 'Uthman (Othman)
the caliph seems to have had no desire to press the conquest along
the coast to Tripoli: but to the early, devout Muslims the principle
of the *jihad*, the holy war, was ever pressing, and 'Amr was a good
soldier. With Mu'awiya, the governor of Muslim Syria, he began
the establishment of a Muslim fleet, using the captured Greek
ships and the great dockyards of Alexandria; with a fleet, advance
along the north coast, largely waterless, was more possible.

The first Arab naval operations were carried out in the same
years as the conquest of Tripoli. Mu'awiya's fleet seized Cyprus in
649, and in 652 the Egyptian Arabs defeated a larger Greek fleet off
Alexandria. In 654 the Syrian fleet pillaged Rhodes, and in 655 the
Syro-Egyptian fleet destroyed some 500 Byzantine ships near
Phoenix, off the Lycian coast: Constans II had led the fight in
person, and he lost, with his ships, the naval supremacy of the
east Mediterranean. The two Arab generals, Mu'awiya of Syria
and Abdullah of Egypt, had proved themselves outstanding sea-
captains, and the Arab word *amir* acquired in the west its sense
of admiral. Nevertheless, the early caliphs distrusted this alien
method of warfare, and both 'Umar and 'Uthman sent messages
to their admirals, emphasizing the need of camping where the
caliph's messenger, or the caliph himself, could reach them riding
the preferred horse or camel. But the fall of Egypt and the existence of an Arab fleet had rendered the Byzantine province of
Tripoli and the great headland of Cyrenaica defenceless; 'Amr
indeed had pushed his raids right along the coast to Barca in
Cyrenaica in 643. The Berber tribes of Tripoli submitted; for the
time being.

The caliph 'Umar died in 644, murdered by a Persian slave. He
had appointed on his deathbed an electoral college or *shura*, which
had elected 'Uthman caliph, deferring to the wishes of the old
leading families of Mecca. The choice was unfortunate, for 'Uthman was weak, incompetent and a nepotist. The impetus of Arab
conquest was stayed, partly through weak leadership, partly
through the old nomad objection to central government, and
largely also because the pressure of population from Arabia had
found sufficient outlet.

The limits of conquest in Africa were, however, not yet fixed.
'Umar had refused permission for advance beyond Tripoli, as
adventure further to the west seemed more dangerous than profit-

able. But the double incentive of loot and the holy war seemed to
demand a fresh field among the Berbers to the west, and 'Uthman
took counsel of the Companions of Muhammad and gave his permission. To the Arabs, Africa, shadowed by trees, as their chroniclers wrote, from Tripoli to Tangier, seemed a rich land: and the
olive trees were indeed a source of wealth as much as of shade.
They raided Carthage, beyond the great gulf, and called the land
round it Ifriqiya (Africa). They plundered the province of its
treasure, sending sacks of it along the road to Medina and Damascus: they wondered at the great number of horses, more than they
had themselves in Arabia; at the camels, at the stores of silver and
plate: and above all at the beautiful slave girls, whom they sent to
be sold in eastern markets for as much as 1,000 pieces of gold
apiece. Some were bought for the harems of Muslim chieftains,
and half Byzantine, half native as they were, became the mothers
of Arab nobles.

Nevertheless, the Berbers proved more easy to defeat than to
conquer. They had a perpetual reservoir of undefeated tribesmen
to the south in the Sahara, and whereas the conquests of Spain took
three years, Egypt three, and that of Palestine and Syria only seven,
it took fifty-three years to make a precarious conquest of these
north-west African tribes. Distances were great: other provinces
mattered more than Africa: the Berbers fighting a guerrilla war
could withdraw into the desert, and since they had never been conquered by Rome or Byzantium submitted the less readily to the
Arabs. It took 150 years before the conquest was complete.

To consolidate the military conquest and facilitate its further
development, the Arab leader Sidi 'Uqba founded Qairawan, south
of Tunis and Carthage, to be not only a military post, but a teaching centre to conciliate the Berbers and convert them to Islam.
After pressing his conquest to the Atlantic, he was finally killed by
a Berber chief, who took Qairawan and remained its master from
683 to 686. In these three years, the old Vandal and Byzantine
province saw its last good days, ruled by an African Jugurtha;
Constantine IV meanwhile kept the Muslim armies in check, and
his garrisons held the coast from Sousse to Bona. But after a seven-
year halt by the Arabs, they advanced under Hassan and regained
Carthage in 695, only to be swept from it by a flood of Berbers led
by an African Boadicea, a Jewish priestess called Kahina. In 698,
they took Carthage for the third time, and this time permanently.
Their rule continued uneasy, but two factors helped them: the
Islamization of the Berbers, not too difficult a task, and the enlist-
ing of Berbers to fight in the armies that conquered Spain.

What accounted for the complete dechristianization of north Africa, the old province of Cyprian and Augustine? For one thing, Romanization had never been complete and between the old Roman towns and villas the Berbers had remained pagan and animist. Judaism indeed had penetrated farther than Christianity. Africa, it is true, had had a large number of bishops' sees, but this fragmentation of authority had favoured local heresy and disunity. Under the Byzantines religious division had risen again: the struggle over Monothelitism disturbed the province at the very moment of the Arab invasions. Moreover, Arab generals, when engaging an enemy, offered as alternatives to fighting conversion to Islam, or a not intolerable tributary status without conversion. Those who thus surrendered might not only keep their religion, but practise their trade or their art (especially medicine), and even hold public office. Severity was only shown to those who treated Islamic rites with disrespect, or lapsed after accepting Islam: the conquered Berbers and provincials might live under a régime of tutelage and tariffs. In all but the fringes of the desert, where the Berber dialects finally prevailed, Arabic superseded Latin and Greek as the language of government and everyday life.

But while the conquest of the Maghreb proceeded, the unity of Islam under a single caliph was lost. The tribal leaders who conquered first Arabia and then Syria and Persia were led by the Companions of Muhammad and had been long trained by him in the stern, simple tenets of early Islam. The close followers of Muhammad at Mecca accepted with passionate fervour the exclusive character of the message of God to Muhammad, and its complete sufficiency. All revelation, all moral teaching, all learning, was completely covered by the Qur'an. But when, by the will of Allah, Syria and Persia had been conquered, with their unheard-of fertility, wealth, buildings, art treasures and learning, the question whether all this richness and knowledge ought to be rejected by the good Muslim was bound to arise. The interests of Syria, of Iraq, even of lesser Arab-ruled dependencies, were bound to conflict, not only with the political dominance of the Meccan party, but with the stricter Muslim attitude towards external luxury, learning and craftsmanship. The personal rivalries of Arab generals after the murder of 'Uthman appeared to divide the caliphate: but provincial interests and religious differences accompanied them.

The question whether succession to the caliphate should be limited to the descendants of the Prophet, or go by election to any pious and suitable Muslim, had been raised even in the time of the first four (elective) caliphs. ʿAli had been Muhammad's first cousin, the husband of his daughter Fatima, and the father of Muhammad's only two surviving descendants; there were those who claimed he should have succeeded Muhammad in 632, instead of giving way to men of greater seniority. ʿAli disposed of rival claimants, except Muʿawiya the Umayyad, the governor of Syria, who led an army against him; but, disliking the mutual shedding of blood by Muslims, he agreed to arbitration of his own and Muʿawiya's claims. The verdict deposed both men from their offices, a verdict pressing the more heavily on ʿAli. When he was later murdered, the party of the Shiʿa, who stood for the rule of Muhammad's descendants, became his partisans, regarded him as a martyr, and refused to accept as binding any teaching except that given by him whom they regarded as the true *imam*, necessarily a descendant of ʿAli, and of greater importance than the caliph himself. The Shiʾites were always a suppressed minority in Islam, and the raisers of numerous rebellions: but the Fatimid dynasty in Egypt was Shiʾite later. Both Umayyad and Abbasid caliphates were Sunnite.

Muʿawiya, the founder of the Umayyad dynasty, relied chiefly on the Arab army in Syria, and the Syrian Christians in the bureaucracy, with whom he was not unpopular; his extension of the Islamite dominions made him regarded as second founder of the caliphate, as well as of a dynasty. Under the Umayyads, however, some of the old Meccan exclusiveness still lingered, and it was left to the Abbasid dynasty (750–850) to abandon the original austerity of Islamic life, and become the patrons of alien learning. Abbasid administration deliberately copied Sassanid practice, and was no longer based on racial exclusiveness. The *mawali*, long full of economic and social discontent, were employed in the ministries and could enjoy high social standing: the change from the Umayyads to the Abbasids meant social revolution. Though the Umayyad caliphate itself had been 'not so much an Arab state as a Persian and Byzantine succession state', with the Abbasids the reliance on Greco-Persian practice and imitation of Greco-Persian absolute sovereignty increased.

The first Abbasid century, beginning with the caliphate of Abuʾl-ʿAbbas (750–754) is reckoned the most splendid in Arab history. The seat of power was now in Iraq, and the ruling circle no longer Arab, but much more international. To preserve Islamic unity, however, the religious aspect of the caliphate was emphasized, in contrast to its secular character under the Umayyads. Government was theocratic and propaganda taught that authority should remain for ever in Abbasid hands. Their government proved as shrewd and worldly as that of the Umayyads. 'The Abbasid was an empire of Neo-Moslems in which the Arabs formed only one of the many component races' (Hitti).

Mansur ('the Victorious'), who ruled from 754 to 775, proved one of the greatest of the Abbasids; all the thirty-five caliphs who succeeded him were his lineal descendants. He contended success-fully with insurrection in Syria, in Khurasan, and by the 'Alid Shi'ites, but he could not subdue or displace the Umayyad amir, 'Abd ar-Rahman, in Spain. The latter was one of the very few Umayyads who had escaped in the general massacre ordered in 750 at the accession of the Abbasids; he had wandered as a fugitive for five years through Syria and Africa, joined by Umayyad partisans, and captured Cordoba in 756. From this year, Islam was divided politically between the Abbasid at Baghdad and the Umayyad at Cordoba, though the Umayyads used at first only the title of amir: Islam was divided also in religion between Sunnites and Shi'ites. The Umayyad amirate (later caliphate) at Cordoba was to last from 756 to 1071: it was Charlemagne's alliance with the Abbasids (though this is disputed), and some invitation to intervene against the Umayyad ruler at Cordoba by certain Arab rebels in north Spain, that prompted his march in 778 through the northern route to Saragossa. (See p. 351.)

But though in Mansur's day it was scarcely possible to hold in one state Spain and the middle east, at least under a single political rule, yet in Syria, Iraq, Persia, Armenia and Khurasan, Islamic rule was glorious. Mansur laid the foundations of his new capital at Baghdad, which he called Dar-al-Salam (abode of peace), in 762. He chose as the site a small Sassanid town just north of Ctesiphon, where the Tigris and Euphrates swing in together nearly to meet, before diverging again in the great oval above their junction at Basra and the river mouth. 'Here', said Mansur, 'is the Tigris, to put us in touch with China and with Mesopotamia, Armenia and their environs.' Here too was the Euphrates, to carry for Mansur all that Iraq, Syria and the adjacent lands could offer; and here, nearby, were the ruins of Ctesiphon, from which he drew his building material. He took four years to build his new city, using vast sums of money, and some 100,000 architects, craftsmen and labourers drawn from Syria, Mesopotamia and the more distant provinces. He built a great Greco-Roman-Persian city, second only to Constantinople in its day, circular in plan, the walls pierced by four equidistant gates. Within, the roads radiated from the caliphal palace and the great, domed mosque in the centre, through the four gates, to the four corners of the empire. From this capital, famous as the city of the *Thousand and One Nights*, the Abbasid caliphs built up the government on the Sassanid model in the time of Chosroes. Persian titles and offices (such as the vizirate), Persian songs, Persian astronomy and Persian learning were adopted; Mansur himself adopted Persian headgear. In all the arts and amenities of life, Persian custom was adopted: but the Arab stamp was given to the new state by the religion of Islam and the retention of Arabic as the official language.

In Baghdad, Damascus, Quairawan, Cordoba and a hundred Islamic cities and villages, the wealth of caliphs and amirs spent itself in the building of palaces, baths, schools, hospitals, caravan-serais and the characteristic mosques and minarets. The ground plan of the Roman villa, with its colonnades and fountain, and the Christian basilica with its roof supported on pillars and its external court, were taken over, and the domed roofing of Mesopotamia. Greco-Roman mosaics supplied a technique, though their mytho-logical figure subjects could not be used by Muslim art, which not only discountenanced a representation of what purported to be other gods than Allah, but even all representations of the human figure and a naturalistic treatment of visible objects. The old Per-sian use of rhythmical pattern as distinguished from naturalistic ornament supplied to the Arabs a decoration accordant with their disallowance of 'images', and became in Arab usage the scrolls and undulant patterns known to us as 'arabesques'. Put very briefly, the points which, arising from her origins, distinguished Islamic art and architecture include:

The mosque, which might be a simple rectangular *cella*, or poly-gonal building dome-centred like the so-called mosque of ʿUmar at Jerusalem, with the *mihrab* or niche, generally arched and decorated, showing the faithful the direction of Mecca.

The minaret, from which the faithful were called to prayer. This was in essence a slender tower, varying in form in the different provinces of Islam, from the ziggurat of ancient Babylon, with its ascending spiral external stairway, to the tower of stages of decreas-ing size from north Africa, the round pillar, decorated and domed, from Persia, the galleried Indian turret and the tall, pointed flèche with its single gallery, from Constantinople.

In the buildings, the use of the horse-shoe arch, especially in Spain; and, especially in eastern Islam, the slightly bulging domed roof. It was used both in the mosque and the madrasa (lecture hall of the theological seminaries). In both the large domes of centrally-focussed buildings, and the small domes of turrets and minarets, these double curved roofs, with the widest part of the dome projecting beyond the supporting walls, needed mathematical knowledge for the supporting scaffolding, and in some cases a roofing by sheets of metal. Whereas in Europe roofing with lead was costly, in this style, born in Asia and on the caravan route to India, roofing with sheets of shining copper even was made possible by the relative plenty of the metals and the riches of Arab princes.

The use of colour in architecture, not only in mosaics and tiles, but in the contrasting colour blocks for arches (as in the mosque at Cordoba) is another feature; as is the use of rich and intricate allover patterns for the covering of large surfaces, like the tomb of the amir Suleiman at Cairo. The use of the allover pattern is itself characteristic of Islamic art: it has neither axial symmetry, like the palmette ornament of the Greeks, nor a central focus, like the spirals of the Celts; it achieved unit and beauty by the balanced repetition of geometrical motifs. Possibly the Persian, Indian and Arab fondness for the allover pattern goes back to its uses in the splendid textiles of the east.

A very characteristic feature of Islamic art is the use of Arabic writing as a form of decoration, whether in buildings, or for textiles, metal work or pottery. The beautiful Arabic script, with its aligned letters of varying height and thickness, formed an admirable banded ornament: while even a few letters could be combined in a pleasant decoration and applied again and again. In the later Islamic mosques and madrasa's, bands of Kufic writing ran in a continuous ornament just where the walls passed into the spring of the dome chamber, binding together walls and dome. In the Fatimid period similar bands of writing were used on the external façade of the great mosque in Cairo. Within the mosques, Arabic writing of the word of Allah adorned the *mihrab*, which was sometimes faced with lustre tiles: the unalterable word of Allah stood out in flat, dark blue against the shining tile (see Farris, *Heritage*). A heavy band of lettering often formed the sole and sufficient ornament to the glazed pottery plates and was inlaid on the bronze vessels.

Another feature of Islamic art springs from its association with the desert. The object ornamented must be such as could be carried on horse or camel back; jewellery and fine metal plate found no place in early Meccan life, and were forbidden to the good Muslim. The craftsman therefore expended his skill on pottery and textiles. The use of very fine design for the adornment of a coarse material is characteristic of Islamic art. In spite of the early Islamic disapproval of luxury and rich materials, however, fine craftsmanship and beautiful design were soon shown in Islamic metal-work and carvings in wood, ivory, rock-crystal, etc.

Eventually the most important contribution of Islam to European civilization was her transmission of Greek and Indian learning, particularly that of the 'Arabic' (early Indian) numerals, which are the basis of all modern calculation. Islam at Baghdad under the Abbasids was a clearing house for Greek, Persian, Syrian, Chaldean and Indian learning, and Arabic the medium of translation of the works of scholars of all these earlier civilizations. In the realm of thought Islam was a carrier, a transmitter, as much as in the realm of trade or art. She used the logic and the science of Aristotle, she gave Europe the numerals of India; and she gave her the Chaldean notions of magic and astrology. If Shakespeare wrote: 'It is the stars, the stars above us, govern our conditions,' the Arabs taught him so.

As to the Arab transmission of Greek learning: it was there awaiting them in the kingdom of the Sassanids. In Justinian's reign, an interest in natural science had flowered again in medicine and mathematics; Aetios of Amida, Paulus of Aegina and Alexander of Tralles investigated too the principles of conics and built ingenious machinery. Alexandria was a centre of Greek culture, and Byzantium now and later had commentators on Aristotle who, in their own line, surpassed the learning of Isidore, Bede or Scotus Erigena in western Europe. Greek learning in Persia met the alien cultures of Persia, Syria and India; the Ptolemaic concept of the universe met the tradition of Babylonian star-worship at Harran, and with it, probably, Babylonian mathematics and astronomy. Harran was the stronghold of the heathen Syrians, and so continued till the thirteenth century: it was also a stronghold of Hellenism and mathematics.

Greek knowledge spread to Mesopotamia and Persia in the fifth century in the wake of religious controversy. The Nestorians were expelled from Constantinople in 431 and fled to Edessa. The now famous schools of Edessa were closed by Zeno in 489, and the Nestorians then migrated to Nisibis in Mesopotamia, and, in the early sixth century, to the Persian medical schools of Jundi-Shapur. Syriac, a Semitic tongue, had long been a literary language, and from the sixth century translations made from Greek treatises passed from Jundi-Shapur into Persia.

When the Umayyad caliphs ruled Persia (661–750), Islam was still intolerant and suspicious of foreign thought: but the Abbasids at Baghdad, especially Mansur and Harun ar-Rashid, and above all Ma'mun, encouraged a revival of learning and its absorption by

Arab scholars. During the years 750–850 the works of Greek authors were found and translated through the agency of Nestorian and Monophysite Christians in Iraq. The works of Galen, Aristotle and Porphyry were already translated into Syriac, and at the schools of Jundi-Shapur three cultures had already met: Jewish-Persian, Syriac-Greek, and Indian. The Monophysite bishop, Georgios, had already translated Aristotle's logical works before 724; Severos Sebokht of Nisibis translated the *Analytics* and wrote on geometry, arithmetic and astronomy; he had already encountered Indian numerals, and helped transfer to the Arabs some knowledge of both Indian and Greek mathematics.

It was the Abbasids, however, who ordered and paid for the methodical collection of Greek and Syrian manuscripts and their translation into Arabic. Mansur invited Nestorian physicians to Baghdad, encouraged them to live there, and to teach and train students; he was the patron of those who translated philosophical and scientific works from Greek, Syriac and Persian into Arabic. But the work of translation was even further encouraged by the caliph Ma'mun (d. 833). Amongst the scholars he collected was the Nestorian Syrian druggist, Hunain bin Isha (809–877), Latinized as Johannitius, who had studied medicine at Jundi-Shapur, learned Greek, learned Arabic at the schools of Basra, learned Persian, entered the service of the physician to the caliph, and finally become superintendent to the great library, collection of manuscripts and school, known as the 'House of Wisdom'. With a staff of translators, he translated great numbers of Syriac, Greek and other manuscripts into Arabic.

The whole work of translation and the dissemination of learning under the Abbasids, as indeed their centralized administration dependent on written orders, was made possible by the new use of paper. This was a much cheaper writing material than parchment, and tougher and more lasting than the old papyrus. Paper was apparently first made in China in the first century B.C. In A.D. 751 the Arabs won a victory over some Chinese forces east of the Sir Darya, on the slopes of the Tien Shan mountains, and captured some Chinese paper makers; under Harun ar-Rashid the craft of paper making was introduced into Iraq and spread rapidly through the Islamic world (Bernard Lewis). By the tenth century, paper was made in Iraq, Syria, Egypt, Arabia, Morocco and, rather later, even at Valencia in Spain: the raw material (rag) was not limited, as with papyrus, to the Nile valley.

Perhaps most notable in the content of Abbasid learning were the mathematical disciplines, absorbed through translations from

India and the Far East. Greco-Roman learning had dealt with 'number' (see p. 87), but without the zero: and with space by means of Euclidean geometry. Indian and Chinese mathematics had meanwhile evolved a system of numerals using the zero, and a science of measurement alternative to geometry in 'algebra'. The first Arabic knowledge of these disciplines seems to have come when an unknown Hindu astronomer came to Baghdad in 772, and brought with him two treatises on mathematics and astronomy. That on astronomy was the early Hindu treatise, the *Siddhanta*, and it was translated by the Persian scholar al-Fazari (d. *c.* 777) under the Arabic title *Sindhind*. The treatise was of twofold importance, for it became fundamental to Arab astronomy, and it introduced the Hindu numerals into Arabic: later, they became known in the west as 'Arabic numerals'. To a Europe using only the Roman numerals, with which simple addition, subtraction, multiplication and division were impossible by written reckoning, the Arabic-Indian use of nine numerals and the zero made possible a revolution in mathematics. Al-Fazari moreover was the first Muslim to construct an astrolabe on the Greek model: both sciences were known to him. The actual transmission of the Arabic-Indian numerals to the west was made through the works of al-Khwarizmi (d. *c.* 850), whose name became in the west the word 'algorism'; the Arabic title of his treatise (meaning *Restoration and Equation* and beginning *al-jabr*) gave us the word *algebra*. This treatise, more than any other Arabic book on mathematics, influenced western thought, though tardily; it was translated by the Englishman, Robert of Chester *c.* 1140, and it was used by Leonardo of Pisa (d. *c.* 1240) and Master Jacob of Florence; the latter's Italian treatise, of 1307, comprises the six types of quadratic equations used by Muslim scholars.

The length of time which elapsed before Arabic numerals reached the west, and the length of time after that before they came into common use, is remarkable. Leonardo Fibonacci in 1202 published in Italy the first book to use the symbols; he had had an Arab master and travelled in north Africa. Italy had Arab colonies in the south in Frederick II's time, and it is not surprising that the numerals should have first obtained a limited use there; they were never in general use in western Europe throughout the middle ages. It should be remembered, however, that Arabic is a difficult language, and Arabs more difficult for Latin scholars to procure as teachers than Jews or Syrians, from whom they could learn Hebrew or Greek; and further, that accounting in western Europe was not merely a matter of book-keeping among the instructed, but of

8

demonstration to the illiterate. The English exchequer table was an abacus to demonstrate to illiterate sheriffs what they owed the king; the notched tally demonstrated at Michaelmas how much they still owed from the earlier session. Even today, the baker in southern France splits a wooden tally with his customer, and putting the two together, his customer watching, makes a cut for every loaf he delivers: there can be no dispute. Similarly, in the middle ages where there was so great a gap between the scholar and the illiterate mass of the population, the adoption of Arabic numerals was incredibly slow, because it lacked the spur of wide, general usefulness. Every accounting was a process of demonstration; the manorial steward, when owed wagon-loads of hay or grain for his lord's court yard, cut notches in a gate post as they were delivered; and royal officials used the abacus, the casting counter and the tally. Meanwhile, in medieval libraries, as evidenced by surviving catalogues, books on algorisms were relatively infrequent and rested beside treatises on hermeneutics, or magic; the position of both pointed to their Arab provenance, for algorism, algebra, astronomy and the science of horoscopes were subjects one and all transmitted in Arabic from Jundi-Shapur, Baghdad and Harran.

As to the Arabs' concept of the physical universe: they absorbed Greek philosophy, embracing as it did a Ptolemaic universe, and an Aristotelianism coloured by the Neoplatonic ideas current in Syria and Persia. One school of Muslim thought accepted, between the one God and the human soul, a ladder of cosmic intelligences inhabiting each of the heavenly spheres down to the lowest, the sphere of the moon. In this lowest sphere there dwelt the one active intellect common to all individual souls, which share in it: with this intellect it is possible to attain a mystical union. It is remarkable that, when the Arab-translated treatises of Aristotle came back to Europe, scholars such as Albertus Magnus and Aquinas should have discarded these Arabic additions and come near to the thought of Aristotle himself.

Arab alchemy similarly was founded on the Aristotelian theory of the elementary composition of matter, and other Greek chemical ideas, but was much coloured by Neoplatonic notions of 'emanation'. There seems to have been a secret sect of natural philosophers or alchemists, who took the title of 'Brethren of Purity'; the first considerable writer on the subject was a somewhat legendary figure, reputed to be a pupil of the Shi'ite *imam*, Jabir ibn-Hayyan (d. 760). Arab alchemy too penetrated to the west.

It may be convenient to recapitulate here the chief landmarks in the astonishing rise and conquests of Islam.

622 July 16   The Hijra, or flight of Muhammad from Mecca to Yathrib or Medina.

632   The death of Muhammad, and the succession of ABU-BAKR as his caliph, or deputy: he ruled at first only the Hijaz, or coastal strip of Arabia by the Red Sea, including Mecca and Medina.
               But he conquered Arabia, al-Hirah and Palestine.

634   The caliphate of ʿUMAR who conquered Persia,

635   conquered Damascus,

636   defeated the Byzantines at Yarmuk

637–8   gained Jerusalem, Aleppo, Antioch, Caesarea and all Syria by 640.

639–42   The Arabs conquered Egypt and Alexandria.

644   ʿUTHMAN succeeded ʿUmar:
               By 650, the Arabs had gained Tripoli: north Africa to the great, waterless gulf of the Syrtes (a notable barrier even in the last war: this was only passed when the Arabs acquired a great fleet).

650   The Arabs occupied Cyprus and reached Crete.

656   ʿALI became fourth caliph: first ruled from Medina, then Kufa: was murdered in 661; was the last of the four 'orthodox' or elective caliphs.

661   MUʿAWIYA founded the UMAYYAD, the second, and hereditary caliphate: the importance of the northern conquests had made Medina no longer suitable as a capital: Kufa in Iraq and Damascus in Syria were rivals as sites of the capital; Muʿawiya was proclaimed caliph at Jerusalem, but adopted Damascus as his capital, where the Umayyads ruled till 750.

670   The Arabs appeared before Constantinople: threatened it intermittently: departed in 677. In Africa, Sidi ʿUqba conquered the Berbers beyond the Syrtes, founded Qairawan (south of Tunis and Carthage), traversed north Africa and rode his horse into the waters of the Atlantic; the Berbers proved hard to subdue.

695   The Arabs took Carthage.

711   The battle of Jerez de la Frontera and Arab conquest of Spain. (Spain and north-west Africa, the Maghreb, were now ruled nominally from Qairawan and were ultimately under the caliph: but Spanish sub-rulers at Cordoba were almost independent.)

717   The last Arab attempt on Constantinople failed.

732   The battle of Tours: the Franks ended the advance of Islam in Europe.

750   The Umayyad caliphate at Damascus was succeeded by the Abbasid (750–1258), which transferred the capital to Baghdad in 762. Meanwhile, in Qairawan, a usurper, ʿAbd ar-Rahman, made himself practically independent of the last Umayyad caliph, and another ʿAbd ar-Rahman, fighting in Spain, became the founder of the western caliphate.

909   The Fatimid caliphate founded in Tunisia.

In assessing the importance of the Arab conquests of the seventh century for modern life, it should not be forgotten that the Arab contribution to mathematical science and the Arab transmissions of the culture of old Persia to Europe were balanced by certain losses. In the Hellenistic east, Greco-Roman culture was permanently eclipsed; in Palestine and Syria 'churches were replaced by mosques, and Greek gave way to Arabic as the *lingua franca* of the caliph's dominions' (W. H. C. Frend). More important still, north Africa in the eighth century was gradually converted from 'a mainly agricultural and Latin-speaking territory to a desert corridor binding Cairo with Cordoba, dominated by Muslim nomads'. Islam sprang from the desert, and in Africa showed herself as ready to control and perpetuate desert life as to change it.

BIBLIOGRAPHICAL NOTE

For an excellent short account of Islam, see B. Lewis's *The Arabs in History*, 1950; for the standard, fuller, account (with descriptions of Arab science and institutions, as well as the political history), P. K. Hitti, *History of the Arabs*, 1949, and the shorter *Mohammedanism* by H. A. R. Gibb, in the H.U.L. A set of illuminating essays by different Arabic scholars, edited by N. A. Faris, called *The Arab Heritage*, was published in 1946 by the Princeton Univ. Press. See also G. E. von Grünebaum, *Medieval Islam*, Chicago Univ. Press, 1945; G. Marçais' *La Berberie Musulmane et l'orient au moyen âge*, 1946; De L. O'Leary's *How Greek Science passed to the Arabs*, 1949; A. Mieli's *La science Arabe*, 1939; F. Sherwood Taylor's 'The Moslem Carriers', in *The Root of Europe*, ed. M. Huxley, p. 44; H. I. Bell, *Egypt from Alexander the Great to the Arab Conquest*, 1948. See also, L. O'Leary, *How Greek Science passed to the Arabs*, London, 1949.

CHAPTER XII

THE EASTERN EMPIRE FROM JUSTINIAN
TO THE ICONOCLASTS: THE HERACLIANS

THE successors of Justinian had to face tasks of great difficulty: above all, that of combining under a single rule the
two halves of the empire. The oriental provinces, in the
matter of culture and society, belonged more to Asia than to
Europe, in spite of their Greco-Roman government and their
Christian faith, and after the Arab onslaught they were to be swept
again under Asiatic rule. But on Justinian's death in 565 the
Asiatic danger still came from Persia.

Justinian's successors were left to deal with a heavily taxed
empire, an uncertain defence against the Persians and the objec-
tions of the east to Chalcedon. Justin II (565–578), who had
married the niece of Theodora, appears to have been mentally
unstable, but he put an end to short-term borrowing by the court,
a measure helpful to the imperial treasury, and was bold enough in
572 to refuse subsidies to Persia, preferring to incur the certainty
of border warfare. He was succeeded by the emperors Tiberius
(578–582) and Maurice (582–602), both of whom ruled with
discretion. Tiberius acquired a reputation for generosity, but
Maurice an evil name for avarice, through his policy of economy,
and that though he was a good soldier, well-educated and charit-
able to the poor.

In the task of imperial defence, Justinian had thrown his
greatest effort into the recovery of the west, and had to content
himself in the east by fighting two frontier wars with Persia,
and regaining control of Lazica. This district, to the eastern end
of the Black Sea, was of moment for military reasons as well as
those of trade, was much desired by Persia, and had recently been
under her control. Otherwise, Justinian's frontier policy was that
of fortifying the *limes* and distributing presents in gold that were
really tribute to the border tribes, and to the kingdom of Persia.

Tiberius and Maurice, however, maintained a passive defence
in the west and, on the other hand, took up the task of active
military defence in the east. They stopped the tributes and sought
to acquire military supremacy in Armenia and the Caucasus: their
aim was to make these hill countries their own recruiting grounds
rather than those of Persia.

The need of defending the eastern frontier in the seventh century led both to a reorganization of the army and, eventually, to a change in provincial government. In Justinian's day, though the general obligation to military service still remained in force, the main strength of the army lay in mercenary troops (*bucellarii*) and federates; many of the former were barbarians, voluntarily enlisted, while the federate bands fought under their own leaders. The penetration of the Balkans by Avars and Slavs, however, made it increasingly difficult for Justinian's successors to obtain mercenaries, and the army with which Maurice fought was raised mainly by conscription. He began the practice of settling his troops in the provinces most threatened by the Persians,[1] notably in Asia Minor: he settled a large army group, a 'theme' in a district, and gave to its general, the *strategos*, both military and civil command. Asia Minor had the three themes of the Anatolikon, the Opsikion and the Armeniakon. Later, the themes were subdivided according to their military composition, and became units of local government; the other provinces of the empire were also eventually reorganized as themes. The change was of considerable social importance, for the soldier in the recruiting province was a small peasant farmer who held his land on condition of military service. Eastern 'feudalism' differed however from the later form in the west, in that the *strategos*, as imperial commander, dealt directly with the peasant. The measure helped to inaugurate and protect a healthy rural society of small-holders, and though the great landowners ceaselessly sought to increase their estates at the expense of the peasants, it was to the government's interest to protect them.

Maurice's attempt to deal with the problem of recruiting was proved vital in the fifty years war with Persia which began in 570 and was to end with the victories of Heraclius. Maurice's most notable early campaign he led himself as *strategos autocrator* under Tiberius. Chosroes invaded Roman Armenia in 578, and Maurice drove him and his Persians back to Lake Van, and in 581 saved Edessa by another victory. When emperor himself, he had the double task of safeguarding the eastern and the Danube frontier, now threatened by Lombards, Gepids and Avars. In the east, a disputed succession gave him the opportunity of success even after a mutiny of the Roman army in 588, due to a reduction of military pay. A Persian chief, Bahraam, rebelled against the claim of Chosroes II to succeed Chosroes I and started a civil war in Persia: Chosroes II fled for refuge to east Rome, was restored by

[1] See Wilhelm Ensslin on the themes, in *Byzantium*, pp. 297–304.

a Roman army, and ceded to Rome, as a price for the recovery of
his kingdom, the fortresses of Dara and Martyropolis. This was
a notable strengthening of the Roman frontier in Armenia.

Maurice's success in the east was balanced by misfortunes
in the west. The Gepids had established themselves as a strong
tribal state in the great southern bend of the Danube, with the
Lombards to the west of them, and the Avars between the Theiss
and the Danube. It would have been wise to treat them as federates
and use them to check the Lombards and Avars: but they had
taken Sirmium (Mitrovica, Yugoslavia) and Justin II had desired
its recapture. After negotiating and failing to bring about its
return, he had allowed the Lombards and Avars to conquer
the Gepid lands. The Avars proved more dangerous than the
Gepids: they took Sirmium, claimed east Roman tribute and
ravaged Dalmatia and Thrace. As akin to the Huns and near-
nomads they commanded great stores of horses and proved brutal
and dangerous raiders. At the same time, the Lombards, who had
shared the destruction of the Gepids, were prevented from settling
there by the Avars, and pushed on towards Italy. In 568, while
the imperial army was engaged with the Avars, the Lombard
people migrated, as once the Ostrogoths had done, to Italy. There
were no imperial troops there to stop them, and only local troops
and the garrisons of a few great towns held out. Nevertheless, their
progress was slow, and Maurice did not at first fear the loss of
Italy or a permanent Lombard settlement there. He could not
however spare an army to drive them out: he was fighting too
hard against the Avars and in Persia. He could only entrust the
defence of the west to new officers, the exarchs of Africa and of
Italy, giving them civil and military powers to act as vice-emperors
in his stead. He also negotiated an alliance with the Franks of
Austrasia, by which they promised to attack the Lombards: there
were five Frankish expeditions to Italy between 584 and 591, but
none with decisive results. Nevertheless, the policy of Maurice,
and the efforts of the Italian cities themselves, prevented the
Lombards from gaining the whole of Italy: that the Lombard
kingdom in the north never gained effective control of the separate
Lombard duchies may be ascribed to the efforts of Maurice and
his successors.

None the less, the not unsuccessful work of the dynasty of
Justinian and Maurice himself, did not save it from an inglorious
end. As the winter of 602 approached, Maurice ordered the army
that had been fighting the Avars on the Danube to remain encamped beyond the river; the army mutinied, raised the rough

and brutal centurion, Phokas, on the shield, proclaimed him exarch, and marched on Constantinople. Maurice fled, Phokas was proclaimed emperor, and Maurice and his five sons were taken and executed.

The seventh century, beginning with the unfortunate reign of Phokas, saw the eastern empire in very grave danger: but also saw it survive the danger. Avars, Persians, Arabs seemed about to submerge *Romanitas* and the Greco-Roman state: the century was a prolonged crisis or day of judgment. To the east as well as the west it seemed that 'the day of the Lord, of the King all just, is at hand, a day of wrath and vengeance, of clouds and thick darkness': but in the end the judgment was favourable and the clouds passed. The empire lost its outlying provinces, was restricted to the east Balkans and Asia Minor, was further Grecized and half orientalized: but found within itself the moral strength to adapt its institutions to its changed circumstances, and to become the medieval state of Byzantium.

For eight years (602–610) Phokas ruled with the support of the inferior ranks of the Army, and the town mobs. Maurice's wish to prevent peaceable acceptance of the Lombards had made him unpopular in Italy and with Gregory the Great: to the latter, Phokas' orthodoxy and disinterest in Italy was highly acceptable. In his own capital however there were revolts, and after the second of these, in 603, Phokas put to death certain leaders and court dignitaries, together with Maurice's widow Constantina and all her daughters. In the provinces government subsided in anarchy: Jews and Christians, Monophysites and orthodox, fought in Syria what amounted to a civil war. In Antioch the Jews massacred the patriarch Anastasius; and across the eastern frontier the Persians under Shahrbaraz gathered their forces to take advantage of the undefended, leaderless empire.

But the generals who had fought with Maurice, the patriarch of Constantinople, whom Phokas had offended, and a number of state officials, looked for help to Heraclius, exarch of Africa, asking him to organize an expedition, seize Alexandria, and save the state. In 610 Heraclius, son of the exarch, brought a fleet to Constantinople, was welcomed and, as Phokas had fled, crowned by the patriarch.

Heraclius' coronation was too late to stop the invasion of the Persians. They took Antioch in 611, spread over Syria, taking Damascus in 613, and in May 614 they captured Jerusalem. They led its patriarch and its inhabitants into captivity, and, to the horror of Christendom, carried off the relic of the true cross, veneration for which had spread from one end of Europe to another in the preceding century: veneration that had inspired the *Vexilla regis prodeunt* of Fortunatus in Gaul, and covered remote Ireland with the early stone crosses. In 619 the Persians took from Heraclius Alexandria, Egypt and the future grain supply. They were ravaging Asia Minor and the Avars pressed down against Constantinople.

Heraclius prepared to regain the lost provinces and the lost treasure with valour and with prudence. He reorganized the army and the imperial finances, the patriarch Sergius aiding him: but all was subordinated to the future attack on Persia. His proclamation to the army represented the future expedition as a holy war, indeed, in one sense, as a first crusade, and by 622 his long preparations were complete. After religious ceremonies imploring a Christian victory over the Persian fire worshippers, Heraclius embarked for Asia Minor, which he liberated from Shahrbaraz, and sought to pass through Armenia to strike at the heart of Persia; he won a victory over Chosroes' generals in the neighbourhood of Lake Van, and one over Shahrbaraz himself. The climax of the campaign came in 626, while Avars and Bulgars were besieging Constantinople.

To leave the capital in face of dangers from these barbarians had been indeed bold. There was a Persian army at Chalcedon, just across the Straits, and the Avar khagan, with his Slav and Bulgarian contingents, concerted with the Persians a double attack. The city was saved by the inspiring leadership of the patriarch Sergius, the prayers and processions of the citizens imploring the help of the holy Mother of God, the city's protectress, and the presence of the Byzantine fleet in the Straits.

In 627 too Heraclius, fighting on the Perso-Armenian border, was enabled to press on into the Persian motherland. He won a victory at Mosul, but could not reach Ctesiphon the capital before winter. In the spring however news came of the collapse of the Sassanids: the Great King was murdered in a palace revolution. His successor made peace, restored Roman Armenia, Egypt, Syria and Asia Minor to the empire in a peace treaty, and allowed the True Cross to be restored to Jerusalem. Holy Cross Day, 14 September, is the liturgical commemoration of 'the Lord's holy cross, found by Helena on Mount Calvary, borne thence by Chosroes king of Persia, and received again by the emperor Heraclius after three victories in Persia'.

The first and glorious period of Heraclius' reign was marked not only by the salvation of the capital and the victory in Persia, but by an effort to reform the empire as important as either. In

view of the ills brought on the empire by the army's elevation of
Phokas to the throne, Heraclius sought to found a dynasty,
associating his two sons with himself from their birth, and giving
office to his brothers and cousins. His second marriage to his niece
Martina in 614 was however disallowed by the canons and caused
difficulty with the patriarch. For strategic reasons, Heraclius considered taking up his residence, at least for a time, in Carthage
where his father had been exarch: but the alarm of the citizens
of Constantinople, and the distance of Carthage from Persia, made
him give up the scheme. That he entertained it at all shows that,
while forced to give up Maurice's hope of regaining Italy, he did
so reluctantly. His measures to raise funds, to restore order, and
above all to create and himself train an army which he could use
against Persia were also notable.

But while the age-old empire of Persia was brought by his
efforts to crashing defeat, away on the Arabian coast of the Red
Sea a new power was rising (see p. 197). When Heraclius was in
622 preparing to lead his army to Persia, Muhammad with a few
followers fled from Mecca to Medina. Heraclius lived till 641:
and before then, in 634, Arab forces had entered Palestine,
routed the soldiery hastily employed by Sergius, governor of
Caesarea, and defeated and killed him. They took Jerusalem in
637 and the caliph 'Umar entered in 638. By 639 the Arabs had
taken Antioch, Edessa, Roman Mesopotamia and penetrated
Egypt. Wasted by illness, Heraclius could only remain inactive
at Constantinople. In contrast to the toilsome years he had once
spent training his army, he had hoped to promote union and
loyalty in Syria, and in Armenia, by conciliating the Jacobites
(the followers of the Monophysite leader, Jacobus Baradaeus
(d. 578)). The religious prestige which he had gained by restoring
the True Cross seemed to promise success to his efforts at conciliation: he and the patriarch Sergius strove to render the doctrine
of the Two Natures acceptable by affirming that in Christ there
was but one 'energy'. The teaching was developed in a doctrinal
statement, the *Ekthesis*, of 638: the human will in Christ was
declared to be so in harmony with the divine will, that He had, in
fact, but one will, and that divine. This *monothelite* doctrine did
nothing to unite Christendom against Islam, for it failed to conciliate the Monophysites, enraged the orthodox, caused strife between Rome and Constantinople, and even led to a pope falling
a prey to heresy (see p. 258).

The Arab invasion followed no systematic plan: its success
was conditioned, no doubt, by the explosive force of a new religion,

but above all by the weakness of the resistance encountered by the raiders. Egypt was a province vital strategically to the empire, and vital also to its revenue and food supply: and its conquest by the Arabs, the unpremeditated result sequence to a raid, took less than three years (December 639–July 642). Away iñ Constantinople, Heraclius was dying, and seeking to provide for the succession; but his second wife Martina and her son Heracleonas were put to death by their rivals.

Constans II succeeded and ruled till 668: he could not halt the Arab advance through north Africa nor the gradual building up of an Arab fleet that took from Byzantium the mastery of the east Mediterranean. But his energetic campaigns in the Balkans secured that when the attack on Constantinople did come, there was no accompanying menace from the Slavs. Meanwhile, the Arab fleets raided Rhodes, Crete, Cos and the Syrian coasts, once even defeating Constans himself in a naval battle: but Constans in the Balkans was strong enough to take up his residence at times in Thessalonica and Athens, to visit pope Vitalian in Rome, to consider an effort to retake either Africa or the Lombard settlements in Italy (he took Benevento in 663). He even resided for five years in Syracuse: but in 668 he was murdered in his bath.

His son, Constantine IV, succeeded: and two years later, in 670, the amir Phandelas led the Arab fleet across the Straits for the attack on Constantinople. But he found the walls of Constantinople restored, and the citizens in possession of a military device just bought from a Syrian architect, Callinicus, the famous Greek fire. Burning naphtha, launched from tubes, was propelled through the air and would even burn on the surface of the water: and it gave the imperial fleet a decisive advantage. Between 672 and 677 the Arabs made an attack on the walls of Constantinople every spring, an attack fruitless and ending finally in a disastrous rout during a storm. The Arab leader Muʿawiya made a peace treaty with the empire for thirty years: a limit had been set to Arab penetration of the northern Mediterranean.

Constantine IV also defended the empire with some success (668–685). He aspired to share the military glories of Heraclius and to restore the empire like his great namesake. In addition, he called his wife Theodora, founded towns called by his own name, restored peace to the church by abandoning the policy of conciliating the eastern sects (whose provinces were now lost to the Arabs) and entering into friendly relations with popes Donus and Agatho. The oecumenical council of Constantinople of 680 restored peace to the church: it was held in the domed palace of the emperor (*in trullo*), presided over by him, and attended by envoys from pope Agatho. In this council, which ranks as the sixth and the last oecumenical, the doctrines of Chalcedon were reaffirmed and the teaching of the one nature, one energy and one will freshly condemned.

Justinian II (685–695: banished ten years and restored from 705 to 711) sought to strengthen the frontiers and to protect Constantinople by defending Thrace, the coast facing her across the Aegean sea: the Slavs and Bulgars (see p. 485) were by now settled in numbers in the Balkans and the country barbarized. To support an army and maintain order, he extended and regularized the organization of the themes, and protected the small, military landowner. Good relations with the papacy were hindered however by his claim that a new council, held in 692 to pass canons dealing with matters of ecclesiastical discipline, and attended only by Greek bishops, should be held oecumenical. The harshness and brutality of Justinian's ministers, and the eccentricities of Justinian himself, led in 695 to revolution: Leontius, the reconqueror of Armenia, was recognized as emperor for three years, and Tiberius III, the choice of the imperial fleet and army after the loss of Carthage to the Arabs, for seven. He too was unsuccessful against the Arabs, and Justinian II was restored to Constantinople by the help of a small Bulgarian force. He was taken and beheaded by revolutionaries in 711: and with him the dynasty of Heraclius ended. Three emperors elected in revolt ruled from 711 till 717: a period of near anarchy had persisted for twenty-two years, from the banishment of Justinian II.

The eastern empire then had from the days of Heraclius to the first fall of Justinian II fought a battle for its very existence. It had lost rich provinces to the Arabs. Its metropolitan lands, however, had defended themselves and barred the ingress of Islam to Europe: the defence of Constantinople in her two sieges were as important to European defence as Charles Martel's victory over the Saracens at Tours. The empire had built up for itself a new army and a new provincial government, and it was this reorganization that eventually held the Arabs and the Bulgars. The emperors led this new army personally in the field, their own position the stronger in the vicissitudes of the empire. In spite of the lost provinces, the Heraclian dynasty clung ever more firmly to the concept of Roman imperial rule as universal, and that though from the age of Heraclius Byzantium was a purely Greek state, using the very title *Basileus* for emperor. 'Heraclius was the creator of medieval Byzantium, whose political thought was

Roman, whose speech and culture Greek, whose faith Christian'
(Ostrogorsky).

But in this century Byzantium was as poor in literature and
the arts as her history was rich in heroic wars and creative political
reform. Byzantine life became precarious and its outlook other
worldly. The imperial titles used were no more the terse, geographical adjectives of conquest: Heraclius was now the 'Deliverer
of the holy land' and the 'Enlightener of the true faith': Justinian II,
the 'servant of God'. The clergy and the patriarch played great
parts in the life of the state, and that at a time of increasing
militarization. 'It was a land of fighters and a land of monks,'
writes Ostrogorsky; but, since armies feed on revenue, and the
Arabs never got the northern shores of the east Mediterranean, it
was also a land of merchants and foreign refugees.

CHAPTER XIII

THE GRECO-ROMAN AND CHRISTIAN HERITAGE

EARLY medieval Europe had many institutions common not only to all the new Germanic states, but to the eastern empire and new Balkan settlements as well; they were her common heritage from the Greco-Roman world and early Christianity. Certain of the most important factors in the transmission of the heritage have already been mentioned: it was scarcely possible to give any picture, however slight, of the Ostrogoths without Cassiodorus, the Franks without Gregory of Tours, or Justinian without his new body of Roman law. Roman learning was mainly transmitted by the Encyclopedists (see pp. 50, 22), till Carolingian monks set to work to copy the texts of the Latin classics. But apart from these great efforts of transmission, there were also the normal channels by which a civilization was passed on to and influenced the new Europe: schools and law courts: the craftsmen who wove silk or set enamel in cloisonné or built the new Christian churches: the bishops who instructed their young clerks and the people and the rulers who elected or appointed the bishops: the papacy whose claims were founded on the promise to St Peter and possession of the precious bodies of the apostles: and the papal curia which followed Byzantine precedent with Byzantine traditionalism.

In the west, the *scholae publicae* came to an end in Gaul in the fifth century, and in Italy after the Ostrogothic régime. The Roman empire had paid the salaries of rhetors who educated boys for the civil service without fee. They lectured on the seven liberal arts, the course on rhetoric including some teaching on Roman law and the exposition of legal formulae: they taught in some *schola*, or *cella*, a room rectangular or irregular in shape, or rectangular with a semi-circular end where the teacher sat. His pupils usually stood: the semi-circular end concentrated attention on the speaker, lending dignity and affording ease in hearing. When the empire in the west collapsed, rhetors in the Rhone valley continued to teach for a time, supporting themselves by fees. Sidonius Apollinaris, bishop of Clermont in Auvergne (d. 489), had the old classical learning, and wrote Latin verse full of mythical allusions: there were other bishops with the old learning in his day, but they were becoming few.

In Italy, where the language continued near enough to classical Latin to make the old literature easily intelligible, lay teachers continued to instruct for fees, certainly till the twelfth century: 'my education', said Benedict of Clusa 'cost my uncle two thousand shillings, which he paid to my masters . . . I indeed am thoroughly learned.' Elsewhere in Europe education after the sixth century became normally the affair of the clergy only: they taught and, in the large majority of cases, they were the pupils. Education was professional, a part of the training of the clergy, secular or regular.

As to the exceptions: in the pre-Carolingian period there were still a few merchants to whom the ability to write, to keep accounts in Latin, was a part of their trade, a skill acquired in their art itself, for there were no schools for traders or any references to lay boys attending schools for such a purpose. In agriculture, the reeves or peasant bailiffs kept their tallies of renders in their head, or made notches on gate posts; though in Sicily Gregory I's bailiffs or *conductores* could understand his many detailed letters of instruction. Among the upper classes, lay boys were sometimes sent for training and learning to some abbey, but this was always by arrangement with the abbot; the boy would usually be trained in deportment in the abbot's household, and his teaching by some individual monk might be arranged by his parent: he was not sent to some 'school' of lay boys maintained at the abbey. The Merovingian kings of Paris often sent their sons for education to Saint-Denis, and some sons of nobles were also educated there: but Saint-Denis was a royal abbey of old and anomalous structure, without St Benedict's reverence for enclosure and non-intercourse with seculars. Mentions of the Merovingian 'palace school' (*schola*) in saints' lives and monastic chronicles do not refer to any school at Saint-Denis; they may refer to instruction given by some bishop or notary of the royal household, but as often the *schola* is the palace guard itself. There were then, in the pre-Carolingian period, no 'schools' intended for laymen.

Yet knowledge of the seven liberal arts, and those other *artes* dealt with by Isidore of Seville, did not perish in Europe: it was preserved by a comparatively small scholar class among the clergy and by the grammarians of Italy: it was possible to revive the same system of education, to cover the same field of learning, in the Carolingian renaissance. The whole of a boy's education for an ecclesiastical career had now to be afforded by the church. The bishop in the days of Gregory of Tours received young boys for training in his *familia*: he gave them the 'first tonsure'. In this small ceremony, an old Roman adoption rite, he cut the boy's hair, repeating with him psalm 16, containing the words: 'the lot is fallen unto me in fair ground: yea, I have a goodly heritage'. The word for 'lot' is Greek (*kleros*) and the boy thus shorn and adopted became one of the clergy: if the rite had been less old, the word for clergy might have been derived from the Latin *sors*. The young clerk was now henceforth the bishop's son: and the bishop must feed, clothe and maintain him till his death: and, equally, the bishop could use him for any ecclesiastical work in his *familia*, his *civitas*, or his diocese. If the boy wished later to be ordained to holy orders and work in another see, he must obtain letters dimissory from his own bishop who, having trained him in the 'clerical servitude' had the right to his services.

The boy's education would include the alphabet, some Latin, enough for the reading of portions of scripture in church, and for the more advanced clerks, a knowledge of the *computus*, ability to understand the ecclesiastical tables that laid down ahead the date of Easter. A young clerk, too, must learn to sing (intone) those portions of the hours or the music of the mass allowed to him: by the time of Gregory of Tours the deacons sang the responsories (the most elaborate musical settings of the mass) and might be expected, on occasion, to show their skill by singing such responsories by royal command at a banquet. A clerk must be trained, that is, when there was as yet no single service book for the office or the eucharist, to follow the ecclesiastical *cursus* for the year, or even (when he had attained to being the senior deacon or presbyter of the *familia*) to prescribe it to the other clerks and ensure that the divine service was rightly performed. He learned to do this, both as regards singing and ceremonial, mainly by sharing in the service himself: but he was also instructed in so much of the old arts as were ancillary to the performance of the rite, and the understanding of scripture. Education was directed towards the *servitium divinum* and narrower in scope than under the pagan empire: but a wonderful liturgy grew up. The Roman church was conservative in her worship, suspicious of new forms in Gaul and northern Europe: but even she finally accepted such Frankish enrichments as the song of the deacon (the deacon, we may note) before the Easter candle: 'Let the crowd of angels rejoice . . . for so great a royal victory. Christ the victor has risen from the lower world. Nothing would it have profited us to be born, had we not profited by redemption . . . This is the night of which it is written: and the night shall be bright as the day.'

All this may go back to the Greek exultation at the Easter mystery, sung by the early Christians in the Rhone valley: and the exhortation to the mother bee who has made the wax for the candle ʾis Vergilian in spirit. Education in pre-Carolingian Gaul was narrow because the country was poor and there was little margin for a leisured class, that is, by definition, for scholars: but out of that selective education grew one of the great arts of the middle ages, the liturgy.

The pages of Gregory of Tours and the letters of the Frankish bishops contain many incidental references to bishops' schools. Bishop Remigius of Reims wrote to Falcon the bishop, upbraiding him for usurping the rights of the church of Reims in that of Mouzon in the Ardennes: Falcon has there (most irregularly) 'made deacons, consecrated presbyters, instituted archdeacons, given a primicery of the school to the militia of the lectors'. An abbot Floretus wrote that Caesarius of Arles, a good classical scholar, had himself instructed him 'in the Latin elements and the alphabet'. Desiderius of Vienne was rebuked by Gregory I for misusing his energies by giving lectures on Latin literature and reading the Latin poets with the young men of the city. Sulpicius of Bourges was second to none in knowledge of rhetoric and poetry. Venantius Fortunatus was an Italian scholar who settled in Gaul under the patronage of St Radegunde of Poitiers; he was made bishop and wrote Latin verses for his patroness. But his finest poems were naturally those written for use in the divine service: the hymns for the Easter procession and the veneration of the relic of the holy cross. Most bishops' schools, however, were not taught by a Desiderius or a Fortunatus.

In the British Isles, the contribution of the Celts to the preservation of classical learning is notable. Ireland, on the edge of Europe, had never received classical paganism and had never been settled by the Germanic barbarians: she was therefore never afraid of a living Greco-Roman paganism, and her minsters from the fifth to the seventh century were undisturbed by outside invasion. She was a fount and reservoir of classical learning, even while her society was still tribal and semi-migratory. Her missionaries preferred nothing to setting out upon the sea in an open boat, they knew not whither, for the love of God: but they often took a book or a roll in their scholar's satchel. The great names are those of Columba, who converted Scotland because of the trouble caused in Ireland by his copying a manuscript without its abbot owner's leave; Columbanus, who planted Celtic monasticism and learning all over western Europe, leaving St Gall and Bobbio to rival Monte Cassino; and Aldhelm, who was *eruditus* by Maeldubh of Malmesbury and Hadrian of Canterbury, wrote fine verse about thunder-storms, diplomas for royal benefactions to minsters in unusually learned and involved phraseology: and taught such scholars as came to him. 'Since I know well,' writes an unknown Scot to Aldhelm, 'that you are eminent in understanding and in Latin speech and the varied flower of letters, even Greek letters; I desire to learn from your own mouth.' He prays Aldhelm to receive and teach him: because many pilgrims and scholars come to him: because he has made the journey to Rome: because he has been brought up 'by a holy man of our own race'. He desires, he says, to read a certain book with the master and he should be able to accomplish in two weeks: not that he would not like to stay longer, but he fears an unlimited request might weary Aldhelm's mind. Education in Bede's day at Monkwearmouth had been fertilized by two traditions of scholarship: that of Celtic Latinity, transmitted through Lindisfarne, and the Greco-Latin learning transmitted by Theodore and Hadrian's school at Canterbury: and by the founder of the monastery himself. Benedict Biscop (d. 690) made six journeys to Gaul and Rome and brought back a large number of books in the panniers of his mule: among them the Vulgate text of the gospels used in the codex Amiatinus (see p. 50).

The fine flower of western scholarship in the early eighth century is represented by the work of Bede, and he acquired it in the library of Monkwearmouth-Jarrow, where he was a monk all his life, and at the hands of its early abbots, whose lives he wrote: as he did lives in prose and verse, of the Celtic saint, Cuthbert of Melrose and Lindisfarne. Since some account of a saint's life, good works and miracles was always read in the night office of his *natalicia*, the material for saints' lives was always available to early historians. Bede's *Ecclesiastical History of the English People*, modelled on Eusebius' *Ecclesiastical History* and like it careful to give the successions of bishops from the foundation of the see (see p. 168), is to us the fine flower of his work. It is marked by a persevering intellectual curiosity, a care to tell the reader the sources of his knowledge, the use of a new scale of chronology, the era of the incarnation, and a Latin clarity in narrative and sobriety of judgment. But to Bede's contemporaries and the scholars of the next generation, it was not the *Ecclesiastical History* but his commentaries on the various books of the Bible that made him a doctor of the church.

St Boniface (680–755) is perhaps the most outstanding figure in the spread of education in western Europe in this period, as Bede is in that of pure scholarship. He brought Christianity to the pagans of central Europe, beyond the Frankish borders, and wherever he planted his little churches, his monks and his nuns, he planted a school of the divine service and a school of Latin learning. He was born at Crediton in Devonshire about 680, and the Saxons of the countryside were still largely pagan, though his parents were Christian. (He wrote to the bishop of Winchester much later, exhorting him to convert the pagans of that see.) There was no church at Crediton: but before his father's house there was set up a large cross, by which Christian missionaries often marked a place where they preached; prayers were wont to be said at this cross in Boniface's childhood. Travelling priests sometimes came and preached there: and at five years of age little Winfrith (Boniface) decided he must be a monk. He was educated at the minster at Exeter and then at Nutcell or Nutshaling near Winchester. When he was thirty he was ordained presbyter, and in 716 he crossed the Channel, and henceforward gave himself to the conversion of the heathen in Frisia, Bavaria, Thuringia, Hesse and all central Europe, as well as to the reform of the Frankish church.

In 742–4 Boniface founded the monastery of Fulda, Sturm becoming the first abbot, and in 746 he set up his chair in the church of Mainz, to be the metropolitan see of Germany. In Fulda and his other monasteries a strict form of the Benedictine rule was observed, but with more emphasis than St Benedict had given to scholarship. Boniface was training not only good monks, but those who should be the future deacons, priests and bishops of the new German church. Till he, with Eobas, bishop of Dokkum and a company of fifty followers, were massacred by pagans at Dokkum on 5 June 755, he was ceaselessly preparing for the building up of a Christian society in Germany, looking in spiritual matters to St Peter and the see of Rome, and for secular protection to the king of the Franks. Shortly before his death Boniface wrote to Fulrad, abbot of Saint-Denis, asking him, as his own life might be drawing to a close, to commend his disciples to king Pepin. His pastoral anxiety shines through his words:

> Almost all of them are pilgrims, strangers to this land. Some are presbyters, duly appointed in many places for ministry to the people; some are monks in our various little cells and children ordained to learn letters; and there are some now old men, who have long lived and worked with me and been my helpers. I am anxious about all of them.

He desires that Lull, his *chorepiscopus* (assistant or suffragan bishop) shall succeed him: he desires the royal patronage for the newly converted lands; he is specially anxious about priests working 'near the march of the pagans': 'they can find bread to eat,' he writes, 'but their clothes they cannot find'.

Boniface's letters are a mine of information about his missions in Germany, and nearly all of them contain thanks for some book or present sent him, or a request for more books. Usually the abbot or abbess to whom Boniface wrote says in reply, either that he and his *pueri* have written the book Boniface asked for, or that he will try to get his *pueri* to write the book for him: in the largest number of cases, the books in question are certain commentaries of Bede. Boniface, in a letter to bishop Egbert of York, mentions an exchange of books and asks for a copy of Bede's commentaries. In another to Daniel, bishop of Winchester, he deplores the latter's blindness, says that his own sight too, is failing, and asks that a certain fine manuscript of the Prophets, clearly written by abbot Winberht of Nutcelling may be sent him: no such fine clear manuscripts are to be had in Germany. Boniface's relative Lioba, the young nun of Wimborne, sent him a small gift and some Latin verses she had composed: he asked her to come out and work for him in Germany. He wrote to Eadburg, abbess of Minster in Thanet, thanking her for her gift of holy books, and, in a later letter, asks her to add to this kindness by 'writing for me in gold the letters of my lord, St Peter the apostle, to the honour and reverence of holy scripture before the eyes of carnal men in my missionary work (*in praedicando:*) because his words sent me on my journey I desire ever to have them with me'. So may Eadburg's work 'shine in letters of gold to the glory of the heavenly Father'. Boniface desired to have, that is, a fine altar book, with the epistles of St Peter, and on certain purple pages the letters written in golden ink: it is such a book as Eddius the presbyter describes Wilfrid as bestowing on his church at Ripon, a *liber purpureus*.

In a letter to his monks at Fritzlar, written 735–7 just after their abbot's death, Boniface gives careful directions about the monks' respective posts, including the teaching of the young monks and children: Tatwine shall be abbot: and 'Let Wigberht the presbyter and Meginbotus the deacon teach them their rule and the spiritual hours and the *cursus* of the church, and admonish the rest and be masters of the children and preach the word of God to the brethren. Let Hiedde be provost and have charge of our serfs and let Hunfrith help him when there is need. Let Sturm be in the kitchen. Let Bernhard be the workman and build our little cells, where there is need. And inquire of Tatwinus the abbot about all things, where there is need, and whatever he bids you, do.' The letter opens a window on to Benedictine life in the eighth century.

The requests for copies of Bede go on. Egbert of York is thanked for the books he has sent Boniface: and asked to send him some of the works of Bede 'who lately, as we have heard, has been endowed by divine grace with spiritual understanding and shone on your province: that thus we also may enjoy, as it were, the light of the candle God has bestowed on you'. He has moreover, he says, sent to Egberht copies of the letters of St Gregory, 'which I have taken from the *scrinium* of the Roman church'. In a letter to abbot Watberht of Monkwearmouth-Jarrow, he again asks for the works of Bede the monk, 'that wisest researcher into holy scripture, who lately, as we have heard, has shone in the house of God like a candle'. Later, Cuthbert, abbot of Monkwearmouth, wrote sending Lull Bede's lives of St Cuthbert in prose and verse: he gently requests that if Lull have any good worker in glassware in his *parochia*, he will send him to him. Lull, himself, wrote home requesting the commentaries of Bede: and when he received Bede's *De Aedificio Templi* returned thanks, and requested yet more copies of the commentaries.

In the eastern empire, though there was more learning, there is less evidence about how it was imparted, and, in particular, about schools. The training here, however much Greco-Roman in tradition, was given purely in Greek. The literature and *artes* of the pagan empire were studied, and not through the veil of the Encyclopedists, and, as far as secular literature was read, it was Greek literature. The schools of, as we should say, 'university' standing survived in the east, whereas nothing quite like them survived in the west.

Education also necessarily had an orthodox foundation: children were grounded in Christian doctrine and the sacred scriptures first of all, in the home of their parents. Then came education by 'grammarians', who might give instruction in the 'sacred writings' as well as profane scriptures, and that at a very early age; or the child might be sent in his native place to learn 'orthography' at a school: the reading and spelling of classical Greek was already an academic study. Unless the boy entered a monastery or entered upon an active life, he would enter a university to acquire 'the higher learning' at about the age of twenty. The course here was 'classical', embracing rhetoric in all its branches, and philosophy, including not only the studies of the *quadrivium* but the philosophical systems of Plato, Aristotle and the Neo-Platonists, Plotinus and Proclus. All these secular studies were underlain by the primary training in the scriptures, and beyond them stretched theology, a separate field of learning. Teaching in this subject was confined to the monasteries, and to the patriarch's school at Constantinople. Neo-Platonism, as was natural, had far more influence in the east than in the west: the eastern monk who about A.D. 500 issued his works under the name of Dionysius the Areopagite defined the godhead by the negative method of the Neo-Platonists; his teaching about the contemplation of God spread, it is true, to the west, and his method appears in medieval writings, e.g. Eckhard's sermons and the English *Cloud of Unknowing*, but in the west they were the mysterious delight of the few. In the Greek east, Dionysius founded a school of thought, and the dispute over Hesychasm in the fourteenth century was partly a dispute between Latin, Aristotle-using theologians and the Greek followers of Dionysius and the Neoplatonists. The word Hesychasm (Hesychia) denotes solitude and contemplation, such as then used by Byzantine hermits and defended by Gregory Palamas and the monks of Mount Athos: the dispute over it concerned these half-Oriental methods of prayer, and the nature of the uncreated light on Mount Tabor. Latin theologians used Aristotelian logic and Thomist theology to oppose Hesychast teaching.

As an outstanding missionary, a counterpart of St Boniface, a word might be said about Theodore of Tarsus (*c.* 602–690). He was born at Tarsus in Asia Minor, and when he was selected for consecration to the see of Canterbury in 667 he was a monk, for he had the monastic tonsure: but he had attended the schools of Athens in his youth, from the age of twenty onwards: Boniface calls him *Greco-Romanus philosophus*. He lived in an age of theological controversy. While he was young, the emperor Heraclius had made an imperial effort to reconcile the east to the Christological position of Chalcedon, which the Monophysites and the Nestorians still regarded as dividing the nature of Christ: he desired especially to conciliate Armenia, now tending to Monophysitism out of opposition to Persia, her military enemy. Heraclius and Sergius, patriarch of Constantinople, put forward to the Armenian church a basis for union affirming in Christ a single 'energy': in 638 an imperial edict, the *Ekthesis*, spoke of Christ as having a single will, the Monothelite position. It was meant to be a new and better *Henotikon* (see p. 156) but it only succeeded in arousing the bitter opposition of the patriarch of Jerusalem, and of orthodox Chalcedonians in Rome and Constantinople. It was on the eve of the Arab Conquests, and Syria, Egypt and Armenia, the provinces whose loyalty it was hoped to win, were soon lost to the Arabs. The controversy over the nature of Christ was however the great theological interest of the orthodox throughout Theodore's youth and middle age; and he would have met many Syrian and Egyptian refugees, fleeing from the Arab invasions. It was this elderly Byzantine gentleman, this Greco-Roman philosopher, whom pope Vitalian consecrated to the see of Canterbury on 26 March 668.

The channel by which he was brought to the papal notice is of interest, as is the Byzantine character of his rule at Canterbury. The pope's choice lit first upon Hadrian, an African by birth and abbot of a monastery near Naples: Hadrian belonged, that is, to the Greco-Roman world of south Italy, to the Byzantine Mediterranean. He was no doubt selected because it was difficult to find an English candidate: there was still rivalry and suspicion between the semi-Celtic Christianity of Lindisfarne and the Latin Christianity of Canterbury, and, though the appointment of Wighard had been agreed upon by the kings Oswy of Northumbria and Ecgberht of Kent, yet Wighard had just died at Rome. On the other hand, appointment to a distant, missionary see does not seem to have been desired by any great ecclesiastic in Rome itself. Hadrian was a monk, as Augustine had been, and Vitalian offered him the see: but he could not be prevailed on to accept it. Did he know from the English companions of Wighard that a Latin monk would be unacceptable to the bretwalda in the north? More probably, he desired the monastic life, and knew himself unqualified by experience for the office of a chief pastor; he never accepted a bishopric later in England, though as the archbishop's chief helper he could doubtless have had one. He suggested in his stead the elderly Byzantine monk Theodore, who had been staying for three years in Rome: it is not known whether he had come on a Byzantine embassy, or whether he was there for devotion or scholarship: it was as an outstandingly good monk and scholar that Hadrian pressed for his appointment, which he obtained.

The Byzantine character of Theodore's rule is easily apparent. He is orthodox, and the young English church must be orthodox: he summons the English bishops (few enough in number) to the synod of Hertford to accept the canons of Nicaea and Chalcedon. Later, at the synod of Hatfield he secures for his own and papal satisfaction their explicit condemnation of Monothelitism, a heresy of but little topical interest to them, but a burning question in the east. Secondly, with an orthodox reverence for the *basileus*

transferred in some measure to the king of Northumbria, he seeks
to work with his approval and obtain from him landed endowments for his new sees: Wilfrid's frank hostility to the king of
Northumbria must have seemed to him almost incomprehensible.
Thirdly, he and Hadrian work for the education of the clergy:
the school at St Augustine's abbey and Theodore's own *familia*
becomes famous for its Greco-Roman learning. The English
church is built up on a territorial basis wherein a learned monasticism plays its due part. It is all very Byzantine and civilized:
Vitalian's appointment justifies itself.

Another heritage was passed on from, or by, the Greco-Roman
world to medieval Europe: the ornament, art-forms and the
techniques that helped to produce them in the different media,
stone, metals, textiles. The art and architecture of medieval
Europe grew out of an inheritance that was, indeed, only partly
Greco-Roman, for in the west the Celtic races made their own
contribution, and the Germanic races passed on the nomadic
art-forms of south Russia; while in the east Iranian influences
contributed their characteristic art-forms and architecture. The
Greco-Roman world had absorbed oriental influences even before
Constantine, and the East Roman empire continued to absorb them:
but it was the Hellenistic, Greco-Roman world that was central,
and that passed on style and techniques from beyond its eastern
frontiers to the Mediterranean and to the west. The most eastern
part of Alexander's empire was conquered by Islam: in 634 the
hard fighting and uncultivated Arabs conquered Persia and settled
down to perpetuate the Hellenistic culture under the sanctions
and prohibitions of the religion of the Prophet. Representations
of the human form were banned as idolatrous, but the east already
loved pattern and abstract ornament, and of this side of her art,
as of her characteristic architecture, there was an efflorescence
under Islam. Muslim art represents, with this modification, the
characteristic art of the successor-states of Alexander's empire;
Greco-Roman art persisted, somewhat under Persian influence,
in the East Roman empire, Italy, and the shores of the Mediterranean; and in the west Celts and Anglo-Saxons, having no advanced architecture of their own, moulded and carved trumpet
spirals and interlacing animals on their brooches and painted them
in their illuminations.

With regard to the history of ornament, it has been pointed
out that originality and association can be better traced in the
lesser features of a design than in the large and obvious aspects:
in the motifs or art-forms of a design, rather than in the whole

composition. Such motifs and art-forms belong to a nation or a civilization and are used by all its craftsmen; they are presupposed and appear in different media. Not only that, but they are passed on from one civilization or race to another: 'ornament is the international currency of art, a medium of exchange in style that commonly ignores all boundaries of region, race or time'.[1] The dragon motif came from China to Wales, and the 'Daniel in the Lions' den' motif was used in an east Mediterranean cult three centuries before Christ and in the ornament of the royal purse at Sutton Hoo: and, indeed, among the Franks and all over early Europe.

In a highly simplified treatment of a vast subject, it is possible to consider three motifs as characteristic of the three parent styles of medieval European art: the palmette, the allover pattern and the spiral. The palmette (or honeysuckle) pattern is a characteristically Greek creation, and is derived from nature: it is, in origin, the tuft of leaves at the top of a palm tree, stylized under a preference for axial symmetry: the leaves, or honeysuckle florets, spring from a point, are symmetrical, and fill a space broadly triangular. The design is self-sufficient and complete.

The allover pattern, on the other hand, came from Persia, was never found in Greek art, has indefinite extension (as often needed in textiles) and, in its simplest form, depended on the pleasant arrangement of simple units like rosettes on a plain ground. There is no axis, and the pattern is not merely an ornamental band, for it can be extended in both directions. It has unity and beauty, but it is that of rhythm and spacing. The allover pattern is characteristic of Islamic art.

The Celtic spiral pattern, used in the trumpet brooches, torcs and illumination, unlike the allover pattern, has a central point, but, like it, is capable of indefinite extension, from the centre outwards. (It was not, however, used to cover large surfaces, like the allover pattern.) Its beauty and interest lies in its specific point of origin or centre, from which the whole pattern whirls and grows: it has been characterized by Professor Morey as 'dynamic'.

These, and numberless other motifs, are useful as criteria in judging the pedigree of the various monuments and beautiful objects of early medieval Europe, because they are found both as ornament on great buildings and monumental sculptures, like those in the Byzantine empire, and also on the jewellery, weapons, ivories and manuscripts of lands that could raise no great stone

[1] See *Medieval Art*, by Professor C. R. Morey, New York, 1942, pp. 7 seqq.

buildings. They were transferred across continents and from one medium to another. The simple, safety-pin brooch from Kerch (south Russia) gave rise to the great square-headed, cruciform and radiate brooches of the Anglo-Saxons, Franks, Visigoths and Lombards; the large, round jewelled brooch, that fastened the *chlamys* of the Greco-Roman emperor, empress or magistrate on the right shoulder, giving the right arm freedom of movement, was copied by the Germanic barbarians, used on both shoulders, and was remotely the ancestor of the Kingston or Faversham brooches. Emperors and popes sent silken vestments of honour, with woven or embroidered figure designs: and though, from the perishable nature of the material, few such textiles have survived from the early middle ages, yet some have, and the sending of others is recorded; they must have been a vehicle for the transmission of art-forms. Early illuminated altar books inspired not only other illuminations in the land of the recipient, but, sometimes figure designs in ivory, or even stone. The late Professor Saxl believed that the sudden arising of a notable school of stone carving in seventh-century Northumbria, of which the grave and splendid figures on the Bewcastle cross were a fruit, was due to the reception of Italian altar books from Italy, in the Byzantine style there current. He suggested that it was the manuscript illuminator who painted the figures on the shaft of the cross in outline and the stone carver, previously unversed in figure sculpture, who did the novel work, with the illumination to guide him.

Christianity, in short, was a great transmitter of art-forms from the east to west. She borrowed the shapes of her early churches mainly from the east (see *infra*); she spread the monasticism of Egypt as far west as Ireland, and with it, possibly, certain art-forms like the *tau* cross for the crozier, and the intricate plait-work of Celtic designs; plait-work that brings to mind the basket making by which the Egyptian monk earned a living, if he did not live on alms; she spread the sign of the cross through Europe. Galla Placidia's tomb house in Ravenna is cruciform in plan, as were many sixth- and seventh-century churches; and the erection of standing crosses, *signa crucis*, in wood or stone, became relatively common. *Signa crucis* were erected at every stage of the carrying of Germanus' body back from Ravenna to Auxerre for burial, crosses were traced on the slabs commemorating the dead built into walls, and standing memorial crosses were erected. In Ireland, the pagan pillar stones became pyramidal shafts for a small, Greek cross at the summit, and in Britain the use of such stone crosses spread. There were two crosses, one large, one small, at the head and foot of the grave of bishop Acca of Durham, and the Ruthwell and Bewcastle crosses are monuments of the eighth-century renaissance in Northumbria, and beautiful beyond others: but fragments of many others remain. Two great crosses near the church at Glastonbury remained till the middle of the nineteenth century, when they were casually disposed of.

Not only was the stone cross used to bless the place of a burial, but to lift, as it were, out of paganism the places where missionaries preached and baptized: the cross was a kind of permanent exorcism and blessing. Boniface used such crosses in his conversion of Germany, and it would seem that where he erected a cross he might expect later to build a church. He wrote a long letter on 4 November 751 to pope Zacharias, asking him *inter alia* to license the setting up of such crosses at special points; the pope wrote in answer 'you have asked us, O most holy brother, what crosses ought to be set up locally in your holy mission (*in sancti canonis praedicatione*)': he had laid down the licensed places in the roll given to Lull the presbyter, Boniface's envoy.

The question of the origin of Christian art-forms has been long debated, though it is accepted that, since Christianity arose in the east, the origin of her art-forms must be looked for in the Hellenistic art of the eastern provinces. Evidence about very early art-forms is necessarily scanty, for the early Christians had an eschatological outlook, distrusted the world of sense, and held the second commandment to forbid representations of its sacred personages. The historian Eusebius assured Constantia, sister of Constantine, his patron, not only that no authentic portraits of Christ had survived, but that it was unlawful to make representations of him, or of his apostles. Moreover, the mere length of time since the earliest days of Christianity has rendered the survival of the very earliest Christian cult objects, or illuminations on papyri unlikely: rich cult objects were subject to looting, and papyrus is all too perishable. Though it has been suspected that the two great Christian schools of Antioch and Alexandria, with their different types of dogmatic teaching, were *foci* also for the spread of two different types of Christian art, the remains from both cities are extremely scanty. There is very little geographical evidence for attaching the names Antioch and Alexandria to the two styles, examples of which occur all over the near east and round the Mediterranean.

It is true, however, that there were two different types of Christian art, and that they go back to two different styles of Hellenistic art: the Attic. and the post-Alexandrian or realistic style. The Attic style had as its examples the classical Greek statuary of Pheidias, Polycleitus, etc., with its typical serene and timeless figure, and its organized, finite treatment of space. Such figures were given no background and they betrayed no struggle, no emotion. The figures on the frieze of the Parthenon, the Attic marbles, move gently forward in the clear, serene air of Greece. The Attic style has been said to express man as master of his circumstances. Intrusion of the outside world, awareness of the background, came with the sculpture of Praxiteles and Scopas: the winged Victories came to express movement through space. But in the period before Alexander, there was still the Attic peace and confidence.

With the post-Alexandrian style, coincident with the fall of the city state, came to the Greeks what has been called 'a loss of nerve', in literature as well as art. The circumstances of man's life became too much for him: the background breaks in upon human serenity, and the Hellenistic sculptor begins to portray scenes of struggle. In the 'school of Pergamum', of which the struggling group, the Laocoon, is an example, actuality is aimed at, not the peace of the gods. Realism, impressionism, begins.

Both these Greek styles survived in the Hellenistic Christian world, the conservative portrayal of the figure without background known as the Neo-Attic style, the realistic and impressionistic style as the Alexandrian. Hence, from the two divergent styles in pagan Hellenistic art, the one two-dimensional, and the other three-dimensional and associated with Alexandria, arose the two styles of early Christian art: and on both of them alien influences imposed modifications.

On the Neo-Attic figures and illuminations (pictures in manuscripts), the influence of Sassanid Persia stressed the immobility and majesty of the sovereign; and also, in illuminations, tended to turn the single figure itself into a pattern: to emphasize the element of decorative space-filling, even though the timeless, serene figure was retained, and in an enclosed, non-realistic background. Byzantine mosaics of Christ the all-ruler, Christ the judge, though without realistic background, laid stress upon the majesty. The figures of the four evangelists in the great seventh-century altar books, on the other hand, represented in the Neo-Attic style without background in an enclosed space, tended to have drapery disposed in patterns: and the derivative Celtic illuminators were even more prone to weave drapery and even hands and feet into pattern. The codex Amiatinus, for instance, now at Florence, is believed to be the codex written at Monkwearmouth-Jarrow by the abbot Ceolfrith, and carried by him as a gift to the pope on his last journey to Rome in 716: the figures of the evangelists are in an enclosed frame, though the drapery and hair show some naturalness, and would appear to show Greco-Roman influence (cf. p. 544). There is a clear connexion between the picture of the monk in the scriptorium here and the St Matthew of the Lindisfarne gospels: but the Lindisfarne gospels are a stage farther from Byzantine influence, and there is much ornament in the shape of abstract pattern and elongated animals which is akin to that found on contemporary Anglo-Saxon ornament. In the Irish Book of Durrow and Book of Kells, again, there are exquisitely drawn pages of abstract ornament, and the evangelists' figures are fantastically bizarre, the faces stiff, solemn and unlifelike, and the hair and drapery arranged in a geometrical pattern. The Book of Kells, with its intricate patterns, beautiful colouring, and incredibly sure and beautiful draughtmanship, is the greatest artistic product of the Irish school.

As to the naturalistic, Alexandrian school, that reproduced in illuminated manuscripts the naturalistic scenes, figures and foliage to be found in Greco-Roman sculpture, low relief and mosaics. Book illustration was of especial importance in the development of Christian art: in spite of the aversion of the east from representations of the godhead by a human figure, in spite of the influence of the second commandment, in spite of the protests of the learned that it was not permissible to make portraits of Christ, such representations and such portraits were made. While the Neo-Attic style was used, as in greater reverence for the great figures of Christ in the mosaics of churches or the solemn portraits of the evangelists, illustrations of both the Old and New Testaments in the Alexandrian style appear to have been made very early. The illustrations of the Joshua Roll (see p. 424), the earliest manuscript of which belongs only to the ninth or tenth century, are naturalistic, Alexandrian in character: Joshua's soldiers wear the military dress of Roman soldiers of the second century, and the scribe appears in places not to understand the detail he is copying. It has been suggested that behind the illustrations of the Joshua Roll, and the naturalistic and roughly contemporary Paris psalter, lie earlier and much earlier manuscript illustrations of the scriptures in the Alexandrian style: that this school of biblical illustration goes back to Jewish illustrations of the Septuagint, and that Christians copied the Alexandrian, traditional style from the Alexandrian text of the Septuagint. Early illustrations of the New Testament, however, as those of the Rossano Codex and the Sinope fragment, though Syrian and Palestinian in origin, are Neo-Attic in style, not Alexandrian: the miniatures have a closed background and are two-dimensional in tendency.

The origin and early history of Christian architecture has also given rise to debate, but here again modern scholarship would tend to find the origin of most types of Christian building in the east. A heritage of architecture was passed on to medieval Europe both in Greco-Roman buildings and Greco-Roman decoration in stone: but in the case of the Christian churches, the heritage was mainly a Hellenistic heritage from beyond the borders of the Roman empire. As to the contribution of the new Germanic settlers, who had contributed so much to the development of art-forms: in the matter of architecture they contributed much less. They were content to copy the Greco-Roman buildings that they found for churches and monuments of importance, though retaining their own irregular mud huts (as at Sutton Courtenay) for their village folk, and rectangular wooden halls of timber or wattle and daub for their chieftains. The art of building in stone they learned from the conquered provincials, using at first provincial stone masons and sculptors.

The type of building for which the empire in the west had afforded no precedent before Constantine was the Christian church: pagan temples had been built for sacrifice, not for the assembly of congregations. There could be no wholesale transformation of the buildings of an earlier cult, when Constantine legalized the Christian society (and Christian worship) by the edict of Milan. It is now accepted that fourth- and fifth-century Christian churches were copied in the main from the Greco-Roman basilica, the Greco-Roman apsidal *schola*, and above all the Christian churches of the east. While Christianity was still unrecognized and sometimes persecuted in the west, it was tolerated in the eastern provinces; it spread early from Edessa to Parthia, and while Christians at Rome or in south Gaul still worshipped in the bishop's own house or the catacombs, Christians both sides of the east Roman border built churches for worship openly, without hindrance.

The elements that went to make up the forms of the early Christian churches in Europe were then as follows: the pagan colonnaded basilica, at first a wall-less building where, on a raised stone platform, approached by steps, rows of columns supported a low-pitched stone roof. The basilica had been used by the senate or ordo of the town, and was designed less for a single meeting than to afford shade and shelter for the transaction of business by small committees or by merchants: The Christian basilica, on the other hand, was meant for the single meeting: was meant to be used by the bishop offering the eucharist before his clergy and people. It usually had a wide centre aisle and two narrower side aisles, the centre aisle often looking towards a semi-circular apse; the small altar, low and pillar-shaped like a Roman pagan altar, stood upon the chord of the apse, and the bishop, up till about A.D. 500, stood at the back of the altar, facing the people. The domed roof was early introduced into Italy, and the apse was roofed with a semi-circular dome.

The form of the small churches of the east was governed by the paucity of such roofing material as was used in the west: timber and stone. In Mesopotamia and the hot eastern provinces, sun-baked brick was used for walls and arches, and the domed roof was evolved: first a flat 'dome' of overlapping ends of timber beams, or overlapping bricks, then a true dome on the same construction principle as the arch. Timber centering would be needed to build the dome, but not in the roof itself. The domed roof would seem to demand a circular wall, a circular church, to support it, and many such small circular churches must have been built in the east; but it was soon found possible to support the dome on a circular ring of columns, with an arcade between them and the containing wall. It was also soon found possible to roof a church square in plan with a circular dome; taking the thrust of the roof down to the square walls by means of the pendentive or the squinch. Octagonal, domed churches were built, and churches cruciform in plan, with barrel vaulting over the limbs of the cross, and a dome over the junction of the nave and transepts. All such constructions could be carried out in brickwork, or where stone was plentiful, churches on these plans could be built of large blocks of stone. The later church at Aghtamar (915–921) on an island in Lake Van, in Armenia, has its walls of large blocks of stone carved in bands of abstract ornament, with figures in relief; the plainness of the walls of brick churches could be relieved, on the outside, by building in bands of different coloured bricks, as in St Sophia, or by using a shallow arcading of recessed arches, or bands of brickwork set slanting, as in the church of the Holy Apostles, Salonika. All these churches, round in plan, square, rectangular and cruciform, originating (except for the basilicas) in Mesopotamia, were after 313 built gradually throughout the Byzantine empire and in Ostrogothic Italy, particularly Ravenna.

Finally, among the institutions, crafts and concepts of the Greco-

Roman heritage, may perhaps be mentioned here the practice of election by recognized procedure, as handed down from classical times, in the case of ecclesiastical elections, episcopal or abbatial. In the case of the Greco-Roman civil service and army, appointment was from above; in the case of the senate's election of the emperor at Byzantium, or the Germanic *gemot's* election of a king, relationship within the royal family, or the family of the deceased emperor, counted for much, and the election was often only the confirmation of a foregone conclusion. In the case of choosing a successor to a deceased bishop or abbot, both celibate, the claims of blood relationship counted theoretically for nothing and in fact for little. The natural field from which to choose a candidate was the senior membership of the bishop's *familia*, or the senior monks of the monastery, and recourse might be had in both cases to outside candidates: the field of choice was relatively large, and some kind of election procedure was gradually adopted. 'Election' in the sixth century and much later meant simply 'a choice': but election in the modern sense, implying some democratic process of choosing, goes back through the middle ages to sixth-century ecclesiastical elections, and thence to classical antiquity. It was pope Leo I (d. 461) who wrote of the appointment of bishops: 'he who governs all should be approved by all', and it was the election canon of 1059 that laid down that the new pope must be elected by a two-thirds majority of the cardinals. This adoption of a simple 'counting of heads' process, and rejection of the process, more normal at the time, of election by the votes of the wiser and weightier voters (the *sanior vel melior pars*), was stated to be without prejudice to such churches as used the method, and had a metropolitan to confirm and decide disputed cases: the church of Rome had no metropolitan or ecclesiastical superior, and since a decisive verdict was above all necessary, the two-third majority was canonically required. It was a step forward in the process of electing, though vaguer requirements that 'the will of the majority should prevail' had appeared in canons before.

It should be noticed that the evolution of election procedure, so important for modern life, lay along a quite different path from the Germanic procedure for making a public choice or decision. The decision by an Anglo-Saxon moot, or a Norman jury of neighbours called together to pronounce on blood guiltiness, was the decision of the countryside or neighbours of the man accused of the crime, and the decision would then necessarily be unanimous. There was no question of a majority: the neighbourhood, who hypothetically best knew, said the man was guilty, or said that he was innocent. Procedure sprung from this old root, requiring the expression of the single will of the whole electorate expressed in a unanimous vote, was long retained in certain medieval diets.

As to the principles governing episcopal elections: by the opening of our period, it was traditional that the election, the choice, should be made by the 'clergy and people' of a bishop's church: by the *laos* or *plebs*, words at first used as including all the Christians of the church, clergy and laity, and later, of the laity, as distinguished from the clergy. There must, further, be the consent of the bishops assembled to conduct the dead bishop's funeral ceremonies, and the confirmation of the election by the metropolitan, who would then proceed to summon at least two bishops, with himself to consecrate (*ordinare, instituere*) the new candidate. The method of choice by 'clergy and people' differed however at different times, and the candidate elected might be set aside by the neighbouring bishops, or the metropolitan, as unsuitable. On the other hand, there were some cases in Merovingian France, where a candidate proposed to the people of the widowed church by the bishops of the province was rejected by them.

On the whole, it appears that the clergy of the widowed church had, in the sixth century, a normally preponderant share in the election, either by the holding of preliminary discussion, or by selecting from a number of candidates 'proposed' to them by the people. As to 'the people' as meaning the laity: by the sixth century, their right of sharing in the choice was already exercised only by the 'nobles' or the 'ordo' (the town council of the late Roman empire: the magistrate), and this right was limited to the formal acceptance, or confirmation, of the candidate. The common folks' acceptance of their new bishop was expressed by acclamation when the candidate was brought out to them. But from whomsoever the initiative, the 'proposition' of the candidate came, clergy or nobles or comprovincial bishops or the pope himself, those who accepted or confirmed him made the choice, in the sixth century use of the term, the 'election'.

In addition to the canonical requirement then, that a bishop must be instituted *electione cleri et populi*, there may be added the oft-quoted dictum of pope Leo I: 'Let no man be reckoned among the bishops who has not been elected by the clergy, postulated by the people, nor consecrated by the comprovincial bishops with the judgment of the metropolitan.' With this principle accords his letter to the bishops of Vienne: 'Those that shall be made bishops shall be asked for (*postulentur*) in peace and quietness. Let the

9

signatures of the clergy, a worthy testimony, the consent of the
ordo and the *plebs* (together) be held binding.'

Further, it should be noted that the Gelasian theory of the two
powers, and the semi-sacred, providential character attributed to
the Byzantine emperor, allowed to that ruler a very large right of
intervention in the affairs of the church, including episcopal
elections. When Theoderic in Italy, and more regularly, Clovis
and the Merovingians in France, intervened in episcopal elections,
they had as *proconsulares* or patricians an apparent claim to be
exercising a delegated right. The Byzantine precedent was, in any
case, there in the background.

Certain landmarks in the history of episcopal elections may also
be noted.

In 483, on the death of pope Simplicius, an assembly of senators
(the Roman *ordo*) and Roman clergy, presided over by the pretorian
prefect in the name of Odovacar, claimed to give his advice on the
succession, and condemned earlier tentative efforts at an election.
The late pope's deacon was elected as Felix III.

In Gaul, the canons of sixth-century councils (Clermont 535,
Orleans 538) required the above-mentioned postulation, election
by the clergy, and the assent of the metropolitan; but in fact the
Merovingian kings interested themselves in episcopal elections
from the first. Clovis proposed his own candidates to the local
clergy for election, his successors nominated them and required
the assent of the local church: the council of Paris of 614 enacted
that bishops must be chosen by the old canonical procedure and
passed over in silence the need for royal assent. But though
Lothar II approved this canon, he added the proviso that the
royal assent was necessary, and the later Merovingians continued
to nominate.

A pope like Gregory I would never have approved the Frankish
kings' arrogation to themselves of the right to nominate, yet his
own letters about episcopal elections carefully safeguarded the
traditional and canonical right of the *plebs*, the *populares*, to 'make
a proposition' and to acclaim. The Frankish kings after Lothar II
used a set of notarial letters to nominate as formal as the Tudor
congé d'élire and letter missive: though they gave the letter nomi-
nating the royal candidate to the candidate himself to deliver to
his future church, instead of sending a letter of nomination direct
to the church. This exercise of royal power over the church
implies a Byzantine conception in the background. Gregory I was
much concerned with the filling of desolate, wasted sees in Italy,
and wrote many letters enjoining the holding of an election and,

sometimes, the sending of the chosen bishop to him for 'ordination' (consecration). He had no strong, single ruler, anxious to put in his own candidate, to deal with: but he frequently mentioned the need of the participation of the local magistrate (*ordo: curia:* late Roman municipal senate) in the election. He usually, when enjoining the filling of a see, wrote *ad clerum, ordinem et plebem* of the local church; he often enjoined some notary, a rector of the patrimony or another local bishop to procure the holding of the election and supervise it; in one case, he ordered that if two priests were chosen, both should be sent to him, together with a delegation of priests to set the affairs of the local church in order. Elections, it appears, were not unanimous, and the character of the candidate weighed with Gregory above the number of his supporters: but the right of the *ordo* to share in the election he recognized.

As regards the manner of making an election, some light is thrown by the Code and the Novels on abbatial elections, which would seem to reflect the varying practice of the day in the east: the use of election by seniority within the monastery, or election by fitness and merit. The *Code*, Bk. I, iii, 46 directs that not the monk next in seniority after the dead abbot, not the second in order, but the monk judged worthy by the whole number of the remaining monks or the majority of them shall be elected, the bishop having given his assent on notification. A *Novel* of 535 (*Novellae* V. cap. 9) throws a little more light on procedure while retaining the main provision of the *Code*: the 'inspection' of each monk as a possible candidate shall be taken in order of seniority, down through the number, and the best chosen, nor should the most senior, nor those next them, claim to succeed as of right. Again, the later *Novel* of 546 (*Novellae* 123) goes further, allowing procedure, when there is not unanimity, by compromise (the classical word for submitting a decision to an arbitrator). *Quem omnes monachi, vel melioris opinionis eligant, . . . eum elegerint* (the bishop ordaining him abbot).[1] This indication that, at one stage, clergy and monks succeeded by seniority accords with our knowledge that the primates of Numidia became metropolitan by seniority, and perhaps by the expostulation of the Gallic priest Cato, who, when in danger of being passed over for the episcopate, cried that he had fulfilled many years in each of the orders of the clerical militia: 'what now remains but for me to be made bishop?'

Election by seniority, however, could not survive for so important an office as bishop or abbot, for, as the *Code* says 'we are conscious that by nature we are not all made equally good or

[1] See Chapman, J.: *Saint Benedict and the Sixth Century*, p. 59.

equally bad'. Throughout the middle ages an election came to be held canonical, first if unanimous or 'by inspiration'; secondly by compromise, or committing the decision to the 'melior vel sanior pars' of the clergy electing; and thirdly, by the vote (voice, *vox*) of the majority.

BIBLIOGRAPHICAL NOTE

For the transmission of learning, see M. L. W. Laistner, *Thought and Letters in Western Europe*, 1931, and *Christianity and Pagan Culture in the Later Roman Empire*, Cornell Univ. Press, 1951: T. Haarhoff, *Schools of Gaul*, 1921: M. Roger, *L'Enseignement des lettres classiques d'Ausone à Alcuin*, 1905: L. Maitre, *Les écoles épiscopales et monastiques*, 1924: N. K. Chadwick, 'Intellectual Contacts between Britain and Gaul in the Fifth Century', in *Studies in Early British History*, ed. N. K. Chadwick, 1954 and *Poetry and Letters in early Christian Gaul* (1954). For the early history of the liturgy, d. Gregory Dix, *The Shape of the Liturgy*, 1943 (to be used with care), and cf. J. A. Jungmann, *Missarum Sollemnia*, Eng. tr. as *The Mass of the Roman Rite* (1951–55), and for early church buildings, G. Baldwin Brown, *From Schola to Cathedral*, 1886, and J. Strzygowski, *Origin of Christian Church Art*, 1923, D. Talbot-Rice, *Manual of Byzantine Art*, Pelican ed. 1954, the illustrations in *Byzantium*, and Sirarpie der Nersessian's *Armenia and the Byzantine Empire*, Harvard Univ. Press, 1947. For Byzantine influence in Britain, see W. C. Collingwood, *Northumbrian Crosses of the pre-Norman Age*, and for the extension of English influence to Central Europe, G. F. Browne, *Boniface of Crediton*, 1910: S. J. Crawford, *Anglo-Saxon influence on Western Christendom*, 1933. See also K. Weitzmann, *The Joshua Roll*, Princeton Univ. Press, 1948: and for early episcopal elections, A. Fliche, *La querelle des investitures*, 1946, pp. 1–10, and Fliche et Martin, *Histoire de l'église*, tom. 7, pp. 191–219. See also E. Barker, *Social and Political Thought from Justinian I to the last Palaeologus*, 1957. See also, for the Roman and curialist views of empire, as opposed to the Germanic and 'hegemonial' views, R. Folz, *L'Idée d'Empire en Occident du Ve au XIVe siècle*, Paris, 1953.

CHAPTER XIV

THE LOMBARDS IN ITALY

THE years of Lombard rule in Italy offer a contrast to those of the Ostrogoths. Both were Germanic invaders, both accounted by the provincials barbarians; but whereas the Ostrogoths settled as federates, under a king appreciative of Roman culture, and with a strong senatorial class anxious to co-operate and make the régime work: the Lombards came merely as enemy soldiery, settled unauthorized in such districts as they could conquer, and only came to value the Greco-Roman inheritance in the last century before their conquest by Charlemagne.

The horror of the Italian provincial and such bishops as Gregory the Great for the 'foul and leprous Lombards' was probably inspired by the original fighting fierceness of the Lombards ('fierce with more than the ordinary fierceness of the Germans') and by the long misery of a protracted and piecemeal conquest. The Lombards, a small Germanic tribe, had come originally from the Bardengau, near the mouth of the Elbe, had settled in Pannonia in the sixth century, wiped out the Gepids with Avar help in the years 565–567 (see p. 215), supplied some 5,000 troops to Narses for the reconquest of Italy, and, as cattle-raisers rather than agriculturalists, were ready for further tribal migration.

Of all the Germanic barbarians, they had progressed least in subjugating their tribes to monarchical rule. The king was only a war-leader, dispensable in times of peace. Society, half nomadic, and mainly pastoral, rested upon the clan and justice was still maintained by the primitive method of the blood feud. At no point in their wanderings had the Lombards had much contact with the Greeks or a settled civilization; they had penetrated to Hungary and fought the Mongol Avars there, and they had acquired some knowledge of Arian Christianity about the time of their contact with the Gepids, though many were still pagans when they entered Italy. They had *duces* as war-leaders of the clan (*fara*), a word which survived in some Lombard place names as did *-engo*, the equivalent of the tribal Anglo-Saxon *-ing*. These *duces* were, at the time of the invasion, united under the war-leader Alboin, as king, as they had been during the earlier period of migration for some 150 years.

As with most Germanic kingships, the Lombards had a royal

family whose members were 'throne-worthy', from whom the folk could choose a king, raising him upon the buckler or shield, if need arose. Members of such a family had no hereditary right to rule, but their chance of selection was privileged. Among the Lombards the descendants of Leth, the Lethings, formed such a dynasty; in the pre-invasion period they held the throne during seven generations, and sixteen of the later kings were of the royal race or married into that house. The royal race, however, was not associated with any legend of divine descent, but only of descent from Leth, or Lethuc, who succeeded in making an elective monarchy into an hereditary one. The king who invaded Italy in 568 was not of the royal race, though representatives of the Lethings had survived. Theodelinda, the famous Lombard queen, was, on her mother's side, a niece of the last Lething king, Waltari; and the strength of her position, and of her daughter Gundeberga, gave them great weight in carrying through the conversion of the Lombards from Arianism to Catholic Christianity. Their influence was due, however, not only to their royal descent, but to their immediate relationship to the duke of Bavaria, a powerful neighbouring ruler. While the hereditary principle counted for something in the Lombard succession, the ease with which candidates from other houses were elected shows that there was nothing approaching a divine right to rule within the membership of a particular family.

The Lombards who entered Italy in 568 under Alboin's leadership were not numerous: they were accompanied by numbers of Saxon and Bulgar auxiliaries. They came by the head of the Adriatic, where Aquileia marked the coast both as port and, by contemporary term, patriarchate, with the old Roman *limes* running north to Forum Julii (the Lombard Friuli or Cividale). From Aquileia, a road ran to Padua, Mantua, Cremona and Pavia, along the line of the Po, while another road ran to Theoderic's Verona and up the valley of the Adige to Trent and the Brenner. From Aquileia again a coast road ran south, crossing the mouths of the Po and its confluents, to Ravenna, there meeting the old Via Flaminia; the Via Flaminia had come across Italy from Rome, crossing the Apennines by the hill town of Spoleto. From Rome the old road ran south through the Campagna, skirting the Cassinese mount and monastery, to Benevento, perched up in a pass in the Apennines and commanding the passage both to the heel and toe of Italy. The Lombard piecemeal settlement was conditioned by strategic needs, and the lie of the old Roman roads.

Lombard rule in Italy lasted for about 200 years, from 568 to 774, and never succeeded in ousting the Greeks from the maritime

regions and great seaports, while the subjugation of the Latin provincials was only completed in 680, by the truce concluded between
Perctarit and Constans II, which gave Perctarit authority over
Rome itself. The protracted struggle with the Greeks, intermarriage, and the final accession of the Lombards to Christianity
explain the preponderance of Greek influence on the new settlers.
Latin leadership in Italy, the remnants of the Latin senatorial
class, had been destroyed in the Gothic wars; the provincials looked
for defence, at least in the first part of the Lombard settlement, to
imperial aid, and though the problem of the defence of the east
Byzantine frontier was even more pressing on the emperors than
the defence of Italy, such help was sometimes given. Greek forces
were sometimes sent, though never in sufficient numbers, and
Greek military officers led the citizen militias in the last periods of
Lombard conquest. The old imperial culture and tradition that had
opposed or sought to shape the Ostrogoths in Italy had been Latin;
that which fought and influenced the Lombards was Greek. The
stream of east Mediterranean and African refugees to Italy after
the Arab conquests increased the Byzantine influence, particularly
as regards ecclesiastical art and liturgy.

The chief source of our knowledge of Lombard origins and history, down to the reign of Liutprand, is the *Historia Langobardorum* of Paul the Deacon, himself a Lombard and one of the
outstanding scholars patronized by Charles the Great. He had
certain earlier written records to use in his history, and he was
familiar with the old tales and heroic poetry of his people. He was
educated at Lombard Pavia, lived for a time at the court of king
Ratchis, and for a longer period at that of duke Arichis at Benevento. Already he had some scholarship and was engaged in historical study: he wrote a *Historia Romana* based on Eutropius. In
775 he entered Monte Cassino and became a monk, writing a commentary on the Benedictine rule, and studying the history of his
own house.

About this time (he wrote later of the period of duke Ariulf of
Benevento's death, at the setting up of the duchy of Benevento), the
coenobium of our blessed father Benedict, situated on Monte Cassino,
was by night attacked by the Lombards. They plundered everything,
but not a single monk did they take, according to the prophecy of the
venerable father Benedict, which he had foreseen of old, and by which
he said: 'Scarcely have I been able to obtain from God, that the lives
of all in this place should be spared to me.' The monks fled to Rome
from this place, taking with them the book of the holy rule, which the

aforesaid father had composed, and certain other writings, and the weight and measure for the daily allowance of bread and wine, and whatever household furniture they could take with them. And after blessed Benedict Constantine and after him Simplicius, and after him Vitalis and lastly Bonitus ruled their congregation, under whom this destruction was accomplished.

In 782, when Paul was already a scholar of note, he went to the land of the Franks, to supplicate Charles's pardon for his brother, implicated in a Lombard rebellion in 776. He was received with honour by Charles, and stayed for some years in the region of the Moselle, writing a *Gesta episcoporum Mettensium*. He returned to Monte Cassino in 786 and there wrote the *Historia Langobardorum*, continuing it to the death of Liutprand in 744. At Charles's suggestion he wrote also a book of homilies. He died in 799.

The period of Lombard rule in Italy has three phases: that of the first conquests and ten years' anarchy or kinglessness: the middle period of struggle for power between king and dukes: and the last century of Lombard rule, when relations between the Byzantine and Lombard states in Italy had become more or less settled, Byzantine churches were being built again, Byzantine art-forms copied and the Lombard conquerors were becoming fused with the Latin provincials in religion and society.

In the first phase, from 568 to 584, Alboin led the tribal *farae* to Aquileia, from which the Greek patriarch retired to the little island of Grado, just to the south. They took Friuli to the north and Verona in the Lombard plain; in 569 they took Milan and in 570 advanced into the Tuscan plain; in 572 they took Pavia. Each tribe settled under its *dux* in a Roman city and its surrounding territory, and by this territorial settlement the *fara* lost some of its old social importance. Some thirty-five of these tribal *duces* reigned almost independently of the king in their own regions. In the time of this first settlement, however, two Lombard leaders left the main body of settlers in Lombardy and led expeditions to the south, each including in his followers a group of tribes; Faroald founded a great super-duchy round Spoleto and Zotto one round Benevento. It was in the course of this foundation that Zotto plundered Monte Cassino. These two great duchies, unlike the lesser ones in the north, included several Roman towns and their territories: they were from the first cut off by distance and physical barriers from royal control.

In the Lombard settlements there was no system of 'thirding' or of conquerors *hospitati* on Roman landowners, as with the Ostrogoths. The Roman landowners had largely perished in the Gothic wars, and the Lombards assumed ownership of the lands they seized. The territories of the fisc passed largely to the king; but in all these cases of expropriation the peasants, the *coloni*, continued to till the land as before. The Lombards during their stay in the northern Balkans had never taken to agriculture, using their conquered peasants to till the land, giving them the half-free status of *aldiones*. They now regarded the Italian *coloni* as *aldiones* and gave them that status. Italian farms were now more largely used for cattle-raising, and the use of the great herds of pigs the Lombards had driven with them from Pannonia; but no great change occurred in the old methods of Italian agriculture. The land, except in certain regions of the Po valley, was unsuited to the use of the Germanic long plough.

As to the civil magistrates: the old curial *ordo* of the towns tended to lose power, under the direction of the Lombard *dux*, though Gregory I's letters dealing with the election of bishops normally ordered that the *ordo* should be consulted. The Catholic clergy were also expropriated in favour of the Arians, or fled. As the patriarch of Aquileia had for long to reside in Grado, so archbishop Honoratus of Milan had to withdraw to Genoa when Alboin captured his city, and his successors continued to reside there.

Alboin ruled for only three years and six months after the invasion and was then assassinated. When he had conquered the Gepids, back in the Balkans, he had killed their king and married his daughter Rosamund. Paul the Deacon, familiar with Lombard heroic poetry, relates the story of the murder of Alboin through his wife's vengeance for her father's death.

> When he had sat longer than was fitting at a banquet in Verona, he ordered the queen to drink from a cup made from the skull of king Cunimund his ally: he invited her 'to drink merrily with her father'. And lest this tale should seem incredible, I say, to show that I speak the truth, that I have seen that cup on a certain feast day and prince Ratchis (at Milan) holding it in his hand and showing it to his guests. The queen therefore conceived a deep hatred in her heart, and plotted with Helmechis, his armour-bearer and foster-brother, to kill him.

Alboin was succeeded, not by Helmechis, but by Cleph, who ruled till he too was assassinated in 574. After this, the nobles decided that no king was necessary: and in the ten years that followed without any central rule the Byzantine cause recovered.

When the Lombards had escaped from the Avars into Italy, only needing henceforth to fight them in the march of Friuli, the Byzantine emperor was left to contend with them in the Balkans. In 570 the Byzantines, however, made a peace with the Avars, and in 575 sent Baduarius as exarch to lead an expedition to reconquer Italy; he landed near Naples and was killed in battle. The emperor Maurice (582–602) now installed an exarch permanently in Ravenna, with the title also of patrician: he was commander-in-chief and had a superiority over all civil magistrates. His forces were not, however, numerous, and could only hold the walled towns, *civitates* and *castra*. Maurice, further, bought the alliance of the Frankish Childebert, king of Austrasia, for 50,000 gold coins, and in 584, 585, 588 and 590 the Franks invaded Italy, without much success. The Byzantines, however, got back Classis, the port of Ravenna, taken by the duke of Spoleto, in 579.

The second phase of Lombard history begins with the decision of the Lombard nobles to restore the monarchy, and should be seen against the background of relative Byzantine success. In 584 the dukes recognized Authari, son of Cleph, as king, and the Byzantine reconquest was halted. In 590, the year of Gregory I's election, Agilulf, duke of Turin, was elected king, and held the throne till his death in 616. His reign was important: for he married the Catholic princess Theodelinda, daughter of the Bavarian duke whose territory stretched down to meet his own at Trent; and he undertook and inspired the dukes to undertake fresh wars against the Byzantines. Arichis, duke of Benevento, threatened Naples; Ariulf of Spoleto marched against Rome in 592, and in 593 Agilulf himself took Perugia and besieged Rome. Pope Gregory made a truce with him, promising, as with Byzantine civil authority, a tribute of 500 pounds of gold a year: terms which the exarch refused to ratify.

For five years the civil war continued, till in 598 Maurice, in difficulties with the Slavs and Avars, sent a new exarch Callinicus, to make an armistice through Gregory's mediations; Agilulf gave up Perugia and withdrew north. With the arrival of a new exarch, however, war began again, and to Lombard advantage; in 602 Padua was taken and Byzantine communications blocked between Ravenna and Istria; Mantua and Cremona fell, and soon Agilulf was again threatening Rome herself. He died, however, in 616.

After ten years' rule by Theodelinda's son Adaloald, the succession passed to a duke of Turin, and in 636 to another notable king, Rothari, duke of Brescia, whose long reign lasted till 652. He married Gundeberga, daughter of Theodelinda, issued a written code of law, and re-opened the offensive against the Byzantines. The imperial army was beaten near Modena, and Genoa fell in 652; a truce followed.

The next two reigns saw a period of Lombard consolidation,

both religious and political. Aribert I (652–661) conciliated both
the provincials and the Byzantines, and authorized the official conversion of the kingdom to Catholicism: the endowment and building of churches and monasteries, the re-assumption of Greco-
Roman culture, could now begin. The old liberal arts began to be
taught again in Milan. The next king, Grimoald, duke of Benevento (662–671) carried through a policy of subjecting the more
independent duchies to himself: Spoleto, Friuli and Benevento
now became an administrative part of the Lombard kingdom.

The Byzantine empire in the seventh century was too concerned
to defend itself, first against the Persians and then against the
Arabs, to be able to defend its possessions in Italy. In the reign of
Heraclius (610–641) the tribute from Italy was not paid and an
exarch was massacred. In Rome, and even in Naples, the defence
and even the civil government of the 'duchies' was entrusted by the
pope to officials of his own naming. Italy was becoming more cut
off from Byzantium, and under the stress of opposition to the
Monothelite policy of the emperors, increasingly hostile. Martin I
(see p. 218) condemned the Monothelite position and died an
exile in the Crimea in 657. When Constans II undertook a fresh
expedition in 663 for the reconquest of Italy, it was defeated by
Grimoald, who proceeded to drive the Greeks even from the heel
of Italy, where they had for so long controlled the entrance to the
Adriatic. Grimoald took Taranto, Brindisi and almost the whole
of Calabria. Before Grimoald's death, Constans II made further
efforts to re-establish the Byzantine position; he made the last
appearance of a Greek emperor in Rome in 665. He constituted the
bishop of Ravenna a metropolitan to balance the effective power
of the pope, and he sought to restrain the Arabs from landing in
Sicily. When he was assassinated in 668, the Arabs attacked Sicily
for the second time, and Constans' successor was responsible for
its defence. Possible danger from the Arabs might have led to co-
operation between Lombards and Byzantines: but the Lombard
kingdom in the north was slow to recognize the danger in the south
from the Arabs.

King Grimoald was succeeded by Perctarit (671–688), who resumed the offensive against the Greeks. In 680 peace was formally
made between Perctarit and the Greeks, on the basis of acknowledgment of the *status quo*, and renunciation by the Lombards of
any further policy of conquest.

The third phase in Lombard history, that of victory and consolidation, is marked by the long reign of Liutprand (713–744).
Just when there was possible danger to the popes that a strong

Lombard king would seek to relegate the papacy to a position of mere equality with his own metropolitans of Milan and Ravenna, the military weakness of the Greeks (rather than the troubles over Iconoclasm) deprived the papacy of the possibility of balancing the emperor against the Lombards. Liutprand had military successes: he took Bologna in 728 and in 732 even entered, though he could not hold, Ravenna. In 739 he besieged Rome, and the Byzantines could send no military help to the pope, Gregory III. In these dangers, Gregory made an appeal for aid to the old ally of the Greeks against the Lombards, the Franks. He sent to Charles Martel, offering to transfer to him the allegiance he owed to the eastern emperor: but Charles Martel, who had received Lombard help against the Saracens, would send no aid. The immediate danger passed when Liutprand withdrew: but the papal appeal to the Franks was a portent.

Liutprand was succeeded in 744 by the weaker Ratchis, who ruled for five years and was succeeded by Aistulf (749–756). Aistulf proved a strong and vigorous king: he took Ravenna in 751 and permanently overthrew the exarchate; the great Greco-Roman stronghold in the north was lost, and the papal patrimony strung out along the Via Flaminia lay open to attack. Aistulf proceeded to seize the patrimony, and even to claim authority over the duchy of Rome.

It was in this acute danger that pope Stephen III, elected by the anti-Lombard party, negotiated with Pepin for an invitation to visit him and Frankish envoys to accompany him. In the autumn of 753 the Frankish duke Autchar and bishop Chrodegang of Metz, referendary to Pepin before his consecration (see p. 62), arrived at Rome with the invitation. Pope Stephen, with an imperial ambassador to accompany him, set out for Francia *via* Pavia; he sought from Aistulf the restoration of the exarchate, was refused, and accorded a reluctant permission to travel on to Pepin's court. The Greek envoy returned to Rome and Stephen and his party in 753 crossed the Alps into Burgundy, where they were met by another duke and abbot Fulrad of Saint-Denis, the great royal abbey of the Merovingians adjoining Paris. Pepin and his two sons came to meet them on the feast of the Epiphany, 754, Pepin prostrating himself before the pope and leading his horse by the bridle, a ceremonial recognition of spiritual or secular superiority. For the rest of the winter Stephen stayed at Saint-Denis, and at Easter he met the king and his Frankish nobles at the royal villa of Quierzy and besought military help against the Lombards. At midsummer, 754, he crowned and anointed Pepin as king of the Franks, confirming the earlier coronation by Boniface in 751, and he crowned with him his two sons, Charles and Carloman, bestowing on Pepin the title of patrician of the Romans.

By what authority he did this is not quite clear, nor is the scope of the title. It is clear, however, that the rite of anointing, as when Samuel took a vial of oil and poured it upon the head of Saul, telling him that the Lord had anointed him to be captain of his inheritance, king instead of the old judges of Israel (1 Sam. X. i), was meant to consecrate a new departure and a new dynasty. It is clear further that, in the weakened condition of Byzantine rule in Italy, earlier popes than Stephen had appointed secular and military officers to the 'duchies': pope Honorius I (625–640) had provided for the government of Naples by appointing a *magister militum* and a notary, and other popes had been required by the emperor to undertake secular responsibilities in Rome and south Italy. Moreover, the title patrician was used at the date both by the recent exarchs at Ravenna and the *duces* of Rome; it is likely that Stephen's conferment of the title 'patrician of the Romans' denoted the limited, contemporary use of patrician, rather than its larger, unlimited use as in the time of Theoderic, nearly three hundred years earlier. In any case, Stephen made Pepin the special protector of the Roman duchy and see. The title was henceforth always used in papal letters to the Frankish king and princes.

The results of this visit were in the end to prove fatal to the Lombard kingdom, and the immediate effect was an Italian expedition of Pepin in 754; the Frankish army escorted the pope back through the Mont Cenis to Lombardy. Aistulf was defeated before the arrival of the main force and retreated to Pavia, where he consented to an unfavourable peace. He acknowledged Pepin as overlord and promised to surrender Ravenna and his other conquests to the pope. Stephen then returned to Rome.

A fresh expedition of the Franks in 756 was needed to enforce the surrenders reluctantly agreed to by Aistulf; and this time the exarchate and the keys of the once captured towns of the patrimony were in effect delivered to Stephen. Moreover, when Aistulf was killed, when out hunting, it was by the aid of Stephen and Frankish influence that Desiderius, duke of Tuscany, was elected king, under oath to make further restitution of Lombard conquests. A policy of acquiescence in Frankish conquest and papal guidance, however, could not be popular with the Lombards; papal independence and Lombard predominance in the peninsula could scarcely be reconciled. Pope Stephen died a year after Desiderius' election, in 757, but his brother Paul succeeded him as pope, and a strong anti-Lombard party persisted among the Roman clergy. Desiderius himself ruled uneasily and without restoring all the lands claimed by the papacy, from 756 till the subjugation of the Lombard kingdom by Charlemagne in 774.

Lombard society and institutions had assumed their characteristic Greco-Germanic forms in the reigns of Liutprand, Aistulf and Desiderius (from 713 till 774): before that period of reconciliation the civil wars had prevented the fusion of hostile populations and the local development of literature and the arts. The Lombard kings, still adding *Flavius* to the royal title, were now not only war-leaders, but guardians of the peace and justiciars. The official title of their court was the Byzantine *sacrum palatium*, and their writing office consisted of the usual notaries headed by a Lombard noble, the referendary; they had a mayor of the palace, like the Franks (see p. 300), a marshal and a sword-bearer. Their councillors, companions (*comites*), capable of being used as envoys or for local rule, were the Germanic *gasindi* (a parallel of the Anglo-Saxon *gesiths*), and, by this final period, they were using their local estate agents, rulers of their demesne, their *praepositi* or *gastaldi*, also in local government. The royal revenue came mainly from the landed demesnes, of which the most important groups were those round Pavia, Milan and Monza. No Roman direct tax was imposed, but Roman tolls and customs were still taken. Some gold and silver money was at first coined by the Lombard kings: but the Arab conquest of the Mediterranean, diminishing the supply of the precious metals, made currency scarce in the last century of Lombard rule.

Lombard society, as at first settled, was tribal: the *centenarius* of the early settlement seems to have been a military group leader. The different classes had their wergelds, as with the Anglo-Saxon and Scandinavian races, and the *aldiones*, bound to the soil by hereditary tenure, continued to till the land. There was no Lombard agriculture or industry, though Lombard craftsmen from the beginning produced brooches and metal work, and later began to undertake building and sculpture.

The primitive, Germanic nature of Lombard society is to be inferred from their law, which, even when coded by Rothari some eighty years after the settlement, still rested on Germanic foundations. In Rothari's *Edict* (643) the chief still exercised a *mundium* or *mund* over his men, a kind of protective, personal jurisdiction not entailing military service. The Lombard kings strove to supersede the old blood feud, which was still legal as between different families, by a system of *wers* and *bots*. Nevertheless, Rothari's *Edict* differs from the laws of Æthelberht of Kent as showing the influence of Roman law, and this became stronger under Grimoald and Liutprand, mainly through the use of written deeds. Liutprand allowed the disposition of land by gift at death, and in donations to churches and monasteries. The influence of Roman law was the stronger in that it was used by the provincials among themselves. In the fused society of the eighth century the Lombards adopted, with the law, the language, customs and clothes of the much more numerous Greco-Roman provincials.

Lombard art and architecture, similarly, was transformed slowly from the Germanic to the Byzantine, and, in the case of decoration and art-forms, a Byzantine not uninfluenced by more eastern elements, Syrian and Arabic. The northern animal-ornament was used by the Lombards in Italy, and the brooches of the grave-finds parallel those of the Visigoths, Franks and Anglo-Saxons: specimens are displayed for comparison with the Sutton Hoo ornaments and the Kingston brooch, for instance in the King Edward galleries of the British Museum. Many radiate brooches have been found, with *kerbschnitt* ornament and the stylized horse's head at the end of the plate: the head becoming more and more stylized and subhuman. The heavy square-ended brooches, the equal armed brooches, and the S-shaped brooch with the biting animal ends are also paralleled by Anglo-Saxon finds: and the round brooches with cloisonné work and those decorated with large stones in raised settings also offer parallels to Anglo-Saxon round brooches, though their workmanship is clumsier. The buckles, shield bosses and swords compare with those of Sutton Hoo; but for the Lombard earrings, with their complex dropped pendants, and the gold crosses from the cemeteries of Nocera Umbra and Castel Trosino with their elaborate interlace, there are no Anglo-Saxon parallels.

The later Lombard art and art-forms survive rather in stone buildings and marble sculpture, capitals and altar slabs, than in metal work. Circular churches were indeed built from the early period of the Lombard conversion, but they were few in number: outstanding Lombard work is later. The round church of St Salvatore at Bagano was apparently built before 600, and seems to belong to the time of Theodelinda: its centralized plan and central dome show the persistence of Byzantine influence in spite of the crudity of the masonry. Basilican churches were also built between 600 and 774, as that of St Stephen at Pavia, with its nave and four aisles; that of St Peter of the Ciel d'Oro at Pavia had capitals of excellent work. Raised choirs were already used, as in the church of St Saviour at Ravenna, with its crypt beneath. But though these Lombard buildings were in plan similar to those of the Christian east and west, the ornament of sarcophagi, lintels and panelled spaces developed a rich, distinctive style. Not only did the Roman vine scroll and rosette ornament persist, but the early interlace and plant trail developed into the arabesque, under eastern influence: and the early Germanic animal ornament became the typical Lombard peacock, lambs and deer, and the fantastic lions, eagles, griffins, dolphins, hippocamps and other kinds of sea monsters. Winged griffins and birds with Sassanian collars show unmistakable east Mediterranean influence, while the stucco figures of Santa Maria in Valle, Cividale, with their stiff-folded drapery, are beautiful pieces of work in the strictly Byzantine style. Though the eighth century was one in which Rome and Constantinople were becoming politically farther and farther apart, Italy was now peculiarly subject to Mediterranean influence, through the crowd of Greek, Syrian and Armenian refugees who fled to her in consequence of the Arab conquests:

Paul the Deacon's references to Lombard churches are of interest. He writes of one:

> And about the same time queen Theodelinda dedicated the basilica of St John Baptist, which she had built in Modicia, which is about twelve miles from Milan, and she adorned it with many ornaments of gold and silver and endowed it with sufficient lands. Now in this place Theoderic, once king of the Goths, had built a summer palace, so that he might dwell more pleasantly and healthfully here in the summer, because it was near to the Alps. Here too the aforesaid queen built herself a palace in which she had certain of the deeds of the Lombards depicted. It was clearly to be seen in this picture, how the Lombards at that time used to shave their hair, and what clothing they used. From the top of the head down to the nape they used to shave, but to have the hair round the face flowing long, and divided in the front of the forehead. They wore loose garments, generally of linen, even as the Anglo-Saxons are wont to have, and these are adorned with broad woven borders, stitched in various colours.

For the papacy, the Lombard period was one of danger finally surmounted. The conquering Lombards threatened the Italian hierarchy by devastating the *civitates* and sweeping away, often, both bishop and *familia*: many of the letters of pope Gregory I deal with the election of a new bishop or the re-establishment of a *familia*. Moreover, the hunger of the populace and the number of war captives called upon a paternal episcopate to feed, visit and redeem: and such calls were most clamant on the holder of Peter's see, the *papa* (father) *par excellence*; Gregory I notably rose to the call. Making provision for such needs was strictly within the vocation of the Christian *pater familias*.

The second danger, that to papal independence, came from both Lombards and the eastern emperors, and this too was notably surmounted, though not without incurring future dangers from the Carolingian empire, and its medieval successors. From the Lombards, the danger was political and material; from the Byzantine empire, political and doctrinal. In the event, and through the Arab conquests of the two other Petrine sees Antioch and Alexandria, Rome came to hold a unique position in the church, in fact as well as in claim. Pope Leo I in the fifth century claimed for the see of Peter a magistral supremacy, a doctrinal authority, as clearly as did any medieval pope later: but the political position of Leo differed from that of the Caroline pope, Hadrian I, who recognized no political superiority in either Lombard king or eastern emperor. While it is true that under the protection and rule of Charlemagne himself, the pope was regarded and even treated almost as a Frankish metropolitan, as almost under the Germanic *mund* of the new emperor, and the gain to papal independence was masked: yet Charles's undivided *imperium* passed to his warring successors, and Rome suffered no permanent Frankish dominance. The foundations of the political independence of the papacy were laid in the Lombard period, when the popes could balance the Lombards in the north against the Greeks in the east and south.

The main landmarks in the growth of papal independence were as follows:

The papacy of Gregory I (see p. 178), who carried through his policy of peace with the Lombards against Byzantine wishes, opposed the emperor Maurice on more than one occasion, but continued always to address him as his humble servant and subject.

The conversion of the Lombards from Arianism through the efforts of Theodelinda and Gundeberga and the re-establishment of the Catholic hierarchy in Lombardy in the year 680; this subjected the whole of Italy again to the apostolic see. Though Celtic missionaries had aided in the conversion of Lombardy, St Columbanus founding the Lombard monastery of Bobbio at the beginning of the seventh century, by the help of a still Arian Agilulf, Celtic influence caused no hindrance to the acceptance of Catholic order, or the supremacy of the papacy. Lombard kings and dukes helped in the founding of monasteries other than Celtic: a duke of Benevento helped re-establish Monte Cassino and Liutprand and the duke of Spoleto founded the famous Lombard monastery of

Farfa. In Lombardy as elsewhere at the time, the foundation of monasteries aided conversion, furthered the growth of written learning, the Greco-Roman arts, and the influence of the papacy, which since the days of Gregory I had become the protector of monks.

The Monothelite controversy, however, issued in a grave discomfiture for the papacy—nothing less than the formal condemnation of a pope on the explicit ground of heresy. Pope Honorius (who reigned from 625 to 638) in reply to a formal query from the patriarch Sergius (see p. 218) eliciting his judgment on the disputed doctrine, had solemnly responded in an unmistakably Monothelite sense. When in 680, during the pontificate of pope Agatho, the emperor Constantine IV summoned what became the Sixth Oecumenical Council, at Constantinople, the assembled bishops, in accepting a list of Monothelites to be condemned, sent by Agatho, added, with good reason, the name of Honorius, which he had discreetly forgotten to include. Modern apologists for Honorius have evolved a theory that the council condemned Honorius 'not as a heretic, but as the supporter of heretics', but the distinction is a purely fictitious one, and it would certainly have been quite incomprehensible to the men of the seventh century. Furthermore, pope Leo II, who confirmed the acts of the council, Agatho having died in the meantime, added a further denunciation of his unfortunate predecessor, explicitly accusing him of having defiled the hitherto spotless faith of the Roman see.

The papal struggle with the Iconoclast emperors, on the other hand, not only succeeded but led to the final emancipation of the popes from the imperial control: it was another landmark in the growth of papal power. In 726 the emperor Leo III forbade image-worship by an imperial edict, and in reaction Venetia and the Pentapolis rose against the exarch, expelled their local Byzantine dukes, and replaced them with elected dukes: all this without papal intervention. In 729 Gregory III, a strong opponent of Iconoclasm, became pope, the last to receive imperial confirmation; he excommunicated the Iconoclasts in a synod of 731. In return, the emperor Leo III removed the dioceses of Illyria, Crete (the Balkans), Sicily and Calabria from the papal jurisdiction and transferred them to that of the patriarch of Constantinople: he also confiscated papal patrimonies in those regions. The breach between pope and emperor seemed to be complete: in 739 Gregory III made his appeal for help to Charles Martel. Two years before the collapse of the Lombard kingdom the notable pope Hadrian I was elected, and he changed the official style for the dating of papal letters by the years of the reign of the Byzantine emperor, and since there was as yet no other, substituted the words: *Regnante Domino nostro Iesu Christo*. The way was cleared for the papal coronation and anointing of a new emperor: even as Samuel had anointed Saul, and Stephen III had anointed Pepin.

BIBLIOGRAPHICAL NOTE

The primary authority for Lombard history is the *Historia Langobardorum* of Paulus Diaconus: *P.L.* 95, col. 541, and *M.G.H.*, ed. G. Waitz, 1878; for trans., see W. D. Foulke, *Paul the Deacon's History of the Langobards*, 1907; T. Hodgkin, *Italy and Her Invaders*. For the recent discovery of the remains of the ancient Christian basilica at Aquileia see *The Times* 11 Oct. 1952. For Lombard archaeology and art, see N. Åberg, *Die Goten und Langobarden in Italien*, Uppsala, 1923, and pt. ii of *The Occident and the Orient in the Art of the Seventh Century: Lombard Italy*, Stockholm, 1945.

CHAPTER XV

THE LATER MEROVINGIANS

THE character of the period 561 to 768 (dealt with in this chapter and that following), is one of violence. From the death of Lothar I in 561 till the accession of Charles the Great in 768 there were struggles, not only between the Frankish kingdoms, but between the Frankish kings and their households, their 'palaces'. The two centuries were marked not only by wars and violence, but by a decline of the Latin tradition in Gaul, of the relatively civilized south of Gaul as against the barbarian, Germanic, north. The *regnum Francorum* in the days of Clovis and his sons had a real unity; afterwards, the kingdoms of Austrasia, Neustria and that successor-state to Burgundy that included part of Aquitaine, tended to become more and more independent, following the interests of their rulers.

The chronological divisions of the period 561–768 run from the death of Lothar I to that of Dagobert in 639, while the Merovingians still ruled France; from 639 to 719, when the Frankish nobility, headed by the mayors of the palace, struggled for the dominance of their respective kingdoms within the *regnum Francorum*, under the cover of nominal Merovingian rule; and from 719 to 768, the period of the growing dominance of Austrasia and her mayors of the palace. From the family of the Arnulfings, descendants of bishop Arnulf of Metz, sprang the Austrasian mayors, Pepin II and Pepin III, and the Carolingian dynasty.

About the curious retrogression in culture and political unity that followed the period of the Frankish conquests, some points may be noted. The first unity of the *regnum Francorum* was due to the personal energy, ability and fighting force of Clovis. He had been no more than the tribal king, the war-leader, of the Salian Franks, and his conquest of the Gallo-Romans had been no more remarkable than his defeat and removal of the other Germanic war-leaders, some of them at first his allies. He had been strong enough to make his residence, not in Tournai or the more Germanic part of his dominions, but in Paris among the Gallo-Romans, and to retain the rule of the north-eastern Franks none the less. The outlet of further conquests had preserved the country of the Franks from over-much internal strife during the lifetime of his sons. But when the natural limits of conquest were reached:

when Frankish aggression was contained by the flowing tide of
the Slav races then pouring into central Europe: the Lombards
then securing themselves in Italy: the Spanish Visigoths, then
with the Pyrenees to guard them: then the warlike energy of the
Franks expended itself in civil war. There was no fund of political
experience to guide a people now territorially settled; the Franks
used certain Roman institutions, but they had no understanding of
the value of centralized government. They did not, like the Arab
conquerors of Persia, seek to understand and assume the culture
they found in the land they conquered; perhaps because, in the
north Frankish regions where they were in greatest strength, there
was no Seleukia-Ctesiphon. Trier had been a great Roman city:
Paris under the later empire had a cross-Channel trade: but
neither was an Antioch or an Alexandria, and neither became a
Frankish Baghdad.

The violence of the period again, the murder of political enemies
and their wives and children, was perhaps no greater than that of
the early Anglo-Saxons across the Channel: but we know more
about it. Gildas, who died *c.* 570, in the *Epistola* attributed to him
speaks about the violence of the tyrants in Britain and of two royal
youths murdered on the altar steps: 'They treat the holy altar as
if it were a pile of dirty stones': but we do not know who the royal
youths were. We know very little of the fate of Britain after
Arthur's defeat in 537 (the *Annales Cambriae* say he died at Cam-
lann in 537), except that Ceawlin of Wessex assumed the bretwaldaship and after him Æthelbert of Kent, in neither case, we
may be sure, without violence. The Anglo-Saxon conquerors with
their oral culture could not transmit their victories and defeats,
their diplomatic marriages and their murders, except by the uncertain medium of heroic poetry. But over in Gaul, where men
used the instrument of writing, there were clerks making entries
in their annals, and a courageous and (for his day) learned bishop
of Tours, well-informed in Merovingian politics, writing down
in his history all that he knew of the deaths of bishops, of miracles
(particularly those of St Martin), of the battles and the murders
and the scandals: and he had much to write.

The disunity of the period was, again, partly due to the clash of
local interests. The four kingdoms of Clovis's sons became the
three kingdoms of Neustria, Austrasia and Burgundy: Aquitaine
was absorbed and divided in portions between these kingdoms.
There was some real difference of culture and economic interest
between the three, beside the personal rivalries of their kings;
and the fact that there were thus three political centres, with the

southern kingdom usually holding the balance between the two northern ones, prolonged the struggle for hegemony.

Finally, the violence and disunity of the period arose, more than from any other cause, from the failure of the Frankish rulers to regard their territories other than as patrimonies, to be divided at death among their sons, legitimate or even illegitimate. There was no sense of 'the state', or of the advisibility of racial cohesion or strategic frontiers or even economic needs in the subdivided patrimony: only of some balancing of assets one against another to each claimant of the inheritance. In the first division of the *regnum Francorum* at least the four sons were provided each with a compact territory or kingdom; but in later ones, three sons shared out Aquitaine and even the port of Marseilles; at another time Paris was divided between claimants. Boundaries fluctuated, and with them those of ecclesiastical provinces; sometimes, when a great city was divided, the king who did not obtain the portion with the bishop's see set up a see for his own bishop in his own share. Not only was authority disastrously subdivided, but the inhabitants, e.g. of Aquitaine, adhered with enthusiasm to their Austrasian or Neustrian sovereigns, and fought amongst themselves.

Only the first part of the history of the period was written by an outstanding historian, namely Gregory of Tours (see p. 57): the last and very well-informed part of the *Historia Francorum* runs down to 591, three years before Gregory's own death. From there onwards, we are dependent on the work of 'Fredegar' and the annalists, historical work of very little merit but composed under the handicap of the non-existence of a common scale of chronology.

Fredegar or *Fredegarius Scholasticus* was, in fact, an anonymous compiler, for no original manuscript mentions his name. The earliest manuscript of the works once ascribed to him, possibly to be dated as between 680 and 725, contains several treatises, all historical in character, including an epitome of the *Historia Francorum*, and a continuation bringing that history down to 768. The first portion of the continuation, from 593 to 642, is our sole source for the struggle connected with the rule of Brunhilde in Austrasia, and incorporates two complete chapters of Jonas' life of Columbanus; after 642 three other writers continued the compilation. All these continuators after 642 belonged to the family or the entourage of Pepin I or his descendants, and hence their narrative is almost an official history of the rise of the Austrasian mayors of the palace.

The writing of 'annals' was at first a year-to-year business of entering episcopal, abbatial and other deaths, and other events of local interest, in an Easter table. In this pre-Carolingian period historical writing was not, apparently, carried much further among the Franks; but in the Carolingian age there was a great recopying and rewriting of annals by scholars of some merit and the outstanding series of annals, the *Royal Annals*, the annals of Lorsch, Reichenau and Corbie and the rest, were all reshaped annals of this kind. The Anglo-Saxon chronicle of 891 was a late and outstanding case of this method of writing history, drawing upon the history of Bede and, as is inferred from entries not drawn from Bede, from two or three early sets of annals. In the late Merovingian period, however, the annals were kept for a practical purpose, chiefly the information of bishops or abbots as to the keeping of the *natalicia* of the saints with mass and office: the relation of the annals to the calendars of the various churches must have been very close. Bede's story of the use of a monastic annal in a Sussex monastery for ascertaining the saint's day of St Oswald of Northumbria illustrates such primitive use of annals as must have existed in the Merovingian churches, after missionaries from England had spread the use of such annals to Gaul.

Bede, in this reference to a monastic annal, relates how, in the monastery of Selsey, during an outbreak of the plague, a boy already stricken with the disease was told by an angel to inform the priest Eappa that none except the boy himself should die. It was then only an hour after sunrise, and that day was the day on which Oswald had been slain in body by the heathen and taken in spirit to eternal joy: 'Let them look', said the angel, 'in their books (*in suis codicibus*) in which is noted the burial of the dead, and they will find that this is the day on which he was taken from this world. Let them celebrate masses in all the oratories of the monastery, either in thanksgiving for the prayers now answered, or in memory of king Oswald.' So the boy called for the priest Eappa to come to him and told him all the angel had said; and the priest believed the boy's words, and he went at once and sought in his annal (*in annale suo*) and found that it was indeed the day on which Oswald had perished. Bede gives no date for this miracle at Selsey, but it must have been later than Wilfrid's foundation of the monastery in 681.

The keeping of Christian annals belongs especially to the Merovingian period in Gaul, but it was part of the Roman inheritance. The origin of annals goes back much earlier, and helps to explain the efforts of these scribes of the dark ages to keep a historical record without a fixed chronology. The primitive form of Roman history was the official writing down of the *Annales Maximi* by the *pontifex maximus*, as described by Cicero. Each year a blank sheet (*tabula*), officially called an album, was set before the *pontifex*, and he wrote at the head of the entry for the year the names of the two consuls, and of the other magistrates: he then briefly entered memorable events as they occurred, during the year. Similar late Roman annals, with lists of consuls, prefects of the city, both for the east and the west, can be seen printed in the *Monumenta Germaniae Historiae*, in the ninth volume of the *Auctorum Antiquissimorum*; and there too can be seen lists of the Roman bishops, with the consuls for the year: Easter tables in Greek with the consuls of the year, Prosper of Aquitaine's epitome of the Latin version of Eusebius' *kronikoi canones*, going down to 433; Victor of Aquitaine's *Cursus Paschalis*, a calendar for the dating of Easter worked out till the year 532 and resting on an Easter cycle of 84 years (see p. 175), and, finally, the Dionysian cycle. Such apparatus as this was, in whole or part, available to the Frankish annalists; but no use was at first made of Dionysius' era of the incarnation.

The Merovingian annals thus belong to the same stage of historical writing as the history of Nennius in Celtic Britain: for general history, where the years of the abbot or bishop of the church were of no avail, only Prosper's epitome and various chronological *memoranda* were at hand. Nennius copied (as part of the historical material which, he said, he had collected together in a heap), the genealogies of Welsh and Anglo-Saxon kings, and such *aides-mémoire* as a note that:

> From the beginning of the world to Constantinus and Rufus are found to be five thousand six hundred and fifty-eight years, etc.

Gregory of Tours, besides using the regnal years of kings and bishops, used similar epochs, writing at the end of his *Historia Francorum*:

> From the beginning to the Flood, 2242 years: from the Flood to the crossing of the Red Sea, 1404: from the crossing of the Red Sea to the Resurrection, 1538: from the Resurrection to the transit of St Martin, 412: from the transit to the afore-mentioned year, the 21st of our ordination, the 5th of pope Gregory, the 31st of Guntram, the 19th of Childebert the younger, 197: altogether, 5792 years.

Such laborious synchronizing of years could not be avoided till a common scale was introduced. The Romans had dated by the indiction, a year's place in a cycle of fifteen years: but knowledge of the consuls or some other historical landmark was needed to distinguish the cycle itself. The reckoning *ab urbe condita* was pagan and, in fact, a literary invention; the reckoning from the Creation (here used by Gregory) had no wide use. Eusebius and Jerome dated from the birth of Abraham; Prosper of Aquitaine dated his epitome in decades from the year of the Passion, and this reckoning was used in 457 by Victor of Aquitaine, who included it in his Easter table. In 525 Dionysius Exiguus (see p. 177) reckoned from the year of grace, the year of the Lord's incarnation, inserting the *annus Domini* in his Easter *tabula*. The headings of his ruled columns, *canones*, ran thus:

> Annus Domini. Indiction. Epact. Concurrents. Moon's cycle: the 14th day of the Easter moon: date of Easter Sunday.

These Dionysian Easter *tabulae* were taken to England and circulated after the synod of Whitby, 664, and an occasional charter has been found dated by the era of the incarnation before the writing of Bede's *Ecclesiastica Historia* in 731: but the popularization of this era was due to the circulation of Bede's history, and, even more, of his *De temporum ratione* by Boniface and the Anglo-Saxon missionaries. The work included too a short world chronicle from the Creation to A.D. 729: it was to be the foundation of the Caroline writing of history, at Saint-Denis, Fulda, Corvey, Reichenau and the other great abbeys.

To run briefly through the political history of the period. When Lothar I died in 561, the more alien among his subjects were no longer dangerous. There were small, unimportant Saxon settlements round Boulogne and at the mouth of the Loire: the Saxons who accompanied the Lombards to Italy made one or two efforts to make fresh settlements in Gaul from Italy, but unsuccessfully. The Bretons were nominally subject to Clovis and his heirs: ecclesiastically, the see of Tours claimed rights over them. The Alemans and Thuringians had been subdued. The Boii of Bohemia had marched south to the eastern Alps and settled there as the Baiovari (people of Bohemia): Garibald, duke of Bavaria, had married a Frankish princess, and the Bavarians were subject to the Franks. The remnants of the Angli who had gone to Britain had been absorbed by the Thuringians, their name remaining in the place-name Engelheim. The Franks were by now the strongest Germanic people in Europe.

At Lothar's death in 561, France was redivided. Charibert got Paris and west Gaul, the 'newest' conquests, the region to be

Neustria; Sigebert, Thierry's kingdom, the valleys of the Meuse
and Rhine, to be Austrasia; Guntram, the old kingdom of Burgundy, with Arles as its episcopal city and Marseilles its valuable
port; and Chilperic, Lothar's son by another mother and not
regarded by his brothers as legitimate, the least valuable share,
the Salian lands round Soissons and Tournai. Gregory of Tours
relates of this division that Chilperic tried to seize the whole
inheritance, laying hands upon Lothar's treasure at Paris, but was
not allowed to hold it long. His brothers forced it from him, and
they made a 'lawful division' of the patrimony. Worse subdivision
followed: for when Charibert died in 567, the three remaining
brothers shared out his inheritance, dividing out Paris in three
portions, giving to Chilperic, Normandy, Toulouse and Bordeaux,
to Sigebert and Guntram shares of Aquitaine. Sigebert got Poitou
and Touraine, Guntram Angoulême, Saintes and Perigueux. So
unreasonable a territorial arrangement brought forty years fighting
to Gaul.

To the territorial complication was added a deadly blood feud
(*faida*) between Sigebert and Chilperic, and their descendants,
involving as well nearly all the Frankish nobles and bishops on one
side or other. Aquitaine had once belonged to Visigothic Spain,
and two Frankish kings thought to safeguard their share of the
southern lands by a Visigothic alliance. Sigebert married the young
Visigothic princess Brunhilde, daughter of Athanagild: the poet
Fortunatus sang the epithalamium at their wedding. Chilperic,
jealous of his brother's honourable marriage, for the Visigothic
court was stately and Byzantine, and he himself aspired to the
old Greco-Roman culture, married Galswintha, sister of Brunhilde,
very splendidly at Reims, temporarily deserting his mistress
Fredegund; he gave Galswintha a dowry of Aquitanian cities,
including Bordeaux. He then returned to Fredegund; and when
Galswintha asked to go back to Spain, she was found strangled on
her bed. The court at Paris mourned her a few days only, and
then Chilperic married Fredegund. Sigebert demanded compensation, and obtained the Aquitanian dowry of Galswintha: but
Brunhilde saw her sister's murder as unemendable, a botless
crime, and she pursued the blood feud as a holy duty. Civil war
between Neustria and Austrasia started in 573, and was almost
uninterrupted for forty years, claiming many royal victims as
the blood price. It created bitter hostility between the Franks of
east and west, and it weakened the monarchy, which had to draw
the *leudes* into the quarrel for their support, and to do it at the
price of concessions and grants.

Chilperic started the war by attempting to seize his brother's cities in Poitou and Touraine: but Sigebert called to his aid the barbarians from beyond the Rhine and a fresh 'barbarian invasion' harried France; Chilperic had to give up his conquests. Again in 575, when Chilperic advanced on Reims, Sigebert called in his trans-Rhenane allies: he drove Chilperic back to Paris, seized the country between Seine and Loire, and was about to be raised on the shield as king by the inhabitants of Tournai, Chilperic's capital, when two of the sons of Fredegund drove their long knives into his side (December 575). Chilperic regained the advantage; he got back Paris, where Brunhilde had been guarding Sigebert's treasure, and sent her to Rouen. Duke Gundobald saved her five-year-old son from death at Chilperic's hands, and the child was recognized as Austrasian king, Childebert II, at Metz, on Christmas Day, 575.

Brunhilde, still under thirty and held to be beautiful, was seized by Merovech, Chilperic's son and her own nephew, and married to him by a complaisant bishop: but the church declared the marriage incestuous. Chilperic sent Brunhilde to Metz, and sent off another son, called Clovis, to take the Aquitanian cities; the Gallo-Roman Mummolus defeated him, and Fredegund, enraged at his attempted marriage to Brunhilde, had him assassinated. Fredegund's own two children now died as infants and she persuaded Chilperic they had been bewitched through Clovis. This prince was also killed.

Guntram, anxious to appease the feud and to ally, as he usually did, with the weaker party, went to negotiate with the Austrasian nobles and Childebert II, and made a solemn alliance with them against Chilperic: he adopted the child as his son. Chilperic at Paris remained unimpressed: he even gave his attention to building circuses at Paris and Soissons and giving spectacles to his people in the Greco-Roman manner. When trouble arose between Guntram and the Austrasians because Guntram would not give up the Austrasian portions of the cities of Marseilles and Angers, Chilperic arranged to seize and adopt Childebert himself. Aegidius, bishop of Reims, arranged the matter in 581: and the Austrasians got their portion of Marseilles and installed their own court and bishop there. Two years later Chilperic ravaged Guntram's lands and forced him to give up to Childebert the Burgundian portion of Marseilles (584): Guntram remade his alliance with the Austrasians, who preferred such an alliance to one with Chilperic: but the young Childebert, when he might have settled with Chilperic, went off to lead a fruitless expedition to Italy.

Meanwhile another son, the future Lothar II, was born to Chilperic, and brought up almost as a prisoner on the Neustrian demesne of Vitry, for Fredegund feared he might be bewitched like his two little brothers; and Chilperic arranged an honourable marriage for his daughter Rigontha. She was sent off from Paris to marry the Visigothic prince Recared, son of Leovigild, and then Chilperic went hunting in the woods surrounding his demesne at Chelles, near Paris. There he was murdered, at dusk, as he was getting off his horse, resting his hand on the shoulder of an attendant: an unknown assassin stabbed him and escaped.

The death of Chilperic in 584 removed a remarkable figure from the Frankish scene. Whereas among the Anglo-Saxons, Lombards and Vandals, a king who admired *Romanitas* usually regarded Christianity as one of its aspects and went down to history as a 'good' king, Chilperic seems to have been inspired by the pagan and despotic possibilities of Roman rule. He was formally Christian: he made offerings to churches and completed the basilica of St Médard at Soissons; he knew enough Latin to perceive that certain Germanic sounds were not expressible in the Latin alphabet and he ordered that four letters should be added. He examined with similar zeal the doctrine of the Holy Trinity, declared it absurd and ordered that three gods should be worshipped. Gregory of Tours could scarcely find words strong enough to condemn him: he called him 'the Nero and Herod of our times', and added:

> For he used to devastate and burn many regions and feel no grief threat but rather pleasure, even as Nero of old used to sing the tragedies while his palace burned. . . . Yet he was not even a good Latin scholar (Gregory continued), for he composed two books in the manner of Sedulius (the fifth-century poet who wrote a long, somewhat rhetorical *Carmen paschale* and also the hymns still sung in the divine office, *A solis ortus cardine* and *Hostis Herodes impie*) and the verses in these books would not even stand on their own feet, for he did not understand metre and put short syllables for long ones and long for short: and other small works or hymns or prose lessons [*missas*] he enjoined to be used, for no reason whatever. He despised the suits of the poor. He was wont to blaspheme bishops and when he was in privacy he used to arrange ridiculous charades and jokes, about the bishops of churches above all. . . . He hated nothing worse than churches. He often used to say: See how poor our fisc is, and how our riches have been transferred to the churches: nobody reigns in this country but bishops: our honour is diminished and transferred to the bishops of the cities.

He used, **Gregory** added, to hold invalid wills made in favour of churches, and there was no kind of evil luxury he did not practise. He used to have the eyes of those who offended him torn out. He added to the protocol of his writs: If any man despise this our precept, let his eyes be put out.

Both the royal husbands of Brunhilde and Fredegund, the chief agents of the blood feud, were now dead, and the political balance of the kingdoms much disturbed. Guntram now stepped in for the second time to protect the weaker side, now that of Fredegund and the Neustrians. Fredegund fled, with her four-month-old son, for sanctuary to the bishop's cathedral, the church of Notre Dame, at Paris, and Guntram came to Paris and tried to allay the resentment of those of Chilperic's subjects whom he had wronged. He recognized bequests to churches which Chilperic had declared invalid and gave alms to the poor, and, addressing the Parisians in the cathedral, asked to be allowed to safeguard and bring up his nephews, Chilperic's sons, himself: at least for three years. The juncture was the more dangerous as an adventurer, Gundobald, claiming to be a son of Lothar I, had gained some success in Aquitaine: he had Toulouse and Bordeaux, and was raised on the shield in the Limousin, with the adherence of Mummolus.

Childebert II, who had just attained the Frankish majority, fifteen years, now came to Guntram and was solemnly re-adopted and declared his heir. He led an expedition to Aquitaine and besieged Gundobald in Comminges, where the latter was taken and killed (585). In the north Brunhilde, enraged at the dukes Ursio, Rauching and Bertefrid who had bluntly opposed her attempt to prolong her regency, had them murdered, together with Aegidius, archbishop of Reims. The queen was, to the Austrasian nobles of the 'palace', a foreigner: the 'palace', the royal officers among whom the mayor of the palace was not as yet the greatest, meant to rule themselves (587).

The treaty of Andelot (28 November 587) set down the terms of alliance made between Brunhilde, Guntram and his nephew, and made a notable re-division of the patrimony of Charibert; the first division had already caused trouble for nearly twenty years. Territorially, Guntram took Sigebert's portion, including a third of the city of Paris, and Childebert II took the remainder: each king left his portion to the survivor. It was also agreed that the *émigrés leudes*, trusted royal servants who had fled to the court of another king in times of danger and there formed a faction hostile to the rulers of their own land, should be expelled from the courts where they had taken refuge; and that grants made to churches and lay lords and hastily resumed on the mere suspicion of disloyalty should be made irrevocable, both for the past and the future. Much resentment had been aroused by the Merovingian resumption of *beneficia*: bishops might grant the life tenure of a piece of land or a vineyard as stipend to a deacon or presbyter of merit, and hope to get it back at death; but the hasty resumption of lay benifices by the kings aroused much opposition by the holder himself, if made before his death, and from his family, if after death. Uncertainty of tenure was one of the chief causes of resentment against the Merovingian kings.

The treaty of Andelot gave Gaul peace for some years, after the recent disturbances of the civil war. Fredegund tried vainly to procure the assassination of Guntram, but 'the good prince' died peaceably in March 592. Childebert II, now holding more than two-thirds of Gaul, tried to make himself master of all: he attacked his cousin, Lothar II, but his forces were defeated near Soissons: Neustria survived. Childebert II died aged twenty-five in 595, and Fredegund in 597.

Brunhilde was now the greatest figure in France; she ruled, at Metz or in Alsace, for her eldest grandson, the child Thibert, while the younger grandson, Thierry, had Burgundy and Orleans as his portion. In 599 Lothar II was again defeated by his cousin, and his realm of Neustria restricted to a few *pagi* round Beauvais, Amiens and Rouen, but this brought no advantage to Brunhilde. Her palace was now strong enough to drive her from Austrasia (599), the mayors of the palace assuming the leadership of the 'government' at this point. Brunhilde took refuge with Thierry in Burgundy: but she still guided the struggle between Austrasia-Burgundy and Neustria.

In 604 a Burgundian mayor of the palace, Bertoald, was surprised with a small army by the Neustrian mayor of Lothar II, Landri. Bertoald fled to Orleans and was besieged till Thierry and a Burgundian army relieved him. Neustrians and Burgundians fought on Christmas Day, 604: Bertoald was killed, but Landri was put to flight, and an infant son of Lothar, Merovech, taken. Thierry was able to enter Paris (605), and was only prevented by his nobles from despatching Lothar; he took this amiss, fought his own Burgundian mayor at the royal villa of Quierzy-sur-Oise, and had the mayor assassinated in Thierry's own tent. He had been hated for his fiscal exactions, and a more prudent mayor was appointed.

Though allies as against Neustria, Thierry in Burgundy and young Thibert in Austrasia (the ruler backed by the Austrasian palace) were now jealous of each other. In 610 Thibert invaded Alsace with a semi-barbarian army, was met by Thierry with a smaller force, and imposed on him cessions of land in Alsace and Champagne. In revenge, Thierry procured the neutrality of Lothar II, led an army to Toul, a city he had had to cede, and defeated Thibert in May 612. Thibert was taken, delivered to his grandmother Brunhilde, forcibly given the tonsure, and soon after assassinated. His infant son Merovech had his skull beaten in.

But again the focus of power shifted, for Thierry died in 613 on the eve of attacking Lothar and making himself master of the *regnum Francorum*. Though quite a young man, he left four sons, of whom Brunhilde wished to recognize the eldest, aged twelve, as king. But this would have made her the regent of a young king for the third time, and the Austrasian palace was willing even to ally with Neustria rather than see this. Bishop Arnulf of Metz and Pepin I (called, though not by contemporaries, of Landen) made alliance for Austrasia with Lothar II: and Brunhilde, after trying in vain to raise the traditional allies of Austrasia, the wild hordes of 'beyond the Rhine', fled to Burgundy. Even Burgundy could no longer be trusted: there, the mayor, secretly allied with Lothar II, was intriguing for support with the 'farons' of Burgundy (*farons* connected with the tribal *farae* and the later old French *baro*), with the bishops and Burgundian *leudes*. The army of Austrasia-Burgundy advanced to meet that of Lothar, and the opposing armies refused to fight: Lothar advanced unopposed down the valley of the Saône, and seized Thierry's four sons. The two eldest he killed; the third, Merovech, he spared, as his own god-son, sending him into retreat: the youngest, a Childebert, disappeared:

In the autumn of 613 the climax came. Brunhilde was seized at the foot of the Jura, accused of causing the death of ten kings (including the death of her own husband actually assassinated by Fredegund), and those of Thierry's grandchildren whom Lothar II had himself killed. The Franks in the now dim past had lived under the Huns, and, with their notable use of the horse in war, had learned from them the terrible and ancient horse-death for criminals. Brunhilde was tortured for three days, and tied alive to the tail of a vicious horse till her body was torn to shreds. Chroniclers, like Fredegar and the adherents of the Austrasian mayors, compared her violent end to that of Jezebel, eaten by dogs. The old queen belonged to her age: she contended for her family and for personal power, with Neustria and with the Austrasian palace. They were too strong for her in the end, mainly through the premature death of her son Childebert II and her grandson, Thierry II.

Against all probability, Lothar II attained in 613 to the sole rule of France, but not to a centralized rule, for that the Merovingians never obtained. He recognized the premier rank in the palace of the mayors, and that by irrevocable act. He confirmed the mayors of Austrasia and Burgundy; in his own Neustria, Landri was succeeded by Gundoland.

The great resettlement of political relations of the three kingdoms was marked by the holding of a reform council in Paris in October 614: 79 prelates were present, and it is notable that they felt themselves strong enough to insert at the head of the canons passed one clearly directed against the royal nomination of bishops.

> When a bishop dies, that man ought to be ordained in his place whom the metropolitan (by whom he is to be consecrated) with his fellow bishops of the province, and the clergy and people (*populus*) of his city shall choose, without any loan or grant of money. And if otherwise he shall get the position by force, or if, by any negligence without the election of the metropolitan and the consent of the clergy and citizens, he shall be introduced into the church, his ordination shall be held null and void according to the ancient statutes of the fathers.

It is notable that Lothar II should have allowed such a canon to be passed: neither he nor his successors observed it. Other canons dealing in particular with the trial of ecclesiastical disputes by the bishop, and the non-trial of clerks by the secular judge, followed.

The canons of this council of Paris were, however, of less constitutional importance than the edict issued by Lothar II in October 614, promising a general reform: it was the price of the general acceptance of his sovereignty. It was the first time any Merovingian king had accepted responsibility to the law: the edict enumerated abuses of the royal power in the past and promised that they should not recur in the future. There was no Magna Carta, no scheme of constitutional government or even a list of detailed reform measures: but the nobles were in a stronger position thereafter. The three palaces of the kingdom, with their officers in present attendance on the king and their past officers domiciled as counts, dukes, domestics, etc. out in the countryside, formed some sort of a 'central government' for each kingdom.

Lothar II's general supremacy from 613 was only exercised at the price of delegation of power. In 616 a diploma granted local concessions to the mayor and the *farons* of Burgundy; and when Lothar's son Dagobert was about ten or twelve, Lothar sent him to live as sub-king in Austrasia, under the tutelage of Arnulf, bishop of Metz and the mayor, Pepin I. Lothar was strong enough, however, to keep the Austrasian share of Aquitaine and the border region of the Vosges; and when Dagobert was fifteen, Lothar made him come to his villa of Clichy, near Paris, for his marriage: a slight to Austrasia. At the marriage, father and son quarrelled, Dagobert claiming all the territories of the old Austrasia; Lothar agreed to accept the arbitration of twelve Frankish doomsmen, who gave to Dagobert the larger Austrasia while leaving Lothar the Austrasian cities in Aquitaine.

In Burgundy, however, Lothar fared better, achieving the suppression of the mayoralty in his own interest. The mayor died in 626 or 627, and Lothar was able to avoid the succession of his son. He assembled the Burgundian nobles and *leudes* at Troyes, and asked them if they wished for a successor to the mayor: they answered that they desired no mayor, and the Burgundian palace henceforth ruled Burgundy under Lothar's distant supervision.

In Neustria, however, Lothar's personal weakness showed itself in failure to punish a murder done at the time of assembly, in the palace itself, a notable breach of the king's peace. Ægyna, one of the Saxons who had settled in the Bessin, murdered Erminarius, the 'governor of the palace of Charibert', the king's younger son. To avoid a fight in his royal villa of Clichy, where the annual assembly was being held, Lothar ordered Ægyna to withdraw to the south bank of the Seine, and many of the nobles who favoured his cause went with him, to the hill of Montmartre. There Charibert's uncle, Produlf, besieged him; but Lothar forbade the *farons* of Burgundy to cross the river, either to defend or attack, and he ordered them to crush those who did. Peace was kept by Lothar's action: but the murder went unavenged, the breach of the king's peace, so far as we know, unemended. Lothar II died in 629, and Fredegar, the Austrasian annalist-compiler, allowed that he had been generous to churches and the poor: but too much given, he said, to the counsels of women. He was buried in the abbey church of St Vincent, later to be Saint-Germain des Prés, then just outside Paris.

The reign of Dagobert I, Lothar's son (629–639), was that of the last Merovingian who really ruled. As Charibert, the eldest son of Lothar, was apparently mentally deficient, Dagobert was recognized as king of Lothar's kingdom, the *regnum francorum*, and Charibert was left with the kingship of a few cities round Toul.

10

To assert his authority, Dagobert in 630 travelled through Burgundy, doing justice, and in 631 he toured Austrasia. Here Arnulf
came from the monastery to which he had retired to give him
counsel, and Pepin the mayor and bishop Humbert of Cologne
were ready to direct Austrasian affairs: it was expected that Dagobert, like his ancestors, would rule from Austrasia. Dagobert
found, however, that Austrasia was too peripheral for the rule of the
regnum francorum; he preferred to rule, like his father Lothar and
like Clovis, from Paris. The Austrasians resented the consequent
pre-eminence of Neustria, and the Burgundian Fredegar dis-
approved: he wrote *c.* 660 and said that Dagobert had forsaken
his earlier love of justice and become too greedy in amassing the
lands of churches and his *leudes*; he had three queens, and really
more concubines than it was fitting to mention. He was generous
of his alms, and might have attained the heavenly kingdom but
for his avarice: even Pepin the mayor dared not remonstrate with
him: his favourite counsellor was Aega, mayor of the Neustrian
palace: the head and front of Dagobert's offending, to an Austrasian sympathizer.

The unfortunate Charibert died in 632: and Dagobert rearranged the rule of his kingdom. To appease the Austrasians,
he sent them his three-year-old son Sigebert, to be installed king
at Metz, confiding him to the tutelage of the bishop of Metz and
duke Adalgisel. After this another son was born to him, called
Clovis: Dagobert made the bishops and nobles swear to accept
him as king of Neustria and Burgundy. To outsiders, Dagobert
seemed respected and strong within his great kingdom: and he
was able to pay some attention to his neighbours.

In 637, the Gascons under their duke Ægyna revolted against
Burgundy and Lothar subdued them. He sent a Burgundian army,
under dukes who were not Burgundian, and under the curious
supreme command of Chadoind the referendary, down into Gascony, and they drove the rebels into the Pyrenees and reduced
their duke to submission.

Dagobert further intervened in Visigothic Spain in favour of
Sisinand: a large tribute in gold was promised him in return. In
Italy even he had sufficient influence to make Rothari give back
a Frankish princess he had imprisoned.

On his eastern frontier Dagobert, however, was less fortunate.
Danger threatened it, and particularly the Franks of Austrasia,
from the Slavs now settled between the Oder and Elbe, in Bohemia and in the eastern Alps: the swaying tide of Slavs was now
half-united by the leadership of Samo, the centre of whose power

was in Bohemia. Frankish merchants were attacked, and *c.* 632 Samo's subjects, called Wends, robbed and killed such a band of Franks, and Dagobert sent Samo an envoy to demand justice. When he was merely chased away, Dagobert declared war, and sought allies among the Lombards and Bavarians. They were old enemies of the Slavs and had some success against them: but a Frankish army was cut to pieces by Wends who invaded Thuringia, and the border tribes who had hitherto obeyed the Franks now, from 632, obeyed Samo.

Dagobert therefore assembled an Austrasian army and retook Mainz, and summoned armies from the other kingdoms to complete the eviction of the Slavs: but at this juncture the Saxons offered to defend the east Frankish frontier, provided the old tribute of 500 cows a year, paid since the time of Lothar I, were remitted. Dagobert accepted: but the result was unfortunate for the Frankish kingdom. Austrasia became increasingly independent under its sub-king, Sigebert; the Saxons grew stronger, and to the Thuringians, in their region south of the Saxons and the Harz mountains, Dagobert had to allow a duke, Radulf. The dukes were always military leaders at the time, and the Thuringians could scarcely defend themselves from the Slavs without one: but he made himself increasingly independent. The needs of frontier defence, as later under the Carolingians, made for local independence. Against Samo himself in Bohemia, Dagobert had led no expedition: but further danger from Slav Bohemia was averted by the collapse of Samo's power on his death.

Dagobert died in 639. He was carried to the basilica of Saint-Denis in his sickness, but found no cure from his holy patron. He confided queen Nantechilde and his son Clovis to Aega the mayor, and on 19 January he died, aged thirty-six, and was buried in the basilica of Saint-Denis. Merovingian monarchy, in its true sense, was buried with him.

From 639 to 721, the death of Dagobert I to that of Chilperic II, some Merovingian shadow ruler, often a child, remained the symbol of the old Frankish unity, and the mayors of the palace of Neustria and Austrasia in effect governed their kingdoms and strove for a general pre-eminence.

At the beginning of this period of shadow Merovingian rule, Clovis II, Dagobert's younger son, ruled Neustria and Burgundy through Aega, and after his death in 641, through Erchinoald, both conciliators of the nobles. Austrasia, under Dagobert's other son, Sigebert III, desired separate government: her palace, headed by Pepin and bishop Humbert, asked for and obtained a share of Dagobert's treasure. Pepin, old and retired, died in 640: but his position had been so strong that his son Grimoald claimed the mayoralty, and obtained it by means of having Otto, mayor of the palace for the child Sigebert III, assassinated (643). Meanwhile in Burgundy, which had had no mayor recently, the regent Nantechilde summoned a council to meet at Orleans, and persuaded it to accept Flaochad, a Frank who had married her niece, as mayor. But the Burgundians feared a strong mayor: they made Flaochad swear to respect the honour and dignities of lay nobles and bishops (642). The mayoralty was thus weak in Burgundy and Neustria, though strong in Austrasia; the strength and turbulence of the Neustrian nobles was shown when Ermanfried, son-in-law and, as he hoped, heir to Aega, a few days before Aega's death assassinated his rival, count Hainulf in full assembly. He then fled to Reims, to take sanctuary in the basilica of Saint-Rémy. Another instance of noble turbulence was the open quarrel in Burgundy of the rich and proud patrician, Willebad, with the mayor, Flaochad: a great plea was held at Chalons-sur-Saône, and the proceedings ended in a kind of ordeal of battle, fought between Willebad and Flaochad and their adherents. Willebad was killed, but when Flaochad died of fever eleven days later, men said it was the judgment of God upon them both for their avarice and ill deeds.

Clovis II died, aged twenty-three, in 657, and Sigebert III, his brother, in 656, aged twenty-seven; he had fought Radulf, duke of the Thuringians, with some success, but government had rested with his mayor, Grimoald.

Grimoald almost overthrew the strong family position of the Arnulfings by an attempt at this point to seize the royal title as well as the substance of power. He desired the throne for his son, and had him adopted by Sigebert III shortly before a son was actually born to Sigebert himself and called Dagobert. Sigebert apparently trusted Grimoald to secure the child Dagobert's succession, but on Sigebert's death Grimoald had his own son enthroned as Childebert III, and had young Dagobert shorn and delivered him to the bishop of Poitiers, with instructions to send him off to some distant monastery. The bishop thought fit to send him to Ireland, where he lived for some twenty years. Meanwhile Grimoald ruled Austrasia for seven years under cover of his son, proclaimed as Childebert III; he was then tricked into going to Paris by the Neustrians, seized, imprisoned, and died (662). His wife was sent off to the cloister under the charge of bishop Robert of

Tours, the young Childebert III disappeared, and for some years the Arnulfings disappeared from the political scene in Austrasia.

The question of the succession in Austrasia in 662 remained open: young Dagobert, away in Ireland was forgotten or his place of refuge unknown. The strongest political personages were Neustrian. Since Clovis II had died there in 657, Balthilde had secured the recognition of her son, Lothar III, as king; she had been a beautiful Anglo-Saxon war captive, a slave girl brought by Erchinoald, mayor of the Neustrian palace. They had had four sons, the eldest now in 657 accepted as Lothar III. Balthilde was known as the patroness of churches and monks: she had given great estates to Saint-Denis, the family abbey of the Neustrian Merovingians, and she had tried to get that early and anomalous foundation, partaking rather of the nature of a house of canons than monks, to accept the strict observance, the subdivision into three choirs for the rendering of perpetual praise to God: the observance of Saint-Riquier. Here she had failed: Saint-Denis was grateful for the endowment but would have nothing to do with perpetual praise. Balthilde now proposed as king to the Austrasian nobles her second son, who became Childeric II (662–675); he was the more acceptable in Austrasia as he reigned under the protection of Himnechilde his aunt (the mother of the absent Dagobert II), and duke Vulfoald, Austrasian mayor of the palace after the fall of the Arnulfings. When Lothar III attained the age of fifteen, in 664–5, Balthilde withdrew to the monastery she had founded on the royal demesne at Chelles, where she died a holy death in 680. Bede speaks of the Anglo-Saxon princesses who in this century were sent to Chelles and other French nunneries for training in the religious life. It appears that many of these royal nunneries in France were 'double', i.e. had a staff of chaplains or monks residing in a separate dwelling within the hedge or fence of the monastic enclosure: and that the so-called Anglo-Saxon 'double monasteries' were copies of the French ones. Such an organization was indeed the only one suited to a house of nuns founded by a princess-abbess; the strange career of the beautiful Balthilde had its results both sides of the Channel in the spread of these 'double' minsters.

Balthilde's son, Lothar III (657–673) ruled as a phantom monarch over Neustria and Burgundy, not as representing her influence but under the tutelage of her enemy, Ebroin, now a powerful mayor of the Neustrian palace. When Lothar III died in 673, Ebroin had his young brother accepted as Thierry III, without even summoning a council to recognize him. This, however, was going too far: the nobles of Neustria and Burgundy, fearing Ebroin's power, appealed to king Childeric II of Austasia for help. He hastened to Paris with his own mayor, Vulfoald, and they seized Thierry III, sheared him and made him a monk at Saint-Denis. Ebroin they captured and nearly killed: but at the prayer of the bishops merely sheared him also and sent him off to be a monk in the distant house of Luxeuil, at the foot of the Jura. It was already clear in 673 that the mayors of the palace were as strong as kings: it was not yet clear whether the mayors of the east or west Franks would achieve predominance.

At the moment, the nobles were in a position to bargain with Childeric II, now sole king in the *regnum Francorum*, about the powers of the mayor: they asked what need there was of a mayor, or at any rate one like Ebroin, who posed as a tyrant and set himself up above the other nobles? Childeric II indeed desired the reality of rule, but could only achieve it by a skilful balancing of personal interests, and in the end his attempt failed; he promised concessions to the nobles, then revoked them and tried to rule by the counsel of Leodegarius, bishop of Autun and Hector, patrician of Marseilles. Both, however, fell into disgrace and had to flee, Leodegarius being sent off to Luxeuil. Childeric II, holding the reins of power, even planned to intervene in Lombardy between rival claimants: but in 675, as he was hunting in the woods of Chelles, he was assassinated. The murderer killed his queen too, and it took some courage for a bishop to come forward to bury them. Audoenus (St Ouen), however, who had been a referendary and was now the revered bishop of Rouen, came forward and buried the royal victims at the abbey of Saint-Vincent. Childeric's mayor, Vulfoald, fled to Austrasia. The vacancy of power in Neustria permitted Ebroin to stage a come-back.

Immediately after Childeric II's murder, the Neustrian and Burgundian nobles took Thierry III out of Saint-Denis and chose for mayor Leudesius, son of the mayor Erchinoald, a move unacceptable to either Leodegarius or Ebroin. The latter succeeded in escaping from Luxeuil. He allied with the nobles of Austrasia, and through their influence, a real (or pretended) son of Thierry III was placed on the throne as Clovis III, and Leudesius was executed. But when Ebroin was firmly in power in Neustria, he thrust away Clovis III and took back Thierry III: and under cover of nominal Merovingian rule tried to deal with over-great nobles, particularly those in non-Neustrian regions. Two bishops of noble origin were trying to make themselves independent in Burgundy: Didier, bishop of Chalons-sur-Saône and Bobbo, bishop of Valence,

who had already been degraded. They were the enemies of Leodegarius in Autun, who was no less Ebroin's own political rival:
they joined forces with the dukes of Champagne and Alsace, and
besieged Leodegarius in Autun. To save his city, he gave himself
up and was brought to Ebroin, who had now survived the threatened
rebellion of the nobles and was supreme in Neustria. Ebroin
confiscated the lands and goods of his enemies, tortured and
blinded Leodegarius, and had him degraded by a complaisant
synod (677 or 679). Leodegarius' brother he had stoned to death,
and all without arousing protest from the mayors of Burgundy and
Austrasia.

Austrasia, however, was not long content with the effective
rule of Ebroin under the shadow king Thierry III: her nobles
remembered the existence in Ireland of Dagobert II. A message
was sent to Wilfrid, bishop of York, inquiring his whereabouts:
Wilfrid took action, sent for him from Ireland, welcomed him in
York and passed him on to the continent. In the early summer of
676 the exile of twenty years was accepted as Dagobert II by the
Austrasian palace, and even by the Austrasian parts of Aquitaine.
A minor war of pillage and raids followed between Thierry III
and Dagobert II, but only till 679. In December that year, by
the initiative of the dukes and the consent of the bishops, Dagobert
was killed out hunting by his own godson: Vulfoald the mayor
disappeared suddenly at the same time. To cover the murder, the
nobles reproached Wilfrid, returning through Gaul at the time,
for helping to bring back to them so bad a king, 'another Rehoboam';
but the populace resorted to his burying place as to that of a saint.

The murder of Dagobert II was the signal for the recovery of
power by the Arnulfings, and this time permanently. They had
been quiescent for fifteen years. Pepin II, who had married
Begga, the sister of Grimoald, now seized power in Austrasia, and
war between the mayors of Austrasia and Neustria was now inevitable. Ebroin and his puppet king, Thierry III, at first defeated
Pepin and the Austrasians near Laon: but he ruled Neustria so
brutally that he was soon murdered. An oppressed *domesticus*
(see p. 297) killed him, *c.* 680, and fled for refuge to Pepin in
Austrasia. The aim of Ebroin had been double, and it had doubly
failed. It had stood for Neustrian supremacy as against Austrasian;
and for the denial of the aristocratic claim to hold all high office in
the palace. Ebroin himself had not been of the old nobility, and
he had dislodged many lay nobles and many aristocratic bishops
from power: he cannot claim any great statesmanship.

An uneasy peace was maintained for a time between Neustria

and Austrasia, largely by the mediation of St Ouen. Two candidates struggled for the mayoralty in Neustria, to the advantage of
Pepin II, who was asked to intervene by the archbishop of Reims.
In 687 Pepin defeated the Neustrians at Tertry, near Saint-
Quentin. The Neustrian mayor, Berchar, was killed, and Thierry III
and the royal treasure fell into Pepin's hand. It was the first military
victory of the Austrasians over the Neustrians for a hundred years,
and it ushered in the dominance of the Austrasian mayors. Pepin II
accepted the suzerainty of Thierry III, but he put in a mayor of
his own choosing at Paris and distributed the confiscated estates
of the nobles at will. When the mayor of his choice, Norbert,
died in 700, he put in one of his own sons, significantly named
Grimoald, as mayor of Neustria.

The real significance of the battle of Tertry is the fall of the
Neustrian palace, as an independent organ of government. Clovis
had been strong enough to rule from Paris, and there the Merovingian tradition had its strongest roots. Lothar I, Lothar II, Dagobert I, Childeric II had all sought to rule the *regnum Francorum*
from Paris, and when Austrasia, the region of Germanic settlement,
of Germanic recruitment, of Germanic frontier defence and the
strongest Frankish armies, became too strong to support the rule
of Neustria, the Merovingian dynasty fell, and the Neustrian
palace with it. Though the public acts and private charters of
Austrasian mayors continued for a time to be dated by the names
of Merovingian kings, these were now indeed phantoms.

Their nominal reigns can be mentioned briefly, as stages in the
increasing power of their mayors. Thierry III died in 690, and
Pepin II imposed as king Clovis, a child who soon died, and in
694.Childebert III (who died in 711) and Dagobert III; all lived
in Neustria at the will of the Austrasian mayors. The Arnulfings
had learned a lesson from the career of Grimoald: they allowed the
last Merovingians, mainly children, to live in an atmosphere of
superstitious reverence: they no longer wished to dispense with a
king whom they regarded as a symbol of Frankish unity. It is
doubtful whether Neustria would in the early part of the sixty
odd years which intervened between Tertry and the coronation of
Pepin III have tolerated the naked rule of an Austrasian noble as
king: Merovingian shadow royalty was a sop to Neustrian pride.

Dangers which menaced the Franks from external enemies were
meanwhile dealt with by the Austrasian mayors.

The Frisians from the coast of the North Sea to the river Weser,
pagan and hostile, had for some years been pressing south: they
had taken from the Franks Utrecht and Durstedt. Their leader

Aldgild, who had allowed Wilfrid to begin the conversion of his people, was now replaced by duke Radbod who was hostile both to Christianity and the Franks. Pepin II fought him for some months: pressed the Frisian army back beyond the Rhine and regained Utrecht and Durstedt. In Utrecht he installed the Anglo-Saxon missionary Willibald as bishop. He sealed an alliance with Radbod by a family alliance, marrying his son Grimoald to Radbod's daughter, newly baptized.

Against the Alemans Pepin also led expeditions: their duke Godefrid had disclaimed the suzerainty of a Frankish mayor of the palace and made himself largely independent. Between 709 and 712 Pepin fought the Alemans under Godefrid's successor and re-established Frankish authority, which was the less difficult in that the Alemans were already Christian.

Against the Bavarians he did the same. Both Irish and Gallo-Roman missionaries had worked here, and for the ultra-Rhenane Franks Pepin founded the see of Salzburg; Christianity was a security for Frankish influence.

In Aquitaine, Pepin was less successful in asserting a general Frankish overlordship: the land had been too much partitioned, and the various groups of cities still adhered to a divided lordship. The Auvergne, Poitou and Touraine were loyal to Austrasia: the Limousin and Toulousain to Neustria, while Le Berry, Perigord and Quercy were Burgundian. Even church councils could not normally be held for the whole of Aquitaine, and counts, dukes and patricians struggled for power with very little reference to Austrasia.

Pepin II (whom modern historians call Pepin of Heristhal) was the first to exercise a general Carolingian power: he prepared the way for Charles Martel, Pepin III and Charles the Great. But the perpetuation of the dynasty at this point hung by a thread: in 708 Pepin II's son Drogo died: in 714 Grimoald was assassinated by a pagan while praying at the tomb of St Lambert at Liége, and when Pepin II himself died in 715, he had no surviving son. He was eighty years old when he died, and his wife Plectrude wished to govern in the name of her grandsons: but the nobles could not tolerate this. The Neustrians rose, beat the Austrasians in a battle in the forest of Compiègne, struck through the woods to the Meuse, made overtures to the still pagan Radbod and to the Saxons across the Rhine. The latter crossed the Rhine and ravaged down to Cologne. In this unheard-of crumbling of the power built up by Pepin, his son by the Lady Alpaïs, Charles, escaped from prison and sought for power.

At the end of 715, Dagobert III also died, and in the absence of an effective mayor, all was confusion and, for Austrasia, danger. The Neustrians took from the cloister a reputed son of Childeric II, a forty-year-old clerk, and when his hair had grown accepted him as Chilperic II. Salvation for Austrasia was to come from Pepin II's grandson Charles, the warlike son of Alpaïs. He gradually retrieved the military position, though he was defeated when he first attacked the Frisians and though the Neustrians and Chilperic II besieged Cologne and required Plectrude to hand over the royal treasure and recognize Chilperic's authority. In 716, however, Charles (Martel), who had been hiding in the Ardennes, surprised the Neustrians and defeated them with great losses. In 717 he again defeated the Neustrians at Vinchy: and he was now strong enough to force Plectrude to give up to him his father's treasure. In 718 he found a descendant of Thierry III, and set him up as the Merovingian king, Lothar IV (718–719). Dealing first with the Frisians and Saxons, he led an expedition which defeated and killed Radbod and established Frankish power over the Frisians. The much weakened mayor of Neustria appealed for help to duke Eudes of Aquitaine, who marched to the Loire, crossed it and joined the Neustrians. He was defeated, however, by Charles, and had to withdraw, first to Paris and then to Aquitaine, taking with him Chilperic II and the Neustrian treasure. By 719 the Neustrian mayor had fled in impotence to the west.

At this juncture, Lothar IV died, and Charles needed another Merovingian shadow king. He negotiated with duke Eudes, who was just then embarrassed by Muslim attack in Aquitaine, for a general peace: it was arranged that Charles should accept Chilperic II and guarantee Eudes' position in Aquitaine. But in 721 Chilperic II also died.

Charles then took from the monastery of Chelles a Merovingian child, the son of Dagobert III and gave him the name of Thierry IV (721–737): though the Neustrian mayor held out at Angers for some time against accepting him, he had in the end to submit. From 719, in spite of the nominal sovereignty of Thierry IV, Charles Martel ruled France, including Burgundy. The death of bishop Savary of Auxerre there in 720 had removed the strongest rival to his rule.

The descendant of bishop Arnulf of Metz and Pepin of Landen had seized power from the Merovingians: the mayor of the Austrasian palace had triumphed over the other mayors. For a short time yet the Arnulfings, though they ruled Francia, were to retain a Merovingian king as a symbol of Frankish unity.

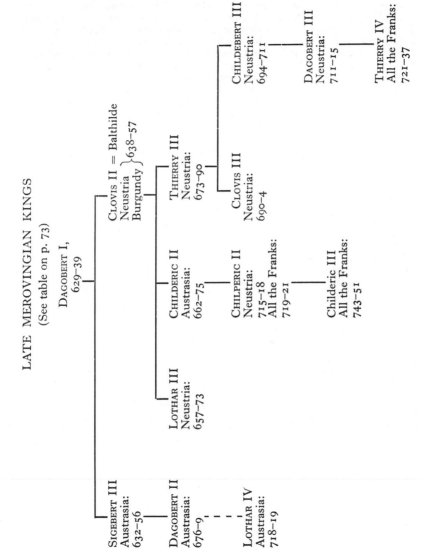

LATE MEROVINGIAN KINGS

(See table on p. 73)

DAGOBERT I,
629–39

SIGEBERT III
Austrasia:
632–56

DAGOBERT II
Austrasia:
676–9

LOTHAR IV
Austrasia:
718–19

CLOVIS II = Balthilde
Neustria ⎰638–57
Burgundy ⎱

LOTHAR III
Neustria:
657–73

CHILDERIC II
Austrasia:
662–75

THIERRY III
Neustria:
673–90

CHILPERIC II
Neustria:
715–18
All the Franks:
719–21

CLOVIS III
Neustria:
690–4

Childeric III
All the Franks:
743–51

CHILDEBERT III
Neustria:
694–711

DAGOBERT III
Neustria:
711–15

THIERRY IV
All the Franks:
721–37

BIBLIOGRAPHICAL NOTE

As for chapter iv: R. L. Poole, *Chronicles and Annals*, 1926; L. Dupraz, *Royaume des Francs*, 1948: see also L. Levillain, *Études sur l'abbaye de Saint-Denis à l'époque mérovingienne, Bibliot. de l'école des chartes*, 1921–30; N. Åberg, *Die Franken und Westgoten*, 1922; G. Behrens, *Merovingerzeit*, 1947 (a comprehensive, illustrated description of early Frankish pottery and grave-finds from the Romisch-Germanischen Museum at Mainz); and L. Dupraz, *Contribution à l'histoire du Regnum Francorum pendant le troisième quart du VII*ᵉ *siècle*, 1948. See also, for the Merovingian bishop Arculf's description of the holy places in the east, D. Meehan, *De locis sanctis*, Dublin, 1958; for the Merovingian *beneficium*, retaining the Roman sense as a concession of privilege, R. W. A. Immink and H. J. Scheltema, *At the Roots of Medieval Society*, Oslo, 1958.

CHAPTER XVI

CHARLES MARTEL AND PEPIN
THE SHORT

WHEN Charles Martel seized power in 719, he had to deal with a condition bordering on anarchy within Francia and the successful encroachment of enemies from without. The struggle between the mayors of Neustria and Austrasia and the bitter resentment of the Austrasian palace at the attempted rule of Plectrude had reduced the *regnum Francorum* to a state of extreme weakness. In the south, Aquitaine under its duke Eudes was nearly independent; the Saracens were pressing beyond the Pyrenees, nearly to Toulouse; on the eastern frontier, Frisians, Alemans, Saxons and Bavarians were preparing to renounce Frankish suzerainty. But in Charles the Franks had found what at this juncture they above all needed, a fine military leader, a hammer (Martel) of their enemies.

His rule accordingly, from 719 to 741, was a period notable chiefly for frontier defence and the defeat of external enemies. Since war is expensive, it was also a period of oppressive rule for ecclesiastics and lay lords alike.

On the eastern frontier in 719 there was danger from the Saxons, Alemans, Suabians and Bavarians. Duke Lantfrid had gone so far towards independence as to issue on his own authority a new version of the old customary *Lex Alemannorum*; in Bavaria, the duke went his own way. Charles now undertook, almost every summer, campaigns for the restoration of his authority in the east. In 720, 722, 724 and 738 there were expeditions against the Saxons and the Alemans; in 730 the Alemannian duchy was reduced to a province. The years 733 and 734 saw what was really a conquest of the northern Frisians. In 725 and 728 Charles intervened in Bavaria, where duke Hucbert recognized his authority: but the duchy was distant and difficult to control from the Rhine mouth, and when Hucbert died Charles allowed his relative, Odilo, to succeed him.

In Aquitaine, duke Eudes aspired to semi-independence, and when Charles made a military expedition there in 731 he did not succeed in getting effective control. But a greater danger now menaced Aquitaine than Austrasian overlordship: that of Muslim conquest from Spain. Between 714 and 717 the Muslim rulers of Spain had been pressing along the Mediterranean coast, and were engaged in conquering the Narbonnaise. In 721 one of them, Asama, attacked Toulouse, but was, however, defeated and killed by duke Eudes. Possession of Toulouse would have given the Arabs command of the valley of the Garonne, the northern frontier of Gascony: and when they turned back from the incorporation of this inland, north Pyrenean, region, they set themselves to gain Septimania, the coastal province that runs from the Pyrenees to the Rhone mouth, with Narbonne as its chief port. In 721 they took its cities of Carcassonne and Nîmes, and in August that year they took Autun.

For the next ten years, 721 to 731, Eudes sought to defend Aquitaine by exploiting the quarrels of Arabs and Berbers in Spain: he made a diplomatic marriage with the daughter of the Berber chief, 'Uthman ben Abi Neza, who commanded the Pyrenean frontier guard of Arab Spain. But in 731 'Uthman rebelled against the Arab ruler 'Abd ar-Rahman and was defeated: and in 732 'Abd ar-Rahman and his troops poured through the passes at the northern end of the Pyrenees and ravaged Gascony. They plundered the country and defeated Eudes at the crossings of the Garonne and the Dordogne: they burned the church of St Hilary at Poitiers, and they prepared to plunder the basilica of St Martin at Tours.

In this extremity, Eudes appealed for help to Charles Martel. He brought an army south to defend Tours, met the Saracens at the outskirts of Poitiers, as they advanced to the attack, and defeated and killed 'Abd ar-Rahman: the Arabs withdrew beyond the Pyrenees. The battle of Poitiers had momentous results: it actually checked Saracen advance north of the Pyrenees, and it led to the submission of Aquitaine to Charles, who pressed his conquering march to the mouth of the Garonne and entered Bordeaux. Eudes' sons showed themselves unwilling to forgo Aquitanian independence and had to be brought to submission by arms: in 736 Charles accepted one of them, Hunaud, as duke and received from him an oath of fidelity. Feudalism had not yet come: the oath taken by Hunaud was that of a *vassus*, a 'recommandé', to a patron.

The duchy of Aquitaine, however, was only a military command, not an administrative unit, and in spite of Hunaud's submission Charles had difficulty in asserting his authority over south-east Gaul. Duke Mauront in Provence, the bishop of Auxerre and others tried to secure a local independence and needed military coercion to keep them subject. Charles led an expedition which held Lyons in 733, and left a garrison: but the local nobles intrigued with the Arabs against him, and in 735 the Arabs were able to enter

Arles and plunder Provence. In 736 Charles had to lead an army south and retake Lyons, Arles and Marseilles: Arab capture of this port would have drawn tighter the economic blockade of western Europe. It is a sign of the difference of culture between the Mediterranean, quasi-Byzantine, south of France and the Germanic north, that in 736–7 duke Mauront and the Provençal nobles delivered to the Saracens Avignon and the left bank of the Rhone: and when Charles and his son Hildebrand in 737 led another army south to drive them out, retook Avignon and blockaded Narbonne, the local leaders were so lukewarm in support that they could not hold the country. They burned Nîmes, Agde, Béziers and other cities to punish the citizens and deprive the Arabs of supplies and retreated north. In 738, while Charles was occupied in a Saxon war, Mauront rebelled again and the Arabs crossed the Rhone: Charles had to ask help from the Lombard Liutprand, and he crossed the Alps and drove the invaders out. Local rebellions broke out again in 739 and 741: the last was suppressed by Hildebrand and his legitimate brother Pepin, son of Charles Martel, a few months before Charles's death.

Charles Martel's defence of the land of the Franks was achieved by ruthlessness to rebels and those who were reluctant to contribute to the cost of campaigns. There was no general measure of secularization of church property, but a long series of confiscations and usurpations as need arose and opportunity offered. Bishops who sided with rebels, as Rigobert of Reims and Wando, abbot of Saint-Wandrille, were deprived of all their lands, and the bishop of Orleans was thus punished for his inactivity against duke Eudes. But even without such a political justification, church lands were often arbitrarily seized and granted as *precariae* to the *vassi* who composed Charles's armies; he needed cavalry and encouraged the growth of their number.

Charles ruled throughout as sovereign of the Franks, and for the last four years of his life, after the death of Thierry IV in 737, he did not create any new Merovingian shadow king. He issued edicts and did justice on his sole authority, that of the *maiordomus* of the palace. When Gregory III wrote to him for help against the Lombards in 739 and 740, he addressed him as *subregulus*: but his request for aid showed that he well knew Charles possessed the reality of Frankish power. Charles's dispositions for the succession were those of an effective sovereign and still in the Merovingian manner, patrimonial. Shortly before his death at the villa of Quierzy in October 741, Charles had drawn up the act which decreed that his eldest son, Carloman, should receive Austrasia,

Alemannia and Thuringia: the younger, Pepin the Short, Neustria, Burgundy and Provence: and a natural son, Grifo, lands in all three kingdoms, without sovereignty. Neither Aquitaine nor Bavaria appear in the act. Both Carloman and Pepin (Pepin the Short, Pepin III) became mayors of the palace, of Neustria and Austrasia respectively.

For ten years, from 741 to 751, the two mayors ruled France, not without opposition from those whose aspirations to independence Charles Martel had suppressed, and from their own half-brother Grifo. The peripheral regions under Frankish rule revolted immediately on the news of Charles's death: the dukes of Aquitaine and Bavaria disclaimed allegiance, Theutbald claimed the position of duke in Bavaria, the Saxons plundered their neighbours, and Grifo rose against the authority of his half-brothers. Carloman and Pepin dealt with all these menaces to the peace in unison. They imprisoned Grifo, wasted Aquitaine in 742, defeating its duke, and in the late summer attacked the Alemans and marched through Alsace to the Danube.

Since some of the rebels had sheltered themselves under an unwillingness to obey a mere mayor of the palace, Carloman and Pepin now (in 743) raised the Merovingian Childeric III to the throne, without any diminution of their own power and dignity. In 743 and 744 Carloman led new expeditions against the Saxons; in 743 Carloman and Pepin jointly brought duke Odilo of Bavaria to submission. They invaded his country and at the peace of 744 deprived him of the Nordgau. The Alemans too were chastised by expeditions in 744 and 746.

While the two mayors were campaigning on the eastern frontier, the duke of Aquitaine again rebelled and even crossed the Loire to attack Neustria. In 745 Carloman and Pepin defeated him and forced his resignation in favour of his son.

Meanwhile, in the frontier regions beyond their effective control, Boniface the Anglo-Saxon missionary had long been working under Frankish and papal encouragement. In 719 he had gone to the pagans of Thuringia and Hesse; in 722 he had obtained episcopal consecration from Gregory II, and been commended by him to Charles Martel for protection; in 732 he had been made archbishop by Gregory III and had founded the sees of Büraburg, Wurzburg, Eichstätt and, in 741, Erfürt, all with Charles's aid. Boniface had summoned helpers, monks and nuns, from England, and had taught the pagans, setting up preaching crosses at places where later churches were built and protecting the setting up of such crosses by obtaining papal licence; he had founded, not only greater monasteries, but small cells of monks for the Christianization of the countryside. In 735 he was summoned to Bavaria to preach and teach, and in 739, with duke Odilo's help, he reorganized the church of that country. He divided the duchy into the four sees of Salzburg, Freising, Regensburg and Passau. He found the two mayors of the palace no less willing to support him in Germany than their father Charles, and anxious also for his help in two matters concerning the Franks: the use of the royal title and the reform of the Frankish church.

Their first action had been to strengthen his own hands in Germany: Carloman granted him the lands to support his great abbey of Fulda in Hesse, of which his disciple and successor, Sturm, was made the first abbot. In 745, to strengthen Boniface's metropolitan authority and allow him to introduce reform into the Austrasian church, Carloman and Pepin sought to erect Cologne into an Austrasian archbishopric for him; but there was noble opposition, and in the end, Boniface was made, by the action of pope Zacharias and the concurrence of the two brothers, metropolitan of Mainz.

The Frankish clergy, both Austrasian and Neustrian, meanwhile stood in need of reform. The Merovingian nomination of bishops had not always produced a satisfactory episcopate and clerical hierarchy, and the recent annexation of episcopal and particularly monastic lands, however necessary in the cause of defence, had produced desolated minsters and wandering and irregular monks.

There were other causes also that made the Frankish church seem to Boniface and his friends, product of the golden age of monastic learning in Northumbria, admirers of Bede and the Benedictine life, very remiss and disorderly. For one thing, the 'false monasteries' that Bede complained of in his letter to archbishop Egbert of York, would seem to have developed in the more barbarian parts of northern Gaul, for the same cause was at work; when land held by tribal custom, not bequeathable at death, could be rendered thus bequeathable only by a written grant, and such grants were made normally to minsters, Germanic lords, Frankish or Anglo-Saxon, sometimes founded 'private monasteries' for the sake of getting bookland, continuing to live there themselves with their wives and families. Again, in an age when the Benedictine rule in Gaul was often used along with the Celtic rule of Columbanus, and not sharply distinguished from that of the *vita apostolica*, or communal apostolic life such as had been practised by Augustine of Hippo, there was cause for confusion in the minds of

Benedictine reformers. Even great monasteries like those of St
Martin at Tours and Saint-Denis were houses of canons rather
than monks, and had old, lay bedesmen entered on their *matriculae*,
and there were other houses of an intermediate and anomalous
nature. Moreover, houses founded as Benedictine were sometimes
allowed to become houses of canons, because canons were not
bound to give up their patrimony, and bishops in times of civil
exaction found it easier to feed canons than starving monks. All
these causes, beside the downright irregularities and immorality
of impoverished and wandering monks and clergy, cried out for
the reform and reorganization of the Frankish church.

As early as 742 Carloman had appealed to Boniface to reform the
manners of the Frankish clergy: with Boniface's advice, Carloman
announced at an Austrasian synod of 742 that lands usurped from
churches should be restored. Pepin also asked Boniface's help in
743. But the question of restoring monastic lands and thus aiding
monastic order could not be solved by a simple decree of restoration, for that would have dispossessed the *vavasores* of the army,
still needed for defence. Hence in an Austrasian synod at Estinnes
in 743, and a Neustrian one at Soissons in 744, it was further laid
down that part only of the lands should be restored and that on the
other part the annual payment (*cens*) for the *precaria*, hitherto paid
to the mayor, should now be paid to the church which had earlier
possessed the land. From 750, moreover, it was ordered that church
lands not hitherto confiscated in whole or part should suffer partial
confiscation. The partial and unequal distribution of the burden of
defence was better equalized.

The six years' joint rule of the two brothers ended in August
747, when Carloman, uncompelled by external pressure, desired to
become a monk. He went to Rome and received the clerical tonsure from pope Zacharias, planning to build himself an abbey on
Mount Soracte: but in 750 he gave up his project and entered as
a simple monk at Monte Cassino.

Pepin from 747 governed the Franks as sole mayor, Pepin III:
he seems to have contemplated using his half-brother Grifo, and
released him from prison, but Grifo departed to the Saxons, made
trouble, and had to be suppressed with them, by an expedition, in
748. And when duke Odilo died at about that time, Grifo escaped
to Bavaria and hoped to make himself independent there with the
help of Lantfrid II, now duke. Pepin, however, marched into
Bavaria, captured Grifo and Lantfrid II, and made Tassilo III,
son of Odilo, duke in Lantfrid's place, keeping a tight hand himself over the government of the duchy. To Grifo he accorded a few

counties in Neustria: but Grifo preferred to leave them and take refuge in Aquitaine.

The single rule of Pepin the Short (751–768) was marked by the taking of the royal title: the Merovingian dynasty was at length changed for the Carolingian. Pepin was now uncontested master of France, with the exception of some small trouble from Carloman's son Drogo. From 749 to 751 there had been a two years' peace: and the omens were favourable for assuming the royal title, for the two great spiritual forces of the day, Boniface and the papacy, were ready to legalize the assumption of kingship, even as Samuel had anointed Saul to be king, changing the rule of Israel.

In 750 Pepin sent Burchard, bishop of Würzburg and Fulrad, abbot of Saint-Denis, to pope Zacharias, asking him which of the two he should judge worthy of the kingdom, Childeric who had the name of king but did nothing, or Pepin, who disposed of all the business of the kingdom? Zacharias answered them and announced by the authority of the blessed Peter the apostle that Pepin was king, and commanded him to be anointed to the kingship by Boniface, archbishop of Mainz, which thing should be done at Soissons. The anointing was performed by Boniface, at the head of a band of bishops in the autumn of 751, after an assembly at Soissons had formally raised Pepin on the shield: the change of dynasty received supernatural sanction.

The strength of Pepin's position at home was now sufficient to enable him to intervene in Italy, and by his successful campaign there to become the dominant power in western Europe: to have a 'foreign policy' and not merely a 'frontier policy'. He became a force to be reckoned with by rulers in Italy, Constantinople, Spain and even Baghdad, after the Italian expedition which he now undertook.

The appeals of pope Stephen II (or III) for help from Pepin have been already noticed (see p. 252 and also p. 322). On 6 January 754, pope Stephen, who had travelled from Italy, was met by Pepin three miles from his villa at Ponthion. The circumstances of the meeting were notable. Pepin acted as *strator* to the pope, dismounting and leading his horse by the bridle, which shows that the famous forgery, the Donation of Constantine (*Constitutum Constantini*) had already been produced in Italy, and studied by the papal *scrinium*. The Donation was a magnificent amplification of the theme of the old *Actus beati Silvestri* (see p. 176). It was addressed by Constantine to pope Silvester I: in its first part, Constantine related his instruction and baptism by pope Silvester

at Rome, and the cure there of his leprosy. In its second part, by
an expansion of Constantine's laying aside of his imperial insignia
in the *Actus*, Constantine conferred all these insignia on the pope
(who refused, however, to wear the diadem, as unfitting to a head
that had received the tonsure and received instead the tall white
cap or *phrygium*), acknowledged his primacy over the four patriarchates of Antioch, Jerusalem, Alexandria and Constantinople
and all other bishops, and conferred on him, among other privileges, the territorial rule of Rome, and all the provinces and towns
of Italy. In sign of the temporal, quasi-imperial power thus conferred, Constantine himself acted as *strator* to Silvester, leading his
horse by the bridle. There was, in fact, in the middle of the eighth
century, a vacancy of power in the old exarchate of Ravenna and
the Byzantine duchy of Rome, which the author of the *Constitutum*
thus filled and more than filled. His work of historical imagination
was to change the climate of opinion in the Latin west as effectively as St Augustine's *De Civitate Dei* had done earlier: and the
beginning of its effectiveness dates from the encounter of pope
Stephen and Pepin at Ponthion.

Two actions of Stephen were dictated by the concept of papal
temporal power lying behind the Donation: the renewed confirmation by the pope of Pepin and his dynasty as kings of the Franks,
and the obligation imposed that they should act as protector of the
papacy against its enemies. After wintering at Saint-Denis, pope
Stephen in June 754, anointed Pepin and his two sons kings in a
great ceremony at Saint-Denis, and conferred on them the title of
patrician of the Romans. The title of patrician had been conferred
on Charles Martel as a simple title of honour which the Byzantine
emperors bestowed on such officers as the exarch of Ravenna, the
(Byzantine) duke of Rome, etc.: the title *patricius Romanorum* was
new and was given as implying the obligation to the protectorate
of the papacy. In pope Stephen's letters, indeed, he spoke of the
unction he had bestowed on Pepin and his sons precisely as making
them protectors of the holy see, as if the office of protector as well
as king was conferred with this sacramental sign. Pepin certainly
understood this new obligation as binding him to defence of the
papacy against the Lombards.

As to the moral question of the sanction conferred by the fabricated and tendencious *Constitutum Constantini*: it should be noticed
that public opinion (or rather, notarial practice) tolerated at the
time the production of written evidence of something held to be
true: certainly the *Constitutum* was accepted by the papal household and *scrinium*, and by the notarially trained monks of Saint-

Denis. This does not imply, however, any general or local tradition of the events related in the *Constitutum*, such as often lay behind the facts in a 'forged' land charter. The *Constitutum* was an able forgery, fine propaganda, the work of a single mind, used with boldness and imagination by Stephen II and his *scrinium*.

Pope Stephen's object in his journey to France in 754 was the obtaining of Pepin's help against the Lombard king Aistulf, the usurper of papal lands. Pepin encountered, however, some opposition from the nobles to the undertaking of an expedition to Italy to restore the papal lands: expeditions to distant Italy had not so far brought the Franks much good, and there had recently been an alliance with the Lombards: Carloman too left Monte Cassino and travelled to France, hoping to prevent the Frankish invasion and maintain peace. Pepin shut him up in a monastery at Vienne, where in 755 he died; and prevailed upon an assembly at Quierzy to accept his Italian project. He had motives other than devotion to the papacy to undertake the war, for Aistulf had been sheltering his enemy, Grifo.

In 755 Pepin fulfilled his promise to the pope by an expedition to Italy. He besieged Pavia and obtained from Aistulf a promise to restore to the *Romani* (i.e. the pope) Ravenna and the other territories of the exarchate. The Byzantine government, belatedly informed in 756, sent an embassy to Pepin to remonstrate, but fruitlessly. After the second expedition to Italy to enforce the Lombard cessions, and a two years' partial rule of the territories by the Franks, Pepin's envoy, Fulrad of Saint-Denis, formally and symbolically 'restored' them to the pope, laying the keys of certain exarchate cities and a written diploma on the altar of St Peter's. The pope ruled the duchy of Rome and the exarchate, the *respublica Romanorum*,[1] as a kind of papal state, under the protection of Pepin: and it was Pepin who arranged the further delimitation of territories between Stephen and the new Lombard king, Desiderius, in 763. Suzerainty over the duchies of Spoleto and Benevento was denied to him; Pepin remained in control of papal relations with the Lombards.

Pepin's conquest of the Lombards had brought him into relations with the Byzantine emperor, Constantine V (Copronymus). He sent an embassy to Constantinople in 756, and received one from Constantine at Compiègne in 757: the envoys brought him an

---

[1] It has been claimed by some historians that 'respublica Romanorum' implied the temporal sovereignty of Latin Christendom: see Dr Ullmann, *Growth of Papal Government:* the phrase had, in any case, a particular application to the lands claimed by the papacy in Italy.

organ as present from the emperor. But the Frankish conquests in
Italy prevented permanently good relations with Byzantium, which
had always valued southern Italy. Greek embassies in 765 and
767 tried in vain to arrange a Franco-Byzantine royal marriage, and
to make trouble between Pepin and the pope on doctrinal issues.

The dominant position of Pepin in western Europe even made
his alliance valuable to the Abbasid caliph of Baghdad, Mansur.
Both he and Pepin seem to have sought to co-operate against the
Umayyads of Spain: a Frankish embassy went to Baghdad in 765
and Arab envoys reached France in 768.

Though Pepin's intervention in Italy stood out to his contemporaries as his most remarkable achievement, it was made during
a long series of summer campaigns to establish or maintain his
power over Aquitaine and the Mediterranean coast, the Saxons
and Bavaria. There was still much fighting to be done with the
Saracens from Spain; Charles Martel had attempted to drive them
from Septimania, but had not succeeded. Various Saracen setbacks
now favoured Pepin's effort to expel them from the Frankish
Mediterranean lands; the Kharijites (seceders) rose in Africa and
caused difficulties to the caliphate after 740; the Berbers revolted
against the Saracens in Spain in 741–2; the Kalbites, another Syro-
Arabian sect in Islam, made difficulties in Spain in 745 and 746;
the establishment of the Abbasid caliphate in Baghdad caused a
rift between the east and west of Islam, and, finally, the Umayyad
amirate, independent of Baghdad, was established by 'Abd ar-
Rahman at Cordoba in 756. The Christian inhabitants of the Septi-
manian cities, with the help of the Visigothic leader Ansemund and
a Frankish army, threw out their Saracen garrisons; the Franks
regained Nîmes, Maguelone, Agde, Béziers and their territories;
the last Saracen stronghold Narbonne, long enabled to hold out by
the Arab fleet, was regained for the Franks in 759. The population
rose and massacred the Saracen garrison.

The Frankish conquest of Septimania had disturbed the duke of
Aquitaine, who had hoped to liberate it from the Saracens himself:
he had attempted to seize Narbonne in 751. Pepin himself, however, was now able to safeguard his conquest of Septimania by
attempting to gain the direct rule of Aquitaine, winning territory
there gradually from the north. As excuse for sending armies to
Aquitaine, he could allege the duke's aid to his enemy, Grifo, and
his confiscation of the lands of Austrasian churches in Aquitaine
and disregard of other Frankish grants of privileges and immunities to churches. Between 760 and 763 he sent an army annually
into Aquitaine, while the duke retaliated by raiding Septimania

and Burgundy. But the Franks had secured themselves a citadel in 756 in Bourges, and from there they pushed eastward into the Auvergne and from 766 south-westward towards the Garonne. Pepin thus gradually won back the Aquitanian lands and had the duke assassinated on 2 June 768. He had secured the direct rule of Aquitaine: he now appointed counts for the territories within the duchy and issued at Saintes a capitulary for Aquitaine. The clauses of the capitulary guaranteed to his subjects personal security and Aquitanian private law, and to his clergy stability of their benefices; from them in return an orderly and regular church life was required.

The Saxons also Pepin brought back to their old relations of tribute and distant subjection. Throughout his reign they had been raiding Hesse and Thuringia: in 753 Pepin marched against them and conquered their lands to the Weser; after another expedition in 768 the Saxons had to promise an annual tribute of 300 horses. It is notable that these border Germanic tribes never paid tribute in money: their early tribute in cows represented the current wealth of the tribe, and the later tribute of horses points to Pepin's military needs.

With Tassilo III, duke of Bavaria, Pepin had for a time good relations. Tassilo ruled under his protection, and in 757 actually came to France and before the assembly at Compiègne took the vassal's oath of fidelity. He fulfilled his obligations of general loyalty and adherence by rendering military service to Pepin in the Italian expedition of 756, and in the first expedition to Aquitaine. The work of Christian missionaries now in Bavaria tended to support Frankish interests: Christianity penetrated at this time to the Slav races of Styria and Carinthia, to the north-east of Bavaria. In this border duchy, however, Frankish control of internal government was very difficult to maintain, and at the end of Pepin's reign Tassilo was becoming more independent and less loyal.

Frankish government and institutions had developed during the 200 odd years since the reign of Lothar I, but without revolutionary change; even the rise to power of the mayors of the Austrasian palace was long prepared. From the first, the Frankish royal power was personal, resting on the astonishing military success of Clovis, and borrowing nothing of the Roman conception of a magistracy within the law. The lands of a tribal king won by conquest were his personal possession, to be divided out among his sons as family land would be divided out by the custom of the folk: hence, throughout Merovingian history, the patrimonial partitions of the *regnum Francorum* at a king's death. The Frankish monarchy was despotic, and the royal orders or bans absolute; the régime has been described as despotism tempered by religion and fear of assassination. The mysterious power of the saint to protect the people of his see, or the clients who resorted to his basilica, was one of the few things feared by the Merovingian king: St Martin, patron saint of the Franks, was strong enough to protect the people of Tours even from the Merovingian tax-surveyors, the makers of *descriptiones*. His miraculous protection more than once availed them and, by the king's orders, they were not 'described'.

As to the king's powers in legislation: the Merovingians allowed private law to be regulated by Germanic folk custom, Roman law, or the curious *ad hoc* mixture of both administered by the *mallus*. Public law, however, they regulated by edicts or precepts issued on their sole authority: announced usually in an assembly but not the work of the assembly. Such edicts dealt with the organization of justice, the relations of the king with bishops, churches and abbeys, and the clerical order. In the royal writing office the notaries copied the rescripts of the late Roman emperors as preambles to the royal writs or letters and issued the diplomas of a privilege and immunity, and the formal series of documents used for royal appointments to bishoprics. In such appointments, contrary as they were to the canons, the kings often nominated from the palace lay, notarial, officers, who were then ordained to the see with or without observance of the canonical 'interstices' between the reception of the various grades of the clerical order. Election by the clergy and people of the see became exceptional in the later Merovingian period and, for the candidate, dangerous. Simony often accompanied the exercise of the royal power of episcopal appointment.

Not only did the king control the appointment of bishops, but the summons to church councils and the passage of canons, for which the royal authority was necessary. There was no firm boundary between matters temporal and spiritual, and kings and bishops lived and ruled from day to day, with no definitions and delimitations made between their powers. When Charles Martel made his heavy confiscations of church lands, there was no effective protest, not only because danger threatened, but because the resumption of benefices and *precaria* was often practised by the kings against lay land holders, and was, indeed, one of the subjects of discontent with their régime. The church was less able to defend herself. Pepin the Short was the patron of church reform and carried through with Boniface an equalization of the burden of his father's confiscations: but he made no fresh grants to churches himself, except in the case of Saint-Denis, where he had been brought up.

The Merovingian secular government was neither specifically Roman nor Germanic: the kings preserved what coincided with their own interests, making innovations at need, but not systematically. No effort was made to preserve the old Roman structure of government in seventeen provinces under the praetorian prefect of the Gauls: but within the provincial structure of the old Roman government there had survived the *civitas*, the small Celtic or Iberian state which had preceded the Roman conquest: and these *civitates* remained. They had been economically ruined, but their territorial boundaries lived on into the period of Frankish rule, partly because each city had a bishop and clergy to serve the area and they knew the boundaries. Sixth-century Gaul had about 120 such 'cities', or sees, and the Merovingians took them over and used them permanently as administrative units. Without modifying their bounds, the king installed his representative in each city, his *comes*: the later emperors had used *comites* for various posts, but had never allotted one to each city and its territory. The Goths and Burgundians were the first to do this and Clovis had followed suit. The count was, in his territory, a real viceroy: he commanded the city's military forces, and had final administrative and judicial power: he also enforced the payment of royal levies. In the south, he was for long chosen from Roman stock.

In the Germanic north, cities were few, and there was no ready-made counterpart to the *comes*: the Frankish *centenarius* or *thunginus* seems to have been an elected tribal officer, military or civil, and as such he soon disappeared. The Merovingian kings introduced counts among their own people in these regions, assimilating their position and work to that of the old *graf* (see p. 63). Little is known of the *graf* in early days: but he seems to have been an estate agent, a reeve, like the Anglo-Saxon *ʒerefa*. The northern graf-count has as his sphere, however, not the territory of a city, but the *pagus*: in the basins of the Scheldt, Meuse and Rhine Christianity had been weak, and the city boundaries had been irrecoverably obliterated by the invasions.

The *graf* was not the only Merovingian estate agent: like the Visigoths and Burgundians the Frankish kings took over the territories of the fisc, and their administration by a *domesticus*. Each royal demesne was an administrative and judicial island of territory within the *pagus* or *civitas*, not under the jurisdiction of the count but of a domestic. The domestic ruled not merely a single demesne but a group and was normally the equal in importance of the count; the produce of the demesne went to the king's treasure and the lodging of the king and court, if the demesne centred in a royal *villa*, or dwelling. In the seventh century, however, the use of domestics lapsed and the kings used a villicus, or steward of a single villa, in their place.

The administration of justice in the later Merovingian period adopted two dissimilar procedures, Roman and Germanic. In the later empire, the court of the *praeses*, the *judex*, of the province, had been held at different places within his wide jurisdiction and rested upon a written procedure. The *judex* had notaries who collected written depositions of evidence and the *judex* himself was sole judge, with wide discretionary powers. Visigoths and Burgundians adopted such a procedure.

Among the Franks, however, there persisted the old Germanic custom of judgment pronounced by a delegation of the freemen of each canton or *pagus*. The 'hundred elder' or hundredman, the *centenarius*, had merely presided over a tribunal of doomsmen, the *mallus*, and was charged with the execution of their sentence. The procedure was oral, formal and symbolic, and judgment followed the testimony of oath-helpers or the judgment of the ordeal.

The Merovingian kings used counts, however, both in the Roman south and the Germanic north, where the supervision of the whole canton or *pagus* by a 'hundred elder' soon lapsed; the count came to preside over the *mallus* in his stead. The count was given the pursuit of the criminal and the direct punishment of the guilty: but not the wide powers of the Roman *praeses*. Where there was a mixed population, Salian procedure was imported into the more Roman parts of Gaul: though it is notable how few references there are to Germanic legal procedure in the pages of Gregory of Tours. The count was not left unaided to pronounce judgment for a mixed population: the kings compelled the Gallo-Romans to appear periodically in each city to speak the law, as the Frankish delegates spoke it for themselves. The count's court was the *mallus*, not now an assembly of freemen, but a bench of assessors or doomsmen, called in Latin *boni homines* (in later French, *prudhommes*), in Germanic *Rachinbergii* or *Rathinbergii*; they gave sentence and the count executed it. When the bishop sat in the count's court, he seems to have been summoned to sit as a doomsman, to speak the law in some suit affecting clerics and laymen: suits between clerics went to his own tribunal.

In the *mallus* Germanic procedure thus predominated, for procedure was oral: by the awarding of *rachat*, (*bot*) or money compensation for crime, or by sworn testimony or by ordeal. Where society had become Germanic, or where the ruling class was Germanic, the more advanced Roman procedure was no longer suitable or available. The church pressed for the assuagement of injuries by *bots*, as preferable to the deadly *faida* or blood feud; the kings also pressed it, for they received a third of the composition money, called the *fredum*; the count collected this money, receiving a small fraction for his trouble. His main recompense for the duties of his office was the proceeds of some royal demesne. The *mallus* thus made its own legal decisions, without reference to legal textbooks: law was local, part Germanic and part Roman, according to territorial custom. The *mallus* was a useful agent of royal government, for the king's orders could be proclaimed there, as also his summons to the army, and his royal edicts.

Franks and Gallo-Romans (Bede in 731 speaks of them as still distinguishable groups) were thus equal before the curious mixed law of the count and the *mallus*: and they were equally subject to royal absolutism. The king could give any office at pleasure: he could free a serf and make of him his vassal or count; he could use the officers of the palace for work outside their proper sphere, sell a bishopric to a Syrian refugee, or use a Jewish merchant to collect his taxes. The old senatorial class, so powerful in the Auvergne in the later empire, still persisted and bishops like Gregory of Tours still worked on lines they would have approved: but their old power as a class had disappeared by the end of the sixth century.

The Frankish nobility were, in historical times, always a nobility of service, a 'thegn' class, not a nobility of birth, like the *eorlcundmen* in early Wessex or Kent. A nobility of landholders and officeholders soon arose: the king's service trebled a man's wergeld. To enter the royal service, a freeman commended himself to the king, became his *cliens*, his *fidelis*, his *leude*, and in the early Carolingian period, his *vassus*. These commended men, these *antrustions*, and the later *vassi*, were no longer solely the war-band of the prince, as earlier: they included royal servants and even ecclesiastical dignitaries. High officers, *proceres*, *optimates*, dukes and counts, were all the king's servants.

Each kingdom, Austrasia, Neustria, Burgundy, had a writing office, a *scrinium* like that of the old Roman king of Soissons and other Roman governors. The notaries of the *scrinia* were trained to receive reports, write letters and supervise accounts; a *cancellarius* was a notary of a special kind (see p. 401). The royal treasure was kept in a chamber adjacent to that in which the king slept, and was in charge of a *camerarius* and *cubicularius*. The officers of the palace (see p. 62) continued as in the early Merovingian period: *pincerna*, *comes stabuli*, seneschal (from the Germanic *sinischalk*, who had jurisdiction over the numerous palace servants), the *capellani* who guarded the royal relics, chief of them the *capa* or *capella* of St Martin, and, in charge of all the departments of the palace, the *maiordomus*. He was charged with the feeding and ordering of the whole body: as *maior palatii* he succeeded an officer of the Roman emperors, who had had the *cura palatii*.

The mayor's court, his palace tribunal, was therefore a supreme court, over which he might preside himself: but for routine cases the *comes palacii* presided. The court was a tribunal for the *leudes* or *vassi* of the king's entourage: it had no formal constitution or regular sessions and its sphere of jurisdiction remained undefined. Its procedure also was undefined: it was less formal and Germanic than that of the *mallus*. It was not a court of appeal: it was the court for the king's clients or vassals: and both for those who formed the palace, and those who had been sent out to hold office in the countryside. With the king's *fideles* the ordinary local courts could not deal; and the king could, at will, summon any case to be tried by the court of the palace.

Though each kingdom in the Merovingian period had thus its palace, its central government with tentacles out in the country-side, though Paris, Soissons, Reims or Orleans were in a sense capital cities, yet the *regnum Francorum* had no capital and no cen-tralized administration. Each king travelled with his palace, partly in order to feed his court at the different *villae*, partly for love of hunting, partly to keep in touch with the different parts of his kingdom. Byzantine terms and ceremonial were to some extent in use: the court physician was the *iatros*, the kings spoke of them-selves as *domini*, spoke of *indulgentia nostra, misericordia nostra*, used a throne and some approximations to Byzantine court cere-monial. But their court was a simple and barbarian imitation of the Byzantine emperor's, their court departments quite unlike the great *officia*, staffed by learned laymen, of the Byzantines.

Allusion has been made (see p. 131) to the mixed economy, so largely a food and services economy, of the later Merovingians. The kings lived on the produce of their demesnes, as did the counts and dukes; the kings had customs and tolls and sometimes levied money taxes, which all went into their treasure. Apart from mili-tary expeditions, the great field of expenditure of the kings' revenue was that of diplomatic presents (Pirenne noted their size, and how it was frequently cheaper to buy loyalty than to fight a border tribe), and the presents made to their own *leudes*, their *fideles*. The kings needed their support, and like the old Germanic 'ring-givers' were forced to secure loyalty by generous giving: in their case of lands and immunities. The royal demesnes were, in time, very much granted out: e.g. what had been originally a complex of royal demesnes round Paris became gradually almost solely church lands: the territories of Saint-Denis, Chelles, Saint-Germain, etc.

The decay of the royal Merovingian power did not arise from popular opposition, or even relative impoverishment, but from eclipse by the Merovingian palace, and its mayor. A narrow ruling class of administrative nobles came to rule France; its members intermarried, and it included not only the 'palace', the royal household, but its once members, the counts, dukes, domestics, etc. out in the countryside. It was these distant members who met in assembly with king and palace once a year, constituting a 'full palace': the old tribal assembly of freemen, the *champs de Mars*, had ceased to meet in Clovis's time. It was the palace who decided the succession, accepting or rejecting partition among the late king's sons: it was the palace which ruled during the frequent minorities. Minorities were indeed so frequent in the Frankish kingdoms that they might almost be considered the normal state of affairs: warlike expeditions were none the less undertaken in them and the palace ruled, even before the power of its mayor became overshadowing. In the seventh century, except for Dagobert's reign, the three kingdoms were ruled by their palaces, even as in the eighth century the *regnum Francorum* was ruled by the mayors.

Circumstances favoured the rise of the mayor of the palace. The palace was strong because it controlled the armed forces; in the sixth century dukes had been rare and counts had sufficed, even for the leading of their local armies. In the course of the forty years of civil war (573–613) dukes appeared, soldiers who commanded armies, the count doing so only exceptionally. Duchies were at first not territories but military commands, dukes being assigned two or three cities for their support; territorial duchies developed only gradually, Champagne being an early example. The kings ceased to be effective leaders of military expeditions, which were now led by dukes: not single commanders but in numbers proportionate to the size of the expedition: one to Lombardy had as many as twenty dukes.

The mayors of the palace came to hold a leading position in the administration, both in peace and war, only after *c.* 550; but by 613 it was clear that in each kingdom the true master of the palace was the mayor. He was responsible for supply and for palace order and cohesion: he headed the king's *antrustions*, his *leudes*. The other nobles now came to fear his power; in 642 the Burgundian nobles ridded themselves of their mayor, and in 673 the Neustrian nobles appealed against Ebroin, their most notable mayor, to the king. From 687 the Austrasian mayor was the real ruler, not only of Austrasia, but of the *regnum Francorum*: he changed his title only in 751, the substance of power he had had before.

Pepin III thus in 751 set the coping-stone in the work of his predecessors, and he equally laid the foundations for the great reign of Charlemagne, his son, and that in almost all the departments of Frankish life and policy. He was not, however, long lived. In 768, after a campaign in Aquitaine, though only fifty-four, he felt death near. He divided his kingdom, as Frankish rulers before him, between his sons, Carloman and Charles. He then died at Saint-Denis on 24 September 768.

Against this background of political struggle, frontier defence and frequent civil war, what happened to Frankish art and architecture in the long Merovingian and early Carolingian periods? They cover the age of Bede, who died in 735, and that of a very splendid period of Northumbrian art. There was peaceful intercourse with the Anglo-Saxons all the time and a parallel social development: yet no monuments of artistic culture like the Northumbrian crosses or the Lindisfarne gospels have come down to us from Merovingian France. The phenomenon deserves some explanation: some consideration as to whether the simple explanation is that there was more fighting among the Merovingians than the Anglo-Saxons, and therefore less margin of creative effort, or whether other causes supervened. In view of the wars in England between the kings struggling for the bretwaldaship, between the Deirans and Bernicians in Northumbria itself, between Northumbria and Mercia and Mercia and Wessex, the Anglo-Saxons would seem to have done as much fighting as the Franks: though not, of course, with external enemies like the Slav tribes, the Lombards and the Arabs.

First then, as to Anglo-Frankish intercourse, tending towards the production of a common culture. On the secular side, merchants crossed the Channel in both directions, to the fair of Saint-Denis, to London which, as Bede says, was a mart and emporium for many nations. The coins in the pouch of the king commemorated at Sutton Hoo in the mid-seventh century were all Frankish. Cross-travel by churchmen was equally frequent; Augustine had taken Frankish interpreters; Felix of Burgundy converted Suffolk, the Frankish Lothere, bishop of Wessex, attended the synod of

Whitby while still unable to speak English; in Dagobert's day Richarius went to preach in England. The Northumbrian Wilfrid was trained by and received the tonsure from Annemund of Lyons. Benedict Biscop took back glass makers from Gaul to glaze the window of his new church at Monkwearmouth and Jarrow. There was no great difficulty in Anglo-Frankish communications, and it might have been expected that the Northumbrian golden age would have extended to Merovingian France without a sixty years' interval and the personal impetus given by Charles the Great.

Eventually, through the work of Boniface and the many Anglo-Saxon missionaries, the Northumbrian renaissance did influence Carolingian learning, art, scripts and illuminations. With Benedictine monks and nuns of Anglo-Saxon stock working in Frisia and among the Saxons, and with the influence of Boniface guiding Pepin the Short in the reform of Frankish clergy and monks, it could hardly have been otherwise. Carolingian art was itself born of the cross fertilization of two cultures: the Northumbrian and the Byzantine, just as the Northumbrian renaissance itself had been born of the fusion of Celtic, Anglian and Byzantine cultures. The Carolingian Franks bordered the Mediterranean, were awed by the remains of Greco-Roman art in Lombard Italy, and were in touch with Greek religion, books, churches and traditions in their new conquests of the middle Danube lands, and the patriarchate of Aquileia at the head of the Adriatic. Byzantium and Byzantine influence was always very close, and Carolingian art was not to be merely a reflowering among the Franks of Northumbrian art, transmitted by the missionaries. Nevertheless, Northumbrian art was one of the springs of Carolingian art, as Northumbrian learning, transmitted through Alcuin and others, was to be one of the sources of Carolingian *sapientia*: reference to it cannot, therefore, be altogether omitted.

It seems, then, that the art and learning of seventh- and eighth-century Northumbria grew out of the fusion of two cultures, the Celtic and the Anglo-Saxon, and that the immediate stimulus to such a flowering was the introduction of yet a third influence: that of Byzantine books, illuminations, textiles and reliquaries, brought by Benedict Biscop in the north, and by Theodore and Hadrian in the south. Benedict Biscop's journeys to the continent and Rome are described in Bede's *Lives of the Abbots* (of Monkwearmouth-Jarrow): he brought back from the continent a very fine library of books, which Bede was to use later: and he died in 690. Theodore and Hadrian founded a school of Greco-Latin learning at Canterbury, from which Aldhelm was to gain his scholarship. Both brought to England altar books and books for the divine office written on vellum, a very expensive material compared to the papyrus rolls and tomes which had so largely served the Roman empire; but a smooth material capable of taking illumination (illustration), as papyrus was not. In the Greco-Roman empire, book illumination was rare, for books were not used in any public ceremonial, as altar books in the Christian churches later, and the very expensive vellum was only used for such solemn tomes as copies of Vergil's works, or, later, the *Digest*. Illumination could only be made on vellum, and there were few vellum books: representations of Vergil, however, were sometimes painted at the beginning of the Aeneid, and very occasionally similar ones of other writers also. The vellum altar books and service books now brought by Benedict Biscop and Theodore may well have had pictures of the four evangelists before their gospel, and of David before the book of psalms: for Byzantine books were sometimes thus illuminated, following the Vergilian precedent.

In one case this certainly happened: an extant manuscript, the Codex Amiatinus, was written in the monastery of Monkwearmouth-Jarrow as a gift for the pope. It has a very early Vulgate text and also pictures of the evangelists and David, in the manner earlier described, and it shows connexions with the biblical text of Cassiodorus at Vivarium. It is accepted as having been copied from a book brought back by Benedict Biscop.

The Lindisfarne Gospels, again, with its evangelists' portraits and its intricately beautiful pages of abstract ornament, has a Latin text founded on the Vulgate text of Codex Amiatinus, not on the old Latin version earlier in use in Britain, and from which the larger part of the text of the Book of Kells is drawn. None of the famous Northumbrian and Irish manuscripts, the Book of Durrow, the Lindisfarne gospels, the Book of Kells, could have been illuminated without access to a Byzantine manuscript or its copies, for reasons of text and ornament. The Northumbrian manuscripts use the typical Anglo-Saxon elongated animal in their ornament, and, even more, the Celtic spiral which had developed from La Tène art-forms, and the Celtic plaitwork. In Northumbria, however, and especially the northern province of Bernicia, the Celtic population far outnumbered the Anglian: it was really a Celtic countryside with an Anglian ruling race. But the ornament indigenous to Northumbria, or to Iona or the Irish monasteries, could not of itself have produced the Evangelists' portraits, which are clearly Byzantine in origin.

The Bewcastle and Ruthwell crosses, again, which may be dated as between 664 and 700, and Acca's cross of *c.* 740, mark a sudden efflorescence of figure-carving in stone, in the Byzantine manner. Here again, as in the illuminations, there is a curious mixture of cultures: Ruthwell, six miles north of the Roman Wall, has the northern, Runic letters and a verse from the Anglo-Saxon poem, the *Dream of the Rood*; Bewcastle has the names of the Anglo-Saxon princess Cyniburg, daughter of Penda, who married Alchfrith, Wilfrid's patron. Both have ornament that looks back to Egyptian monasticism, the monasticism of the desert; Bewcastle has as one of its three main figures the Baptist, peculiarly a saint of the desert, and Ruthwell has the figure of Christ treading upon the asp and the basilisk, from the verse in psalm 90, the desert psalm (*super aspidem et basiliscum ambulabis et conculcabis leonem et draconem*). Yet both crosses have as their dominant figure subject the Byzantine representation of Christ in majesty, and the naturalistic rendering of the other figures can only be Byzantine in origin. The late Professor Saxl conjectured that illuminators familiar with the Byzantine treatment of figures drew the outline in paint upon the flat stone face of the cross's shaft, and that the stone carver then worked upon them. He might well have known stone figures in the round of Roman emperors or matrons or soldiers; but here on the crosses is a figure of the Byzantine Christ such as could only have been designed by someone familiar with imported books, textiles or reliquaries.

All this flowering of Northumbrian art was due to royal patronage, but made at the instance or by the work of the church. No secular works of art, no palaces, have come down to us, though the Sutton Hoo finds have provided us with the personal equipment of a great East Anglian king of the middle of the seventh century. It is difficult to believe that such art flourished only in Northumbria, and that such churches as that of St Augustine's, Canterbury, had, say in the late eighth century, nothing to equal it. As to memorial crosses like bishop Acca's, William of Malmesbury tells us that two survived in the cemetery adjoining the church at Glastonbury in his time; and parts of an Anglo-Saxon cross, around which the Anglo-Saxon church of Reculver was most probably built, and many fragments of other crosses survive. The sixth-century illuminated manuscript known as the Gospels of St Augustine's, Canterbury, a manuscript of Corpus Christi College, Cambridge, is now believed by experts to have been an altar book actually brought with him by St Augustine, and can scarcely have been without influence on Canterbury scribes. It has a miniature of St Luke in the Byzantine manner, and probably once had others of St Mark and St John; it has also a series of small pictures of the life of Christ, and had probably, as manuscript evidence suggests, very many more. The gospels are written in two columns to each page and in uncials; the tradition of large, clear lettering for an altar book recalls the request of Boniface in Germany that his friend should send him out such a book. Indeed Boniface's almost wearisomely reiterated requests for books for his mission is evidence that the southern Anglo-Saxons were writing many manuscripts at the time, though few have survived. All this suggests that though the chief focus of the renaissance of Byzantine art in the early eighth century was in Northumbria, and though conditions in this remote part favoured survival because there was less rebuilding than in the south, yet the renaissance was not confined to Northumbria. With so many channels of communication open, it might have spread to the *regnum Francorum*.

In contrast to this outburst of Anglo-Saxon art and architecture, however, building and its attendant arts saw no such flowering among the later Merovingians and early Carolingians. No great Frankish buildings or monuments, at any rate, remain. It is likely that, in the south especially, some churches or even palaces, were built, for descriptions of buildings with colonnades and mosaics have come down to us (like those which Eddius Stephanus wrote about Wilfrid's churches of Ripon and Hexham): but seventh- and eighth-century Frankish art survives for us in altar and personal ornaments and the remains of small churches rather than in the colonnaded buildings described by a few Merovingian writers.

There is some indication indeed that wood was used for the building of late Merovingian churches and houses, and such would not, of course, have survived. Wood was plentiful, particularly in the north-eastern lands of the Franks, where Christianity and the building of churches came late, and for building wood sufficed. Fortunatus (d. 670), writing of the country round Poitiers, has one poem about a wooden house: he doesn't, he says, want a wall built of hewn stone, he prefers the craftsman's timber work: the massive timber palaces reach up to the sky, and never a crack in their solid surface. Whatever protection rocks or gravel or limestone or clay may afford, here a nice little woodland has built a house all by itself: and loftier and greater than the stone ones, and surrounded on all sides by porticoes, and the wood carver has given his fancy free play in his sculptures. The *Lex Burgundionum* too rates a woodcarver higher than a blacksmith; while a goldsmith's wer is 200 *solidi* and a silversmith's 100, the woodcarver's is 60 and the blacksmith's 50. The reappearance in Carolingian art of Greco-Roman naturalistic sculpture, and also of a few features of Germanic pattern, seem to indicate that they were transmitted by the rustic woodcarver.

The treasuries of churches have transmitted a few illuminated manuscripts (not in the same class as the famous Northumbrian ones), ornaments and even textiles from the late Merovingian period. The treasury of the cathedral of Sens has a curious picture of the Assumption embroidered on linen, where the unskilled Frankish workers have tried to imitate the figures of an eastern silken brocade; the museum at Lyons has a silken tissue from the tomb of St Merry, who died at Paris c. 700, embroidered in gold and coloured silks with scrolls and fantastic little animals such as are found in manuscripts of the period. Part of a chasuble with silken embroidery like cloisonné metal work has survived to us from Balthilde's abbey of Chelles (see p. 277).

The monasteries too of this period would seem to have been simply built, with church and domestic buildings within a hedged enclosure: the buildings themselves of wood and roofed with thatch. St Benedict of Aniane, according to his *Vita*, finding the valley in which he had at first settled too narrow, began to build a new monastery outside its limits. He and his brethren used to carry planks of timber on their own shoulders through lack of oxen to draw them . . . He ordained that the houses should not be made or roofed with shining or pictured walls and tiles, but with straw and other cheap material. He would not have vessels for the making of Christ's body of silver, but first of all he had them of wood, and then of glass. Thatched roofs, however, involved risk of fire, and when the monastery was rebuilt in 782 tiles were used.

Some large abbeys still, however, in the Greco-Roman tradition had churches and oratories of stone, like that of Jumièges, built c. 684 on a cruciform plan; here the monastic enclosure was square, with ramparts and turrets. The abbey of St Riquier (Centula) near Abbeville is the only Frankish house of which we know the ground plan and buildings in the early Carolingian period, and this through a seventeenth-century drawing made from a very ancient miniature. The abbey had already an honourable history when Charlemagne presented the abbey to his son-in-law Angilbert in 792, together with new endowment for its rebuilding. Angilbert completely rebuilt church and cloister, in stone; there had in the days of Balthilde been three choirs in the abbey, singing the office in three chapels at successive hours. Angilbert rebuilt the great church of St Riquier, with the rectangular cloister stretching from its southern wall, and the small churches of St Benedict and St Mary at angles of the cloister. The interest of the main church lies in its equal emphasis on the east and west ends, where the nave is crossed by transepts surmounted by lantern towers: an arrangement of which the fundamental feature, the provision of two chancels, is not uncommon in great romanesque churches of monastic or capitular foundations. Several explanations of this plan are possible: some would ascribe it to the prevailing fashion of orientation, as opposed to the more common practice of occidentation in previous ages, in which case the old altar would not be abandoned, but retained in addition to the new; such was the case at Canterbury, where, upon the building of the eastern apse and new high altar by archbishop Odo (961–988), the altar in the western apse became the Lady altar. Another theory would find the desire to provide a grand parochial altar in addition to the monastic or conventual altar. These theories are not mutually exclusive, and the answer is probably that there were a variety of

FRANKISH MAYORS OF THE PALACE

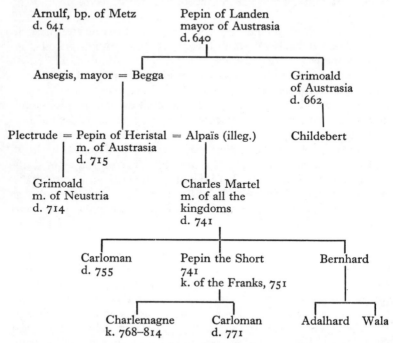

reasons for this development. Whatever the cause, the result was extremely imposing, as may be seen from the several magnificent minsters erected on this plan which survive in Germany.

BIBLIOGRAPHICAL NOTE

As for chapter iv: and see W. Levison, *England and the Continent in the Eighth Century*, 1946; L. Levillain, *De l'authenticité de la clausula Pippins*, *Bibliot. de l'école des chartes*, tom. lxxxviii (1927), and *L'avènement de la dynastie Carolingienne*, in above series tom. xciv (1933). See also G. Ellard, *Ordination Anointings in the Western Church*, 1933, Cambridge, Mass; *Sankt Bonifatius, Gedenkgabe züm zwölfkundertsten Todestag*, Fulda, 1954. See also, W. Levison and H. Löwe, *Deutschlands Geschictsquellen im Mittelalter : Die Karolinger von Anfang des 8 Jahrhunderts bis zum Tode Karls des Grosses*, vol. I, Weimar, 1953; L. Dupraz, *Le royaume der Francs et l'ascension politique des maires du palais au déclin du VIIᵉ siècle (656–880)* Freibourg, 1948.

CHAPTER XVII

THE CAROLINGIAN POLITICAL SCENE

THE Carolingian age marked a new epoch in the history of Europe, and it is worth considering for a moment the setting and the actors of the new scene: the scene that was beginning when Pepin the Short died at Saint-Denis on 24 September 768, and left his kingdom divided between his sons Charles and Carloman.

If an observer in an aeroplane had passed above Europe at the time, flying from Thames mouth to Rhine mouth, and then along the Rhine–Danube frontier that had once bordered the Roman empire: or above Gaul, now the land of the Franks and called Francia in the north and Aquitania south of the Loire: he would have seen a land still, in the main, wooded. Among the woods, small strips of ploughed fields followed the river valleys and the foothills, with small villages set in small clearings. He would have seen the vineyards of Italy and Francia, and very good vineyards too along the Rhine where the Roman army contractors had first planted them; but in the main he would have seen a land uncleared of forest, with large, undrained swamps: country abounding in game, wild fowl and fresh-water fish. The thirteenth century, the century of the great forest clearings, the *défrichements*, was still far ahead.

The old Roman towns, laid out by the *gromaticus*, the army surveyor, were still inhabited, and on the same town plan: not as in Britain set aside (or used as stone quarries) by invading barbarians. There were also other towns, *municipia, castra, castella*, small by our reckoning, but affording a market for the produce of the countryside. In such towns, the old Roman *civitates* for choice, the bishop had his seat, his cathedral church, the symbol of his teaching office, and the count had his *mallus*, his court.

The towns, however, were not rich, as certain towns of the empire had been through the eastern trade, and as the towns of north Italy and the Danube and Rhine valleys were to be again in the twelfth century through its renewal; for there was now little eastern trade, only a trickle that came up the Russian rivers to the Baltic, and a smaller trickle of silks and spices and luxury goods that came somehow up the Rhone to Charles's court and the great churches that would buy silken cloths and ivories and vestments: for the Arab fleet largely blocked the Mediterranean.

It was the countryside that counted: that produced the food on the great landed estates or villas and the small *vici* of free peasants. It was the peasant who tilled the ground that the Carolingian kings had to protect against raiders from across the frontier or oppressive landholders near by: and some of the Carolingian capitularies did seek to protect the peasant. It was the peasant who grew the food and from the land and the peasant came the royal revenue, chiefly from the lands or villas of the fisc; there was little other regular royal income. Though Charlemagne and his sons got rich through war plunder, they did not get their main revenue from customs or direct taxes, though such were still levied.

The observer in the aeroplane, flying over western Europe, would have seen then, besides the towns, the vills, the *vici*, and the royal palaces.

The vills were semi-manorial villages, whose name went back possibly to some Roman villa of the fourth or fifth century, and whose organization in any case resembled it. It was the estate of some royal or noble landowner with the peasants who worked it, the successors of the *coloni*; it was focussed in a house, perhaps the Germanic version of a Roman villa house, with an inward-looking square court or courts, with colonnades and ranges of two-storeyed buildings. This formed the dwelling of some Frankish noble, *antrustion* or *vassus*, or of some royal bailiff or steward, the *villicus*; its half free peasants looked to the villa and paid their rent in services and in kind.

The observer would have seen villages (*vici*) of Germanic free-holders, and free villages even in Aquitania, with the houses running alongside the road: or clustered at a cross road, beginning to develop naturally, without benefit of surveyor, into a spider-web road plan.

Then, too, he would have seen some of those princely villas, built on the same inward-looking plan, with the same colonnaded courtyards, that Charlemagne and his successors had as their palaces. The word *palatium*, a royal residence, had originally, and still had in Carolingian times, an imperial association: the original *palatium* was the villa on one of the seven hills of Rome, the Palatine. Here Augustus had built his royal residence, and later Caesars added ranges of buildings to his *palatium* till the royal residence covered the whole Palatine mount. The first *palatium* then was a royal villa in a great city: and Charlemagne's *palatium* at Aix-la-Chapelle inspired the growth of a city around it, though

originally there had been no city and no Roman roads converging
on it: it was joined to the Roman roads only by secondary byways.
But for the most part, the Carolingian palaces were great villas
out on the countryside, the focus of some demesne that had once
belonged to the imperial fisc. They might be near some town, but,
as it were, accidentally. Not all of them grew into medieval towns:
for the court resided in any one of them (except Aix) but a small
portion of the year. The Carolingian court was nomadic, and
passed from villa to villa, whose food supply could maintain it
only for a short time.

As to the appearance of these Carolingian palaces: they must have
looked like extensive dwellings, something between the Lateran
palace and a good sized farm. Fundamentally, they were all villas,
the urban ones (as at Mainz, Worms), with grounds enclosed by
a wall pierced by two gates: those in the countryside among
extensive orchards, gardens and fields, enclosed only by hedges or
an earthen bank. The royal residence was built round an *atrium*,
with an assembly hall (the *casa, sala regalis*), rooms for the family
and officers, a chapel, often with an apsidal end for the altar, just
as the great hall sometimes had an apse as framework for the king
or speaker, and beyond, or on the opposite side of the main court,
a farmyard or *basse-cour*, with hens, geese, cowstalls and pigsties,
storechambers and barns. The palaces would differ from the
royal villas out on the countryside only in the richness of the
materials used, the Byzantine character of the ornament, the use
of stone as against wood for buildings.

It is important for the understanding of the Carolingian period
to notice the change in the centre of gravity within the *regnum
Francorum*. Whereas the Merovingian kings and Pepin the Short
lived in and ruled from a hall near the royal abbey of Saint-Denis
outside Paris: or from one of the royal villas on the Oise or the
Aisne: Charles made his three great new palaces on the Rhine. He
swung the centre of gravity in his kingdom from the Seine to the
Rhine. His father, Pepin, had been preoccupied with uniting the
Franks of Paris and the Seine valley with those of Aquitaine, and
the Seine valley was the focus of his power, as it had been of the
Merovingians; but when Charles became engaged in the conquest
of Saxony, he made use of dwellings nearer and nearer to the
Rhine: Héristal in the valley of the Meuse: Thionville in that of
the Moselle: Nymwegen on the Waal: Aix, between the Rhine and
the Meuse: Ingelheim near Mainz, and Worms to the south of
Mainz. Here there were villas, half-ruined palaces, that could
be reconditioned for court use. Finally, as an outward sign of his

Saxon conquests, and to provide a political focus for a power pushed farther to the east, to show that the Rhine was no longer a frontier but a Frankish river, Charles built himself three great new palaces: at Nymwegen, at Ingelheim and at Aix (*Aquisgranum*). The Merovingians had ruled from the Seine: the Capetians would return to the Seine: but Charles ruled from the Rhine.

With this transfer of power to the north-east went a change in the economic position of the land south of the Rhine mouth and west of the Meuse, the modern Belgium. Under the old empire, the needs of the Roman army had stimulated the production of food, clothes and arms, and the local Morini had traded with the war-fleet stationed at Itium (? Boulogne). Wheat from the Rhine valley went by the wheatships down the Meuse to Tongres and to Fectio (Vechten), near Utrecht: there were depots also at Nymwegen and Cologne. The Meuse valley had metal workers that produced arms and tools for the Roman army; Flemish wool was woven into cloaks for the legionaries; enamelled brooches were made between Sambre and Meuse; there were several local mints.

Merovingian Belgium, however, had become again an agrarian country: the barbarous Frisians took and held the lower course of the Rhine, Meuse and Scheldt: no more is heard of Boulogne, Fectio and Tongres as important marts. Clovis and his Franks took Soissons but passed on to Paris. In the lower Rhine country, coins were minted and customs levied at new *vici*, Dinant, Namur, Huy, Arras, Térouanne, Cambrai, Antwerp. Trade with the Baltic was renewed, but in a new set of ports; Maestricht replaced Tongres, Durstedt replaced Fectio, Quentovic replaced Boulogne for trade with Great Britain and Ireland. And now, under the Carolings, these new young towns, *bourgades*, continued relatively prosperous, with mints and a weaving industry in the valley of the Meuse, and even a few Jewish and Syrian merchants arriving from the Rhone valley and the Mediterranean. The Carolingian abbeys bought some of their food, and clothes, and spices, from a distance; Stavelot and Malmédy had depots on the Loire; Corbie, on the Somme, asked from the king at the end of the eighth century the privilege of purchasing its supplies of spice, perfumes, and papyrus directly from those of the fisc, at Marseilles and Fos (the two Mediterranean ports where the kings kept buyers and a store), and to be allowed to send its own men there to fetch them. Commerce grew with the growth of the slave trade with Britain, and slaves were sold in the markets of Arras and Tournai. The Carolingian shift of power could not bring to the Rhine mouth the trade and wealth it had enjoyed in Roman days, for there was little long distance trade and a continuing scarcity of currency: but it brought a relative prosperity.

As to the political groupings in the days of Charlemagne: no concept of the nation state was as yet in use, even though for two centuries the different kingdoms of Merovingian co-rulers had loosely been described as the *regnum Francorum*. Five political forces, however, may be singled out among the Franks and their neighbours in western Europe.

There were first the Germanic peoples, led now by the Franks, whose Carolingian dynasty was descended from the mayors of the palace of Austrasia, the most Germanic and least Romanized Frankish territory. The Franks had long conquered and assimilated the Gallic Celts and Germanic Burgundians and the more distantly connected Visigoths of southern France. Aquitania had engaged his father's and was to engage much of Charles's attention, and to be none too obedient to his rule. The Germanic Alemanni and Bavarians to the east were also none too submissive; but they were all substantially akin to Charles himself. Their nobles, like Charles, wore an adaptation of Roman dress, the short tunic and long, shoulder-pinned cloak: they wore the quite un-Roman moustache, the relic, apparently, of the barbarian beard: they had the same old Germanic folk poetry. There were the Lombards too, in north Italy, where Desiderius sat upon the throne of Theoderic in Ravenna and lived in his palace. They had a smaller territory than the Franks, but they had secured, as it were, a more distinguished position. They were now orthodox, but the pope hated and feared them, all the more since Desiderius had encroached upon the territories given to the papacy by Pepin the Short.

Then, there were the Saracens, holding nearly all Spain, and dangerous neighbours to the Franks along the Mediterranean coast. The first followers of Muhammad had not been cultured, but the second generation had taken Syria and Persia: the caliph of Baghdad was now, as it were, a ghost who sat, robed and crowned, upon the throne of Alexander. In Spain, Cordoba, seat of the Umayyad caliph, had become a near eastern city, civilized, luxurious, learned. The Moors in Spain were a fighting race, an alien culture and a danger to the Franks; but from 755 they were divided from the caliphs of Baghdad by the institution of a caliphate of their own. Charles's intervention in Moorish affairs was conditioned by rivalries between the two caliphates, and an invitation to help the rebels against the Umayyads.

There was, thirdly, the Scandinavian culture of the countries bordering the Baltic: still heathen: still land-hungry: still using an oral learning and embodying their history in heroic poetry: still slightly contemptuous of the written word and using the Runic alphabet when there was (infrequently) a need for inscriptions or writing. There was a great similarity of life between the Scandinavian peoples and the still pagan and unconquered Saxons; they were disturbed by Charles's conquest of Saxony and by Saxon refugees. They became, from the end of the Saxon conquest in 786, and throughout the ninth century, an increasing danger to Europe. In these Viking raids an alien, northern civilization can be seen breaking in waves upon western and even eastern Europe.

There was, again, the submerged Roman civilizations of Italy, less deeply submerged than that of Gaul, persisting in the natural homeland of the Roman empire. In Lombard Italy Roman law, rather in the form of the Theodosian than Justinian's code, still ran, and in the centre of the peninsula the see of Peter preserved the old Roman gravity, prudence, and regard for law; preserved relics of the Roman provincial system in the territorial episcopate; preserved some of the substance and much of the phraseology of Roman Law in the sacred canons.

Finally, there was the Byzantine civilization of Constantinople, always influential in Italy, and always permeating the countries bordering the Mediterranean. The days of Justinian and the dream of a restored Roman empire centring in Byzantium were long past; Slavs and Avars had for two hundred years been settling in the Balkans, barbarizing the countryside, and partly reducing Greek Christianity there to ignorance and impotence. The zeal of the iconoclast emperors, which claimed to lead a crusade against superstition, was to attract the notice of Charlemagne and Alcuin and have its repercussions on the restoration of the empire in the west; but the Carolingian tradition in sculpture, illumination and architecture continued to model itself upon the Byzantine east.

Of these five cultures then, Charles extended the half Germanic, half Roman one of the Franks; the Muslim one he held at bay; the Latin culture of Italy he further depressed in Lombardy though protecting its expression in the papacy; the Byzantine power he held at bay by his peace of 812, while the Scandinavian attack, provoked partly by his own conquest of Saxony, was to wreck the empire of his successors.

Our knowledge of the Carolingian scene, material and political, rests largely upon written sources. Written records and historical writing for this period are more plentiful than in earlier centuries, and of greater importance as compared to archaeological evidence; though the excavation of some of Charlemagne's palaces and the survival of Carolingian jewellery, coins and illuminated manuscripts throw light on the material environment.

Of the written sources, two pieces of historical writing stand out: the *Royal Annals* and Einhard's *Vita Karoli Magni*. The Carolingian period saw indeed the high-water mark in the writing of annals and the *Royal Annals*, written by a succession of learned scribes of the king's chapel, were only the best informed of a number of annals kept in monasteries or by the clergy of great churches; but for Einhard's work, written by a layman and in good Latin, there was no parallel.

The keeping of annals and the day-to-day observance of calendars in the Merovingian period had prepared the material for the Carolingian annalists to work upon in their rewriting of past history; and the royal insistence on learning had now provided scholars better equipped to record the events of their own day. The *Royal Annals* (earlier called the annals of Lorsch or Laurisheim, an abbey near Worms) cover the years 741 to 829. They say nothing of Charles's or Louis the Pious' personal life or of the machinery of government: but, faithful to the Latin tradition, they record the events of each year as they occurred. The portion for 741 to 788 was apparently written all at once, by an editor and redactor who used Fredegar's continuator, some small, older annals, and supplied certain information of his own. The annals from 789 to 829 were apparently written from year to year, or as the events occurred, by three annalists distinguishable by their style: the annalist of 795 to 813 wrote a particularly correct Latin. The preoccupation of the annalists with Charles and his son Louis and the royal prestige, together with the exact information of royal affairs they directed, suggest strongly that the annalists were personages of the royal palace and (since good Latin writing by lay courtiers was rare) that they were members of the royal chapel, such men as archbishop Arn of Salzburg, or the archchaplain Hildebald. They must have been, in any case, men who had access to official documents and the royal correspondence; their dating is sure, and their knowledge of campaigns, embassies and treaties exact. As might be expected, the *Royal Annals* glide over the Frankish disaster at Roncesvalles and certain other defeats in the course of the long Saxon wars; nor do they mention certain rebellions against Charles, nor the Donation of 774 to the papacy, which brought him inconvenience. These omissions to favour royal prestige were, however, remedied in a very careful version of the *Royal Annals* (called by Kleinclausz the *Remaniement*) by an exact but anonymous editor. Earlier historians have conjectured him to have been Einhard, but there is no certain evidence.

Other Carolingian annals smaller in bulk and less well informed, but throwing light on certain aspects of the reign, include the annals of Saint-Nazaire (or Lorsch); the annals of Metz, of Saint-Maximin and the chronicles of Lorsch and of Moissac, both useful for the fall of the Lombard kingdoms and the imperial coronation.

Einhard himself, though not as commanding a figure at Charles's court as Alcuin or Angilbert, was nevertheless one of the inner circle of his officers and friends. He was born *c.* 770 in the Maingau, and *enutritus* at Boniface's abbey of Fulda under abbot Baugulf. He was not an oblate, but stayed in the abbot's household till some time after 791, when Baugulf thought so well of his character and ability that he took him to Charles's palace for the royal service. Alcuin, another heir of the Northumbrian renaissance, was still with Charles, and speaks of Einhard in a letter to Charles as 'Bezeleel, your and my own familiar helper': which must imply that, like the Bezeleel of the thirty-first chapter of Exodus, he was skilled in gold and silver work, the cutting of precious stones and in wood carving, all arts that, like his appreciation of Latin literature, he would have gained at Fulda. His friends, recognizing his powers, called him *Einhardus Magnus*, though in person he was short and slight. Alcuin, in one of his letters, wrote with a heavy playfulness of this contrast between Einhard's physical and intellectual stature: his name, to contemporaries, would have had the accent on the last syllable, and the *h* silent; Ei-nárd. 'Nard [spikenard]', wrote Alcuin, 'in however small a quantity, throws a sweet scent far and wide . . . Nardulus [my little Ei-nárd], all hail to thee!' He goes on to explain that size is no measure of worth: the tiny bee brings the honey, the eye though small directs the whole body. From all this, we infer that the diminutive Ei-nárd was learned, vigorous and fit to be entrusted with rule.

Einhard remained, as he said himself, 'in unbroken friendship with Charles himself and his children', for about twenty years. Charles sent him as his envoy to Rome in 806, and, when he asked his magnates' counsel about the succession in 813, the magnates chose Einhard as their spokesman. On Charles's death, he stayed sixteen more years at the court of Louis the Pious, still loved and trusted and, indeed, provided for on a very generous scale by appointment as lay abbot of Blandinium, Fontanelle, Saint-Bavon the Great and Saint-Servais of Maestricht and finally, in the troubles of the reign, he retired to an abbey he had built in his native country, Mulinheim (Seligenstatt). On this abbey he conferred the relics of St Marcellinus and St Peter, writing an account of the miracles wrought at the saints' intercession in his *Translatio SS. Marcellini et Petri*. (The solemn translation of relics of saints buried hitherto in the churchyard, or brought from a distance, and now literally 'raised to the altars', was now a great solemnity in some cases amounting to a canonization: and often reckoned as the day on which the saint was annually commemorated.) Einhard lived ten years more as a distinguished and devout scholar at Mulinheim, supported by the income of his other lay abbacies, and died in 840. He seems to have written his life of Charles soon after the latter's death, between 817 and 821; besides his personal memories of Charles, he could make use of the *Royal Annals* and doubtless other annals, and monastic libraries.

As to the historical value of his work: Einhard wrote in the manner of Suetonius' biographies of the Caesars, desiring to give an account of the 'amplification and adornment of Francia' through Charles's efforts, rather than to give an exact chronological account of campaigns and embassies; he gave an invaluable account of Charles's manner of life and his family: of his character, as it appeared to him. The work is not a mere panegyric and does mention some facts unfavourable to the royal prestige; moreover, when Einhard knows nothing of a matter, he says so. His personal account of Charles, and the *Royal Annals*, are complementary in the information supplied.

Three other biographies, much less valuable than Einhard's, throw some light on Charles's reign: the life of Louis the Pious, by Thegan, bishop of Trier and the clerk called the Astronomer; the life of Adalard, abbot of Corbie, by the monk, Paschasius Radbert; and the life of Alcuin, by an anonymous monk, the friend of Alcuin's pupil, Sigulf. Moreover, certain saints' lives, though composed rather for edification than historical information, have some useful detail: e.g. the lives of Sturm, abbot of Fulda, and Willehad, his successor, and that of Liudger, first bishop of Münster and missionary among the conquered Saxons. Moreover, the lives of popes Stephen III, Hadrian and Leo III in the *Liber Pontificalis* are valuable for Charles's relations with the papacy, and for the coronation in 800.

Besides these historical sources for the life of Charlemagne, it is possible to trace the first stage in the development of his legend in the poem of the anonymous Monk of Saint-Gall. The work is unfinished, and deals with the careers of the victorious and warlike Pepin the Short, the great emperor himself as the central figure, and the holy and merciful Louis the Pious. It deals not only with victories and conquests but with Charles's measures of ecclesiastical administration and his daily life: it is the work of an admirer. The author says of himself that he spoke German, had never been to Francia, that he stammered, and was now old and toothless. He was a monk at Saint-Gall in the time of abbot Grimbald and abbot Hartmud, and wrote his poem at the order of Charles the Fat, just when Hartmud had resigned his abbacy, which occurred on 6 December 883. Charles the Fat was deposed in November 887, so that the book must have been written between these two dates. A point of interest about the author is the probability that he was the ninth-century authority on the chant, Notker Balbulus, monk of Saint-Gall under Hartmud, who was 'assiduous in prayer, reading and copying', versed in *scientia*, a master of the chant and friend of Charles the Fat, and the recipient of an oral tradition about Charles in the monastery. He lived on till 912, and wrote his book some sixty-five years after Charles's death, when his victorious and single rule had begun to seem a golden age to those who lived in the alarms and civil wars of his successors. The Monk of Saint-Gall, in any case, used the *Royal Annals* and Einhard's *Vita*, and derived some information from Adalbert, one of Charles's officers who fought under Gerold, the king's brother-in-law, against Avars, Saxons and Slavs. He knew also Werinbert, son of Adalbert, a priest, and drew from him information about Charles's relations with the church; from these two men he may also have drawn his description of Charles's palace at Aix, and the bridge he built at Mainz. But the poem, though valuable, has numerous anachronisms and errors: the Charlemagne he describes is already the Charlemagne of legend, not history.

In addition to annals and historical narratives, there are more surviving letters, and *acta* turned out in the course of central and local government, than in the Merovingian period, largely through the adoption of parchment in place of papyrus as a writing material. The Arab fleet blocking the Mediterranean did good service to historians, for it led to a most remarkable increase in the chances of survival of a written archive, or indeed of correspondence, or any treatise written on vellum; papyrus was a friable material, cheap, light, and quite capable of lasting in readable condition for ten years or so, which was all that was necessary for the accounts and mercantile records so plentifully used under the Roman empire. But for permanent record, papyrus needed quite

exceptional conditions of protection from damp and fire risks, as
well as from theft; a very small proportion of papyrus records
have survived, and those in a partly perished condition, with holes
and missing words and passages, such as would be less likely to
occur in a parchment record, if it survived at all.

Charles, on his many campaigns and journeys, wrote letters to
his family and the officials left at home, and twenty-three of his
letters have survived. There was no system of posts, as in the
Roman empire: letters were entrusted to the traveller who happened to be going in the right direction, or to a special messenger;
many letters must never have arrived. Even as regards royal letters,
twenty-three must have been only a small proportion of those sent.
Moreover, in 791 Charles noticed the bad condition of the letters
addressed to his father and grandfather, and still preserved by the
chapel: many must have been on papyrus. He ordered them to be
'renewed and recopied', necessarily on parchment. This copy took
the form of the *Codex Carolinus*, a volume with abstracts of some
fifty-seven letters, with the datings and other protocol omitted.
(The formal opening of the letter was the first protocol, the formal
ending the final protocol.) The letters nevertheless throw useful
light, from specimens sent to Charles himself, on events in Italy
and relations with the holy see. Certain letters of the popes to
Charles have also survived independently: some letters of Einhard,
written during the latter part of his life, and a few letters sent to
Paul the Deacon, Angilram, bishop of Metz, Paulinus of Aquileia,
Arn of Salzburg, etc., and three from Alcuin himself. Alcuin seems
to have written many letters after his retirement to Tours, demanding news of the king and his movements and of all his friends at
court. The *Libri Carolini*, however, are not letters, but a redaction
by Alcuin about Charles's own views on images, attacking both
iconoclasm on the one hand, and the cult of images on the other.

Besides letters, however, records of the Carolingian capitularies,
conciliar *acta*, and diplomas offer plentiful information. A royal
edict, published in an assembly of spiritual and temporal magnates,
and consisting of a number of brief paragraphs dealing with
matters of spiritual or secular order, not arranged in any logical
plan, was a 'capitulary'. The name implies a miscellaneous schedule
of enactments, though sometimes the schedule has a general
subject of legislation, like the capitulary *De Villis* or *De Banno
Dominico*, or *De Judaeis*, or *De missis Dominicis*, or those for local
areas. Besides these capitularies, conciliar *acta*, drawn up by a
notary, record the canons passed by some synod of bishops or
abbots: such canons also were often issued under royal authority.

Diplomas, on the other hand, were records, written down at the time or later, of the oral acts of an assembly: generally grants or concessions to church or monastery made publicly before the assembly. Whereas the royal letters, or writs, were authenticated, as in Merovingian times, by the signature of a royal issuing officer (see p. 62), and (since the adoption of parchment for letters) by the regular use of the royal seal, diplomas were issued on the authority of the assembly before whom the donation or disposition was publicly made, and required the signature of those prepared to attest it. While the earliest extant Merovingian diploma, of 656, is actually witnessed by the signatures of those attesting, in their own and widely differing hands, in the Carolingian period the name, cross and subscribing phrase were all made by the scribe who wrote the document.

The political scene, viewed through the eyes of these witnesses then, centres in the court, and in Charles himself. The court is the *palatium*, and Charles's officers his *palatini*, his paladins to a later age. The palace travels with the king, Charles's family, his chapel and his lay officers: it is the old Merovingian palace, but on a larger scale.

Of Charles himself, we know from Einhard that he was of tall stature: the bronze equestrian statue of the Musée Carnavalet (now in the Louvre), a ninth-century piece of work if not a contemporary portrait, represents him (or a later Carolingian king) as not immoderately tall, with a long, curved moustache; he is wearing the short, Frankish tunic and a long cloak fastened with a brooch on the right shoulder. As he is crowned and bears the orb in his left hand, the intention of the artist is to represent him as riding in a ceremonial procession: and whether or not such a crowned and orbed progress ever took place, it is fitting enough that the monarch who ruled his great empire on horseback should be so represented.

Charles was the eldest son of king Pepin and queen Bertrada, whom the annals of Saint-Bertin represent as the daughter of Caribert, count of Laon; the Carolingian fisc had great estates round Laon. Einhard's rather strange profession of complete ignorance about Charles's birth and early years, together with the indisputable fact of the bad feeling between Charles and his brother Carloman, has suggested that Charles was born out of wedlock, but legitimated by the subsequent marriage of his parents. Kleinclausz suggests from certain inferences that he was born on 2 April 742, and that his parents married between 744 and 749;

he had two brothers, Carloman, about four years younger, and Pepin, who died in infancy or childhood.

His devout mother, Bertrada, had him brought up in piety, and his father Pepin had him trained to be king: which, at that date, implied not the acquisition of book-learning, but the long discipline of horsemanship, hunting, travelling, fighting, the doing of justice and securing of order, and the leadership of a very tough band of illiterate but not uncivilized magnates and vassals. When Pepin and his court and family were keeping the Christmas feasts at Thionville (753) and the news came that pope Stephen III had crossed the Alps and was coming to seek Frankish help, Pepin sent young Charles to meet him and bring him to the palace of Ponthion. Charles saw his father dismount and lead the pope's horse by the bridle, and he saw the pope received in the chapel of the palace with hymns and chanting. He was certainly present on the 14th April following, at the interview between his father and Stephen at the villa of Quierzy, when Pepin promised to grant to St Peter for ever certain cities and territories in Italy; and on Sunday, 28 July 754, he was, with his father and brother, in the basilica of Saint-Denis for a great papal ceremony. Stephen blessed a new altar dedicated to the twelve apostles, and then, before the mass, Charles received at the pope's hand, together with his father and brother, the anointing to be king of the Franks, and the title of patrician of the Romans. Charles fought with his father in the Aquitanian wars of 761, witnessing two of his father's grants to abbeys, and in 764, like Carloman his brother, he was granted the administration of a group of counties. He was twenty-six years old when his father died; he was acquainted with the problem of relations with Italy and the papacy and of local rebellion: but the general control of the *regnum Francorum* had remained firmly in his father's hands.

Pepin's death at Saint-Denis in 768 was unexpected and preceded by only a short illness: there had been no opportunity for intrigue between Charles and his brother about the succession. Pepin had been anxious enough himself for sole rule, but in the short time left him now for decision he could not set aside the traditional Frankish custom of partition of the inheritance between sons, at least without great risk of civil war. The partition that he arranged was curious. He did not follow any Merovingian precedent, except in that the two sons had capitals near together, for mutual convenience in the government of the *regnum Francorum*. Charles had Noyon and Carloman, Soissons: the Carolingian shift of power from the Seine valley towards the Rhine was already indicated. Carloman, the younger son, got a compact block of territory stretching from Soissons to the Mediterranean and from Orleans and Toulouse to the Alps, and his south-eastern frontiers marched with those of the duchy of Bavaria and the Lombard kingdom; he thus held southern Austrasia, southern Neustria, Burgundy, most of Aquitania, Provence and Septimania; Charles's land lay in a great crescent round this block. One horn of the crescent extended along the Slav frontier of the Böhmerwald, its outer edge then sweeping northward and westward along the northern frontiers of Austrasia and Neustria, the Channel, the Biscayan coast of Aquitaine and Gascony. Of the great towns and palaces, Carloman obtained Soissons, Reims, Trier, Paris and Orleans; Charles got Aix (not yet important), Noyon, Rouen and Tours. Pepin's curious division, which gave apparently the more desirable portion to Carloman, has been held to suggest that the younger son, born after marriage, had a claim at least equal to that of the elder son; but it can perhaps be more plausibly explained as entrusting the frontiers needing military defence, and the lands where rebellion might be looked for in Aquitania, to the better, more experienced, fighter.

Both sons maintained a full court of Frankish officers: but these were, after all, as much needed for the rule of their estates as for political purposes. Both appear to have been guided in their external relations by their mother, Bertrada, both had been crowned by Stephen and named patrician; both were bound by their father's policy of benevolent protection of the papacy. That this might involve restraining Desiderius, king of the Lombards, from further encroachments on the lands promised in the Donation of Pepin to the pope, neither Bertrada nor her sons as yet realized. To Bertrada indeed, a firm alliance with the Lombards, cemented by royal marriages, seemed the clue to future peace. Charles's relations with his brother were, from the first, bad: but in these early years he showed no distrust of the family policy, inspired by Bertrada. A man with his training was no theorist, but dealt with problems as they came.

As to Charles himself, with his firm step and manly carriage, his beautiful fair hair, his blue cloak, his sword, which (Einhard says) he always wore: the impression he gives is one of great intelligence and enormous energy. Intelligence he had himself and sought for in others: he could read Latin with some facility (it was, after all, the administrative language), Greek he understood better than he could speak. He was interested in the structure of the physical universe, and used to ask his learned councillors questions about the reasons of eclipses that they could not answer. He used to have a book read at meals: either some pleasant or instructive discourse, or history and things done of old (*antiquorum res gestae*): he liked Augustine's holy books, and specially those entitled *De civitate Dei*. He cherished the liberal arts, and the great teachers of these subjects he loaded with honours. Of these arts, he studied Latin literature as a middle-aged man with Peter of Pisa; for the other arts he had Albinus, surnamed Alcuin, also a deacon, a Saxon by race and from Britain, a most learned man in all subjects, as his teacher; he learned rhetoric and dialectic with him, and he gave the better part of his time and labour to the study of the physical universe (astronomy: the Ptolemaic universe). Indeed, he learned the art of reckoning, and curiously and intelligently pondered the course of the stars. He used even to practise writing and to have letter sheets and small books carried round (on pack horses) in his bed along with the pillows, and when he had free time, he used to train his hand to make letters; but in this labour, which Einhard calls 'preposterous' because it was that of a professional scribe, not a king, he was not very successful.

Charles acquired, that is to say, what was in those days the highest form of education, a certain competence in *sapientia*, *sophia*, the liberal arts, mainly orally, and during the course of an active and nomadic life. His intelligence is shown in the value which he, a good fighter and general himself, attributed to book learning: he was a good Christian and as such reverenced the clergy, but he saw them also as possible agents for the spread of learning; he warned the young clerks of his palace school, the juniors of the *capella*, that it was those who minded their books who were going to get bishoprics and abbeys from him.

Charles himself not only spent a very large proportion of his life in the saddle: but constrained his court to do so too. Only in the very worst of the winter months was his court comparatively at rest in Francia, and even then their stay at one villa or palace was, at longest, a matter of a week or two. This was necessary for reasons of supply, and it also made possible a supervision of the local counts by Charles and his palace: but it was not the life for weaklings, either ecclesiastics or vassals. Nevertheless, Charles drove them on, wherever his presence was needed, counts and household and scholars and chapel, even, except on campaigns, his wife and the princesses, from Rhine mouth to Rome, and from Tours to Passau. Even on campaigns, some of his chapel must accompany his own expedition or that of his 'prefect' or duke: Charles's capitulary of *c.* 769, it is true, forbade bishops and *sacerdotes* (a word including bishops and priests) to bear arms: but excepted those who went with the army to accomplish the solemnities of the mass or bear with them the protection of the saints, i.e. carry the king's holy relics: the original *capella* was a relic chest and a chaplain a custodian of relics. The prince, the capitulary goes on to stipulate, shall have with him two bishops with priests of the chapel, and each prefect on an expedition one priest, to hear confessions. Alcuin endured this hard, migrant life for long enough: but in 796 he at length obtained permission to retire to the abbacy of Tours, which had an excellent library, and the cuckoo singing in the garden in spring. Having reached this scholarly haven, however, he could scarcely bear to be without news of Charles and his still migrant court. Charles ordered, in the capitulary *De Villis*, that the villas should all be supplied with benches and tables and cushions and bedding and pots and pans and all things needed for the arrival and brief residence of the court: but none the less, it must have taken a lot of horses to transport Charles and his court from villa to villa. The Franks were skilled horsemen and made much use of the horse: and they had need to, to make any kind of central rule of Charles's dominions possible. Charles 'constantly took exercise, both by riding and hunting', says Einhard. 'This was a national habit, for there is hardly any race that can be placed on an equality with the Franks in this respect.' All the economic historians stress the extent to which the Franks used the horse; and one explanation why it was the Franks and not the more centrally placed Lombards who founded an empire, is probably the very old Frankish association with the horse-using nomads, their predilection for the horse, and Charles's energy on horseback. He rode into his empire on horseback and he governed it on horseback.

Charles had then physical strength, great intelligence, and an enormous, driving energy. To conceive his own strategy, to plan his campaigns, assemble his armies, one year in Spain, the next in Saxony, to conquer Italy and the Avars and in the winter season, between campaigns, to keep touch with his Frankish counts by means of riding with his palace from one villa to another: all this would seem enough for one man. But to be in addition the driving force behind the movement to re-establish the Greco-Roman learning in the west, the arbiter on theology, the protector of the papacy: it is astonishing to find a man of mental and physical vigour equal to all these tasks.

As to the other members of his family: Charles's mother, Bertrada, influenced the policy of both her sons at the beginning of the reign. She desired both a firm Lombard alliance and the good-will of the papacy, not facing the fact that the interests of her two would-be allies were opposed. She desired peace. 'Pacificus' as a royal title in those days implied, however, not 'pacifist' but a maintainer of peace: it implied the intention of maintaining peace in Christendom as a strong sovereign power. Bertrada's desire for the Lombard alliance, perhaps mainly for the sake of her younger son whose territories marched with Lombardy and to whom access to Italy was easiest, was not to lead to the peace she desired. Desiderius' sister Liutberg was already married to Tassilo, duke of Bavaria: Bertrada arranged for Charles to marry another daughter of Desiderius (Desideria ?), and for Charles's sister, Gisela, to marry Desiderius' son, Adalgis; Bertrada herself went to Pavia to arrange the marriages. Charles was compliant, despite the remonstrances of pope Stephen III, to whom a Franco-Lombard alliance was repugnant; he had moreover already parted with Amodru, a Frankish lady to whom he had not been married. He married the Lombard princess at Christmas, 770, at Mainz: she was the first of his four wives.

As to Carloman, Charles's brother, Einhard represents him as having desired to upset the mutual concord which his father had desired maintained in Francia between the brothers: but before any open dispute broke out, Carloman died, in 771. He had married Gerberga, a Frankish lady, and left two baby sons. With the consent of all the Franks, even of those of Carloman's household officers, Charles assumed the government of the whole *regnum Francorum* and Gerberga fled with her infant sons to the protection of the Lombard court.

Charles's first marriage, with the Lombard princess, was a political alliance of short duration, but his later wives were personages at the Frankish court. When he repudiated Desideria (Desirée) in 771, he married Hildegard, a princess of the ducal house of Alemannia, and had by her his sons Charles, Louis (and his twin Lothar, who soon died), and Pepin (called Carloman at first). Hildegard died in 783 and was honourably buried at Metz; Paul the Deacon wrote a lament for her: Frank, Sueve and German mourn her, he cried: yes, even the Briton and the Goth and the Irishman. Charles at her death married Fastrada, who was his queen from 783 till in 794 'death with his cold flower bore her from their midst'. Charles then married another Alemannian lady, Liutgard, who was probably his favourite wife; she died in 800 at Tours, while Charles was staying there and debating with Alcuin the difficulties of the charges brought against Leo III.

Alcuin mourned her, and Charles had no more wives: though he had children later by three mistresses.

The lay magnates of Charles's court were both his household officers and sharers in the government of his dominions. The organization of the household was still Merovingian, though Charles modified it at will. There was no chief minister and there were no favourites: Charles really governed, with the help of his *vassi regales*. These permanently in residence formed his palace, some contemporaries speaking of them as his *aulici*, the members of his hall (*aula*): only later was the palace spoken of as the court (*curia*). Occasionally too, and mainly by the poets, the adjective 'sacred' was applied to a royal officer or to the palace itself, in imitation of Byzantine usage: but the word gained no entry in the language of Charles's official documents.

Though the lay magnates were certainly as important agents of Charles as his clerical ministers, his *capellani*, less is known of them personally than of the latter. Clerks like Alcuin and Theodulf and the rest wrote letters to each other and to Charles, letters full of greetings for the individual members at that time with Charles in his palace, and sometimes with brief descriptions of their qualities and character: the *praefecti* and *duces* on campaign wrote fewer letters: at any rate, fewer of a literary character. The clerks in their letters sent more and longer greetings to the clerical members of the palace than to the lay officers, probably as being more familiar with them. Brief references to the lay magnates come rather from accounts in the annals of the expeditions they led, from Einhard, and from diplomatic sources: their signatures to diplomas, and their names at the head of mandates addressed to them by Charles. No such source gives much personal detail.

From such contemporary sources we hear of count Roland, prefect of the Breton March, who fell at Roncesvalles (see p. 352). He is mentioned with the seneschals Eggihard and Anselm, in an epitaph for Eggihard: one of those stately and romantic Latin verses, which Carolingian poets loved to write and wrote so well: 'Here he lies in the tomb', the verse runs, 'who was chief in the royal hall: in God's hall he lives now.' All these Frankish lay nobles (*magnates, proceres*) served some time as part of Charles's household, where they had often been trained (*enutriti*) since boyhood; they were then sent on missions, or put in charge of military expeditions and at some early or later period they would be given lands or charge of some county, and planted out in the countryside. Such men shared with Charles the burden of government, of conquest, and the making of policy, during and after their permanent attachment to the palace; they were often members of his council (see p. 397). William, son of count Thierry of Toulouse, was brought up at the palace before being made councillor and count (see p. 403). Gerold, an Aleman and brother of queen Hildegard, was made count and given the defence of Bavaria and the frontier bordering on the lands of the Huns, and in 799 he 'met death's savage sword' in its defence (see p. 368). He fought, said his epitaph, for the peace of the Pannonian lands, and a faithful Saxon rescued his body and brought it home for burial; he was succeeded by the seneschal, count Audulf, who had earlier succeeded Roland as count of the Breton March when he too was killed on campaign. Of Meginfrid, chamberlain 791–796, we know that Alcuin wrote to him as his friend and as treasurer (*arcarius*) of the royal palace; he blamed the harshness in the exaction of tithe which followed Charles's capitulary for the Saxons, and he blames the hasty and forcible conversion of pagans: 'the Christian faith should first be taught, and then may sacraments of baptism be received'; in these matters Meginfrid, attached to the palace, had influence. Of the royal butler, Eberhard, the chamberlain Adalgis (782) and the constables Geilo (782) and Burchard (807) little but their names is known.

Two of the councillors who were closest to Charles were of Carolingian stock, and began their career as lay nobles: Adalhard and Angilbert; Adalard ended his as a cleric and Angilbert as a layman, but a great prince-abbot. Of these we have more information. Adalard, Charles's cousin, was the son of a half-brother of Pepin the Short; he was *enutritus* at the palace and as a young *vassus* became count of the palace (see p. 391). When twenty years old, however, he entered the monastery of Corbie in Picardy, and passed on from there to Monte Cassino. Charles however ordered him to return to Corbie, where he was elected abbot, and when in 774 Charles's three-year old son Pepin was left as king of Italy, Charles committed the actual government of Italy to Adalhard and a lay noble, Rotchild. When king Pepin died in 810, Charles again left the government and defence of Italy to Adalhard and his brother Wala; only limiting their powers in 813 by naming Bernard, Pepin's son, as king of Italy. Adalhard thus, after his palace training, mainly served Charles as his agent in Italian affairs; the Lombard, Paul the Deacon, loved him and wrote that sooner should Rhine and Moselle flow backward to their source than the dear name of Adalard find no place in his heart.

Angilbert, also, was *enutritus* at Charles's palace, and taught by Alcuin himself; he received the old notarial training, and in 782 accompanied the young king Pepin to Italy as *primicerius palatii*. In this post he would have worked with the palace chaplains, but would scarcely have been termed *capellanus* himself. Besides the writing of notarial *acta*, however, he could write *carmina* worthy of his masters, Peter of Pisa and Paul the Deacon and Alcuin: he would write to Peter in his epistolatary *carmina* (Charles's circle were fond of writing letter-poems) as to his *dulci doctoque magistro*, and Peter in return termed him his 'divine poet'. Charles's *academia* indeed surnamed him 'Homer', apparently from a Latin epic that he wrote about Charles and pope Leo. In 790 Charles presented him, while still a layman, to the abbacy of Centula on the Somme, the abbey of St Richarius (Saint-Riquier). Angilbert received with the grant considerable new endowments for the abbey, with which he proceeded to rebuild it on a splendid scale (see p. 308). In 795 he was so trusted a councillor that Charles sent him to the newly elected pope, Leo III, to confer with him on his own position, his relations with the Franks, and the affairs of the church. He long ruled his abbey as prince-abbot, and for a time he had an intrigue with Charles's unmarried daughter, Berta, and was the father of her two children (one of them the chronicler, Nithard); there is no evidence that he lost the favour of Charles over the matter, though Alcuin blamed him. He was a notable councillor of Charles, writing him many letters as 'David', some other *carmina* and one poem where, as Homer the prophet, he sings at great length of David, the glory of prophets, with the curious refrain:

> *David amat vates: vatorum est gloria David.*

He died in 814, very soon after Charles himself, and was understandably canonized for his great work at Saint-Riquier. 'I am thy servant', his dedicatory poem for the abbey church runs, 'thy servant, O Richarius, great shepherd: here have I built thee this small house, O father!' He ordered that when he died, he should be buried on the threshold, that the feet of all entering might pass over him, and wrote this verse for his gravestone:

> I, as the abbot, have laid this lowly pavement,
> For I am Angilbert: led by the love of God:
> That when I die, Christ who is my life and salvation
> May grant to me at last his holy rest.

But his friends were not content with such lines, and had carved round the tomb they raised for him upon the pavement another epitaph:

O king: give rest to Angilbert: who art father and kindly king!
O law: give him the eternal life of law: for thou art law!
O light: forever give him light: thou art that kindly light!
O peace: forever give him peace, for thou art peace!

Charles's ecclesiastical councillors also had great weight with him, and not only as repositories of the best learning of the day, but as now the heirs of all the traditions of the old Greco-Roman civil service. Christian clerics in the sixth, seventh and eighth centuries acquired the technique of Roman government and Roman law: the bishop's and the count's notaries, and the notaries of the palace had long worked with clerks, and the clerks were now ready to take over. But they had had, in addition to notarial training, long years of clerical attendance at the divine office, which was in effect, a year-long communal meditation on the Bible, and particularly the psalms. There was very little in the day office except the scriptures, and in the night office there were, beyond the passages of Old and New Testaments, and a saint's life if his *natalicia* was to be celebrated the day following, only the patristic homilies and comments. A cleric who had followed the office from boyhood would know the New Testament, passages of the Old, and something of church history: and now promising young clerics knew something of *lex Romana* as well. They were ready to run a Christian empire; to act as advisers to a *basileus*; and they lived in a climate of opinion that was Christian and Roman. There was no 'lay' climate of opinion apart from theirs, or opposed to theirs.

Among Charles's clerical counsellors, the Englishman, Alcuin, was perhaps the most outstanding; both for his influence in foreign relations and the affairs of the Frankish church. He was already fifty years old when, in 781, he was transferred by his bishop, Æthelbert of York, and entered Charlemagne's service. He had been born in or near York, round about the time of Bede's death in 735, of noble family and akin to Willibrord, the apostle of Frisia: he actually inherited in later life the lay patronage of the monastery at Humber mouth built by Willibrord's father. He was called Albinus, after the martyr saint of Britain(?) and sent as a small boy to receive the clerical tonsure and be brought up in the *familia* of the great and learned archbishop, Egbert of York. He passed up the different grades of the clerical order, being promoted to a different grade in the cathedral schools with each, and winning the praise of archbishop Egbert and Æthelbert, the master of the schools, for his learning. He studied the liberal arts, and the mysteries of holy scripture: 'my master', he wrote afterwards, 'told me to rise with all that was in me to the defence of the Catholic faith if anywhere I should hear of the springing up of strange sects, opposed to apostolic doctrines'. He read Pliny, Cassiodorus, Gregory the Great, Isidore and Bede; he also learned to read Greek.

He was once taken by Æthelbert to Italy and to Francia, on one of the expeditions when Æthelbert was seeking manuscripts and contact with Italian and Frankish scholars; he heard Peter of Pisa, the classical scholar, disputing at Pavia; he visited and long remembered the monks of Murbach; he came to succeed Æthelbert as master of the York schools himself. He was made deacon at the age of about thirty-five, but never priest; the deacon was, at the time, the chief administrative officer, and often the right-hand man, of the bishop or archbishop; had he remained at York, he was in line to succeed his master Æthelbert, as Æthelbert had succeeded Egbert. He had however a friend, possibly slightly senior to himself in the York *familia*, the cleric Eanbald: and when Æthelbert, feeling his end near, resigned his see (he died that same year, in 780), Eanbald was elected to succeed him, and the king of Northumbria sent Alcuin to the pope to ask for the pallium for the new archbishop. Alcuin, on his return journey, met Charles and his court at Pavia, just before Easter in the year 781; he had actually met the king before, when Æthelbert had sent him to Charles on some mission. There were already connexions between the English mission in Saxony, its homeland and supporters in England, and the Frankish court; Charles desired to attach the Northumbrian scholar to his service, and prevailed upon the king of Northumbria and Eanbald to release him. Charles had already collected a band of learned clerks at his palace, Peter of Pisa, and Paulinus, soon to be patriarch of Aquileia: Alcuin would represent that other bright source of the classical renaissance, Bede's Northumbria.

Alcuin was now a senior scholar: he entered Charles's service, and after a brief return to York with Eanbald's pallium, he joined the Frankish court in or about 782. He was invaluable to Charles as the senior tutor of himself and his household: as the supporter of his warlike yet still missionary advance in Saxony, for with the affairs of the English teachers in Saxony Alcuin was very well acquainted: and as a distinguished Christian authority for consultation about Frankish relations with the papacy and the eastern emperor. He was ready, indeed, to guide Charles's policy in the difficult matter of the trial of pope Leo III with gravity, discretion, and a due knowledge of canon law; ready to guide the reform of the Frankish church, begun under Pepin and Boniface, ready to write the *Libri Carolini*, sustaining with all his learning Charles's views on the question of iconoclasm. From the time when Charles had established his palace at Aix, Charles frequented the curious and learned postprandial sessions where Alcuin taught the liberal arts, as in an *academia*, mainly by way of question and answer. Alcuin wrote of this informal school, attended not only by the young lay vassals and clerks, but by the senior officials, the royal princes and Charles himself; Pepin and Charles are represented as among the questioners in the dialogue. The Frankish palace, however, was never stationary, even at Aix, and Alcuin yearned for a more settled existence, with books at hand, such as he had had at York. Moreover, there was much bustle and business encompassing those who lived at the palace, as he wrote to Samuel, archbishop of Sens: 'Alcuin is bound in servitude: he dines at a fixed hour: now, here is the seneschal, here the butler, here the cook, the brewer, the stableman; here is the launderer and here the man who sweeps up the hearth: and merchants who will not be put off waste a lot of time.' He had long given up, however, any idea of return to York; he loved his 'laurel-wreathed David', and his children and all his friends of the palace, too much. Charles, in return, loved him: but by 794 Alcuin was sixty-four and old for the migratory life of the palace, and Charles gave him charge therefore of the holiest relics and abbey in the kingdom: the abbey of St Martin of Tours. Here he ruled the canons from his little cell in the garden, and sometimes entertained Angilbert and even Charles himself: and never ceased writing letters and demanding news of them. To his friends at the palace he wrote: saying he would send letters more often if he had a dove or a raven who could be trusted to bear them. 'What happy days they were, when we did acrostics together' (*pariter lusimus litteraliter seria*). He was ready in any case to direct his friends' reading and offer learned counsel to Charles; he was sad only at his friends' absence and at the drying up of his own powers of writing *carmina*. He ruled his abbey from 794 till his death in 806: 'sadly the children wail in their song for Flaccus': Fridugis his scholar lamented in lovely verse the emptiness of the little cell in the garden at Tours.

As Charles had sought in Alcuin a representative of Northumbrian learning, so he summoned to his palace from Italy three scholars: Paul the Deacon (see p. 247), Peter of Pisa and Paulinus of Aquileia. Like Alcuin and Paul, Peter of Pisa remained in deacon's orders, which suggests that those who held themselves primarily dedicated to scholarship and teaching did not, at the date, go on to the priesthood. Born or educated at Pisa, in the land of Latin scholarship, between *c.* 720 and 725, Peter the deacon had won renown for his teaching of Latin literature, his power of academic debate, when Charles summoned him to his palace; and at the palace school he spent the greater part of his life, returning to Italy shortly before his death, *c.* 799. He taught Charles Latin, and apparently enough rhetoric, which included the study of metre, to appreciate the many *carmina* addressed to him by his scholarly friends. He taught Angilbert, he was the friend of Alcuin and Paul the Deacon, and his regular charge was the instruction of the boys of the chapel, and the young lay nobles *enutriti* at the palace. Some of the *carmina* and verse letters which he exchanged with his friends, some of the epitaphs which he composed, still survive.

Charles kept Peter of Pisa always at his palace, for the teaching of the boys demanded a permanent *scholasticus*, but Paulinus of Aquileia he sent out, after a time of service in the chapel, to be one of the most important of his agents in Italy. What Adalhard was to him in central Italy, Paulinus was in the north, for he knew its affairs as a native and by education. He had been born near Cividale (Friuli in the eighth century: the old Forum Julii), and educated at the patriarchal schools of Old Aquileia, at the time there located.

The patriarchate of Aquileia had had a strange and stormy history, for the city of Aquileia, at the head of the Adriatic, had stood in the path of invaders of Italy from the middle Danube and the Balkans: Huns, Ostrogoths, Lombards. Aquileia had, in fact, been completely wiped out by the Huns in 451–2, and left desolate, her citizens taking refuge with the Veneti in their lagoons. She had been held a patriarchate as the great mother church of the region, with jurisdiction to the north and over the Roman cities of Trent, Treviso and Pavia to the west, and with an old tradition of foundation by Mark the Evangelist before his teaching at Alexandria: reverence for and patronage by St Mark was taken by the Aquileians to what was to be, in future, Venice. At the beginning of the sixth century Aquileia had been rebuilt and her church recognized as a patriarchate by Ostrogoths and the pope; the bishops of Trent, Treviso and Pavia were her suffragans, and her influence was the greater because she stood for *Romanitas* and orthodox Christianity, while the Ostrogoths, who held Milan and Ravenna, were Arian.

The Ostrogoths, however, fell: the Lombards overran Italy and Aquileia, and the patriarch now fled for refuge to Grado, a little island near Trieste and a last remnant of the East Roman emperor's territories in north Italy. In the years following, Aquileia was for fifty years in schism from Rome, and when her patriarch was finally reconciled, with some of his suffragans, in 606, others remained unreconciled: there were thus two very small patriarchates for a time, that of Old Aquileia in Friuli, supported by the Lombards and in schism, and that of Aquileia in Grado, in communion with Rome. That of Old Aquileia was in time also reconciled, and it was with this see at Friuli that Paulinus had a lifelong association.

Paulinus came of a Roman family that had survived under the Lombard occupation near Friuli and become reconciled to the régime. When the Lombard kingdom fell in 774, Paulinus had long been lecturing in the schools of Friuli and had acquired a reputation for learning both in the field of Latin literature and biblical scholarship: Charles invited him therefore to his palace, and he became the friend of Peter of Pisa, Alcuin, Arn, Fulrad of Saint-Denis, Einhard, and the other learned gentlemen of Charles's circle. He was assigned estates in Lombardy by Charles, and in 787 made patriarch of Aquileia. By so doing Charles secured the loyalty of what had been the old mother church of Bavaria and the middle Danube, before Boniface and his helpers came into these semi-pagan lands from the north; and he secured control of a great Latin church bordering on the Greek obedience. The see of Aquileia in Grado was subject to both papal and Greek influence, and Charles had good reason to favour the rival see.

Paulinus wrote a great deal of Latin verse: but he also made a good, reforming bishop, holding synods, of which some of the canons have survived, and defending the rights of his see. He obtained from Charles a diploma securing the free election of the patriarch of Aquileia, and various privileges and immunities for churches, monasteries and hospitals. He was a weighty theologian and summoned by Charles in 794 to the assembly at Frankfurt which condemned Adoptianism, but also gained an unenviable notoriety by attacking the veneration of images as defined by the recent Council of Nicaea. Paulinus wrote a treatise against the Adoptianist position and it was sent to Spain as the official declaration of the council. He accompanied Charles later in the campaign against the Avars, reckoned to be in the religious hinterland of his own metropolitan see and wrote a poem about the Avar war afterwards; and he presided at the synod of Salzburg which debated the evangelization of these pagan peoples. In 796 Paulinus summoned his own synod at Friuli, passed canons on ecclesiastical discipline and again dealt with Adoptianism and the *Filioque* clause: a matter of importance to a church part of whose old territories on the Adriatic were well disposed to the Greeks. A copy of these canons was sent to the emperor. In 798 Charles used Paulinus, with Arn of Salzburg, as *missi* at Pistoia, and again as imperial legate at Rome.

But though Paulinus was thus an active and successful metropolitan of Aquileia, always loyal to the Frankish interest, Charles would not support his claim that the newly conquered and converted lands in Carinthia and the Avar country should be placed under his jurisdiction, as having in the past belonged to the old patriarchate of Aquileia. Paulinus himself died in 802, before the matter was decided; but the see of Salzburg in Carinthia was created at the expense of the old patriarchate and Charles, called in to arbitrate between the patriarchate and the new see as to boundaries, gave to Salzburg all Carinthia north of the Drava.

Paulinus' works, beside his dogmatic treatises against Elipandus and Felix (see p. 334), included many occasional *carmina*, elegies, a long poem *De regula fidei*, a song on the old city of Aquileia, destroyed and never rebuilt, and some noble hymns for the chief feasts of the church, for use in his own basilica of Aquileia in Friuli. Here in 802 he died and in the patriarchal basilica he rests.

Paulinus was scholar, poet, theologian and man of affairs, but the next place in scholarly renown to that of Alcuin was probably accorded to the Spaniard, Theodulf: *scientia praerogativa . . . pollebat*. Theodulf, as he records himself in one of his poems, was born in Spain (Hesperia), a Goth: but he was an *alumnus* of Narbonne. He seems to have been involved in some kind of political trouble before, at the age of about thirty-four, he was invited to Charles's palace around 794, and there he became the most distinguished poet of the royal circle: part of his hymn for Palm Sunday is still sung in the liturgy:

> *Gloria, laus et honor tibi sit, rex Christe redemptor,*
> *Cui puerile decus prompsit osanna pium.*

In 798 Charles found work for him outside the palace: he made him bishop of Orleans and gave him several abbeys, among them Fleury-on-the-Loire, where St Benedict's bones had been brought to rest. He also appointed Theodulf *missus* to tour southern Aquitaine. Though, by the efforts of the count of Toulouse, Aquitaine was now fairly safe from Saracen attack, Visigothic refugees were arriving in some numbers and settling in the country, and there was likelihood that they would bring with them 'the Spanish heresy' of Adoptianism. Theodulf, at Charles's command, defended the *Filioque* clause in a treatise, *De Spiritu Sancto*. Apparently he also showed readiness to defend Charles's subjects from the severity of the courts and judges; in a long poem, *Versus contra judices*, he gave some account of his experiences as *missus* and complained of the severity of Frankish law. He wrote also at Charles's request an account of the baptismal ceremonies (*De ordine baptismi*), and again and again he despatched *carmina*, to Charles himself, to Fardulf, abbot of Saint-Denis (with some small presents), to the queen (asking that she would send him balsam for making the chrism that would go out to anoint the people), to Gisela the princess (with a psalter 'shining with gold and silver'), and to others. He wrote too occasional verses, about the coming of king Louis to Orleans, a poem to be written in his Bible, describing the contents of each book, and one about the patristic tomes he has been used to read and also the *gentilia scripta*, Vergil and Ovid and the rest of them: in their sayings are many frivolous matters (the naked boy, Cupid, and his bow and arrows, indeed): yet these sayings, under their false wrappings, hide many truths; the pen writes down the false words of poets, the true ones of sophists, and yet can often turn the words of poets into truth.

Theodulf enjoyed Charles's favour all his life, and his name appears among the signatories of Charles's will; but he became involved in the conspiracy against Bernard, king of Italy, and was exiled by the emperor Louis to the monastery of Angers, where he spent the last seven years of his life, dying on 18 December 821.

Finally, Theodulf sang the praises of Charles, his fame and his family in a long poem which is, in some respects, the best contemporary picture of Charles, his courtiers, and his family circle. The whole world, he says, rings with Charles's praises, and though he could say much, never could he say all. Let men measure the Meuse, the Rhine, the Saône, the Rhone, the Tiber and the Po, and they will have measured the bounds of Charles's fame. No man could measure his prudent statesmanship for that is wider than Nile and icy Danube, greater than Euphrates, no smaller than Ganges. The people whom Charles has beckoned have come in readiness to serve Christ: the pig-tailed Hun, the Arab with flowing hair: Arabs and nomads, both have come. Legates come from Charles in peace: in his hall is held honourable council: where the great building of his hall arises, there his paladins sit in their high seats; through the long *atrium* the people come and go.

A fair progeny surrounds the king, the boys on this side, the girls on that, like young branches of the vine. The young Charles and Louis stand together, the one approaching manhood, the other with the face of youth. The king glances at them, and then at the crowd of maidens, none fairer than the other, in dress, beauty, body, heart and faith. There is Berta and Rohtrud, Gisela and Liutgard: they are kindly to all men, and trained in study and the liberal arts. The maidens bring flowers and fruit to the king, Berta roses, Rohtrud violets and Gisela lilies: they shine with gems and gold, and their father speaks gently to them and jokes with them. The vassals draw nigh and are glad, fulfilling each his service.

Let Flaccus (Alcuin) draw near: he is the glory of our prophets, a mighty sophist and a maker of melody. He can set forth true dogma from the scriptures, and solve the problems of mathematics. Flaccus' question now seems simple, now rugged and rock-sharp: now he deals with the secular arts, now the divine: the king himself is one of those who seek to answer his questions: he's a very lucky man who can answer all these *Flaccidica*.

Then there is Riculf, of mighty voice, senses alert, polished in speech: noble both in learning and faith: if he go far, he will not return empty handed.

A sweet song would I sing thee, wert thou not absent, my Homer (Angilbert): but since thou art, my muse is silent.

Yet Ercambald's prudent presence lacks not (he was 797–812 notary in Charles's court): he whose faithful hand holds twin tablets; Lentulus is here, bearing sweet apples;—see he is hurrying round too fast: be slower, brave Lenticulus!

Here too Nardulus hastens swiftly in and out: he scurries here and there like a little ant. The small house of his body shelters a mighty guest: the small cavern of his breast protects a mighty spirit. Now he bears books, now the work of his handicraft: now he prepares darts well fitted to slay the Scot (name not known).

Theodulf goes on to say that this letter, the third in its series, shall be borne to him whose name begins with the letter that is first in 'caelo', second in 'scando' and third in 'ascensu', fourth in 'amicitiis': there will be no doubt who is meant! Let it go where the Levite Fridugis stands with Osulf and Nardus and Ercanbald: where Eppin the butler pours the wine at the royal feast, where father Alcuin sits ready to bless the meal.

BIBLIOGRAPHICAL NOTE

(to chapters xvii, xviii, xix and xx)

The Latin text of Einhard's *Life of Charlemagne* was published, with introduction and notes, by H. W. Garrod and R. B. Mowat, in 1915. A good modern work on Charlemagne is that of L. Halphen, *Charlemagne et l'empire Carolingien*, 1947, but the most detailed study, with quotations of contemporary sources, is still that of A. Kleinclausz, *Charlemagne*, 1934. A more popular book, with good illustrations and some footnotes, is J. Calmette's *Charlemagne: sa vie et son œuvre*, 1945. For Alcuin, see E. S. Duckett's *Alcuin, Friend of Charlemagne*, 1951 (with a full bibliography), Kleinclausz, *Alcuin*, 1948, and 'Alcuin: Lettres', in *Annales de l'Univ. de Lyons*, Ser. 3, Lettres, fasc. 15. For the Carolingian court circle, Hincmar of Rheims' 'De ordine palatii', in *Bibliot. de l'école des chartes . . . sciences phil. et hist.*, fasc. 58, 1869. See also W. Levison, *England and the Continent in the Eighth Century*, 1946, and M. L. W. Laistner, *Thought and Letters in Western Europe, A.D. 500–900*, 1931. For recent studies, see L. Wallach, *Alcuin and Charlemagne*, 1959; R. Boutruche, *Seigneurie et Féodalité*, 1959; H. F. Haefele, *Notkeri Balbuli Gesta Karoli*, 1959; J. M. Wallace-Hadrill, *The fourth book of the Chronicle of Fredegar*, 1960. See also, L. Wallach, *Alcuin et Charlemagne*, Cornell Univ. Press, 1959, which portrays Charles as the conscious heir of the Roman tradition; L. Halphen's collected essays *A travers l'histoire du Moyen Age*, Paris, 1950.

CHAPTER XVIII

THE CAROLINGIAN CONQUESTS

THE restoration of the empire in the west in the year 800 was certainly conditioned by the conquests of Charlemagne. He had then conquered the Lombards and gained Rome; he had conquered the Saxons and Avars; he had made of his conquests an opportunity to extend Christianity, to convert the barbarians, and this was an essential function of the Christian emperor. All these favourable conditions had been produced by military conquest, and the history of these conquests is the most important strand in the history of the reign. Charles was hailed as *Pacificus* in 800, and contemporaries saw nothing startling in so hailing a ruler who had fought more campaigns and won more battles than any general since Belisarius, or perhaps even Caesar: for unity of rule was conceived of as the preliminary to peace, and the pacific sovereign was he who enforced law and quiet order, almost necessarily in this early and violent age, by the sword.

Charles's army was the instrument of his conquests, and the organization which made its use possible at and beyond all the different frontiers of the *regnum Francorum* was simple: and yet it was surprisingly successful. The Frankish armies crossed the Rhine, the Alps, the Pyrenees; passed the Elbe to the north east, and the Bavarian plateau towards the river Enns: they passed the Danube and the Tisza (Theiss) to attack the land of the Avars: they passed the Po and the Apennines and reached the Tuscan cities and Rome herself. The Frankish army fought with men of very different races, employing different techniques of fighting: Lombards: Saxons: Avars: Arabs: Greeks: and everywhere it pressed, the frontiers of Francia were in time extended.

As to the composition of the army: the old tradition that every freeman owed military service still held, but could not be literally fulfilled, for the Frankish army was now a cavalry army, and the small freeholder could not have afforded the war horse, shod and saddled, and the equipment necessary. It was once assumed that the change in the Frankish army from a mainly infantry to a mainly cavalry force took place with some suddenness about the year 755, when Pepin ordered the assembly of the army he was going to lead into Italy for May, instead of at the traditional date, the kalends of March; presumably to allow the growth of wayside grass for the

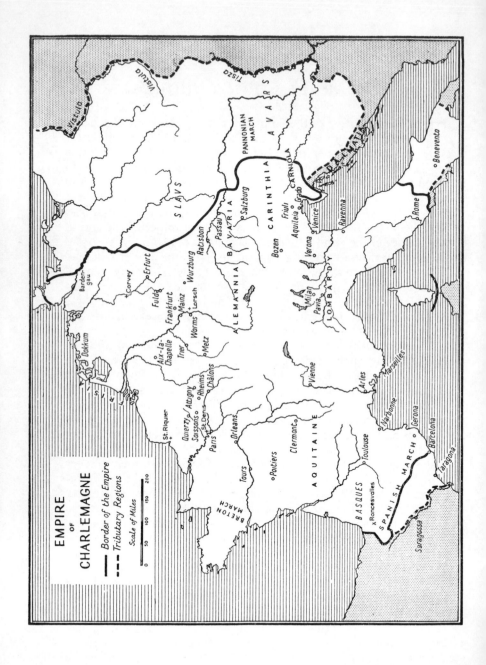

EMPIRE
OF
CHARLEMAGNE

Border of the Empire
Tributary Regions

Scale of Miles
0 50 100 150 200

VISTULA

SLAVS

TISZA

PANNONIAN
MARCH

AVARS

DALMATIA

Benevento

CARINTHIA

Salzburg

CARNIOLA

Friuli

BAVARIA

Bozen

Aquileia Grado

Ravenna

Rome

Venice

Verona

Passau

Ratisbon

Wurzburg

ALEMANNIA

Milan

LOMBARDY

Bardengau

Corvey

Erfurt

Fulda

Frankfurt

Mainz

Worms

Lorsch

Pavia

Dokkum

FRISIA

Aix-la-Chapelle

Trier

Metz

Vienne

Arles

Marseilles

St. Riquer

Quierzy

Attigny

Rheims

Soissons

St. Denis

Chalons

Paris

Orleans

Narbonne

Gerona

Barcelona

Tarragona

Saragossa

Tours

Poitiers

Clermont

AQUITAINE

Toulouse

BASQUES

Roncesvalles

SPANISH MARCH

BRETON
MARCH

horses. It is now held, however, that the cavalry element in the Frankish army had long been growing, and that the May starting date was decided upon to allow the snow to melt in the Alpine passes, rather than for the growth of grass. In any case, the cavalry element was now of predominant importance. By custom, the land-holders (whether proprietors or holders of a benefice) only owed personal service in the field if their holding amounted to four *mansae* (holdings of from 25 to 37 acres): landholders of smaller areas could not, in fact, serve as horse soldiers. In 808 Charle-magne, however, ordered that a holder of three *mansae* must serve, using the help of a stay-at-home holder of a single *mansa* to equip himself; one, moreover, out of every four holders of a single *mansa* must serve. The principle of mutual responsibility for the equip-ping of a horse soldier was thus laid down: in fact, nothing like this proportion of horse soldiers to landholders could ever have been raised in a single campaign as casual references to the numbers engaged in battle show. Nevertheless, the change to a cavalry army was made: with great social repercussions.

The obligation on landholders to join the army for the summer campaign, when summoned, was general and strictly enforced: the fine for non attendance was the *heribannum*, a composition fee of sixty *solidi*: but not all freemen were summoned every year; only landowners in provinces adjacent to the campaign planned. The peasants who tilled the land were not, in the main, freemen, but on these too the obligation to provide for the army pressed, for the landowners of the different regions were bound to provision the expedition and received letters enjoining them to do so from Charles, well beforehand. Clerks did not owe military service (save the few who accompanied the armies): but bishops and abbots, as landowners, were all bound to send their quota of horsemen. Since Charles's heaviest wars lay beyond the eastern frontier, the eastern Franks usually formed the spearhead of the army; all those called up had to bring with them food for three months, arms, tools, etc. Even abbots and abbesses had to send food supplies, including live cattle, driven along behind the wagon train of the expedition. This had also to be provided.

This army of horsemen not only rode to the battlefield, but charged and fought on horseback. As was usually the case in the middle ages, campaigning occupied the summer months; but with Charles's army the starting date was determined by the earliest time at which the horses and cattle could find pasture along the route. Behind the armed horsemen went the baggage wagons, with spare armour, clothes and food, wagons drawn by horses or oxen.

The rivers that lay across the line of march were forded by bridges of boats, and where possible the river itself was used for transport by boat: small boats with sails and a cabin.

The strategic unit of the army was the *turma* or army corps, and the tactical unit the *scara*. The horsemen were armed with a long lance and buckler: the lance with a narrow, leaf shaped head and cross bar beneath (to prevent its being too deeply embedded), and the buckler round, painted red or blue, with a heavy, central boss. The horsemen carried also a heavy, two-edged sword (*spatha*), and a short sword with a single cutting edge, like the original Germanic *scramaseax*; they wore a cuirass sewn with metal rings or plates (*broigne*). By a new departure, unknown to the Merovingians and in imitation of Byzantine cavalry, the Carolingian horsemen carried also a yew-bow and quiver, shooting from the saddle. These horsemen were far the more numerous part of the army and did most of the fighting; army servants about equal in numbers were needed to drive the baggage wagons and cattle, act as smiths, cooks, etc. There was also a small proportion of infantry, transported on horseback but fighting on foot: the *fantassins*. They too were armed with lance and buckler, and had special uses, such as battering in the gates of defended places with axes and trying to fire the wooden towers and superstructures in siege warfare; a few such infantry-men formed part of each *scara*. While the cavalry wore a casque, or helmet, the *fantassins* were bareheaded. Fighting, after the dis-charge of arrows and the shock of the cavalry charge, was mainly individual, and the possession of an especially heavy, well-worked sword or other weapon counted for much; such weapons, wrought by skilled smiths in the Frankish countryside, were expensive. The standards of the Carolingian army were almost the only feature that recalled Greco-Roman warfare: they were light, that horsemen might carry them on lances, and included the old *vexillum* of the Roman cavalry, now a small three-pointed banner, and the *draco*, a hollow, light *vexillum* in form of a dragon. The influence of Vegetius' *Art of War* still survived, and the definitions (founded on Vegetius) given in Isidore of Seville's *Etymologies*.

As for Charles's share in the victories of the Frankish army, he seldom fought in the battles themselves, but he was remarkable as a strategist and a planner of campaigns. As Kleinclausz has noted, he had a genius for bringing an overpowering force to the critical spot at exactly the right time. He conceived large operations: he prepared by collecting exact information about the nature of the country, possibilities of supplies, fodder and water (individual loot-ing for food was forbidden, but the army as such had the right to take *fodrum*, forage, water and pasture, in prescribed quantities while on the march); information about the climate, rivers, ways, harvest times, and the disposition and resources of the enemy. He usually rode with his army, and if some vassal led it, he remained in the near neighbourhood; he inspired great confidence. All the army officers and leaders were those of peace time, who on campaign expected, as part of their service, to fight for their king: counts palatine, constables, chamberlains, even local counts: Carolingian marshals seem to have been of lesser importance, and rode in charge of horses and transport wagons. Neither Charles nor his officers were professional soldiers; but they fought summer after summer, the annalists noting as exceptional the years when the king stayed at home, *sine hoste*; probably both Charles and his paladins reckoned the summer campaigns to be the most serious business of the year.

As to the general history of Charles's campaigns and conquests: he was first occupied in holding the sum of the Frankish lands against internal rebellion, and later in extending the Frankish borders beyond the limits won for them by Charles Martel and Pepin the Short.

His first campaign, in 769, was to suppress the Aquitanian rebellion, for which Charles asked the help of Carloman and was refused. He summoned Lupus, the duke of Gascony, to give up the duke of Aquitaine, who had fled to him for refuge, crossed the Garonne into Gascony, forced Lupus to give up the rebel, and restored his own authority in Aquitaine.

In 770, through the mediation of Bertrada and abbot Sturm, Boniface's successor at Fulda, he allowed himself to be reconciled to Carloman, and to make the Lombard marriage.

Meanwhile, the papacy was in difficulties. In June 767 Paul I had died, and the duke of Tuscany had prevailed on the electors at Rome to choose his brother Constantine, a layman, and to have him pushed hastily through the grades of the clerical militia and consecrated as pope, on 5 July. The *schola* of Roman notaries, themselves laymen, usually of noble Roman birth, were affronted at this exercise of external influence: and Christopher the primicery, asking for Lombard help, deposed Constantine and had his eyes put out; he next had a Roman priest consecrated as Stephen III. In 768 a council at the Lateran, with twelve Frankish bishops present, passed a canon allowing the election of none but a Roman priest or deacon as pope, and forbidding any layman to take part in the election. The situation was precarious, and when Bertrada herself came to Rome, Desiderius marched there in the Lent of 771, had Christopher and his son killed, and refused to restore the lands promised to the papacy by the Donation of Pepin. This flouting of an act of submission promised to the Franks might have been tolerated by the queen mother and Carloman; but it went too far for Charles: he repudiated his Lombard wife, an open insult to Desiderius, in the summer of 771. He had taken upon himself to enforce the terms his father had imposed on Desiderius, and to protect the papacy. In December of that year, Carloman died.

Charles's own intervention in Italy was now possible, for he commanded the Franco-Lombard frontier. On 3 February 772 Stephen III died, and the deacon Hadrian, who had long worked as papal notary at the Lateran, was elected pope. He had had great administrative experience and was strongly anti-Lombard. When Desiderius demanded that he should crown Carloman's two sons, seizing the towns of the old exarchate right up to Ravenna, Hadrian refused; Desiderius marched into Tuscany and prepared to besiege Rome itself. Hadrian then sent envoys, appealing to Charles for aid.

The moment was inconvenient to Charles: he received the papal envoys in his palace at Thionville (January 773) while planning an immediate campaign against the Saxons: he did not want an Italian war. He even offered Desiderius the large sum of 14,000 gold *solidi* if he would restore the lands taken from the pope: but Desiderius preferred to march on Rome, where Hadrian was prepared to withstand attack or siege. Moreover, the Lombards were Catholics, and when Hadrian prohibited further approach and launched an excommunication, Desiderius was unsure of their support and retired to Viterbo.

Charles, however, decided that the potential threat from Desiderius as protector of his own two nephews was too great. He collected two armies for the invasion of Italy. One, commanded by Bernard his uncle, was to go by the Great St Bernard: the other, led by himself, took the Mont Cenis. The two armies met in the plain of the Po, to find that Desiderius was holding Pavia, and his son Adalgis, with Carloman's widow and her two children, Verona. This city was easily taken by the Franks: Adalgis fled to Byzantium and Charles took possession of his brother's widow and the children. Pavia stood a siege from September 773 till the following spring. Before Pavia fell, however, Charles left his army and travelled to Rome to keep the Easter feast. On 2 April Hadrian received him as patrician of the Romans, according him a ceremonial greeting hardly given in the past even to the exarch: mutual oaths of loyalty were solemnly exchanged.

It was during this Easter visit of 774 that Charles, according to the *Vita Hadriani* in the *Liber Pontificalis*, made his famous Donation of territories to the pope. The document itself has not survived, and would seem to have promised territories that Charles was not then in a position to give and never, in fact, gave. Yet the reference to the making of the Donation in the form of a solemn diploma, drawn up by Charles's chaplain and notary, Hitherius, and signed by Charles himself and those of his nobles present at Rome, is explicit and now generally accepted. The lands given are said to have included the ancient exarchate of Ravenna, the provinces of Venetia and Istria, and the duchies of Spoleto and Benevento. The implementing of the grant would have involved war with the Greeks over Venetia, and with the Lombards of south Italy: it would have left the pope with the temporal rule of central Italy, from Ravenna to Benevento, not merely restored to him the landed estates of the old patrimony, of some of which the Lombards had deprived him. It has been suggested that the *Vita Hadriani* overstressed the comprehensiveness of the grant or the precision with which it was made; and, more recently, that Charles in 774 was swayed by the atmosphere and traditions of Rome, and regained a greater sense of practical possibilities later, when uninfluenced by the 'Roman ambiance'.

There is much to support this view, including the history of the so-called 'Donation of Constantine'. In the climate of opinion of the eighth century, Constantine, the apostle of Christianity for Europe, was a name to conjure with (see p. 146). When Charles made his Donation in 774, as the *Vita Hadriani* states, there was produced for his confirmation the Donation which his father Pepin had made at Quierzy to pope Stephen III, and which Charles himself and all the Frankish leaders had signed: it is now accepted that the Donation of Constantine had been produced by the papal notaries as a *pièce justificative*, at Quierzy. This strange document related a tale quite unconnected with history, of how Constantine as a pagan had been healed of leprosy by pope Sylvester, been then converted, placed upon Sylvester's head the white tiara and given him the city of Rome and all the provinces and towns of Italy: given him an authority that antedated both Lombard and Greek rule in Italy. The language of this 'Donation of Constantine' accords with that of the papal *scrinium* in the time of Stephen III, a reason for connecting it with Stephen's visit to Pepin.

The *Vita Hadriani*, in any case, states that Charles in 774 had three copies of his Donation made 'in the same pattern' as Pepin's Donation at Quierzy; some knowledge of the 'Donation of

Constantine' may have spread from Saint-Denis among the Franks, for Fulrad of Saint-Denis had been Stephen III's host on this same visit, and also preserved a copy of the 'Donation'; the *scrinium* at Rome must have had knowledge of it. Charles's confirmation of the grant is one expression of reverence for the 'Romulean city', the city of Peter; and the atmosphere of reverence for Rome is expressed also in the noble Latin hymns of the Frankish court poets of this generation. Charles was a pilgrim at Rome at Easter, 774, and Paulinus of Aquileia or some courtier expressed his own and perhaps Charles's wonder in the hymn:

> *O felix Roma, quae tantorum principum*
> *Es purpurata preciosa sanguine:*
> *Non laude tua, sed ipsorum meritis*
> *Excellis omnem mundi pulchritudinem.*

The Carolingian poets had too much learning and too much historical conscience to have produced the Donation of Constantine: but the same impulse of enthusiastic, if unhistorical and unscrupulous, piety for Rome produced their hymns, the Donation of Constantine, and the Donations of the two Frankish rulers.

After his Roman Easter, Charles went north again, and in June 774 took Pavia, sending Desiderius and his family captive to Liége. From July 774 he used the title: *Carolus, gratia dei rex Francorum et Langobardorum atque patricius Romanorum*: he claimed and meant to keep control of Lombardy, while leaving the Lombards, in the main, local self-government. He put a Frankish garrison in Pavia and appointed a few Frankish counts. He took over some royal Lombard lands and bestowed certain estates on great Frankish churches. A larger measure was to restore to the pope the lands recently usurped by Desiderius, and with them Bologna and Imola, promised by Pepin in 756 but never actually given up. When archbishop Leo of Ravenna claimed to exercise all ecclesiastical jurisdiction in the lands now transferred to the pope, Charles allowed him to retain them till his death; with the pope's very old claim to appoint the archbishop of Ravenna, the matter should solve itself.

The Lombard dukes and the Greeks in Italy were not willing, however, to acquiesce in Charles's annexation of the Lombard crown. Hadrian reported to Charles that Adalgis, with the dukes of Friuli, Spoleto, Benevento and others, were planning revolt, with possible help from the Greeks. Charles in 775 suppressed the revolt, killing the duke of Friuli in battle: this duchy, at the head of the Adriatic, would be dangerous if open to the Greeks. The duchy of Friuli was suppressed, and the number of Frankish counts in Lombardy increased.

The papal struggle with Lombards and Greeks in south Italy was less easily dealt with: Greek colonization and influence had increased there in the seventh century. The duke of Benevento had encroached on the southern patrimony, and the patrician of Sicily, arrogating to himself the title of *basileus* and viceroy to the emperor, and using the royal title not only in Sicily, but in south Italy, seized Terracina from the pope. Hadrian's forces recaptured it in 778, but could not hold it. Hadrian then wrote to Charles for help, urging that without it the Greeks and Lombards would seize the whole plain of the Campagna, from Rome to Naples. Duke Arichis of Benevento, a son-in-law of Desiderius, was now calling himself *princeps*, minting his own coins, dating his *acta* by the years of his principate, and seeking the lordship of all south Italy.

Charles made his second journey to Rome in 780 to deal with this situation. He made further arrangements for the Lombard kingdom on his way, kept Easter at Rome, and dealt with Hadrian's large claims arising out of his own Donation of 774. Hadrian claimed in virtue of this grant Spoleto and Benevento themselves, as well as the Spoletan and Beneventan patrimonies: and also the duchy of Tuscany. Charles could only have allowed his claims, justified or not, by a costly campaign in south Italy. He therefore restored to Hadrian the Neapolitan patrimony, but not Terracina, nor would he give him Spoleto or Tuscany.

Charles's agreement with Byzantium was rendered the easier because the emperor Leo IV had died in 780, and the empress Irene was now in power, ruling as regent for his son, Constantine VI: Irene, moreover, was no iconoclast (see p. 412). Good relations seemed possible, and in 781 Charles's daughter Rohtrud was even betrothed to the young emperor Constantine. Peace with the Greeks in Italy seemed reasonably secure, and Hadrian's old patrimonies had been restored to him, though he had been disappointed at the meagre fulfilment of Charles's and Pepin's large Donations. He had baptized Charles's three-year-old son, Pepin, and had anointed him and his elder brother Louis as kings. Charles left little Pepin as nominal king of Lombardy, with Frankish deputies to rule for him and guide the external and military policy of the kingdom; in home affairs the Lombards were left to rule themselves.

A third visit by Charles to Rome was however necessitated in 786 by the ambitions of Arichis, duke of Benevento: he had seized Amalfi from the Byzantine duke of Naples. Charles arrived in

Rome at Hadrian's invitation at the end of 786, and in 787 he invaded Arichis' duchy and brought him to submission. He demanded an oath of fidelity, the giving of hostages and future tribute, while he restored to Hadrian the Beneventan patrimony. While Charles was at Capua, an embassy arrived from Irene to express indignation at the Frankish intervention in south Italy, and break off the betrothal of Rohtrud and Constantine. Irene's stern measures to the iconoclasts at the council of Nicaea, 787, had improved her relations with Hadrian, and Charles too felt it necessary to conciliate Hadrian; he therefore promised him Orvieto in Tuscany and certain towns in Benevento. When in 787 duke Arichis died, Charles allowed Grimoald his son to succeed him, and, to prevent a possible Beneventan-Byzantine alliance, did not force him to give up the towns promised to Hadrian. In spite of these efforts to avoid war in Italy, war actually broke out between Franks and Byzantines in 788: but in the north.

Charles was always loath to intervene in south Italy, when intervention meant war so far from his base; but frontier disputes between Franks and Greeks at the head of the Adriatic were bound to occur when their mutual relations were bad. Here, moreover, it was easier for the Franks to fight, and the more expedient in that Byzantium might try to stir up trouble in the adjacent Frankish duchy of Bavaria.

In 788 Adalgis, the Lombard heir, fought with the Byzantines against an army led by the Frankish *missus*, Winigis. He was defeated, and the Franks conquered the Byzantine province of Istria, expelling the pro-Byzantine Venetian merchants from the exarchate. One cause of this minor war may have been the non-invitation of Charles or Frankish bishops to the council of Nicaea in 787 (see p. 412).

For seven years more pope Hadrian continued to rule Rome and the patrimonies and retain good relations with Charles. His pontificate was perhaps the most notable since that of Gregory the Great for the Roman see. He had been swept to power, like Stephen III, by the Roman, anti-Lombard party, headed by the *scrinium*, and he was by training very closely tied to them. His uncle, Theodotus, had been primicery of the notaries and 'once consul and duke'; Hadrian himself, though not a member of the *scrinium*, had been regional notary. He had been made subdeacon and deacon, serving the poor by whom he was beloved and esteemed pious; he had conducted papal business from the Lateran palace. He had both a high notion of the position of the apostolic see, and the toughness of the well-trained lawyer. He would not tolerate being bullied by Desiderius, nor would he acquiesce in the iconoclasm of the eastern empire. The shadow of the great name of Constantine, it is true, fell over the word emperor, but Hadrian found the Greek emperors of very little use to him.

His most notable work was the severance he accomplished in the old relations between the apostolic see and Constantinople. It was he who stopped using the regnal year of the eastern emperor for the dating of his letters, using instead the phrase: *Regnante domino nostro Jesu Christo* (see p. 384); from 781 he dated his letters by the years of his own pontificate. Without renouncing East Roman sovereignty, he ignored it: he wrote with deference to the ruler at Constantinople, but without the old formal acknowledgment of sovereignty. He minted coins with his own name, and issued orders to the old imperial agents in Italy. It was not to be he who should crown a new emperor at Rome: but, more than any man, he made that coronation possible.

As regards the patrimony, he showed himself a good administrator; and he was, moreover, able to rebuild the walls and water-conduits of Rome. As regards his new protector, the patrician, however, he found himself increasingly powerless in large issues, though both he and Charles continued to treat each other with courtesy and deference. Hadrian certainly contended for a much wider fulfilment of the Donations of Pepin and Charles than the latter was willing to undertake: Charles never in fact gave up, that is, what he had solemnly offered at the confession of St Peter. He seems to have held that since his intervention in Italy was undertaken to secure the papacy from Lombard aggression, and since he had now himself become king of the Lombards and averted the original danger, there was no need to implement the Donation.

Beyond this disappointment, Hadrian could not prevent Charles's exercising a practical suzerainty in the duchy of Rome and in the patrimony. Charles demanded that the inhabitants should swear loyalty to himself as well as the pope: he coined money at Rome: he received complaints against the papal government. Hadrian had to acquiesce in the direction of papal foreign relations by Charles, and, if he had avoided submission to the Lombard king, he found himself, in secular matters, powerless before his own protector. Yet Charles had the greatest respect for Hadrian and frequently wrote him news of himself, his queen and his children. He knew Hadrian's needs, and sent him presents of horses and church ornaments, and wood and tin much needed for the repair of the roofs of St Peter's and other churches. Hadrian for his part sent Charles marbles and mosaics for his new villas and basilicas, and saw that all Italian bishops and abbots recognized his authority; his letters were most useful to Charles as a source of information. He died on Christmas Day, 795, and when the news of his death arrived, Charles wept for him as for a father.

Hadrian had not been the only Roman to find the Frankish protectorate overpowering. When a priest of his *familia*, of low birth and no experience outside the papal household, was elected on his death as Leo III, the choice was unacceptable to the Roman knights, and particularly to the *scrinium*. As so often later, there was jealousy between the clerks and priests of the papal *familia* and the lay notaries of the *scrinium*, who were married and associated by birth with the class of Roman nobles. Hadrian had united notarial and clerical experience and been a candidate acceptable to the nobles; Leo was not. Leo at once showed himself pro-Frankish by sending Charles, in open acknowledgment of the protectorate, the standard of Rome and the keys of the sepulchre of St Peter's: Charles was acknowledged *defensor* and *advocatus* of city and see, with all that that implied in canon law of the lay patronage of a church, even a great church. Charles, in acknowledgment of the tidings, sent Angilbert to Rome to receive the oath of loyalty from the Roman people. Angilbert was an honourable and acceptable Frankish envoy, and the oath-taking at Rome passed off without disturbance. Leo's enemies at Rome held their hand for a time.

Charles's conquests were in no case completed in a year, or in groups of consecutive summer campaigns. He fought beyond the frontiers of his kingdom, and often before he could complete the summer's conquest or organize the conquered territory, news would come of danger on some other frontier. Thus, an early campaign meant to safeguard Aquitaine from Moorish attack ended in disaster in 778, and danger from the Saxons was so urgent that no revenge could be taken by Charles in the summer following: but in the end the Franks established a March beyond the Pyrenees.

Danger from the Saracens in Spain had much decreased with Pepin's vigorous measures against them in Aquitaine, and with the divisions in Spain between the Abbasids and the Umayyads; but the Umayyads had now united the Saracens by the creation of their amirate of Cordoba. Moreover, the southern road from Spain to Aquitaine lay open to advance from the fortress of Saragossa on the Ebro, and the Saracen outposts of Barcelona and Huesca. The small Christian kingdom of the Asturias, in the corner of the Bay of Biscay, was well disposed towards the Franks, but much too weak to engage the whole military attention of the Saracens.

Charles moreover was attracted to some intervention in Spain for the sake of aiding the submerged Christian population. When the chance came, he was inclined to take it.

In 768 envoys from the caliph of Baghdad had been sent with presents to Pepin, and it was possible for Charles to regard the Abbasids as the lawful rulers of Spain, and the Umayyads as usurpers. Between 770 and 777 'Abd ar-Rahman, the Umayyad caliph, had had to subdue internal risings fomented by the Abbasid caliph, and in 777 a group of conspirators, led by the Yemenite Sulaiman ben Alarabi, governor of Barcelona, made overtures to Charles for help, promising to deliver to him certain towns in the north of Spain. Sulaiman actually made the journey to Charles himself, reaching him at Paderborn in Saxony, where Charles had been leading an expedition. He promised him the loyalty and eventual submission of all his followers. Charles appeared to have brought Saxony to submission, and he could raise a large army next spring; he hoped that a Spanish war would at least bring better terms to the Spanish Christians.

Charles therefore kept the Easter feast at his villa of Chasseneuil, and, leaving his wife Hildegard there, collected an army of Austrasians, Burgundians, Bavarians, Septimanians and Lombards, and ordered the advance by both northern and southern roads into Spain. The southern division of his army marched through Septimania towards Barcelona: the northern, commanded by Charles himself, through the difficult Pyrenean gorges, and possibly through the pass of Roncesvalles, into Navarre: Pampeluna, its chief city, was the appointed meeting place for the Frankish armies. Navarre was difficult country, for its inhabitants were mainly Basques (Gascons), and they were used to fighting the Moors, the Asturians and the Franks, indiscriminately. The local Saracen chiefs offered their submission to Charles in Pampeluna: and he heard there that his ally Sulaiman had taken Saragossa. But when he arrived before Saragossa, meeting the other Frankish army before the walls, he found that another Saracen chief was holding it against him. He was, on the whole, disappointed of the Abbasid help promised to him. He left Saragossa, marched south and was, however, able to take Huesca, Barcelona and Gerona. He then led his forces back up the Ebro to Pampeluna, and since he could not hold it as an isolated outpost beyond the Pyrenees, he razed its walls to the ground. The Basques of Navarre were enraged, and though they could not fight a pitched battle with Charles's well-armed cavalry, they lay in wait for him in the mountains when he returned by the northern route to Aquitania. Even now, they acted rather as pillagers than patriots, hoping to loot the baggage train that followed the Frankish cavalry. They lay in ambush on the heavily wooded cliffs that lay above the pass of Roncesvalles, and let the advance guard and Charles himself pass. The rearguard was led by Eggihard the seneschal, the count palatine Anselm, and Roland, prefect of the march of Brittany; the whole rearguard fought and was cut down, to the last man, on 15 August 778. The *Royal Annals* pass over the matter in silence, but all men knew, as a ninth-century historian states casually, the names of Charles's paladins who died fighting: the memory lies behind the eleventh-century poem, the *Chanson de Roland*. As another annalist wrote briefly of the year 778: This year the lord king Charles went to Spain, and there he suffered a great disaster.

There was no immediate sequel to the expedition. Sulaiman fought a rival for the leadership of the Abbasid party and his con-spiracy came to nothing: 'Abd ar-Rahman retook Saragossa and asserted his authority over the Basques; and Charles had news of urgent dangers in Saxony. He left his account with the Saracens for the time unsettled, and went off to Saxony. Christian refugees from Spain passed the Pyrenees and founded little colonies in Septimania.

Frankish authority in Aquitania now needed strengthening in view of a renewal of Saracen attack, and in spite of his preoccupa-tion with Saxony, Charles found energy to deal with the matter. Nine new Frankish counts were established in the principal Aqui-tanian cities, with some lesser officers; many Frankish vassals were planted out in the countryside, and Franks or specially trusted clerics were established as bishops and abbots. Aquitanian patriots still regarded themselves as having more *Romanitas* and *civilitas* than the semi-barbarous northerners, and some show of respect and autonomy had to be granted them; Charles therefore in 781 made his year-old son Louis, born in Aquitania while Charles was away fighting the Moors, king of Aquitania. The new kingdom in-cluded Aquitania proper, within the great sweep of the Loire to the north (but not including Tours, still the holiest shrine and church in Francia), Septimania and Gascony (north of the Pyrenees). Louis' two regents, Arnold and Meginarius, ruled Aquitania in his minority, exercising only a limited supervision of Gascony. Charles continued to direct all the external relations of Aquitania himself, appointing his officers, and enjoining the acceptance of his capitu-laries; the young king's powers were limited to enforcing their acceptance, and supporting Charles's *missi*.

Enforcement of order among the Basques of Gascony was still

difficult: Basque tribes continued to fight each other, and to intrigue with the northern Saracens. Wasconia (Gascony) now had its duke and counts, appointed by Charles, but, though these had taken oaths of vassalage, they frequently rebelled. In 785 attack from the Saracens seemed so imminent that harsh security measures were enjoined. In 790 the Basque chieftain Adelric nevertheless attacked and captured the greatest Frankish leader in southern Aquitania, Chorso, duke of Toulouse, and at this insult Charles himself was driven to intervene. He summoned Adelric to the assembly at Worms in 790, which was so much resented by the Basques that William, count of Toulouse, and successor to his father Chorso, had to intervene in Gascony. The Basques had entered into negotiations with the Saracens, and from 785 to 790 Frankish troops had gradually occupied Gerona and other posts beyond the Pyrenees, till they held some three hundred miles of the Mediterranean coastline of Spain.

ʿAbd ar-Rahman, the founder of the Cordoban amirate, had died in October 788, in old age. He was succeeded by his son Hisham, young, able, and a devout Muslim; he desired to incite his subjects to a holy war and extend the bounds of Islam. He exhorted his followers in 791 to exalt the glories of Islam by the sword, and by 793 he had collected a strong army to invade and ravage Gaul. They advanced to Narbonne, burned the suburbs without the walls, took numerous captives and much plunder, and marched on Carcassonne. William, count of Toulouse, intervened to stop them but was defeated: the Saracens bore off their plunder and hung spoils on the walls of the great mosque of Cordoba. It was a great humiliation to the Franks, the less avoidable because Charles at the time was preparing his expedition against the Avars.

In 796 the tide turned. A small Frankish raiding force sent to Spain by Charles reached their objectives and returned safely; Hisham died in 801; the new amir, al Hakam, quarrelled with his uncle and the Saracen governors of the northern towns. Discontented Saracen chieftains sent to Charles at Aix-la-Chapelle, inviting his help; young Louis arrived at Aix; the discontented Saracens had conversations with Charles and his son both at Aix and Heristal. In 799 Huesca was placed by its chieftain in Charles's hand, but the other vague promises of submission in return for help Charles distrusted. Meanwhile the Aquitanian chiefs had of necessity undertaken the defence of their frontier district, their March, and contemporaries began to speak of them as *marchiones* (marquises).

The Spanish March was formally constituted in 795, when king Louis garrisoned certain fortresses beyond the Pyrenees, committing them to the charge of count Borrel and count Rostaing. He used also, in defence of the March, a roving band of mixed Christian and refugee Saracens and with these helpers conquered a narrow strip of territory stretching from the coast beneath the crest of the Pyrenees northwards to Navarre. This brought the Frankish power reasonably near to the Christian kingdom of the Asturias, and king Alfonso II twice sent embassies to Charles, bearing presents and pressing for an alliance; in 798 Alfonso sent to Heristal a third embassy, with Moorish prisoners, arms, mules, and spoils taken from the city of Lisbon. At the southern end of the Spanish March, the Balearics too were captured and brought under Frankish rule: hard fighting advanced Frankish conquests along the coast. A revolt against the Franks in 800 was followed by the death of Hisham, and during the Saracen divisions at his death, count William led the Franks on to the capture of Barcelona: the March had been doubled in extent. Fresh campaigns followed every year from 809 to 812, and in 813 king Louis himself appears to have led the Franks on to the capture of Navarre. He left a skeleton government in Pampeluna, and had to return without taking the fortress of Huesca.

By the end of Charles's reign the Spanish March had been attached to the kingdom of Aquitania, as part of the duchy and 'March of Toulouse', whose count William had been so largely responsible for its conquest. The land, as elsewhere among the Franks, was divided into counties, under the general authority of the count of Toulouse. Colonies of refugee Christians from Spain were allowed to settle in the war-wasted territories. Count William himself, long the friend and patron of monks, in 806 retired to the abbey of Gellona which he had himself founded, and which became known from its founder as 'Count William of the Desert'. He died in 812, and his great deeds were sung in the 'Cycle of William of Orange'. The Spanish March, which later became the province of Catalonia, proved a Christian bastion for north-east Spain, and a basis for a Christian *reconquista*.

For comparison with the Spanish March, the smaller March of Brittany may be noted. The Celts of Brittany, always hostile to the Franks, had been pressed gradually westward, and in 753 Pepin had made his way as far as Vannes, claiming tribute. By 778 there was a March of Brittany, with count Roland as its prefect, comprising the adjacent counties of Nantes and Rennes. The Bretons were never, however, willingly submissive: in 786 the seneschal

Audulf had to be sent to compel the payment of tribute, and in 799 Guy, prefect of the March, invaded their lands and made the greater part of independent Brittany submit. Frankish authority, however, was never well or easily maintained; there was another rebellion in 811.

BIBLIOGRAPHICAL NOTE

For Charles' agents in the rule of the Lombard kingdom after his conquest, see D. A. Bullough, in *'Baiuli' in the Carolingian regnum Langobardoruns', and the career of Abbot Waldo* (†813), E.H.R. 1962, p. 625.

CHAPTER XIX

THE CAROLINGIAN CONQUESTS:
CONTINUED

THE heaviest and the most protracted of Charlemagne's conquests, and the one most important for the civilization of Europe, was the conquest of Saxony. From the time of Clovis I's sons the Franks had attempted to draw these Germanic tribes within their own orbit, and Charles Martel and his sons had made no less than ten attacks on the Saxons, but they still, at the time of Charles's accession, remained independent, pagan, and unfriendly. Charles Martel's wars had been, not serious attempts at conquests, but punitive expeditions accompanied by massacres, looting and the capture of prisoners. Frontier incidents and minor Saxon raids had been the only disturbance of the peace for fifteen years before 768.

As to the territory of the Saxon tribes, who had no federation, over-king or royal family: they inhabited the country south of the Heligoland Bight and the North Sea to the Harz mountains and the wooded hills running from the Harz westward: they held, that is, the Lüneburg heath, where the prototypes of the earliest Anglo-Saxon brooches and pots have been found, and the rising ground to the south. The frontier of the *regnum Francorum* included a fairly narrow corridor east of the Rhine from the Frankish province of Hesse nearly to Deventer: Christian Frisia, the modern Holland, was under Frankish rule, and bordered on Saxony. Pagan Frisia, a strip of coast to the north, including the mouth of the Ems, stretched to the mouth of the Weser: these northern Frisians were independent of either Franks or Saxons: the northernmost part of the Frankish frontier lay between Christian and pagan Frisia. The coastline of the Saxons included the mouths of the Weser and Elbe as far as the river Eider, at the base of the Danish peninsula. The Saxons included three main tribes: the West-phalians, settled along the Ems valley and the slopes of the Teutoburgerwald, which bordered the valley and ended to the south in the hill fortress of Eresburg; the Angarians, who lived along the valley of the Weser, one of whose upper tributaries was the Fulda, rising south in Frankish Hesse; and the Eastphalians, who lived between the Harz mountains and the Elbe. The Nordal-bingians, reckoned a Saxon tribe, lived to the north, between the

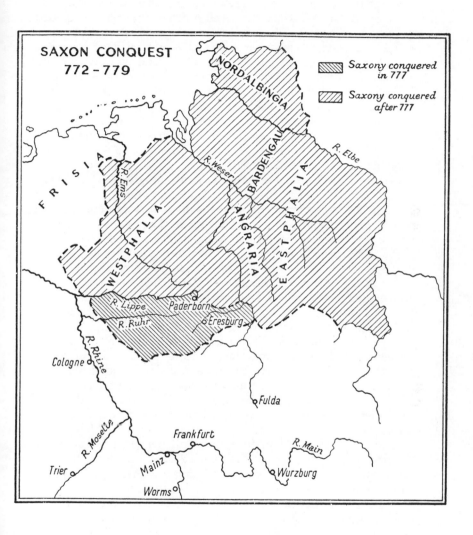

SAXON CONQUEST
772–779

Saxony conquered
in 777

Saxony conquered
after 777

NORDALBINGIA

FRISIA

R. Elbe

R. Ems

R. Weser

BARDENGAU

WESTPHALIA

ANGRARIA

EASTPHALIA

R. Lippe

Paderborn

R. Ruhr

Eresburg

Cologne

R. Rhine

Fulda

R. Moselle

Frankfurt

R. Main

Trier

Mainz

Wurzburg

Worms

Elbe and the Eider. Beyond the Elbe lay the various Slav peoples.

The Saxons, akin in language and social structure to the early Franks and Anglo-Saxons, still lived much as the tribes described in Tacitus' *Germania*. They were farmers, growing crops of barley and coarse grain, keeping herds of cattle, and raising horses: the sale of horses was their chief trade. Their land was divided into cantons (hundreds), and they observed their own customary law.

Besides the difficulty of maintaining an ill-marked frontier between the Franks and neighbours of the same race who remained free outside, Charles and the Frankish leaders were moved by missionary zeal to convert the Saxons to Christianity. The Saxons regarded their traditional paganism as synonymous with political independence: they had sacred springs, groves and woods, cremated their dead, practised augury, and offered animal and even human sacrifice. They had sacred buildings, fanes, of wood or stone, sometimes circular in shape, and with some cult symbol within, generally shaped like a tree-trunk: the famous Irminsul in its hill sanctuary seems to have been such. Boniface himself had, at the risk of his life, begun the conversion of the Saxons, and his disciple, the noble Bavarian Sturm, had founded the abbey of Fulda in 744, where Benedictine monks trained future missionaries and maintained a great Christian outpost as near to the pagan Saxons as they dared. In Christian Frisia, the abbey of St Martin at Utrecht sent out missionaries, and the Anglo-Saxon Willehad worked among the pagan Frisians, with the church of Dokkum as his centre, and pushed on to the mouth of the Ems, between 770 and 780: Frankish, Frisian, Bavarian and Anglo-Saxon missionaries were already working among the Saxons themselves. In particular, the native priest Liudger carried on from 780 the work of Willehad: he was to push on, behind the Frankish armies, during the Saxon wars, and to try even to convert Heligoland. But the Saxons feared to lose their independence by adopting Christianity, as indeed the Christian Frisians had done: the attitude towards conversion was hardening, and Alcuin reflects the Frankish estimate of the Saxons by calling them fierce and warlike and suggesting that their name was derived from the Latin *saxa* (rocks). Etymologically he was wrong; the derivation from *seax* (knife people) would have suited his argument equally well.

Charles began the Saxon wars in 772, to punish recent raids on Hesse. Conquest was not intended, but the Irminsul was destroyed, and the Westphalian stronghold of the Eresburg was seized and held for the defence of Hesse. Charles took hostages and returned to Francia; but in 773, while he was in Italy, the Angarians invaded Hesse, desecrating Boniface's church of Fritzlar, and the Westphalians raided Frisia. In September 774 Charles sent punitive bands across Saxony, to ravage and plunder: and he prepared a large scale attack on the Saxons for 775. He held a council of bishops and vassals at his villa of Quierzy in January of that year, announcing his intention of waging war against the Saxons as perfidious treaty breakers: he intended to conquer and convert them. He started from Düren in the spring, taking monks with his army for the intended conversion, crossed the Rhine, took the castle of Sigiburg, building a church there, and gained the bank of the Weser. There he defeated a Saxon army and pressed on into the land of the Eastphalians; he forced Westphalians, Angarians and Eastphalians to submit, and when he returned to Düren in October 775 he left Frankish garrisons in the Saxon fortresses and an apparently conquered country.

The year 776, however, saw a fresh Saxon revolt, when Charles was engaged in dealing with trouble in Friuli; but he returned in high summer, led a Frankish army from Worms, retook and rebuilt his forts of Eresburg and Sigiburg, which the Saxons had destroyed, and a third *castrum* at Karlsburg. Many were baptized and took oaths of fidelity to Charles. Not the whole of Saxony, but the lands to the north of Hesse and Thuringia, seemed reasonably secure; the northern plain, between the Rhine and the Elbe, remained outside Frankish control. Yet at this point Charles seems to have hoped to bring the Saxon wars, with their pillage, burnings, massacres by both contendents, to an end.

In the summer following, therefore, he appeared with a large Frankish army at Paderborn, in the fertile plain between the Lippe and the Teutobergerwald, on the northern limit of conquered Saxony, and there he held a great assembly. Saracen envoys appeared asking for an alliance, and crowds of Saxons came to receive baptism and solemnly enter into engagements of loyalty to Charles: the five years' war seemed to have been brought to a close. At the least, a Saxon March seemed to have been created, guarding Hesse and the missionary centres of Fulda, Fritzlar and Hersfeld. Sturm, abbot of Fulda for the last thirty years, came to Paderborn to convert the Saxons, baptize, and build churches. He had worked almost continuously all his life in Hesse and none knew the Saxons better; under his guidance Charles divided the country into missionary districts. There is no evidence that, when Charles returned to Francia in December 777, he intended any further conquest of the Saxons. He thought he had 'changed cruel wolves into gentle lambs': in reality, he had only conquered half a people.

The very next year, in 778, the Westphalian noble, Widukind, led a violent Saxon reaction: he led raiding parties that pillaged and burned the countryside right up to the Rhine. The news was brought to Charles at Auxerre, on his return from a campaign in Spain ending in the disaster at Roncesvalles. Charles sent a Frankish force to destroy the Saxon raiders, if possible while they were still in Francia: but they escaped to their own country, ambushed their Frankish pursuers at a river crossing, killed most of them and put the rest to flight. Another Saxon band which had marched on Fulda, causing such alarm that St Boniface's relics had been taken from the tomb for hasty transit to the south, heard of the Saxon victory and returned to share the jubilation: Fulda was saved.

Charles wintered at his villa at Heristal and in the spring of 779 held an assembly at Düren, and marched to the upper waters of the Lippe, crossing at Lippeham. He traversed the land of the Westphalians, raiding and burning in his turn, reached the Weser, and received oaths and hostages from Angarians and Eastphalians, who were unwilling to fight a pitched battle. He returned to Heristal and wintered at Worms, planning to renew the Saxon wars next year. In 780, accordingly, he led his army from Eresburg to the sources of the Lippe: held an assembly: marched on to the Bardengau on the eastern bank of the Elbe: ordered large numbers to receive baptism, and pushed on to the frontier of Slavs and Saxons beyond the Elbe; he had, for the first time, reached the further limits of Saxony. Trusting to the security of the protectorate he had established in these wild regions, he sent yet more abbots and priests to convert the conquered; but his best apostle, the aged Sturm, had died at Fulda the December previous. His work was taken up by the learned Anglo-Saxon missionary Willehad, who had begun his missionary work in Frisia. While Liudger still worked among the pagan Frisians, Willehad pushed farther along the coast to the mouth of the Elbe, and there were many conversions.

So far, Charles's armies and his missionaries seemed to have attained their ends in Saxony. Charles felt able to winter in Italy in 780-1, and, to keep control of the situation, held another great assembly at Lippspringe in 782, similar to the splendid gathering at Paderborn; he received there embassies from the king of Denmark and the khan of the Avars. He undertook the defence of the Saxon-Slav frontier, ordering his chamberlain, Adalgis, his constable, Geilo, and a count palatine, Worad, to raise a force of east Franks and Saxons and suppress the Slavs. He divided northern Saxony into counties; and appointed as counts not only Franks but Saxons (782).

Charles, however, had reckoned without Widukind, who had taken refuge in the remote parts of Denmark and bided his time. He now appeared in Saxony, leading a national movement and calling for the destruction of the Frankish missionaries and their churches. In Wihmodia, between Elbe mouth and Weser mouth, his followers punished the newly converted for their forsaking of the old gods, killed many priests, and drove Willehad to flee the country. Similar anti-Christian outrages occurred in Frisia, and Liudger too was driven out: Widukind realized only too clearly that Christianity and Frankish rule went together. The new converts in Frisia and Saxony returned to the worship of idols. Charles's officers, Adalgis, Geilo and Worad, without waiting to be joined by count Thierry and Frankish reinforcements, marched to the Süntelgebirge, a range parallel to but east of the Teutoburgerwald. Here, in the heart of Saxony, Widukind and the rebels had gathered, and here the Franks attacked them in the mountains, and were disastrously defeated. Adalgis, Geilo, four Frankish counts and many officers were killed: there was so great a slaughter of Franks that Charles could not afford to overlook it. In spite of the lateness of the season, he led a large army into Eastphalia, to where the Weser borders the Bardengau, and demanded that the Saxons should give up to him the rebel leaders. Widukind had fled: but the Saxons delivered to Charles a great number of rebels, and Charles had no less than 4,500 of them beheaded at Verden, besides taking away with him great numbers of prisoners. It was a terrible vengeance: the measure of the damage done to Frankish prestige at the Süntelgebirge. Sympathy for nationalist aspirations was no part of the climate of opinion of the day: the Saxons appeared to the Franks simply as oath breakers.

In conformity with the gravity of the Saxon danger, and the crisis provoking the massacre of Verden, was the *Capitulatio de partibus Saxoniae*, now generally believed to date from the year 782. The Saxons were subjected universally to the authority of Frankish counts: they were forbidden to hold public gatherings (moots), and the count only might henceforward administer the *bannum* (composition) for the blood feud (*faida*), and the lesser offences atoned for by a lesser *bannum*. The death penalty was enjoined for all disloyalty to the king, injury to Christian missionaries, and offences shewing hostility to the Christian religion.

Death followed refusal to take the oath of fidelity to Charles, or
the breach of it when taken; for the murder of bishop, priest or
deacon, theft from a church, not keeping the Lenten fast, and
refusal to be baptized; it followed also on the offering of human
sacrifice, and the disposal of the dead by burning, in the heathen
manner.

Whereas heretofore the missionaries had mainly been left to
accomplish the work of conversion, though Charles had exacted
compulsory baptism from large numbers just as he had exacted the
oath of fidelity: now, the whole practice and apparatus of the pagan
rites were to be destroyed wholesale and replaced by those of the
Christian church. Churches were to have the same honour and
respect as the old pagan temples, together with rights of sanctuary, and only in their cemeteries were Christian Saxons to receive
burial, not in a *tumulus paganorum*. Each local church was to be
endowed with two *mansae* and a court (*curte*), the endowment
among the Saxons of the pagan priest; a *mansa* is held to have been
the land and complex of customary rights of the Saxon villager,
two of them being needed for the priest and the peasant or peasants
who worked them for him: the word *curte* is elsewhere used of the
farmyard, or yard for the storing of hay and fodder. The Christian
priest with his double peasant's holding was to be accorded a
peasant or peasants to work his land, according to the number of
villagers the church served. This measure meant the expropriation of an influential class and must have brought disturbance and
unpopularity among the Saxons. Boniface had lamented the poverty
of his missionaries, hardly able to feed, much less clothe themselves: now they were to be compulsorily provided for, at the
pagan priest's expense. The measure is thought to have been the
means by which Christian parish churches first became endowed
with glebe land: and to have been responsible also for the introduction of certain rural obligations on the parish priest, such as
keeping the boar for the village, obligations which are found
to be customary later in some districts, and which originated in
the relation of the villagers to their pagan priest. Not only were
the pagan priests expropriated, but all the Saxons, great and small,
were ordered to pay a tithe of their harvest and the young of beasts:
a very heavy tax. Christianity was thus enforced and provided for:
but at the price of bitter resentment. Charles, spending his winter
at his villa of Thionville, heard of more troubles in Saxony.

In May 783, while he was preparing further wars in Saxony,
queen Hildegard died. Charles buried her at Metz and then led
part of the army to Detmold, near Paderborn, defeated a Saxon

force, and went to Paderborn to await the rest of his forces. He defeated the Saxons again at the Haase, and advanced from the Weser to the Elbe, ravaging the country. He married a new queen, Fastrada, at Worms and wintered at Heristal: and scarcely was the winter past when he heard of yet another rising of Frisians and Saxons. In 784 he ravaged the country from the Rhine to the Weser, left his son Charles in Westphalia with part of the army, fought his way again to the Elbe, and returned to Worms. Though the season was so late, he would not return to Francia for the winter, but made his way again, plundering and burning, to Steinführt on the Ohre, kept Christmas in the Weissgau, and returned to the Eresburg. He summoned to him there his queen Fastrada and his sons and daughters, strengthened the castle and had a church built: he would keep his court there among the Westphalians, when he wished. Willehad was sent for and told to go off to Wihmodia and build more churches. While Charles stayed at the Eresburg, he sent out columns to pull down Saxon fortifications and keep the countryside in terror, and in the spring he held an assembly of Franks and Saxons at Paderborn. None dared withstand him now, wherever he should march: he was able to go to the Bardengau and summon Widukind from his retreat in Denmark to come to him and make his submission.

Knowing that the Saxon resistance was hopelessly broken, Widukind and his lieutenant Abbio were prepared to submit. They demanded hostages for their safe conduct, and Charles sent them in charge of a Frankish officer, who was also to lead Widukind to him. The Saxon leaders followed this officer through Saxony right to Attigny and there received baptism, Charles himself standing godfather and bestowing the christening presents (785). Nothing is known of Widukind's later fate: but the news of the christening was received with joy in Francia, and in Rome the pope ordered a three days' thanksgiving.

The incorporation of Saxony in the *regnum Francorum* could not be accomplished however by punitive expeditions, the savage *Capitulatio* and the baptism of Widukind: years of missionary work were needed to wear down Saxon resentment. In 785 Charles had the old customary *Lex Saxonum* edited, written down in Latin and published, which must have been intended to further the better doing of justice by the Frankish counts and bishops. The laws consisted mainly of lists of money compositions for physical injuries, and graded the Saxons in four social classes, the noble, the freeman, the litus (or freedman) and the slave (servus): but the laws now provided for offences against new

Christian classes, bishops, priests, etc. While death was enjoined as of old for a killing through the blood feud or the stealing of a war horse, it was also enjoined for conspiracy to kill the king of the Franks or his sons or a killing in a church: there were moreover new penalties connected with the Frankish conquest, as the doing of any evil to a man making his journey to the *palatium*. Though the compositions or fines were stated in terms of money (*solidi*), it is clear that they must normally have been paid in cattle or sheep, for one clause sets down relative values. The *solidus*, it is stated, is of two kinds, one worth two tremisses, which is the worth of an ox of twelve months, or a sheep with her lamb: the other *solidus* is worth three tremisses. Compositions for homicide are paid for with the lesser *solidus* (this mitigated the very heavy fine), for lesser offences with the greater *solidus*. Then follows a long list of the worth at which the different farm animals are to be reckoned: two plough oxen at five shillings, a very good ox at three shillings, etc. Though the issue of the laws may have meant better justice, they enforced harshly both Frankish rule and the new religion.

Away at Charles's court, Alcuin distrusted all this policy of forcible conversion, accompanied as it was by the payment of tithe by men who might indeed have been baptized but could scarcely, as he hints in his letters, have been taught the Christian faith; in another letter he speaks of tithe as having destroyed the faith of the Saxons; and, indeed, such payment in a country for twenty-two years ravaged by war must have been a heavy and incomprehensible burden. 'If only', wrote Alcuin, 'Christ's gentle yoke and his light burden had been preached to these people with as much zeal as tithe has been demanded! . . . What, did Christ's apostles go into all the world levying tithe and asking presents? Certainly, to give tithe is a good practice: but it is better that tithe should be lost rather than that their faith.'

Meanwhile, Charles in July 787 entrusted Willehad, bishop elect but not yet consecrated, with the charge of preaching the faith in Wihmodia and the shores of the North Sea: Willehad fixed the site of his new see at Bremen, and there built a beautiful basilican church; a week after its consecration he died, and was buried in it. His disciple, Willerich, succeeded to his labours, though he was not made bishop till 805. Liudger did a parallel work among the Frisians and the Westphalians; he founded there the first monastery among the Saxons, later called Münster. Charles made him a bishop in 802, and he took up residence in Münster, dying there in 809. Bishoprics in these years were also founded at Paderborn, Verden and Minden.

Incorporation in the Frankish kingdom meant liability to serve with the Frankish army, and the Saxons in 789 did in fact fight with the Franks against the Slav Wilzes, eastern neighbours of the allied Nordalbingians; they took and fortified the passage of the Elbe. But there was no certain Saxon loyalty: in 792, when Charles was preparing an expedition against the Avars, some Saxons killed a band of Franks near Elbe mouth, and though punishment followed, so did other minor revolts.

In 793 the Saxon rebellion became general and dangerous, and war followed till 799. Some troops of count Thierry were massacred near the mouth of the Weser, and general burnings of churches and outrages against Christians followed. Charles and his son gradually suppressed the revolts in yearly campaigns between 794 and 797, even wintering in Saxony, at Herstelle on the Weser, in 797–8. The years were miserable ones for the Saxons, for there were now two parties among them, and sometimes those faithful to Charles were dispossessed and driven from their homes by the rebels, and _vice versa_, with very little hope of recovery. To enforce peace and order, Charles had thousands of Saxons carried away into Francia and there settled, while their place was taken by colonies of Franks; and in time, Frankish order was enforced, and Frankish counts, together with such Saxon ones as proved themselves faithful, became the new aristocracy of the Saxons. Large Saxon estates were, moreover, incorporated with the Frankish fisc, and military posts set up to guard them. In time, the Saxons, as Einhard wrote with some truth, 'were united to the Franks and formed with them henceward one people'.

The legal foundation for this amalgamation was the replacement of the fierce _Capitulatio Saxonum_ by the more pacific _Capitulare Saxonicum_ in October 797. In general, the death penalty was here replaced by a heavy fine, the _bannum_, and a tariff of lesser fines for less serious offences. Whereas, under the _Capitulatio_, the Saxons had been living, as it were, under military law, offences against Frankish rule or Frankish religion were now brought under a general system of money composition, became a part of Saxon common law. Frankish arms were only needed after 797 for the subjugation of the Nordalbingians, whose country had not as yet been occupied. In 797, 802 and 804 expeditions were made along the lower Elbe, and beyond the Elbe, and the lands thus subdued held by the policy of mass deportations and colonization by Franks tried earlier in Saxony.

Charles's subjugation of Bavaria differed from that of Saxony, because the great duchy of Bavaria had long ago been conquered by the Merovingians; the Bavarians were Christian and already part of the *regnum Francorum*. But their distance from the main seats of Frankish rule, and their common frontier with the Lombards, offering as it did the possibility of an alliance to offset the strength of Frankish overlordship, rendered the duchy unwilling to submit to more than a nominal rule by Charles. Bavaria included the valley of the middle Danube; her northern frontier ran along the Böhmerwald, turned south-west by Regensburg (Ratisbon) on the Danube, and passed along the Lech, its tributary, to the slopes of the Alps: within its southern frontier were the Brenner pass and Bolzano. The frontier then turned northward along the Alpine crests, till it met the Danube again; the duchy was, as it were, trumpet shaped, the trumpet mouth along the Danube, and the throat, the Brenner pass. It was a land of forests, sandy warrens and marshes, with the Alps towering to the south; but it had been long colonized and its society was no less advanced and civilized than that of the Franks.

It was also the seat of a flourishing Christianity, planted in the past by Boniface; Frankish and Irish missionaries had pressed down from the upper Danube and the Bavarian church had now six sees, the greatest of them Salzburg, Regensburg, the capital, and Passau, and the church was the richer in that tithes were customarily paid. In the regions where missionary monks had planted Christianity, the monasteries of Chiemsee, Mondsee and Kremsmünster flourished under ducal patronage and claimed to control and rule the rural parishes which they had founded: this was a subject of contention with the Bavarian bishops. Salzburg itself was for thirty-three years a centre of missionary activity under the Irishman Vergilius, and from 785 under the Bavarian Arn: many Slav tribes of the eastern Alps were converted. The Bavarian duchy was very much the secular aspect of the Bavarian church, which had spread the Frankish influence among the heathen Slav tribes. On its secular side, the duchy was divided into counties in the Frankish manner, and the duke issued semi-royal edicts or capitularies in his assemblies.

The vassalage of the Bavarian dukes to the Carolingians had nevertheless been maintained. Carloman, Charles's uncle, had made Odilo, the Agilolfing duke, give up part of the Nordgau, which lay along its northern frontier, and recognize his supremacy. Tassilo, the grandson of Pepin by Hiltrud his mother, had become duke in 748 and taken an oath of vassalage to Pepin at Compiègne in 757: had later marched as his vassal to Pavia. But twenty years after his accession he had married Liutberg, daughter of Desiderius, and now maintained a pro-Lombard policy. He did not renounce his Frankish vassalage, but he disregarded it. He had sent his eldest son Theodo to Rome in 772 to receive papal baptism and possibly royal unction; he united the province of Carinthia, with its Slav tribes, to the duchy; he kept a splendid court at Ratisbon, and Frankish annalists, as if in anticipation, sometimes even spoke of Bavaria as a kingdom.

For ten years after 768 Charles made no claim for the recognition of his supremacy; the Bavarian Sturm influenced his counsels, seeing in his home duchy a bastion of the church, and the fight to convert the heathen as one. Charles, however, had ecclesiastical friends in Bavaria who kept him informed: one of them, the bishop of Freising, was deprived of his see for over-friendship with Charles: and Charles intended, when he could, to have his supremacy recognized. He knew the Bavarian army to consist only of *fantassins*, not cavalry, and when he had himself become king of Lombardy, his territories almost encircled Bavaria.

In 781, when Charles was in Rome, he prepared to deal with Tassilo. He persuaded Hadrian to send with him a joint embassy to Tassilo, reminding him of the oaths he had sworn to Pepin: the pope sent two bishops and Charles the deacon Riculf and a butler, Eberhard. Tassilo agreed to come to Charles to renew his oath, provided hostages were sent him to guarantee his safe conduct: when these arrived, he travelled to meet Charles at Worms, renewed the ancient oaths, and gave hostages for their keeping. The bishop of Regensburg himself was taken off at their head to Quierzy.

After this oath-taking, however, Charles was too much occupied by trouble in Saxony to make Tassilo keep his oath. The duke his vassal lent him no aid, and in 785 one of Charles's counts in Lombardy was even killed in a frontier incident with the Bavarians. In 787, with trouble obviously brewing, Tassilo sent to pope Hadrian Arn of Salzburg and the abbot of Mondsee, to ask him to intercede with Charles for the pious duchy; but though Hadrian wished for peace between the cousins, he was in no position to withstand Charles. He urged Tassilo therefore to submit to Charles's requirements and even threatened him with excommunication if he refused. In 787, after the double surrender of Widukind in Saxony and Arichis in Benevento, Charles summoned Tassilo to appear before him in Worms: and Tassilo refused.

Charles therefore prepared to invade Bavaria by a notable

operation, in which three armies converged on the duchy. He led one army himself up the Rhine and to the Lech, marching nearly to Augsburg; the second army came by the Danube, and the third, under king Pepin, marched up from Italy by Bolzano. Tassilo was weakened by the existence of a pro-Frankish party, and by the general horror of his subjects at disregarding a papal interdict. In 787 Tassilo was forced, without a battle, to appear before Charles at the Lechfeld, near Augsburg, and surrender his duchy. He then received it again, but as a benefice, kneeling before Charles, putting his hands between Charles's hands, and swearing the oath of vassalage. His subjects too were made to swear loyalty to Charles, and among the hostages demanded was Theodo, his son and heir. Charles returned to Francia 'with peace and joy', but Tassilo returned in humiliation, to be persuaded by Liutberg to rebel yet again. He allied himself with the pagan Avars on his eastern frontier, and apparently with the Greeks in Italy, who were preparing an offensive; but his own subjects now denounced him to Charles. He was driven in 788 to appear at Ingelheim before a great court of Franks, Bavarians, Lombards and Saxons, and was condemned to death for a long past crime of *herisliz*, withdrawal from one of Pepin's expeditions. Charles spared his life: but he meant to have done with the Agilolfings. Tassilo was forced to receive the tonsure and become a monk at Jumièges, and later at Worms: Liutberg and their two daughters at the same time were made nuns and their other two sons monks. God the all-powerful, said the Franks, had given Bavaria to Charles without a battle; but for some time yet some Bavarians resented the ousting of the ducal family, and in 794 Charles made Tassilo appear before an assembly at Worms in his monastic habit, and solemnly renounce all claim to the duchy.

The reorganization of Bavaria, with Carinthia annexed, was actually carried out by Charles during some months that he spent in Ratisbon in the autumn of 788. No new duke was appointed, but count Gerold, brother of Charles's Alemanian queen, Hildegard, was left with chief power, as *prefectus* of the mark reaching to the Enns which Charles organized against the Avars, to the east of Bavaria. Gerold's function was military: he commanded the Bavarian forces, and was succeeded on his death in 799 by Audulf, a Frank. The old ducal demesnes became part of the Frankish fisc; Frankish capitularies were enforced, and some of Charles's judicial reforms also. The old territorial *gaue* were however maintained, and the old Bavarian customary law, now issued as the *Lex Baiuwariorum*. On the spiritual side, Arn of Salzburg worked for the incorporation of Bavaria in the Frankish church; in 798 Charles obtained from the pope the erection of the see of Salzburg into an archbishopric, with authority over the other Bavarian sees. Under the rule of Arn, the clergy became learned and zealous, and the rural churches of the great abbeys were placed under the bishops. The abbeys themselves became firm supporters of the royal power, for they received as abbots some of the most learned clerks of Charles's court: Hildebald of Cologne received Mondsee, while Chiemsee was assigned to Angilram of Metz.

Charles finally pressed his south-eastern frontier beyond Bavaria by conquering the Avars and setting up a new mark. The Avar ruling caste was Turco-Tatar by race, of the same steppe stock as the Huns, though the population of their territories consisted largely of conquered Slavic tribes. Frankish description of the 'tressed' hair of the Avars suggests that they were, in fact, pig-tailed Mongolians. They still lived mainly on and by their horses and were widely feared for their savagery and the swiftness of their plundering raids; they were professional pillagers and had accumulated great stores of gold and silver ornaments and precious vestments, largely from the plunder of churches. Their tribes were ruled by a khan and his second-in-command, the *iugur*, and their headquarters and treasure store was a great fortified camp, the Ring. The monk of Saint-Gall describes it as having nine concentric ramparts of wood and stone, with houses and gardens filling the slopes between the ramparts. Though his description has been described as purely imaginative, yet hill forts with multiple ramparts existed in Europe from what archaeologists call Iron Age B: while the older Hallstatt culture based defence and attack on the thrown spear, not many of which could be carried and for which a single earthen bank and palisade sufficed, the La Tène people had a more effective long-range weapon in the sling and the beach pebble; they began to use forts with multiple ramparts, the slopes within the ramparts acting as a glacis. The Avars were light horsemen using the bow, with a longer range than the sling; they would have found an old multiple fort like Maiden Castle well suited to their defence needs; they even knew something of throwing up fortifications themselves. If the Monk of Saint-Gall used his imagination in describing the Ring, he drew a not improbable picture.

With such people, Charles had in Bavaria a long and somewhat uncertain frontier; the Avars were moreover ever ready to ally with any of his enemies, Bavarian, Lombard or Saxon, or to

13

shelter refugees; and they were a very dangerous type of pagan, needing conversion. In 788 Charles began an eight-year war against them, a war which Einhard says was the fiercest of all his wars except the Saxon. The fighting in 788 was defensive and successful: the Avars had thrown one army down against the Frankish count of Friuli, and two into Bavaria, hoping to be helped by a Bavarian resistance movement which was, in fact, already crushed.

In 791, after careful preparation by Charles at Regensburg, a notable combined operation was launched against the Avars. Charles led the Frankish army by the right bank of the Danube to the Enns, where a three days' halt was made for the saying of masses *contra paganos* and the singing of litanies. Charles then divided his force, leading one column himself by the right bank of the Danube while count Thierry led the other by the left bank; between them a fleet of Bavarian boats, laden with troops, food and munitions, was commanded by the *prefectus* Gerold and maintained communication between the two Frankish armies. Marching thus down the Danube into Avar country, Charles meant to hold both banks and the river itself. Meanwhile, his Lombard forces were led up from Italy by king Pepin, through the small province of Carniola to the south of Carinthia, to the Avar frontier. Though the Avars had thrown up some fortifications against invasion, they could do nothing against Charles's cavalry and *fantassins*, and fled. Charles camped in victory at the confluence of the Danube and the Raab: but the Avars were saved from destruction at the time by an epidemic that attacked Charles's horses. Some nine-tenths of them are said to have perished and Charles withdrew his army in two columns, reaching Regensburg himself in early winter. Pepin's army retired to Italy, laden with booty recovered from the Avars.

Charles hoped to attack the Avars again next year: it was for this purpose that he had a canal, 300 feet broad, dug for some 2,000 feet between Altmühl and Redmitz, to facilitate the passage of provisions from the Rhine to the Danube. But trouble in Spain and Benevento, and rebellion in Saxony, prevented an immediate invasion; he ordered Pepin to try to surround the Avars and prevent intrigues between them and the Saxons. In 795 one section of the Avars, under the *tudun*, decided that submission was best: they came to Charles in the Bardengau and offered to receive baptism, but they came too late to prevent an expedition which Pepin was already leading into their territory. By the end of 796 the khan had been killed in strife between the different Avar parties, and an attacking force, commanded by Eric, duke of Friuli, and the Slav chieftain Woynimir, had forced its way into the Ring and seized much treasure. This was sent to Charles at Aix, and part distributed as diplomatic presents to the pope, king Offa of the Mercians, etc. The *tudun* himself came also to Aix and received baptism, Charles standing godfather. This campaign of 796 was really decisive: the khan and the *iugur* were dead and the new khan ready to submit: those Avars still unwilling to submit could only flee to the country beyond the Tisza, to the Bulgarians. The remaining Avar risings, in 797 to 803, were not dangerous, though Gerold the prefect was actually killed in 799; Eric, duke of Friuli and his co-conqueror of the Avars, was killed in a Slav ambush the same year.

The Avar country was not all taken over by Charles; that on the right bank of the Danube, lying in the angle where the Danube makes its great southward bend, became the Bavarian Mark, to defend Carinthia: that on the left bank, between the Danube and the Tisza, was left unoccupied. This Bavarian Mark, limited on the south by the Drava, was definitely organized in 803 to include certain Bavarian frontier counties, the Danubian country between the Enns and the Raab (the future Ostmark), and the southern part of Carinthia, with Carniola. The people subject to the Avars in these lands had included two main divisions of the Slav races: Slovene in the Pannonian lands and Carniola, Croatian between the Drava and the Sava. All were pushed from the greater valleys, particularly that of the Danube itself, by the Alemanian colonization that followed immediately upon Charles's conquest; the Slav tribes were driven into the lesser valleys or the less desirable mountainous regions. Politically, what had been Avar land was now ruled by two chiefs: the northern part went to the prefect of Bavaria, the southern came under count Eric and became part of the Mark of Friuli.

The conversion of the Slav and Avar peoples was undertaken on more experienced, gentler lines than that of the Saxons; the influence of Alcuin and Paulinus of Aquileia was exerted in their favour. Arn of Salzburg was charged with the conversion of the northern Pannonian lands; he had a *chorepiscopus*, or rural bishop, to help him, and new rural parishes were founded. North of the Raab, the bishop of Passau undertook the same task. The patriarch of Aquileia similarly undertook the Christianizing of the pagans of the Mark of Friuli, and even claimed jurisdiction of Christians in Carinthia, on the ground that missionaries from the south had been there before the Lombards came and long before Boniface.

This interesting claim was opposed by the bishop of Passau, and Charles had to intervene to settle the dispute.

The final result of the destruction of Avar power on the Danube was the conversion of Slovenes and Croats, but also their subjection in the middle Danube plain to another steppe people from the east, the Hungarians. The Alemanian settlers and the Slovenes were too weak and too unorganized to resist this new Asiatic people, nor were Charles's descendants strong enough to hold the country for them. The Hungarians established themselves towards the end of the ninth century and became for some seventy years as much a centre of raiders and pillagers as the Avars themselves had been.

Charles's war with the Greeks in north Italy differed from his earlier wars of conquest, in that it was inspired mainly by the need of Byzantine recognition of his imperial title (see p. 387); there was none the less a need to delimit the Franco-Byzantine frontier at the head of the Adriatic. Carinthia and Carniola, now Frankish provinces, stretched far to the east of Friuli and the head of the Adriatic: the prolongation of the eastern frontier of Carniola southward to the Adriatic would have given the Franks supremacy over some of the southern Slavs of Croatia and Dalmatia, as well as the whole head of the Adriatic. The Dalmatian coast, however, was still part of the Byzantine empire; and the whole Adriatic was indeed a Byzantine lake: at the head of the Adriatic, west of the old Aquileia, the Greek emperor still claimed sovereignty over the Venetians and their narrow strip of coastline. Just south of old Aquileia, on the little island of Grado, the patriarch of Grado (see p. 334) looked to Byzantium and claimed the allegiance of local bishops. The sea coast and the trade of the Adriatic, that is, were Byzantine: the hinterland round the whole head of the Adriatic Frankish. A state of war between Franks and Greeks lasted for fourteen years, from 800 to 814, and at the end of it the situation was approximately the same; but the Franks gained from the Greeks recognition of the western imperial title as the price of peace.

As to the fighting: Venice and her trade was the most valuable pawn in the game. Since the Franks had conquered Istria in 788, Franco-Byzantine relations had improved: embassies from the empress Irene were well received by Charles in 798 and 799, though no territorial settlement was reached. Good relations were, however, shattered when the news of Charles's coronation reached Constantinople (see p. 387); from that time, settlement of the boundary question in Venetia and Istria was of no use to Charles without Byzantine recognition. He set about winning over the Venetians.

The latter were still Byzantine subjects, though the old Byzantine officers, the tribunes, had become a local aristocracy, since 742, with a duke or doge at their head; the power of the tribunician nobles had declined, however, before the officers of the doge, whose policy aimed at local independence under the distant, ineffective sovereignty of Byzantium. The Venetian merchants were rich, for in their island of Torcello they had a great market where they imported from the Greeks silks, purple and luxury goods, selling to them in exchange the war captives (slaves: Slavs) brought down by the Franks from their Danubian lands, together with corn and metals. With Lombardy also they did a thriving trade in salt and the merchandise transported from the east. There was a very close connexion between Byzantium and Venice, which might almost be reckoned a Byzantine colony or outpost; for geographical and economic reasons Venice would be very valuable also to the Franks. Charles tried from 800 onwards to win over the local bishops and particularly the patriarch John, their head. In 802, however, John was accused by the doge Maurice II, to whom the Byzantine connexion was worth much more than the Frankish, of treachery in conspiracy with Charles; the patriarch was seized and murdered. Fortunatus, his successor, proved also pro-Frankish and was forced to fly to Charles at Salzburg for refuge in 803. Negotiations had been proceeding between Charles and the Greeks for recognition, and Charles in 803 had too much else on his hands to send an expedition against the Venetians, where the pro-Frankish and pro-Greek parties continued to struggle with each other. At Christmas, 805, however, two newly elected doges presented themselves at Charles's villa at Thionville, and at the same time there arrived the duke and bishop of Zara, the chief port of Dalmatia: all desired a peaceful settlement. Charles was accepted as sovereign both by the Venetians and Dalmatians.

In 806, however, the Greeks were strong enough to reverse the position. A Greek army defeated king Pepin and a fleet under Nicetas exacted from Venetians and Dalmatians a fresh acknowledgment of Byzantine sovereignty; Fortunatus had to leave his patriarchate of Grado and set up his *cathedra* at Pola. The two pro-Frankish doges went over to the Greeks. In 809 another Greek fleet under Paul, prefect of Cephalonia, not only dominated the head of the Adriatic, but attacked Comacchio in the exarchate of Ravenna; while the Sicilian Greeks ravaged Populonia on the Tuscan coast.

Though the Franks had thus proved, however, the general danger to Italy of fighting the Greek navy, the real centre of dispute was the head of the Adriatic and Venice. The Venetians had shown themselves anxious only for their own peace and autonomy, and unwilling to fight either Greeks or Franks effectively. At Charles's orders, king Pepin in 810 reconquered Venetia, and this was a strong bargaining counter in the negotiations for a settlement that Charles's envoys (Aio, count of Friuli, among them) were conducting with the Greeks. When the Frankish envoys arrived at Constantinople in October 811 they offered, in return for imperial recognition, the cession of Venetia to the Greeks, with a Frankish guarantee of security for the doges, bishops and such Venetian merchants as should travel in Charles's empire. Fortunatus was already restored to Grado and the Franks recognized Greek sovereignty over Dalmatia; northern Croatia and Istria were to remain Frankish. Though the ratification of the treaty was delayed by the deaths of two Greek emperors and of Charles himself (see p. 406), these territorial terms were finally accepted in 814, along with the mutual recognition of the two emperors.

Before the final negotiations were reached, however, Charles had secured the Frankish position in south Italy. He had concluded a firm treaty of peace with Grimoald, duke of Benevento (always a possible ally of the Greeks), and had delivered a copy of the treaty to his son Louis. In fact, when Charles died, Italy was at peace, and the Greeks willing to recognize the *status quo*. The Franks had retained the head of the Adriatic, with Friuli, Carniola and Istria: they had returned Venice to its Byzantine overlordship. In the extreme south, the Greeks held only the heel and toe of Italy (Calabria), and the rich island of Sicily.

For the other Mediterranean islands, Sardinia, Corsica and the Balearics, the Franks had to contend with the Saracens. Charles sent naval expeditions at times against the raiders of the islands, largely to protect the Frankish and Italian coasts: but they also in fact rendered the Greeks uneasy. Both Arabs and Greeks had formidable fleets in the Mediterranean, whereas Charles's strength lay mainly in his land army; but he could collect at times Frankish and Italian ships from the ports, man them with fighting men, put a count in charge and send out a considerable offensive fleet. The Greeks at the time held the theme of Sicily and, nominally, Sardinia as part of it; Corsica and the Balearics, which they had once held, they had left undefended to Saracen attack. The Arab

pirates sailed to their objective, bringing with them aboard ship
their small horses, which they then used in raiding parties for the
capture of slaves. The use of horses would seem to have supplied
a model to the Viking raiders of the ninth century, though the
northmen brought no horses but collected them immediately on
landing from a strategic point up river. Since the successful extension of the Spanish march in 799, Charles had claimed the
protectorate of the Balearics; and he and Pepin fought an almost
continuous naval war of defence with the Arab raiders who sought
to make Corsica their base for raiding the shores both of Aquitania and Italy. They used the island itself as a field for slave raids
and to obtain the timber they needed for their ships: and they
hoped to make Corsica a permanent base. In 806 Pepin collected
a fleet from the Italian ports and chased the Arabs from Corsica:
but his officer, Hadumar, count of Genoa, was killed. Charles sent
also a Frankish fleet under the constable Burchard; they defeated
the Arabs, who lost some thirty vessels. But while such Frankish
naval expeditions needed special efforts, the Arab slave raids were
a routine mercantile venture, paid for themselves and were soon
renewed: Leo III in 808 complained to Charles that the Italian
coast was not safe from raids, and besought him to deal with
Corsica again. On Easter Saturday, 809, the Arabs raided a town
and carried off all the inhabitants but the bishop, the old and the
sick; in 810 they twice found Corsica defenceless and ravaged it,
using 'the great fleet of all Spain'. Sardinia too they used as a
naval base.

The naval war became, however, more intense when the Arab
fleets from north Africa joined in. A certain Ibrahim ben Aglab
conquered the African tribes loosely organized by Islam, and
founded the Aglabite dynasty, under the supremacy of the caliph
of Baghdad, Harun ar-Rashid. A strong fleet based upon the ports
of Tunis issued out to harry the Mediterranean, competing with
the Spanish raiders for Christian vessels and undefended coasts.
Sicily itself was endangered and a Byzantine fleet arrived, commanded by a patrician who commandeered the ships of Gaeta and
Amalfi for use against the Arabs; the African pirates none the less
ravaged the coasts of south Italy and made off with considerable
plunder. Pope Leo III, Charles and the Greeks were all disturbed
by rumours of a great joint attack planned by the Arabs from
Spain and Africa: Charles sent his cousin Wala to help Leo defend
the Tuscan coast. He wrote also to George, the patrician of Sicily,
suggesting a common defence against the Arabs: but George
found it more expedient to make a ten years' truce with the caliph

of Baghdad. Neither the Spanish nor African chieftains, however, paid the least attention to the caliph of Baghdad; the raids continued. In 813 the African fleet sailed on Sardinia but was shattered by a storm; the Spanish raiders seized booty and 500 prisoners from Corsica, were met at sea near Majorca and forced to give them up by a Frankish count in command of a fleet, and then sailed back and recompensed themselves by pillaging Civita Vecchia. In short, while the Christian population of the islands profited very little from Charles's efforts at defence, the raiders were, in the main, restrained from attacking the coastlines of France and Italy, both by the efforts of the Frankish fleet to hold the enemy at the islands, and by the series of defensive posts set up by Charles and Pepin along the coast of the mainland. These Arab-Frankish 'combined operations' were, in any case, of interest as seeking to delimit the Muslim and Christian spheres of influence in the Mediterranean, and as serving as a model, both for the attack and the defence, in the raids which Europe was to suffer later from the northmen.

BIBLIOGRAPHICAL NOTE

As for chapter xvii: the clearest and most detailed account of the conquest of Saxony is to be found in Kleinclausz' *Charlemagne*; see also M. Lintzel, *Der sächische Stammestaat und seine Eroberung durch die Franken*, Berlin, 1933. See also, for the political circumstances in which the Carolingian empire was founded: Halphen, *L. Charlemagne et l'Empire Carolingien*, Paris, 1947.

CHAPTER XX

THE CHRISTIAN EMPIRE

WHEN Leo III crowned Charles emperor on Christmas Day in the year 800, his action may well have been immediately unexpected to Charles, but it was the climax to which events had been long tending. It is improbable that it was the result of a manœuvre on the part of the great Frankish clerics to whom it was highly acceptable, much less that it resulted from a manœuvre of Charles's own: he had no need to manœuvre: but it accorded both with the needs of the time and the climate of opinion of the day.[1]

Of all the precedent circumstances rendering possible the revival of the title by Charles, his conquests were the most important: *ampliavit regnum Francorum*: he ruled much more than a kingdom. He held all that Clovis and his sons had held, all that Pepin had held, and in addition, he ruled part of Spain, the Lombard kingdom, Frisia, the lands of the Saxons with a mark beyond the Elbe, and all the plain of the middle Danube that he had taken from the Avars. He had passed far beyond the Rhine-Danube frontier of the old empire. Wide conquests suggested to learned writers before Charlemagne's day the word empire and emperor; Adamnan called Oswald, the conqueror of Scottish and Welsh Britons 'emperor', and Bede, in 731, with a more exact scholarship, hesitating to call the bretwaldas (overkings) 'emperors', said 'they had this kind of an empire'. Not many men in eighth century Europe read books or knew much about the Romans: but many could see, even in a thinly Romanized province like Britain, the Roman wall or the multiangular tower at York or some ruined baths or amphitheatre, buildings that had belonged to an old empire. In Aquitania and Italy men still passed daily in the shadow of Roman buildings. The Anglo-Saxon thegn might see in them only wondrous wall-stones, shattered cities, a wall standing goat-grey and red-stained through king's reign after king's reign: he could not give those who feasted in these halls a name: but he knew very great men had lived in them of old, till Wyrd

[1] Prof. F. L. Ganshof, in *The Imperial Coronation of Charlemagne: theories and facts*, Glasgow, 1949, inclines to Frankish initiative for the coronation.

overthrew them. Every young clerk, however, following the office as a boy in his bishop's household or his minster, knew the word 'Roman' and 'empire': for he read of how 'Helena, the mother of Constantine, after the wonderful victory which Constantine the emperor, divinely accepting the sign of the Lord's cross, won over Maxentius, came to Jerusalem seeking that cross'. And she found it, and men sang *Vexilla regis prodeunt*, and built the high crosses and venerated the names of Helena and Constantine the emperor all over Europe.

The learned clerics of Charles's court knew, however, much more about the old empire. They recopied classical texts, sometimes from papyrus, on to vellum, in the new, beautiful, Carolingian minuscule (see p. 528): they read Vergil and Suetonius. They were not ill-informed about Roman antiquity; besides the texts of Caesar and Tacitus and Livy, they used reference books like Vegetius' *Art of War*, and Isidore's *Etymologies*, which preserved snippets of Roman history and Roman knowledge. They used the Eusebian tables translated by Jerome. They knew as a matter of everyday knowledge what a *vir illustris* was, and a consul and a patrician and an emperor. As has been said, a historical and an antiquarian wind was blowing strongly through the palace of Aix and the Carolingian monasteries and may have played its part in the revival of the imperial office.

But though Charles was to be acclaimed *Augustus*, the emperor he was to stand for in the year 800 was not Augustus, but Constantine. The empire connoted the Christian empire, where the emperor had a truly apostolic office: was not Constantine by right of his great conversion a thirteenth apostle? The emperor, to the eighth-century mind, was associated with the great college, as was the pope himself at Rome. The emperor must spread the faith among the heathen, protect it from distortion by heretics, rule and protect the church. In all these functions Charles had shown himself, while king of the Franks, an emperor in fact. He had fought the pagan Saracens and the pagan Saxons and the pagan Avars, and always consciously for the propagation of the faith, like any eastern *basileus*. He had disputed with the Adoptianists; he had involved himself in the iconoclastic controversy; he was ardently interested in maintaining the purity of the faith, as he saw it, even though he got his theological expert, Alcuin, to write the appropriate books and letters. The eighth-century Latin mind expected an emperor to be at once a missionary and a theologian, besides defending his empire and keeping order: Charles notably fulfilled the conditions.

MM. Kleinclausz and Calmette both stress, and rightly, the emergence of the term 'the Christian empire' in the years before and after Charlemagne's coronation. The Christian empire, as Augustine had taught, was the end to which the historical process moved: the emperor (as the Byzantines knew) existed providentially to help the church and promote the spread of the kingdom of God: to establish peace. The concept was part of the climate of opinion of the age. It appeared in Hadrian's apostrophe to Charles: 'Behold, a new Constantine, that most Christian of God's emperors, has arisen' and it appeared often in the writings of Charles's courtiers, Alcuin above all.

Alcuin wrote of Charles *inter alia*: 'On him alone has rested all the safety of the church.' In June 799 he wrote in a famous letter that three persons held the highest position in this world: the pope: the emperor: and the king of the Franks; the papacy was in distress and the empire fallen, for it was held by a woman through an abominable crime; Charles, king of the Franks, was now the strongest and wisest of the three powers: Jesus had made him the protector and leader of Christendom.

Yet, in fact, while Charles and his advisers were moving towards a monarchical protectorate of Latin Christianity, the equivalent of the Byzantine emperor's protectorate of Greek Christianity, the papacy at Rome was preparing to accept Charles as the protector, in a very different sense, of the whole of Christendom. The *patricius Romanorum* might well become the *imperator Romanorum*. The old danger to the papacy from imperial supremacy at Byzantium would be thus avoided: possible future danger from the setting up of a quasi-Byzantine court at Aix would be safeguarded: the protectorate of Christendom would be geographically linked with Rome. While Charles desired a position the equivalent of that of the eastern emperor, the papacy desired to make him the protector of the universal church, and as such the instrument of the Roman see.[1]

Another circumstance predisposing to the reception of the imperial title was the 'vacancy' in the eastern empire. Irene, empress regent, fearing that her energetic and warlike son, Constantine VI, would soon assume full power, had him arrested and imprisoned in the palace: by Irene's orders, his eyes were put out (17 July 797). From that time she styled herself, not *basilissa*, but *basileus*. To the west, the title as held by a woman seemed a contradiction in terms; by her shocking act, the empire at Byzantium appeared vacant. When Charles was crowned emperor, it

[1] See Dr W. Ullman's important chapter iii, in his *The Growth of Papal Government in the Middle Ages*, 1955.

was as the single Roman emperor, like Constantine: only later was the co-existence of two emperors found useful as the diplomatic formula for peace with the Greeks.

Charles's elevation to the empire hinged upon his possession of Italy and the patriciate of the Romans, neither of which in themselves constituted an affront to Byzantium. Charles held a by no means orthodox doctrine of images, but till 793 his relations with Irene and Constantine VI had been good; two Byzantine envoys in 797 had been well received at Aix. Even when in 798 other envoys from Irene announced that Constantine had been blinded and deposed for his evil living, there was no open breach between Franks and Greeks: the envoys were politely treated at Paderborn. It was reported that Irene appeared in a golden chariot drawn by four white horses, each led by an officer of patrician rank, while she threw alms to the people 'after the consular manner': but no one at Aix at the time thought the matter, though shocking, was of any direct importance to the Franks.

Charles's intervention in Roman affairs arose rather from an appeal of pope Leo III for help. Charles had received from him the standard of the city, and his envoys had received an oath of loyalty from Leo's subjects in the patrimony: Charles had recognized Leo as pope and could not be disinterested. He had indeed sent him a letter of good advice more appropriate as coming from a supreme overlord than a mere *defensor civitatis* and patrician: he had called upon him to live according to the canons, to extirpate simony, with which he had heard the church in Italy was stained, and to root out heresy: Leo accepted the advice with a meekness that might have come from a Frankish metropolitan. He summoned a council to Rome to deal with the Adoptianist heresy, as requested, in 798. Between the years 796–799 he had his great new reception hall or *triclinium* at the Lateran palace decorated with mosaics that expressed the contemporary Roman view of the relations between the spiritual and temporal powers. The splendid hall ended in an apse, trefoil in plan: on the vault of the central apse was represented Christ standing on a rock from which flowed the four rivers of Paradise, with this inscription: 'Go, teach all nations', while on the side vaults were represented the apostles fulfilling the command and teaching the distant peoples. On each side of the chief apse with its supreme figure of Christ were two groups: one of Constantine and Sylvester at the feet of the Saviour: one of Charlemagne and pope Leo III kneeling before St Peter. While to Charles Peter extended the standard, a banner with red roses on a blue ground, attached to a light spear; to Leo he extended the stole of priesthood; Peter himself wore the pallium. While the apparent equality and divine origin of the spiritual and temporal powers has often been remarked, the main *motif* of the mosaics after all was the apostolic commission to teach all the world: the stress was on teaching rather than on jurisdiction. The empire was to be Christian, and teach.

On 25 April 799 Leo's enemies tried to get rid of him. He was riding from the Lateran palace on the day of the Greater Litanies to put himself at the head of the procession starting from St Lawrence in Lucina, when he was ambushed by ruffians hired by the primicery Paul and Campulus the sacellarius (the notary paymaster): they represented the hostile Roman nobles. They dragged him from his horse, tried to put out his eyes or cut out his tongue, and dragged him injured and bleeding, to a cell in the monastery of St Erasmus. From there he was rescued by the two Frankish *missi*, abbot Wirundus and Winigis, duke of Spoleto, who took him to Spoleto. Their intervention shows that they held the violence shown to Leo a criminal offence, possibly backed by anti-Frankish jealousy. Charles was aware from the reports of Arn of Salzburg that trouble was brewing at Rome, and he sent off count Germer from Saxony to escort Leo to him at Paderborn. When he heard that Leo was near, he sent the arch-chaplain Hildebald and another count to meet him, and when he was nearer yet, Pepin and some other counts. When the cortège arrived at Paderborn, Charles greeted and kissed Leo, led him to be received in the chapel with hymns and chants, and next day made a great feast. Leo for his part blessed a new altar and laid in it relics of St Stephen the first martyr. All could see his own half healed wounds.

Letters from Leo's enemies now arrived, however, charging him explicitly with immorality, adultery and perjury: the matter could not be ignored, though the men who made the charges were themselves responsible for Leo's injuries. Alcuin, away in his monastery at Tours, was very troubled: he deprecated the scandal but saw that measures must be taken to clear Leo's character in Rome: how to do this without appearing to sit in judgment on him was very difficult. The pope, he wrote to Charles, was the chosen of God, the vicar of the apostles, the heir of the Fathers, the prince of the church: his innocence must be established. Alcuin wrote also to Arn at Rome, warning him to be very cautious: *apostolicam sedem judiciariam esse non judicandam.* When Arn wrote back about the scandals current about Leo, Alcuin burned the letter as private

to himself, warning Arn again to support the authority of the holy
see and the integrity of the Catholic faith.

Only Charles however could adequately deal with the problem
and only in Rome. He wintered at Aix, spent Easter at Saint-
Riquier and went on, with queen Liutgard and his three sons, to
Tours, where he had long conferences with Alcuin. One of Charles's
reasons for coming to Tours was to pray at the shrine of St
Martin for queen Liutgard, who was sick; but she died at Tours
and was buried near the shrine, after which Charles made no legal
marriage. In the autumn he travelled to Rome: Alcuin sent him
a little poem, addressing him as his 'dear David' and the protector
of Rome, capital of the world, and praying that as Charles guides
the head of the church, the Lord may guide him with his almighty
power; so too did bishop Theodulf of Orleans, crying that surely
Peter himself had sent him to save the pope.

On 24 November[1] Charles solemnly entered Rome, and was
welcomed by Leo on the steps of St Peter's; on 1 December he
presided at St Peter's over a great assembly of ecclesiastics and
laymen, Franks and Romans, which considered the complaints
brought against the pope. It was, in fact, a judicial inquiry: and at
the end of three weeks Leo submitted to take the oath of purgation which Charles demanded. On 23 December in St Peter's,
before an assembly composed as before and presided over by
Charles, he took a solemn oath, as being neither judged nor
constrained, but by a spontaneous act, before God and his angels
and blessed Peter, prince of the apostles, that he had never perpetrated nor ordered to be perpetrated the crimes and evil deeds
laid to his charge. In spite of the assertion that the act of purgation
was voluntary, all men in the city knew that Charles and the bishops
had required it. But the pope had a counter-stroke in store.

Two days later, on Christmas Day, Charles returned to St
Peter's to hear the pope celebrate the Christmas mass, and see his
son Charles anointed king. As he knelt in prayer before the
Confession of St Peter, before the mass, the pope approached and
crowned him with a diadem, at which the Roman people gave him
the official acclamation: *Carolo augusto a Deo coronato, magno et
pacifico imperatore, vita et victoria!* The pope then adored him,
as the patriarch in Santa Sophia adored the *basileus*, kneeling with
forehead bowed to the ground: the ceremony was clearly copied
from the Byzantine rite. While coronation with a diadem usually
accompanied the making of an emperor, acclamation by the

[1] For the beginning of the *annus incarnationis* on 25 December, see
F. M. Powicke, *Handbook of British Chronology*, 374.

Roman people was the collative act, the relic of the old homage to the emperor as triumphing: *vita et victoria!* It was clear to the congregation in St Peter's and to the city of Rome that Charles who had been patrician of the Romans left St Peter's as emperor.

As to the matter of the acclamations or *laudes* received by Charles from the Roman people in St Peter's, Dr E. H. Kantorowicz has shown in his *Laudes Regiae* that the old Greco-Roman acclamations to the ruler had long in the east become associated with liturgical acclamations to *Christus Victor*; and with liturgical acclamations to the Christian ruler and his agents. Such liturgical acclamations were sung by the clergy, whereas the collative acclamations at a Byzantine imperial election were made by the laity, the Roman people. Dr Kantorowicz considers it difficult to be sure whether the acclamations on Christmas Day, 800, were liturgical acclamations, or elective ones: 'The festival *laudes* were combined with the emperor's coronation. It seems useless to try to find out whether the chant represented festival or elective *laudes*, for probably they were both.' They must, indeed, have included elective *laudes*, for they were chanted by the Roman people, seculars; but Dr Kantorowicz's work illuminates yet another manner in which the Frankish palace and people were moving towards a Greco-Christian attitude to their ruler, for the first Carolingian form of the liturgical *laudes* goes back to the period between 783 and 787. Two points are of interest.

First, the very old use in Italy and the west, not only of penitential processions, litanies, with responses to each petition in the form *ora pro nobis, libera nos, audi nos,* etc. (of such processions the western Litany of the Saints is one form which has crystallized and survived), but of litanies of exultation, beginning with the words

Christus vincit: Christus regnat: Christus imperat.

to which the responses were, not petitions, but acclamations, *laudes,* the crowd singing *Christus vincit.* While Christ was acclaimed as ruler and commander, with him were acclaimed his royal vicars on earth, popes and bishops, his royal house, his judges, his army: the present and the transcendental world 'dissolving one into the other'. The acclamations were the pith of the chant; they were also, on occasion, made to the victorious cross, the *signum* of Christ's victory; to rulers and bishops on arrival at a city; to Charles on his coming to Rome in 781; they were associated with the Easter *Exultet* and with the words ending a liturgical prayer

to Christ, *qui vivit et regnat in saecula saculorum.* Liturgical
acclamation of Charles as Christ's vicar was thus familiar to the
Frankish palace long before A.D. 800.

Secondly (though this is not referred to by Dr Kantorowicz),
the liturgical use of the triad at the beginning of the acclamations

Christus vincit, Christus regnat, Christus imperat,

in Italy and among the Franks, throws light on Hadrian I's
change of protocol in the dating of his *acta.* Where before 781
the dating clause had included the regnal year of the eastern
emperor, Hadrian's notaries in 781 (the year of Charles's Roman
visit) wrote: *Regnante domino deo et Salvatore nostro Jesu Christo,*
adopting a phrase used earlier among the Franks and Gallo-
Romans.

Charles, within a few months of his coronation, used the imperial title at the head of his *acta* and the news of his 'honour and
elevation' was received with qualified joy at the Frankish court and
by Alcuin: and, indeed, the imperial dignity had been dearly
bought. The matter was only briefly alluded to, though the *Royal
Annals* recorded the terms of the acclamation carefully. No change
of ceremonial was made at the court of Aix, nor any attempt to
follow Byzantine court precedent. Charles still ruled as king of
the Franks and king of the Lombards, though the imperial title
was useful to him as a single title covering all his subjects, and
more particularly as increasing his power in the city of Rome itself.
Here his orders now ran unquestioned and his residence could
prolong itself to any limit. More particularly, the title covered
and confirmed the protectorate he already exercised over the
holy see.

About the question as to the initiative behind the act of coronation: Einhard said that Charles himself declared that had he
known about the pope's intention beforehand, he would not even
have entered the church, though it were Christmas Day. Certainly
'the Roman people' in the church were ready with their acclamations, which were made carefully and in due form, which suggests
papal initiative. There seem to have been no other special preparations: but the Byzantine ceremony scarcely required them. There
are no grounds for thinking that the pope was obeying an order
privately made to him beforehand by the Franks; it would appear
that he was trying subtly to gain an advantage for the papacy in
future by bestowing the diadem on a barbarian emperor. He was
following Byzantine precedent, and while no one in Byzantium

held that the patriarch bestowed the empire because he crowned the emperor, coronation was practically essential for elevation to the empire (see p. 150). In the present case, however, it could well be held that the imperial dignity was actually bestowed by the pope, for other title to it Charles had none; and what the pope could give he could also take away. The new emperor was to be the protector, but also the instrument of the pope.

On the other hand, Leo must have known that Frankish statesmen held that Charles was already acting as Christian emperor, in fact if not in name, and that his action could not be refused by Charles and his advisers, however awkward the position in which it placed them. The coronation appeared also to be a personal advantage to himself: as justifying retrospectively the fact that Charles had passed judgment upon him. It strengthened his pro-Frankish policy as against the possibly pro-Lombard or pro-Byzantine one of his enemies, the Roman nobles and the *scrinium*. Certainly it delivered the papacy itself from the old fear of Byzantine overlordship: it achieved the end of pope Hadrian.

It was not apparent to Leo at the time that it would probably have been more advantageous to the papacy to have continued to accept the distant and nominal overlordship of the eastern emperor. Professor Dvornik has stressed that thus the unity of the Christian empire would have been preserved, and the western church saved from the abuses connected with the Germanic institution of the *eigenkirche*. The papacy moreover would have avoided becoming involved in the efforts of the Frankish bishops on the middle Danube to depress the Slav races and disallow the use of the Slav liturgy. Such considerations, however, could not weigh as heavily with Leo in the year 800 as did his determination to lay a sure foundation for papal temporal sovereignty. This policy was, perhaps, the biggest miscalculation of all, but one can hardly criticize Leo for not foreseeing its disastrous results seven centuries in advance.

Charles's own words about the coronation, that he would not have entered St Peter's had he known the pope's intention to crown him, may also be explained by the diplomatic situation. Charles may have expected no great reaction from the Greeks while Irene was claiming to be *basileus*: and Constantine VI in 800 had no unquestioned successor in Constantinople. Byzantium, however, settled her own difficulties by accepting the logothete Nicephoras (see p. 413) as emperor; and, this settled, was in a much stronger position to protest at Charles's usurpation of the imperial title. Tension between Franks and Greeks in Italy at once became acute; the Greeks would not recognize Charles, and a state of war in Italy was protracted till 814. It is not difficult, then, to understand Charles's disclaimer: his relations with Byzantium, difficult enough already, were now gravely affected by his assumption of the imperial style; an assumption adroitly forced upon him at an inconvenient moment and in a most compromising manner. The pope had brilliantly revenged his enforced purgation. The only course left to Charles was to use the advantages of his new dignity to the full and to overcome the disadvantages, in which he succeeded very well.

In consequence of the coronation, Charles henceforward used the imperial title, acted as the protector of the holy see according to his own interpretation, and fought a long, if minor, war with the Greeks till a diplomatic *modus vivendi* was arrived at.

While continuing to govern his territories as king of the Franks and king of the Lombards, he used the title:

> *Carolus, serenissimus augustus, a Deo coronatus, pacificus, imperator Romanum gubernans imperium, qui et per misericordiam Dei rex Francorum et Langobardorum.*

The title implied his succession to Constantine and Theodosius and all the emperors so familiar to his notaries and the *archicapellanus* from the extracts from their edicts in the Theodosian code. A leaden seal, detached from one of Charles's diplomas, has the inscription: *Renovatio imperii*. The reverse of the new *denarii* which Charles struck in Italy referred to the Christian empire, for it had a device of a temple surmounted by a cross (probably representing St Peter's at Rome), with the inscription *christiana religio*. In his coin device, and constantly in his interventions in the matter of theology and heresy, he claimed the Constantinian appellation of *isapostolos*; the exercise of such a function was in itself imperial.

In his relations with Leo III moreover Charles constantly acted as emperor, which implied the defence and guidance of the holy see. His first act after his coronation was to banish Leo's accusers. Leo he treated always with personal kindness and deference. When he heard in 804 that Leo desired to spend Christmas with him, he sent his eldest son Charles to meet him on the northern descent from the Alps, welcomed him himself in the basilica of Saint-Rémi at Reims, celebrated Christmas with him at Quierzy, and the feast of the Epiphany on 6 January at Aix. In the Act of Thionville he charged his three sons to defend the holy see as their father and grandfather had done: he wrote to consult Leo on matters of doctrine and ecclesiastical discipline.

In Italy, however, he succeeded in acting as Leo's overlord, and particularly in Leo's relations with Pepin, king of Italy, relations which were sometimes troublesome. On one or two occasions Leo pleaded with Charles for support against Pepin, but did not find Charles's *missi* very helpful. It was further a sign of the acceptance of Frankish overlordship that Leo, from the end of 800, dated his letters not only by the years of his pontificate but by those of Charles's reign, and that he struck new coins bearing on one side his own name, and on the other that of Charles the emperor.

The difficulty of Charles's relations with Byzantium after his coronation, however, did not prove easy of solution. When the news had been brought to Constantinople, though the empress Irene had been old, ill and surrounded by intriguing favourites, it was felt that Byzantine prestige itself had received a great blow. To all Greeks in the year 800 the empire was one and indivisible, and Charles's claim to empire could only be a usurpation; his view that a second empire might be set up beside that of Byzantium was completely unacceptable. Though the western part of the empire had long been lost, the Byzantine world had never recognized the loss as irrecoverable; it was far from clear at the time that Christendom had, in fact, split into two portions. To Charles, however, acceptance of this fact, which involved his own recognition as emperor by Byzantium, was necessary to the peace and stability of his dominions. Non-recognition by the Greeks involved war in Italy and the Adriatic coasts: but the war was not merely a territorial dispute.

In 802 an embassy from Charles was received by Irene in Constantinople, and in answer she despatched the *spathiarius* Leo to Charles. According to the Greek historian Theophanes, a marriage was even projected between Charles and Irene to restore the unitary character of the empire, but the evidence for such a project is insufficient. In any case, Irene was dethroned by a palace revolution in October 802, and it was left for her successors, Nicephoras and Michael I, to negotiate for a settlement with Charles. Nicephoras sent envoys to Charles at Salzburg in 803: but the Frankish written proposal which they took back, a proposal for the mutual recognition of the two sovereigns as ruling an eastern and a western empire, was still unacceptable. Nicephoras preferred to continue the fighting in the Adriatic to the loss of prestige which such a recognition would have brought him. He was hard pressed at the time by both Arabs and Bulgarians and he feared a Frankish attack on Sicily: but he sent no reply to Charles's proposal and the war continued. Charles, for his part, looked to Byzantine difficulties to secure him eventual recognition.

Pepin's reconquest of Venetia in 810 (see p. 374) at last made Nicephoras anxious to find a formula for peace. He sent the *spathiarius* Assafius to Charles at Aix, and in October of that year Charles gave him honourable reception. The outline of a peace treaty was agreed and in 811 Charles sent Hugh, count of Tours, the count of Friuli and a Frankish bishop to bear it to Constantinople. The text of the treaty has not survived, but it is known to have been a *foedus*, a pact between equals. It recognized an eastern and western empire (*orientale atque occidentale imperium*), headed by two sovereigns each terming the other brother and emperor. In return for this substantial concession, Charles had been willing to yield Venetia and Dalmatia. When the Frankish envoys reached Constantinople, however, it was to learn that Nicephoras had just been killed in battle with the Bulgars (October 811); but though the mission as accredited to Nicephoras could not fulfil its purposes it found the new emperor, Michael I, friendly. Fresh Greek envoy, came to Charles, gave him the imperial acclamations in the Greek tongue, and furthered the despatch of a fresh Frankish mission which, in its turn, was to find that the emperor Michael had been deposed by Leo V, the Armenian. Leo sent yet another Greek mission to ratify the peace treaty, and it arrived at Aix to find Charles just dead and to deliver the treaty for ratification to his son Louis. They saluted the new emperor as *basileus*, and the coexistence of the two emperors, eastern and western, within the Roman empire, was recognized. The Italian war, and the blows of other enemies, had led Byzantium to make the concession, so convenient for Charles in his dealings with the papacy.

Though Charles continued to rule his dominions after 800 with the same officers and institutions as he had before, without any attempt to set up a civil service or a centralised government on the Byzantine pattern (as to which he had very little information and certainly not the means of imitation), yet in one or two respects he acted as Christian emperor, beyond merely using the imperial style and exercising the protectorate over the holy see. He issued capitularies applicable to all his dominions: he sent out *missi* to enforce them and prevent, if possible, misgovernment by his counts and vassals and he held great councils of churchmen and lay officers to regulate the affairs of the church and enforce the discipline of the clergy as much as of his secular officers.

In March 802 he issued general instructions to the *missi dominici*, who should, it is laid down, be men of high standing, inaccessible to bribes or other influence. He usually chose two great officers, one clerical and one secular, to perambulate a region familiar to them; thus in 802 he sent Fardulf, abbot of Saint-Denis and Stephen, count of Paris, to visit the Paris region. Maginard, archbishop of Reims, and count Madelgald were chosen for the region south of the Channel, while Magnus, archbishop of Sens and count Godfrey travelled by way of Orleans, Troyes, Langres, Besançon and Autun. Each year certain pairs of *missi* made their journeys through portions of the empire. They were always chosen as men of affairs, bishops and abbots as rulers of great estates or holders of immunities, and counts actually in office: their own office and functions did not lapse while they thus acted for some weeks as perambulating inspectors. They visited in pairs a group of counties, perhaps half a dozen, bearing the instructions of the emperor, general or particular: they were competent to try suits of laymen or clerks, since they comprised always at least one bishop or abbot and one count. They inquired into the behaviour of royal servants of all grades, into the holding of the local tribunals, the administration and keeping of oaths of fidelity; they received complaints; they could deal with the worship of God and matters pertaining to Christian salvation; they delivered royal instructions, oral and written. They were ordered to see that justice was done 'fully, correctly and equitably' to all churches, widows and orphans, and to all men, and without delay: they were ordered to send the emperor a report on how they had executed his orders on their mission.

The instructions were admirable, but the work was heavy, and the time which could be allotted to each town inadequate to the number of suits and complaints brought before them. The old customary laws, now written, differed in the different regions, which is doubtless why *missi* were chosen to operate in their own neighbourhood: they were men, however, of the same class and family connexions with the officers they were sent to supervise. Their own functions were difficult to reconcile with their work as *missi*, with their summonses to general assemblies, and, on the part of the counts, to military expeditions. The weeks of their missions were all too short, and the interests of the inspectors too much the same as the interests of the officials inspected. Nevertheless, they must have filled a need, for the number of missions sent out by Charles at the end of his reign increased, though he would also send for suitors, or the disobedient, to appear before him personally. Perhaps the most important work of the *missi* was the publication of the capitularies and their enforcement in the different regions and sub-kingdoms.

Charles in October 802 held an important assembly at Aix of high ecclesiastics and secular officers, for the better keeping of law in the empire. To the secular clergy, the bishops, priests and deacons, the rules of canon law and the decrees of the pontiffs were read aloud; abbots and monks heard the rule of St Benedict read, and were exhorted to keep it themselves and see that their subjects kept it when they returned home; while the counts were told to do good justice to rich and poor. Charles himself explained to the highest officers assembled and those in charge of duchies and counties the different laws of his dominions, and ordered the officers of regions where the local customary law was still un-written to have them written down on their return. As a conse-quence of this assembly, there was a great writing down of local codes, Thuringian, Frisian and other: and presumably a recopying for the different counties of local codes already written, like the law of the Saxons, Bavarians, etc. The law of the Ripuarian Franks had certain old Germanic terms deleted, even as the law of the Salian Franks had been re-edited some twenty years earlier. The Roman law of the Visigoths, the Breviary of Alaric, was officially copied by the palace notaries for Frankish use.

The capitularies issued after 800 do not differ in character from those issued before, though they were now to be generally enforced. They dealt before and after with the discipline and endowment of clergy and monks (p. 505); with the administration of the estates of the fisc (the *De Villis* of *c.* 800, see p. 325); with the payment of tithe from the royal villas to the churches on the respective demesne of the fisc; with the owners of four manses who owed service with the army, with their summons by count, vicar or *centenarius*, and the payment of the ban by those who absented themselves (808); with the conduct of justice, in Charles's presence, or that of the count of the palace, or the count, or the *centenarius*, or before the *missi* (811 and 813); with the cherishing of letters in bishops' schools and in monasteries (see p. 504). Many of the capitularies were also issued for particular regions, as for Saxony (see pp. 361, 363); the pagus of Sens; Bavaria, the Spanish March, Italy, etc.

For the issue and publication of capitularies Charles would summon a great council, with more than the normal number of members. One such 'great council' or 'general assembly' was normally summoned at the end of each winter, to hold a kind of stocktaking of the events of the past year and to deliberate with him on his plans, often military, for that coming. To such an assembly, when a capitulary was to be issued, Charles would summon jurists not regular members of the council: Hincmar (see p. 396) speaks of these assemblies sometimes as a *placitum*. In them Charles did justice: he alone made decisions about any business or suits that were deliberated, and to them he published the capitularies that were additional to the local codes in his dominions.

Charles was not only supreme law-giver, but supreme judge in his empire: he could summon any plea before him and his sentence was definitive. Certain enormous crimes were necessarily judged by him or in his presence, and appeal lay to him in both lay and clerical suits. Clerks, however, might not appeal to him without the consent of the bishops. Charles gave judgment immediately on dressing or, if he were not out hunting or travelling, in the course of the day. The count of the palace, however, judged the pleas of the lesser people, only the pleas of magnates going before Charles himself.

Most of the cases known to us to have been heard by Charles himself were, in fact, pleas about property in land between great ecclesiastics. The dispute between Fulrad of Saint-Denis and bishop Herchenrad of Paris, in July 775, is of interest for the procedure, reported as normal. Written documents were first normally presented as evidence, and the contestants might bring also oral testimony; but when, as here, the evidence was indecisive, recourse was had to the judgment of God. Charles ordered that a man from each of the contesting parties should go to the chapel of the villa and there stand, his arms crossed, in the sight of all: God then made plain his judgment, because the man of the bishop of Paris began to tremble and appear convicted. Charles then consulted his faithful, including the count of the palace, and gave judgment for Fulrad, and the notary Theudegarius wrote down the judgment. Of the counts of the palace who thus assisted Charles in judgment we know the names only of a few: Anselm in 775, Worad in 781–2, Adalard in 800, Amalric in 812: they had, it appears, helpers.

The problem of the succession to his royal and imperial dignities needed settlement from A.D. 800 onwards. Charles passed the last years of his life more and more at his palace of Aix, a great Frankish ruler, with the Saracens and the Slavs, the Greeks and

even the Romans on the horizon of his life. The mere fact of age
diminished the extraordinary energy and power to travel which
had made his conquests possible. His sons were grown men:
Charles, the eldest, whom he kept normally with him, who was
as closely in touch with the east Frankish vassals and army as he
was himself: in touch, that is, with the fighting men who were the
backbone of Charlemagne's empire; then, Louis, who had been
sent off as a child to rule Aquitaine, who had been brought up in
a different, an Aquitanian, tradition, whose youth, sheltered by
Charlemagne's middle-aged councillors, had known none of the
difficulties of his father's; then, Pepin, who ruled Italy, was equally
guided by his father's councillors, but who had the early Carolingian ability to get an army to a strategic area, and to fight. Charles
had also younger children: but he had not married any woman
after his fourth wife's death: and in view of the difficulties caused
later by Louis the Pious' late marriage to Judith, his conduct must
be judged politically prudent, though at the time it was held uncanonical and, by some, scandalous. It was almost certainly the
same motive, the wish to avoid entangling alliances and the need
for the territorial endowment of imperial grandchildren, that
made Charles keep his daughters unmarried: though he claimed
that he did this because he liked their company. The question of the
succession to empire and kingdoms was now due for settlement:
and Charles made a formal *ordinatio*, or act of settlement: at his
villa of Thionville, on 6 February 806. This took the form of a
divisio regnorum to follow on Charles's death: succession to the
empire was not dealt with.

At the beginning of this *Ordinatio*, read to the general assembly,
Charles was styled emperor and it was specified that, during his
lifetime, he should continue his royal and imperial power over
his *regnum atque imperium*: but that, on his death Pepin, as king,
should rule Italy, Bavaria, part of Alemannia, and Rhaetia; Louis,
as king, Aquitania (less Tours, shrine of the great patron saint of
the Franks), Gascony, Septimania, Provence and Burgundy; while
Charles, the eldest son, should rule the heart of the Carolingian
patrimony: eastern Francia, part of Burgundy, part of Alemannia,
Neustria, Austrasia, part of Thuringia, Saxony, Frisia and the
Bavarian Nordgau. Some provision was made for 'confraternal
government', in that each son was to defend his own external
frontiers and keep charity with his brothers. It was further laid
down that all three brothers should defend the church of St Peter
at Rome: that each should have access, by a specified route, to and
from Italy. Should any of the sons die, his share of territory should

be divided in a specified manner between the remaining two brothers: but if he himself had a son whom his people wished to succeed, he should inherit his father's rights and territories. It is a comment on the brutality of the age and Charles's strong family feeling that he forbade that any of his grandsons should ever be put to death, be forced to enter a religious house or suffer mutilation, without a lawful judgment: and that the order was later disobeyed.

Every effort was made by Charles to buttress the authority of the act of Thionville, so as to secure a peaceable succession; the magnates swore to observe it, and the new oaths of fidelity now taken to Charles included promises to respect the act. Furthermore, Einhard travelled with a copy of the act to pope Leo, to obtain his recognition and signature. The act, however, did not become effective because both the brothers, Charles and Pepin, died before their father, and Louis, by the accident of survival, became in 814 sole ruler of all his father's territories. Meanwhile, Charlemagne remained in complete control of his sons and of his empire, continuing to style himself king of the Lombards, though Pepin was a king in Italy. He sent *missi* into his sons' kingdoms and minted coins both in Italy and Aquitaine.

Though the act of Thionville never became effective, it has received much comment as showing that Charles regarded his territories as a Frankish patrimony rather than an indivisible empire. With regard to this, some points should be noted.

First, that the act was a *divisio regnorum*, but made no division of the empire, and designated no successor to the empire or the patriciate. There was ample Byzantine precedent for designating a son, or an adopted son, as future emperor, but designation by will had usually been preceded by association in office. In any case, Byzantine constitutional precedent, if known to Charles, was of less importance than practical considerations. In 806, apparently, Charles was not ready to name any of his sons emperor, nor was the question of the succession urgent. Besides the possibility of arousing quarrels, there was an obvious difficulty in making the elder son emperor: he would have Aix and the Carolingian homelands, but he would not have Rome. An emperor should have both Aix and Rome. It is notable that Charles divided the particular duty of the patriciate, the protectorate of the holy see, between the three brothers, not assigning it in particular to Pepin, king of Italy. The question of succession to the empire and the patriciate was, in 806, passed over for future settlement.

Secondly, it has been argued from the act of Thionville and

the eventual failure of Charles's 'empire' to survive as a territorial unit, that Charles used and regarded the term 'emperor' merely as a personal title.[1] It is indeed arguable that Charles was 'emperor' only in the sense that Clovis I was 'consul', and Pepin the Short *vir illustris* and *patricius*. Such a view, however, leaves out of account the twelve years of war fought with the Greeks in Italy, wars that were not fought about the use of a mere personal title: wars that continued for some years after Charles had arranged for the *divisio regnorum* at his death.

Such a view leaves out of account also Charles's aim at unitary rule of his dominions so far as the conditions of his day allowed. Government depends on communications, and the very great economic change in the four hundred years between A.D. 400 and 800 had brought about a new 'culture' in western Europe. There was no longer an imperial posting service, and the old imperial civil service (with its advantages and its very heavy cost) had been replaced by the services of the Merovingian palace, and the Carolingian palace and vassals. By no possible chance could a Frankish ruler in Charles's position have replaced the relatively primitive government of Pepin the Short with a complex civil service and developed money economy, as in the later Roman empire; but to admit this is not to admit that Charles was using the title emperor as a mere personal decoration, a title of protocol and prestige only. It was in the Greco-Roman tradition that the empire existed for peace, and Charles and his palace had come to accept the tradition as much as Dante later. To exercise unitary rule of the empire Charles could use only his palace, his family and his vassals: the division of kingdoms among his sons in 806 was a compromise with circumstance, not a formal renunciation of future imperial rule.

The machine of government of Charles's large empire sufficed during his own life-time to hold it together; the Carolingian palace and the vassals in the countryside, slight enough governmental links as they seemed, proved sufficient to build up a Franco-Greco-Roman, a Carolingian, culture that persisted even when the quarrels of Charles's descendants destroyed unity of government at the top. There was, in Charles's empire, no scientific road-making on the Roman scale: Roman roads, after all, were designed for the passage of the legions, infantry regiments, and Charles's army and his messengers were horsemen. For them

[1] See *The Medieval Empire: Idea and Reality*, by Professor G. Barra-clough.

metalled roads were not essential, though the army sometimes used old Roman roads. Carolingian government depended on the horse; the palace rode from villa to villa and wherever the king went judgments were given; counts and vassals rode to Charles's general assemblies; the *missi* rode upon their tours. Many horses were needed, and many were bred on the lands of the fisc, by bishops and abbots and the vassals; many were bought from the Saxons.

Government at the centre rested with the *palatium*: the making of policy rested with Charles and his council (see p. 397) some of whom accompanied him. The palace was also the nerve-centre of the fiscal system: it had charge of the royal treasure, and revenue was brought to it by the counts from their counties. Some money taxes were still collected: the old *cens*, a direct tax on lands and individuals collected by the counts: the customs, collected by *telonarii* at ports, and tolls collected on certain rivers, roads and bridges. Annual gifts, really compulsory, brought in considerable revenue in precious metals and in kind, and the profits of justice were considerable. Lands, armour, horses, golden ornaments came in as the estates of the disinherited; there were fines for duties not performed; the third of treasure trove went to the king. Tribute from conquered nations came to the palace, and great wealth accrued to Charles as war plunder: gold and silver, mainly in ingots or ornaments, precious vestments, armour, horses, oxen. Diplomatic presents swelled the revenue, and the different customary laws had long lists of offences emendable by money compostions, which were shared between the king and the local count (and usually paid in farm animals). It was the count's duty to collect the revenue and bring it to the palace at Aix, from which large government payments had to be disbursed.

The maintenance of Charles's household and the entertainment of guests were mainly met by the exploitation of his villas, found all over his empire. He had inherited those of the Merovingian fisc and though he granted some of his lands to abbeys and churches, he did not make proportionately so many grants as the Merovingians. From the villas came grain, oxen, pigs, salt, horses, forage, wine and beer in relative abundance; for the villas had arable fields, meadows, woods, the right to the fish in the rivers, high Alpine pastures, vineyards by the Rhine and in Italy, olive groves and salt-pans. Charles's conquests brought him in many more villas: those of the Lombard king in Italy and the duke of Bavaria: many Saxon lands. He could reward his young vassals and the officers of his court from this source, without diminishing the lands of the fisc in the Frankish home country, and this contributed to the royal wealth.

As to the spending of the royal revenue: there was of course no distinction between Charles's private and public expenses. The revenue had to provide for the daily living of the palace, the maintenance of royal buildings, and the building and adornment of new villas, palaces, bridges, etc.; it had also to supply diplomatic presents. There were great barns and storehouses at Aix, as well as the royal treasure. The chamberlain (*camerarius*) had charge of the *sacellum fisci*, and by the end of the reign had as assistants the *sacellarius* who guarded the treasure and the *scapoardus*, who guarded the royal plate and ornaments. They made payments, in so far as money payments were necessary, to the royal chaplains for expenses or alms, to the *missi* for expenses and diplomatic gifts, to the seneschal, butler and constable for expenses connected with Charles's household. These three household officers were charged respectively with the provision of food, wine and horses, and in general with making the arrangement for Charles's travel from villa to villa. The queen, as mistress of a household, seems to have had a nominal charge over them and the right to consult them; she had also the right to consult the local stewards in charge of villas which the court intended to visit. She had, that is, her own place in the household, which included Charles's daughters and their women attendants: this may explain the very short interval between the death of Charles's wives, to one or two of whom he seems to have been attached, and his marriage within weeks to another queen.

Charles's travelling household always included, as Hincmar tells us (see p. 533), three of his wisest councillors. This council, the list of whose membership was definite, met, not at fixed times or places, but solely at Charles's will; he himself presided over it. He consulted it on all important matters, again, solely at his own will. The obligation on members to secrecy was strict and derived from the tradition of the Roman notaries, for the great clerks of the chapel had received notarial training and some of them were members of the council. Apart from the three councillors travelling with the household, the other members, clerical and lay, attended when summoned. Charles's choice of those summoned to a particular council depended on their adjacency at the moment to the travelling palace, or their possession of some special qualification: a normal council meeting would not include the full number of members. Not only royal vassals and abbots but bishops also were on the list of councillors, for in 794 the council of Frankfurt, with the authority of pope Hadrian, dispensed Charles from pope Gregory's ruling that bishops should be occupied solely with the affairs of their bishopric.

Our chief authority for the officers of the Carolingian palace is Hincmar's *De ordine palatii*, a treatise written not long before his death in 882, but which incorporates information derived orally from members of Charles's palace. The picture it draws applies properly to the court of Charles's great-great-grandson, but the information it gives about the officers of the earlier period can be checked by the signatures of Charles's *acta* and tallies fairly well.

The *De ordine palatii* was composed by archbishop Hincmar of Reims shortly after the death of Louis III, for the direction of his brother, king Carloman. Hincmar was born in 806, trained as a young monk in the royal abbey of Saint-Denis, which had long been closely connected with the royal writing office, and was familiar with the court of Louis the Pious (d. 840): he was much in Louis's confidence. He was later the chief minister of Charles the Bald, from 845 archbishop of Reims, and from 845 to 876 he directed the church of France. Though he did not write the *De Ordine Palatii* till 882, he based it on a work of Adalard, abbot of Corbie (d. 826), and his chapters on the palace officials appear to rest closely on Adalard's work.

The *De Ordine Palatii* describes the services of the palace as consisting of six bureaux, headed by the arch-chaplain, whom Hincmar calls the *apocrysarius* (Greek for secretary). The term must be derived from Adalard's earlier work, for it was a Byzantine court title which he or the small learned circle of court scribes applied to Charles's writing officer, after Charles's assumption of the imperial title: a usage which did not become accepted at the Frankish court. No Frankish diplomas are known to have been witnessed by an *apocrysarius*.

But the *apocrysarius* (says Hincmar) whom they nowadays call the *capellanus*, or the *custos palatii*, rules all the palace clergy under his charge (*cura*) and disposition. With him is associated the chancellor (*cancellarius*), called after the secrecy of the screens (*cancellae*); and there were subject to him prudent, wise and faithful men who wrote out the royal precepts without immoderate greed of gain, and faithfully preserved secrecy. After these two officers, the sacred palace (sacred is another Byzantine touch) is served by these ministers: namely, the chamberlain, the count of the palace, the seneschal, the butler, the count of the stable (constable), the lodgings officer (*mansionarius*), the four chief huntsmen, and one falconer.

And although beneath them or beside them there were other ministers as, the porter, paymaster, the plate-warden (*scapoardus*) and the
juniors of some of them called deans (*decani*): or even of others beyond
these, like the hedge-wardens, the houndsmen, the beaver-wardens
and others: though, indeed, each of these according to his degree was
intent on his work: yet not to these as to the other chief officers belonged the rule of the confederation of the whole kingdom in the great
and small things that occur daily, together with that over the whole
assembly of the palace. . . . Those high officers would not, nor might
they absent themselves from the palace.

In other chapters of his treatise Hincmar says again that the
apocrysarius, 'who is called among us the *capellanus* or *custos
palatii*', was responsible for all ecclesiastical business and the
service of the church, for all monastic and canonical disputes and
for the foreign relations of the church. He does not elaborate
further on the relation of the chaplain (*apocrysarius*) to the chancellor and notaries: but the passage quoted shows the chaplain in
charge of those who wrote the royal deeds.

Hincmar's information about the royal secretariat confirms the
documentary evidence about a very important change in the
latter carried through by the early Carolingians: the change from
the use of a lay to a clerical secretariat. The Merovingians had
used a *schola* of notaries, headed by a referendary, generally
of noble birth: the early Carolingians used their palace chaplains,
headed by an 'arch-chaplain', and the later Carolingians applied to
this officer, Hincmar's *apocrysarius*, the old, notarial title of
chancellor. It was to be a change very important to the church and
governments of medieval Europe.

The Merovingian kings had signed very few documents themselves and those only of the greatest importance: authenticity
was afforded by the signature of the referendary, and the old
legal form of 'recognition'. The referendary offered (*optulit*) the
written document to the king for his inspection, and then wrote
recognovit or *recognovi* and his signature at the end; the recognition of the referendary gave an authenticity equal to the signature
of the king himself. Late in the Merovingian period, and increasingly as parchment was used instead of papyrus, a wax impression
from the royal seal ring was used in addition to the notarial signature of the referendary, for authentication. Parchment was
a tougher material than papyrus to sustain and retain a wax seal;
though the Roman gentleman of old had fastened his papyrus
letter with wax and sealed it with his seal ring, such letters were
not intended for permanent record; the authentication of public

and private deeds was then always made by the elaborate notarial signature which would not by its weight drag a hole in the papyrus. With the Carolingian use of parchment for all deeds, the seal became a double means of authentification, though the notarial signature was not disused.

Meanwhile, another set of palace officials, the *capellani*, were acquiring in the late Merovingian period a knowledge of *formulae* and Roman law similar to that possessed by the lay notaries of the Frankish *scrinium*. It was a parallel development to that by which the bishop's deacons had taken over the work of his notary or notaries. The chaplains had, by definition, charge of the king's sacred relics, especially that most sacred relic, the short cloak or *capella* of St Martin of Tours. They lived with the palace and added to their primary duty of guarding the relics that of saying mass for the king on feast days and writing such documents as might be required. They worked in conjunction with the royal notaries, and when the Carolingians desired to change their writing officer, they could find among their royal chaplains a substitute for the referendary.

Charles Martel and Pepin the Short made the change, and their usage was followed by Charles the Great and the later Carolingians. Charles Martel, ruling the Franks under the nominal kingship of Thierry IV (721–737), first used the royal referendary, Chrodegang: but, from the death of Thierry IV in 737 till his own death in 741, he ruled France as sole mayor of the palace, and as mayor authenticated his own documents in his own name. From 741 till 747 Charles's sons, Pepin and Carloman, ruled respectively as mayors of Neustria and Austrasia, authenticating their own *acta*, but from 747 Pepin ruled alone and in 751 was anointed king by Boniface, now archbishop of Mainz. He did not revert to the use of a lay authenticating officer, for he and his father had used their position as authenticating officer as steps to the throne, and such a course might have had its dangers. He used instead the clerks of his chapel: in 752 he issued at Compiègne a diploma which Boniface recognized as *archicancellarius*: but normally Pepin used one of his palace chaplains. The names of Chrodingus, Widmarus, Winiramus and Baddilo appear on documents over a number of years, and then that of Hitherius. Hitherius as chaplain three times wrote out documents for Baddilo's recognition, and in 768 he recognized a document himself. In the language of Charles's day, he had become *archicapellanus*: the first of those authenticating officers who would later be called 'chancellors'. In 768 he authenticated three documents, all dated from the abbey of Saint-Denis, and he became himself later abbot of St Martin of Tours.

The arch-chaplain had thus stepped into the shoes of the old referendary and from henceforth the Carolingians always used such an arch-chaplain, priest or bishop, to authenticate their *acta*. 'Hitherius', says the diplomatist and palaeographer Breslau, 'is the first royal chancery official whom we can with certainty recognize as a cleric. From then on, for many hundred years, there are no lay chancery officials. The change of custom was linked, and not accidentally, with the change of dynasty.'

The duties of the *apocrysarius*, however, were not only 'secretarial'. He was still called chaplain of the palace, archbishop of the sacred palace, arch-priest, as well as primicery of the palace or chapel, the word primicery having a notarial association. He ruled the palace clergy, had charge of the rites and offices of the chapel, supplied clergy to the royal villas and himself said grace for Charles at meals and gave him the last sacraments. He had also a general charge of divine worship in the empire, and all ecclesiastical suits and business came before him.

An additional advantage in the use of clerics as writing officers was that they could be rewarded or supported by appointment to a clerical benefice, instead of by the grant of some villa or demesne of the fisc. The early Carolingians had some scruple about taking bishops for long periods from their sees, before and even after the ruling of the council of Frankfurt: they tended to provide for their chief notarial officer by the grant of an abbey: Saint-Denis, St Martin's of Tours, Corbie, etc. The grant of a monastic or clerical benefice was in any case an economical form of payment. The royal abbey of Saint-Denis had a particularly close connexion with the early Carolingian writing office. Fulrad, abbot of Saint-Denis, seems to have been arch-chaplain at times under Pepin, and he acted as such for Charles, up till 784. Hincmar's master, Hilduin, was abbot of Saint-Denis from *c.* 814 and of Saint-Germain des Prés in 819: he became arch-chaplain in 822. He fell into disgrace in 830 and was sent off to the abbey of Corvey in Saxony, taking Hincmar with him. Hilduin had his abbey of Saint-Denis restored to him eventually, though not his arch-chaplaincy. He was succeeded as abbot of Saint-Denis by Louis, not a monk of Saint-Denis, but a young noble connected with the Caorlingian house who had been trained in the royal writing office and was acting as arch-chancellor. Besides Saint-Denis, however, other abbeys and bishoprics were held by the arch-chaplain: from 784 to 791 Angilram, bishop of Metz, famous for his knowledge of letters and the church chant, was arch-chaplain; from 791, Hildebald, archbishop of Cologne.

The palace chaplains then were responsible for all documents written for Charles, for letters of appointment to office, letters of instruction to officials and the *missi* and ordinary correspondence. They wrote and issued royal donations, to churches and private individuals, and ecclesiastical privileges: all documents with a rigorous protocol, in the old notarial tradition; the form of Charles's titles and that of dating were all precise. For the latter, the day and month of the calendar in use at the time at Rome were given, the indiction, and the regnal year of Charles as king of the Franks, or as king of Lombardy. The royal seal affixed to their documents was an ancient cameo with the head of a Roman emperor, or, at times, of the Egyptian Serapis.

As to the *cancellarius*, who, Hincmar says, was associated with the *apocrysarius*: the term had been in use in the Merovingian palace (see p. 299), and was familiar to all notaries and ecclesiastics from its use in the Theodosian Code and the Breviary of Alaric, which to all eighth-century lawyers constituted 'Roman law'. In these sources the chancellor, originally no more than a palace usher at Byzantium, had come to mean the notary who admitted witnesses to the law court of Merovingian count or duke, and took down their depositions and issued documents. The chancellor had come to mean a special sort of notary and an important one: but employed out in the countryside, not in the Merovingian palace. When a term was needed for a chief notary among the palace scribes, it was there at hand to supply that of referendary, whose office had been allowed to lapse. Nevertheless, the term chancellor was not taken over at once to designate the arch-chaplain: it was hardly important enough. When Boniface recognized an important diploma for Pepin, performing a notarial act, he was designated 'arch-chancellor'. Moreover, chancellor in the eighth century denoted a notary who could marry, and was hardly suitable as the title for a palace chaplain, however excellent his notarial training and knowledge. It was only gradually, in the ninth century, that the notarial character of the documents written and issued by the authority of the arch-chaplain led to his normal designation as chancellor.

Meanwhile, the use of chancellor for a local notary was not discontinued. They still, as they were stated to have done in the old *Lex Ripuaria*, attended local tribunals and registered *acta*: they were called *cancellarii in iudicio sedentes*. Not only the count in his *mallus* had his chancellor or amanuensis, but counts, bishops

and abbots in their private capacity sought to have such a legal
scribe, called indifferently chancellor, notary or amanuensis. They
authenticated by notarial subscription, often with the formula,
ego N. *rogatus*. Sometimes priests acted as these local chancellors:
whether clerical or lay, the chancellor was *rogatus* to read the act
aloud, affirm its validity and sign it. These chancellors had been
gradually increasing in numbers for nearly two centuries, and a
capitulary of Charlemagne in 803 extended both their numbers
and their activities: the *missi* were enjoined in the capitulary to
create notaries in all places as needed, and to bring a list of them
to the palace. As to the count's chancellor, he disappeared with the
disappearance of the *mallus* in the feudalized society of the tenth
century.

But at the Carolingian court the term chancellor was to survive.
In Hincmar's time the lay notariat had given place to a bureau of
chaplains and a few notaries, headed by an arch-chaplain and
chancellor. The chancellor's name proclaimed him a lawyer, but,
in fact, he too was now usually a priest. Ithier, protonotary or
chancellor, held this post till 776, and was abbot of St Martin of
Tours; Rado and Ercanbald, who was chancellor 797 till 813, were
in the notarial bureau and became higher clergy; Jeremie, with
a similar career behind him, became archbishop of Sens. The
arch-chaplain had, in Charles's day, been monk or cleric by
career and risen to be abbot or bishop, but he had had a notarial
training as specialized and precise as that of the chancellor who
was, in fact, his subordinate. The arch-chaplain was, indeed, a
lawyer, and the chancellor in the royal writing office was, in fact,
a priest. In the course of the ninth century the title of arch-chaplain gave way to that of chancellor, who was normally a bishop,
and always the royal authenticating officer. He kept the king's
ring for sealing, a technical means of authenticating proper to
the king as layman, perhaps more suitable to a chancellor not
technically a notary, and possibly easier of general administration
when documents became more numerous. When the royal writing
office, which it is now proper to call a chancery since its head was
the episcopal chancellor, issued a large number of documents,
some of them not of the first importance, the royal seal could be
affixed by a subordinate in the department without requiring the
authenticating signature of the chancellor. The old notarial tradition continued, however, to dictate the terms of the protocol.

Charles's provincial government in the old *regnum Francorum*,
and in his newly conquered lands, rested upon the count and the
county. The Latin *comes* appears in grants and codes in the Ger-

manic form of *graf*, Latinized as *grafio*. The county (*comitatus*)
was synonymous with the Merovingian *pagus*, the Germanic *gau*,
and ancestor of the modern French *pays*. Counts are found from
one end of the empire to another. Other sharers in local government were also addressed by Charles at the head of his capitularies
and letters, some as holders of immunities, others as lesser officials,
subordinate to the count. In his preambles Charles thus addresses
bishops, abbots, dukes, counts, vicars, *centenarii* or hundredmen.

Bishops and abbots had great estates and immunities which
forbade to the count the right of entry: within them the spiritual
holder of the immunity did justice and collected certain royal
taxes, keeping them for himself. Bishops and abbots were, in a
sense, royal officers, for Charles appointed them, though he could
not remove them, as he could the count: he could, however,
transfer bishops from one see to another. Bishops and abbots
had not merely a spiritual charge: they had great experience of
affairs.

As to the secular officers: the word 'duke' still connoted military
leadership, and only in Italy was a duchy a territorial unit, except
in the case of Le Mans, which Charles created in 790 for his son
Charles. The old administrative unit, the *pagus*, was everywhere
headed by a great noble called in Italy the *gasthold*, in Aquitania
the *saio*, and elsewhere the count; where Charles introduced
Frankish officers in newly conquered lands, Lombard, Saxon or
Spanish, these were always termed counts. Within his county the
count was Charles's deputy, with all the powers and obligations
such an office implied: fiscal and judicial authority, and the administration of the royal ban. The count was responsible for delivering
to the treasury the product of direct taxes and tolls, and the money
compositions for offences, as also for publishing capitularies and
royal instructions, carrying out public works and levying troops.
He had to help him a *vice-comes* whom he appointed but the
emperor approved, and vicars or *centenarii*, who administered
smaller regions within the county: the term vicars was used of
his agents in the central Frankish regions, *centenarii* among the
eastern Franks. To render his accounts and bring with him the
funds collected the count spent some weeks annually at the palace,
and this, apart from attending the general assembly. His office,
finally, was revocable at will, though such revocations were exceptional and the same count might well hold office for twenty or
thirty years. Sometimes his son, or a member of his family, succeeded him, but not as of right. Occasionally, though rarely, a
count would hold more than one county.

The end of Charles's reign was shadowed not only by advancing age, but the loss of two of his sons in the prime of life: men who had been trained for kingship in the tough, Carolingian school. The Act of Thionville for the division of the kingdom proved useless. In the summer of 810 Charles's sister Gisela and his daughter Rohtrud both died: on 8 July, his son Pepin, thirty-three years old and a good fighter, and in December 811, his eldest son, Charles. For Pepin's kingdom of Italy, Charles provided by sending Adalard, abbot of Corbie and his brother, Wala; to Charles he had given no sub-kingdom, destining him to rule on his own death the heart of the Frankish lands. In that summer of 811 Charles had made his own will, bequeathing his personal possessions; two-thirds of these precious objects, then stored in his *camera*, were bequeathed to twenty-one cities of his empire and were to be retained in the *camera* deposited in twenty-one coffers with the name of the city-legatee on each, till his death. The remaining third, whose use Charles reserved to himself for life and which included his personal robes, ornaments, tapestries and the silver table engraved with the map of the world, were to be shared between Charles's descendants and the metropolitan churches; Charles's library of manuscript books was to be sold for the benefit of the poor. Twenty-seven bishops, counts and abbots signed the will and became its executors. To provide adequately for the division of the empire was, however, less simple. Charles deferred the decision till increasing illness made it imperative in 813.

In the autumn of the year 813, the matter of his recognition as emperor had been settled: the Greek envoys had saluted him emperor; the Frankish lay nobles, using Einhard as their spokesman, urged him to settle the succession. Accordingly, on Sunday, 11 September, Charles crowned his son Louis in the chapel of the palace of Aix; he took the crown placed ready upon the altar, made the thirty-five-year-old son Louis a homily on the duties of Christian sovereignty, and placed the crown upon his head. The crowd acclaimed Louis as emperor, the mass was celebrated and the day finished with a royal banquet; at the same assembly at Aix Charles also formally recognized Pepin's young son, Bernhard, as king of Italy. Some days later, he commanded Louis, while preserving his imperial title, to return to his duties as king of Aquitania; Charles intended to continue till his death the central rule of his empire. The succession seemed reasonably secure, for though Charles had had children by Frankish ladies since the death of his wife Liutgard (children including Drogo,

THE CAROLINGIANS

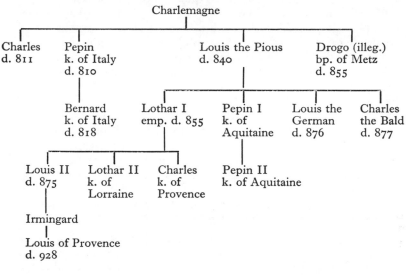

Charlemagne

Charles	Pepin	Louis the Pious	Drogo (illeg.)
d. 811	k. of Italy	d. 840	bp. of Metz
	d. 810		d. 855

Bernard	Lothar I	Pepin I	Louis the	Charles
k. of Italy	emp. d. 855	k. of	German	the Bald
d. 818		Aquitaine	d. 876	d. 877

Louis II	Lothar II	Charles	Pepin II
d. 875	k. of	k. of	k. of Aquitaine
	Lorraine	Provence	

Irmingard

Louis of Provence
d. 928

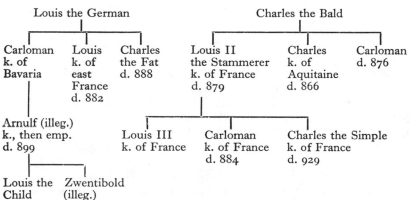

Louis the German — Charles the Bald

Carloman	Louis	Charles	Louis II	Charles	Carloman
k. of	k. of	the Fat	the Stammerer	k. of	d. 876
Bavaria	east	d. 888	k. of France	Aquitaine	
	France		d. 879	d. 866	
	d. 882				

Arnulf (illeg.)
k., then emp.
d. 899

Louis III	Carloman	Charles the Simple
k. of France	k. of France	k. of France
	d. 884	d. 929

Louis the	Zwentibold
Child	(illeg.)

the future archbishop of Metz, and Thierry, born when Charles was sixty-five years old), they were illegitimate and too young to endanger a peaceful succession. Charles lived, however, only a few months after the ceremony of September 813: he was gravely ill from November onwards, on 27 January 814, he sent for Hildebald, his arch-chaplain, to give him the last sacraments, and he died the day following.

Funerals followed rapidly on death in the middle ages: Louis was in Aquitania and there was no question of waiting: Charles was buried the day he died. The church had long followed Roman law in prohibiting burial within a building or church, but in 813 a council of Aix had relaxed the prohibition in favour of bishops, abbots, good priests and the faithful laity; it was decided to bury Charles in the chapel of the palace at Aix. A great white marble sarcophagus, its side carved in deep relief with the raising of Proserpine by Pluto assisted by Minerva (according to the poem by Claudian), was selected for Charles's tomb: it was a very fine monument, and its subject, with its classical parable of the resurrection, not too unfitting. A grave was dug beneath the tiled floor of the chapel, the sarcophagus lowered into it, the ceremony concluded according to Alcuin's sacramentary, and the flooring replaced. A month later, when Louis arrived from Aquitaine, he ordered a monument to be raised above the tomb, with a figure of Charles and this inscription:

> Beneath this tomb rests the body of Charles the great and orthodox emperor who nobly extended the kingdom of the Franks and ruled prosperously for forty-seven years. He died seventy years old in the year 814 A.D., the seventh of the indiction, the fifth day before the kalends of February.

Time has not spared, however, the monument raised by Louis (probably the model of a small classical building, with columns, in gilded wood or stone, and with an inscription: Einhard speaks of its 'gilded arch'). Even the exact place of burial is unknown, though the grave would probably have been made in the centre of the basilica, as the most honourable position. The northmen sacked and burned Aix in 881, and the monument with the inscription to the great emperor would not have escaped them.

BIBLIOGRAPHICAL NOTE

As for chapter xvii: see also F. L. Ganshof, *The Imperial Coronation of Charlemagne: Theories and Facts*, 1949: G. Barraclough, *The Mediaeval Empire: Idea and Reality*, 1950: E. H. Kantorowicz, 'Laudes Regiae', *Univ. of California Publications in History*, vol. xxxiii (1946): P. E. Schramm, *Herrschaftszeichen und Staatssymbolik*, in Schrifter der Mon. Germ. Hist. Bd. 13, 1954–: R. Folz, *L'Idée d'Empire en Occident du Ve au XVIc siècle*, 1953: H. Fichtenau, *The Carolingian Empire*, 1957. See also, W. Ullmann on the translation of the Roman Empire from east to west, in E.H.R. 1957, p. 522, and his views on the *Renovatio Romani Imperii*, E.H.R. 1956, p. 635; also H. Fichtenau, *Das Karolingische Imperium : sociale und geistige Problematik eines Grossreiches*, Zurich, 1949; H. F. Haefele, *Notkeri Balbuli Gesta Karoli Magni*, M. G. H. Scriptores, Berlin, 1959; D. Obolensky, *The Bogomils; a study of Balkan Neo-Manichaeism*, Cambridge, 1948 (for link with Cathars).

CHAPTER XXI

THE BYZANTINE EMPIRE FROM 711 TO 912: THE ISAURIAN EMPERORS, THE AMORIANS AND THE RISE OF THE MACEDONIAN DYNASTY

THE Heraclian dynasty in the seventh century had halted the advance of Islam: it had saved eastern Europe for the Greco-Roman tradition and afforded a barrier behind which the new barbarian nations of the west could be taught the Christian faith and Latin civilization; it had defended in Byzantium itself that hearth of light and fire that was to irradiate the Balkan Slavs, Bulgars and Russians. The East Roman empire had been in this respect an effective guardian to the new Europe. But while in the seventh century the Heraclian emperors had been forced to concentrate on the defence of their eastern frontier, the Slav races had infiltrated the Balkans (see p. 485) and settled there, a heathen population. They had had no civilizing contacts with the old Roman empire, with the Frankish empire mainly the contacts of frontier wars and raids, and with the Byzantine empire none at all. The Huns and the Avars had imposed a massive barrier. The seventh century, therefore, the century of the Slav immigration into Illyricum and the Balkan provinces, had brought to those lands and even to Constantinople a certain deterioration in culture. In Constantinople, towards the end of the seventh century, revolutions succeeded one another, after the assassination of Justinian II as well as before, and in the Balkans massacres and the capture of towns multiplied.

Help was at hand, however, with the advent to power of Leo, *strategos* of Anatolia, at a moment of extreme danger to the capital. The Arab army had invaded Asia Minor and was closing in on the Straits and Constantinople; but Leo also marched on the city, had himself proclaimed emperor in 717, and was at once supported by the senate, the court officials and the army. Leo III's family had its origins in northern Syria: he proved not only a great general, but the founder of a dynasty, the Isaurian, whose rulers' outlook was to some extent concentrated on the eastern frontier. Though they did attempt to check the Slavs on the north, Leo III and his successors all saw as the greatest of Byzantine problems the need of defence against, and advance against, the Arab forces of Baghdad, Mosul and Egypt.

Leo III's first action after his coronation was to deliver the city of Constantinople from the third and last of the Arab attacks, in the summer of 717. The Arab general Maslamah actually crossed the Hellespont and brought a force against the walls of Constantinople, while a great Arab fleet besieged it by sea. The use of the new Greek fire, and the death of the Arab admiral, defeated the naval attack: while hunger, and a final intervention of Bulgarians on the Greek side, defeated the Arab land forces. In Asia Minor also the Byzantine army persevered in hard fighting, repelling an Arab invasion every year till Leo and his son Constantine won the decisive victory at Akroinon in 739, after which the Arabs were expelled from Asia Minor once for all. Constantine V (741–775) carried the wars against the Arabs beyond the frontiers of Asia Minor, the establishment of the Abbasid dynasty in 750 causing strife in Islam and favouring his offensive. He entered Arab territory in Syria in 746, and established the Greco-Arab frontier on a line running roughly from the south-eastern angle of the Black Sea to the Gulf of Antioch, thus holding for the Greeks the cities of Melitene and Mopsuestia: moreover, the Greeks had reconquered Cyprus, and Constantine's fleet cleared the seas surrounding it, and those of the east Mediterranean, of Arab pirate shipping. He and his father had thus stabilized the situation on the eastern frontier and safeguarded the Asiatic themes; guerilla warfare continued, but for 200 years the Greek frontier in Asia Minor was substantially the same.

In the Balkans also the Isaurians fought hard, though less successfully. The Bulgars had established themselves south of the great bend of the Danube (see p. 487) and in 755 Constantine V found himself at leisure to deal with them. He planted in Thrace colonies of Armenians and Syrians, taken from the captured cities of Melitene and Theodosiopolis: he built a line of frontier fortresses, including Philippopolis and Sardica, and he led many campaigns against the Bulgars, who were themselves at times divided by faction. In 777 the Bulgar khan himself fled to Constantinople and accepted baptism: a vigorous offensive might have made the Bulgars permanently subject to the emperor: but danger from them seemed at the time small, and the opportunity was missed. The early Isaurians kept the Bulgars in check, but never established complete control over them.

The internal administration of the empire also profited from Isaurian measures. The dangerous frequency of attempts to seize the throne before their rise to power led Leo and Constantine to make every effort to establish a dynastic succession in their own family. Leo associated Constantine with him on the throne as early as 720, and had him crowned by the patriarch; Constantine in his turn associated with him his son Leo IV, while he had his four other sons made caesars. Imperial edicts also dealt with the law, the army and finance. Leo III issued a new legal code, the *Ecloga*, which sought to modify certain principles of Roman law by applying Christian standards to private morals and family life; this code not only became the working code of the Byzantines at the time but, mainly through translations, was influential later among the Slavs. To secure also the safety of the frontiers and the recruitment of the army, Leo III extended and reorganized the system of themes. In Asia Minor, to diminish possible danger from an overstrong *strategos* in charge of too large a theme, and to secure better administration, he subdivided the Anatolian theme, and the Opsikion (which faced the capital across the Straits). Soon afterwards, themes were created for Macedonia and Cephallenia in the Balkans, and, at the beginning of the ninth century, for the Peloponnese and Thessalonica. Measures were also taken to fill the empty treasury, such as the 'doubling of the indiction', which secured in the year September 727–8 a double payment of all levies collected at the indiction. (The indiction was originally a corn tax levied by the emperor Constantine I in 312, and reassessed every fifteen years: for its use as a dating cycle, see p. 13.) New taxes were also imposed and collected with a harshness that filled the treasury. The army was better paid and better disciplined; contingents from all the themes were welded into a single imperial army. The peasant of the eastern provinces also profited from the Isaurians' solicitude for recruitment: efforts were made to halt the development of the great demesnes and prevent the disappearance of the small freeholder, and also the communities of free peasants working their village lands collectively for their own profit. The condition of the peasant population improved under Isaurian rule.

The iconoclast controversy begun under the Isaurian emperors is now recognized as not merely a quarrel about the use of icons (religious pictures or statues, as of Christ or the saints), but as a symptom of the orientalization of the eastern empire in the eighth century. Byzantium now faced east. The Arab invasions had deprived her of certain eastern provinces, and, in the seventh century, had even menaced Asia Minor; Arab fleets threatened Byzantine sea trade in the east Mediterranean. The danger of attack on

Constantinople was real. Imperial attention was focussed on the
defence of the eastern frontier, and though the danger from religious dissidence in Egypt and the once Byzantine parts of Syria and
Armenia was lessened by their permanent loss to Islam, yet the
religious views of the endangered and fighting provinces of the
eastern frontier acquired a peculiar importance, with the advent of
the Isaurian dynasty even a dominant importance, at Constantinople.

The question of the use of icons to the Christians of Asia Minor,
Syria and Armenia was not merely a question of the superstitious
use of icons, but of the use of icons at all. It involved deep questions of theology as well as the Persian and west Asiatic use of
abstract art-forms and pattern, rather than naturalistic representation of the external world. For the dispute about icons was in one
respect a continuation of the old Christological controversy; the
east had farther found it easy to worship the godhead of Christ,
the one nature and that divine, and had not accepted readily the
Christological decisions of Chalcedon. The use of the sacred icons
stressed the human nature of Christ as against the divine, which
could not, as the iconoclasts claimed, be represented at all. Two
centuries earlier, the mosaics of St Apollinare-in-Classe had represented the transfigured Christ on Mount Tabor by the symbolic
cross, not by the human figure: but had not hesitated to represent
St Apollinare and the apostles as men, according to the artist's
imagination. The iconoclasts now desired to ban all such humanistic representation. The influence of Arab practice and Persian art
on the iconoclasts is now accepted; the buildings of the Isaurian
emperors were inspired by the architects and influence of Baghdad.
The emperor Theophilus (829–842) built himself a new palace on
the Asiatic side of the Bosphorus in imitation of the caliph's palace
at Baghdad, and eighth- and ninth-century Constantinople came
to rival Baghdad in general appearance. Moreover Islamic monotheism and the prohibition of the use of the human figure in the
mosque and in Islamic art could not but influence the Christians
in the eastern provinces: it has been claimed that the caliph's
ban (723) on the use of icons in Christian churches in his lands
occasioned the iconoclastic movement in the empire.

Apart from the general persecution of those who defended the
use of images (called iconodules by the iconoclasts), the movement
had other important results. It involved a particular struggle of
the emperors with the monks throughout the greater part of the
empire: some monasteries had icons to which the populace were
peculiarly devoted, and the monks defended the devotion: more-

over, the question of military recruitment was affected by the traditional freedom to join a monastery: all these causes explain the iconoclasts' efforts as directed peculiarly against the monks. The movement blackened the reputation of the Isaurian emperors, in spite of the fact that their military exploits saved Europe. It delayed also attempts at the conversion of the Slav races by the Greek church: and it contributed to the drifting apart of the churches of Rome and Constantinople. The Greek church was rendered all but helpless by the bitter imperial persecution: the Roman church openly reprobated the Isaurian emperors for their ban on images. When the long controversy was over, the process of estrangement had gone far; the popes were no longer, in the secular sphere, the subjects of the Byzantine emperor and synods in the western empire they had erected were attacking the cult of images at the very moment of the orthodox victory in the east.

The struggle began with a public pronouncement of Leo III against images in 726, and the removal and breaking of images of Christ in the capital and elsewhere. Popular riots followed in Greece and the Cyclades, and pope Gregory II openly protested, excommunicating the Italian exarch and denouncing iconoclasm as heresy. In 730 the emperor Leo III issued a formal edict against image worship, and deposed the patriarch Germanus when he refused to sign it; he replaced him by the *syncellus* Anastasius, and persecution began. The patriarchal schools, as likely to prove obstinate, were closed. In Italy, opposition was general, and a Roman synod of 731 excommunicated the iconoclasts. Leo III replied by transferring to the jurisdiction of the patriarch of Constantinople those dioceses which hitherto had been under the secular rule of Byzantium but the spiritual jurisdiction of the pope, i.e. Calabria, Sicily, Crete and Illyricum. This action was peculiarly resented at Rome, and for several centuries proved an obstacle to the restoration of good relations between the two patriarchates: for when the iconoclast quarrel was at length ended, the papacy had acknowledged the Frankish emperor, and the east Roman sovereign refused, not unnaturally, to restore the dioceses.

Constantine V continued the struggle by an astute use of propaganda, patronage and persecution. He transported to Thrace colonies of Syrian and Armenian iconoclasts, he brought others to Constantinople, he wrote theological treatises himself. The army, mainly recruited in the eastern provinces, supported him, as did many of the secular clergy, including a number of bishops. In 753 more than 300 bishops assembled at the palace of Hieria across the Bosphorus (they did not however include the patriarchs of

Alexandria, Antioch, Jerusalem or Rome), condemned devotion to icons as 'a thing hateful and abominable', and excommunicated those who defended it. Fierce persecution followed next year: at Constantinople images in churches were broken, frescoes painted over, mosaics destroyed, paintings on wood scraped down and writing defending the use of icons burnt. Image worshippers, and particularly the monks, suffered arrest, imprisonment, exile, physical injury and in some cases, death. The monastic order seemed destroyed in Constantinople; but the iconoclast victory cost the empire the loss of all but southern Italy. In 751 the Lombard Aistulf had taken Ravenna and the exarchate, and was about to threaten Rome; the pope could get no help from the iconoclast Constantine V and in 754 made his journey to Pepin, seeking help. The Franco-Roman alliance that was to break the old relations of Rome and Byzantium was initiated. When the old emperor Constantine died in 775, nothing had been done to retrieve the position in Italy and the internal struggle over the icons still reft the empire.

Leo IV, surnamed after his mother, a princess of the Khazars of south Russia, Leo the Khazar, continued with some success his father's wars against the Arabs, and against the image-worshippers: though here he was affected by the as yet secret devotion of his Athenian wife, Irene, to the cause of the monks, and used less violence. He died in 780, leaving the succession to his ten-year-old son, Constantine VI (780–797) and the regency to Irene (797–802).

The orthodox reaction under Irene could not come as a sudden *volte-face*, for the army and many officials were still iconoclast, the emperor's brothers, the caesars, the puppets of ambitious rivals, and the need of military action against the Arabs still acute. Irene intrigued against her rivals, made peace with the Arabs in 783, approached Charlemagne with the offer of the marriage of his daughter to the young Constantine, and sent the logothete Staurakios to lead an expedition to Greece against the Slavs. The campaign had some success and Staurakios celebrated a triumph at Constantinople and remained Irene's principal adviser.

Meanwhile the empress prepared for the holding of a council which should disavow iconoclasm: she approached pope Hadrian I, who promised to send legates: she sought to win over the army. In 787 the council met at Nicaea, vindicated the monks, and restored the cult of images, distinguishing however between the veneration (*proskunesis*) which might be offered to them, and the adoration (*latreia*) which might be offered only to God. The empress signed the canons and there were shouts of acclamation for the new Constantine and the new Helena. But the reversal of iconoclast policy was only part of Irene's personal struggle for power, and for that she needed the removal of her son Constantine, who was now seventeen and showing himself a vigorous leader in wars against Arabs and Bulgars. She persuaded Constantine to disgrace and blind one of the generals, which lost him the support of the army: she inspired him with distrust of his brothers, and suggested to him the blinding of the eldest and the cutting out of the tongues of the other four: she encouraged him to send his wife into a convent and form an illicit union with his mistress: the monks and the devout were scandalized. In July 797 she had Constantine himself seized and blinded, and was herself proclaimed empress. As empress, she could lavish favours on the monks, but could not control the intrigues for the succession that seethed in the palace (see p. 419). The treasury was exhausted, the realm disturbed and disorderly, and when Irene died in 802, her successor, the logothete Nicephoras, found it necessary to carry through a reorganization of the finances which involved the return of many monastic lands to the fisc and the abolition of many immunities.

Neither Nicephoras I (802–811) nor Michael I (811–813) openly renewed the campaign against images: this was left for Leo V (813–820), who proved an able defender of the empire. He defeated the Bulgars at Mesembria in 813, and after the death of the terrible khan, Krum, made peace with his successor. Confident through his military success, and doubtlessly encouraged by the news of the anti-iconodule synods of the west, pre-eminent among them the council of Frankfurt, which had denounced the council of 787, he now openly declared for iconoclasm. The cult of images was still, in fact, displeasing to the army; but when Leo ordered the acts of the council of 753 to be put in force again, he met with opposition, especially from the monks. That of Theodore, abbot of the Studite house in Constantinople, was particularly notable: he was a learned man, and respected as a good spiritual father to his monks and the upholder of the tradition of St Basil. He was to be the spearhead of the opposition to the later iconoclast emperors and four times exiled in the course of the struggle. He now declared at a palace conference that ecclesiastical matters were the proper business of priests and monks, and secular administration that of the emperor. This was a notable denial of the dominant interpretation of the imperial ruler as another Constantine, a thirteenth apostle, ruler in things secular and sacred. A claim for ecclesiastical independence, as such, was not new, for it had been made by Maximus the Confessor; but Theodore's exposition of it was notable and evidence of the long bitterness of the quarrel over the icons: evidence also of the dislike of the church of Constantinople of being ruled by emperors who held views, not of the old Greco-Roman church, but of her more Asiatic provinces.

Though Theodore the Studite was exiled in 814 for his violent opposition to imperial iconoclasm, this policy was, in fact, less intransigent than it had been earlier. When the council of Constantinople met in 815, it proscribed image worship, but affirmed that the icons were not idols, thus echoing, consciously or otherwise, the doctrine of Charlemagne and his council of Frankfurt. Michael II (820–829) was iconoclast in background and outlook; but he desired to mitigate the sharpness of controversy and therefore banned all discussion of the veneration of images. His son and successor, Theophilus (829–842), was intelligent, learned, and ready to become the patron of art and letters; he enriched the capital and fostered the higher studies at his court. In his reign the example and influence of the caliph's court at Baghdad was strong in Constantinople, and with regard for Arab learning and science went regard for Arab hostility to images. In 837 Theophilus appointed his son's tutor, the greatest of the Byzantine scholars who admired Baghdad and deprecated veneration paid to the icons, John the Grammarian, to the patriarchal throne, and a short persecution of the iconodules followed. But when Theophilus died in 842, iconoclasm was found to have died with him. Michael III (842–867) succeeded his father while still a child, and it fell to the empress-regent, Theodora, to accept her counsellors' advice and restore the orthodox teaching about images. The patriarch John refused to countenance such a move and was accused of sorcery. He was sent off to a monastery, the monk Methodius was made patriarch, and a council was held in February 843. The polite fiction that the late emperor had renounced his errors on his deathbed was accepted by the bishops, the veneration of images solemnly re-established, the exiles returned, prisoners were set free, and a triumphal procession made on the first Sunday in Lent, to the church of Santa Sophia, to offer thanksgiving for the return to orthodoxy. The day closed with a great feast given by Theodora at the palace. The orthodox church still keeps the first Sunday in Lent as the festival of orthodoxy.

The Isaurian and early Macedonian emperors were all confronted by a double enemy: the Slavs, now penetrating their Balkan provinces and settling in great numbers, and the fiercely hostile Islamic forces of the east, north Africa and the Mediterranean islands, the bases of their pirate fleet. Byzantine relations with the

Slavs are mainly dealt with in chapter xxv: the wars of the Amorians and the early Macedonians with the Arabs were felt at the time to counter the greater danger and to be the supreme Byzantine task: their history is for a time a main strand in the skein of Byzantine foreign policy.

The wars of Byzantium with the Arabs in the first half of the ninth century were nevertheless affected by her relations with the Bulgars, whom she found a desperate enemy up till 820, but with whom she then made a thirty years' peace. Since the death of Harun ar-Rashid in 809, the Abbasid empire had been weakened by civil war and revolts against the heterodox caliph, al-Ma'mun, but Theophilus' forces were still no greater than those of the Arabs, and a struggle over the eastern provinces lasted most of his reign. The caliph's army invaded Cappadocia in 831, and al-Ma'mun, three times invaded Asia Minor and took the passes in the Taurus that commanded access to the Anatolian themes. Possession of the passes in the Taurus and Anti-Taurus was, throughout these frontier wars, of the greatest strategic importance to both sides. Against al-Mu'tasim, al-Ma'mun's successor, Theophilus had more success, invading the country round the head waters of the Euphrates; but in 838 the Saracens retaliated by launching a great expedition and taking Theophilus' birthplace, Amorium, on the borders of the Opsikion theme and Anatolia; the Byzantines, however, pushed them back beyond the Taurus. When Michael III succeeded Theophilus in 842 as a boy of four, the eastern war languished: his ministers were no generals, but the caliphate also was weak. Four caliphs were murdered between 861 and 869: but the emperor Michael himself was also murdered by his favourite, Basil the Macedonian, in 867. The twenty-five years of his reign had helped to heal the wounds of the iconoclastic struggle, and had seen the beginning of a revival of letters and secular science at Constantinople: but no great military success.

Basil I (867–886) had climbed to power by violence and treachery; but his accession marks the spring and flowering time of the medieval Byzantine empire. He founded a dynasty that ruled the empire for nearly 200 years (867–1056). The religious troubles were over: learning flourished through fresh study of the old Greek masters and access to the mathematical knowledge of Baghdad: buildings, mosaics, painting, illumination took on a peculiar beauty: and the military skill of the Macedonian emperors and their generals recovered some of the provinces lost to the caliphs and added military glory to internal recovery. The Macedonian period in Byzantine history saw the fine flower of a culture. Byzantium was a buttress to Europe: and if she was in less direct contact with the west than she had been in the age of Justinian, she was increasingly in a position to pass on Greco-Roman civilization to the Slavs.

Basil I was of Armenian stock, though his family had settled in Macedonia. He had been groom to caesar Bardas, and murdered his friend and patron in 866: he had been made associate emperor by Michael, and in 867 he had Michael murdered by a companion when he was in a drunken sleep. Basil was fifty-five years old and a hard drinker himself, a fine man to look at, though of only mediocre education. As emperor he proved intelligent, hardworking, a good administrator and a fine military leader. The empire found economic prosperity under his rule: successful warfare in those days paid immediate dividends in loot, tribute and ransoms, and Basil's wars against the Saracens were successful. In the reigns of Basil I and his son Leo VI the eastern frontier was pushed eastwards: in Basil's reign Egypt and Khurasan had become independent of the caliph of Baghdad, as had some small principalities on the frontier, like the amirates of Tarsus and Melitene; and the Byzantines profited from their enemies' divisions. Between 871 and 882 they reconquered the passes in the Taurus which enabled them to pour into Syria; in 872 Basil defeated the Paulicians of the upper Euphrates country: they were an iconoclast sect who had not returned to orthodoxy and their position on the frontier made them potential allies of the Saracens. Basil suffered a Saracen defeat in 873: but when he died in 886 he had extended his frontier, thrown a bridge over the upper Euphrates and much improved the Greek strategic position. Byzantium was to gain also from the caliph's recognition in 886 of Ashot Bagratuni as king of Armenia; he sent him a royal crown and saluted him as 'king of kings'. An independent Armenia would be a useful buffer state for Byzantium, and soon after Basil also sent Ashot the Great splendid gifts and a royal crown. While the Byzantine emperor professed particular friendship for Armenia, he usually intrigued with the small principalities subject to her, with a view to the possible future annexation of Armenia.

In the west, Basil's efforts against the Saracens met with mixed success: he could do little against them in Sicily, but in the Adriatic he defended the small Slav states of Dalmatia and kept the allegiance of Venice. Through the alliance of Basil, the western emperor Louis II, and the pope, the Franks were enabled to take Bari in 871; but the Saracens took Malta in 870, and in Sicily they held all the fortified towns except Taormina and Syracuse. When Louis II died the Byzantines took over the defence of Bari (876). The struggle with the Arabs was hard, though the Greeks in 880 regained Tarentum. It was on the cards that south Italy, Sicily, the southern shores of the Adriatic, the Aegean islands and Cyprus might all pass permanently to Islam, like the southern and eastern coasts of the Mediterranean, and it was mainly the hard fighting of the Byzantine empire under the Macedonians that prevented this further Arab conquest, though the Greeks fought for a time with varying success. In Sicily, Syracuse fell to the Arabs after a long siege in 878: but the Byzantine fleet appeared in the Tyrrhenian Sea and won so resounding a victory over the Arab fleet near Lipari that Capua, Naples, Salerno and Benevento accepted the Byzantine protectorate. In 885 the Greek general Nicephorus Phokas, grandfather of the future emperor, campaigned in Calabria and Apulia, winning many towns from the Saracens, and attaching the small Lombard states more firmly to Byzantium; two new themes, the themes of Lombardy and of Calabria, were created in south Italy. In 887 the Greek fleet captured Cyprus and held it for seven years.

On the shore of the Adriatic, Basil's success was no less important for the future. He had sent a Greek fleet in 868 to deliver Ragusa (Dubrovnik) from the Arabs, and with the co-operation of Venice the small towns and Slav settlements of the Dalmatian coast were defended and restored to order. The Croats and other Dalmatian Slavs returned to Byzantine Christianity and Byzantine vassalage; the orthodox bishoprics founded in south Italy contributed to the Byzantinization of south Italy, and to the spread of Greek Christianity among the Slavs. On a smaller scale, and contending with an alien civilization, Basil I, like Justinian, had made a reconquest of Italy.

Basil I died in 886, and was succeeded by Leo VI, 'the Wise' (886–912): he continued the Saracen struggle, though with less success than his father. The Saracens had held Crete since 826, and from this base in particular their raiding fleets harried the Aegean islands, now deserted by their inhabitants, and the coasts of the Peloponnese, Macedonia and Thrace. They had retaken Cyprus, and in 902 a fleet of corsairs penetrated the straits and threatened to attack Constantinople. Then, hesitating to embark on an attack that could scarcely have succeeded without an army and a long siege, they sailed on to the rich port of Thessalonica and took it with a brief assault. Besides an enormous plunder, they carried off many thousands of young men and women and sold them as slaves in the markets of Chandax (Crete) or Tripoli. So great a disaster necessitated the manning of a Byzantine fleet specially to retrieve it. It was led by Himerius: but nothing was achieved, for the corsairs, taking Thessalonica, had taken many more ships. The Byzantine fleet was again defeated in 911 near Samos, and left the Saracens in command of the Aegean, while the loss of Reggio had given them control of the straits of Messina in 901. They took Taormina in 902 and ruled undisputed in Sicily; the amir of Qairawan even spoke derisively of undertaking a new expedition against the city of 'this foolish old Peter'. Byzantium was too busy with Bulgaria to play the part of protector of Italy: but the wave of Saracen success had, as it proved, reached its high water mark. Their eventual defeat in south Italy and Sicily was to be at the hands, however, not of the Byzantine emperor, but of the Normans.

Meantime, at home, the Hellenized Byzantine empire had stable government, economic prosperity and a splendid court. The *basileus*, still the Roman *imperator*, was the supreme war leader and the authoritative guardian and exponent of the law. He was the *autokrator*: his power, regarded as of divine origin, was absolute, although the empire was never totalitarian, and ecclesiastical and constitutional limitations of the imperial will developed in course of time. The emperor, when he appeared in public at the solemn seasons, wore the ceremonial garments prescribed by a rigid court etiquette: a long, straight robe stiff with embroidery and sparkling with precious stones, a jewelled crown and purple sandals. 'By the beauty of ceremonial', wrote Constantine Porphyrogenitus, 'the imperial power appears more splendid, as in a surrounding glory, and strikes with awe and wonder both strangers and subjects.' Around the emperor, the officials of palace and empire moved in a splendid circle: the old civil hierarchy of the Roman emperors and Justinian had never been abolished but had developed, in the 300 years between Justinian and the Macedonians, and become orientalized. Titles of honour and of official rank were now most often in Greek, though Latin ones like *caesar*, *magister*, *protoasecretis*, *cartularius*, and so on, also survived. The central government was organized in departments; in the countryside the old provinces had been replaced by the new organization of the themes. The civil servants of central and local government were well trained and well disciplined, and recruited for the most part from the senatorial class into which all holders of office passed. Greek was the sole administrative language.

A splendid industry and foreign trade made the empire rich, and Constantinople, to men of the ninth century, a city of almost fabulous beauty and riches. From the workshops and markets of the capital flowed a stream of luxury goods and articles of the finest workmanship, to Venice and north Italy and the Franks, to Naples and Rome and Marseilles, to Thessalonica, second greatest city of the empire; to the Slav hinterlands, and, by the Russian rivers to Kiev and the Baltic. A no less important trade flowed eastward, to Alexandria and, through Asia Minor, to Syria, Armenia and Baghdad, bearing the furs of Russia and Scandinavia, amber and slaves, the fine linens of Egypt, and cargoes of timber and grain for the east Mediterranean ports. Constantinople, with her merchants and her sea captains and her bankers, was the nodal point in all this web of trade. The industrial gilds of the city, the metal workers, painters, builders, workers in marble, the silversmiths, the craftsmen who worked in gold or silver or cloisonné ornaments, the weavers and embroiderers of silken textiles and ceremonial garments, the illuminators of manuscripts, each gild with its strict monopoly and each regulated by the prefect of the city, were at once evidence and creators of wealth. Economic prosperity went side by side with the efflorescence of letters in the ninth century.

The first two Macedonian sovereigns gave much attention to the restoration of orderly government and the reform of the law. Basil I sometimes himself presided in his supreme law court, supervised the recruitment to the civil service and sought to protect the small landholder. He found the laws of Justinian old and unsuited to his times, and those of the *Ecloga* in some respects useless and even bad: he desired to carry through a great new codification of Roman law, but only succeeded in issuing two preparatory manuals, the *Prochiron* (879) and the *Epanagogè* (886). In his desire to secure the succession of his dynasty, and not entirely for selfish reasons, Basil's vindication of the imperial authority gave rise, for the first time in Byzantine history, to the idea of 'legitimate' succession, i.e. through an imperial family whose members were *porphyrogeniti*, born in the porphyry palace of the emperors, a condition which no usurper could satisfy.

Both this new insistence on hereditary succession to the empire, and the effort at administrative and legal reform, were carried further by Basil's son, Leo VI. He married four times to secure a legal male heir, though both the Byzantine church and civil law reprobated a third marriage, and forbade a fourth. Plots to secure the succession had, however, developed, and in 903 Leo narrowly escaped assassination; when his mistress, the 'black-eyed' Zoe, gave him a son in 905, he married her and had her crowned empress, though this cost a struggle with the patriarch, Nicholas, whom he had to depose. He appealed to the pope about his marriage, and Rome did not condemn this fourth imperial marriage; the child, Constantine Porphyrogenitus, was crowned co-emperor in 911, and succeeded his father in 912 as Constantine VII. Leo VI's reign saw an outburst of legal activity: he issued a complete new code, the *Basilics*, in sixty books, between 887 and 893, together with many novels. One of these, the *Book of the Prefect*, regulated the status of the industrial gilds at Constantinople, and is evidence both of the complex organization of the city and its centralized control by the government. The themes, henceforth twenty-five in number, were organized and the salary of their governors fixed. Even the Byzantine hierarchy was reorganized, and the metropolitans made dependent on the patriarch of Constantinople, who was appointed, and in practice could be deposed, by the emperor. The imperial edict stated the number of metropolitans and autocephalous archbishoprics as fifty-one each, and listed the bishoprics in their respective provinces.

In the intellectual and religious sphere above all, the Macedonian period was the daybreak of a new age. The iconoclast movement had been a spiritual invasion from the east: its defeat had cost many battles and sacrifices, but it had brought about the victory of orthodox Greek Christianity at Byzantium. Byzantium was now ready to take up a commanding and independent position, midway between the east and the west. She was also to be the scene, not merely of a renaissance of the old Greco-Roman learning and art, such as was illuminating the court of the Carolingians, but of Greek classical literature and also Greek learning as fertilized by Arab studies at Baghdad. While in language and literature her scholars remained purely Greek, their addiction to the secular arts and particularly the mathematical arts show Arab influence. The Arabs studied astrology as the work of the *magi*, and it was not for nothing that certain Byzantine scholars were surnamed 'the magician' (Lecapenus): throughout the early middle ages, a zeal for the higher mathematics was apt to give rise to accusations of the practice of sorcery. The beginnings of the new era of Byzantine enlightenment preceded, indeed, the advent of the Macedonian dynasty: the three greatest exponents of the new learning, Bardas, Photius and Constantine, the apostle of the Slavs, were trained under the Amorians, but their work bore fruit under the Macedonians. The defeat of iconoclasm had, by allaying something of party bitterness, made possible this enthusiasm for the Greek past and present splendour of Byzantium, the emergence of the medieval Byzantine empire, individual, independent and Greek. Iconoclasm had also brought about, however, the end of Byzantine universalism, in practice if not in theory: there was now a western and an eastern instead of a single Christian empire, and the see of Old Rome, to which all Byzantine theologians had been willing to accord a primacy of honour, was under the protectorate of the western empire. It was a situation in which the Latin and the Greek churches might easily drift further apart.

The brilliant revival of Greek studies is linked with the name of Bardas, chief counsellor and power behind the throne in the reign of Michael III: what Theoktistus had been to the empress-regent Theodora, he was to his nephew Michael. The conferment of the title *caesar* gave him a commanding position in the imperial family itself, and in the state, and he used his position for the revival of Greek literature and learning. The old Greco-Roman *artes* had not yet been formally assessed as seven in the east, as they had been in the west: but the mathematical *artes*, and beyond them 'philosophy' or the explanation of the physical universe and what lay behind its manifestation as apprehended by the senses, together with medicine and law, had been estimated as higher studies. These had languished at Constantinople under the iconoclast emperors. Under Bardas' patronage and continuous supervision and support a school of these higher studies was founded in the Magnaura palace at Constantinople, whither the most illustrious masters in philosophy were summoned to teach. At its head was placed Leo of Thessalonica, the pupil of John the Grammarian, a man of outstanding learning in mathematics, medicine and philosophy, and reputed a magician; geometry, astronomy, including the study of the earth and planets, and philology, were all taught in the schools. Among the most outstanding of the scholars of this lay university were Constantine, also from Thessalonica, and Photius, the most brilliant of them all. The classical, pagan and scientific character of the studies did not go unattacked at the time: there were those who deprecated them as leading to a return to paganism, and who attacked Leo of Thessalonica as impious, and likely to go to hell with his friends Homer and Hesiod, Aristotle and Plato. The movement however could not be hindered; for that matter, Christian philosophers were too deeply in debt to Plato and the Neoplatonists, particularly in the east. As to Aristotle, he was in rather a different category. His logic was to prove a sharp instrument in the pursuit of knowledge later in the west; but he was known to be as much studied in Baghdad as Byzantium: his later philosophical teaching was determinist, and those who sought to account for certain phenomena not easy to explain on a determinist basis found acceptance of the Arab teaching on the influence of the stars useful. In the Byzantine empire as in the west astrology and magic fascinated many scientific minds in the early middle ages, and not only as a possible source of power through the plotting of the course of a man's life beforehand or the summoning of demons by incantation, but as supplying a possible explanation of phenomena otherwise inexplicable. But while certain scholars fell under popular suspicion of sorcery, far the more important cause of the suspicion incurred by the 'new learning' was its preoccupation with a pagan literature. The foundation of the Magnaura schools as a centre for higher studies was not unprecedented, for Theodosius II had founded a similar university at Constantinople in 425: but here again there was a difference. The earlier scholars had expounded a literature that was Latin as well as Greek: the scholars of the Magnaura devoted their energies to the Greek classics and the literature of Hellenism, though a hint of Latin studies remained now and even in the eleventh-century university.

Beside this renaissance of Greek scholarship and the lay spirit, religious learning also was cherished, particularly in the monasteries. Orthodoxy had been defended by the monks, and intellectual activity was valued, particularly in the Studite house in Constantinople. The famous monastic rule (*typicon*) of Theodore the Studite gave due honour to the acquirement of all sorts of knowledge by the monks: grammar, philosophy and theology were taught there, as were the writing and illumination of manuscripts and the sacred chant and writing of hymns for liturgy and office. The monastery had a fine library, to which other than monks might have recourse, and a *scriptorium*, where manuscripts were assiduously copied. Saint's lives were written, of use to the secular as well as the ecclesiastical historian: the ninth century is the golden age of Byzantine hagiography. If the central fact of Byzantine church history in the ninth and tenth centuries was the existence of two ecclesiastical parties: the moderates, who would admit the ex-iconoclasts to office, and, while not denying the Roman primacy, strongly resisted papal intervention in the internal affairs of the church of Constantinople, and the rigorists, led by the Studite monks, who suspected the ex-iconoclasts, and, for the support of orthodoxy, as they saw it, welcomed such intervention from Rome: then it must be admitted that both these ecclesiastical parties cherished a learning and literature of their own. That of the Magnaura was the more novel and the more brilliant.

Along with the revived interest in classical literature at Constantinople went a development of the art of illumination. While this word originally meant the brightening of manuscripts by the use of silver and gold leaf for initials or paintings, it has come to be used of any kind of decoration of manuscript texts (vellum of course affording a better surface for such decoration than other materials). Even line drawings can be described as illumination. The word 'illustration' had a similar history. Surviving Greek illuminated manuscripts are rare before the ninth century, and there is evidence that the Byzantine illuminators then increasingly practised the art so as to combine the traditions of the Syriac, Coptic and other near eastern scribes. They produced manuscripts with mixed oriental features but with the Greco-Roman tradition emphasized. Sometimes this was done by introducing into the background of figure compositions rustic villas, temples, altars, etc. from bucolic manuscripts, or collections of mythological figures: there was now some classicizing of the illumination of holy books, as well as of wall decorations.

The earliest extant illuminated early Christian rolls or books (*rotuli* or *codices*) are few, but they are nearly all of near eastern provenance. From the end of the fourth century Christian holy books began to supersede illuminated rolls. The old Itala manuscript in pre-Vulgate Latin was illustrated in the classical manner; the Cotton Genesis (a Greek, sixth-century work), has a more developed classical tradition; and the codex Rossanensis, the Greek text of the first two Gospels, is believed to have been produced in Antioch about 500, but with more splendid materials; on leaves stained purple the text runs in silver, and, for the opening lines, in gold. The illuminated episodes in the life of Christ in the Rossano gospels are very early in type, with evenly spaced lines of figures and very little suggestion of background; the codex Sinopensis and the Vienna Genesis are in style very closely related. The Rabula gospel book, signed by Rabula its scribe and dated as written in 589, is a Syriac text, written in Mesopotamia. It has very early canon tables (see p. 265) in a decorative architectural setting; its ornament is similar to that of the Rossano gospels, but less finished. Several pages of illumination similar to that of Rabula are bound up with the Echmiadzin gospels, an Armenian text.

Of the ninth-, or early tenth-century Byzantine illuminated manuscripts, the Joshua Roll in the Vatican Library, the Paris psalter and the Homilies of Gregory of Nazianzus are perhaps the

most interesting. The provenance of the Joshua Roll is much disputed. Professor Boase dates it as possibly sixth century restored
in the ninth century, and some scholars have seen in it a ninth-
century copy of an archetype of the earlier date. It has lines of
figures such as those found in early near eastern rolls or picture
cycles, but they are here joined by incidental scenery to make a
continuous illustrated band. Dr Kurt Weitzmann, however, sees
in the Joshua Roll a work of the tenth century, not the copy of an
archetype, but composed newly as a roll from two elements: early
Christian or Jewish figure cycles, and 'insertion motives' (mountains, temples, rustic villas, etc.) from classical pagan *codices*; he
regards it as a work of the Constantinople *scriptorium* under Constantine VII, Porphyrogenitus. The tenth-century Paris psalter he
regards as also a work from that *scriptorium*. Whatever their origin,
the lively Hellenism of the treatment (in the Paris psalter the verse:
Why sleepest thou, O Lord? is accompanied by a drawing of the
Lord actually awakened and hastily getting out of the oval glory in
which he was traditionally painted, in order to pursue his enemies),
and the conventionally classical background sketches appear to
show the revived influence of antiquity. All this classical detail in
Byzantium influenced painting in Italy: as did the illuminated
commentary on four of the Homilies of Gregory of Nazianzus
(d. 390). This work was unique among patristic commentaries in
that it explained Gregory's classical references in marginal *historiae*, with illustration. The name of the commentator is actually
unknown, but he seems to have lived in Syria or Palestine, and is
usually known as the Pseudo-Nonnus, from an ascription to a
nonnus (not necessarily a proper name, but a senior monk) in a
late manuscript.

Among the scholars of this Greek renaissance, the following were
of special eminence. John the Grammarian, surnamed Lecono-
mantes, and by his opponents Jambres, Jamares, and Jannes, had
won the special confidence of the emperor Michael II, who had
entrusted him with the education of his son. He was actually sent
as imperial envoy to the caliph of Baghdad, and his zeal for Arabic
learning accounts for the suspicions held of him as sorcerer. With
his brother Asbestas and their friends, he had built a special house
for the pursuit of such studies (or of the mysteries of the occult),
and held conferences there with scholars similarly interested. He
was patriarch at Constantinople from 830 to 842; but he had no
public teaching post.

An important step towards the public teaching of the secular sciences was taken when the emperor Theophilus became the patron of Michael Psellus (the elder), who became the chief instructor of Leo the Philosopher. So far famed was Leo's mathematical learning, that the caliph Ma'mun invited him to come and teach in his house of Wisdom at Baghdad. Leo showed the invitation to the emperor Theophilus, who forbade him to go, but appointed him to lecture on mathematics at the church of the Forty Martyrs. Later he had Leo ordained bishop for the see of Thessalonica, where he continued his studies both of applied mathematics and the occult. After the 'return to orthodoxy', in 843, he was deposed by the new patriarch Methodius: but not before he had appointed the young Constantine, the future apostle of the Slavs, professor of mathematics at the cathedral school. On leaving Thessalonica, Leo returned to Constantinople and continued to teach until, about the year 864, Bardas founded the Magnaura schools, making Leo rector, and his pupils, Theodore and Theodegius, lecturers in geometry and astronomy.

While Leo had been the centre of one circle of scholars before his appointment to the Magnaura, another surrounded the young Photius (c. 820–891), who was related to the imperial Macedonian house. His family had been friendly to the monks and even suffered persecution from the iconoclasts, but the young Photius was fascinated by the new studies and the new, lay scholarship. He read in great libraries, heard famous scholars, and while still without official post taught in his own house and acquired a reputation for scholarship. He was at the centre of the movement which restudied the Greek classics; his labours were immense in the whole field of Greek literature and he soon attracted a band of young scholars: he taught grammar, logic and theology, and, even when employed in the imperial chancery and later when patriarch, he never gave up his scholarly interest in manuscripts and his pupils' work. His *Myriobiblion* attested the width of his reading: his book on the Manichees his ability as a historian. Unlike Leo the Philosopher who was, in part at least, attracted to an alien learning, he gloried in Byzantine literature as a quasi-national inheritance from the Greek past. The Tiber had flowed into the Bosphorus, but it was so long ago that the Tiber was forgotten. The Homeric literature had long been and remained for the Byzantine citizen the heroic poetry of his own past, scarcely less familiar than the Christian scriptures.

It was the fate of the scholar Photius, the fine flower of the ninth-century Byzantine renaissance, to become both the patron of the Moravian mission which extended Byzantine Christianity and culture to the Slav races and the cause of a schism between the Greek and Latin churches. This latter was temporary only, but it preceded the increasing misunderstandings which led eventually to the disastrous schism between Rome and Constantinople. It showed the difficulties likely to arise over ecclesiastical jurisdiction when the patriarch of old Rome looked for protection to the western emperor and the patriarch of new Rome to the *basileus*. The immediate dispute in the Photian schism was over the validity of the election of Photius as patriarch of Constantinople, a matter of canon law; but the issue was complicated by the rival claims to jurisdiction in the Balkans involved in the question of the Christian missionaries in Bulgaria.

Modern scholarship has modified the views held thirty years ago about this schism, the character of Photius and his place in church history. The work of Byzantinists has now established that much of the older history of the Photian schism was based on the writings of medieval controversialists in the west: that, in fact, a western legend grew up about the Photian schism, which failed to give due weight to the existence of two parties at Constantinople itself in the ninth century, one willing to grant to the Roman patriarch a primacy of honour, the other a primacy of jurisdiction. The difficulties over the Bulgarian mission were not (the newer view says) allowed due weight; nor did the older view take into account the regard in which the eastern church held Photius, for his moral character as well as his learning: he was, in fact, canonized, like his opponent, Ignatius. Finally, the older view increased the length of the Photian schism by regarding it as one with the dispute of Leo VI with the patriarch Nicholas over his fourth marriage, a dispute ended in 920. The Photian schism is now held to have lasted from 867 to 869–70, and the 'second' Photian schism which pope Formosus tried to heal to have been a schism within the Byzantine church itself, between the moderates and the rigorists (now the extreme Ignatians).

The existence of the two parties in the Byzantine church preceded the struggle over Photius' appointment as patriarch, and conditioned it. At the opening of 858, Photius was head of the imperial chancery (*protoasecretis*) and esteemed the leading scholar of the day; the patriarch Methodius, who had largely allayed the bitterness of parties during his tenure of the patriarchal throne, had been succeeded by the monk Ignatius, a son of Michael I. This devout and ascetic bishop commanded the respect of the Studites, and of those who accepted the Amorian dynasty only of necessity: he was especially hostile to Bardas, who had engineered the murder of Theodora's chief minister, Theoktistus, driven Theodora into a nunnery (856), and placed his nephew, the eighteen-year-old Michael III, on the throne. Bardas for ten years (856–866) governed the empire in his nephew's name, as *magister*, domestic of the schools, curopalate, and (from 862) as caesar: Ignatius remained loyal to Theodora and her memory. The young emperor led an irresponsible and (reputedly) a disedifying life; disedifying rumours as to Bardas also reached Ignatius. On the feast of the Epiphany, 858, Ignatius refused to receive Bardas to communion in Santa Sophia: a public humiliation. Bardas in return exiled Ignatius on a charge of treason, and had Photius (still a layman, though unmarried) elected by a synod to the patriarchate, no objection being raised. It is not clear whether Ignatius had, at the moment of removal, been willing to resign: if so, he withdrew his resignation and claimed that he was still patriarch; the Studites, and some of the rigorists, supported him. Bardas held a second synod, which accepted Photius, and within five days he was made a monk, received all the minor and holy orders and was consecrated patriarch; he celebrated on 25 December 858, in Santa Sophia. A great party struggle between the followers of Ignatius and Photius had begun, and Photius himself, to secure his position, notified his succession to the patriarchate to pope Nicholas I.

Nicholas showed himself ready, not to accept Photius, but to inquire into the validity of the appointment. His two legates summoned Ignatius to appear before them in a synod held at the church of the Holy Apostles (861), declared him deposed and accepted the election of Photius. The great majority of the Byzantine clergy did, indeed, accept Photius: but pope Nicholas, on the legates' return, and on receipt of further information about Ignatius, declared his legates to have been bribed. They had, in fact, been very sumptuously treated by the emperor. At a Lateran synod of 863 Nicholas excommunicated Photius and his supporters and declared Ignatius still patriarch.

The quarrel between Nicholas and Photius, who disregarded the decision of the Lateran synod, was embittered by the rival claims of the two churches to jurisdiction in Bulgaria: and further, by Photius' denouncement to the church in Bulgaria, and to the other eastern churches (866), of the doctrinal errors of the western church, especially her teaching on the celibacy of the clergy and the addition of the *Filioque* clause (see p. 102) to the creed. A council at Constantinople (867) excommunicated Nicholas, making the schism formal: the emperor Michael himself presided at the council. Byzantine feeling rallied to Photius as to a national hero opposing foreign intervention both in Bulgaria and the capital, while the other eastern patriarchs supported him.

The murder of the emperor Michael III (867) by the Macedonian, Basil I, however, brought about the fall of Photius. The new emperor had had Bardas murdered also, and could scarcely rely on the support of Photius, whom he therefore deposed, recalling Ignatius. He anticipated papal support, and papal legates, sent by Hadrian II, presided at a synod in Constantinople (Eighth Oecumenical Council of the Latins, 869–70) and declared Ignatius patriarch. The schism was ended; but the papacy found Ignatius as obdurate over Bulgaria as Photius had been, and relations deteriorated. The Byzantine clergy still favoured Photius: Basil recalled him from exile, he was reconciled to Ignatius, and when Ignatius died in 877, he succeeded him as patriarch. Pope John VIII, at Basil's request, sent legates who in a synod of 879–80 solemnly accepted Photius and declared peace with the church of Constantinople.

Photius' final deposition (887) was again due to a change of sovereign, and to the hostility of the young emperor Leo VI to his father Basil's memory and his father's ministers. To secure peace between moderates and rigorists, a peace likely to be disturbed by his action, he made his own brother Stephen patriarch, and exiled Photius. The extreme rigorists were, however, unappeased: they denounced Photius till his death in exile in 891 and demanded from the pope a further condemnation. They were actually in schism with the official church at Constantinople, refusing to communicate with her, but no 'second schism' occurred between Constantinople and Rome. Photius died in his distant monastery, reviled by the rigorists of his own church, but still in communion with Rome.

The cause of the next struggle within the Byzantine church was the affair of the emperor Leo VI's fourth marriage, to his mistress Zoë. He had placed on the patriarchal throne in 901, Nicholas Mysticus (the imperial secretary) and expected complaisance; but Nicholas, though willing to baptize the child, Constantine Porphyrogenitus, would not recognize the marriage to Zoë, and twice forbade the emperor to enter Santa Sophia. Leo deposed Nicholas and replaced him with his own confessor Euthymius, a pious but simple monk, who, for the sake of peace between parties was willing to recognize the marriage and crown the young Constantine. Schism followed between the Nicolaites and Euthymian parties in the church. Nicholas Mysticus was re-established in 912, when Leo VI was succeeded by Constantine VII, and during the minority he struggled for influence with the empress Zoë and other rivals for power. He succeeded in humiliating the young emperor and vindicating his reprobation of Constantine's parents' marriage in 920, as also in mitigating the bitterness between parties in Constantinople. He published the *tomus unionis*, in which he legitimated the fourth marriage of the sovereign in this case, while severely castigating such a marriage in normal cases. Nicholas, the pupil of Photius, had vindicated the patriarch's right to act as censor of the emperor's morals. 'Men grew accustomed to think that in all questions falling within his sphere, and above all, when any moral issue was at stake, the patriarch had undisputed rights against his master, the emperor.' (*Byzantium*, p. 113.) And in this dispute at least, the patriarchal legitimation of the marriage was in accord with an earlier judgment given by the papal see.

The end of the Carolingian dynasty in the west, best marked perhaps by the accession of the Capetians as rulers of the west Franks, came thus when the Byzantine empire had entered upon a very splendid period of her history, from 842 (the return to orthodoxy) to 1025 (the death of Basil II). Successes in the administrative, military and naval fields, accompanied by the marked intellectual and artistic activities which had also been a feature of Byzantine life under the Amorians, came to full fruition in the tenth and eleventh centuries under the Macedonians. On the eastern frontier, the initial work of Michael III's generals had brought stabilization, and this was followed in the tenth century by an interesting Byzantine offensive which recaptured Cilicia, northern Syria and even Antioch, the seat of the patriarch. Of equal importance was the recapture from the Arabs of the naval bases, Crete (960–1) and Cyprus (965). In the Balkans, the danger to Byzantium in the possible setting up of an independent Slav empire and patriarchate ended with Basil II's victory over the Bulgarians in 1014: Bulgaria was organized as a province of the empire, its church Greek but semi-autonomous. Meanwhile, while in western Europe the Vikings raided far up the rivers, while defence was local and urgent and even the kings' courts filled more with warriors than administrators or scholars: while learning had its home in the monastic libraries and was even there endangered: civilization, learning, the arts, even sophistication reigned in Constantinople. Byzantium in these centuries was the splendid heir of the Greek tradition.

ADDITIONAL NOTE
concerning the Council of Constantinople, 869–70

Professor Dvornik, after thorough research, concludes that this council came to be reckoned oecumenical only by the blunder of certain Latin canonists in the late eleventh century, and that so to regard it was not in accord with the official tradition of the Roman see. See pt. ii, ch. ii, *The Oecumenicity of the Eighth Council in Medieval Western Tradition* in his work *The Photian Schism* mentioned in the bibliography.

BIBLIOGRAPHICAL NOTE

As for chapter viii: see also J. B. Bury, *A History of the Eastern Roman Empire (A.D. 802–867)*, 1912; S. Runciman, *Byzantine Civilisation*, 1933; K. Weitzmann, *The Joshua Roll*, Princeton Univ. Press, 1948; G. Every, *The Byzantine Patriarchate, 451–1204*, 1947; F. Dvornik, *Les Slaves, Byzance et Rome au ix* siècle, and *The Photian Schism: History and Legend*, 1948; for iconoclasm, see E. J. Martin, *A History of the Iconoclastic Controversy*, 1932, and the account and references in *The Photian Schism*, p. 8 ff; P. J. Alexander, *The patriarch Nicephorus of Constantinople*, 1958. See also, G. Mathew, *Byzantine Painting*, 1950. See also, for the role of the Byzantine emperor as universal ruler, but never the successful dictator in doctrinal matters to the Orthodox Church, L. Bréhier, *Le Monde byzantin*, No. 2, Paris, 1949; for a revised view of the patriarch Photius, F. Dvornik, *The Photian Schism*, Cambridge, 1948; for relationship of the eastern and western emperors, W. Ohnsorge, *Das Zweikaiserproblem im fruheren Mittelalter*, Hildesheim, 1947.

CHAPTER XXII

THE DIVISIONS OF THE CAROLINGIAN EMPIRE: 814-843

CHARLEMAGNE'S empire had been something more than an enlarged *regnum Francorum*: it had found in the old Greco-Roman tradition of *imperium* a pattern for a more civilized, centralized, peaceful rule of western Europe; but nevertheless the basis of Charlemagne's power was his command of the Frankish army, and its spearhead, the east Frankish host. Charlemagne's empire was to break up, not because there were, after his death, no counsellors to value imperial, unitary rule, and not even because Charlemagne's descendants each fought for his own hand and to secure and increase his territories: but because none succeeded to undivided command of the Frankish host. Charlemagne had ruled Italy and Rome through his counts and *missi*: but he had lived at Aix, in the east Frankish homeland, among his vassals; his son Louis succeeded to his empire, but his youth had been spent in Aquitaine, and in Aquitaine were his personal councillors and vassals; he could never command the same personal loyalty of the east Frankish host. Lothar, his son, ruled Italy: and Italy, not the old Austrasia, was the centre of his power. Imperial rule could only continue under the shield of the undivided loyalty of the Frankish host: and this was lacking. Certain imperial theorists, including mainly scholar clerks but also the cold and brutal layman, the emperor Lothar himself, failed to recognize this.

Other causes have been held responsible for the break-up of the Carolingian empire, and did, indeed, contribute to it. Too much of the emperor Louis the Pious' attention was given to the question of church reform; and though reform of the monasteries and clergy was a service to learning, provided a leisured class, and directly affected the civil service of the empire, yet it could not take the place of the military defence and policing of the empire. These, at the time, were a ruler's primary duty.

Then again, the growing strength of the external enemies of the Frankish empire contributed to the defeat and discredit of Charlemagne's descendants. The Slavs and the Bulgars were restive on the eastern frontier. The Saracens from Spain, Africa and the Mediterranean islands harried the southern coast of Aquitaine,

the western coast of Italy, and Sicily itself. And above all, the
northern pirates from Denmark and the Scandinavian peninsula
developed a technique of rapid sea raiding with which the Frankish
army was quite unfitted to cope. The Frankish army could be
moved great distances and fight great battles: but the campaign
needed a lot of planning and could only start when there was
enough spring grass for the horses. Reception of the news that
the northmen had sacked Durstedt or Quentovic meant that
their fleet had already sailed away with their plunder, and no
defence or even retaliation was possible. Undivided command of
the Frankish host by a young and vigorous ruler might have led
to the only possible centralized defence against the northmen:
the military conquest of Denmark and southern Scandinavia.

Though the history of the Carolingian empire can thus be
considered under many aspects, that of its political divisions and
subdivisions is primary and can be briefly stated. The partitions
were nearly all impermanent and occasioned, not by the interests
of different racial or economic groups, but by the personal ambitions and struggles of Charlemagne's heirs; but out of them the
old Merovingian kingdoms of Neustria and Austrasia, merged
in Charlemagne's empire, were to become distinct again by the
end of the ninth century as the kingdoms of the west Franks and
the east Franks: in the tenth century, Capetian France and the
Ottonian empire. The landmarks in the century of impermanent
partition are: the rule of Louis the Pious as emperor, from 814
till 840; the notable partition of Verdun in 843, between Louis
the Pious' three sons; and the worst period of Danish raids, from
855 till 888, ending with the deposition of the last Carolingian
emperor, Charles the Fat, in 888.

The reign of Louis the Pious was, as it were, an epilogue to that
of Charlemagne, for there was still one emperor, the *missi* were
still sent out, and capitularies passed applying to the whole empire.
But in the character and ability of the ruler there was a great
change. Louis was thirty-six years old in 814, impulsive, passionate and weak. He entered Aix on 27 February 814, and proceeded
to rule by the advice of his own Aquitanian councillors; his
chancellor, Helisachar, became head of the palace chapel, the
much trusted Burgundian monk, Benedict of Aniane, was given
a new monastery, founded for him at Inda, near the palace itself.
Louis proceeded to get rid of his father's councillors and reform
the disorderly conduct of the palace. Adalard had retired to his
abbey of Corbie, from which he was now exiled to Noirmoutier
at the mouth of the Loire; his brother Wala was sent to be a monk

at Corbie. The princesses, Charles's daughters, were sent off to nunneries, and a new ordinance issued about the conduct of the palace and the palace police. Louis' nephew, Bernard, whose succession to the kingdom of Italy Charlemagne had sanctioned, was summoned to Aix to take a new oath of fidelity to Louis; and from the heading of his *acta* Louis dropped the titles of king of the Franks and king of the Lombards, which Charles had always retained, and described himself now simply as 'Louis, by the order of divine providence, emperor and Augustus'. The ideal of imperial unity, raceless and Christian, found a yet more explicit expression in a letter of Agobard, bishop of Lyons: while making the facile demand that the old customary laws should be abolished, and only one law, the code of the Salian Franks, observed throughout the empire, he described as shocking the differences of procedure still to be found there: 'where in name there was now neither Jew nor Gentile, barbarian nor Scythian, Aquitanian nor Lombard, Burgundian nor Aleman, bond nor free: there should be one Frankish law for all'.

No effort was made to follow such exuberant counsel: but in two respects Louis' policy was guided by Frankish churchmen: he undertook a programme of church reform, and he loosened the Frankish control of the papacy.

Not only had Charlemagne provided for the officers of his chapel, and his clerical *missi*, by endowing them with abbeys and bishoprics: but military needs had brought about in many cases the granting out of church lands to lay vassals and there were complaints of impoverishment. Between 814 and 816 Louis made many new donations to churches; in 816 he summoned a council to Aix, and required the secular clergy to live according to the canons; in 817, under the presidency of Benedict of Aniane, monks were required to keep the Benedictine rule with a primitive strictness (see p. 52). In 819 these reforming measures were enforced in a general capitulary.

Away in Rome, Leo III neglected to take the oath of obedience to the new emperor, as required by Charlemagne's ordinance: and Louis let the omission pass without protest. Leo III died in June 816, and the new pope, Stephen IV, though he required the Roman people to swear fealty to Louis as emperor, did not defer his coronation till he should have received Louis' confirmation. There was no imperial protest: nor was there when Pascal I was consecrated without confirmation in January 817. Nevertheless, the traditional Franco-papal alliance was not broken, for the papal household needed defence against the Roman nobles: Stephen IV travelled to Reims and formally crowned Louis emperor, supplementing with the religious rite the lay coronation by Charles in 813: and in 817 Pascal sent the nomenclator Theodore to renew the traditional alliance. The new privilege granted by Louis on this occasion not only confirmed the pope in all his territories, but renounced imperial jurisdiction in Rome and all intervention in papal elections.

In the same year, 817, Louis made an *Ordinatio* or disposition of the empire. He had three sons, Lothar, aged about twenty-two, and two younger ones, Pepin and Louis, neither of whom had yet attained their majority, which the Carolingians reckoned according to Ripuarian law, as fifteen. At the general assembly which was engaged in reforming the monasteries of men, Louis announced his intention of issuing the *Ordinatio*, after three days of prayers and fasts. By its terms he ordained that:

Lothar should be associated with him as emperor forthwith, and should be the sole inheritor of the empire at his father's death. The kingdom of Italy, adjudged to Bernard, Louis' nephew, by Charlemagne, remained his, however.

Pepin should keep the kingdom of Aquitaine, given him by his father in 814: on attaining his majority, he should have also Gascony, the March of Toulouse and certain counties in northwest Francia.

Louis should rule Bavaria as king: both young kings acting under the general control of the emperor.

It was further laid down, that when Lothar should be sole emperor, he should allow his brothers the internal government of their kingdoms, together with the disposition of 'honours', and the right to taxes and revenue; he should, nevertheless, control their general policy. They must make him the customary annual gifts, and he must afford them military protection when necessary.

In Italy, however, no provision had been worked out to accommodate the positions of Bernard as king and Lothar as emperor, and Bernard felt his position imperilled. As the beginning of troubles, Bernard and his supporters made an unsuccessful rebellion. Louis set out with an army for Italy, but he was met at Chalons-sur-Saône by Bernard, who there made his submission. He was condemned to death, but though the sentence was commuted to blinding, he died (818) of the torment inflicted. In the same fit of panic over the Italian rebellion, Louis ordered Charles's illegitimate children, Drogo, Hugh and Thierry, to be sent off to monasteries. The way was now clear for Lothar's rule of Italy and the fulfilment of the *Ordinatio* of 817: but at this juncture Louis' queen, Irmengard, died, and Louis married the beautiful and accomplished Alemannian princess, Judith. Her father, Welf, had great possessions in Bavaria and on the eastern frontier, and the match seemed politic; but long years of civil war were to befall the empire through Louis' desire to upset the *Ordinatio* of 817 in order to provide his late-born child Charles, Judith's son, with a portion at least equal to those of his brothers. Judith's sole endeavour was directed to this end, and she soon had a predominating influence over her husband, especially after the death of Benedict of Aniane in 821. The very name given to the child hinted at his succession to Charlemagne; he has come down to history, however, with a disastrous record, as Charles the Bald.

When the immediate danger from Bernard's rebellion had ended with his death, Louis was gradually reconciled to those whom he had condemned as Bernard's supporters. Adalard, the trusted counsellor of Charlemagne, was recalled from exile, given back his abbey of Corbie, and in 822, at the assembly of Attigny, Drogo and Hugh, Charlemagne's sons, were recalled from banishment. Drogo was made bishop of Metz in 823: Hugh was given several abbeys. The influence of this little group, all imperialists in intention and standing for a return to the unitary rule of Charlemagne, seem to have inspired Louis' surprising and disastrous penance at Attigny: their personal loyalty to Bernard blinded them to the harm likely to follow to imperial prestige. As the *Royal Annals* wrote under the year 822:

> The lord emperor, having held council with his bishops and nobles, was reconciled with his brothers, whom he had made to receive the tonsure against their will: and for this deed and for those things that were done to Bernard, his brother Pepin's son, and towards abbot Adalard and his brother Wala, he made a public confession and did penance. And this he did in the assembly which was held in August that same year (822) at Attigny, in the presence of his whole people.

In Italy, disorders had not ceased at Bernard's death, and Louis' son Lothar was now sent there to deal with them. As the eldest son, his interests coincided with the desires of the imperialists, and the tie was strengthened by his marriage to Irmengard, daughter of the count of Tours, one of the imperial group but not of the same ability or honesty as Adalard and Wala. Lothar had been trained to rule under the tutorship of Einhard, and under his guidance his stay in Italy between 822 and 823, and from 824 to 825, was marked by certain reforms in administration.

It was marked also by steps to restore the Frankish control of the papacy.

In April 823 Lothar was crowned emperor by the pope: and immediately after he sat in judgment in a suit between the Lombard monastery of Farfa and the pope, giving his decision for the abbot of Farfa: the act asserted imperial jurisdiction over the patrimony.

A more startling act was to follow. Pope Pascal died in May 824, and through Wala's influence the pro-Frankish party at Rome succeeded in electing Eugenius II. Lothar, on receipt of the news, set out for Rome, held an inquiry into the election, and issued the *Constitutio Romana* of 824, dealing with imperial relations with the holy see. A quasi-Byzantine control was asserted over it, explicable in the light of the contemporary imperialists' view of the empire as one aspect of the Christian church and the emperor, by virtue of his office, another Constantine. The *Constitutio* thus asserted the inviolability of those under the protection of pope or emperor; imposed on each newly elected pope an oath of fealty (fidelity) to be made at the hands of an imperial *missus*, while requiring from all Romans at each election an oath of fealty to the emperor. It also placed the papal *curia* permanently in the charge of two Frankish *missi*, one of whom was expressly given the right of intervention if the pope failed to do justice. Imperialist policy had succeeded in Italy, and in August 825, imperialist counsels obtained the appearance of Lothar's name, together with his father's, at the head of all imperial *acta*.

Meanwhile, dangers to the imperialists were arising in other quarters. The *Ordinatio* of 817 had weakened the Frankish defence on the Spanish frontier by separating the Spanish March from the duchy of Toulouse; this trans-Pyrenean March, now called Septimania, was increasingly attacked by the Saracens. A Frankish force, attempting to extricate themselves from a fruitless attack on Pampeluna by the northern route, was in 824 attacked by the hostile Gascons in the pass of Roncesvalles. In 826 the Saracens besieged Barcelona: a Frankish army sent in charge of the chancellor Helisachar failed to relieve it, and the Frankish and imperialist counts, Hugh of Tours and Matfrid of Orleans, sent by Louis in a further relief expedition, accomplished nothing. It fell to Bernard of Septimania, son of the count William who had retired to Gellona, to retrieve the situation. The two Frankish counts were deprived of their counties and fell into disgrace.

Moreover, on 13 June 823 Judith gave birth to her son, Charles. Lothar was requested to stand godfather, and even made to promise not to oppose his future territorial endowment. Nevertheless, while all Louis' sons felt their interests threatened by Charles, Lothar and the imperialists were particularly uneasy. Hugh of Tours and Wala now attended Lothar's court instead of that of Louis. While men like Wala, Adalard and Agobard of Lyons had far-sighted, if impracticable, views on the unity of the empire, Hugh and Matfrid were selfish scoundrels, and in addition, incapable. Material for opposition to Louis was, however, increasing: the Franks had received several checks from the Danes, the Slavs and the Bulgars, and the *pagenses* complained of the hardship of long campaigns and of bad harvests. Lands were misappropriated and there were complaints against lay abbots; Louis in 825 sent out a general admonition to all orders in connexion with these abuses and ordered a general inquiry. Nothing was achieved however and in 828 Wala reproached the emperor for the continuance of abuses. Synods at Mainz, Lyons, Paris and Toulouse uttered the same complaints in 829: Louis in that same summer issued from Worms three capitularies dealing with the abuses complained of and sent out more *missi*: but he had too little control over the territorial counts and dukes in his sons' kingdoms to enforce reform.

At the assembly at Worms, in August 829, Louis made his first open move against the imperialists: he sent Lothar back to Italy, summoned count Bernard from Barcelona to be an imperial chamberlain, and, without consulting the assembly, endowed his son Charles with a territory in Alemannia including the family lands of Welf, sure to be loyal to Judith, and also Rhaetia, Alsace and part of Burgundy. Young Charles's share was inferior to that of his brothers, nor was the royal title accorded to him; but suspicion was aroused because of the simultaneous enforced retirement of Lothar and the omission of his name henceforward from the imperial *acta*. Wala protested and was exiled to Corbie, from where he apparently led an opposition which went as far as accusing Louis and Judith of practising black magic and other scandalous crimes. After Wala's death, Paschasius wrote an apology for him under the thin disguise of an *Epitaph for Arsenius* (whom the emperor Theodosius had appointed as tutor to his sons, Arcadius and Honorius). Wala, Paschasius wrote, was not accused by the good of not loving the king's glory and the extension of his kingdom, but of loving them too much. 'For he wished to secure that so glorious and Christian a kingdom should not be divided in parts, for the Saviour saith: *Every kingdom divided against itself shall be brought to nought*. For he wished to secure the unity and dignity of the whole empire, for the defence of the *patria* (Bede's favourite word), and the liberties of the churches.' Nevertheless, in spite of protests, Louis succeeded in clearing the palace of friends of the imperialists and giving their offices to friends of Judith and the chamberlain Bernard.

The following spring revolt broke out. An expedition against the rebellious Bretons had been planned to start unwontedly early, actually on 14 April 830, the day following on Holy Thursday, while it was still Lent. The host was to meet at Rennes, and there were complaints of the inconvenience and unsuitability of such a date and starting point; it was even murmured that an unnecessary campaign was being staged to Bernard's advantage, and that efforts must be made to deliver Louis from his evil councillors. Lothar came hurrying from Italy, Pepin and Louis came to join, not the host, but the rebels. Bernard fled to Septimania, Judith took refuge in the convent of Laon: the rebels seized her and took her along with them to meet Louis at Compiègne. They pressed Louis to abdicate, and when he asked time for consideration sent Judith along to the nunnery of St Radegund at Poitiers and constrained her to take the veil. Lothar and Wala, however, judged the forcible deposition of Louis inopportune: they required from him promises of better government, had Lothar's name restored to the *acta*, and withdrew. The only result of the revolt of 830 was that one court faction replaced another: east Frankish resistance to dominance by Lothar, whose real interests lay in Italy, had proved too strong for radical change.

Later that summer, in October 830, reaction set in, in favour of Louis. He held an assembly at Nymwegen, in the heart of the east Frankish lands, bade all his vassals to come unarmed, and was strong enough to dismiss Lothar's adherents, sending the arch-chaplain Hilduin into exile at Paderborn and Wala back to Corbie. By the spring following, Louis' supporters were yet stronger. He convened an assembly to meet at Aix on 2 February 831, and he had the empress Judith brought back to him at the palace, sending her son Charles and bishop Drogo to meet her. Before the assembly Judith swore to her own innocence, and Louis accused the authors of the plot of 830 as traitors: the assembly upheld him. Wala was sent off to the wilds of Rhaetia: Lothar was required to return to Italy and not to leave it again without special permission; his name again disappeared from the *acta*. Bernard was reinstated.

A new act of partition was now issued, setting aside the *Ordinatio* of 817. In this instrument, all reference to Lothar as emperor was omitted, as was indeed his position in Italy; apart from Italy, tacitly ignored, the empire was divided between the emperor's three sons, Pepin, Louis and young Charles. Pepin's kingdom of Aquitaine was enlarged by the addition of a series of Neustrian counties north of the Seine, while to Louis' share, the kingdom of Bavaria, was added all the north German lands, the modern Netherlands, and certain districts of north France. Charles received, in addition to the lands allocated to him in 829, more of Burgundy, Provence, Gothia (which gave him a corridor to Bernard's March of Septimania) and certain important districts in north France, where the Carolingian fisc had great estates: regions round Laon, Reims, Trier, etc. The emperor himself appeared to be left with very slender resources: but this partition was only, in fact, to come into force at his death. Charles was still only seven years old: his elder brothers distrusted him, each other, and the emperor. At the end of 831 Pepin was openly in revolt; in 832 Louis of Bavaria invaded Alemannia without success; and Louis the Pious, after an abortive expedition into Aquitaine, declared Pepin deposed and Charles king of Aquitaine. From henceforth, whatever civil wars agitated the empire, the inhabitants of Aquitaine were divided in their adherence to the two claimants, Charles and Pepin.

In 833 the exasperated imperialists broke into a second revolt, under the leadership this time of Louis the Bavarian, Pepin and Lothar; to give an appearance of legitimacy to the rebellion, Lothar induced pope Gregory IV to intervene in the cause of peace and the unity of Christendom: the supporters of the emperor were disturbed in their loyalty to Louis by that owed to the pope, who in his letters in the cause of peace appeared to be supporting Lothar and the rebels. Louis collected his army at Worms and the German bishops wrote reproaching Gregory for forgetting his loyalty to the emperor: the pope and the imperialists wrote letters accusing Louis of breaking the peace by upsetting the *Ordinatio* of 817. On 24 June the imperial and the rebel hosts met at Rotfeld near Colmar; Louis made the mistake of negotiating instead of fighting and gradually his vassals melted away and joined the other camp, breaking their solemn oath of vassalage and turning what should have been a field of battle into a field of lies (Lügenfeld). Louis was left alone and surrendered: Lothar proclaimed his father's downfall and announced a new partition of the empire —Louis the Bavarian's German lands were increased; Pepin received, beside Aquitaine, the counties between Loire and Seine;

Charles was left portionless, and shut up at Prüm; the emperor
Louis was kept a prisoner at Saint-Médard and exhorted to take
the monastic habit in penitence; Judith was sent off to Italy, and
pope Gregory went sadly back to Rome.

In the late autumn, however, the indignities suffered by Louis
provoked a reaction, especially among the Germans: Raban Maur,
abbot of Fulda, wrote in Louis' favour. In 834 Louis of Bavaria,
'Louis the German', led an army to rescue his father; Pepin was
won over, and Bernard of Septimania brought help. Lothar now
had his father and young Charles at Aix: but he was not strong
enough to prevent Louis' reconciliation with the church, and
after a summer's campaigning against his brothers, he withdrew
to Italy. From the autumn of 834 till his death in 840 Louis ruled
the empire outside Italy nominally as emperor: he was recrowned
at Metz in 835: his whole ambition was to secure from the two
sons who had supported him a worthy kingdom for his son
Charles.

In 837 Louis felt himself strong enough to make a fresh parti-
tion in favour of Charles, whose original estates had by now mainly
passed into the control of Louis the German. He gave him a
peripheral territory stretching from Frisia, the lands on the lower
Rhine, and the Meuse to the Seine, and beyond the Seine to
Auxerre and Troyes. Louis the German protested and attacked
Frankfurt: his father in return invaded Bavaria in 839. Young
Charles had come of age in 838 and been crowned by his father;
Pepin of Aquitaine had died that same year: but the old emperor
did not feel himself or Charles secure. He made overtures of
peace to Lothar, who came to him at Worms in the spring of 840
and made with him the last partition of Louis' reign. While Louis
the German was restricted to Bavaria alone (from which it would
have needed a serious war to dislodge him), the rest of the empire
was divided between Lothar and Charles. Lothar's share, outside
Italy, was to lie to the east of the Rhone, Saône and Meuse:
Charles's to the west of these rivers. Charlemagne's empire, when
Louis died in the summer of 840 on an island in the river by
Ingelheim, seemed hopelessly divided. In Italy, Lothar ruled
with some security, but in his trans-alpine territories his brother
Louis was firmly ensconced in Bavaria: while Charles (the Bald)
had no security in Aquitaine, because some of the vassals supported
Pepin's son, now king Pepin II.

The internal divisions of the Frankish lands were not unnoticed
by outside enemies. In 837 the noble Breton, Nominoë, had risen
in rebellion and a Frankish army had occupied his territory; on

the eastern frontier, the Slavs penetrated Saxony, and in 838 Frankish armies had to march against the Wilzes and the Obotrites, the Sorbs and the Bulgars, while the most dangerous enemies of all, the *Nortmanni* or northmen, had made bad raids from 830 to 840 along the coast of the North Sea and the Channel. Frisia was the special object of their expeditions; Durstedt, the chief port for the sea trade of western Europe, was sacked four times between 834 and 837, and never recovered.

The partition arranged by Louis the Pious before his death could never be enforced: it took three years of struggle between his sons before the more famous Partition of Verdun could be agreed upon. In the shifting fortunes of the campaigns between Lothar and his two brothers, and also between them and their rebellious vassals and rivals for power, two factors remained constant. Lothar openly proclaimed his right to empire, as in the *Ordinatio* of 817, in disregard of all the engagements that he had made since for territorial partition: such a claim opened the door for Louis the German to claim much larger territories than he had been allowed in 840. The whole question of partition was reopened and had more practical importance for the combatants than any claim of Lothar to unitary rule, which must, in any case, have been a matter of prestige and protocol only. Secondly, the structure of society had by now come to depend upon the oath of vassalage (see p. 557): the palace officials, the local counts and a great number of holders of benefices out in the countryside were held to their king (or to some great lord) by this personal oath, accompanied by the ceremony of homage: the vassal's oath was utterly solemn and binding. Yet the obligations of the vassal to his lord when they conflicted with his obligations to the king (unless the vassal were a king's vassal) had not as yet been worked out: still less the vassal's obligation to the emperor when they ran counter to his obligations to his own king. In Charlemagne's day, vassalage to one of his sons had not conflicted with a superior obligation to the emperor; now, such a final obligation had become shadowy as compared to the vassal's personal oath to his king. It followed that in this, as in the earlier struggles between Charlemagne's descendants, it was possible for a vassal to interpret his obligations to emperor or king according to his own interests, and the promises of reward held out to him. The claims put forward by Lothar and his brothers were made in the hope that a sufficient number of vassals would support them. As it turned out, while Lothar could rely on his Italian vassals and those round

Aix and the Rhine mouth where the imperial tradition coincided with local prosperity: and while Louis the German retained the loyalty of the east Franks and Germans: Charles the Bald had no territories of proved loyalty. Aquitaine was loyal to Pepin II, despite his youth: Paris and Neustria had no personal loyalty to Charles, though large estates of the Carolingian fisc had long been administered by the officials of Louis the Pious, who were ready to regard Charles as Louis' successor; these demesnes were useful supports of his power, but did not supply him with good, fighting vassals.

On the receipt of news of his father's death, Lothar at once sent messengers to Germany claiming the imperial supremacy, as provided for in 817. Three learned· ecclesiastics supported his claim: bishop Drogo of Metz, Raban Maur, abbot of Fulda, and Walafrid Strabo of Reichenau: they upheld the old Carolingian tradition. Lothar tried to restore his supporter, bishop Ebbo to the archbishopric of Reims, vacant since his deposition by Louis the Pious in 835; but the pope would not confirm the restoration. Lothar had more success, however, in winning a number of lay vassals over from their allegiance to Louis the German, who was likely to prove his chief enemy. Lothar had to face, nevertheless, the need to defeat two armies: those of Louis the German and Charles the Bald. He crossed the Rhine to attack Louis at Frankfurt: but Louis' army was strong, stronger, Lothar reckoned, than that of Charles. He therefore made an armistice with Louis, hoping to defeat Charles first; he drove him back from the Quierzy region to the banks of the Loire, and received the submission of many of Charles's vassals, including that of Nominoë of Brittany. He met Charles's army near Orleans: but again both leaders feared to exhaust their armies in a battle which would leave the advantage to the third leader whose forces would be still intact. Another armistice was made: but the triangular campaign was at once renewed. Lothar attacked Louis and tried to confine him to Bavaria; Charles crossed the Seine and by May 841 had retaken Paris, Troyes and Châlons-sur-Marne. He sent a message to Louis that he was coming to his help, and the armies of the two younger brothers met near the Rhine. Lothar meanwhile had joined forces with Pepin II, the rival of Charles the Bald in Aquitaine: the chances of victory in a decisive battle seemed relatively even. On 25 June 841 the opposing forces met at Fontenoy, near Auxerre, and after an exhausting battle, the advantage lay with Charles and Louis. Even now, Lothar did not recognize defeat, and continued to intrigue with his brothers' vassals, plan a new campaign, try to stir up the old spirit of pagan resistance among the Saxons against Louis, and win the adherence of the northmen by giving the island of Walcheren as a benefice to their leader, Harald; but the autumn and winter of 841 showed that strength was too evenly divided for an imperial victory.

The two younger brothers realized the need for a particularly solemn alliance, if they were to withstand the arms and the intrigues of Lothar. On 14 February 842 they made to each other the famous oath of Strasbourg, binding themselves in a solemn alliance against Lothar. The language of the east Franks was now distinguishable from that of the west Franks as the ancestor of modern German as against modern French; each brother swore before the other's host, and in the tongue of that host, that he would, for their common safety, succour and help his brother in all respects, as was just: and that he would never make with Lothar any arrangement that might be harmful to his brother. After which, a representative of each host swore in his own language that he would never aid the brother who should break this oath, even if the oath-breaker were his own lord; the oath of Strasbourg was made more binding than the oath of vassalage itself.

In March 842 Charles and Louis had some military success against Lothar, who withdrew to Lyons, possibly *en route* for Italy; after which the two younger brothers prevailed upon the clergy to declare Lothar deposed. But to enforce a complete deposition and expropriation was beyond their power. They followed Lothar to the Rhone valley, and there met Eberhard, count of Friuli, who proposed partition. The Frankish magnates indeed were by now anxious for peace; the campaigns had left the Franks weak against their external enemies and Fontenoy had been a very bloody battle. Yet another partition was planned: its terms to be decided, not merely by the three brothers, but by 120 commissioners, who were to meet at Metz. Lothar still resisted such an acknowledgment of the defeat of his claim to empire; but Louis strengthened himself by crushing the Saxon resistance, Charles raided the garrisons of Pepin II in Aquitaine, and Lothar had finally to allow the commissioners to meet at Verdun. The danger from the northmen was by now acute: they had sacked Quentovic and Rouen, and in the summer of 843 they sacked Nantes and raided the mouth of the Loire, fortifying the island of Noirmoutier as a base.

The partition conference was held at Verdun in August 843. It was agreed that Lothar should hold Italy, the Carolingian homelands round Aix and the Rhine mouth, and a corridor joining the two territories: its western frontier to run from Antwerp to the Somme, up the banks of the Meuse to the headwaters of the Saône and down the Saône and Rhone to Arles, while the eastern frontier skirted Frisia to the Rhine, up the Rhine to Rhaetia, eastward along the Alpine crests to Bozen, and southwards to include in Lothar's territory Istria and Aquileia. Charles the Bald received the Frankish lands to the west of Lothar's corridor, and Louis the German those to the east. Though the corridor was to form no later state itself, its existence for even a short period tended to separate the eastern and western kingdoms of the Franks. The curious territorial division was due to the fact that each brother was actually in possession of the lands composing his share, or the greater part of them, at the time, and to the desire for equality of revenue. No share had racial unity, identity of language, or natural frontiers. No further unity of the *populus Christianus* could be postulated after the Partition of Verdun: the deacon Florus of Lyons wrote in sorrow that there was no more an emperor, only kinglets: no more a *regnum*, only *fragmina regni*. The bishops still yearned for at least a semblance of unity, for 'confraternal rule', for conference and co-operation: but when, on occasion, such conferences were held, only declarations in the most general terms were issued: scarcely even in the pressing danger of the raids of the northmen were definite defensive measures taken in common.

CHAPTER XXIII

THE CAROLINGIAN EMPIRE FROM 843 TILL THE DEATH OF CHARLES THE FAT, 888

THE Carolingian empire in this period was not effectively ruled by a single government, but it was still ruled by members of the same royal house. There was still an emperor with power real in some portion of the empire and titular in the rest, and the Frankish 'culture' still prevailed from beyond the Pyrenees to Moravia, and from Hamburg to Benevento. There was more than one administrative palace, but government was carried on as before by palace, dukes, counts and marquesses, and in learning and art Frankish scholars lived on a tradition Greco-Roman in origin but now rather Latin than Byzantine. The question of territorial partition among Charlemagne's descendants was rivalled in importance only by the raids of Saracens, Slavs, and above all, the northmen.

Lothar I, from 843 till his death in 855, still used the imperial title, but the only imperial prerogative which he made effective was his protectorate of the holy see. In the recent civil wars the papacy had sought to escape from Frankish tutelage; when Gregory IV died in 844, Sergius II was consecrated without notification of an imperial *missus* or the taking of the promised oath of fidelity. Lothar however sent his son, Louis, to Italy as king; he came to Rome, and the pope made formal excuses for the recent procedure at the election, made the Romans take the oath to the *missus*, and crowned the prince as Louis II. After this assertion of imperial rights, Louis received the homage of Siconolf, prince of Salerno, now claiming the whole duchy of Benevento: war was already threatened among the claimants to the small Lombard states in south Italy. In another effort to assert imperial authority, Lothar asked pope Sergius to make his half-brother, Drogo, bishop of Metz, papal vicar for all the transalpine lands of the Franks, but the west Frankish bishops objected, and at the synod of Ver asked king Charles the Bald to provide to the see of Reims, still unfilled since the deposition of Ebbo. In consequence, Hincmar, a learned monk of Saint-Denis, was elected, and was to prove himself not only a good administrator of the west Frankish church, but a great supporter of west Frankish independence against the imperial pretensions of Lothar:

and also of his own rights as a metropolitan against the holy see. He was, in short, a great servant of west Francia, against any claims to superior power, spiritual or secular.

Lothar's activities were mainly exercised in Italy, to build up the royal position there. He confirmed the patriarch of Aquileia in his position in 845, to strengthen him against the patriarch of Grado, now allied to Byzantine interests. He tried also to defend the Tyrrhenian coasts against the raids of the Saracens: in the south, Naples also was trying to organize a defence with Gaëta, Amalfi and Sorrento. The raids however got worse: in 846 the Saracens pushed northward up the coast and raided Rome herself, profaning St Peter's basilica and carrying off rich plunder: Christians shuddered at the sacrilege and the prospect of future danger; Lothar was much disturbed. Attack was needed in the south, where the Saracens already held Benevento, and Louis II in 847 led an expedition south and recaptured it. To end the weakness of the duchy, divided between the adherents of the two claimants, Siconolf and Radelchis, Louis awarded Salerno to Siconolf and the duchy of Benevento to Radelchis: but both proved useless as defenders of south Italy against the Saracens. In 852 Louis himself tried to take Bari, the chief Saracen base, but his expedition failed.

The next pope proved himself a better leader against the Saracens. Sergius II had died in 847, and Leo IV been consecrated without waiting for imperial confirmation. He proceeded to have Rome on the right bank of the river, including St Peter's, defended by a wall, for defence against the Saracens: the enclosed area thus became known as the Leonine city. His efforts were justified, for in 849 a raid by a Saracen fleet was beaten off. But in Provence the Saracens plundered Arles in 850. Frisia too between 845 and 852 suffered continuous raids, in her case from the northmen. Lothar found it expedient to grant a great Danish duchy, at the mouths of the Rhine, Meuse and Scheldt, to Rurik and his nephew, Godefrid the Yngling, king of Denmark, and for a time relative peace followed.

In 850 Lothar raised Louis II to the imperial dignity, and the pope had him acclaimed emperor in Rome, and crowned him. The young emperor's rule was effective only in Italy; when Leo IV died and Benedict III was elected, he sought and received confirmation from the imperial *missi* before consecration.

Meanwhile Neustria suffered even worse disorders from raiders and from rebels against Charles the Bald, who had very little authority in Aquitaine, Brittany or the Breton March. A selfish and uncontrolled vassalage sought to retain church lands, use their private churches as sources of revenue, and increase their estates at the expense of their neighbours. Charles the Bald, to whom their fidelity was owed, was not a prince without valour or initiative, as the events of his troubled reign were to show; he had imbibed learning at his father's learned court, he had an almost Byzantine interest in theological problems and a dogged persistence in the face of misfortune; but his resources were too small to support his position and his claims. He was no general, and it took him nearly twenty years to realize that a new strategy was needed against the attacks of the northmen. At the beginning of his reign his other enemies seemed more dangerous. In 843 he led a campaign against Nominoë, and a more successful one into Aquitaine in 844: he besieged Toulouse, captured Bernard, marquess of Septimania, and had him executed. But in the Breton March he was defeated. In 845 things went worse; Charles had to allow Pepin II the effective rule of Aquitaine, receiving him as his vassal: and Nominoë defeated him. He had to acknowledge Nominoë as independent ruler of Brittany in 846.

Meanwhile, the raids of the *Nortmanni* had wrecked Quentovic and Paris (see p. 443) and only the payment of a large 'geld' procured their departure. In Brittany, Nominoë chased off four bishops as pro-Frankish, invaded the March, took Nantes, and asserted Breton independence of the mother church of Tours. When he died in 851, Charles tried to claim fealty from his son, Erispoë, without success; he had to recognize him as king and cede to him the Breton March in return for an oath of fidelity unlikely to be observed. The year 850 was one of ill omen for defence against the Danish raids, for in that year a Danish partition was arranged between the claimants to that kingdom, and this for a few years ended the Danish civil wars, leaving many adventurers free to fight elsewhere. External raiding, rather than maritime commerce, now became the main occupation of the Scandinavian peoples, and the Frankish lands were plundered from three chief Scandinavian bases. From their headquarters in the Gironde, the Danes sacked Bordeaux in 855; they fortified an island in the Seine which was vainly besieged in 852 by both Lothar and Louis: they abandoned it for a heavy price in 853, burned Nantes in 854, ravaged the district of Perche in 855 and reoccupied their headquarters on the Seine. They held similarly an island in the Loire and in 853 issued from it and sacked St Martin's city of Tours, holier than any place in Gaul. No effective measures were taken against them, though at Servais in 853 a capitulary tried to protect refugees: 'concerning strangers who have taken refuge in these parts of our kingdom through the oppression of the northmen or the Bretons, it has been ordained that they suffer no harm from any public servant, but be allowed safe passage until they can return to their homes'.

The kingdom of Louis the German was, from its inland character, less troubled by Danish raids: Louis' military energies were directed to keeping his eastern frontier against incursions of the Slavs and the Bulgars. Bohemia was nominally subject to him, but it needed expeditions between 846 and 855 to secure this submission: missionaries from Passau had little success in converting the Bohemians. In Moravia, to the south of Bohemia, Louis' authority was also weak, but in 846 he replaced duke Moimir with the more well-disposed Rastislav, who was ready to support the Christian teachers from Passau; in 855 Louis found it necessary however to march against him too. German colonization and mission work from Salzburg prospered better in Pannonia; in lower Pannonia the Slav prince Priwina was converted and set about converting his subjects. Peace on the eastern frontier was only disturbed when Charles the Bald stirred up the Bulgars to invade Pannonia in order to hinder Louis the German from invading Aquitaine. Towards the north of Louis' frontier, expeditions were needed against the Obodrites in 844, and the Sorbs in 851; but against the Danes Liudolf, count of the east mark of the Saxons and the mark set up against the Danes, kept the frontier for Louis, till king Rurik burned Hamburg in 845. There was another Danish raid up the Elbe in 851 and Bremen was sacked in 858; but as these were the only raids of the northmen in more than thirty years, the east Franks were fortunate as compared with the subjects of Charles the Bald.

The emperor Lothar I died at the monastery of Prüm in 855, leaving his territories divided between his three sons: Louis II, Lothar (II) and Charles. Louis II kept Italy, with the imperial crown, Lothar II had Frisia and Francia, Charles (still a child, and an epileptic) Provence and the Rhone counties. Not only was Lothar I's corridor separated from Italy, but the northern part of the corridor, the future Lorraine, was separated from the southern; further subdivision was to follow. Aix was no longer an imperial capital: Lothar II, by title emperor and king, ruled *Francia media*, middle France, but scarcely a middle kingdom, so ill-defined and shifting were its frontiers: the region was geographically nameless, and hence designated *Lotharii regnum* or *Lothariense regnum*: in short, Lorraine.

The period between the death of the emperor Lothar I, in 855, and that of the emperor Louis II in 875 was one of internal confusion and external danger. Two of the sons of Louis the Pious remained alive in 855, ruling the old empire with their three nephews; though the Alps made a satisfactory northern frontier to Italy, there were no satisfactory natural frontiers between the kingdoms of Charles the Bald and Louis the German, and both might fairly hope to despoil their young nephews to their own advantage. A special opportunity offered itself over Lothar II's desire to divorce his wife Theutberga; if he failed in this, he would probably die childless, and the *regnum Lothariense* might be divided between the kings of the west or east Franks, or absorbed by either of them. The Lorraine divorce involved a serious issue in canon law, but it was even more important in the sphere of Frankish politics. Acute difficulties over the divorce did not however arise till 860.

The first five years of Lothar II's reign brought further troubles to the kingdom of Charles the Bald, and further fighting in south Italy. To balance the support Pepin II was receiving in Aquitaine, Charles the Bald betrothed his son Louis the Stammerer to Erispoë's daughter; but when Erispoë was assassinated in 857, Solomon his heir expelled Louis from the province of Maine. Moreover, the *Nortmanni* burned Paris in 856, and Bayeux and Chartres in 858: while Danes from the isle of Noirmoutier burned Orleans in 856, and in 857 Tours and Blois. In 859 other northmen ravaged Noyon, Amiens and the mouth of the Scheldt, while those of the Loire sailed round Spain and attacked Septimania and Provence. Count Gerard, who ruled this region for Charles the Bald, however, defeated them; it was becoming clear that defence against the raiders depended on the energy and ability of the local count or marquess, rather than on the king: for in Neustria and the Rhine mouth, where the local vassals made no preparations against the raiders, there was no successful resistance. In 858 Charles the Bald met Lothar of Lorraine at St Quentin to concert defence, and an attempt was made to block the Seine to the invaders by fortifying the island of Oissel near Rouen, but no more than this beginning could be made, for this summer Charles was all but pushed from his throne. The Aquitanian supporters of Pepin II joined with the Burgundians in inviting Louis the German to invade his brother's dominions. Louis' own position was secure at the time, for his lands were sheltered from the raiders, his son Carloman proving an effective commander in Pannonia and Carinthia, and the northern Slavs prepared for defence rather than attack. Louis led his army against Charles, whose lay vassals mainly abandoned him and fled. His throne was saved for him by the fidelity of the west Frankish clergy, and particularly by archbishop Hincmar of Reims. When Louis convoked a synod of clergy to Reims, hoping to be crowned there king of the west as well as of the east Franks, Hincmar boldly withstood him; the lay vassals came to doubt his ultimate success and abandoned his cause; Louis had to recross the Rhine in January 859. Peace was made between Louis and Charles at the conference of Coblentz, summoned by Lothar II in June 860. The territorial *status quo* was maintained, but Louis the German had lost prestige and Charles the Bald correspondingly gained; Hincmar, who had saved his crown for Charles, and also west Frankish independence of Louis, now held a very strong position.

Meanwhile, in south Italy, there was fighting between Salerno and Benevento, between Salerno and Capua, and also between the duke of Benevento and Louis II himself: the Saracens profited by these internal wars. They sacked Naples in 856, ravaged Capua and the Campagna, and put Monte Cassino to ransom; in 860 a fleet of northmen sailed from Provence and sacked Pisa. Though Louis II could do little for the defence of south Italy he strengthened the Frankish position at the head of the Adriatic by making a useful alliance with the Venetians, and he maintained Frankish authority in Rome. When Benedict III died in 858, Louis secured the election and consecration in his own presence of Nicholas I, who was to prove a greater pope than any since Hadrian I.

After the year 860, Frankish politics centred on the repudiation of Theutberga by Lothar II (of Lorraine). Theutberga had had no child and Lothar believed her sterile; on the other hand, he had had children by Waldrada, his mistress, before he married Theutberga, and he now alleged that he had actually concluded a marriage with her before the ceremony with Theutberga, which was therefore no marriage. He summoned a synod to Aix in 860, and when this synod refused to accept his plea, he summoned a second, to meet on 15 February 860, using all his efforts to have the marriage with Theutberga declared invalid. The archbishops of Trier and Cologne refused to be pushed the whole way: they forbade future relations with Theutberga, but did not declare the marriage null and void. Archbishop Hincmar, however, wrote and vehemently defended Theutberga and the marriage: he had good moral and canonical grounds for his action, but these coincided with the interests of his master, Charles the Bald, who was strongly opposed to Lothar's 'divorce', and wished to see him die still married to Theutberga and still childless: he or his heirs might then hope to annex Lorraine. Theutberga in 860 fled to Hincmar and Charles for protection, and obtained their support for the petition she addressed to pope Nicholas I. Lothar sought to counterbalance this move by making an agreement with Louis the German at Coblenz for present support in return for a promise of the succession in Alsace, after which he summoned a third synod to Aix (862) and obtained from it the decision that Theutberga's marriage was invalid and that he was free to marry again. He at once married Waldrada and had her crowned queen.

Pope Nicholas, however, had been apprised of the decision of Aix, 862, and at once sent off two Italian bishops as his legates to convene a great synod and inquire into the matter of Lothar's marriage, thus asserting his jurisdiction at the same time over the Frankish clergy (in disagreement over a matter of canon law) and a Frankish king. A synod of Lotharingian clergy met at Metz: and the legates, who presided over it, were bought over by Lothar and concurred in the verdict that Waldrada had been married to Lothar before his irregular union with Theutberga, which was in fact no marriage. But when news of the verdict, and his legates' conduct, was brought to Nicholas, he quashed the proceedings of the synod of Metz: summoned a Lateran synod: deprived the two archbishops who had borne him news of the synod of their sees, and forbade Lothar's further relations with Waldrada. Even when Louis II appeared in Rome with an army in 864, Nicholas would not yield in the respect of Lothar's marriage, and his firmness seemed victorious when in that year Lothar, in great difficulties with the northmen in Frisia, heard the papal decision and sent to Nicholas signifying his submission. He hoped, however, that such submission need be temporary only, and to weaken Theutberga's support by her brother Hubert, who commanded an Alpine region between his own southern lands and the Rhone counties of his brother Charles, he gave the *ducatus* (still a military office) of the region to a vassal who had abandoned Charles the Bald for his own service. This vassal became Conrad II, and Theutberga's brother died soon after. In 863 the epileptic Charles of Provence died, and Lothar and Louis shared his kingdom, Louis taking Provence and part of Burgundy and Lothar the duchy of Lyons, adjoining his own southern lands. Charles the Bald got nothing: and the prospect that, through the energetic action of pope Nicholas, Lothar's now considerable kingdom would have no inheritor, induced him to make overtures to his old enemy, Louis the German. The two kings met and conferred at Tusey in February 865, and called upon Lothar to accept the papal pronouncement; at the same time, in some disquiet at Nicholas' claim to final jurisdiction, they forbade their bishops to attend the general council at Rome which Nicholas was summoning to hear the disputes about Lothar's marriage. Lothar in alarm, sent messengers to Nicholas protesting his submission and asking papal protection from his uncles.

The strength of Nicholas' position appeared in the mission, headed by his legate Arsenius, bishop of Orta, which he sent to the western Franks, with command to compel Lothar to take back Theutberga as his wife, to warn Charles and Louis to forbear to attack Lothar, now submissive, and to replace Rothad, bishop of Soissons, in his see: Hincmar, Rothad's archbishop, with Charles's support, had deposed him. By such action Nicholas challenged the authority of metropolitans to depose their provincial bishops on any grounds, without recourse to the holy see, and upheld Rothad, who had appealed to him. Rothad, to support his claim, had brought to Rome the important collection of decretals, largely unauthentic (see p. 538), now known as the Pseudo-Isidorian or False Decretals, though it is not proved that Nicholas had taken cognizance of them when he ordered Rothad's reinstatement to his see of Soissons. Charles the Bald was humiliated over the matter, as was Hincmar, who had striven vigorously to show that the deposition of Rothad in a synod presided over by his metropolitan had followed all the rules of canonical procedure. Hincmar had earlier done good service to Charles the Bald, but Charles, in deference to apostolic authority, now withdrew his favour from him, and in 867, in spite of Hincmar's opposition, also had the papally appointed clerk Vulfad ordained priest and appointed to the see of Bourges. When Nicholas I died in 867, his decisions stood unchallenged: he had vindicated his claim to the control of the metropolitans by the papacy, and to the subjection of the emperor himself on a moral issue.

In their desire to partition Lotharingia at Lothar's death, Charles and Louis the German had paid too little attention to the raids of the northmen and other external enemies. In the eastern kingdom, Louis' son Carloman had rebelled in 861, and sought to rule the valley of the Inn in alliance with the Moravians; he was replaced as ruler of the eastern frontier lands in 863 by Gundachar, made marquess of Carinthia. The Obodrites attacked the more northern frontier in 862, and at the same time Hungarian horsemen, migrants from the steppes and more recently from the banks of the Dnieper, swept for the first time against the eastern frontiers of Bavaria. The eastern frontier of Louis stood always in need of defence, and he was too suspicious of his brother's intention to concert with him any serious defence against the northmen. Moreover, he feared the mutual jealousy of his own sons, and arranged in 865 a partition of his own kingdom to become effective after his death: Carloman was to inherit Bavaria, the Danubian marches and the eastern lands peopled mainly by the Slavs: Louis, Franconia and Saxony: and Charles, Rhaetia and Suabia.

Charles the Bald, however, made a beginning in the defence of his lands against the northmen. Since it was clear the host could not reach the raiders in time to force them to give battle, it was now realized that the blocking of the great rivers by some fortification of an island or bridge offered the best hope of defence. There was difficulty in bridging rivers like the Seine or the Loire anywhere near their mouth, but the strategy was sound and the pirates had already pointed the way to such defence by fortifying their own base camps on the rivers. They would make, as the Anglo-Saxon Chronicle was to write later, a 'wearc'. Charles the Bald and his Neustrians were now to try the expedient of making a bridge or a similar 'wearc' to hold the Seine, an attempt on the same lines as the fortifying of Oissel in 858. Assemblies were held at Pitres on the Seine farther up river, near Mantes, in 862 and 864, measures taken for the building of a bridge at Pitres, and a long, miscellaneous edict issued at Pitres, in 864 referring in some clauses to the harm done by the northmen and Charles's other enemies, and the need of preparations against them. No man, it was decreed, must, without the royal permission, sell or give his armour (*brogne*, Anglo-Saxon *byrnie*, *brunia*) or weapons to a stranger, either for a price or in ransom to the northmen; all the Frankish *pagenses* who had horses or who could obtain them, must ride with the count against the enemy (this is not the summons to the host, but the sudden call to repel raiders): freemen who remained at home when they were needed for the defence of the *patria* must be brought before the inquest of the *missi*: freemen must come without excuse for the fortifying of new towns and the making of bridges and causeways across the marsh; counts and bishops must protect refugees from 'the persecution of the northmen'. Moreover, those who in times like these have made without royal permission forts and entrenchments and hedges (*castella et firmitates et haias*), these (i.e. the northmen or the king's enemies like the Bretons) must by the first of August pull them down again, 'for they inflict plunder and harm on the villages and dwellers near by'.

The fortifications begun after the edict of Pitres were not at once successful in stopping the northmen. In 865 these burned Poitiers and Orleans on the Loire: but count Robert the Strong fought them and prevented their pressing into Neustria. Even on the Seine, raiders got by and plundered the environs of Saint-Denis. In 866 the Neustrians again fought these raiders of the Seine, without driving them away: Charles the Bald had to buy them off; at which they sailed for England. The same year the northmen of the Loire killed count Robert the Strong and the count of Poitiers. The eastern Frank, Hugh, in this extremity was made duke of the region between Seine and Loire and also lay abbot of Saint-Martin of Tours and of Noirmoutier; all the resources of the countryside were placed at his disposal, but even so he could scarcely defend Neustria from the raiders of the two rivers. In such circumstances, Charles had to make peace with the Bretons, yielding them the county of Coutances, but though their king Solomon gained this advantage over Charles, he could not persuade pope Nicholas to confirm his own erection of Dol to be the archdiocese for Brittany.

Charles the Bald's difficulties with pope Nicholas had already led to his agreement with Louis the German at Tusey; in 867 he met him again at Metz and confirmed their agreement to partition Lotharingia on Lothar's death, which occurred in August 868, in Italy. At the moment, Louis the German's attention was engaged by a rising of his son Louis and dangers from the Slavs on the eastern frontier: he himself was at Ratisbon, a sick man. Charles, on the contrary, was momentarily in a strong position: abbot Hugh, by means of the new fortifications, was holding his own against the northmen of the Loire: Charles hoped to gain all Lotharingia, in spite of the pledges for partition which he had given at Metz. In 869 he marched into Lotharingia, was supported by Rurik the Northman, duke of Frisia, and on 9 September had himself crowned king of Lotharingia by Hincmar, at Metz. But Louis the German could not be ousted from his share of Lotharingia by a mere diplomatic move: he warned Charles that he would not accept such a disposition of his brother's lands, and Charles preferred negotiation to fighting. On 8 August 870 a partition treaty was signed at Meersen, and Lotharingia was divided; Charles received Frisia and the lands west of the Meuse, Moselle, Marne, Saône and the Jura, Louis the eastern parts of Lotharingia. Charles was strong enough to take the duchy of Lyons from count Gerard and confer it on his supporter, count Boso, and to hold his share of Lotharingia against the remonstrances of Nicholas' successor, pope Hadrian, who denounced the violation of the emperor Louis II's right to succeed in Lotharingia.

The emperor Louis II was, however, in 870, nearing the end of his reign. He had had to contend in south Italy with the Saracens, the internal struggles of Salerno, Benevento and Capua, and finally, with the Greeks. Louis had made a great effort against the Saracens in 867, using a fleet lent by the Venetians: by 867 the Saracens were holding only Bari and Taranto. Bari was besieged in 869, with the help of a Byzantine squadron which blockaded it by sea: the siege was long, but Bari surrendered to the Franks in 871. The Greeks, however, expected to keep the city which had once been their headquarters on the Adriatic, and the allies quarrelled so sharply that the emperor Basil I would address Louis II only as *rex*, not as *imperator augustus*: Louis fiercely asserted his right to the imperial title. Whereas Basil had asserted that Louis was not emperor, since he did not rule all the Frankish lands, Louis asserted that he did so rule, 'for we may be said to rule those territories which are held by those of the same flesh and blood as ourselves': Louis' words, that is, asserted the indivisibility of the Carolingian empire, though his actual power extended no further than the Alps. Louis further besieged Saracen Taranto, but the duke of Benevento captured him, denied his right to operate in Beneventan territory, and allowed the Saracens to keep their city rather than let Louis take it.

Another long-term blow to the unity of the Frankish dominions on the eastern frontier was the introduction of Greek missionaries into Moravia; up till this time the conversion of the Moravian Slavs had been carried out by Bavarian clergy, and with conversion went German colonization; Rastislav, prince of Greater Moravia, however, was hostile to the Bavarian clergy, and applied for missionaries to the Byzantine emperor, Michael III, who sent him Cyril and Methodius (see p. 497). Rastislav, however, was defeated by the Franks between 867 and 870 and the Frankish clergy returned with the victors.

Moravia and Bulgaria indeed contended successively for leadership of the Slav tribes and the setting up of a third, a Slav, empire in the Balkans, to hold a position midway between east and west: their aspirations for leadership helped to dictate the form of Christianity they adopted, eastern or western. Eventually, Moravia fell into the orbit of the Franks and Latin Christianity: Bulgaria to Byzantium and the Greek church. But though the Franks retained their supremacy in Moravia, in the last years of the emperor Louis II, in Italy and on the eastern frontier they suffered misfortunes. Louis himself died near Brescia on 12 August 875, and without a male heir; he bore the imperial title but his effective rule had extended only to Italy.

Charles the Bald and Louis the German had for some years both hoped to succeed to the empire; but Louis' position was temporarily weak. He had had to repel a Danish raid in east Frisia in 873, and fight the northern Sorbs: but the situation in the southern part of his eastern frontier was more dangerous. His son Carloman now ruled Moravia, the Ostmark of Bavaria and upper Pannonia, while lower Pannonia, the country between Drava and Sava, and Carinthia were under the rule of Arnulf, Carloman's bastard son. The Moravians however had revolted in 873 and were now merely tributary, inspiring the Czechs of Bohemia with aspirations to independence; in both the Moravian and Pannonian churches German influence had been excluded in favour of that of Methodius with his more favourable attitude to the use of Slav as a liturgical language. Louis the German was ill-placed at the moment to contend for the imperial succession.

Charles the Bald, on the other hand, was relatively unhindered. The northmen of the Loire had in 873 been driven from Angers; a Breton war of succession followed on Solomon's death in 874 and removed danger from that quarter; in Aquitaine, Bernard, count of the Auvergne, Bernard, marquis of Gothia (now separated from Septimania), and count Boso, were loyal. Charles's reconciliation with Hincmar strengthened him as against pope John VIII who, though an astute diplomatist, was less outstanding a statesman than Nicholas I. On the news of the emperor's death Charles set out for Italy with papal approbation. The Saracen fleets held command of the Adriatic and the Tyrrhenian seas, and even raided papal territories; south Italy was in a state of war and confusion, and it was even hoped that Charles the Bald, who had been so helpless against his own pirate enemies, might bring salvation to Italy. On Christmas Day, 875, pope John had Charles acclaimed at Rome and crowned him emperor: he then named the bishop of Sens, Ansegis, papal vicar for Gaul and Germany, and received from Charles a renunciation of his right to keep an imperial *missus* in Rome, together with a generous confirmation of all earlier privileges made to the holy see. This Franco-papal alliance struck, Charles went to Pavia, had himself elected king of Italy, entrusted to count Boso the government of the Italian kingdom, and recrossed the Alps. He had done nothing for the peace or security of Italy.

He secured for his own rule the part of Provence which had belonged to Louis II, and on the strength of his Italian successes, convened an assembly at Ponthion for June 876, and received from his nobles fresh oaths of fidelity, made to him as emperor. Fifty bishops from Francia and Lotharingia attended the assembly at Ponthion, both to swear fidelity and to hear the papal letters of admonition read to the assembly by the two papal legates: Charles's accession to the empire and the kingdom of Italy were solemnly recited, as ushering in a new era of imperial peace and splendour for the Franks; at the end of the session Charles presided, clad in the ceremonial garments of a Byzantine emperor. Nevertheless, the representatives of the east Franks and Louis the German were confined to a single bishop and two counts, and those sent, not to share in the deliberations of the assembly, but to protest on Louis' behalf at the annexation of the late Louis II's lands by the king of the western Franks. Moreover, through the influence of Hincmar, the bishops were not ready to accept Ansegis as papal vicar, protesting rather their acceptance of the rights reserved to metropolitans by the sacred canons. The papal vicariat remained a dead letter.

About a month after the assembly at Ponthion, on 26 August 876, Louis the German died at Frankfurt. Charles, now emperor, immediately possessed himself of the left bank of the Rhine, hoping that the jealousies of Louis' three sons, and the campaign against the Moravians on which Carloman was engaged, would allow him to gain power over the east Franks. One of the three brothers, Louis the Young, however, defeated him at Andernach, and forced him to abandon his hopes of German rule: by a partition made in the Reissgau, the three sons shared out Louis the German's kingdom: Carloman took Bavaria, Pannonia, Carinthia and the suzerainty of the tributary Slav lands; Louis had Franconia, Saxony and Thuringia and Charles Suabia. Lorraine remained undivided.

In Italy, pope John VIII proved himself a loyal ally of Charles and an able administrator and even strategist. He reclaimed parts of the patrimony from the encroachments of the nobles and had his measures ratified in 877 by a synod of Ravenna. He ranged the south Italian princes against the Saracens, drew the Italian seaports from entangling alliances with the Muslims and achieved a limited success, for the Saracens still raided at times even up to the walls of Rome. In north Italy he had little help from Charles or his officers; count Boso abandoned his rule of Italy to Berengar, count of Friuli, and went off to marry Louis II's daughter; but in the south, the emperor Basil I in 876 put a Greek garrison in Bari, and was recognized as emperor by the Dalmatians.

In 877, at John VIII's urgent invitation, the emperor Charles decided to return to Italy. A fleet of *Nortmanni* had again entered the Seine and Charles bought them off with a large sum. He then took measures at an assembly held at his villa of Quierzy in June 877 to secure stable government during his Italian visit, and these measures were of lasting importance in the history of vassalage and feudal society (see p. 558). The contract initiated by the vassal's oath had been terminable at death, or indeed, in some circumstances, even before; a vassal's sons did not automatically become vassals of the same lord or king, and the vassal's office (palace office or county) did not pass to his son. The vassalage at Quierzy, however, feared that Charles's son, Louis the Stammerer, whom he proposed to leave as his regent in his absence, might disregard the traditional practice by which 'honours' or benefices did pass to a vassal's son on his father's death; several clauses of the capitulary passed at Quierzy therefore were intended as safe-guards against such usurpation or interference by the regent. It was laid down that, if a count died while the emperor was in Italy, his son could not be thrust from his father's office or benefice till the emperor's return. The presumption was established that the vassal's son inherited his father's position and lands. Charles made his second Italian expedition in August, and it brought his reign to an inglorious end. He learned at Pavia that Carloman was marching against him, and that the counts on whose loyalty he had reason to count, abbot Hugh whom he had appointed to guard west Francia from the Vikings, and count Boso and the two Bernards, had revolted against him. Charles recrossed the Alps, and died on the road from the Mont-Cenis on 6 October 877.

The worst period of internal confusion and external attack in the history of the Carolingians followed on the death of Charles the Bald and lasted till the deposition of Charles the Fat (877 till 887). It was also a period of extreme misery for England, for the northmen used the Channel as a waterway and pressed their attacks now on one side, now on another. Succession to Charles the Bald's kingdom and empire was, in 877, very uncertain. His eldest son, Louis the Stammerer, swore to respect the rights of the clergy and nobles, and was crowned king at Compiègne on 8 December 877. The warlike lay abbot, Hugh, advised negotia-tions with his German cousins, especially Louis the Young, and a peace of mutual acceptance of the other's rights was made;

Louis the Stammerer could now attend to the threatened revolts of Bernard of Gothia and other Frankish counts. Louis the Young was left free to negotiate with Carloman for the partition of Lotharingia: Carloman had been accepted as king of Italy, and was willing to relinquish his share of Lotharingia to Louis, even though it meant the relinquishing of the palace of Aix, the focus of Carolingian prestige. Louis, king of Italy, was sick, and returned to Bavaria at the end of 877.

He left a situation in Italy very dangerous for the pope, for Frankish counts in the north and the rulers of the small Lombard states in south Italy were quite without control. Marquess Lambert of Spoleto and Adalbert, marquess of Tuscany, entered Rome in Carloman's name in 878, restored certain of John VIII's enemies, whom he had banished, and, instead of introducing strong rule in Rome, left the city in anarchy. In the south, the Saracens fought and intrigued successfully; they bought over Sergius, ruler of Naples, and when the pope paid Amalfi to protect his southern territories against them, the city took the money but gave no protection. The pope had to agree to pay the Saracens an annual tribute of 25,000 'mangons' (Arabic coins) almost as a rent for his own territories. In May 878, therefore, pope John VIII set off to get help from the Franks; he reached Arles by sea, and made his way to Troyes, where he had invited Louis the Stammerer and the Fankish bishops to meet him. Memories of the successful Frankish visits of Stephen II and Stephen IV inspired him, and, like them, he recrowned the Frankish king: but neither Louis the Stammerer nor the Frankish bishops could bring him help. In this strait, he offered to make Boso, count of Provence, king of Italy: but though Boso accompanied him back to Pavia, he found the hostility of the Italian counts and bishops too strong and went back across the Alps. John VIII's position in Italy remained for some years unprotected and precarious.

When Louis the Stammerer died on 10 April 879 he left two sons, Louis III and Carloman. The great Frankish nobles, abbot Hugh, Bernard and Boso, had them both acclaimed as kings: but a section of the Frankish nobles, led by the Paris abbots of Saint-Germain-des-Prés and Saint-Denis, and Conrad, count of Paris, offered the west Frankish crown to the German king, Louis the Young. The latter did indeed advance into western Francia, but used his claim to the crown as a bargaining counter to obtain that part of Lotharingia which Charles the Bald had obtained by partition in 870. The two young west Frankish kings went off to fight the northmen of the Loire: Louis the Young in 880 possessed himself of the whole of Lotharingia, while the two young west Frankish kings partitioned their territories, Louis III taking Francia and Neustria, Carloman, Burgundy and Aquitaine.

Meanwhile, it was a misfortune for the Franks that king Alfred fought so well against the northmen in England, that between the years 871 and 878 he had confined them to a Danelaw consisting of northern England and East Anglia; some of the 'Danes' settled with their fighting men to exploit the English 'harrowers and plowers', but a large band of professional fighting men sailed for further plunder to the Scheldt and the Rhine mouth. A great host of northmen landed in Flanders in 879, burned Térouanne and Saint-Bertin and fixed their base at Ghent; in 880 they plundered Tournai. The same spring another band of northmen plundered Hamburg and wiped out a Saxon army: the Danish mark, beyond the Elbe was lost. Sorbs and Czechs, encouraged by this Saxon defeat, raided Thuringia. Yet another Danish fleet sailed up the Waal and took Nymwegen, once a Carolingian palace; when Louis the Young besieged them there, they burned the place and sailed away.

While such misfortunes befell the Franks of the Baltic and the Rhine mouth, an adventurer not of Carolingian stock for the first time set himself up as independent ruler in Aquitaine. In October 879 Boso, duke of Provence, had himself elected king by lay nobles and clergy at the council of Mantaille; the bishops present crowned him king of a territory including the basin of the Rhone, from Arles to Lyons. Such revolt against rule that was at least Carolingian, however much divided in exercise, could not be passed over; the lay abbot Hugh, moreover, threatened to be as dangerous as Boso. In June 880 Louis III, Carloman, and Charles of Suabia (only surnamed Charles the Fat in the thirteenth century) took the field against their rebellious nobles: Louis the Young sent a detachment to help. They crushed lay abbot Hugh, took part of his kingdom from Boso, but failed to take Vienne. In 882, however, Carloman sent them further reinforcements from Italy, and Boso's new kingdom was overthrown; Boso was limited to a small territory round Vienne, Charles the Fat and Carloman divided the rest.

In Italy, John VIII was so hard pressed by the Saracens, that he invited Charles the Fat, whose Suabian territories opened on to the Lombard plain, to come to his help. In 879 Charles came to Italy: had himself recognized king of Italy, as the heir of his brother, without any intervention from John VIII, and returned to Suabia having done nothing to aid the pope. So necessary was some aid to John, that he approached the emperor Basil in 879 for help: the Byzantines took Taranto in 880, their fleet beat the Saracens in the Tyrrhenian sea, but no military aid was forthcoming to defend John against his immediate enemies. Again John appealed to Charles the Fat: who came to Rome in February 881, was crowned emperor, and again departed without any measures of defence for the holy see. Louis the Young died at Frankfurt in 882, and Charles the Fat was more interested in trying to get his own authority recognized in Germany.

In south Italy, however, the wars against the Saracens took a turn for the better: Naples, Salerno and Capua laid aside their quarrels and made common cause against them. They drove the Saracens back into defended positions, from which, however, they continued to send plundering raids, and it was while they were keeping Rome in a state of demi-siege, that John VIII himself was murdered by conspirators within the Lateran.

In Francia, the raids of the northmen were at their worst. The great Danish army within its fortifications at Ghent stood a siege by the abbot Gozelin, and in 880 burned the country between the Scheldt and the Somme. Arras and Cambrai went up in flames; in 881 Amiens and Corbie were destroyed by fire: but in August Louis III won a victory in the field that sent the invaders back to the Meuse. The scene of devastation was merely shifted farther east: Maastricht and Liége, on the Meuse, were burned: so were Cologne and Bonn on the Rhine, together with the palace of Aix, Stavelot, Malmedy, Prüm, Trier and Metz. The northmen of the Loire were no less active: here, Louis III fought them and drove them to leave his lands, for a time, for the coasts of Britain; but in August 882 an accident led to the young king's death at Saint-Denis. His brother Carloman succeeded Louis III, and Hincmar addressed to him his treatise *De Ordine Palatii* as a memorandum for orderly government.

As to the great Danish army of the Rhine mouth: Charles the Fat marched against it once again in 882, but instead of carrying through the siege of Asselt, he preferred to rid himself of the danger by paying a heavy geld and granting Godefrid, one of their leaders, a great benefice in Frisia, in return for Godefrid's baptism. Nevertheless, the Danish raids continued: Deventer and Duisberg were taken, and it was left for count Henry of Lorraine and the bishop of Hamburg, Rimbert, to struggle against the marauders in the north-east; while the great army itself moved to the Scheldt, in 882 sacked the valley of the Somme, Laon and Reims, and chased before it the aged prelate Hincmar, who died in December at Épernay. Lay abbot Hugh and Carloman won a few victòries over the Danes, but could not prevent the great army from taking up winter quarters at Amiens; in 884 Carloman's vassals refused to fight the Danes and he had to buy them off, shortly before his own death in December of that year. Charles the Fat was accepted by the west Frankish nobles as his successor in 885, and theoretically Carolingian unity was re-established; but in western Francia Charles the Fat's authority was shadowy, and his rule (in so far as it existed) exercised by lay abbot Hugh and Bernard Plantevelue.

The reign of Charles the Fat saw failure after failure against the northmen. They moved from Amiens to Louvain, and an expedition of west Franks in 885 failed to expel them. A certain Hugh the Bastard concerted with the Dane Godefrid a rising in Lorraine in the same year; Charles the Fat succeeded in arresting Hugh and having his eyes put out, while the assassination of Godefrid was successfully arranged by count Henry: all of which brought about the end of Godefrid's Danish duchy of Frisia. But the same summer of 885 the great Danish army moved to the Seine and besieged Paris, which was defended by abbot Gozelin, now its bishop. Gozelin had been abbot of Saint-Germain-des-Prés, the basilica with the sacred relics of Germanus, bishop of Paris; the abbey of Saint-Germain-des-Prés had been twice before sacked by the Danes, but the relics of St Germain had been hastily removed beforehand. This siege of Paris was the greatest of the Danish attacks: the city stood a year's siege and was defended by count Eudes of Paris, later to be king, and by abbot Gozelin, who died upon the walls in the midst of the siege. Messages calling for aid were sent to Charles the Fat, who made his way to the Seine: but all he could do was to promise the Danes a large geld, and permission to pass through the city and up the head waters of the Seine in order to plunder the upper Rhone and Burgundy. The citizens of Paris, however, refused the Danes passage up-river on either side of the Ile de la Cité, and the Danes had to drag their boats overland along the river bank. The glory of successful resistance fell to count Eudes and Saint-Germain: not to the emperor. Charles made count Eudes duke of Paris and gave him the abbeys of lay abbot Hugh, lately dead: he then withdrew and left the Danes to ravage the valley of the Oise and in the winter, Burgundy. In this winter of desolation, Dijon held out, and Tours: their fortifications stood them in good stead.

The incompetence and inertia of Charles the Fat, whose great bulk seems to have been due to disease, were no less apparent in his German and Italian dominions than in Frisia, the Rhine mouth and western Francia. The east Frankish counts and dukes disregarded the royal authority and settled their own quarrels by force of arms; a specially dangerous struggle occurred in Bavaria and its eastern mark between rival claimants for local rule, and beyond the east mark the Moravians pillaged the Frankish frontier lands and Pannonia. In Moravia Methodius continued to teach his converts under great difficulties, and after his death in 885 his followers were expelled from Moravia. Moravia was out of Frankish, or Roman, control. Similarly, in Italy imperial authority was at a discount. Pope Marinus I (882–884) appealed to Charles for help against count Guy of Spoleto, and Charles came to Italy, declared Guy's estates confiscated, and made a treaty with Venice. But the sentence against Guy could not be executed, even by the faithful Berengar of Friuli, and in 885 Charles had to pardon him. The papacy remained unaided through the short pontificate of Hadrian III (884–885), though an imperial *missus* had been re-established in Rome, and the next pope, Stephen V (885–891) relinquished all hope of help from the Carolingians, and adopted a policy of relying on the small, south Italian states for help against the Saracens, and of an alliance with Byzantium. The Saracens burned Monte Cassino and other Italian monasteries in 883, and Stephen called for help upon Basil I, whose Greek troops chased the Muslims from Calabria, and in south-west Italy established his authority over Naples and Salerno. Meanwhile Stephen made a firm peace with Guy of Spoleto by 'adopting' him, and encouraging him to attack the Saracens and conquer Capua and Benevento, all of which he did. These local forces in Italy proved much more useful to the holy see than the distant Carolingians.

One offence against Carolingian unity ceased when Boso of Vienne died in January 887. His son Louis did homage to Charles the Fat and the emperor, reverting to the old Greco-Roman expedient, 'adopted' him: Provence was restored in appearance to Carolingian rule. Charles's incapacity and deterioration, physical, mental and moral, was now, however, apparent to all: his authority was openly set at nought. In July 887 he was forced to disgrace his counsellor and arch-chancellor, Liutward; in the autumn his nephew, Arnold of Carinthia, the son of Carloman rose and, a month or two later, proclaimed himself king at Frankfurt; Charles the Fat found himself bereft of all support, renounced the imperial dignity and died on 13 January 888. Carolingian unity had finally been dissolved. Count Eudes and Guy of Spoleto both in 888

claimed the title of king of *Francia Occidentalis*, and Eudes easily
maintained himself against his rival.

Guy went off to dispute for the crown of Italy with Berengar of
Friuli: and another claim to kingship was put forward by a
Welf, Rudolf of Burgundy, who claimed the corridor kingdom of
Lothar II. Louis seized power in Provence. The claimants for
local power had long, in fact, divided the empire of Charlemagne,
but they had all been Carolingian by family. From 888 even this
phantasmal Carolingian unity disappeared: the new local rulers
were of other stock.

CHAPTER XXIV

CELTS AND SCANDINAVIANS

O F the peoples who inhabited the fringes of Europe farthest
from the two *foci* of light and learning, Rome and Constantinople, only a short account can be given here. The
Celtic and Scandinavian peoples had in early days no written literature: it is therefore difficult to reconstruct a chronological account
of their early history from written sources, generally the chance
references of alien peoples, often their enemies. The archaeological
evidence about these early peoples, their ornaments, weapons, their
burial places, sometimes their peasant huts and occasionally their
chieftain's halls, is relatively plentiful and often shows fine artistic
skill. Both these races made their contribution to the history of
early medieval Europe.

The Celts, like the Scandinavians, spoke an Indo-European language. Their earliest home was in central Europe, between the
North Sea, the Alps and the Carpathians; they had as their neighbours the Latin and Sabellic tribes who soon passed south into
Italy. There would seem at an early period to have been a common
Italo-Celtic language. From central Europe, however, the Celtic
peoples dispersed, not only into Italy, but from the middle Danube
south into the Balkans and Asia Minor, westward into Gaul, and
northward into Britain and Ireland. These early migrants settled
among the iron age people of the Hallstatt culture (named from the
famous cemetery near Salzburg), and brought to these metal
workers Greek and other Mediterranean influences and techniques.

The early megalithic monuments, such as, for instance, Ave-
bury, or Stonehenge with its outer ring of wooden posts, its inner
circle of lintelled stones (and the rest of the stone complex), had
been set up by the earlier peoples of the stone, bronze and early
iron age: they were already very old at the time of the early Celtic
wanderings and settlements, very old in the time of the Hallstatt
people. The Celts were metal workers, and their distinctive contribution to civilization lay, not in the raising of monuments, but
rather in the smelting and casting of iron, and the social changes
that followed the new techniques. In the fifth century B.C. increased
Italian influence produced the second great iron age society, the
specifically Celtic or La Tène culture, called after the pile-built

16 465

settlement at La Tène on lake Neuchatel. The Celts now worked in bronze or gold for their chieftains' ornaments, sometimes using a red enamel. Already the characteristic trumpet ornament appeared upon their brooches, buckles, mirrors and other metal work, together with the Greco-Roman palmette. The distinctively Celtic ornament in, for instance, the Book of Kells or the Lindisfarne gospels, had its ancestry in the iron age art of Gaul, the Danubian territories and Asia Minor.

The Celtic populations of northern Italy, Roman Gaul, central Europe and Britain underwent conquest by the Romans and by the Germanic peoples who migrated in the fifth and sixth century A.D., but the Celts remained a large, and sometimes the largest element in the population. In Gaul, their place-names remained in the countryside, their craftsmen continued to use the spiral decoration and plaitwork, sometimes alone, sometimes in conjunction with the Germanic animal ornament. In Wales, Cornwall, and their colony, Brittany, the Celtic language survived; in Ireland above all a Celtic, tribal society developed, uninfluenced by Roman or Germanic conquest.

Among the Celtic peoples of western Europe, living in tribal settlements and ruled by tribal chieftains, the Druidic priesthood was a common link. It has been suggested indeed that the Druids originated not with the Celts but with the mesolithic or neolithic peoples who made the great stone monuments, but the evidence shows rather that the Druids were a characteristic order of Celtic society. There is no evidence at all that they used the megalithic monuments in their rites and sacrifices. The word Druid, once thought to be connected with an old Irish word for the oak tree, is now held to be derived from another Irish word meaning 'the wise one', 'the soothsayer'. There is, however, evidence that the Druidic rites included a ceremonial cutting and offering by the Druids of the mistletoe that grows upon the oak; the old Irish feast of Samhain, at the beginning of November, was marked by such a ceremony. But of the old stone age gods for whose offerings Stonehenge (and the smaller, wooden 'henges' which air photography has discovered in Britain) were built, we have no knowledge.

Since the Celtic peoples were spread over western Europe for some 500 years before Caesar, and continued as the subject population, not completely Romanized or Christianized, for some 400 years after him in Gaul, Britain and Ireland, it is unlikely that their customs remained uniform and undeveloped; evidence (nearly all from alien observers) that the Celts did or did not practise sacrifice and even human sacrifice: that the Druids were 'philosophers', and the like, may refer to different periods in their long history. It seems fairly certain, however, that when Greek and Roman writers like Ammianus, Clement of Alexandria and Origen spoke of the Druids as 'philosophers', they were speaking of Celts who had had contact with the empire, and possibly even with Greco-Roman thought: relatively late Celts. It is of interest that, of all the pagan cults encountered by the Romans in the west, that of the Celts alone had a teaching priesthood, and one that linked the race groups in Gaul, Britain and Ireland.

There is a good deal of evidence about these Druids, and their secondary order of *filid* (teachers) and *vates* (bards or soothsayers), in the writings of Caesar, Strabo, Ammianus and those old Irish writings about the struggles of Patrick and his helpers with the Druids (the *filid* and their schools they tolerated). The Druids of Roman Gaul used to visit Britain as part of their training, and there was also communication between the Druids of Ireland and Wales. It seems that these priest-diviners, who also acted as judges and as the repositories of the long-stored oral knowledge of the tribes, must have been a cohesive force in Celtic society. There was, in fact, a common Celtic culture, and the Druids, *filid* and bards helped maintain it. They educated the young and they passed freely among the tribes: in Ireland, even when those tribes were at war. There were Druid colleges, which chose and trained new members: and there were also Druidic families, for certain chieftains, or even fifth-century Christian saints, are said to have sprung from Druidic stock.

Apart from Ireland, no independent Celtic state survived the Germanic migrations and conquests: though Wales and Brittany long continued Celtic in language and culture. But the Celts made, nevertheless, their own contribution to the new Europe. The Celtic tribal province or canton survived both the Roman and Frankish conquests of Gaul, and the Roman town, the old tribal headquarters, became the seat of the Roman magistrate and the Frankish count. Medieval local government in France rested upon a framework ultimately Celtic. Celtic linear pattern combined with Greco-Roman naturalism in the eighth and ninth centuries to give birth to the brilliant illuminations and sculpture of Ireland, Celtic Scotland and Northumbria. The names of Celtic gods and goddesses survived in many of the place-names of Gaul and Britain: Lug, the sun-god, gave his name to Lugdunum (Lyons) and Luguvallum (Carlisle): the goddess Brigantia gave hers to the tribes of Roman Yorkshire; Camulos, a Gallic and British god, to Camelodunum. The large group of Celtic stories of a voyage to the country of the blest, or the dead (like that of Bran, son of Cuchulainn) had their Christian counterparts in the voyage of St Brendan and others which seem to foreshadow the passing of Dante to hell, purgatory and heaven. And again, Celtic life, still half nomadic and tribal, and yet with its curiously strong organization for the preservation of a common learning, developed not unnaturally its peculiar form of Christianity, its peculiar Latin learning, and its peculiar missionary genius.

St Patrick (c. 385–461) planted in Ireland the Latin Christianity in which he had, it would seem, been trained at Auxerre, the see of St Germanus, and the primitive, eastern monasticism he had learned at Lérins, at the mouth of the Rhone. He was able to teach an Irish clergy to recite the Latin office, and, because Latin had never been a spoken language in Ireland, the clergy studied grammar and kept the Latin inflexions pure. It is however possible that the remarkable spread of Latin learning among the Celts was not due solely to the missionaries: a vernacular account of the work of St Patrick speaks of the *retorici* with whom St Patrick contended: these he may have met in Gaul, or they may possibly have been refugees from fifth-century Gaul.

St Patrick would naturally have sought to reproduce in Ireland the Christian organization with which he was familiar. He therefore established for himself a territorial archbishopric of Armagh; but the tribal and pastoral nature of society, and the lack of 'towns', soon led to the service of the Irish church by tribal monasteries of clergy, headed by abbots. Irish clerics could pass among the small villages of the tribe, accompany the chieftain, or go on pilgrimage for the love of God, not knowing where their voyage would end. In the monasteries, to which the ridged and cheap papyrus barely came, a beautiful Celtic script developed, written with quill or reed pen upon the smooth surface of vellum: the beautiful Irish illumination developed from the astonishingly sure Irish penmanship. The creed preserved the one Christian faith, although the Latin services had a character all their own; and the essential function of the bishop in ordination, the dedication of churches and other rites was preserved, without, however, jurisdictional authority. Every Irish monastery had its bishop, or even several bishops, to perform the traditional ceremonies: but authority came to lie, not with these bishops, but with the abbots. It was this lack of a territorial episcopate that roused the later suspicion of Celtic Christianity as unorthodox, and the isolation of Christian Ireland was perpetuated by the paganism of the Anglo-Saxons who invaded Britain in the fifth century. Nevertheless, the Irish monasteries were esteemed for their learning, and frequented by travelling scholars both from Britain and the Continent.

Irish Christianity, learning and art, moreover, extended themselves to Britain and the Continent. Columba (d. 597), a relation of the Irish high-king and pupil of Finnian of Moville and Finnian of Clonard, sailed with twelve disciples and founded a monastery on the little island of Hy (now Iona). Irish daughter houses spread over Scotland, and the monk-bishop Aidan brought Irish Christianity from Iona to Lindisfarne. Meanwhile Columbanus, a monk of the great *bangor* (monastery) in county Down, went off with twelve companions *c.* 590 to convert the half-heathen people of the Vosges; he founded Celtic monasteries, keeping his own severely ascetic rule, at Luxeuil and Fontaines. He taught among the Alemanni and left his pupil, Gallus, in a monastery founded in Switzerland; he himself passed on into Lombardy and in 613 founded the monastery of Bobbio in north Italy, dying there in 615. Columbanus, Finnian of Clonard and Gildas (? author of the *De Excidio*), were all known to each other, all Celtic scholar-abbots, and some of their letters and writings have survived. When Columbanus died, the Celtic form of monasticism was more widely extended than the Benedictine in western Europe: and for some time later, founders of monasteries often laid upon their monks the obligation to follow both monastic rules. The Celtic missionary monks, sprung from a mainly pastoral society whose only large, settled communities were the monasteries themselves, made admirable missionaries to western Europe, and contributed to the passing on to heathen and illiterate peoples of the Greco-Roman heritage.

The Celts, despite the diminishing importance of their small kingdoms or tribal groups to the political history of western Europe, nevertheless made their own contribution to her early literature and art. They helped to pass on the Greco-Roman tradition in the field of literature, while making use of some distinctively Celtic forms of their own; in the art of writing, illumination, metal work and sculpture the Celtic genius remained undominated by Byzantine influence, and became one of the factors of the Carolingian renaissance.

In the field of learning the Irish monasteries commanded respect, especially in the sixth and seventh centuries, when Ireland was untroubled by invasion, Britain settled by a barbarian and only slowly converted people, and northern Francia, from the Seine to the Rhine mouth, had little learning, and no leisured class except the relatively few monks of Columbanus' houses. (The double minsters of Francia and Gaul, referred to by Bede as places to which Anglo-Saxon princesses were sent for training, seem to have produced no literature.) The Breton, Welsh and Irish monasteries of the sixth century clung to the study of Latin to secure an enlightened saying of the office and study of the scriptures; Armagh, the see of Patrick, and Clonmacnois, founded in 548, were notable schools of Latinity. The Irish monks revered the name of Vergil, and though he was no Christian, named their promising clerics after him: but they would seem to have been more familiar with the great fifth-century glossators and grammarians, like Nonus or Servius or Donatus, than with the Vergilian text. Gildas, for instance, was one of those scholars who belonged to the second period of Irish church history (the first being the Patrician, and the third that of Maelruainn, propagandist of the anchoretic life). This second period was dominated by the figure of the *sapiens*, exponent of the Latin written learning in a population knowing only the oral, vernacular learning of the Celts. Columbanus, Finnian of Clonard, Gildas and others were *sapientes*: but Gildas' classical learning was limited. He quotes Vergil from memory six times, but inaccurately; he knew something of Persius and Martial and Claudian and Porphyry. He also knew Jerome's letters and his *De Scriptoribus Ecclesiae*, and, as a good abbot, he was acquainted with the old canons of the church: Columbanus refers to him as an authority in his subject. But in the field of classical literature, his delight in the rarer Latin words indicates that the great glossaries were his favourite, or only accessible, texts: 'otherwise', says Mommsen, 'he could not have written so obscurely'.

The work of the two Columbas contributed also to the passing on of the Greco-Roman heritage by the establishment in peasant societies of a class of literate clerics. Columba's (Columcille's) foundation of Iona in 565 was to prove the mother house of Melrose, of a number of houses in Caledonia, of the great minsters of Iona and, eventually, York. Of Columba's own writings, only a few hymns, chief among them the *Altus Prosator*, survive; but his work helped to establish a leisured class of literate Scottish monks, and lay behind the outstanding work of Adamnan, abbot of Iona from 679 to 704. Adamnan's *Life of Columba*, indeed, was a fine piece of Latin rhetoric, bringing the actions, aspect and qualities of the great abbot clearly before the reader: it was the first piece of fine historical writing in these islands before Bede. Adamnan also wrote a commentary on Vergil, but his finest work in the Latin tongue and tradition was his *De locis sanctis*, presented to his friend and pupil, king Aldfrid of Northumbria. Adamnan here compared the oral information of his guest, the Frankish pilgrim bishop, Arculf, about the holy places in Palestine and about Constantinople, with the evidence he could get from Jerome, Sulpicius Severus and other Latin writers. His book has all the freshness and detail of a traveller's tale, and is of interest as showing the knowledge of Byzantium and even Damascus which might be available to a seventh-century Scottish abbot. The Latin learning of Iona and Lindisfarne was available to Bede, and he, like Adamnan, compiled a Life of Columba: but it is likely that his resources, the great library of manuscripts laboriously brought back by Benedict Biscop for his monastery of Jarrow, were greater than those of Iona or Lindisfarne.

Columbanus, like Columba, increased the number of Celtic scholar monks, and of his own writings more is known than of Columba's. Six of his letters have survived, one of them defending the Irish method of reckoning Easter, and a collection of verses unremarkable in themselves but showing a good knowledge of Vergil. His three dogmatic treatises are lost, but some short addresses to monks have survived, and his monastic rule, a *regula coenobialis patrum*, notable for the austerities enjoined on the monks. Just as the Irish method of reckoning Easter was the survival of an old method conditioned by Irish isolation, so in the Columban *regula* the spirit of Pachomius and the desert fathers survived less modified by Latin familial tradition than in that of Benedict.

A curious Celtic *jeu d'esprit*, unimportant as literature but perhaps indicative of the extent to which the Celtic monk could get access to the great glossaries rather than Latin texts, was the *Hisperica Famina*, used in a few short Celtic poems, one or two tracts, and a few passages of scholars who, like Aldhelm, could write good Latin prose and verse. The vocabulary of this conceit was collected from the rarest and most obscure Latin words, and some invented ones: *famina* is such a word for speech, *Hisperica* from Hesper, the evening star; the expression would mean 'western (Latin) speech'.

When Irish scholar monks drifted to the Continent as missionaries, each perhaps with a single Latin text in his book satchel, they joined for the most part a Columban house, or the household of some missionary Frankish bishop. They took their Celtic enthusiasm for Latin literature, their Celtic ability to write fine verse, to Frisia and the land of the Saxons, to the middle Danube and to Lombardy. But the very fact that they had now at their disposal all the manuscript riches of Italy and the Adriatic, Latin and even Greek manuscripts, merged their studies in the rising wave of the Carolingian renaissance, and deprived it of distinctive character;

Irish classical learning had always been derivative of its source. In
the later Carolingian period the greatest scholar at the court of
Charles the Bald, John Scotus Erigena (see p. 515) was an Irishman: but he wrote as a Byzantine Neoplatonist.

In the field of art, however, the Celts remained undominated by
the Greco-Roman tradition, though their illuminated gospel books,
like the Book of Durrow and the Book of Kells, adopted the custom
of inserting a picture of the evangelist and his symbol from some
Byzantine prototype. In Scandinavia, barbarian art persisted because the country remained long unconverted; in Ireland, however,
early converted by the Patrician mission, the barbarian style with
its abstract ornament, its trumpet pattern, its double spirals,
triumphed in the main over Greco-Roman naturalism. The spiral-
and-trumpet pattern, in which the thickened trumpet ends continued to form focal points from which other spirals sprang in
radiating directions, was purely Celtic: but other motifs, like the
interlaces borrowed originally from Roman pavements in Britain,
the key pattern of Latin origin, and the 'lacertines' of interlacing
ornament, all adapted themselves to the Celtic love of abstract
ornament and dynamic design. They are all found in Celtic illumination, the ornament on the side panels of the Celtic crosses, the
goldsmith's work, and the Irish 'shrines' or reliquaries so often
looted by Norse raiders and carried off to Scandinavia.

Research into the history of Irish illumination has now penetrated beyond the Book of Durrow, the earliest of the Irish illuminated gospel books, and it appears that the earliest Irish missionaries knew nothing of the later, Insular, system of decorating
the gospels. There is in Trinity College, Dublin, a gospel of the
late antique style of the fifth century (*codex Usserianus primus*): it
was not written in Ireland, but imported there in the finished state.
The old Latin psalter known as the Cathach of St Columba was
however written in Ireland: it is the earliest extant example of the
Irish national script: each psalm has an initial in Roman capitals,
the thick strokes decorated: the ornament is ultimately La Tène,
translated from stone carving and metal to illumination, and
'showing the age-long Celtic predilection for curvilinear ornament'. The Irish minuscule and art-forms were carried to Europe
by the missionaries, and only gave way to the Carolingian minuscule and Greco-Roman naturalism in the renewed enthusiasm of
the ninth-century renaissance.

The Scandinavian peoples (Norwegians, Swedes, Danes, and
for cultural purposes, Icelanders) were always outside the Roman

empire, although the remains of their civilization show many traces of Roman influence. The early Scandinavian languages were not very different from those of the Teutonic peoples of northern Europe: the primitive Scandinavian language, that is, belonged to the Teutonic branch of the Indo-European speech family. This primitive language, however, the language of the earliest northern runic inscriptions dating from *c*. A.D. 300, had been transformed before the beginning of the Viking period (*c*. A.D. 800) into different dialects; in which probably the Danish-Swedish tongue differed from the Norwegian, though these northern peoples still thought of their language as one, the 'Danish tongue'. Scandinavian civilization also seems to have been, roughly, undifferentiated, though the evidence comes mainly from burial finds and is scanty about the habitations of the living. Inhumation and cremation of the dead were practised, and the personal ornaments buried with the dead were rich; they included square-headed and cruciform brooches, inlaid garnet ornament and those pendants peculiar to the Scandinavians with a coin device rather barbarously copied on one side only, bracteates. Ship burial within a mound was sometimes afforded to chieftains, as in the Vandel graves near Uppsala (and the cenotaph discovered in 1939 at Sutton Hoo). The practice of ship burial points however to the normality of travel by sea along the Scandinavian waterways, and to some belief in another life beyond the troublesome waves of this world. The Scandinavian peoples in their native lands did not officially accept Christianity till *c*. A.D. 1000.

The landmark in the history of the Scandinavian peoples comes at the end of the eighth century, with the beginning of the 'Viking' age, when the Scandinavians broke out of the isolation of their northern world, and sailed across the North Sea and the Baltic to make pirate raids on adjacent countries. They had long been sailing in the Baltic and trading with the Slav races, and were already fine boat-builders, seamen, metal workers and fighters. The word Viking is of Nordic origin, and possibly derived from a word meaning sea-roving: the term would apply to sea traders as well as sea pirates, for the Vikings practised both trade and piracy: but in the ninth and tenth centuries they found piracy the more profitable. The Viking period is one when a northern culture broke in upon one that was southern and more civilized. The Vikings wanted 'a place in the sun', and had a warlike technique that enabled some of them to get it, and all of them to enrich themselves by plunder. To some, fighting would seem to have been an end in itself, like dangerous sports throughout the ages, for the

battle of the crew of a Viking ship usually resolved itself into a
series of hand-to-hand encounters; sagas speak of the kind of rage
of battle into which the northern warriors passed as 'going ber-
serk'. Prayers to be delivered from the fury of the *Nortmanni* were
soon included in Christian litanies.

The northern civilization from which the Vikings came was that
of peasant farmers, where the crops that could be grown in the
short, northern summer were supplemented by fishing. Each patriarchal farmstead was self-supporting, and every man had some
knowledge of farming, stock breeding, fishing and smithy work,
though some smiths and metal workers practised a special craft.
The iron axe had been used for forest clearing since the Celts
brought the iron-working techniques to western Europe; but forest
clearing by fire had still been easier, and the potash in the wood ash
useful for the growing of a few successive crops. But now, in the
Viking period, planks were needed for the clinker (nail) built
Viking ships, and the iron axe had become a more useful tool: an
impetus was given to wood felling, and the Viking period saw
great forest clearance in Scandinavia.

The 'long houses' of the Viking homestead were perhaps 100 feet
in length, with a series of log fires down the centre; the women
spun and wove, cooked, made blankets, cheese, beer and everything needed in domestic life. Pairs of oval, convex, 'tortoise'
brooches, beads, mosaic ornaments, combs, and shears and scissors
for weaving, have often been found in women's graves. No writing
on vellum or papyrus was practised, though runic inscriptions were
occasionally cut on stone or metal work; literature was oral, and the
long northern nights favoured entertainment by heroic poetry and,
in Iceland, the prose 'saga'. For the northern peoples, contact with
civilization came not by land but by sea: the iron axe had made the
building of the wooden ships possible. The new skill in iron smelting and forging provided the spears, swords and battleaxes for
warfare, as also the coat of mail, the *brynja* or byrnie, made of
linked iron rings.

The beginning of the Viking raids was probably not unconnected with Charlemagne's wars against the Saxons: the Anglo-
Saxon Chronicle speaks also of a raid made on Wessex in the days
of king Beorhtric of Wessex (786–802). Great Britain, Ireland, and
Charlemagne's empire were henceforth attacked by Norwegians
and Danes, while Swedes mainly found an outlet through the
Baltic and down the Russian rivers. The raids were not mass
migrations, but expeditions led by individual chieftains or kings;
there are some signs, however, of more or less peaceful settlement

in the Hebrides and northern Scotland. While the earliest raids were summer campaigns, it was soon found advisable for the 'host' to winter at some river mouth as a base for further raiding.

As to the rise of kingdoms in these northern lands (the area covered by the modern Denmark, Norway, south Sweden and the Baltic coast beyond Jutland): a whole world of legendary history about their kings, some of it founded on fact, is represented in *Beowulf* and other early heroic poetry. The poets and their hearers knew of Eormanric, king of the Goths (indeed, a sixth-century king of Kent was called Eormanric): Heremod, king of the Danes, and the Swedish king Ohthere, both mentioned in *Beowulf*, probably actually existed. But the earliest Scandinavian king to have relations of some importance with Charlemagne's empire was Godefrid, mentioned as king in 804 by Saxo Grammaticus. Godefrid came into conflict with Charles and brought an army to the Schlei, the Baltic creek which lies to the south of Jutland. Relations with the Franks remained uneasy and Godefrid was preparing to fight them when he was killed by one of his own men in 810; he had been king also of southern Norway. War broke out in 812 between the followers of Godefrid and those of a former king, Harald. Eventually Harald, a descendant of the earlier Harald, won a temporary victory, and agreed to divide the Danish lands with the sons of Godefrid, chief of whom was Horic. Both sides desired the help of Louis the Pious, and in 826 Harald came to Ingelheim, near Mainz, and was baptized with four hundred of his followers: he had just anticipated the arrival of Godefrid's followers, asking for Frankish support. He then returned to Denmark with Anskar, the *scolasticus* of Corvey, as his chaplain, but was expelled in 828 from his kingdom; he retreated to the lands in Frisia earlier granted him by the emperor. In the year of the grant, 826, Louis the Pious granted lands in Frisia also to Harald's brother: it was imperial policy to make the Danes converted allies. Their conversion was, however, slow: the first of the Danish wooden churches was built only about 850. The political relations of the Scandinavian lands, however, remained confused, and with the later Carolingians hostile, through the Danish raids and occupation of northern Frisia.

Meanwhile the Norwegians, besides colonizing (usually after warlike attack) northern Scotland, Ireland, northern England and Normandy, had been increasing the area of cultivable land in their own country with the axe; the fjords and valleys of their deeply indented coast had long been forest covered. Population now increased and also the wealth brought in by traders and sea-rovers; the loose overlordship of the Danes was challenged. King Harald

Fairhair of eastern Norway at length conquered all the Norwegian petty kings and nobles by his crowning victory of Haforsfjord (*c.* 900). The subject of a fine poem, *The Lay of Harald*, he reigned for about fifty years, and founded a Norwegian dynasty, finding it useful to ally with the English king Æthelstan against the Danes. He is thought to have died *c.* 931–2 (Turville-Petre). The country was already beginning to be organized for sea-warfare into districts, each bound to produce a ship with a crew of 80–100 warriors for two months in the summer; even as, in the Carolingian empire, the provision of armed fighting men fell upon landed proprietors.

Of the early history of Sweden, little is known: Tacitus mentions the Suiones and their kings. The Goths appear to have migrated, before the middle of the second century, from the region in southern Sweden now known as Gothland. Various north Germanic tribes appear to have made independent tribal settlements in Sweden, the Swedes themselves inhabiting Uppland. Uppsala, with its king and great heathen temple, was the focus of their settlement: the discoveries of Swedish archaeologists have established that three Swedish kings mentioned in *Beowulf* were laid in the mound in old Uppsala in 575, 510 (?) and 500 respectively. The Geatas of south Sweden were overrun or absorbed by the Swedes, possibly subsequently to the date of *Beowulf*, and, in their expansion now and later, the Swedes sent out also Viking raids against the Slavs. The conversion of Sweden, however, was begun at about the same time as that of Denmark: king Björn of Denmark sent emissaries to Louis the Pious desiring Christian teachers in 829. Anskar, whose earlier missions to the Danes had failed with the exile of Harald his protector, was now sent to Sweden, and many converts, some noble, received baptism; Anskar was consecrated first archbishop of Hamburg in 831. He also received, with bishop Ebbo of Reims, a papal legateship to the northern peoples.

The early Scandinavian peoples and the Goths in south Russia before Wulfila taught them, had one thing in common: some form of primitive runic script. They used it for inscriptions in stone or whalebone, in metal work, and according to one theory, for the cutting of brief messages on sticks. The forms of the letters, where straight lines replace the curves of Greek (or Latin?) capital or cursive letters, suggest either the cutting of the letters with a small knife on a rounded twig or the carving of an inscription in stone by a craftsman less skilled than those responsible for inscriptions in the Greco-Roman world. Runes are known to have been in use in the Scandinavian north in the third century A.D., and the runic script appears in inscriptions found all over Europe, from Rumania and western Russia to the east of France, Frisia and England. Some of the inscriptions are believed to have magical significance, for they consist of groups of runic symbols not forming words. The runic alphabet consisted of twenty-four symbols, divided up into three groups of eight. The oldest decipherable runic inscriptions were found in south-western Denmark and date from the mid-third century: the area round Schleswig and Fyn appears to have been a cradle of the Scandinavian form of runes, which spread from there to Sweden and Norway, and, with the invading Anglo-Saxons, to England. Other inscriptions sited on a line running through Pomerania, Brandenburg and Rumania, and found in conjunction with archaic objects, show that runes were early used along the northern coast of the Black Sea and along the lower Danube: 'this line gives an immediate indication, if not of the runes' earliest home, at least of the first spreading of the runic writing' (Sketelig and Falk).

When Wulfila began teaching the Goths in Dacia and Moesia, they would have been using a runic script. Wulfila, however, rejected the runic script as a medium for his new translation of the gospels into Gothic, possibly as associated with paganism and magic, possibly as less suitable phonetically than signs resting ultimately on the Greek alphabet. He certainly made his translation from a Greek manuscript and used the Greek capital and cursive letters with which he was familiar as the basis of his new Gothic alphabet, which he wrote with a straight-cut reed or quill pen; he made use of only one or two runic signs. There is no evidence, however, that the Goths at this early stage used runes for writing on papyrus or vellum, any more than the Scandinavians: these early people handed down their heroic poetry, and the genealogies of their kings, in the memories of their bards or *scopas*. The runes were used for inscriptions: 'I, Viv, engraved the runes to my master (Vodurid).' 'Rolf raised this stone.' 'Hlewagast from Holt made this horn.'

The ogham writing, the earliest and most numerous examples of which were found in Ireland, appears to have been a primitive, inscription-writing practised by the Celts. The technique and purpose is similar to that of the runes, though the alphabet itself is different. Its structure implies a knowledge of the Latin alphabet, not of the Greek: its characters consist of groups of straight lines, cut right or left or diagonally along the arris (edge between two planes) of a pillar stone. The inscription runs up the arris, and, if long, down another edge. The place of origin of the script is thought to have been Ireland itself; but the language of the oldest ogham inscriptions is so old a form of Celtic that the Irish had not yet become distinct from the British form of it. The use of the script is generally believed to have developed after Patrick introduced the Latin language to Ireland; the primitive nature of the language, and the analogy to the use of runes, suggest to others that ogham was a script used by the Celts, near neighbours to the Latins, even in their earlier home on the Continent. The reading of ogham was facilitated by two bi-lingual inscriptions, in ogham and Latin, found in Wales; other ogham inscriptions occur in Scotland, Devon and Cornwall, and one at Silchester in Hampshire.

Runic writing and other features of the distinctive northern, Scandinavian culture persisted throughout the Viking period and down, indeed, to the eleventh and twelfth centuries. The Viking raids and conquests brought the northmen within the sphere of the old Greco-Roman influence: but, because the Scandinavian countries remained pagan, they were not penetrated in the ninth century by southern traditions and techniques. The northmen were wood users: their ships and their halls were built of wood: their richest ornament was carved woodwork, often deeply undercut or even hollowed out within like the carved posts of the Oseberg ship: and they used a barbaric animal ornament developed by carving in wood; the bodies of the animals, highly stylized, were sometimes covered by a design of raised or embossed texture, produced by the wood-carver's tool, not the brush of the Hiberno-Saxon illuminator. On the whole, the influence of Greco-Roman art-forms was surprisingly small in Scandinavia or Denmark in the ninth century; there were no carved Greco-Roman figures in pagan Scandinavia: fierce beasts or twining dragons continued to decorate wooden ships and halls in a manner reminiscent rather of the steppes and even China. There are more ninth- and tenth-century carvings showing Viking influence in Britain, Ireland and the land of the Franks than there are carvings in Scandinavia showing Greco-Roman influence.

Wood perishes: but literary evidence shows that in the Carolingian empire and much more in Scandinavia wood was the most widely used building material. While timber was still very plentiful, 'blockwork' building was used in eastern Europe with the timber balks or planks lying horizontally one on the other and fitted into each other at the angles of the building by means of cut notches: the ends of the balks protruded externally. Not much ornament was used in such 'block' buildings nor were they used in the far north: the technique was used where oak was plentiful.

When timber was rather less abundant, and when, as in Scandinavia, there was much pine forest capable of producing long beams, framework or half-timber construction was used: this is apparently referred to by Bede as building *more Scottorum*. In such a building, timber uprights supporting the roof or cross beams were set some distance apart, and the space between them filled, sometimes with plaster, clay or a different timber, and sometimes with a diagonal framework of the same timber as the uprights, filled in with clay or plaster. In this half-timber work, the timber frame itself had artistic value and displayed a technique developed quite independently of the Greco-Roman tradition.

The third style of timber building, characteristic above all of Norway, was that used in the later mast-churches, which clearly derived from the structure used by ship builders. No pagan, secular building of this type is extant, even in Norway, its home: the fine, early mast-church of St Andrew at Borgund (near Bergen) dates from *c.* 1150. This church has successive tiers of roofing ascending to a central spire, the roof gables ending in long, curved dragons derived from old pagan tradition: as in all mast-churches, the accent is on height, not length. Such a church implies a long preparatory stage in this style of building: though the mast-churches certainly derive their origin from ship building, and the need for a strongly-stayed central mast to support the great, square sail, yet it would seem that some intermediate stage must have intervened between the ships and the extant mast-churches: some simpler form of mast and sleeper building than those now extant. In pagan, ninth-century Norway, such a technique may have been used for the halls of kings and earls. The essence of the construction was the laying of four great, interlocked beams or sleepers under the floor (as at Borgund); these formed a square or rectangle, and in the intersecting corner beams four masts were set, with two more masts intermediately on each side. Above this tall, two-storeyed structure other frameworks of sleepers and masts were raised, rising to a central wooden spire: and, around the central rectangle of mast-columns, light external screens or walls were built to a height of one or two storeys, supporting light, outlying roofs and increasing the floor space. Thus, externally, the Borgund church looks like a cluster of descending roofs, separated by short spaces of wall. In such mast-churches, the carpenter's experience in nail-building a ship, and setting the mast in a central sleeper laid across it, lay at the root of the development.

While the mast-built halls of the Vikings in the ninth century are only an inference from the later churches, two of their richly carved ships have survived, because laid up in burial mounds. The Oseberg ship, found in a mound not far from the Oslo fjord, was built c. 800: it was already old when used for the funeral rites of Asa, the wife of Gudröd, in the mid-ninth century. The ship was not built for raiding on the open sea: it had a high prow and stern post, both beautifully carved, but its sides were low. Within it were laid the lady's ceremonial wagon, and two wooden beds, all beautifully carved, her cloth of gold coverings and household paraphernalia: and with all this furniture to accompany her in death there were also laid the bodies of thirteen horses, six dogs and a woman, slain in sacrifice. While the Oseberg ship appears to have been built as a royal pleasure barge, that found in the mound at Gokstad was an ocean-going vessel, used for piracy or distant trading, built about 900. It was clinker-built and undecked, with an external keel, and a strong block, capable of supporting a mast, fitted into the ship's frame. It had sixteen oars a side, and, instead of a steering oar, a rudder-board and a tiller. On such ships the Vikings could even cross the Atlantic: and their narrowness in proportion to their length allowed them to be rowed far up-river.

The Oseberg and the Gokstad ships have, as it were, survived by accident, and but for them we should have little knowledge of the richest ornament of the Viking period. The desire to commemorate the dead, before the period of Scandinavian expansion, took the form of barrows erected on the skyline rather than of carved stone monuments. In the ninth century, however, carved tombstones and metal horse furniture and jewellery came into use, decorated by craftsmen less highly skilled than the wood carvers, but showing the same tumultuous vigour in the form of their decorations. The earliest style of this animal design is called after Jellinge, the royal residence of the Danish kings in Jutland. It has two types of animal ornament, both showing foreign influence: connexions between the Danes settled in Ireland and Britain with those still in Scandinavia continued close. The first Jellinge style, shown in the richly decorated Copenhagen horse collars, has a Hiberno-Saxon interlaced pattern, with a 'loosely knit confusion of violently racing creatures' (Kendrick). Similar in the rugged and violent confusion of the design is that of the second Jellinge style, so-called from the sculptured boulder or memorial stone of Harald Gormson at Jellinge (set up c. 980). This has a runic inscription, an Anglian 'great beast' or lion, struggling with an intertwined serpent, and on another side what may be a crucifixion, with the half-pagan figure of Christ struggling with interlacing bands or serpents. The theme of a central human or animal figure struggling with twining serpents must indeed be old, far older than the tenth-century versions of it that remain. It suggests in Scandinavian-Anglian terms descent from the ancient Daniel-in-the-lions'-den motif, and its violence, profusion and struggle are indeed symbolic of Viking art and life at the period.

There are two later styles of Viking art: the Ringerike style, which copied in stone and metal the illuminated acanthus work of the tenth-century Winchester school and belongs to the period when Svein and Cnut ruled an empire ringing the North Sea: and the Urnes style, in which ingenious and intricate animal-patterns were used to adorn small metal objects used even in Christian worship. Both these styles, however, belong to the mid-tenth and eleventh centuries: they show increasing Greco-Roman influence.

BIBLIOGRAPHICAL NOTE

FOR THE CELTS, see II. Hubert, *Les celtes depuis l'époque de la Tène et la civilisation celtique*, 1950, with a full bibliography, dealing with the topographical, linguistic, archaeological and literary sides of Celtic history: for trans., see M. R. Dobie, *Greatness and Decline of the Celts*, 1934: A. Longnon, *Noms des lieux anciens de la France*, 1890: d. Gougaud, *Les chrétientés celtiques*, 1911: R. Flower, *The Irish Tradition*, 1947: F. Henry, *Irish Art in the Early Christian Period*, 1940. For Gildas, the dating of his life, and his whole or partial authorship of the *De excidio Britanniae*, the publication of Père Paul Grosjean's work on the sources of Bede must be awaited: the brief references to Gildas on pp. 469–470 are merely provisional. For Columbanus, see G. S. M. Walker, *Sancti Columbani Opera* (with translation), 1957; for the *Hisperica Famina*, P. Grosjean's 'Confusa Caligo', in *Celtica*, vol. iii (1955).

FOR THE SCANDINAVIANS, see G. Turville-Petre, *The Heroic Age in Scandinavia* as a necessary preliminary to Scandinavian studies: H. M. Chadwick, *The Heroic Age*, 1912: A. Mawer, *The Vikings*, 1913: T. D. Kendrick, *A History of the Vikings*, 1930: B. S. Phillpotts, *Edda and Saga*, 1931: H. Sketelig and H. Falk, *Scandinavian Archaeology*, trans. E. V. Gordon, 1937: C. A. J. Nordenfalk, *Before the Book of Durrow*, 1947: T. D. Kendrick, *Late Saxon and Viking Art*, for Scandinavian influence on Anglo-Saxon sculpture and timber constructions. See also, L. Bieler, *Ireland, Harbinger of the Middle Ages*, London, 1963; J. Brønsted, *The Vikings*, Penguin, 1961; L. Musset, *Les Peuples Scandinaves au Moyen Age*, Paris, 1951; P. H. Sawyer, *The Age of the Vikings*, London, 1962.

CHAPTER XXV

THE SLAVS

THE migrations of the Celtic and Germanic tribes lasted through several generations and were paralleled by those of the Slavs: but while Celts and Germans were early brought into touch with the cultures of old and new Rome, the Slavs were brought late into these civilizing contacts. When they eventually settled in central and eastern Europe they acquired their share of the Greco-Roman heritage mainly from Byzantium: they were, eventually, to be her heirs. For Europe and for the future their massive settlement, their nascent states, and the form of their civilization were to be of the greatest importance.

For the prehistory and early history of the Slavs our information rests on archaeological and linguistic evidence, and incidental passages in Greek and Latin historians and geographers: the Slavs had no writing, and therefore no account of their own origins, before their conversion to Christianity. It would appear that in the first 400 years of the Christian era the Slav peoples were living in the area bounded by the Carpathians in the south, the middle Dnieper in the east, the Beresina and Bulgarian lakes in the north, and a vague line between the Vistula and the Oder in the west. What was Poland from 1923 to 1939 seems to have been the area where the Slavs lived longest: perhaps since their differentiation from the Balts in prehistoric times. But of this their earliest annalists were ignorant: the eleventh-century writer of the Russian *Primary Chronicle* could only say that for many years the Slavs lived beside the Danube, 'where the Hungarian and Bulgarian lands now lie'.

As to their name: the Slavs called themselves *Slovene*, and the Germans called them *Vendi*, *Venethi* or *Wends*. The Greeks called the southern Slavs *Sklabénoi* or Slavs, and the eastern Slavs *Antes* or *Antai*, though these last may well have been an Iranian tribe who made themselves masters of the Slavs of south-west Russia. Jordanes (*fl. c.* 550), indeed, writing of the Goths, describes the Slavs as the same people as the Baltic Venedae (Wends): 'From the source of the Vistula river immense areas are occupied by the population of the Venethae, who, though their appellations may change in various clans and districts, are mainly called *Sclaveni* and Antae.' Any identification of these Slav *Wendi* or

Venethae with the *Venethae* of Venetia is, however, very dubious: there were Slav settlements at the head of the Adriatic from about A.D. 550, but the Germans called the Slavs *Wendi* or *Venethae* long before that. The Serbs and Sorbs were also Slavs: a ninth-century Latin writer, describing the cities and regions on the north bank of the Danube, speaks of the land of the *Seruiani*, 'which is so great a realm that from it, as their tradition relates, all the tribes of the Slavs are sprung'.

The Slav language itself is Indo-European, and the early location of the Slavs between the Baltic and the Carpathians is attested by its many resemblances to the Baltic group of that speech family: Lithuanian, Latvian and Old Prussian. In very early times, however, the Slavs spread to the basin of the Pripet, which flows eastward and joins the Dnieper north of Kiev: they were for long exposed to the repeated impacts of alien peoples from Asia. They spread northwards to the source of the Dnieper and the rivers that flow into Lake Ladoga and the eastern end of the Baltic, but their route southwards to the Black Sea was for long blocked successively by the Scythians, the Goths and the Huns.

Thus, instead of early contacts with the Greco-Roman civilization of the Roman empire, the Slavs were for many centuries in contact with quite another culture: that of the northern nomads (see pp. 21–27). The belt of Eurasian steppes runs north of the deserts and the mountains from Manchuria to the Carpathians: it passes north of the Altai mountains and the Himalayas, north of the Aral sea, the Caspian and the Euxine. It is cut by the valleys of the Volga, the Don, the Dnieper, the Bug, and the Dniester, all flowing down from the north into inland seas, and it extends into the great southward bend of the Danube, and across to the Carpathians. The extension of this steppe belt explains why the earliest races in command of the south and centre of modern 'Russia' were not the Slavs, but the Tatar nomads: or populations dominated by the nomads.

Back in prehistory, the bronze age Cimmerians of south Russia had been conquered and replaced by the Scythians, fierce, horse-riding, predatory tribes who brought with them the use of iron for swords and tools: they came from Kasakstan and were the first Eurasian nomads from the east of whom we have real knowledge. Herodotus used the word Scythians loosely for almost any barbarians north of the Euxine, but 'the true Scythians', he said, were the nomads. This is supported by the selection for

portrayal in their metal work of predominantly wild animals
and beasts of prey: the panther, tiger, deer, as well as the horse
and bull. The Scythians traded with the Greek towns of the
Bosphorus and the Euxine, dominated the Ukraine and advanced
up the Volga. Among the tribes encircling them to the north-east
were the Iranian Sarmatians, and by the third century B.C. these
new nomads had displaced the Scythians and pushed across the
Don. The hegemony of the tribes of central Russia passed also
from the Scythians to the Sarmatians and it was the Sarmatians
who opposed the Romans on the Danube in the fourth century A.D.
They had, by then, advanced along the steppes into Hungary.
Already in the third century, however, certain Gothic tribes from
the Baltic and the Pripet had established themselves north of
the Euxine (see p. 26): Ermanaric was king of the Ostrogoths
c. 350–370, and Sarmatian power was in decay, even in the Crimea
and round the Sea of Azov. With Ermanaric there appear to have
settled certain Slav tribes, and the connexion of Goths and Slavs
in south Russia lasted some two centuries. The end of the Sarmatian era came, however, not with the Gothic encroachments,
but with the fifth-century attack of the Huns: they attacked the
Alans, the most easterly of the Sarmatian tribes first, and accomplished through first the establishment and then the downfall
of the Hunnic khanate a general movement and re-diffusion of
Sarmatians, Slavs, and Goths. The Slavs moved gradually into
central and south Russia (as well as into the Balkans), but there
were layers of nomad population there before them, and this
Eurasian element in the population, the remnants of Scythians,
Sarmatians and Avars, was to be increased by the settlement of
Bulgarian tribes, the Kutriguri and the Utiguri, round the Sea of
Azov. The massive Slav (Antic) settlement over central and southern Russia meant the predominance of a mainly Indo-European
population over a mainly Tatar one, to whom some of the Slavs
had earlier been agricultural serfs; it substituted the rule of an
agricultural and trading people for that of the nomads.

To Procopius and other Byzantine writers of the sixth, seventh
and eighth centuries the Slavs seemed a kindly, hospitable people,
who treated prisoners of war well, but who were very little
civilized. They lived as much by hunting and fishing as by agriculture: they were fair-haired, tall and hardy. They had little
military skill, fought without fortifications, and retreated into
the great forests when endangered. It seems clear that the primitive
Slav group was a rural community united largely by common

descent and, when the migratory period was over, possessing fields and woodlands in common. Tribal complexes with remote ties of kinship might number several thousands, but the Slav village was normally small. The houses were log cabins, disposed in line along either sides of the way, or grouped around a central space. The villagers practised a simple, semi-nomadic agriculture and cattle raising: they had a reasonable knowledge of metal working, weaving and the making of pots. The early Slav vocabulary shows they had barley, wheat, rye and oats, and such fruit as apples, pears and plums; but they had a long, cold, continental winter and for their dress used mainly furs. Civilization came to them late. Not only were they without immediate contacts with east or west Rome, but the cold climate, undrained marshes and unfelled forests made the economic margin of life small.

The primary reason of the great Slav expansion to the west and south was the evacuation of Germany by many Teutonic tribes (the Suevi, Vandals, Rugians, Salian Franks, Heruls) in the first half of the fifth century, and the pressing after them of other Teutonic tribes (the *Marcomanni*, the *Quadi*, the *Langobardi*); a partial vacuum was thus created in eastern Germany and central Europe and into this the Slavs were attracted. Pressure on them from the Balts, Finns, Huns, Avars and Khazars also helped to move them, and a great part in Slav expansion was played by the fact that Huns, Avars, and nomadic Iranians (*Jazuges*, *Roxolani*, Alans), and possibly *Antae*, Croats and Serbs, took subjected Slavonic tribes with them in their westward advance. In the northwest, they pressed beyond the base of the Danish peninsula, where the Obodrites settled, and lived in small communities along the Elbe from Magdeburg to Hamburg and beyond to Fulda and Erfurt. But here the Germanic population was already equal to the food supply, and the main Slavonic push was made to the south and the east.

The Czechs who settled in Bohemia and Moravia were only one of a score of Slav tribes. The tribes who were the ancestors of the Slovaks settled in northern Hungary south of the northern ridge of the Carpathians, in the valleys of the Hron (Gran), Nitra, Váh (Waag), and the upper basin of the Tisza (Theiss). It is now believed that in this region of Hungary not all the *Marcomanni* had departed for Bavaria before the coming of the Slavs: archaeology shows no sudden break between the Teutonic and Slavonic remains. What happened to the Teutonic *Quadi* of Moravia is not known: many of them may have been subdued and absorbed by the Slavonic invaders.

In the sixth century the Slavs pressed into the Balkans, the Croats and Serbs penetrating Istria and Dalmatia, and other Slav tribes Illyricum. The whole problem of the origin of the Croats and Serbs and their advent to the Balkans has been confused by the statement of Constantine Porphyrogenitus, who puts it in the days of Heraclius, obviously much too late. It seems that among the innumerable small tribes who took part in the invasion of the sixth and seventh centuries were those called Croats and Serbs. They, like the Czech tribes in Bohemia, probably gradually established some sort of hegemony over the other Slav tribes in their neighbourhood and ultimately gave their name to the whole group. In any case, the southern Slavs by 527 had crossed the Danube in some numbers; in Justinian's reign they were pillaging within the frontiers of the Byzantine provinces; they joined the tribes pressing forward to Constantinople in 559.

Conquest of the Slavs by the Avars then followed: the Avars took Belgrade (Singidunum) in 582, and henceforward, till Charlemagne conquered them, the Avars appear as the overlords of the Slavs. By 597 Avars and Slavs (the Slavs in far greater numbers but the Avars as a conquering caste) had pressed down to the outskirts of Thessalonica, the second greatest city in the Byzantine empire; but in 601, after defeat by the imperial army, a peace fixed the Danube again as the frontier line between the Greeks and Avar-ruled Slavs. Such repulse could not, however, be maintained: the revolts in Phokas' reign compelled him to withdraw all Greek troops from the Danube frontier, and the Slavs and Avars poured again into the provinces of Moesia, that lay south of the great southern bend of the Danube: into Dacia and Thrace, that lay to the south again: and into Macedonia, with Thessalonica as its great seaport. On her the Slavs crowded their attack.

Meanwhile, to the west of the Balkans, the Slavs of Pannonia had poured into Istria and Dalmatia, the hinterland of the Adriatic. They took Salona in 536 and other old Latin towns and the old Latin hierarchy went down before them; though a Christian remnant in the population still looked across the Adriatic for help from Rome. Among these Dalmatian Slavs the Croats established their ascendency; they may have originated as a Sarmatian tribe in south Russia, but they had long lived among the Slav tribes of Bohemia and Silesia. The Adriatic coast south of Istria became especially associated with their name.

The great Slav-Avar push southwards culminated in the siege of Constantinople in 626, in the failure of which the Avars suffered more than the Slavs. The Avar supremacy was already weakened, though the Byzantines could not push either Avars or Slavs out of the Balkan provinces altogether. In 623 some of the western and south-western tribes had thrown off the Avar yoke under the leadership of one Samo, who according to the pseudo-Fredegar was a Frankish merchant who ruled a Slav confederation for some thirty years, and kept at bay not only the Avars but also Dagobert, the Frankish king. His lead was followed by the Slavs of the Danube valley, also under the leadership of a foreigner, a baptized Bulgar chief named Kuvrat. In 650 the Avars were confined to western Hungary, where they remained, so weakened as to be comparatively innocuous, until their last remnants were conquered by Charlemagne and his sons (see p. 371). The Avar hegemony among the Slavs was in fact replaced by that of the Bulgars, a Turco-Tatar tribe who had come into the Balkans from the steppe country, fought indeed under Heraclius' leadership in the siege of the capital in 626, and then settled among and afforded leadership to the Moesian Slavs. The Danube as the northern frontier of the Byzantine empire was now permanently lost and the Slavonic flood overwhelmed, for a time, even the greater part of the Peloponnese.

The gradual Slav advance southwards, in small bands, continued all through the seventh century: their numbers were great and continually reinforced by fresh tribes from beyond the Danube. They had no supra-tribal organization, till the Moesian Slavs found it under the Bulgarian khan Asperuch [Isperich]; he and his horde taught their Slav subjects the use of fortification against the Byzantines: they had themselves learned it from Greek prisoners of war. By 813 they had brought the Thracian Slavs under their rule as well as the Moesian. Though the Bulgars themselves were small in number, and soon Slavised in language, they were numerous enough to form in Bulgaria the military and official class; by the ninth century the original race difference had disappeared and the Bulgars were reckoned a Slav people. In what had once been 'Greece', however, the Peloponnese, Thessaly, Epirus and the coasts of Macedonia and Thrace, Byzantine supremacy was gradually restored, and the Slav population Hellenized: though the Slav language was still spoken in Macedonia, and specially round Thessalonica.

Comparing the areas settled by these south-western Slavs with their modern territorial names, it would seem that by about 900 the Slavs of the Slovene linguistic group held Austria, Styria and Carinthia (then collectively known as Carentania), and present-day

Slovenia down to Grado (then known as Carniola). From about 800 onwards this area was subject, directly or indirectly, to the Franks, and the Carentanian part was by 900 in process of being Germanized. Secondly, Slavs of a Croatian type of speech held Upper and Lower Pannonia, now known as western Hungary (the area between the lower Drava and lower Sava), together with Illyricum and Dalmatia as far south as Cetinje. The northern part of this Croatian area was a client state of the eastern Carolingians; but 'Dalmatian Croatia' threw off the Frankish yoke in the latter part of Louis the Pious' reign, and under an independent line of Slav princes developed into the Croatian land of the tenth century. By the treaty of 810 between Charlemagne and Nicephoras the Greeks retained some of the islands and coastal towns. Thirdly, present-day Serbia, Bosnia, Hercegovina, Montenegro and Macedonia (and, till Asperuch's invasion, Bulgaria) were inhabited by many separate tribes whose Slavonic dialects shaded off from old Serbian in the west to old Bulgarian in the east. Before 900 they had achieved little unity.

By the mid-ninth century, the Slav populations had largely completed their settlements, and can be grouped as western, southern and eastern. Outside this grouping, the Slav population of the Baltic regions had as yet formed no states. The forefathers of the Poles, a Slav tribe referred to in the Russian *Primary Chronicle* as the Polyanians or Lyakhs, were relatively few in number and lived in the Oder basin and the Vistula basin west of modern Warsaw: there was as yet no 'Poland'. But there was certainly the beginnings of political life in Little Poland (round Cracow) much earlier than the ninth century: the Cracow annals have memories of a series of 'bishops' who well may have been clergy instituted by Methodius in the mid-ninth century (see p. 497). But south of these unfederated Slav tribes the western Slavs included the Czech and other Slav tribes of Bohemia, to be conquered for a time by Charlemagne, Louis the German and Carloman and won for the Latin church, the Slovaks, and the Slovenes of Carniola and Istria: the Moravian Slavs of the middle Danube were also threatened for a time with Frankish penetration, religious and political, but from such influence Byzantine policy saved them. The southern Slavs are sometimes reckoned to include those settled in Istria, and, normally, the Croats of southwest Hungary, Slavonia and Dalmatia: these, the wars of Charlemagne made subject for a time to the count of Friuli. Their princes did homage to Louis the Pious in 814, but several revolts against the Franks followed and subjection was uneasy. Besides these Slavs of the Adriatic coast lands there were the more numerous Serbs and Slavized Bulgars occupying the Balkan lands between the great bend of the Danube and the old Hellas.

The eastern Slavs had been numerically a large group, who had early passed from the Pripet basin and the western slopes of the Carpathians to the Dnieper just north of Kiev, where the river Desna flowed into the Dnieper from the north-east. Expansion was easy along this waterway to the headwaters of the Volga and the Don, and also up the Dnieper, by an easy portage, to the headwaters of the western Dvina, which flows into the Gulf of Riga. The rivers opened an easy system of communications in all directions, but the steppes between the Don and the Dnieper exposed the east Slavs themselves to various waves of attack from the Turco-Tatar races. The Avars had been such: but by the eighth century they were being pressed westwards by the Khazars. These blocked the way of the eastern Slavs (the future Russians) to the sea of Azov and the Black Sea by their empire which centred on the Volga, a unique waterway. The Khazars traded with the Arabs of Baghdad, exchanging with the city of the caliphs the furs of the north and slaves for her luxurious textiles, jewellery and sword blades. The Khazars traded with Jews, Arabs, Slavs and Greeks, and were the chief carriers between the interior of modern Russia, the Black Sea, and the camel routes to the Caspian, Baghdad and India. The great Khazar towns of Itil at the mouth of the Volga, Sarbel on the Don (as well as the Bulgar town of Bulgar on the upper Volga) played a vital part in the civilization of the future Russia; it seems probable that their trading connexions with the Swedes began very early, earlier than the Kiev chronicler indicates.

The trade with Asia had once, in the days of the Roman empire, passed to the Mediterranean: but now in the ninth century its passage to western Europe was blocked by Arab pirate fleets. The great Slav state of Russia grew out of a diversion of part of the eastern trade up the Russian rivers to the Baltic, whence it was passed on to western Europe: but the creators of the diversion were not the Slavs themselves but the Scandinavian boat builders and sailors. Sweden appears at this time to have been known to the Finns as Roslagen, and when the northmen from Sweden came down, it would appear, under Rurik [1] from the Bay of Finland and Lake Ladoga and settled in Novgorod as their rulers, the Finns turned

[1] Vernadsky holds Rurik to have been, not a Swede, but a Low German, who spent part of his life in England.

the invaders' Scandinavian place-name into Ruotsi. The Arabs called the northmen 'Rus' and the Byzantines called them 'Rhos'. These Scandinavian merchants or raiders were not numerous: it would appear that the Slav inhabitants of the Don and Volga valleys had already, under Khazar influence, reached some level of political and economic development. Nor were the Scandinavians all Swedes: for the two followers of Rurik who sailed down the Dnieper and first settled in Kiev (according to the Kiev chronicle) were Norse Varyags (Varangians); Oleg, the son of Rurik, followed them some twenty years later. Kiev was, from this time, the capital of a 'Russian' state. The Rhos in their long, swift boats were able by 865 to sail down the Dnieper, through the lands of the Khazars, and ravage the shores of the Sea of Marmora and the Black Sea. They attacked Constantinople itself (see p. 493) in 860 and later: but even more important than the alarm they inspired as pirates was the trade they established with the great city. They opened a commercial waterway linking the north with the Black Sea and the world of Byzantine culture. They saw the stone-built Byzantine cities and villas, the carved capitals, the stone fortifications; they met Byzantine merchants and at times received Byzantine envoys, dressed according to their rank and always well-supplied with honorific gifts and large sums for diplomatic presents. They saw, on their voyages to the Black Sea, Christian churches, their icons and their carved reliquaries; Christianity was the religion of this rich, learned, civilized, splendid empire. Before there was any question of alliance or the reception of baptism, they had an apprehension of the Byzantine, Christian culture.

The conversion of the Slav races to Christianity was, nevertheless, a landmark not only in their own, but in European history, for it brought them fully into the orbit of Greco-Roman culture and the Christian religion. It was only unfortunate for the Slavs that already in the ninth century, the century of their conversion, the single *imperium* had been divided, in practice at any rate, between the Byzantines and the Franks. The Latin Christians and the popes were, in fact, under the secular jurisdiction of the Frankish empire: the Greek Christians of the *basileus*. While most of the Slavs were converted eventually to Greek Christianity, those in the west were taught by Frankish, Bavarian, Irish and Italian missionaries and professed Latin Christianity. In the century of their first conversion the eastern and western churches were still undivided, even the Photian schism being short.

Latin Christianity was taught in the ninth century to the

Slovenes of Carniola and Istria, the Moravian Slavs, and the Croats of Dalmatia who were subject to the count of Friuli. Frankish missionaries from Salzburg worked in Moravia, while the priests of the Latin patriarchate of Aquileia preached in Istria and among the Dalmatian Croats. Moravia, a large region lying beyond the eastern frontier of the Frankish empire and with fluctuating boundaries, embraced a large number of Slav tribes once ruled by the Avars: it stretched from the Carpathians in the north, over the basins of the middle Danube and Tisza, and to the south of the Danube. The Magyars were later, perhaps between 890 and 910, to overrun the greater part of Moravia, conquering the Slav population as once the Avars in the same region had conquered the Latin provincials; north of Magyar Hungary a relic of the ninth-century Moravia was cut off by this Magyar wedge, and survived as the province of Moravia, to the south-east of Bohemia.

As to the Slavs of Dalmatia: a remarkable symbiosis of Slavs and Latins resulted from the Slav settlements, while in Moravia both Byzantines and Latins were to make rival attempts to intro-duce their own religion and culture. It is now realized that the civilizing conversion of the Slavs in the Balkans was to be of great importance for the future of Europe, for the split between the eastern and western cultures was in fact to come in the Balkans, at a line drawn down the eastern frontier of the Dalmatian Croats and Serbs: 'the gate between east and west stands forever on this Croatian frontier'. It is Professor Novak's, Professor Dvornik's and other Byzantinists' view that, if an independent Slav empire, using the Slav vernacular for its liturgy, could have been allowed to develop from Greater Moravia, this third empire would have been a bridge between east and west, the Slavs would have had a reasonably early share in the Greco-Roman heritage, schism between Rome and Constantinople might have been avoided, and Europe strengthened in its defence against Islam. Before the emperor Leo III's subtraction of Illyricum from the jurisdiction of the papacy, emperor and pope worked together for the con-version of the Slavs: afterwards, the question of these subtracted provinces embittered the relations between Byzantines and Latins, and their missionaries worked in rivalry: sometimes in hostility.

As to Dalmatia: as early as 599 pope Gregory I heard of and grieved over the inroads of the Slavs, and their destruction of the many old Roman settlements on the Dalmatian coast. Heraclius requested pope John IV (640–642) to send missionaries to convert the Croats and Serbs: Illyricum was in the Roman jurisdiction and relations between pope and emperor were good. Both knew that the sees of the Illyrian bishops who had attended the council of Grado in 579 had been destroyed; Sirmium, in Pannonia, had been an important see: Salona had been the metropolitan see of Dalmatia. Pope John, in answer to Heraclius' request, sent the abbot Martin to buy Christian slaves in Dalmatia and bring them to Rome, together with the relics from the ruined churches. A limited success attended these missionary efforts: some sees were revived, including Ragusa (Dubrovnik), some intermarriage took place between Slavs and Romans in the towns of Croatia, some understanding was gained of the Slav language: economic and social relations gradually improved. The see of Salona was revived, and c. 750 transferred to the old palace of Diocletian at Spalato (Split). The liturgy used was Latin, for the Slav language was as yet without an alphabet and unwritable at any length. Some Slav sounds were difficult to write in a Greek or Latin script, though the Slavs themselves used runes for their as yet infrequent inscriptions. Whereas the Germanic barbarians who had once conquered the west had been few, and the provincials who imparted the Greco-Roman culture many: in the Balkans, the Slav conquerors were very numerous and the civilized, conquered population few: assimilation was slow.

The rate was quickened with Charlemagne's conquest of Istria and northern Dalmatia: in the ninth century the Franks dominated Dalmatia: bishop John of Ravenna restored the old Latin hierarchy in the north, and the Latin language came into use in Croatia, both for public documents and private letters. Later in the ninth century, when Constantine-Cyril and Methodius had introduced a Slav alphabet into Moravia, whence its use had spread to Croatia and Dalmatia, two scripts were used: the Caroline script from the *scriptorium* of the monks of Benevento for Latin manuscripts, and the glagolitic or the Cyrillic scripts (see p. 495) for manuscripts in the Slav tongue. In economic life too there was interchange of goods between Slavs, Italians and Franks, an interchange which affected even the Dalmatian hinterlands through Dubrovnik, which became a *focus* of Slav culture, and from which many manuscripts have survived. While the earliest of these documents are in Latin, those slightly later are in Latin with a Slav signature and those later still completely in Slav. From the *scriptoria* of Benevento and Monte Cassino the Slavs learned the art of illumination, and from their own Latin background, and from Italy, the classical styles and art-forms. They took over the achievements of antiquity, attaining in some arts a noble harmony of the old and the new; they achieved, that is, a mixed Slav-Latin art parallel to the mixed Anglian-Celtic-

Byzantine art of Northumbria in the eighth century. The importance of Split and Dubrovnik as *foci* of Slav influence was due partly to papal uneasiness at the possible extension of the jurisdiction of Salzburg through the work of Frankish missionaries, supported as it was by the heavy weight of secular authority: Rome therefore created for the Slavs an independent see, by raising Split to metropolitan rank. The Latin liturgy was used in the see, now under the spiritual authority of the pope and the secular jurisdiction of Constantinople.

At the height of the ninth-century renaissance, the court at Constantinople was seeking to extend Byzantine influence by the conversion of her barbarian neighbours and invaders, as well as by diplomacy; the most famous of the missionaries sent out were among her leading scholars, Constantine 'the philosopher' and Methodius his brother, both of them friends and protégés of Photius and Bardas. The function of the Byzantine emperor had always been conceived of as apostolic, and, now that the worst bitterness of the iconoclast struggle had been allayed, both emperor and patriarch were ready to support missionary effort. Even before the sending of formal missions for conversion, the relations of barbarians with Byzantium had led to acquaintance with Christianity, not only through the reception of diplomatic missions, but by contact with Byzantine priests, merchants and prisoners of war: a port like Thessalonica had churches, a cathedral, schools, and many Christians of Slav origin. Prince Rastislav of Moravia, the khan of Bulgaria, the khan of the Khazars, the Russians of Kiev, had all heard of the great caesar of Constantinople (the Russians called his city Tsargrad) and the religion of his court.

The first mission of the Photian renaissance went to the distant Khazars. In 860 a Russian fleet had raided Byzantium, and the danger had been sufficient to show the advisability of making these new enemies fellow Christians and allies. Photius' mind was already turned to the Crimea, as appears in one of his letters; as was that of his disciple and successor, Nicholas Mysticus, later. With the Khazars of the lower reaches of the Dnieper, imperial relations were friendly: for Justinian II and Constantine V had already married daughters of their khan: but the Jews, who had numerous colonies in the Crimea, were also trying to win the khan to their faith and alliance. A letter from the khan, received about 860, however, gave the emperor his chance: the letter said that, while the khan and most of his subjects were pagan, they were in contact with three great religions, Islam, Judaism and Christianity, and were undecided which to accept: would the emperor send the khan a Christian scholar, who could expound the Christian faith before the Jews and Saracens? In answer, a mission as much diplomatic as missionary was sent and led by the brothers Constantine and Methodius.

Bardas' choice of these scholars, the sons of a probably Greek *drungarios* of Thessalonica, was natural, from their ability to speak Slav: the Khazars ruled over several Slav tribes. Constantine had gone high in the civil service and had a great reputation for learning; Methodius, now a monk, had been the Byzantine governor of a Slav province. Constantine, moreover, had already been sent on a diplomatic mission *c.* 851 to the Arab Mutawakkil, to discuss with his scholars the Christian doctrine of the Trinity. The brothers landed at Cherson, in the Crimea, and there Constantine, according to his *legend* (the account of his life to be read at night office of his feast day), found a psalter and the gospels 'in the Russian language': with the help of a native, he was enabled to read them. Unless the passage is apocryphal, it must refer to some writing in the runic script, which was in use at the time, though hardly for so long a book as the gospels or else to some gospel book in Syriac or Armenian, reaching the Khazars as the property of a foreign priest or merchant. It was in a script hitherto unknown to Constantine, but he deciphered it with the help of some dweller in the peninsula. The language of the Magyars, however, many of whom lived at the time in the neighbourhood of Cherson, was too much for Constantine, for they 'howled like wolves'. In his journey to the Khazars he found, however, a Christian village: the Khazars and the Rhos also had found some such on the Crimea and the northern coasts of the Black Sea, and a Christian remnant survived. Constantine held his debate with the Jews and Saracens: the khan wrote politely about him to the emperor and sent back with him 200 Byzantine prisoners of war: but was actually won over later by the Jews, and with his subjects accepted Judaism. Such acceptance involved no political tutelage, as would the acceptance of Greek Christianity, or Islam. Arab sources confirm the account of Constantine's mission and debate.

The next request for Christian teachers came from Rastislav, prince of Moravia, and marks the first attempt (Samo's principality apart) to set up a Slav state, independent of either the eastern or western empire, along the slopes of the Carpathians: in Greater Moravia as distinguished from the later, diminished, Moravia. This request for teachers, not surprising in view of the need of political support against the Franks, reached Bardas and Photius in 862. The Byzantine palace had had as yet no relations with the Moravians; it would have been preferable to win over their Slav neighbours, the Bulgars, to alliance, conversion and possibly allegiance, but the Byzantine leaders realised that it would be useful, meanwhile, to convert the more distant Moravians, whom the Franks had been trying for some time to win over. Nor was the motive of the mission merely diplomatic: the conversion of pagans to Christianity had always been one of the imperial responsibilities.

Rastislav at this time was the virtual chief of all the Slav tribes, north to the Carpathians and Bohemia as well as south to Belgrade, and he desired independence for the Slavs. Conversion by the Frankish, the German, bishops might lead to complete loss of independence. Rastislav turned therefore to the tsar of Constantinople; he had some knowledge of the Byzantines, for an old Roman trade route, still frequented, had run from Byzantium, through Adrianople and Nish, to Belgrade; it also continued by way of Carnuntum, up the Morava through the Oder gap to the Baltic: it was part of the amber route of prehistoric times and went straight through Rastislav's dominions. The Venetians also traded with the Slavs of the Danubian plain. Byzantine money found its way into Moravia, and some knowledge of Greek Christianity. Rastislav may have known the more liberal attitude of the Greek church to the use of the vernacular in her liturgy compared with that of the Latins; the Frankish missionaries in his countries used the Latin mass, and apparently could not even explain the faith in the Slav languages: he asked the emperor to send him from Byzantium teachers who understood the Slav tongue. The *Life* of Methodius states that Rastislav had made the same request to Rome first, saying that he desired a bishop: the pope, however, had apparently no Slav teachers to send.

The emperor Michael then told Constantine to undertake the mission: 'You must go, for no one but you can accomplish the work': to which Constantine replied that he would go, but he must first have a writing suitable to the Slav tongue. The emperor answered that his father, his grandfather and many others had sought such a writing, but it did not exist: God, however, always supplied necessities to his servants! Constantine then went away and composed the glagolitic alphabet: a fine phonetic instrument with forty letters, twenty-one apparently following Greek models and the others representing Slav sounds, either by oriental letters or a combination of Byzantine and runic signs. The emperor bade him take with him his brother, the abbot Methodius, and the two set out, bringing with them certain passages from the gospels which the philosopher had already at Constantinople translated and written in Slavonic. They received Photius' blessing before starting with a caravan of priests, monks, craftsmen and traders, along the old Roman road to the Danubian plain. They were welcomed by Rastislav in the spring of 863, presented the emperor's letter and presents and began their teaching; but both their presence and their ability to teach in Slavonic were at once resented by the Frankish missionaries. Constantine and his brother celebrated mass in Slavonic, using the passages from the Slav gospels they had prepared: they completed their Slav gospels in Moravia. They preached in Slavonic: they translated liturgy and office into Slavonic and used them: they prepared to educate a Slav clergy. Constantine contended with the Latin clergy, who argued that God had chosen three languages only for the lawful rendering of the divine praise to God, Hebrew, Greek and Latin: he called them 'Pilate's pupils', because Pilate had had the inscription over the cross written in these three tongues. But though Constantine used and defended the use of Slavonic for the mass, he used the Latin rite to which his Moravian converts were accustomed.

The brothers stayed three years in this, the first, Moravian mission (864–867) and then travelled, by way of Venice, to Rome, where charges had been preferred against them. Recourse to the pope was natural, for he had the right to control their Frankish opponents; moreover, like all Byzantines, they accepted the primacy of the Roman church. Nicholas I, whose relations with Photius were bad, who had, indeed, excommunicated him, was just dead; news of the palace revolution (23 September 867), the murder of the emperor Michael and fall of Photius, had not yet reached Rome. Nicholas died on 13 November 867, and was succeeded by Hadrian II. Not only was a favourable reception of Constantine and Methodius doubtful through their connexion with Photius, but it was complicated by the negotiations of Boris of Bulgaria ith the holy see for the establishment of a Latin church in Bulgaria (see p. 411). The Illyrican jurisdiction had never been returned by the Greek emperor to the pope: and Rome naturally desired, in its place, the conversion of Moravia and Bulgaria by Latin priests, and the establishment of new hierarchies under her own authority. She was opposed, however, to the setting up of Frankish-Latin hierarchies, which would extend Frankish secular fluence into the Balkans.

Hadrian II therefore inquired into the character, learning and practices of the two brothers, finding them to be holy and learned men. He was well-disposed to them, moreover, as they brought to him the relics supposedly those of his great predecessor, St Clement of Rome. It was difficult, however, to accede to their desire to use a 'barbarous' language in the liturgy, a very different matter from the use of Greek, which was perfectly familiar at Rome. Byzantine pilgrims came to Rome, and there was a permanent colony of Byzantines there and several Byzantine churches. The need, however, to confirm Latin authority in Moravia, especially as Boris withdrew the expected invitation to set up a hierarchy in Bulgaria, outweighed the novelty of approving the liturgical use of Slavonic. Hadrian II formally approved the work of Constantine and Methodius and their methods; Constantine became a monk, and received the honourable name of Cyril: monastic profession was necessary in the Greek church before ordination to the episcopate. Constantine-Cyril, however, died in a Greek monastery at Rome in February 869; he was buried in the church of St Clement, whose relics he believed himself to have found among the Khazars, and brought with him to Rome. Constantine's death and the precarious position of Rastislav, now at war with Louis the German, decided Hadrian to send back Methodius to Moravia only as a simple priest. When, however, Rastislav was defeated by the Franks and Bulgaria accepted missionaries and an archbishop from Byzantium, Hadrian's successor, John VIII, made a bid to retain the Roman influence in Greater Moravia. Methodius was still working in southern Moravia and John created him (arch)bishop of Pannonia, apparently without an urban centre as his *sedes episcopi* (*c.* 870): he also made him papal legate for all the Slav races. Certain limitations, however, were enjoined on the liturgical use of Slavonic.

Rastislav's defeat by the Franks restored the German clergy to Moravia, but the dispersed Slav teachers and their pupils in other Slav lands continued the use of the vernacular for teaching and the liturgy. 'Glagolitism', the movement for a vernacular liturgy, remained through the centuries, and especially among the Dalmatian Slavs, a permanent religious factor, though the original glagolitic alphabet gave way, under the influence of the Beneventan script, to the Cyrillic. This second Slav alphabet was used by all the Slavs and became the foundation of the Russian alphabet.

While Moravia returned to Latin Christianity, her neighbour Bulgaria soon adopted both the Byzantine alliance and the teaching of Methodius and his helpers. Bulgaria had long been a dangerous neighbour to the Byzantines, inflicting upon them defeats and humiliations. Constantine V had fought many campaigns against them, dying at the beginning of one of them in 775. Charlemagne's destruction of the Avar empire in 796 had allowed the Bulgars to spread from Bessarabia into Pannonia. When Nicephoras attacked the khan Krum in 807, a terrible war followed: the Byzantines took the Bulgarian capital in one campaign, and reoccupied it in 811, but were defeated in the Balkan mountains as they returned for the winter: Nicephoras was killed and his skull used as a drinking cup by Krum: the Bulgars then ravaged Thrace unchecked. Leo IV defeated the Bulgars at Mesembria in 813, and Krum's son and successor, Omurtag, signed a thirty years' peace with the Byzantines in 815–16, and respected the treaty. The Bulgars now had peace and learned some Byzantine arts: Omurtag built a fine palace at Pliska, another on the Danube and a third, a fortress palace at Preslav, 100 years later the capital of Bulgaria. Greek was used for Omurtag's inscriptions: and civilization and Christianity made their appearance in Bulgaria, though Christianity was suspect.

The thirty years' peace with the Bulgars expired in 845–6 and was not renewed. The Bulgars even invaded Macedonia, took Philippopolis and threatened Thessalonica: but the exploits of Krum could not be repeated. Bulgaria had now to reckon with the warlike Franks as well as the Byzantines. The Bulgars made peace with the regent Theodora, and when the tsar Boris succeeded in 852, peace was maintained: and even so, it was becoming clear that Bulgaria would have to choose between a Frankish and a Byzantine alliance. The Frankish prince, Louis the German, desiring to encircle Rastislav of Moravia, made alliances with the Bulgars in 845, 852 and 862; but in 863 he attacked Bulgaria, and the Byzantines, who had been approached for an alliance, sent a Greek force to her aid.

Boris decided therefore to throw in his lot with Byzantium. He came to Constantinople for baptism (864), was given the name Michael and received from the font by the emperor himself. Photius made the newly baptized a homily of welcome. Boris, however, found that his godfather expected too much subordination from Bulgaria: he therefore wrote to pope Nicholas I asking for a Latin bishop and priests, and Rome sent a mission under Formosus; but after 869 Boris aligned himself, after all, with Byzantium, and it was in Bulgaria that the dispersed Moravian missionaries found their fruit. The Slav pupils of Methodius also penetrated north into Bohemia and the adjacent lands: some of the Czechs were now first converted to Greek Christianity and a vernacular liturgy, though most remained pagan. The Slav rite never had a more than insecure hold on Bohemia, though it lingered on, with interruptions, in St Prokop's monastery at Sázava till the eleventh century. The conversion of the Bohemians was pre-eminently an achievement of the German clergy, who were encouraged, but not introduced, by Wenceslas, duke of Bohemia. He was martyred on 28 September 929, but medieval Bohemia, like the Dalmatian Slavs, retained Latin Christianity. Nevertheless, the Czechs venerated the memory of Methodius and their first instructors in Christianity.

In Bulgaria, the pope had hoped to establish a Latin church through the help of Boris, and he expected the support of the patriarch Ignatius, whom he had recognized in the council of February 870. Ignatius, however, proved as much the defender of Byzantine claims as Photius had been. He consecrated an archbishop for Bulgaria with ten Greek bishops under him: the Latin clergy had to withdraw.

A period of advancing civilization and extension of the Bulgarian frontiers followed, both to the west, and to the north of the Danube up to Poland. Slavs and Bulgars had long been one people with one language; the old struggles of the monarchy with the Bulgarian nobles, the boïars, had ended in favour of the tsar. The Bulgars were now civilized, Christian, and the rulers of wide territories, and Boris desired to rule a Slav empire which should control the Balkans and be the equal of the eastern and western empires. After a long reign, he withdrew to a monastery in 893, living on till 907, and dying a saint.

The tsar Symeon (893–927), Boris's son, aimed also at leadership of the Slavs in the Balkans, and with apparently more chance of success than the earlier state of Moravia, though her territories had been even wider, and she might have drawn the Czechs also into a single Slav empire. Bulgaria, however, was more centralized. Symeon had been for many years in his youth a hostage at Byzantium: he had studied Demosthenes and Aristotle and become, as they said of him, 'half a Greek'. He desired even to conquer Constantinople, and in 894, on the occasion of an injury done to his merchants by the removal of their market from Constantinople to Thessalonica, he declared war. The Byzantines and Slavs began a hundred year struggle for the dominance of the Balkans. The emperor Leo VI had an Asiatic war on his hands, and, to counter Symeon, invited the Magyars into eastern Europe: they first defeated Symeon and then themselves suffered defeat. But while Magyar encroachments disturbed Symeon, Arab successes alarmed Leo, and in 904 a treaty was signed fixing the Bulgarian frontier far to the south in Macedonia, and ceding to her supremacy over several Slav tribes. In his long reign, Symeon possessed himself of Thrace, and in 924 he all but succeeded in taking Constantinople: his victories and the splendour of his capital and his court have led to a comparison of his work for the Slavs to that of Charlemagne for the Franks.

BIBLIOGRAPHICAL NOTE

See S. H. Cross and O. P. Sherbowitz-Wetzor, 'The Russian Primary Chronicle', in The Med. Acad. of America, no. 60, 1953: G. Vernadsky, *A History of Russia*, Yale Univ. Press, 1951 ed.: S. H. Cross, *Slavic Civilisation through the Ages*, 1948: F. Dvornik, *Les Slaves, Byzance et Rome au IXe siècle*, 1926, and *The Making of Central and Eastern Europe*, 1949: A. A. Vasiliev, *The Russian Attack on Constantinople*, 1946: S. Runciman, *A History of the First Bulgarian Empire*, 1930: G. Every, *The Byzantine Patriarchate, 451–1204*, 1947. For Ancient and Kievan Russia, see also, G. Vernadsky, *The Origins of Russia*, 1959. See also, O. Hoetzsch, *The Evolution of Russia*, London, 1966; G. Vernadsky, *The Origins of Russia*, Oxford, 1959: *Kievan Russia*, 1948: *The Mongols in Russia*, 1953; F. Dvornik, *Les Slaves, Byzance, et Rome au IXe siècle*, 1926, and *The Making of Central and Eastern Europe*, London, 1949; for Cyril and Methodius, Z. R. Dittrich, *Christianity in Great-Moravia*, Gröningen, 1962.

CHAPTER XXVI

THE CAROLINGIAN RENAISSANCE:
SCHOOLS AND SCHOLARS

THE ninth century saw a great renaissance of learning and the arts both in eastern and western Europe, the latter usually known as the Carolingian renaissance. The two flowerings of letters and culture were, however, very different in character. In the Byzantine empire the revival occurred in an old, or at least, a mature civilization; where the inheritance of Latin learning had never been lost, where there had always been a large class of learned laymen; where the citizens of Constantinople and other great cities still lived their lives under Roman law and among Justinian's buildings; where an educated class was no stranger to fine Latin poetry, the liberal arts and Greek philosophy. To such a people the ninth-century renaissance brought a change in the field of study: a turning back to Greek literature rather than Latin, but not a first introduction to fine literature and abstract thought as such. Moreover, to some small extent there was a meeting of two streams of culture, always a factor in the history of thought and the throwing up of a wave of new learning, architecture and art: the learning and the art of Baghdad met that of Constantinople. Whereas Greco-Roman mathematicians had used as an instrument only Euclidean geometry, an arithmetic that had to be demonstrated with an abacus, and an astronomy resting mainly on Ptolemy, Arabic scholars could use algebra as an instrument as well as geometry, Indian numerals for written calculation instead of the abacus, and a more developed astronomy. Byzantine scholars could advance their mathematical knowledge beyond the old *quadrivium*, if they had contact with Arabic thought, and a few had (see p. 209). At Constantinople much more attention was, in fact, given to the *quadrivium* than in the Latin west.

The Carolingian renaissance originated under different conditions, had a different character, and brought quite different results. It was more purely a renaissance: a re-birth of the old Greco-Roman learning: there was only a limited mingling of different streams of culture. It was again, in contrast to the revival at Constantinople, the appropriation by a much younger, more 'barbarian' people of an old learning, and an art more developed than their own. It was also a partial democratization, by means of monastic and episcopal schools, of the intellectual heritage that only a few giants, like Bede and Boniface and their immediate followers, had had before. This democratization did not mean that a class of learned laymen came into being, as in the Byzantine empire: but it meant a great extension of the clerical order, and its better education.

Moreover, in the days of oral teaching, the existence of a better educated clergy meant a less superstitious laity: the economic margin of life was still too small to permit of the extension of literacy generally to the laity, nor was this possible in fact for another thousand years; but in the peasant society of western Europe, it was something that the church, through her oral teaching, her yearly succession of fasts and festivals, her rogations, her blessings, her Christian sacraments, introduced men's minds to thoughts of another order than those connected with the toil of work on the land. To teach illiterate Germanic or Celtic peasants the Christian faith, either by oral instruction or church paintings or the carved crosses, was to introduce them to a new philosophy of life and one lived and passed on now for some hundreds of years since Constantine by Greco-Roman scholars and administrators. Lay buildings of any splendour, or any material but wood, were few and far between in the Carolingian west: the houses of common men in the countryside, or even in the small towns, were mere lath and plaster shacks, thatched with straw and frequently destroyed by fire: but the village church, even when not of stone, would be larger than any villager's house, and have a stone altar and some kind of altar vessels and books and candlesticks and harness (as the Anglo-Saxons said) for the priest, and a lamp to burn before the relics: all things precious and belonging to another world. The village priest might be by birth just a peasant, like the villager himself, but he should be able to read and write: literacy made him, in a sense, a citizen of the Greco-Roman world. Hence, the extension and better education of the clerical order, for which the Carolingian rulers pressed, meant the opening of a window even for the villagers on to a different world.

Again, the Carolingian renaissance contrasts with that in contemporary Byzantium in that it produced scholars with a young and almost naïf admiration for Vergil and Ovid, and the cadences of Latin poetry, as against the new Byzantine rediscovery of the Iliad and the Odyssey. Compared to its volume, Carolingian poetry was not, in the main, great poetry: but all Carolingian scholars were poets of a sort. They wrote verses with their frequent and delightful letters; they wrote epitaphs in verse; they wrote verses in honour of newly-built churches or altars; they wrote honorific verses to rulers, and just occasionally, when they were moved by 'the tears of things', or some circumstance of their own life, the verse they wrote was poignant and unforgettable. Alcuin wrote of the cuckoo, Fredugis, his scholar, of the loneliness of Alcuin's little cell at Tours without him, and Paulinus probably wrote the hymn used later for the foot-washing on Maundy Thursday: *Ubi caritas et amor, Deus ibi est:*

congregavit nos in unum	*Christi amor,*
exultemus et in ipso	*iucundemur,*
timeamus et amemus	*deum vivum*
et ex corde diligamus	*nos sincero:*
ubi caritas et amor,	*deus ibi est.*

The chant for the *Mandatum* was as beautiful as the words.

One striking feature in all this proliferation of Latin verse was the writers' delight in the mere arrangement of words, in acrostics and anagrams and riddles, in the making of verses in which the initial letters of each line formed words, and sometimes where letters taken diagonally across the verse formed words also. In fact, the typical Carolingian scholar had a crossword-puzzle mind, and the Irish verses found in the manuscript from Reichenau seize upon this Carolingian appreciation of verbal dexterity. Translated from the Irish by Robin Flower, the well-known verses run

> I and Pangur Bán my cat
> 'Tis a like task we are at:
> Hunting mice is his delight,
> Hunting words I sit all night
>
> When a mouse darts from its den,
> O how glad is Pangur then!
> O what gladness do I prove
> When I solve the doubts I love.
>
> So in peace our tasks we ply,
> Pangur Bán, my cat and I;
> In our arts we find our bliss,
> I have mine and he has his.

The white Pangur and the Irish monk often caught their prey they were highly skilled hunters. But all this verbal dexterity, this delight in Latin verse, was not merely frivolous and useless: it accompanied ability to rewrite, digest and pass on the Latin classics. Realization of this is shown in those verses of Theodulf of Orleans which describe the liberal arts pictorially, as a tree 'decorating' the whole world: Grammar, a draped female figure, sits at the root of the tree, no art without her, and at her side Rhetoric and Dialectic; aloft in the boughs of the tree sits Measurement (Moderatio), embracing the art of numbers: she stands with both feet on a branch, holding in one hand number and the other volume, 'whose mother is physics'. But Grammar sits at the root: the Carolingians were sure of that.

Apart from their delight in Latin verse, what did the Carolingians achieve in appreciation or extension of the Greco-Roman field of knowledge, the liberal arts? The study of these arts was assumed by all the Carolingian rulers to be the natural goal of education; western Europe, since the fall of the Roman empire, had had no contact with any learning more advanced than that then lost, her relations with Islam having been, in the main, hostile. It was natural that a desire for knowledge should take the form of an effort to repossess what had been lost and only partially recovered. It is true that these secular studies were now made professedly for the better understanding of the scriptures and the Christian faith and that some of the most voluminous Carolingian writings were in the sphere of theology; but, apart from theology and the old learning, ninth-century scholars explored few new fields. Many had a glossarial knowledge of Greek, and a few, notably John the Scot, Erigena, read Greek easily; a few studied medicine; there was some effort (less than might have been expected, with the great Frankish push to the east in progress) to use the German vernacular to teach the life of Christ; but the only study regularly promoted by imperial capitulary and the canons of councils was the study of the liberal arts and the ecclesiastical disciplines.

The great instruments for the promotion of such studies were the monastic and cathedral schools: the monastic schools above all. A bishop from Merovingian times had been bound to train boy clerks for the future clergy of his see, either himself, or through a *scholasticus* who was also his own secretary, and in Carolingian times the need remained. In 789 a capitulary of Charlemagne enjoined that there should be schools of young clerks (*lectors*) in every monastery and bishop's house: 'let them read psalms, notes, chants, the *computus* and grammar'. The *computus* meant more than just 'reckoning': Raban Maur's treatise on the *computus* covered the whole field of the *quadrivium* except music, (see p. 521). For so general a command, the aim was high: and later imperial injunctions and the canons of councils show that it was not reached: the rural clergy in general never attained to this standard of education: but cathedral schools there were in the ninth century, from the famous schools of the canons of Tours, directed by Alcuin himself from 794 to 804, to those of small cathedrals 'ruled' by a single *scholasticus*. The council of Châlons, 813, again ordered that cathedral schools must be established, and the council of Aix-la-Chapelle, 817, in ordering that cathedral clergy should live communally (or 'canonically') required them to keep a school. The old rule of Chrodegang had ordered that the rulers of churches should appoint a canon to supervise and teach the children committed to the community, so that they might be duly promoted to the different grades of the clerical order: the *regula Aquisgranensis* of 817 enjoined that *scholastici* should strive after Latinity rather than rusticity: 'in such lectures, the taking of written notes about the scriptures is sometimes more illuminating than mere reading, and the use of dictation should be learnt and the mind sharpened for study'. The council of Paris, 824, ordered each bishop to be more zealous for the education of the clerical militia, and to have schools for young clerks: but the financial difficulty of providing a good *scholasticus*, and maintaining the young clerks, still hindered the universal provision of good cathedral schools.

Monastic schools in the late eighth and ninth century produced riper scholars. They taught only the oblate children and young monks: only in a few cases, and in missionary lands, did the Benedictine monastery have a second and extern school to educate young secular clergy (as at Fulda). In the normal monastic schools there was not the difficulty of 'providing a benefice' for the *scholasticus*, for he would be a monk himself, spending his whole life in the community. Learning was also promoted by abbots, who sent their promising young monks to study at other abbeys under some famous *scholasticus*, which contributed to the wider influence of exceptional scholars, and also made the provision of a learned *scholasticus* easier for the smaller abbeys.

An endowment at least moderate and the maintenance of regular discipline were an indispensable background for monastic study, and the reform movement led by Benedict of Aniane helped to secure regularity and order. Benedict had been born near Dijon *c.* 751, and though trained for knighthood, he had thrown up his career in obedience to a monastic vocation. He looked back to the monks of Egypt, regarded the rule of St Benedict as professedly 'only for beginners' and the infirm, and 'strove to ascend by the rules of Basil and Pachomius'. When he founded his own monastery at Aniane in Aquitaine, he turned, however, to the Benedictine rule, insisting only on its strict and primitive observance. Before his death in 821 he had, under the patronage of Louis the Pious, extended this observance to many older houses not hitherto professing the Benedictine rule, enjoined the *capitulare monasticum* for such observance on the abbots who assembled at the council of Aix in 817, and composed the *Concordia Regularum* and *Codex Regularum* for the further instruction of the Benedictine abbots and monks. Though Benedict had not set out to make the monks learned, the order and regularity he secured did, in fact, condition the success of the great monastic schools in the ninth century. The foundation of the abbey of Cluny in 911 was to perpetuate such conditions in the tenth.

Each great Benedictine abbey became thus, in the ninth century, a focus of scholarship. Moving across the empire from east to west, Fulda, founded in Franconia by Boniface in 744, had the highest reputation: it was a channel through which the earlier, Northumbrian learning passed to the empire. Corvey in Saxony, daughter house of Corbie in Picardy, was a storehouse of Frankish learning set down, like Fulda, in a country recently pagan. On the shores of Lake Constance, the abbey of Saint-Gall retained, even in the ninth century, the Columbanian traditions of its founder, and Reichenau, at the other end of the lake, under the rule of Walafrid Strabo, was reputed a very learned abbey; it had been founded by an Irish missionary, St Pirnin, and Old Irish must once have been spoken there (see p. 503). The humanist scholar, Sedulius Scottus, founded his monastery at Liége in 848, and with his fellow Irishmen made it a famous school. Prüm, a few miles south-east of Liége, was a learned abbey, as was Wissembourg, farther south and near the Rhine. In Burgundy, the abbey of Lyons fostered scholars and controversialists: at the beginning of the ninth century it lay in the southern portion of the central Frankish kingdom, and the precariousness of its position was reflected in the bitterness of its academic disputes.

In the reign of Charles the Bald, the traditions of a learned palace entourage, a palace school, were transferred from Aix-la-Chapelle to Paris and the royal residences near the Seine among which the court moved. Similarly, the academic palm passed from the schools of Tours after Alcuin's death to other schools; for a time to Ferrières under Servatus Lupus, and also to a ring of abbeys round Paris on the lower Seine: Jumièges, Saint-Wandrille and Saint-Riquier, where Angilbert, the Carolingian Homer, had died in 814. In Picardy, Saint-Vaast just outside Arras, Saint-

Bertin (the nucleus of the town of Saint-Omer), and above all Corbie, were renowned for their learning. Wala and Adalard, Charlemagne's sons, took refuge at Corbie in adversity, and there Paschasius Radbert taught, and the monk Ratramnus, who answered the attacks of Photius on the Latin church.

Some great cathedral schools shared the fame of the monasteries: Reims, Orleans and Metz were notable examples. Laon, later to be the school of the calculators and abacists, was now a hearth of Irish learning.

Among the abbeys founded by Columbanian scholars, Luxeuil and Bobbio continued to copy and study classical and patristic manuscripts: they were reinforced by a continuous flow of postulants from Ireland. The young Irish scholars appear to have struck the Franks and Italians as indefatigable travellers, enthusiastic for learning, but somewhat noisy and contentious. They became assiduous copyists at Bobbio, and their capacity for work outran the abbey's supply of writing material. 'This is the plain meaning', writes Dr E. A. Lowe, 'of the (abbey's) imposing series of seventh- and eighth-century palimpsests.' The number of these washed down and rewritten vellum manuscripts runs into dozens, even among those that still survive. The oldest of these extant palimpsests was made up of a discarded fifth- or sixth-century Gothic Bible. Bobbio had been built in the old country of the Ostrogoths, and it was, after all, natural that so much of the scanty literary remains of the Gothic tongue should have survived in the library at Bobbio. Apart from the very important copy of Wulfila's gospels, the Codex Argenteus, which after its travels remains now at Uppsala, the remnants of Gothic manuscripts are nearly all buried in palimpsests, and, with the exception of a Milan palimpsest, 'the burying was done by Bobbio monks' (Lowe). They buried some Gothic gospels to rewrite them in Latin, and they equally buried certain classical Latin works which they held of no particular importance, to use the vellum for patristic works.

Charlemagne's efforts for the maintenance of schools were clearly aimed less at the improvement of learning for its own sake than at the better education of the clerical order, which, incidentally, was now providing him with a civil service. That considerable success was obtained is witnessed by the proliferation of the clerical order itself, and the organization of the rural clergy in deaneries and archdeaconries in the Carolingian period; by efforts to extinguish pagan superstitions, and by the exercise of more effective scrutiny in the process of canonization.

That pagan practices still survived in the countryside is clear from imperial and conciliar legislation. Charlemagne had received from pope Hadrian on his visit to Rome in 774 the collection of canons known as the *Dionysio-Hadriana*, the canon law as it was observed at that time in the Roman church, and he sought to obtain its general observance among the Franks. Even in his first capitulary he had re-enacted an edict of Carloman, 742, against pagan practices.

We have decreed that each bishop, according to the canons, shall take heed in his parochia, the *grafio* who is the *defensor ecclesiae* helping him, that the people of God do no pagan rites, but cast away and scorn all the evil deeds of paganism, whether it be the profane offerings for the dead, or sortilege and divining, or phylacteries and auguries or incantations, or the sacrifice of victims, which fools perform near the churches with pagan ritual in the name of the holy martyrs and saints of God: which provoke the saints rather to wrath than to mercy.

In the *Admonitio Generalis* of March 789, which was in fact a short digest of the *Dionysio-Hadriana* with the addition of a few African canons, the prohibition of pagan rites was repeated: 'there must be no more enchanters nor weavers of spells nor weather magicians: and where there are trees or rocks or springs where fools are wont to carry lights and other rites, such evil customs must be altogether removed and destroyed wherever found'. The capitularies for Saxony, newly converted, naturally prohibited heathen rites in several passages: canonical authority must be obtained for the cutting down of (sacred) trees and groves. But that pagan practices lingered on in the whole Carolingian empire is attested by the repetition of prohibitions in the later capitularies. A ninth-century Vatican manuscript gives a full list of pagan practices, auguries and rites, including celebrations for Woden and Thor. The canons of church councils forbade the giving of Christian serf-girls to pagans, pagan witchcraft, auguries, phylacteries, etc., the making of pagan vows, pagan dancing and leaping and singing by women on Christian festivals, etc.

The efforts in the Carolingian period to procure a more effective supervision of the process of canonization may be also accounted a sign of the better education of the clergy. Canonization had hitherto been popular and little supervised. From the earliest days of the church special reverence had been shown for the bodies of the martyrs and their *natalicia*, or anniversaries, had been celebrated: this was a matter for the local church. In Africa, however, after the Donatist schism, doubts arose about the veneration paid to local *martyria*, little altars in the fields or at the roadside, believed to have been erected over the relics of Catholic martyrs: a council of Carthage, 401, ordered that no memorials of doubtful martyrdoms should be made 'except where there is a body or relics, or the origin of any such habitation or site of martyrdom is most faithfully known: for completely untrustworthy altars are widely set up attested only by vain dreams accounted as revelations'. The local bishop was charged with ascertaining the authenticity or otherwise of these altars. This African canon of 401 was embodied in both the collections of Dionysius Exiguus and the *Hispana* (see p. 537): but Merovingian canonists in the centuries before Charlemagne were less concerned with the subject of canonization than ecclesiastical penance, and practice in the veneration of the relics of the saints changed.

The great factor in this change was the barbarian invasion of western Europe: it became necessary in very many cases to transport the relics of saints to a place of safety, and the honour paid to martyrs, and now also to men of known holy life, confessors, became dissociated from the place of burial: very many early 'translations' were made under fear of desecration. But such removal of relics led to confusion and doubts about authenticity: in the days of Gregory of Tours, for instance, and later, 'when the history of the saint was unknown, or the cult of some early martyr was revived, there was always a great danger of inadequate investigation and of uncritical reliance upon visions' (E. Kemp). Local devotion seems to have led to the translation and veneration of new saints, usually without sanction from any high ecclesiastical authority, and certainly without any recognition that episcopal permission must be obtained before such translation and veneration. While the Merovingian church was expanding into the countryside, the finding that a martyr's bones were buried in an adjacent cemetery, even if his identity were only attested in a dream, made possible their translation to the altar of the new church and an increase of offerings.

In the reign of Charlemagne, however, the bishops were no longer willing to allow this practice, and their reforming efforts were expressed in the royal capitularies. The *Admonitio Generalis* of 789 forbade new saints to be venerated or invoked, or have memorials to them erected by the wayside: except those known by the authority of their passions (attested accounts of their martyrdoms) or the merit of their life. In 802 a capitulary ordered that the spurious names of martyrs be not venerated; in 813 the council of Mainz forbade that the bodies of saints should be translated from place to place, and, further, that any man should

presume to translate the bodies of saints from place to place without the council of the prince or the leave of the holy synod of
bishops. A yet more explicit ruling of 811 had reprobated the
practice by which the relics of saints were translated where new
basilicas were being built, and 'men were urgently invited to endow
the new church with their property, in so far as they were able.
Those who made such a translation seemed to themselves to
perform a meritorious action, deserving well of God: but let
them persuade the bishops of this and let all things be done
openly.'

In short, a new stage was reached in the process of canonization
in the ninth century: episcopal and even metropolitan inquiry
came to precede translation and the raising to the altar of the
saint's body or relics. Iso, *scholasticus* of Saint-Gall (see p. 541),
gives an account of the canonization of St Othmar, who died in
759. The monks, revering his memory and led by certain signs,
compiled a book containing accounts of his holiness by the saint's
contemporaries: they submitted the book to Salomon, bishop of
Constance, and though he was much edified, he in turn laid the
matter before the diocesan synod. The synod assembled, heard
the life of St Othmar described by the bishop, fasted for three
days, and authorized the translation (864). Translation was, by
this date, the act of canonization. The care for verification shown
in this new process of episcopal or synodal inquiry compares
with the care taken by scholars like Servatus Lupus in the collation
of texts, and attests a general improvement in clerical education.

The harvest of Charlemagne's efforts to foster monastic and
episcopal schools can be seen best in the work of particular ninth-
century scholars. Raban Maur, one of the greatest of them, was
intellectually the child of Alcuin, who had died at Tours in 804.
Raban was born at Mainz in 784, made an oblate monk at Fulda,
and sent by his abbot to complete his studies at Tours under
Alcuin, who called him Maurus after the favourite pupil of St
Benedict. He returned to Fulda and at no long interval was made
the monastic *scholasticus*: under his care, the schools at Fulda in the
days of Louis the Pious came to eclipse even those of Tours.
Raban was made abbot of Fulda in 822, adhered to the emperor
Lothar I in the troubles between him and his brothers, and in 842
after Lothar's defeat, was dispossessed of his abbey and retired
to that of Petersburg. Louis the German, esteeming his character
and learning, made him archbishop of Mainz in 847, and he died
in that position in 856. Apart from many scriptural commentaries

and a great encyclopedia of Christian knowledge about the universe that betrays no recent contacts with Byzantine science or
theology (see p. 421), Raban's most interesting work was his *De
institutione clericorum*, written while he was still responsible at
Fulda for the schools not only of oblate monks but of secular
clerks. For the young clerks he desired instruction in both the
ecclesiastical disciplines and the old Greco-Roman learning: the
trivium and *quadrivium*. He himself produced no work of striking
originality: but men called him the *praeceptor Germaniae primus*
and he did as much as any man to form the climate of opinion of
the early middle ages.

What Raban Maur had been to Alcuin, Walafrid Strabo was
to Raban Maur. He was twenty years younger, received his
monastic training at Reichenau, with its Irish traditions, and was
then sent to Fulda to study under Raban Maur. While still under
twenty he wrote the tract foreshadowing Dante's *Inferno*, the
Visio Wettini. In 829 he went from Fulda to Aix-la-Chapelle, to
instruct the young Charles (the Bald), and when this task was
completed, he was made abbot of Reichenau, though not yet
thirty. He lost his abbey in the troubled year, 840, but recovered it
in 842; he died in 849 at the court of Charles the Bald.

It was held till recently that he actually compiled the *Glosa
Ordinaria*, a great catena of marginal and interlinear glosses on
every verse of the Old and New Testaments: a work which
digested the comments and exegesis of patristic and early students
of the biblical text. Dr Beryl Smalley has shown, however, that
Raban Maur was concerned only in the early stage of the gradual
accretion of these glosses; Bede had supplied commentaries which
presented the barbarians with patristic teaching on the scriptures
simply but faithfully; Alcuin had supervised the revision of the
text of the Bible and presented it to Charlemagne as a present
for his coronation; Raban Maur had made further commentaries
on certain biblical books. Walafrid Strabo commented on the
Psalms and Canonical Epistles: and later scholars continued the
work. The *Glosa Ordinaria* was not completed till the twelfth
century, not, in fact, till, by a parallel development, the sciences
of civil and canon law had also produced for themselves a *Glosa
Ordinaria*. The brief, terse gloss, marginal or interlinear, was in
fact a legal rather than a theological technique: the *Glosa Ordinaria*
on the scriptures could scarcely have been completed in that
form before the twelfth century legal commentators at Bologna
had done their work. For the rest, Walafrid Strabo's reputation
rested on some saints' lives, some Latin verses in the humanist

Carolingian tradition (addressed, for instance, to the emperor or describing the equestrian statue of Theoderic at Aix), on a mainly liturgical tract entitled *De ecclesiasticarum rerum exordiis et elementis*, and on an interesting verse tract about his garden (*Hortulus*). In this, passing among his flowers and herbs, he lingered lovingly over the description of rue, with its sharp, blue-green leaves: his rounded pumpkins, dyed yellow by the summer sun: horehound, which smells sweet but does not taste sweet: fennel and gladiolus, lily and poppy, betony and agrimony and the rose: 'and may the eternal God grant us green-springing virtue and the palm of life unwithering'.

Just before Walafrid Strabo's death an Irishman, Sedulius Scottus, came to Liége with some companions (848), and made of it a famous school. He wrote graceful Latin verses to the great, commentaries on the epistles of St Paul and a political treatise entitled *Liber de Rectoribus Christianis*, in which he showed acquaintance with the political theorists of antiquity. He knew some Greek, like most Irish scholars. Just south of Liége, the poet Wandalbert used a variety of Latin metres with great skill and pleasant effect in his *Martyrologe*.

Meanwhile another scholar, Servatus Lupus (805–862), abbot of Ferrières, was illustrating the Carolingian thirst for learning less by his treatises than by the assiduity with which he collected and collated manuscripts for the abbey library, particularly the works of classical writers. He entered at Ferrières under an abbot third in succession and tradition to Sigulf, a pupil of Alcuin, but the house was poor and there was little teaching of the liberal arts. When Lupus was twenty-five, he was sent to Fulda to study under Raban Maur, and became one of the circle of scholars who corresponded with him and each other. He himself wrote to Einhard, and began that series of letters by which he is chiefly known, containing so many requests for the loan or gifts of books. Lupus was a sedulous copyist of classical manuscripts, and frequently importuned his friends for the loan of a second copy so that he might correct the *lacunae* in his first; he had his own system in copying a manuscript of leaving a gap for a word where he suspected his text to be corrupt. He borrowed Cicero from Einhard, and several patristic manuscripts from Alcuin at Tours; he wrote to the archbishop of York for books, to pope Benedict III, and many others. The sending of books from monastery to monastery was, he knew, dangerous unless the book was small enough to conceal in the messenger's clothes or satchel, and he would not send any larger book from his own library. He collected most of

Cicero's works, which were less generally accessible than those of Vergil, which he also possessed: some Livy, Caesar, Sallust, Suetonius, the Latin Josephus, and Boethius' *De Arithmetica*. He was a great teacher and a very great librarian. The greatest of his pupils, Heiric of Auxerre, who studied not only at Ferrières but with the Irishmen of Laon and at Soissons, has left a collection of long passages from classical writers taken down from Lupus' dictation: and also a long poem on the life of Germanus of Auxerre.

Meanwhile, two efforts were made to supply a life of Christ in the vernacular for the instruction and use of priests out in the countryside, or possibly for presentation to some great lay noble: the peasants themselves, of course, could neither read nor afford the great cost of books. The *Heliand* (*Saviour*) was written in Old Saxon, in the alliterative metre used by Caedmon in England long before; the author is unknown, but a Latin preface states that the work was commissioned by Louis the Pious, and the poem appears to date from the second quarter of the ninth century. The preface quotes Bede's story of Caedmon's inspired poems: it would seem that Anglo-Saxon tradition occasioned the work. Whether the actual writer was a missionary, familiar with Old Saxon, or an old Saxon skóp, or an old Saxon monk who well remembered the songs heard in his youth, is not clear. Somewhere behind the poem was a man of learning, for the material of the poem was the old gospel harmony (*Diatessaron*) of Tatian; the commentaries of Bede, Alcuin and Raban Maur were also familiar to the poet, or supplied to him by the said man of learning. Rather later, *c*. 865, Otfrid, monk of Wissembourg in Alemania, made a prose digest of the gospels in 'the tongue of the Franks', i.e. German. He was a native of the country, but trained at Fulda under Raban Maur, and in his German *Liber Evangeliorum* he loaded his digest of the life and teaching of Christ so heavily with comment that all freshness and directness was lost: it does not appear that the work was widely known.

Lyons in Burgundy had been a great pre-Carolingian school and *scriptorium*, with natural contacts with the Byzantine Mediterranean, as is shown by some surviving leaves of Greco-Latin grammars and glossaries on papyrus, a few papyrus leaves of the breviary of Alaric, and a fine sixth-century vellum copy of the Theodosian Code, probably written there, as well as other indications. In the early ninth century it was still an intellectual centre: the Visigothic archbishop, Agobard of Lyons, in spite of the struggles of 833 in which he was involved, wrote a treatise *De modo regiminis ecclesiastici*, engaged in the controversy with the Spanish Adoptianists, and with archbishop Amalaric who had replaced him during the period (835–838) when he had been dispossessed of his see. Amalaric, a liturgist with a considerable reputation, had in 820 presented Louis the Pious with his treatise, *De ecclesiasticis officiis*; a considerable struggle against Amalaric's interpretation of the ceremonies of the mass had been maintained in Agobard's absence by the learned archdeacon, Florus.

In western France, in the reign of Charles the Bald, the most renowned of all the Irishmen, John the Scot, outshone not only the other Carolingian scholars, but those of some centuries to come. He was, in fact, in touch with Byzantine learning. That such contact was not impossible is shown by the fragmentary Greco-Latin vocabularies and grammars of the pre-Carolingian period that have survived, as by, for instance, a Greco-Latin psalter beautifully written in uncials (see p. 527), certainly produced in some important Frankish centre where the Greek caligraphy was still practised, and before the eighth century. There must have been many more such vellum manuscripts in the ninth century than now survive, for the Carolingian scribes were prone to wash down such little-used manuscripts for palimpsests. The list of Carolingian scholars who knew some Greek from glossaries is long, particularly in the case of the Irishmen: but apart from Erigena there were few interested in Greek literature. The works of the Greek fathers, the lives of the desert fathers, the canons of Greek councils, were all accessible in Latin versions: it was easier to use them in a language with which all were familiar. It took a fine and far-ranging mind like John the Scot's to read the Greek theological literature as yet untranslated: to read, that is, the theology long studied and accepted at Byzantium, but as yet unknown in the west. That he in no way dispensed himself from the normal field of Greco-Roman study is shown by his commentary on Martianus Capella's treatise on the arts (see p. 86).

The place of John's early studies in Ireland is unknown; he is first found attached to the palace school of Charles the Bald, which he directed. At the request of Hincmar of Reims, then engaged in his controversy on predestination with Gottschalk, he wrote his *De Predestinatione* in 850–1; and till 860 he seems to have contented himself with the study of Latin philosophy and theology; in that year, however, he began his series of translations from Greek theologians. His knowledge of Greek had gone far beyond the meaning of names and terms, such as his contemporaries gleaned from the glossaries and Isidore. His most important work was to popularize the Neoplatonist but orthodox teaching of Dionysius 'the Areopagite' long esteemed in Byzantine thought. The *nom-de-plume* of Dionysius the Areopagite had been adopted *c.* 500 by a Christian disciple of the Neoplatonist philosopher Proclus; this disciple was ascetic, orthodox, and possibly a bishop in Syria. In the struggle over the Christological decisions of Chalcedon then agitating the east, he appears to have been a moderate Chalcedonian, not actively hostile to the Monophysites; he wrote treatises *On the divine names, Mystical theology, The Celestial Hierarchy, The Ecclesiastical Hierarchy*, and certain epistles to the disciples of the apostles. These works taught the approach of the Christian soul to God by *ascesis* and the *via negativa:* they were of massive importance in the development of Byzantine theology, and they were never, from the time of John the Scot's translation of them, completely unknown in the west. Such works as Meister Eckhart's sermons, and the English *Cloud of Unknowing* show their influence, as do other western tracts.

The works of the Pseudo-Dionysius were not completely unknown in the west before John the Scot: pope Gregory the Great knew them, and pope Martin I knew Maximus the Confessor, their great exponent and commentator: he was present at the Lateran council of 649. The works of Dionysius were known at Saint-Denis in 827, and translated into Latin. John the Scot retranslated them all before 862, and in the years following he translated also the *Ambigua* of Maximus the Confessor, Gregory of Nyssa's *De Imagine* and Epiphanius' *Ancoratus*: he commented on the *Celestial Hierarchy*. All this mystical theology, carefully aligned with orthodox teaching, was commonly accepted in the Byzantine church, and the work of John the Scot made a notable contribution towards keeping western theology in line with that of the east.

After thus steeping himself in the Dionysiac literature, John produced between 862 and 866 his chief philosophical-theological treatise, the *Peri Physeon* or *De Divisione Naturae*, an exposition of the 'how' as well as 'why' of the universe after which Raban Maur had been merely groping. He attempted a synthesis of the Latin and Greek sources of knowledge available to him, and even, though his Latin theological vocabulary was insufficient to the task, he produced a reasoned synthesis. From God, uncreated and the creator, come the (platonic) Ideas, created and yet creative, eternal like the creator, 'for so, coming from God, they are eternal and created, for they are eternal in the Word of God'. From them all creation comes into being, and, coming from God, shall return to him again. Quoting Maximus' *De Ambiguis*, he wrote: 'All that is moved according to its nature is moved by the cause of all things: and the end to which each moves is that cause by which it is moved and to which it is drawn back again.' The Dionysiac teaching had been received with surprise in the east when it first appeared, but after examination its orthodoxy had been approved. Erigena's version, with its less subtle Latin vocabulary, gave rise to some suspicion of pantheism: but Erigena was, in fact, no monist, and a papal condemnation of his teaching as pantheist was given only after some centuries, an intervention in a controversy then current. He died about 875, the year Charles the Bald was crowned at Rome and came back to preside over his bishops in Byzantine ceremonial robes: Charles was no defender of the Frankish monasteries from the northmen, but his court was not uninterested in Byzantine learning.

Some of the finest Carolingian verse came from a near contemporary of John the Scot, the unhappy Gottschalk, who died in his silent prison, desiring the last sacrament and unreconciled, in 870. He was the son of a Saxon knight, offered as an oblate at Fulda, and at sixteen passionately anxious for release. A council of bishops granted it him: but such dispensation was novel, for the vows taken by the parents who offered their son were then held as binding as those taken by a novice himself. Gottschalk's abbot, Raban Maur, appealed against the conciliar decision, and Hincmar, archbishop of Reims, submitted the case for the emperor's decision: Gottschalk's plea for release was disallowed, but he was not sent back to Fulda. Corbie and abbot Ratramnus first received him, and then Orbais, where he long studied the doctrine of Augustine about man and sin and the prevenient grace of God (see p. 90). The doctrine of predestination became henceforth the sheet anchor and absorbing interest of his life, but while all his prose works on his subject have perished or been destroyed, the Latin verse that he wrote so effortlessly has survived. He tells us in one place that he spent only a year on the study of rhetoric, perhaps with Ratramnus to whom he wrote a poem: but he spent years wandering in Italy, land of grammarians, and came to write the old, familiar language in the new metres. The use of rhyme in Christian Latin verse is said to have sprung from the example of rhetorical rhymed prose, but Irish influence probably gave it a further impetus.[1] Gottschalk's use of rhyme, as in those

[1] See P. Grosjean's important article mentioned in the bibliography on p. 519.

flute-like sounds of his lines to a friend who had asked him, an exile, for a song, is remarkable:

> Ut quid iubes, pusiole,
> quare mandas, filiole,
> carmen dulce me cantare
> cum sim longe exul valde
> intra mare?
> O cur iubes canere?

If the Carolingian period was notable in the history of Latin poetry for the change from measured verse to verse with the stress accent, it was notable also for its use of rhyme and for the introduction of the sequence into the liturgy. The ninth century saw increased use of the Roman chant among the Franks, but even more significant were the developments which were to come from the sequence itself; this liturgical sequence was to be a factor of the greatest importance in the history of western Latin poetry, vernacular poetry and the first dawn of medieval drama. The history of the sequence belongs both to those of western Latin poetry and of music, as one of the liberal arts: it is connected also with those of the monastic schools and of a scholar long considered its originator, Notker Balbulus, *scholasticus* of Saint-Gall. While the general subject of Frankish plain chant is briefly treated in the next chapter (see p. 541), that of the liturgical sequence may be mentioned here, for its use marked a beginning. The Easter sequence

> Victimae paschali laudes
> immolent Christiani

with the ceremonial actions that accompanied it, have been considered the germ of medieval drama.

What then was the sequence? It sprang from the wordless prolongation of the last syllable of the Alleluia sung before the gospel at mass, already very old. Gregory I had stated that in the time of pope Damasus (d. 384) the Alleluia had been prolonged by the singing of a *iubilus* or *iubilatio*, a melody without words (*melisma*). A direction in the Roman *Ordo* ran: *Sequitur iubilatio quam sequentiam vocant*. When words were added to the *iubilus*, the sung passage was called a *versus*, or, among the Franks, a *prosa* (*prosa ad sequentiam*). The term sequentia, in Byzantine music *akolouthia*, soon came to be used, however, of the words and music together: the singing of such sequences in the Carolingian empire was certainly in imitation of Byzantine practice, and illustrates the relation of western music to eastern music at the time. The singing of the long *iubilus* after the Alleluia was eastern and had appeared in the Ambrosian Alleluia before the days of Gregory I: it was sung twice, with a verse of scripture set to a melody in between.

The Ambrosian rite had only a small number of these Alleluia melodies, sung at the different feasts, but they were long. Dr E. Wellesz has shown that in Gregory I's day the singing of the Alleluia with verse was introduced at Rome into all the masses of the ecclesiastical year, save those of the penitential seasons: but at the same time the first singing of the *iubilus* was shortened and, in the verse, the melody was brought into closer relation to the words. Gregory said of the singing of the Alleluia at Rome: 'We have cut short this custom, which in this matter had been handed down from the Greeks.' Dr Wellesz believes that the Gallican Alleluia up till the eighth century had had the same structure as the Ambrosian, the Mozarabic and other pre-Gregorian types, and that the older, longer, pre-Gregorian form was still used by the Franks till the sequence poems, such as those composed by Notker Balbulus, began to be widely used among them.

It was once believed, on the strength of the *incipit* of the *Liber Hymnorum*, that Notker was himself the originator of the sequence, at least among the Franks: this is now discredited. Notker was the younger *scholasticus* in charge of the oblates' school at Saint-Gall, and worked under his master Iso (d. 871) towards the end of the ninth century. Saint-Gall had certainly a rich treasury of chants, transmitted in its tropers (*troparia*) or hymn-books. Notker himself tells us in the *Prooemium* to his *Liber Hymnorum* that a priest of Jumièges, fleeing to Saint-Gall after his abbey had been sacked by the *Nortmanni*, had come, bringing with him his antiphoner, in which were certain verses sung at the sequences, 'but already corrupted'. Delighted at these verses, but disapproving of certain features of them, Notker himself wrote two new verse sequences. Since Saint-Gall was not the monastery where the writing of sequences originated: claims have been put forward for other monasteries, on the Continent or in England, but no certain conclusions have been reached. What is certain, from Notker's own words in the *Prooemium*, is that Iso, Notker's master, knew of such music in the older, Ambrosian manner, with the words of the sequences sung to melodic phrases more or less elaborate, and knew also of the more succinct, Roman chant applied to the verses of the Alleluia: he approved Notker's first two sequences, but recommended him to write his hymns with one note to each syllable (in the Roman manner), and Notker complied. Though Notker was not the originator of the sequence, he is the first western *cantor* whose name is connected with it: and he and the choir of Saint-Gall, using Byzantine prototypes, did for Frankish music what the scribes of the *schola Palatina* did for the illumination of western manuscripts.

BIBLIOGRAPHICAL NOTE

For Carolingian abbeys, see under 'La Renaissance carolingienne', E. Amann, *L'époque Carolingienne*, pp. 93–106, and references, and J. M. Clark, *The Abbey of St. Gall*. For a list and résumé of Carolingian writings on the liberal arts as well as 'science' in its modern sense, see G. Sarton, *Introduction to the History of Science*, vol. i, 1950. For Carolingian thought, see the earlier portions of J. de Ghellinck, *Literature latine au moyen âge*, 1939, and E. Gilson, *La philosophie au moyen âge*, 1944. See *supra*, bibliog. note to chapter xvii, on Alcuin: and W. S. Howell, 'The Rhetoric of Alcuin and Charlemagne', 1941, *Princeton Studies in English*, vol. 23. See also M. Cappuyns, 'Jean Scot Erigène', 1933, Louvain dissert, in fac. theol., Ser. 2, tom. 26, and C. E. Lutz, *Iohannis Scotti Annotationes in Marcianum*, Med. Acad. of America, 1939: for the pseudo-Dionysian writings, used by John the Scot, see E. Amann, *L'époque carolingienne*, p. 313 and refs. For Carolingian verse, see E. Duemmler's *Poetae Latini aevi Carolini*, tom. i, 1881: C. U. J. Chevalier's *Repertorium hymnologicum*, 6 tomes, 1892–1920: F. J. E. Raby, *A History of Secular Latin Poetry*, 2 vols., 1934, and H. Waddell, *The Wandering Scholars*, 1927. For the Irish influence on rhyme, see P. Grosjean, S.J., 'Confusa Caligo', in *Celtica*, vol. iii (1955): an article on the *Hisperica Famina*. See also, D. Knowles, *The Evolution of Medieval Thought*, London, 1962 (from Plato and Aristotle); G. Leff, *Medieval Thought from Saint Augustine to Ockham*, Pelican, 1958; P. Renucci, *L'Aventure de l'Humanisme européen au Moyen Age*, Paris, 1953; B. Smalley, *The Study of the Bible in the Middle Ages*, Paris, 1953, for the rejection of Walafrid Strabo's authorship of the Gloss; P. McGurk, *Latin Gospel Books from A.D. 400–800*, Ghent, 1961, for Carolingian debt both to Latin antiquity and Irish Learning.

CHAPTER XXVII

THE CAROLINGIAN RENAISSANCE: THE CONTRIBUTION TO KNOWLEDGE

WHILE the Carolingian imperial encouragement of schools tended to produce more educated and intelligent clergy, the product of new and original works in the field of the liberal arts was small. Here there was very little fertilizing contact with Byzantine or Arabic learning: only, in fact, in the case of music, and the Neoplatonist teaching about the structure of the universe. Only in the first case was there a real efflorescence of an art, when Byzantine music, Rome reformed, was introduced to the fine instrument of the monastic choirs, and the ninth and tenth centuries heard the first and most beautiful cadences of liturgical plainchant. Otherwise, while the greatest ninth-century teachers maintained that Greco-Roman learning was a most desirable part of clerical education, new and original works in the field of the liberal arts were few.

Alcuin was the first scholar to mark the non-mathematical off from the mathematical arts by the use of the term *trivium* and *quadrivium*, but he himself made no contribution to the *quadrivium* as great as Bede's *De temporum ratione*. His teaching must have been largely oral and informal, and his treatises on the arts were cast into the form of dialogues. That on grammar was set forth as between Alcuin himself as *magister* and two boys, one Saxon and one Frankish, in his school; they had just 'burst into the thorny thicket of grammar', and had to be taught about nouns, genders, cases, verbs, etc. The dialogues on rhetoric and dialectic were written as between Alcuin and Charlemagne: that on rhetoric dealt with the art of speaking well, and mainly in the law courts. These three treatises covered the *trivium*, but for the *quadrivium* Alcuin supplied no comprehensive treatises, but only two short tracts: *On the full moon and the moon's course* and *On leap year* ('What causes leap year? the tardiness of the sun in his course', etc.). Alcuin had nothing apparently to add to Bede.

The prose works of Raban Maur bulked much larger than those of Alcuin, and if in his writings he contributed nothing new in the field of the *quadrivium*, at least he insisted that all seven arts should be included in the education of clerics, and he wrote two treatises dealing with the *quadrivium* himself. In the third book of his *De institutione clericorum* he insisted that the young cleric must be fully trained both in *sapientia* (the seven liberal arts) and *caritas*: it was not safe for a future ruler of souls to be ignorant of anything. He devoted a chapter each to grammar, rhetoric, dialectic, mathematics, arithmetic, geometry, music and 'the books of the philosophers'. He wrote also a treatise, *De computo* in dialogue form. 'Number', he wrote, 'has existed since the beginning of the world: take away number, and all is enveloped in blind ignorance: nor could we differ from the animals without it, for they know not how to reckon.' But in this treatise the science of reckoning is not taken beyond the teaching of Boethius and Bede, though Raban passes in it beyond arithmetic to an exposition of the earth and the planets. 'The heaven (*coelum*) is by nature subtle and fiery (clear and bright) and distant everywhere from the earth its centre by equal spaces.' Wise men (*sapientes*) say that it 'spins round with unspeakable swiftness each day, so that it would rush to destruction were it not restrained and moderated by the influence of the planets striving in their starry argument: for they fly round ever on a fixed course, performing their smaller gyrations each upon its hinge (*cardo*). And the ends of the earth's axis, on which it turns in its revolution, we call the poles, which languish in icy stiffness.' He goes on to deal with the five bands or climates of the earth, with comets, solstices, equinoxes, the waxing of the moon and leap-year, with the year of the Lord's incarnation, and Dionysius' exposition of the cycle of nineteen years by which Easter is reckoned, with epacts and the courses of the stars, with the moon's cycle and the Easter moon. The treatise *De computo* thus covered much of the field of the *quadrivium*, and added to what the encyclopedists had taught only the application of arithmetical and astronomical knowledge for the problem of determining Easter and the rest of the church's calendar.

More notable and longer than the *De Computo* was Raban Maur's treatise on the universe, written about 844 (*De Universo libri viginti duo*). This was not merely a description of the physical universe, as known in the ninth century, but an effort to estimate its intention, its *ratio*. The early medieval mind was not empiricist: where modern inquiry insists on the 'how' of natural phenomena, the medieval mind concentrated on the 'why'. Coming to the Greco-Latin description and explanation of the physical universe from a state of Germanic ignorance, the early medieval scholar was not predisposed to question such descriptions. Whether he was dealing with the old Greco-Roman science, or the Christian explanation of the creation, maintenance and rule of the universe

he did not question assertions founded on knowledge much pro-
founder than his own. The universe was as the *sapientes* described
it, and its general purpose as the Christian doctors taught: but
about the working of the universe they taught very little. To what
purpose, he asked, did the planets, local thickenings or bosses, as
it were, of their own crystal spheres, swing round the earth as their
hinge and centre? All things below the sphere of the moon were
mutable, compounded of earth, water, air and fire, and above the
sphere of the moon immutable, where the planets swung on their
individual spheres and the fixed stars on the sphere of the empy-
rean, of *coelum* itself. To what purpose was all this elaborate
apparatus, behind which lay the Ideas, surely purposive, in the
mind of God?

It would seem that Raban Maur, fumbling after an answer to
the question 'why', thinking as a philosopher, not a physicist,
hoped to find it by applying to the known universe and its parts
the method of interpretation which had long been applied to the
Christian scriptures. By a fourfold interpretation, each scriptural
passage might be understood literally, historically (*tropologice*),
allegorically and mystically (*anagogice*). Raban, availing himself of
the patristic and later commentaries on the Bible in the fine library
of Fulda, seems to have desired to set down all he could find out
about the how and why of the universe, using as a clue an allegorical,
historical or mystical interpretation of the facts, such as the
commentators used on the scriptural text: and using etymology
as the first clue for such interpretation. In many sections of the
De Universo Raban was thus led to incorporate much of Isidore's
Etymologies: but the work included theological explanations as
well. In his preface, addressed to Louis the Pious, Raban explained
that he has earlier sent his commentary on the scriptures to Louis,
and that, when he was lately in the emperor's presence, Louis
had said that he had heard Raban had compiled works on the
meaning of words and their mystical significance, and he had
asked Raban to send it to him. This he has willingly done, dividing
the work into twenty-two books, so that Louis might, if he wished,
have it read before him, and so that he and his wisest readers
might, if reason demanded, emend it.

> For many things are there explained of the nature of things, and
> the meanings of words and even of their mystical significance. For I
> reasoned that it ought to be drawn up in order, so that the prudent
> reader might find continuously set forth the historical and mystical
> explanation of things, and thus satisfy his desire for the making plain
> of history and allegory.

Raban's work, in fact, always noting the etymology of the term discussed, ranged over the whole field of knowledge. It discussed the nature of God, the holy Trinity, Adam, the patriarchs and great figures of the Old Testament, the prophets and the Wisdom books, the canon of the gospels, conciliar canons, the Easter cycle, the canonical hours and sacraments, the six ages of man, portents (as Varro describes them), domestic animals and how Adam named them, wild beasts, small animals like mice, serpents and fishes, dragons, and birds (including the phoenix, which is an Arabic bird, and the green parrot, which is an Italian bird with a loud voice, and can be taught to say, *Cesar, ave!*). By book ix, Raban is describing atoms, as the very smallest parts of the physical world, which cannot be seen or divided: 'these in the early morning of the world flew in restless motion, even as the finest dust is seen when transfused by the sun's rays pouring through a window. . . . Out of these atoms arose all trees and grass and fruits and fire and water: the philosophers have reckoned that out of atoms all things have been produced and do remain. Atoms exist either in the mass (*in corpore*) or in time or in number . . . the atom is that which cannot be divided, as the point in geometry . . . For the indivisible unity in things exists to have a mystical significance . . . the one God and Father of all.'

There is a great deal besides this; about elements, the heaven or firmament of the fixed stars: the stars, sun, moon, geographical terms, the phenomena of the weather, public buildings, ports, sewers, baths, prisons, windows, philosophers, poets, sibyls, *magi*, the pagan gods, racial names (the Scots are so called from a word in their own tongue meaning that they have painted bodies, pricked with sharp needles dipped in dyes), rocks, precious stones and metals, weights and measures, numbers and their allegorical significance, music and medicine, agriculture and trees, warfare and weapons, horses and chariots and hunting, the art of building and woodwork, weaving wool and garments, drinking vessels and kitchen vessels, and much else. The *De Universo* is not great literature, but its reader gains a good impression of the mind of the man called the *praeceptor primus Germaniae*, the most orderly and capacious mind of the ninth century in the west.

A few other ninth-century works in the field of the *quadrivium* have come down to us. The anonymous *De mundi caelestis terrestrisque constitutione liber* appears to be founded on the work of a disciple of the Neoplatonist philosopher Macrobius, but also on eastern and non-Christian material. After descriptions of geographical and climatic phenomena, and one of the planets which quotes the *Historia Caroli* as stating that Mercury was once seen for nine days as a spot on the sun, and an assertion that the spheres of the most distant planets take longest to move around the earth, it goes on to deal with the origin of the human soul, according to the diverse teachings of Anaxagoras, Thales of Miletus, the Stoics, Plato and Aristotle, and, finally, the Hebrews. Moreover, 'it is the teaching of the philosophers that souls freed from the body desire to be, should be, and can be reincorporated'. Another astronomical treatise composed probably in Gaul early in the ninth century was entitled *De forma caeli et quomodo decurrit inclinatum* (or, *Sphera caeli*). Agobard of Lyons (d. 840) again, while he composed no general treatises in the field of the *quadrivium*, wrote one *Liber de grandine et tonitruis* where he denounced the common belief that storms were caused by incantations and magic, and explained them as natural phenomena: in his other writings he was ready to denounce superstition.

Apart from treatises on the seven arts, or in their field, various verse descriptions attest the Carolingian adoption of their study as the normal field of higher education. They were apparently also represented pictorially, though no Carolingian examples survive today: a poem of Theodulf of Orleans suggests the description of an actual picture or carving, as do others. It has been suggested that the representation of each art as a draped woman, carrying a symbol of her particular skill, goes back to Martianus Capella's imagery of the arts as the seven bridesmaids, and certainly Martianus' treatise had been continuously used in Gaul and was much esteemed by the Carolingians: but the allegorical use of the draped female figure with an emblem was much older than Martianus. The west Roman emperors had frequently used the reverse of their coins as a means of propaganda, depicting a draped female figure and emblem: Augustus used such figures of *Virtus, Victoria, Clementia, Iustitia*, and *Pietas*: and later imperial coins stressed the emperor's *Providentia*, and his subjects' *Securitas, Tranquillitas* and *Hilaritas*. The allegorical Roman lady was long familiar before Martianus dealt with the arts as bridesmaids, and the Carolingian use of her in decoration went back probably to archaeological models rather than Martianus. The Irish monk, Dungal (d. 826), who knew some Greek, wrote a poem on the seven arts and medicine, apparently describing the arts thus figuratively painted, and a poem in a Saint-Gall manuscript similarly described a scene where wisdom (*sapientia*) sits in a circle formed by her seven daughters, the arts.

All these works on the *quadrivium*, and indications about the teaching of the seven arts down to the mid-ninth century, are little more than digests of the work of the encyclopedists, but with the comments or notes of John the Scot on Martianus Capella's treatise there is a significant change. His comments have survived only in a single manuscript from Corbie, though there are two others which give his text together with additional notes by Remigius of Auxerre; Erigena's explanation of the physical universe had no wide influence. Whereas the sixth-century encyclopedists and their Carolingian successors accepted a scheme of the planetary universe going back to Pliny the Elder and Ptolemy, a scheme in which the spheres of the moon, sun and planets swing round a central earth, Erigena followed Heracleides, Macrobius and Chalcidius in teaching that Venus and Mercury followed courses round the sun, while the sun, moon and the other planetary spheres revolved round the earth. In the *De Divisione Naturae* (see p. 515) he went further than Macrobius and Chalcidius and taught that Mercury, Venus, Mars and Jupiter revolved round the sun, which was midway between the earth and the fixed stars: 'for the Platonists', he wrote in his comments, 'do not say that the course (*circulum*) of Saturn, Jupiter, Mars and the moon revolve round the earth, but only that Saturn revolves round the earth'. The earth, to Erigena, was not the centre of the whole planetary system: the sun swung round it with its own satellite planets.

His teaching about the 'antipodes' also was not that current in the ninth century. The *antoikoi*, he says, are those who live on this earth in the eastern sphere; the *antichthones* are so-called because they possess the opposite (contrary) part of the earth. 'There are therefore four sets of people, that is: we and our antipodes, the *antoikoi* and their *antichthones*.' The summer and winter seasons, and the length of day and night, differ for these four sets of people.

Erigena's teaching on the other arts contains no such exceptional teaching as his above comments on 'geometry'. It is now recognized, however, that already in this commentary on the arts he was leaning towards Neoplatonist teaching, and the position he expounded in the *De Divisione Naturae*.

It may fairly be said then, that the Carolingian renaissance was not an advance in the old Greco-Roman knowledge, but a great extension in the field of those who used it. One agent in this extension, the schools, has been mentioned, but there were two more, of the greatest importance and closely connected: the industrious recopying on vellum of Latin works, classical, patristic and legal, and the evolution of a fine, clear handwriting generally known as the Caroline minuscule. The monastic *scriptorium* did as much for the spread of knowledge in this period as the monastic *scholasticus*.

To take the fundamental advance in the technique of writing manuscripts first. There were, perhaps, two chief reasons for this technical change which conditioned the spread of knowledge and gave a certain shape to medieval culture from the ninth century onwards. One was the change from papyrus as a writing material to vellum (see p. 137), the other the need to economize space in so expensive a material and yet to use a script that, though smaller, could be clearly followed by the eye.

In the old Greco-Roman empire a great deal of writing had been done on papyrus, and some *codices* of great literary or legal works, and the Christian scriptures, had also been written on vellum. For the mass of temporary papers, letters, mercantile memoranda, the records of government collectors, etc., papyrus had been material that lasted long enough: ordinarily, some few years. The hand used on it was known as cursive and had been developed from the straight strokes used by those who took notes with a stylus on waxed tablets: but by the fifth century A.D. cursive documents had letters run together and curved forms. There was even a cursive book hand, more formal than that used in documents. But on the ridged surface of papyrus no difference could be made between thick and thin strokes, and no such decorative hand evolved as was possible on vellum: the meaning of 'cursive' indeed was 'running', and this implied both rapidity of writing and the running together of the letters: the scribes who used it were traders, officials and, pre-eminently, the notaries. The association between the cursive hand, the notaries and the law courts was very close, and remained so in the new barbarian kingdoms. Papyrus *codices*, bound books, were occasionally written, particularly legal tomes, but the great mass of papyrus manuscripts, written in the cursive hand, must have been in the form of loose *schedulae* or rolls.

For the great vellum *codices* of the Latin west from the fourth to the seventh centuries, two other hands were used: rustic capitals, derived from the lettering of Latin inscriptions, with every letter separate and the same height, but much narrower than the square capitals of the inscriptions: it was necessary to get very much more writing in a book than an inscription and the narrowing of the letters was an economy measure to save vellum by getting many more letters into the line. The other variety of script was the uncial or half-uncial, a hand evolved apparently in the fourth century as a papyrus book-hand: in this fine, rounded hand the letters were formed separately, but the shape of the Roman capitals had been modified to expedite writing. Half-uncial is the characteristic script of Christian writings till the mid-seventh century. Words in both scripts were undivided by spaces longer than those that separated each letter, and the eye had very little help from punctuation or a regular use of capital letters; the beginning of an important paragraph in a gospel book was however sometimes illuminated. The script, following in the tradition of uncial writing and stone inscriptions, was still large, though it had gone as far in the direction of narrow letters and economy as it could go. Though they were clear to look at, neither uncial lettering nor rustic capitals were particularly easy to read.

The Germanic nations when they settled had therefore two types of writing to choose from: that derived from Roman capitals, and the cursive used by the notaries. They then developed writings of their own, called by modern palaeographers 'national hands'. The Irish developed the most distinctive hand; they used it for the scriptures, office books, and such works as they could afford the vellum and time to copy. There is linguistic evidence that papyrus was not unknown in Ireland, but from the fifth century the Irish must have had to rely almost entirely on vellum, and it is not apparent that they had any notaries. They evolved a beautiful Irish book-hand, the Irish minuscule, and even an Irish majuscule, a rounder and more solemn hand, and both these scripts were carried to England and eventually to the continent by Irish missionaries. Among the Merovingian Franks, where the royal writing office changed quite suddenly from the use of papyrus to parchment (see p. 398), the royal notaries continued to use the cursive hand to which they were accustomed, evolving the ugly 'Merovingian cursive'. The Visigoths in Spain developed a minuscule script founded on the half-uncial letters but with cursive elements; and in south Italy the *scriptorium* of Monte Cassino developed a beautiful parchment book-hand founded on cursive, the Beneventan script: the only 'national hand', indeed, founded on cursive.

Vellum had always been a scarce and expensive material, and the multiplication of monastic and episcopal *scriptoria*, together with the needs of the Carolingian palace and the writers of legal documents, made it even more difficult to get a sufficient supply. Vellum was from the end of the seventh century the only writing material, for all purposes: and the sheet prepared from the skin of a sheep, goat or calf, made only a single folio (folded sheet) of a *codex*. It was just not possible for the Carolingian scholars to write out the Latin Bible in capitals taking nine large folio volumes, as Cassiodorus had done. The Irish and Anglo-Saxon missionaries had worked out a much more economical minuscule script and used one or two varieties of it, but none of them, even the Irish script of Luxeuil, was very easy to read. In these circumstances, it was the distinctive contribution of the Franks to evolve a minuscule founded on cursive: it was the monks of Corbie who were the first to use the delightful, small, clear, rounded script that was to spread over Europe as the Caroline minuscule. It was in use in the palace school when Alcuin came there as director, and he appears to have promoted its use in the monastery of Tours when he went there: the beautiful ninth-century hand of Tours was a Caroline minuscule. Alcuin's revised text of the Bible was written in this hand, and Charlemagne's control of the Frankish church promoted its spread. He sent for an authentic copy of the Benedictine rule from Monte Cassino, and the copies of this document made for the use of Frankish abbeys seem to have been made in this hand and been a particular agent in the extension of its use; and his receipt of the *Dionysio-Hadriana* and the making of Frankish copies, together with his requirement that the Frankish liturgy and rite should conform to those of the Roman church, meant the further dispersion of many manuscripts using the new minuscule to all parts of the empire, and even outside the empire. The new script separated the words, connected the letters of the word by ligatures, and used a four-line system of letter-heights. Some letters reached a certain height or depth below the line and most were aligned within the two central lines. Some punctuation was used and a few abbreviations. This is the script which the fifteenth-century humanists called *littera antiqua*, because the earliest versions of classical writers that they could find were written in it and they believed it to be the original old Latin writing.

The Carolingian scholars were on the whole agreed that the reading of good Latin books (though pagan) was necessary for those aspiring to write good Latin themselves, and this led them to copy the Latin classics on vellum in the new minuscule. There must have been many papyrus copies of the works of Latin writers of the second rank now perished, for in many cases the oldest extant manuscripts of such works are on Carolingian vellum.

Some of the works of Vergil and the greatest writers had always been written on vellum, in rustic capitals or uncials: but our knowledge of Latin literature would be very incomplete but for the Caroline manuscripts that fill the gaps. Not all Caroline efforts were praiseworthy from the palaeographical viewpoint, for vellum was in such demand that even the Irish scribes, who had a particular admiration for Vergil and Latin pagan literature, frequently washed down classical manuscripts to write copies of the Vulgate, etc.: the monks of Bobbio, for instance, used manuscripts of Cicero's speeches, Plautus and the Letters of Fronto as palimpsests: they still survive at Milan. Saint-Gall, however, preserved its fourth- or fifth-century Vergil manuscript, and its monks copied Valerius Flaccus and the Verrine Orations. The monks of Rebais, near Paris, copied Terence, Cicero, Vergil and Horace, as well as books which might be termed textbooks for the liberal arts, Donatus on grammar, Priscian on rhetoric, and Boethius. Fulda preserved copies of Suetonius, Tacitus and Ammianus Marcellinus; the scribes of Saint-Gall, Bobbio, Reichenau, Fleury, Tours, Monte Cassino, Corbie, Reims, Saint-Denis, Mainz, Laon and the other Carolingian houses, very many more. While the works of Vergil, Terence and Livy have survived to us in the main on vellum manuscripts copied in the classical period, those of Caesar, Lucretius, Juvenal, both Plinies, Tacitus, Lucan, Martial, and other writers of the second class have survived only in Carolingian copies. They had possibly survived so far mainly as papyrus copies, difficult to read, fragile, and not thought worthy of retention once they were transcribed on vellum, or possibly the need for vellum, so generously used for vellum copies in the old, large hand of the classical period, occasioned the washing down of the works of some of these pagan writers of the second rank for palimpsests, once they had been copied in the Caroline minuscule. In any case, Europe was indebted to the Carolingian scribes for the preservation of the greater part of Latin literature.

It is in connexion with the enthusiasm of the Caroline scholars for copying old manuscripts, for preserving ancient texts, for having recourse to a written authority, that another of their activities should be considered: the compiling of forgeries and near forgeries. The Forged Decretals and the Forged Capitularies do not stand alone: they were the outstanding examples of documents fabricated by a scribe or an atelier of scribes, anxious to supply evidence to promote some worthy and desirable end. No real forgery was ever made without a purpose, whether it was that

18

of a privilege or immunity for an abbey, the re-writing of an old and meagre saint's life with many additional miracles, or the compilation of a set of conciliar canons with a tendentious mixture of authentic and dubious material.

It is, at a first glance, surprising that this tolerance of dubious or fictitious material by the mid-ninth-century Frankish compilers should have followed upon the careful sifting of historical material by a writer like Bede. Why had Bede a high standard of historical integrity and writers like Hincmar of Reims and those of the atelier that composed the False Decretals so little regard for it? There is one obvious reason: Bede was a good Benedictine monk, who lived all his life in his monastery, who certainly had a high regard for king Ceolwulf of Northumbria, but who was not engaged in any political struggle between kings: or with a turbulent and anticlerical court circle. Bede does mention in his letter to archbishop Egbert of York that certain 'false monasteries' have been founded by lay thegns who wished to secure the privileges and exemptions of land booked to a minster; he recommends Egbert to take them over on the ground of the uncanonical or unmonastic character of the life lived there. The need of any new written deed did not occur to him. In short, Bede lived before abbots and bishops had been drawn into the court circle and the royal service: there was apparently no urgent need for fabricated authorities to support good causes. Bede, again, had no notarial training.

Certain factors explain the climate of opinion with regard to 'forgery' in the Carolingian empire. In the first place, this drawing of the higher clergy into the service of the rulers of Austrasia, Francia, Italy and the dukes and counts who served them necessarily drew them into the rivalries and enmities of their masters. Secondly, these scholars had now perfected themselves in the art of the notariat: they knew how to draw up charters and privileges: they knew the *formulae* of capitularies and canons: they knew all the protocol. Thirdly, they were well aware that written authorities were now held desirable as proof of legal ownership or the right to inherit, and that it was lawful, when a document had been destroyed by fire, to supply a copy from memory and get it attested publicly by notarial signature. Such record of perished charters was a precedent for the writing down of grants originally oral, when it was believed that the new charter recorded a true oral tradition. Fourthly, the traditional material used by the notaries down to the last quarter of the seventh century had always been papyrus, and papyrus perished easily in western Europe. There was a movement in the late eighth and ninth century to copy old grants, and treatises written on papyrus, on to parchment, and in such copying it was possible to expand or clarify some clauses or slip in others not thought necessary in the originals: or to modernize the method of dating. Such manipulation of old material was not reprehended.

A halfway stage between making a slightly changed copy of old material, and making a frankly 'forged' grant of tendentious import, was the making of a 'copie figurée', when not only the old Latin forms (or Merovingian forms of liquescent Latin) were copied, but even the archaic lettering. To distinguish between a 'copie figurée', perhaps with interpolations, and an outright forgery, was difficult: the way for the tendentious forgery was prepared. Then too, the movement to rewrite and expand the old, brief *acta* of the martyrs and saints for the glory and financial advantage of particular churches must have lowered the standard of historical integrity in other writing.

Perhaps most important of all the factors making for the ninth-century tolerance of tendentious forgery was the general scribal fondness for *les exercices à l'antique*, both in the reproduction of script and illumination. The exact reproduction of old manuscripts, the making of facsimiles, has only been made possible by modern techniques of photography and printing: but some ninth-century scribes, both in Constantinople and the west, delighted in writing and illuminating in the antique manner, and even in producing an 'antique text' with script and illumination taken from different originals (F. Wormald). But even in such cases, their division of the words, their abbreviations, or perhaps their intrusion of an insular *b* in a text of rustic capitals, or some other current usage of their own day, would often show that the manuscript in question, purporting to have been written in the fifth or sixth century, was actually written in the ninth. To write a psalter, perhaps in three narrow columns in the antique manner, perhaps in rustic capitals, served no tendentious purpose, but was apparently a delight to the scribe who wrote it and the abbey for whom it was written. It is within this general atmosphere of admiration for the antique that the forged papyri of Saint-Denis, Hincmar's life of St Rémi, or the collection known as the Forged Decretals should be viewed. They also were *exercices à l'antique*: tendentious ones.

Two of these instances of the ninth-century *expertise* in the re-editing or fabricating of written evidence may be briefly noted. The abbey of Saint-Denis had a long-continued tradition of skill in this kind of work. A famous study of the manuscripts of this

abbey, particularly of the Saint-Denis cartulary, has been made by
M. Léon Levillain: he found that for a certain period 'an office
of forgery functioned regularly at Saint-Denis'. Till 658 the church
of Saint-Denis, with the shrine of the famous martyr and his
companions, Eleutherius and Rusticus, was always described as
a 'basilica', not an abbey: the strict enclosure enjoined in the rule
of St Benedict was not prescribed or observed: connexion with the
court was close. King Dagobert (623–639) may, however, be said
to have refounded Saint-Denis as an abbey: he certainly made it
large grants, probably written ones. This refounding of Saint-
Denis took place between 623 and 625; later, queen Balthilde
encouraged the *fratres* of the abbey to accept the Columban-
Benedictine rule and granted the house an immunity. In 654
her husband, Clovis II, confirmed a privilege which bishop
Landri made to the abbey at Balthilde's request, and this original
papyrus survives. But in the ninth century the abbey produced
also a pseudo-original privilege of bishop Landri, purporting to
have been written in 653: it was written on the back of a genuine
seventh-century papyrus document, but some of its clauses are
anachronisms in a document purporting to be seventh century.
Other documents written in Merovingian hands on papyrus and
with seals taken from old charters affixed were also treasured at
Saint-Denis: they had a notable collection of fabricated documents.
M. Levillain demonstrated both the authenticity of Landri's
privilege, dated 22 June 654, and the fabrication of several later
documents. As to why Saint-Denis embarked so successfully on
the practice of fabricating evidence, the answer probably lies in
the nearness of the abbey to Paris and its association with the
court, together with the fact that its priest members were not
originally Benedictine, and from early times were used for the
writing of royal grants: they were early trained in notarial usage.
The Carolingian kings continued to use the abbot and his well-
trained monastic scribes. The needs of a great house and the
exigencies of royal business must have made life at Saint-Denis
very different from that at Monkwearmouth, and account for
its fine collection of forged diplomas.

Archbishop Hincmar of Reims, again, had been trained in
historical method at Saint-Denis. He was a great political bishop,
the greatest in western Europe in the mid-ninth century; he was
a good canonist, a good palaeographer well able to distinguish
authentic from fabricated manuscripts, and he used his scholarly
knowledge in the interests of Saint-Denis, his church of Reims,
Charles the Bald and the church at large, regardless if necessary of

historical integrity. Again, it should be noted that Hincmar and the ninth-century climate of opinion did not countenance the production of evidence to prove falsehood, but only to support what was believed to be most true and right when no written evidence existed; or existed only in old manuscript fragments or scattered allusions in annals: or of which there were only hints in pictorial representations.

Hincmar entered Saint-Denis as a canon, but when, by two synods held there in 829 and 832, the *ordo monastica* was ordered to be re-established, he gladly received the habit. He became the *custos* of the treasures and relics of the abbey and the assistant of his abbot Hilduin. 'This intimacy not only introduced him to the elaborate mechanism of forged diplomas and falsified history by which the abbey sustained its territorial claims, but ultimately saddled him with the delicate task of attempting to reconcile the emperor Louis the Pious with Hilduin.' It has been suggested that it was in the interests of this reconciliation that he compiled the *Miracula Sancti Dionysii*, and the larger study, the *Gesta Dagoberti Regis*, in which Hilduin seems to have collaborated with him. Dagobert was the great patron of Saint-Denis, and both tracts invited Louis the Pious to a further patronage of the abbey and to reconciliation with Hilduin. Levillain's analysis of the *Gesta Dagoberti* shows that it is a *marqueterie de textes* of older abbey grants and saints' lives, adding nothing new to their information: an illustration of the normal practice of these ninth-century compilers. They did not invent new incidents: what they said can be found in some other source. When the whole compilation was termed, as here, the *Deeds* of some saint or hero, the word 'forgery' need scarcely be used, though facts from unreliable sources were given equal weight with those from reliable ones. When, however, such a compilation took the form of a capitulary or set of canons attributed to particular kings or councils or canonists, or the letters of historical personages, the word forgery can hardly be avoided.

In 845 Hincmar moved from Saint-Denis to Reims: he had already served Charles the Bald on several missions, and when the council of Ver asked Charles to provide the church of Reims with a pastor, Charles appointed Hincmar. He took with him not only the historical technique learned at Saint-Denis, but copies of the *Gesta Dagoberti*: his characteristic style and constructions marked his new *Vita Remigii*, which was meant to do for Reims what the *Gesta Dagoberti* had done for Saint-Denis.

The publication of the *Vita Remigii* was the occasion of pope

Nicholas I's rebuke of Hincmar as the fabricator of evidence, the issue of clever forgeries to deceive the papacy about the metropolitical powers of the see of Reims. He wrote in 866 to the synod of Reims that Hincmar had used his astonishing astuteness for his own ends, and to Hincmar himself, that he could, if he had chosen, have legally accused Hincmar of fraud (*fraudis aliquid in talibus committere fatere possemus*). The allusion must have been to Hincmar's drawing up of this life of St Rémi, meant to emphasize the position of St Rémi as the bishop who had baptized Clovis and brought the Franks from the darkness of paganism into the Christian church. The church of Reims could hardly claim to be of apostolic foundation, like Rome or Aquileia: but the *Vita Remigii* emphasized the parallel between John who had baptized Christ and Rémi who had baptized Clovis. John was no apostle: but among them that are born of women, who had arisen greater than John the Baptist? The Lord had said: No man. The church of Remigius was the baptismal church of the Frankish nation and, by inference, the rights of her bishop quasi-patriarchal.

The material used by Hincmar for the *Vita Remigii* is of great interest. He admitted that he was editing an older life of St Rémi, which he says was in a book that 'like others, was so perished partly by damp, partly by the gnawings of mice, partly by the cutting out of leaves, that only a few scattered leaves of it could be found'. Nevertheless, some form of the *acta* and *miracula* of St Rémi must have been used in the choir at Reims, for the lessons of the night office before his feast, some form other than the few scattered mouse-eaten leaves of the old life, and to this Hincmar would have had access. Some political *pièce justificative* was needed when, on the emperor Lothar's death in 869, Charles the Bald seized Lorraine and was crowned emperor by Hincmar at Metz: something to show that the anointing and coronation conferred on Charles a claim to wider rule than that of the west Franks. Hence, the Remigius in Hincmar's new life is not merely the bishop who, as in Gregory of Tours' history, baptized Clovis with fitting solemnity, hanging the space before the church with white cloths, and using much incense, but a Rémi who has been himself miraculously anointed at his own ordination with chrism sent from heaven, and who anointed Clovis with oil from an *ampulla* borne down by the Holy Spirit in the form of a dove.

Since there is such variation in the story of the baptism of Clovis as related by Gregory of Tours, a splendid ceremony only, and by Hincmar, it is of interest that it has been recently suggested that Hincmar did not simply invent the miraculous anointings of

Rémi and Clovis, however excellently the two miracles served his purpose of exalting the more than metropolitan position of the church of Reims. He may have used iconographical and archaeological evidence, or suggestion. It was usual from the early seventh century to represent the baptism of Christ in Jordan with the holy dove descending head downwards above his head, giving an impression of great swiftness. In the tympanum of the church of Monza, where the Lombard Theodelinda's little son was baptized, the down-rushing dove bears an *ampulla* of oil for the anointing of Christ at his baptism, anticipating the anointing with which the early church accompanied the immersion or effusion of water in the baptismal rite. The dove bearing the *ampulla* was probably a normal feature of the iconography of the Lord's baptism, and Hincmar must have been familiar with it. He had also himself assisted at the (second) examination of the relics of St Rémi, and seen that by the bones of the bishop were laid two *ampullae*, or flasks. A chalice was often buried with a priest, as a symbol of his priesthood, and the two flasks (presumably for the holy oil and the chrism, that priests must seek from the bishop) may well have been buried as episcopal emblems. That they were so found is attested in the *Life*. Hincmar's imagination, or perhaps older tradition, associated them with the miraculous descent of the holy dove bearing the *ampulla* on the old mosaics and carvings. The influence of Hincmar's life of St Rémi was shown in the popularity of representations of the dove with the *ampulla* in the Reims school (see p. 547), from the second half of the ninth century onwards. Hincmar's coronation and anointing of Charles the Bald with the chrism from the *ampulla* of St Rémi established the tradition that the kings of France must always be anointed from the Sainte Ampoule. The Sainte Ampoule no longer exists: the Convention of the French Revolution in 1793 ordered it to be destroyed; but descriptions of the object then destroyed suggest that it was of immemorial antiquity: a flask of old Roman glass.

The fabrication of a group of forged canons and capitularies, of which the Pseudo-Isidorian decretals had far the most permanent importance, was the work of a group of reformers alarmed at the condition of the Frankish church in the mid ninth century. The civil wars among the successors of Charlemagne and the raids of the northmen had not only plundered churches and abbeys of their treasures, but occasioned heavy financial demands by rulers and local counts, and, above all, widespread alienation of church lands to laymen. Conditions had become similar to those when Charles Martel, to support his wars, had impoverished the church and alienated her lands to laymen (see p. 287). Moreover, Frankish sees, especially east of the Rhine, had been originally missionary sees, and very large compared to the older sees of the Franks in Aquitaine, and the loose grouping of parishes under an archpriest did not suffice to keep church life zealous and orderly in these disturbed times: through the influence of the Irish monks, the country bishop (*chorepiscopus*) who had no see in a city and was a kind of rural missionary helped to keep church life going, but was much distrusted by the territorial bishops [as he had been earlier in the east]. In these circumstances, the episcopate of Charles the Bald took the normal procedure of protesting at the violence done to clerics and disregard of the canons and the rights of churches, and passing reforming canons at the councils of Loire, near Angers (843), Coulaines, near Le Mans (843), Meaux (845) and Paris (846). The bishops desired to declare excommunicate the usurpers of church lands and despoilers of the poor; they criticized royal demands on ecclesiastical treasure: they asked for an inquiry into alienations. When the royal assent was not accorded to the demands put forward in the councils, they presented them again to Charles the Bald at the general assembly at Épernay in June 846: and received a sharp rebuff. The lay nobles, whose interests were threatened, contended so vigorously against the proposals, and in such terms, that the bishops left the assembly in humiliation and despair; at which the assembly passed a mere twenty of the eighty-three *capita* proposed, choosing those most easily evaded.

The episcopal affront at Épernay inspired a group of scholars to compile what was apparently to be taken as a newly discovered and very full and helpful version of the old Isidorian canons (see p. 537): at least, the very strange ascription of them in one manuscript to 'Isidore Mercator' would seem to have implied some association with the great seventh-century canonist. The intention of the atelier of reforming scholars who composed them was to do what the council of Épernay had failed to do: safeguard the position of the bishop, himself the guardian of orderly church life, against the lay rulers who had humiliated him, and against the Celtic *chorepiscopus*. While the pseudo-Isidorian collection covered the whole field of western canon law, its purpose was especially to protect the territorial bishop, and this by emphasizing the position and rights of the papacy as the final authority in the church and the final court of appeal. The Christian empire of

Charlemagne, with its Byzantine concept of the emperor's rights over the western church, had proved unable to protect the church and had, in its financial necessities, plundered bishoprics and abbeys: the reformers invoked in counterbalance the intervention and protection of the papacy. In so doing, they exalted papal rights, not only over lay rulers but over the metropolitan bishops.

There was, in the ninth century, no single authoritative, exclusive collection of canons and decretals (papal letters giving a legislative decision or direction). For the Carolingian church the *Dionysio-Hadriana* (see p. 508) had a particular authority: the other great collection was the *Hispana* of the Visigothic church, which included some old African and early Frankish canons. The *Pseudo-Isidoriana* made use of both these collections, and supplemented them by non-authentic material. It was a collection involving much labour, and it was the last and finest of a series of fake capitularies and canons.

The *Hispana* was already widely used in the Frankish church, and in two forms. In one, the groups of canons were recorded chronologically: in the other rearranged in subjects ('systematically'). This old *Hispana-Gallica* was already a severer code than the *Dionysiano-Hadriana*, and some Carolingian additions were made to it in a manuscript from Autun and copied in other manuscripts (the *Hispana-Augustodunensis*).

Again, the *Capitula Angilramni* was a partial summary of Roman practice purporting to have been sent by Hadrian I to bishop Angilram of Metz: it drew on the Theodosian Code, the Breviary of Alaric, and some non-authentic sources.

The *False Capitularies* were occasioned apparently by the refusal of Charles the Bald to issue the reforms suggested by the bishops at Épernay as new capitularies. The preface stated that Benedict the Deacon (Benedictus Levita) had been asked by Autcar, bishop of Metz, to complete the collections of (genuine) capitularies made by Ansegis; he had therefore collected in three supplementary books certain capitularies of Pepin, Charlemagne and Louis the Pious that Ansegis had overlooked. He had found them in loose sheets (*schedulae*) in divers libraries, particularly that of the church of Metz. The name of the author and the attribution to Metz were false; the material, secular and canon laws, was wide and both authentic and fictitious. There were borrowings from a council attributed to St Patrick, from the so-called Penitential of Theodore of Canterbury and various Carolingian councils, including an address of the bishops to Louis the Pious in 829. The work was too voluminous to have been the work of one compiler: the *schedulae* mentioned were actually the digests and excerpts made by a circle of collaborators from various historical sources. Very many changes were made, however, in the wording of the sources to make them harmonize with the views of the reformers: some diminished the authority of the metropolitan, some anathematized the secularization of church goods, some were directed against the *chorepiscopi*.

Internal evidence and method suggest that the False Decretals were the work of the same atelier of reformers as the compilers of the False Capitularies. They were preserved in five groups of manuscripts, the most widely copied of which was that ascribed to Isidore Mercator. This was in three parts, the first of which contained, among some fabricated and some authentic matter, a long series of apocryphal letters from the early popes of Rome, from St Clement of Rome (d. 100) to pope Melchiades (d. 314). No authentic collection has any knowledge of these letters, but the compilers of Pseudo-Isidore knew from the *Liber Pontificalis* that certain popes had taken part in doctrinal controversies or had issued liturgical or disciplinary canons: they therefore supplied apocryphal letters to lend the authority of venerable antiquity to their new collection. The second part contained the canons of early councils given in the *Hispana*, and Greek and African canons: it was headed by the apocryphal Donation of Constantine. The third part contained the decretals of thirty-three popes from Sylvester to Gregory II, with certain apocryphal canons, some earlier than the Pseudo-Isidorian compilers, some their work.

The *Pseudo-Isidoriana* was thus founded upon the *Hispana*, but stuffed with apocrypha and interpolations: the reformers had found the *Hispana* of Autun insufficient. It was a larger and more far-reaching work than the False Capitularies; and it represented the programme of the ninth-century reformers as rooted in antiquity. Of these reforming scribes, Fournier and Le Bras write in their great history of western collections of canons: 'Il faut reconnaître qu'ils ont sur ce point accompli leur œuvre à l'aide d'un véritable luxe de textes faux.' It is now accepted from internal evidence that they accomplished their work between 847 and 850: the ascription of the atelier of compilers to Le Mans, in the diocese of Tours, is less certain.

As to the influence of the False Decretals: they were not widely copied in the ninth century, or accepted by all canonists as genuine in their own day. In 852 Hincmar of Reims twice quoted from them: but would not accept all parts as genuine. The papacy was slow in accepting them. Their widest influence was when they were used as sources by the reformers of the eleventh century.

BIBLIOGRAPHICAL NOTE

For the Carolingian and earlier scripts, see E. A. Lowe, [Loew], *Codices Latini Antiquiores*, part v, 1940, and his article on 'Handwriting', in *The Legacy of the Middle Ages*: A de Bouärd, *Manuel de diplomatique, française et pontificale* (with portfolio of reproduction of manuscripts), 1929, and *L'acte privé*, 1948: A. Giry, *Manuel de Diplomatique*, 1894: for the False Capitularies and False Decretals, see P. Fournier and G. Le Bras, *Histoire des collections canoniques en occident*, 2 vols., 1931: W. Levison, 'Constantinische Schenkung und Silvester-Legende', in *Miscellanea Francesco Ehrle*, tom. ii (1924), p. 159, and his article in *Aus Rheinischer und Frankischer Frühzeit*, 1948: W. Ullmann, *The Growth of Papal Government in the Middle Ages*, 1954. See also for Merovingian and Carolingian forgery, G. Tessier, 'Les derniers travaux de M. Levillain sur l'abbaye de Saint-Denis', in *Le Moyen Age*, 1929, p. 36 ff. For Carolingian learning, see Laistner, M. L. W., *The Intellectual Heritage of the Early Middle Ages*, 1957; R. Taton, *La Science antique et médiévale*, 1957.

CHAPTER XXVIII

THE CAROLINGIAN RENAISSANCE:
MUSIC AND ART

ONE field in which the Carolingians made an advance had long since been taught theoretically as within the circle of the liberal arts, namely, music. But a theory of music, even a scientific one, is not the same thing as the practice of music, and it was in sung music the Carolingians made so notable a contribution. The ninth century saw a musical efflorescence due both to the fusion of an oriental tradition with Greco-Roman music, and to the existence of a great musical instrument, the monastic choirs. Benedictine monks were bound to a recitation of the divine office as the *opus dei*, and, since St Benedict's own day, to a more frequent or even daily attendance at the solemnities of the mass. A body of men cannot recite the psalms or canticles intelligibly unless they make a 'voiced' sound, that is, unless they chant them (not necessarily with variation of musical notes): a multiple use of the ordinary speaking voice produces only a confused murmur. Even the single cantor or lector, reading a prayer, must make a voiced sound, i.e. chant, for his voice to carry across a quite moderate sized *cella* or chapel. Hence, from the days of the public celebration of the Christian mysteries at least, and presumably from the very earliest days when Jewish and Syrian and Greek and Persian Christians gathered themselves together, there had always been some chanting. Throughout the middle ages the parish priest and his little altar boy were always said to 'chant' the mass, i.e. sing it, though this might mean no more than that the priest said the audible portions of the rite on a note. But while, in the Carolingian period, the rural or town priest would be conservative about such chanting, the monastic and cathedral choirs, singing mass and office day in, day out, would tend towards musical enrichment of the office as naturally as towards the adornment of the chapel and altar. Not only the monks but the cathedral clergy now sang the mass and office: for Charlemagne had ordered that

the clergy shall have a good knowledge of the Roman chant, and use it in the night office and the gradual office [the singing at mass], even as our father Pepin of blessed memory decreed when he did away with the Gallican (office) for the sake of uniformity with the apostolic see.

Much light has been thrown in recent years by the Byzantinists on the origin of church music; like Byzantine music in general, it was entirely vocal and homophonic (without parts). While the Greek philosophers from the time of Pythagoras in the sixth century B.C. had discussed musical intervals and the octave and the whole scientific connexion of music with mathematics, and while by the time of Constantine the rhetors were teaching a classical arrangement of Greco-Roman music in fifteen modes or scales, cult music was, in fact, mainly local. The succession of intervals in the mode, and the melodies of the mode, that is, were local. The Christian musical phrases and the method of chanting antiphonally went back to eastern origins: to the antiphonal chanting in the synagogue, and possibly to the melodies and intervals used by peoples outside the eastern frontier of the Roman empire. This was not strange: since the Christians continued the liturgical reading of the Old Testament scriptures, and the traditional form of the worship of the synagogue for the first part of the Eucharist, it was natural that antiphonal chanting should form part of Christian worship: Eusebius in his *Ecclesiastical History* assumes that this was so.

It is also natural that in the west, where Christian worship was necessarily brief and private, information about early chanting is lacking. The only churches built for public Christian worship were outside the empire, in the east; here, the remains of such churches, built before Constantine, still survive. There was no persecution in the Persian kingdom, and a good deal is known about the church of Seleukia-Ctesiphon (see p. 170). It therefore fits into the historical picture that our first reference to antiphonal chanting should come from eastern sources. It appears that the congregation formed two choirs, the one of men and the other of women and children, and that when each choir had sung a verse, a short refrain was chanted by both choirs. When Ambrose died in 397, such antiphonal chanting at Christian worship had already passed from the Greek east to the Latin west, like the forms of the centrally-planned Christian churches: music in Milan was Greek or oriental.

Gregory the Great forbade the deacon to sing more than the gospel at mass (595), and gave the cantor the charge of the singing in churches; he cut down (see p. 518) the Ambrosian *iubilus* and other melodic *formulae*. In the singing of the creed the music became 'syllabic', one note to each syllable, which, as Iso at

Saint-Gall knew, was the Roman musical rule. There was in the west a real reform, redirection and pruning of the church music then in general use in the Byzantine empire. But further musical advance waited upon the discovery of some method of writing music; in this respect too the west borrowed from the Byzantines.[1]

Up till the Carolingian period, music in the west had been unwritten, dependent on the memory of the cantor: there had been no notation above the words to be sung in books used for the mass or office. Nevertheless, the Byzantines by about 500 had developed a system of writing music from the old prosodic signs described by the sixth-century encyclopedists. These signs had denoted voice-inflexions, a rise or fall in the pitch of the notes, as well as time duration, a long or short pause. They were used for secular music, in the acclamations required by court ceremonial, and in ecclesiastical music, and by about 500 the Byzantines were using two sets of signs, the ecphonetic signs, used in reading the lessons, and the musical signs proper. While the ecphonetic signs were set at the beginning or end of a group of words, the musical signs were set over the syllables of the text. The ecphonetic signs included the high tone or acute (rising) accent, the low-pitched tone or grave (falling) accent, and the ligature or circumflex, consisting of a rising and falling accent; they included also marks of quantity, for long and short syllables, rough and smooth breathings, and certain declamation marks. The musical signs proper at this early stage had no distinct interval value: they were called neums (*pneumata*). In form, both sets of signs consisted of lines and dots, single or grouped, the lines set at an angle and sometimes hooked. Their use appears to have spread throughout the Mediterranean countries. Isidore of Seville, at the far end of the Mediterranean, denied that music could be written: music, he said, 'is a thing of sense: it passes along into past time and is impressed on the memory. For unless sounds are held in the memory of man they perish, because they cannot be written'. Yet elsewhere he implied that music could be written, when he wrote of one or two churchmen that they made and published musical compositions, and of his brother Leander that 'he made many compositions of sweet melody, for the offertory of the mass, and the sacrifice and the alleluia's and the psalms'. It would seem that Leander used the Byzantine notation; but no western liturgical manuscripts using such notation have survived.

When pope Hadrian (772–795) sent to Charlemagne at his

[1] For a very clear description of Byzantine musical notation, see Egon Wellesz' *History of Byzantine Music and Hymnography*, 1949, pp. 216–64.

request musicians to teach his prelates the Roman use and liturgical practice for the course of the year, they brought with them books which the Franks said 'signified the notes by letters of the alphabet, either upright or inverted or forward or backward', i.e. had the Byzantine ecphonetic and musical signs. Though for long after the eighth century this system was too difficult for most western singers, and antiphoners and tropers continued to be written with the words only, leaving the melody to be passed on by the memory of the singers, yet there were some cantors in the song schools who understood the notation and began to write it. The prosodic signs had originally been written in lines of equal thickness on papyrus; but when the Caroline scribes wrote with their quill pens on vellum, the up strokes became long and thin and the down strokes short and fat: the *virga, punctum* and *circumflex* became musical notes, and, in combination, groups of notes. From this system of 'neums' our own musical notation has developed. There is no manuscript evidence of its use among the Franks in Charlemagne's own day, though its introduction must date from the copying of liturgical books with the new Roman rite; but it was certainly in use in the ninth century in the song schools of Jumièges and Limoges, Corbie and Saint-Gall and the rest. Its use is especially associated with the ninth-century singers of Saint-Gall.

Neither in east or west was there as yet, apparently, an exact interval notation. The old Greek music discussed by the rhetors had depended upon an arrangement of intervals, tones and hemitones, in the fifteen Greek modes or scales. Smaller intervals and different arrangements would seem to have been used in local music within the empire and oriental music beyond the eastern frontiers; but by the sixth century the smaller intervals were not used in Greek music, nor were they used in the later Byzantine music or transmitted to the west. By the eighth century the old fifteen Greek modes had been reduced to the eight modes of Byzantine church music, and were so transmitted (with the *tonus peregrinus*) to the west: they were known as the *oktoékos* and were set in a compass of two full octaves known as the 'greater complete system'. The Arabs learned the eight modes from Christian churches and monasteries in the east and gave the system an Arabic name. In the early tenth century the monk Hucbald of Saint-Amand wrote or revised a notable hand-book explaining the system in a work entitled the *Musica Enchiriadis*.

The interval system in western chant was now firmly established: but it was not yet exactly indicated in the notation. The western system developed independently of Byzantine music: the use of a staff line above the written words, the position of the note groups on, above or below the staff, and, finally, the addition of three other lines to the staff (now distinguished by a clef) made possible the exact recording of the intervals used in the melody. This method was in use in the west in the early tenth century, for it is described in the *Musica Enchiriadis*. The golden age of the liturgical chanting of mass and office, with the year-long communal meditation on the mysteries of the life of Christ, had come.

In the sphere of art, the Carolingian renaissance produced few large monuments and almost no sculpture in the round. Artistic skill found outlet rather in objects of comparatively small size, particularly those used in the service of the church. As in the case of learning, there was an effort to recover and imitate the Greco-Roman past, or rather, since architectural and art-forms could not be completely recovered from old manuscripts like classical texts, to imitate such Byzantine buildings, ivories and reliquaries as could be seen in Italy or brought from the east Mediterranean. Byzantine and eastern influence tended to oust the abstract art of the Celt and the old remnants of Germanic animal ornament. Of the two Hellenistic styles of east Mediterranean art, the Celts and Northumbrians had adopted the neo-Attic in the portraits of the evangelists in their gospel books (see p. 237): from the time when the Alexandrian style, with its impressionistic figures and landscape, had become domesticated in Italy, it had grown more popular than the space-circumscribed, timeless, passionless neo-Attic. 'Hellenistic', when used of ninth-century east Mediterranean art, usually implies a lively, naturalistic use of the human figure and an impressionist rendering of incident and of the background. It was this form of east Mediterranean art that the Carolingians finally chose, in place of the stylized, abstract art of the Celt.

Though the Franks thus revered the Greco-Roman past and the Byzantine present, they had neither the slave labour nor the numbers of skilled craftsmen to build many great stone buildings, with carved capitals and colonnaded halls, as the Greeks and Romans had done, nor did their public life demand municipal basilicas, libraries and temples. It did however demand a few *palatia* for their rulers, some stone churches, many fine ivory chests and reliquaries, and fine church books: which the Greco-Roman pagan temples had not needed at all.

With regard to architecture: it was natural that Charlemagne and his court, with their eyes on the re-establishment of a Christian empire, should have planned the imperial chapel at Aix in imitation of a fine Greco-Roman church, St Vitale at Ravenna: of imperial buildings in Constantinople they had no first-hand knowledge. St Vitale had been built for Justinian and completed in 547: it was an octagon with a two-storeyed octagonal ambulatory and a chancel and apse at the east end. The niches enclosing the central space beneath the dome were not enclosed with walls but opened into arcades on both ground and first floor, and thence into ambulatories: 'the central space flows into the ambulatory', creating 'a sensation of uncertainty, a timeless floating' (N. Pevsner). On the walls, the glowing surface of the mosaics with austere figures in sombre tints seemed just as immaterial. These spatial sublettes and complexions were however beyond the understanding of Charlemagne's architects. The Frankish builders copied the octagonal plan of St Vitale for their chapel: but they flattened the curved-out niches, eliminated the columns on the ground floor, and built simple openings with short, sturdy piers. Yet for the upper floor they provided polished antique columns superimposed in two orders, which 're-echo something of the transparency, and the floating of space from one unit into another, which make the beauty of Justinian's churches'. They placed an equestrian statue of Theoderic, looted from Ravenna, in the colonnaded forecourt of Aix: they believed it to be a figure of Constantine, the Christian emperor.

Italy provided models, not only for royal villas in the classical, inward-looking Roman house, but for important early Christian churches and basilicas, particularly those of Rome. The churches of Saint-Denis and Fulda, begun in 760 and 802 respectively, were planned on the model of St Peter's and the other Roman basilicas. The unusual plan of the church at Saint-Riquier surviving in a vellum copy made c. 835, shows it as having two transepts, one at the east end and one at the west, the crossings with the nave crowned by towers in both cases. The opening of the ninth century saw the building or enlargement of many abbey churches in stone; for the country churches and the rural villas or halls of the nobles and officials wood must have been largely used.

With regard to sculpture in the round: the only surviving specimen is the equestrian statuette, in bronze, now in the Louvre. Critics accept this as ninth-century work, an effigy either of Charlemagne himself or of one of the later Carolingian kings. It is surprising that when Byzantine illuminated gospel books reached

Northumbria and inspired a sudden efflorescence of figure sculpture on the Ruthwell and Bewcastle crosses (though, as far as we know, no figure in the round), no such efflorescence of figure work in stone was inspired among the ninth-century Franks. Possibly the Northumbrians, working with a north Germanic tradition of timber architecture, had wood carvers who could turn their skill to sculpting the stone crosses; while the Franks, who had long looked to the Mediterranean for inspiration, had no such artistically skilled wood carvers to turn into stone masons. The Franks had armourers, metal workers, and their single surviving figure in the round is this bronze. It looks as if the timber halls and boats of Northumbria may have had much more decorative carving than the halls of the Franks.

For illuminated gospel books and psalters, used in every abbey and great church in the solemn celebration of the liturgy, there was a great demand in the Frankish empire, and the Caroline illuminators evolved a style of their own. They used mainly Byzantine models, which were at hand in Italy, adding something of their own less civilized vigour and directness. The Irish monasteries on the continent still provided decorated manuscripts with pages of richly coloured 'abstract' design, and their stiff, formalized figures of evangelists. The gospel books of Saint-Gall and Echternach, and the Book of Bobbio, were all the work of Irish scribes, and as Celtic in character as the Book of Kells. The influence of the Celtic style survived, however, in the great majority of Caroline manuscripts only in detail: in borderings, interlaces and solemn initials. Caroline illumination as a whole was modelled on Byzantine and east Mediterranean forms (see p. 423).

The work of the Caroline illuminators is usually considered in schools, though these have no sharply dividing lines. The earliest, the so-called Palatine or Aix group, of which the Vienna, Brussels and Aix gospel books are examples, all belong to the reign of Charlemagne himself; they represent the evangelists as clothed in white togas carefully modelled by shading, and usually without their symbols, as was customary in Byzantine painting. The Vienna gospels used a border of the classical acanthus, and is said to have been the book found on the knees of the dead Charlemagne by Otto III, when he had the tomb opened in 1001; it is the book on which the German kings took their coronation oath. The Berlin and Aix gospel books have conformed to western usage in providing symbols for their evangelists: but there is still an impressionist sense of sky and landscape, with which the evangelists still have some relation.

The manuscripts of the so-called Ada group (from a dedicatory inscription in one of them to a supposed sister of Charlemagne) show more Celtic influence in borders and decorations; the group seems to have been focussed at Trier. An example of the work of this school, made at the end of the eighth century, was the gospels of Godescalc, who had (apparently) been to Ravenna and copied the representation of the Saviour from the walls of St Vitale: the classical shoulder-curls of the figure became however in Godescalc's painting the stringy locks of the northern warrior (R. Morey). The text was written (781–783) in gold on purple vellum, as in models from Constantinople: all the Ada books made apparently for Charlemagne or royal patrons, used rich and luxurious material, like the Harley Gospels in the British Museum, and the early ninth-century Codex Aureus. The evangelists of this school sit within a circumscribed architectural frame, often in an apsidal niche between two columns, with their symbols above their heads; they are, as it were, effigies, like the Celtic evangelists, but the treatment is more humanistic, and the colour very rich. The later Ada manuscripts became increasingly Byzantine.

The work of the school of Tours flourished under the abbacy of Alcuin in the two monasteries of St Martin: that within the city of Tours, and Marmoutier (see p. 71). Alcuin's chief preoccupation was the revision of the text of the Vulgate, not its decoration, but in his time the beautiful Caroline minuscule came into use at Tours and was associated with an illumination of mixed insular and Merovingian type. Under his successors it reached its peak of beauty, as in the Bible presented by the lay abbot of St Martin's, count Vivian, to the emperor Charles the Bald (875–877): and the Bamberg Bible, which reverts to the method of continuous narrative in narrow strips. The interest of these and other Caroline manuscripts lies partly in the evidence that they were inspired by some antique model. The illuminated scenes in Genesis and Exodus in count Vivian's Bible are reminiscent of some late fifth-century model like the Vatican Vergil, for instance in the clumsy rendering of an antique, graduated sky and, in the background of the group representing the delivery of the Law by Moses, the placing of an antique temple (cf. p. 423).

The school of Tours had been eclectic in its use of material: that of Reims, perhaps the largest and most important of the Caroline groups, produced purer examples of the antique style, more nervous and linear than the illumination of Tours. It is not certain that all the books of this school were actually produced in Reims itself: the style is named after one of its examples, the gospel book of Ebbo, archbishop of Reims (816–835). He had been librarian at Aix earlier, and seems to have brought skilled illuminators or fine books from the palace school to Reims. The Utrecht psalter is a fine example of the work of this school: it has the words of the psalm illustrated by bands of small scenes, interspersed with lines of the text (in rustic capitals). Compared with the illumination of the palace school, the figures have exchanged a meditative calm for a lively, almost agitated rendering: the small pictures are literal, lively and sometimes poignant. The artist has made a complete break-through from the stiff, stylized treatment to an Alexandrian naturalism. The Drogo sacramentary from Metz has beautiful examples of storiated initials.

Round the court of Charles the Bald a new school of illumination developed, perhaps focussed in the scriptorium of Saint-Denis. Most of the manuscripts were written and decorated for Charles, who personally assumed the function of lay abbot there in 867. The library or treasury of the abbey now included count Vivian's Bible and some of the Ada manuscripts, and doubtless specimens from other schools, all of which lent models to the Saint-Denis illuminators. They used both Franco-Saxon initials and the fine, humanistic drawing of the Reims school and its acanthus borders: they borrowed and adapted from all Caroline styles: they completely filled whole vellum pages with rich, illuminated ornament. Fulda was another eclectic school which used line drawing on a larger scale than the Utrecht psalter, and also the massively elaborate compositions of the Ada school.

Caroline decoration was not confined to vellum books, but used also in the minor arts, goldsmith's work and ivory carving particularly. Surviving examples include the gold covers of gospel books, e.g. the Ashburnham gospels, in the Reims style as handled at Saint-Denis, in Charles the Bald's golden gospels: and the portable altar presented by Odo, count of Paris to Arnulf of Carinthia, a precious object he had taken from the treasury of Saint-Denis. The late ninth-century golden altars show the Caroline love of linear effect and 'instinct for material splendour' (R. Hinks). They can be compared only with the Byzantine diptychs in their use on the same surface of gold, silver, coloured enamels and figure work in relief. The golden altar of Sant' Ambrogio in Milan, given by archbishop Angilbert about 835, and the cover of the Munich Codex Argenteus, produced at Saint-Denis about 870, both show a mixture of Byzantine and Frankish art. The figures are distinctively Frankish, the jewelled footstools and architectural detail, among which they move, distinctively Byzantine; in all this modelled figure work the fluttering drapery, the craning necks, the expressive gesture all suggest movement, and even violent disturbance. Similarly, in the engraved crystal disc eight inches across, in the British Museum, which bears the name of the emperor Lothar, the story of Susanna and the Elders is engraved in a series of lively episodes; they are like the sketches in Hellenistic illumination, not connected in any coherent design.

The earliest Caroline ivories come from c. 800, and are parallel to the early Ada manuscripts in design: they merely imitate old Italo-Gallic models, though with more emphasis on line than plastic form. A book cover in the Bodleian Library has Christ treading upon the lion and the adder; the beautiful pierced ivory cover of a gospel book of the Metz school, now in the Bibliothèque Nationale, has on one side three gospel scenes, the figures beautifully modelled, with fluttering drapery and limbs in motion; even the shepherds here presenting their gifts to the infant Christ are represented half-kneeling, as if in a movement caught by a camera; the whole cover is bordered by a rich, undercut and pierced design of growing grape-clustered vines.

Of Carolingian wall-painting north of the Alps nothing has survived, though there is plenty of literary evidence that its subjects were both scriptural and drawn from classical antiquity. The murals of some ninth-century Italian churches have survived, and can perhaps be taken as evidence of the general character of Frankish wall-painting, if only because their landscape and figure work share the general character of scenes in contemporary illuminations and ivories, which would have supplied models for some of the Frankish palace wall-paintings; contemporary writers speak also of the painted *palatia* of bishops and great abbots. In the lower church of San Clemente at Rome a fresco of the Ascension includes a group of apostles obviously amazed, and showing their wonder by hiding their eyes or waving their arms. It is all very fluttery: and it is possibly the work of Benedictines dispersed from Monte Cassino; the refugees from iconoclasm had spread a Byzantine style in Italy rather earlier. In any case, the great Benedictine abbeys north of the Alps, possessors of ivories and miniatures, would seem to have been the chief agents in the development of late Carolingian wall-painting and figure work. The Carolingian rulers were their patrons: but the artists in many cases were monks.

Written references to Frankish murals show that all doubtfulness at mentioning or depicting the old pagan gods had completely disappeared: gone were the days when Augustine had apologized for referring to a pagan goddess because it might have implied that he believed in her existence. The paganism which Frankish capitularies and canons condemned was the Germanic or Scandinavian paganism of a people recently converted, not the old gods of Greece and Rome. The very constellations in the night sky had been named after the old gods and heroes who were now painted on the walls even of episcopal palaces: Mercury and Jupiter, Perseus and Andromeda and Hercules. It was fashionable to paint on palace walls the Biblical personages with their pagan antetypes: but sometimes the pagan personages appeared without any antetypal excuse.

The episcopal palace of Theodulf at Germigny-des-Prés had a lively painting of Earth on the refectory walls: she was represented as a strong, vigorous woman among a profusion of chariots, animals and serpents. The palace of Saint-Denis had paintings of the seasons as women, and Saint-Riquier had figures representing the different parts of the world (R. Crozet). At Saint-Gall the sages of Greece faced the Christian saints. The palace at Ingelheim had paintings in a great historical cycle: the pagan conquerors, Cyprus, Ninus, Romulus, Alexander, Hannibal, etc. were set over against Constantine, Theodosius, Charles Martel, Pepin and Charlemagne. Some monastic walls had paintings of the occupations of the months (those from Cosimo de' Medici's study at the Victoria and Albert Museum had a very long ancestry), Æsop's fables and hunting scenes with deer and dogs, all in the Byzantine manner. There must have been many more than those whose memory is preserved in literary reference, and the choice of pagan subjects was natural when so many Carolingian scholars were studying Vergil and Ovid, and when manuscript illuminators of liturgical books even slipped into the detail of decorative borders Bellerophon mounted on Pegasus or the chimaera, Apollo the healer, or a laurel-wreathed bacchante. The sacramentary of Drogo had Earth as a woman suckling two children: and Ocean, riding a dolphin. Even in subjects not directly pagan, the traditions of antiquity intruded: some manuscripts from Tours have the apostle John as an old man with a wing-filled banner above his head, in a manner in which pagan deities used to be portrayed. As to detail: towns were represented as women crowned with a walled and towered headdress, and antique weapons, costume, standards, temples, columns, the masked actor and the paraphernalia of the theatre all appeared in pictured landscape and scenery. Together with the allegorical draped women, feeling for plastic form and fluttering drapery, there was transmitted from pagan antiquity 'the sense of grandeur and the sense of humanity' (R. Crozet).

BIBLIOGRAPHICAL NOTE

For Carolingian music, see E. Wellesz, *Eastern Elements in Western Chant*, 1947, and *History of Byzantine Music and Hymnography*, 1949: for Carolingian architecture, N. Pevsner, *An Outline of European Architecture*, 1948 ed.: J. Pijoan, *History of Art*, vol. ii, 1933; for art, R. Hinks, *Carolingian Art*, 1935: R. Crozet, 'Les survivances de la pensée et de l'art antiques dans la peinture Carolingienne', in *Mélanges d'hist. du moyen âge dédiés à la mém. de Louis Halphen*.

CHAPTER XXIX

THE END OF THE CAROLINGIAN EMPIRE

THE break-up of the Carolingian empire gave birth to new national groupings and a new political structure in western Europe: it was the occasion also of the rise of a new kind of society: feudal society. The years 888 to 911 were years of political insecurity and military chaos: not only were the claims of new aspirants to rule, of Carolingian descent or otherwise, liable to provoke civil war, but, even more, the attacks of outside enemies, raiders by sea and by land, rendered life and property insecure. The northmen had already by 888 penetrated and plundered the land of the west Franks and to a less extent that of the east Franks: the Saracens had raided Italy; but as great a danger was now to threaten the land of the east Franks, the raids of the nomad horsemen from the steppes, the Magyars who were later to be called Hungarians. Pannonia, Bavaria, Suabia, Franconia and even Saxony in the north of Germany were to suffer from raids as cruel as those of the Vikings; in the raids on Saxony in 906, women were driven away naked from their homes, tied to one another by their hair. The Carolingian counts and dukes of Germany made a better showing in defence than the Carolingian emperors and kings had done earlier in the west against the northmen: they fought grim battles, but met with heavy defeats. Military insecurity in Merovingian times had made bands of fighting retainers necessary to the Frankish kings; but the wars of the Carolingians, and above all those of the latter part of the ninth century, made the need of such armed retainers even more urgent. The origins of feudal society, and 'feudalism' as a legal system, have been the subject of prolonged research, and the weightiest modern historical opinion now sees in this need of armed local defence, this need by kings, dukes and counts for armed retainers, for vassals, the factor that produced the new social order. Professor F. L. Ganshof in his *Qu'est-ce-que la feodalité?* (translated by Professor P. Grierson under the title *Feudalism*), has set forth the rise and consequences of the institution of vassalage so clearly and convincingly, that the matter can here be treated briefly.

In the period between the collapse of the Roman empire and the rise of a feudal society in the ninth century, certain institutions and terms were in use that can properly be called 'pre-feudal':

they foreshadowed the personal relationship between a freeman and his *dominus* that was to be the heart of vassalage. There was in the period a shortage of coined money such as precluded the payment of high officials by a cash salary, such as had been possible under the Roman empire: such officials must needs be rewarded by maintenance at the lord's court, or some kind of a lease or grant of land. There was also a need for order and local peace: for the opportunity for peasants and townsmen to till the land and pursue their affairs with safety to life and harvest. There was need for better justice, for better and more modern courts than the old *mallus*, presided over by the counts, or the rare circuits of the Carolingian *missi*. The penal clause in an old Roman will of land had begun: *Si quis*, and laid down that *If anyone* tried to prove this testament ineffective, let him pay so much to the Roman fisc and lose his case; but when there was no longer a Roman fisc to protect testaments, the notaries tried to substitute a Christian penalty: *Si quis* (they wrote): *If anyone* try to upset this my last will, or prevent these lands being given to my wife, or to such and such an abbey for the remedy of my soul: let him be cut off from the communion of the faithful in this life: and let him hear the words of the Lord when he comes to judge the world by fire:

Depart, ye accursed.

A terrible tribunal this, and a terrible penalty: but, as all notaries knew, less efficacious than the certainty of having to render so much to the fisc. The need of secure justice, which in the weakness of central power had to be local justice, reinforced the more pressing need of bands of armed warriors for local and personal defence.

The pre-feudal institutions of Merovingian times had an ancestry going back both to the Roman and Germanic past. By the Roman institution of patronage (*patrocinium*) the head of a patrician family had absolute rights over his own family and descendants, and also over a train of outsiders, *clientes*; the Roman senator, too, exercised a *patrocinium*. He was bound to protect these *clientes* in the law courts, and they gave him social deference; by the end of the fourth century they had come to include also small rural proprietors, who afforded protection to their villagers from the extortions of the tax collector. The emperor had his own *clientes*, and they, as his companions and friends (*comites* and *amici*) formed his entourage (*comitiva*). These clients, however, incurred no military obligation.

The *beneficium* again, so important an institution in feudal society, had a Roman origin. It was the free gift (either of land or office) by a donor not bound by any contract to make such a gift, and as such it could be recalled by the donor. Roman law enforced all contracts freely made, as it enforced all promises made before legal witnesses in the courts; but in some cases, and especially after the fall of the empire, it was desirable to afford protection, or to promise services, without the making of a legal contract: that is, to enter into a personal relationship where the circumstances were unsuitable for the making of a legal contract. Similarly, a revocable grant of land, a *precarium*, was extra-legal. Ulpian in the *Digest* defined it as 'that which is granted at the prayer of a petitioner to his use'. The holder of a *precarium* got, not the ownership, but the use of the land. Neither the *beneficium* nor the *precarium* was hereditary. The grantor of the *precarium* profited by his right to take part of the produce of the land, and, by joining these precarial tenancies to his own estate, increase his lands and defend them more advantageously from the tax-collector. No military service was involved. Both *beneficium* and *precarium* were in use in the Frankish kingdoms in Merovingian times.

The Germanic elements of feudalism came with the invaders of the west, and had their new development in the kingdoms of the Merovingian Franks: they should be looked for (as Professor Ganshof points out) 'more particularly in the heart of the Merovingian kingdom between the Loire and the Rhine'. Gaul was rarely united under a single descendant of Clovis and family partitions brought frequent wars. Even when a civil war was not raging, the Frankish officials were too few to secure public peace and safety: magnates and kings sought retainers for protection as well as prestige, retainers who should fulfil the function of the old Germanic *comitatus*. The Frankish *trustis* appears to have corresponded to the *comitatus*, and the freemen who thus served the king were his *antrustiones* and had a wergeld threefold that of the ordinary freeman. They were also termed *fideles*, *leudes* and, in Italy, *gasindi*: and they were essentially picked fighting men. Only the (Frankish) kings and queens had *antrustions*: they had also servants of lesser social rank to whom the Latinized Celtic word *vassus* was applied: it came from *gwas*, a boy, servant or slave. Those under the king's protection, his *patrocinium*, were now said to be under his *mundeburdis* or *mundium*: a freeman might place himself voluntarily under the *mundium* of king or another, and such an act was made by a specific formula and had legal force. The petitioner asked for protection and maintenance, and entered into a lifelong relationship: he 'commended' himself to his new *dominus*, but he remained a freeman. Clerks sometimes sought the *tuitio* or patronage of a layman, which made the bishops fear they would be withdrawn from their own authority; and, on the other hand, bishops often maintained a household whom they supported, including laymen, and these formed, as it were, an episcopal *comitiva*. Commendation among laymen was in fact a contract made by two partners: the earliest extant *formulae* of commendation do not specify the services required from the *vassus* in any precise terms: they might be military or domestic or agricultural, according to the social status of the petitioner. The social rank of the *vassus* in early Merovingian times was low, for the word implied slavery: but the status of the *vassus* was to rise and to include men of high rank in the king's service.

To the end of Merovingian times there was no necessary and normal connexion between the benefice, the *precaria* (Merovingian for *precarium*) and the *vassus*. The king might bestow a benefice, secular or spiritual office or land, without endowing the recipient with precarial land: he might and often did maintain him in his own entourage till he had performed many years of service, and then make him a grant of land, absolutely or as a *precaria*. The churches and abbeys often granted precarial land, expecting in return a part of the produce. Benefice and the *precaria* were still separate. Nor did the grant of either necessarily accompany commendation and the entry into the state of vassalage: the would-be *vassus* might commend himself for protection only. Professor Ganshof holds that beneficial tenements were sometimes granted in this period to vassals to ensure their maintenance: but that there is not enough evidence to show that the practice was very widespread before the middle of the eighth century.

Under the Carolingians, however, vassalage and benefice are commonly found united and in extended use. The century from *c.* 750 to *c.* 850 was one of almost continuous wars, first aggressive wars against the Alemanni, Bavarians, Aquitanians, Lombards and Saxons, and then wars of defence against northmen, Saracens, and later, the Hungarians. The early Carolingians increased the number of their vassals and maintained them by landed grants, in some cases from their own estates but mainly from lands once the property of churches and abbeys. Complaints of injustice and of clerical irregularity consequent on these confiscations followed (see p. 290), and Pepin the Short and Boniface had to reconcile military needs with the demands for ecclesiastical reform: their solution marked a great increase in beneficial tenure. It was arranged that all secularized lands should be held by the mayor of the palace (744) and later by the king, and that he should grant them as benefices to their present holders; at the same time, the holders, the king's vassals, should pay a precarial rent to the church who originally owned the land. Further, in the mid-century Pepin the Short ordained a *divisio* of the land of all the west Frankish churches: a part remained in their effective possession, but the larger part remained to the mayor of the palace or the king to grant as benefices to his vassals. It was as a sort of compensation to the west Frankish church that Pepin ordered that tithe should be paid to the church by all his subjects. Even this treatment of the secularized lands was insufficient to secure Pepin enough military support, and he and the great magnates, dukes, counts, margraves, etc., granted many benefices to their vassals from their own or conquered lands. By the accession of Charlemagne, the union of benefice and vassalage had become common: and there was a marked rise in the social status of the vassal.

Under Charlemagne and his successors there was a further extension of vassalage, normally now beneficed vassalage. The institution spread from the region between Loire and Rhine into Franconia, Aquitaine, Alemannia and Bavaria; in Lombardy it was influenced by the position of the Lombard *gasindus*. Great estates bestowed by the king (*villae: maneria*) were sublet to the grantee's own sub-vassals, and cultivated by peasants rendering food and labour services. The Carolingian rulers encouraged this great spread of vassalage, for it gave them military support: the *vassi* were horsemen, cavalry, the spearhead of the Frankish army; the Frankish kings now, moreover, had vassals planted out in all the countryside forming a local governing class whom they could have paid in no other way. They could correspond with counts and other vassals and get their orders carried out locally; the importance of the vassals' work and their increase in numbers is attested by the frequent reference to them in capitularies, charters and annals. Even in the creation of sub-vassals, owing fidelity to their immediate lords, the Frankish rulers saw no danger.

The word vassal was now in general use, and as covering dukes, counts and the lesser vassals and sub-vassals: it embraced a large class, including all those who had put their joined hands between their lord's hands in the rite of homage (the *inmixtio manuum*). The word *homo* was often used in the technical sense of vassal, as was the term *miles* (soldier and knight) from the second half of the ninth century; the vassal might owe his lord administrative and other services, but the military obligation had become paramount. The wars of Charlemagne increased not only the number of the vassals, but their rise in status, for the heads of the subjugated states themselves signified their submission, and the incorporation of their land in Charles's kingdom, by becoming his vassals. Tassilo III, duke of Bavaria, had become the vassal of Pepin the Short in 757, commending himself into his hands and swearing oaths on holy relics; a Danish king became the vassal of Louis the Pious, etc.

The act of commendation was accompanied, as is shown in a contemporary reference to that of Tassilo III, by the swearing of the vassal's oath of fidelity or fealty. The magnates of the provinces between Seine and Loire are said to have commended themselves to the future Charles the Bald by the giving of hands and binding themselves with the oath of fidelity: other references show that the *inmixtio manuum* and the taking of the oath of fidelity constituted the legal bond of vassalage. The words of the vassal's oath after A.D. 800 ran:

> By this oath I promise to be faithful to the lord Charles, the most pious emperor, as a vassal should rightfully be to his lord, for the preservation of his kingdom and his rights.

Vassals to the magnates took similar oaths, and Professor Ganshof explains that, in theory, they owed military service to their immediate lord only so long as the lord was serving the emperor or king; but from the time of Louis the Pious magnates in rebellion against the emperor were in fact able to take the field at the head of their vassals (and see *supra*, p. 443). The swearing of the oath upon the relics gave the vassal's oath a religious character and a peculiar solemnity: to the old Germanic obligation to serve the chieftain to the death in battle was added the sacredness of the Christian oath, taken in public before witnesses, before the saints in heaven, and under the protection (*patrocinium*) in particular of the saint on whose enshrined relics the vassal laid his hand.

The size of the benefice with which the vassal was endowed now varied greatly, from a duchy or even sub-kingdom to the small estate with which churches and abbeys were forced to endow their *milites* from their own lands; but by the mid-ninth century the legal union of vassalage and benefice was assumed. Vassalage was not yet hereditary: the grant of the benefice (later called fief) lapsed at the death of either lord or vassal: but from the year 877, when Charles the Bald made certain rulings at Quierzy-sur-Oise about the fate of benefices if their holders died during the expedition he was planning to make to Italy, the hereditary nature

of benefices was recognized as normal (see p. 458). Some benefices consisted of offices, supported normally by landed estates,
such as duchies and counties, and in such cases the complex of
rights, obligations and territories were known as *honores*; by 877
such 'honours' had been assimilated to benefices and were covered
by the rulings of Quierzy-sur-Oise. The son of a count, like the
son of a landed vassal, was presumed to succeed to his father's
honour: the all-important Carolingian count became a hereditary
official, and the lands of the county became a family inheritance.
This assimilation of the honour to the benefice was more complete
among the west Franks than the east Franks; but here too assimilation was often accepted. When the old pre-Carolingian tribal
areas in Germany regained their local independence after the
death of Louis the Child in 911, they were not headed by some
descendant of the old Germanic kingly families, but by some
strong Carolingian count in the area who had amassed lands and
rights within the two generations since 877, and was strong
enough to get himself accepted as duke of a 'national' duchy.

It is of interest that the vassal's oath of fidelity was also used by
Charlemagne as a model for the oath of fidelity that he demanded
that all his male subjects should take to him after he had become
emperor. A subject's loyalty before Charlemagne's day was implicit, and not attested by any oath-taking, but even before
Charlemagne became emperor his conquests had occasioned his
demand that certain of his newly incorporated subjects should
swear fidelity to him individually.

In a recent essay,[1] Professor Ganshof has explained the relation
between the general oath of fidelity, finally imposed by Charlemagne on all his subjects, and the oath of the vassal. An oath was
so sacred that Charlemagne not only came to demand one from
all his subjects, as a safeguard against local rebellion, but even
distrusted the practice of oath-taking by the members of any
association, such as the gilds: the members of an association might
plead justification in following their alderman or leader in civil
or military disobedience to the king's orders. An oath-bound
subject sharing in a rebellion incurred, however, the penalties not
only of infidelity, but perjury; it was clearly expedient that newly
conquered subjects should take such an oath. Moreover, it enabled
Charlemagne to require from cathedral chapters petitioning leave
to make a free election of a bishop, the insertion in the diploma

[1] In *Mélanges d'histoire du moyen âge dédiés à la mémoire de Louis
Halphen*, p. 779.

issued of a clause requiring the candidate to be in all points *fidelis* to the king.

Charles was influenced in his policy of requiring a general oath of fidelity to be taken by all his subjects by the conspiracy of count Hardre and other Thuringian nobles in 785, where the rebels swore each other a mutual oath; Charles quelled the rebels, made its leaders take a solemn oath of fidelity to him, and then, curiously, condemned them to death for oath-breach. In 789 he enjoined a general oath-taking on all his subjects by capitulary, the subject promising to be faithful to king Charles and his sons all the days of his life, *sine fraude et malo ingenio*. The *missi* were commissioned to exact the oath: but were not numerous enough or strong enough to compel the oath to be taken in all cases. In 792 some counts made another rebellion led by Philip le Bossu, a bastard son of Charles: they denied having taken the oath of fidelity, and Charles accordingly enjoined more effective measures. The Frankish and Lombard kingdoms were divided into circuits, and *missi* appointed to take the oath themselves from all officials, lay and ecclesiastical, and to see that the local counts made all the remaining males of twelve years old and over to take it. The oath-taking of 793 was generally enforced, and a written record made; the sub-vassals of other lords took it as well as the king's vassals and the general population.

In 802, when Charles was emperor, a general oath-taking was again required, and made both more detailed and more solemn by direct allusion to the vassal's oath: a man should be *fidelis* to Charles 'as a vassal (*homo*) should be of right to his lord'. The earlier oath-forms had been negative, an oath not to do certain things disloyal in a subject: now it was explicitly laid down that he should not usurp royal lands or serfs, or aid usurpers, or do wrong to churches, widows or orphans or despoil a benefice granted by the king; not to neglect a summons to the army or an imperial order; not to hinder justice or tolerate its hindrance. Charles was seeking to use the oath now not merely to prevent the giving of aid to rebels, but for the elimination of abuses. Three kinds of oath-taking and three only were legal, as was laid down in 805: this oath of fidelity to the king: the vassal's oath: and the judicial oath. All other oath-taking was conspiracy, and forbidden.

The political submergence of the Carolingian empire after 888 resulted from there being no single survivor of Carolingian stock who could command sufficient respect from east and west Franks and the papacy to attain the imperial title, and at least nominal rule. The urgent needs of defence made local rulers in command of their own army and of what had been imperial resources a first necessity, even though the tradition of Carolingian rule still had great weight with the secular magnates and very strong support from the church. The ninth-century papacy, scholars and episcopate never ceased to deplore what they regarded as the usurpations of local rulers of non-Carolingian stock: they desired unitary rule as consonant with St Augustine's teaching about the City of God: they anticipated Dante in believing that the empire exists for peace. They had doubtless also approved the Carolingian willingness to support the church and use her rulers and scholars: there was self-interested regret at the lessening of their own political influence and the confiscation of church lands in the wars; but this was not all. A pale Byzantine splendour had suffused the Carolingian background, and the Byzantine concept of the emperor as another Constantine had largely been accepted by the Frankish episcopate. After 888 the bishops were left with the unacceptable situation that Carolingian and non-Carolingian rulers, often at odds with each other and helpless as defenders of the Christian empire from the pagans, yet exercised the old imperial, Byzantine control of episcopal elections and the right to dispose of church lands; the ninth-century bishops and abbots had all the disadvantages of the Byzantine system without its advantages. By their fostering of vassalage, moreover, the new rulers had passed on to local kings, dukes, barons, counts and margraves their own rights of patronage and control over the local churches and abbeys. Lay control, which had arisen from a passing on of Byzantine and then Frankish imperial powers to local magnates, was to lead to many abuses in the tenth and eleventh centuries, and it was suspect to the Frankish bishops from the ninth. The Carolingian tradition had naturally no stronger supporters than the episcopate.

Charles the Fat was deposed by the diet of Tribur in November 887, and died on 13 January 888. The abbot Regino of Prüm, a famous annalist, recognized the change his death brought, and wrote

After his death the kingdoms that obeyed his sway, as if deprived of a lawful heir, dissolved into their component parts: and now they waited not upon their natural lord, but were disposed to create for themselves a king from their own stock.

This, he continued, led to great wars, not because these regions lacked Frankish princes fit to rule a kingdom through their nobility, fortitude and wisdom, but because their equality in generosity (noble birth), dignity and power fomented discord: 'for no one so much excelled the rest that these others would deign to submit themselves to his dominion'. The land of the Franks gave birth to many princes fit for the government of the kingdom; but chance, through natural jealousy, armed them to their mutual destruction.

There was, in fact, only one lawful Carolingian claimant to rule in 888: he was the seven-year-old Charles, the posthumous son of Louis II, the Stammerer (see p. 459). Louis the Stammerer's cousin, the Bavarian Carloman, had only an illegitimate son, Arnulf, now duke of Carinthia; Arnulf's mother was a noble lady, and he himself was energetic, able, and a good fighter, but his illegitimacy was against him. When he was only twenty-five he had been put in charge of the marches of Pannonia and Carinthia, and the German nobles knew his personal qualities: he had even administered the duchy of Bavaria during the illness that preceded his father, Carloman's, death. His cousin, Louis III, succeeded to the duchy of Bavaria, and Arnulf found Charles the Fat unfriendly and suspicious; but on his deposition in 887 the German magnates elected Arnulf king of Germany. Only the stain on his birth prevented his election to the empire, for he inherited the loyalty due to the Carolingians: but, as it was, the west Franks, who had just undergone the dreadful siege of Paris in 885-6, and who could not hope for leadership from a seven-year-old Carolingian boy, elected as king Odo, count of Paris. Count Robert the Strong, his father, had defended Paris, and Odo had distinguished himself fighting against the northmen. He and Arnulf, however, had not been the only claimants to the west Frankish throne. Fulk, archbishop of Reims had intrigued to crown Guy II of Spoleto king of the west Franks: Guy came of a Frankish family which had settled in Italy and had pretensions on the Italian crown and even the empire. But the Frankish nobles preferred Odo. Guy II, conspiring with some north French bishops and Baldwin II, count of Flanders (grandson of Charles the Bald), then went to Arnulf at Worms, asking him to claim the kingdom of the west Franks and the empire, denying any part of it to Odo, who was unconnected with the Carolingian stock. Odo, however, had just defeated the northmen and his prestige was high: Arnulf in 888 met him at Worms, recognized him as king of the west Franks and received from him some kind of profession of loyalty: not, however, the oath of vassalage. The west and east Franks now had their separate kings, the line of Arnulf holding Germany till the death

19

of his son, Louis the Child, in 911, and that of Odo alternating with a Carolingian descendant and others till his own line, the line of the counts of Paris, gained the permanent rule of 'France' in the person of Hugh Capet in 987.

But the Carolingian empire in 888 was split into more than two kingdoms: the smaller kingdoms of Provence, Burgundy and Lorraine now attained their independence without serious dispute, and the crown of Italy was claimed by two candidates, who fought a civil war for some years.

Provence, long separate in tradition and language from north France, had tried more than once since the emperor Lothar I's death in 855 to gain her independence. Count Boso had ruled as king from 863 till his death in 887, and left a young son, Louis, and an ambitious wife, Ermingarde, who fought for her son's rights to succeed eventually. Arnulf had few supporters in this distant province and allowed Ermingarde to summon an assembly at Valence, which early in 890 elected Louis king and had him anointed. Ermingarde ruled as regent till her death in 897. She had hoped Arnulf would support her son's claim to the whole of the old corridor kingdom of Lotharingia: but this Arnulf was unwilling to do. He installed his illegitimate son Zwentibold as king of Lorraine (in the north of the old Lotharingia), and allowed count Rudolf I to make himself king of Burgundy in the middle portion of the old corridor.

The Jura mountains lie between the Lake of Geneva and the Saône, and count Rudolf had ruled this region for some years as marquess when the magnates of the old province of Transjurania met and elected him king of Burgundy, in 888. He also was ambitious, and desired to become king of the old Lotharingia: he at once occupied Alsace and part of Lorraine, but the magnates held aloof, and he had to be content with Arnulf's recognition of him as king of Transjurane Burgundy only. His small kingdom embraced the archdiocese of Besançon and the towns of Basle and Geneva.

The northern part of the old corridor, now Lorraine, accepted the royal rule of Arnulf from 888 till 895, losing its independence. When Arnulf's queen in that year gave birth to a son Louis (the Child), he wished to provide for his bastard son, Zwentibold, and at an assembly at Worms persuaded the magnates of Lorraine to elect him their king. Like his father, Zwentibold was able and energetic, but he was arrogant and no statesman. Zwentibold's unpopularity was shown when certain Lotharingian counts stole church lands from the bishops of Toul and Trier, and Zwentibold forced them to restore them, rousing such bitter opposition from the magnates that Arnulf had to intervene to bring about a reconciliation. Zwentibold roused fresh opposition when in 898 he exiled count Renier (Renard) of the Long Neck, on which Renier appealed to the then king of France, Charles the Simple. Charles invaded Lorraine, but received little support; he negotiated a peace near Prüm and retired. The final struggle came for Zwentibold on Arnulf's death in 899: Louis the Child was elected king of Germany, and Zwentibold's own subjects elected Louis king of Lorraine also. The armies of the two half-brothers, Louis and Zwentibold, fought near the Meuse in August, 900, and Zwentibold was killed. Louis the Child was recognized as king by all Lorraine, to which he granted a local autonomy; he appointed Gebhard, count of Franconia, duke of Lorraine, and the land had no more kings.

The succession to the kingdom of Italy was long disputed after 888 between representatives of the families of two Frankish counts associated with the Carolingian conquest of Italy. In the north, the margraves (marquesses) of Friuli had long defended a Frankish march against the Slavs, an assembly at Pavia, now, with its palace the capital of northern Italy, in 888 elected Berengar, marquess of Friuli and also a grandson of Louis the Pious on his mother's side, to be king of Italy. He had no supporters however in central or southern Italy.

Guy II, duke of Spoleto, whose old Lombard duchy straddled the Alps and who also ruled Naples, was better placed strategically to command central Italy: the south, in any case, was still held by Byzantines and Saracens. The Frankish dukes of Spoleto came from a family of the Moselle region, but by 888 they had Italianized themselves by long settlement and prudent intermarriage. Guy's father, the first duke, had gained the duchy in 879, and passed it on to his eldest son Lambert, while Guy held the county of Camerino. In 882 Lambert died, and Guy II succeeded; he was an able intriguer, ready to ally with Saracens or Byzantines when it suited him. Both pope and emperor distrusted him and he was declared a traitor; Charles the Fat commanded Berengar to seize both his person and his lands, but he failed. In 885 Guy made his peace with Charles.

In 888, his first reaction to Charles's death was to intrigue with archbishop Fulk to gain the French crown, and when this scheme failed he fought again with Berengar near Brescia, but indecisively. Berengar vainly hoped for help from Arnulf, whom he had recognized as king of Germany, but no sufficient help came; at a fierce battle on the Trebbia in 889 he was completely defeated by Guy's forces. The Italian bishops, before the battle, had just concluded an agreement with Guy to elect him king in return for promises to respect their rights and those of the papacy: but they were ready to accept his possible defeat as the judgment of God between the two contestants: Guy, however, maintained his predominance.

In south Italy the Byzantines were anxious to regain their old territories. They held Bari from 876, and in 888–889 repelled a Saracen attack from Sicily. The Saracen admiral had actually landed on the continent and been forced to return with his troops to Sicily. The Byzantines might have regained all south Italy: they temporarily gained Benevento: but no help came from Constantinople and the Lombard princes were as hostile to them as to the Saracens. They could hold only the coastal region from Siponto to Bari.

Between 888 and 890, therefore, six kings had established themselves in regions covering the old Carolingian empire: but there had been no revival of the imperial title. The strongest possible claimant, in lands and ability and Carolingian parentage, was illegitimate; but pope Stephen V was in difficulties with the Roman nobles, and had noted how Arnulf had maintained the Carolingian tradition in his expedition of May 889 against the pagan Obodrites. In 890, therefore, he invited Arnulf to come to Rome and deliver Italy from 'bad Christians and menacing pagans': it was clear that he would be ready to crown Arnulf as emperor. But Arnulf in the years 890–894 was withheld from any Italian expedition by rebellions in Germany and what he deemed to be the menace of the great Slav empire of Moravia on his eastern frontier; the northmen, moreover, were still riding through Lorraine and plundering even Aix-la-Chapelle. In spite of the papal invitation, any Italian expedition was deferred. In 891 Arnulf won a victory over the northmen near Louvain, and the year following he marched into Bavaria to interview the Moravian prince, Svatopluk, who failed, however, to meet him. Though Arnulf led an army into Moravia, he could take no towns or strongholds, and, after plundering the countryside, returned to Germany leaving his relations with the Slavs unsettled by treaty. Had either the Slavs or Arnulf known of the imminent menace from the Hungarians, their true policy would have been one of alliance.

Stephen V meanwhile, in default of Arnulf, had sought another protector in Guy II, whom he had long distrusted both for the fear of encirclement between Spoleto and Naples, and Guy's willingness to ally with the Saracens. In February 891 Stephen broke with the long tradition of Franco-papal friendship and crowned Guy emperor in St Peter's. Guy henceforward claimed the imperial title and issued capitularies on the Carolingian model: in 892 he effected the coronation of his son Lambert by the new pope, Formosus. But his power did not even extend over all Italy; Berengar in the north was hostile; Odo of the west Franks and the three small kingdoms of the old Lotharingia, all disregarded him; in Germany, Arnulf bided his time to reckon with him.

In 893, at pope Formosus' invitation, Arnulf sent an army under king Zwentibold to help Berengar in a campaign against Guy. Zwentibold reached Pavia, where Guy had taken refuge, and then unaccountably retired to Germany. Very early in 894 Arnulf himself led an expedition into Italy and with Berengar marched on Bergamo, held against them by its count and bishop. They took Bergamo, hanged the count, and sent off the bishop to Mainz; most of the Lombard towns, including Milan and Pavia, made their submission. All seemed favourable for an advance on Rome, for the Tuscan princes had submitted to Arnulf and the pope was ready to welcome him: yet he hesitated and then for some unknown reason, returned to Germany. Possibly he returned because the plague had ravaged his army: possibly because the marquess of Tuscany was unreliable, or because Rudolf, king of Burgundy, was hostile to his acquiring the imperial title: both rulers could endanger his communications with Germany.

Arnulf chose indeed to return by the Brenner, and encountered Rudolf's open hostility in the form of a contingent sent to aid the marquess Anchiar, a relation of Guy of Spoleto: they were defending a town besieged by Arnulf. Arnulf's power was strong in Germany: but he could not prevail in Italy or prevent Rudolf of Burgundy from reigning there till his death in 912.

Arnulf's second expedition to Italy was no more successful: Guy of Spoleto died in 894, his son Lambert was too young to be dangerous, and the pope Formosus again invited Arnulf to come to Rome. Accordingly, he marched for Rome in December 895, through country foodless and wasted by the Spoletan army, which retreated before him. He reached Rome with an exhausted army and found the gates closed, and Rome held against them by Guy's widow, Agiltrude. Arnulf and his Germans forced the gates, and he was crowned emperor in St Peter's by Formosus on 22 February 896: the Romans gave him the oath of fidelity. Even now, however, the situation was dangerous, for neither Agiltrude nor the young king Lambert would submit. Arnulf marched northward to take Spoleto, held against him by Agiltrude, but was struck with paralysis on the way: he was carried back to Germany and lived there helpless till 899: his army had evacuated Italy.

When Arnulf died, in December 899, his son Louis, to whom the German magnates had already sworn fidelity, was only six years old; the descriptive title, Louis the Child, was used of him till his death in 911. He was Arnulf's only legitimate heir, and an assembly at Forchheim in February 900 proclaimed him king of Germany. The crown of Lorraine was disputed between Zwentibold and Charles the Simple of France, but both accepted the succession of the young Louis III, though Zwentibold did so unwillingly. Louis came to Thionville to receive their oath of fidelity, but Zwentibold rebelled, was defeated, and killed. Lorraine was merged in the German kingdom.

The Forchheim assembly had appointed a council of regency, on which two bishops, Arnulf's closest friends and counsellors, had the chief place; they were assisted by some lay barons and the marquess of Bavaria. There was no general disposition to upset this regency government inaugurated by respect for the Carolingian tradition, but real Carolingian rule was threatened by two great dangers, external and internal: attack from the Slavs and Magyars on the eastern frontier, and the drift to decentralization of power in order to deal with swiftly moving land and sea raiders. The danger from the northmen was not over: and in this reign it was to be matched by the swift, terrible raids of the Hungarian horsemen from the south-east.

The Magyar horsemen from the steppes, later to be called Hungarians, had settled around 860 between the Don and the Dnieper. Pushed by the arrival of new eastern tribes, they had crossed the Dnieper and then the Dniester, remained a short time in Wallachia, and in 895 crossed the Carpathians and settled on the middle Danube, attacking both the Slovenes and the Moravians. The plain of the middle Danube was inviting to these half-nomad horsemen, and while Arnulf intrigued with them against the Moravians, divided leadership among the Moravians themselves made defence impossible. The Magyars took the plain but were not ready to settle and practise agriculture: they used the rich plain for horse-breeding, to support their plundering raids on Italy and Germany. Away in Germany the paralysed Arnulf could do nothing against them. Moravia, which should have formed a buttress protecting Germany, was now weak and divided; when her strong duke, Svatopluk, died in 894, the jealousy of his two sons, Moimir and Svatopluk II, was fomented by the intrigues of Arnulf, and led to open war between them in 898. Arnulf was helpless and the Magyars overran Moravia; in 899 they raided the Lombard plain, and in 900 Pannonia. In November, 900, bishop Richer of Passau and count Liutpold raised an army and fought the invaders in a bloody battle; the Magyars retreated, but their offensive strength remained.

The German regents in 901 now made formal peace with the Moravians, but too late to stop the Magyar invasion. In 901 the Magyars invaded the German province of Carinthia: in the years 905–906 they bore down all Moravian resistance, and the Moravian state collapsed.

Germany was now directly threatened: in 906 and 907 strong Magyar forces ravaged the valleys of the Danube and the Elbe. The Bohemian Czechs had granted the raiders passage through their lands and in the high summer of 906 they passed by the Elbe valley through the northern mountain frontier of Bohemia and barbarously ravaged Saxony. In 907 they raided an almost undefended Bavaria: only Innsbrück was strong enough to withstand them. The next spring an assembly of German magnates sitting under the young king Louis, tried to raise an army that should protect Bavaria, a province with access both to Germany and Italy: but in July 907 this army was almost destroyed and its leader, duke Liutpold, killed in battle. In 908 the raiders ravaged Saxony again, defeating an army of Franconians and Thuringians, and killing the bishop of Würzburg and the marquess of Thuringia in battle. The next year the Magyar horsemen again raided south Germany, penetrating Suabia, a province hitherto unravaged: they took much plunder. On their way back, the invaders were surprised near the river Inn by Arnulf, the young marquess of Bavaria and the son-in-law of count Liutpold: in the ensuing battle, July 909, he avenged Liutpold's death. In 910 Louis the Child collected with difficulty an army of Suabians, Franconians and Bavarians: but the invaders won a victory over them near Augsburg; the defeat of so much effort was a catastrophe. When Louis the Child died in 911, Germany was exhausted and the situation desperate. The Magyar Hungarians had established themselves as a permanent danger to the German frontier in the south east, and the possible plunderers of almost any part of Germany. The burning of villages, the pillage and profanation of churches were as common a sight now in the south and east of Germany as they long had

been in the north and east from the Viking raids. Defence had
to be local: well-timbered burgs in the Alfredian manner, or
mound-and-bailey castles, were the only places of refuge.

The need of a strong local power in the general anarchy explains
the second outstanding feature of the reign of Louis the Child:
the rise of the so-called 'national duchies'. Louis the Child's
efforts to halt the Magyars, or to deal with confusion amounting
to anarchy, drove each region to set about its own defence: the
old tribal groups, with a common historical provenance and a
common dialectal form of the old Germanic language, regained
their pre-Carolingian independence. Their leaders, however, were
in no case the descendants of the old pre-Carolingian tribal kings
or dukes, but the descendants of the Frankish officers appointed
by Charlemagne or his successors to rule the region. Out of the
families of the many Frankish counts and margraves, and the
comparatively few (military) dukes, the most able, fortunate, or
diplomatic made themselves rulers of territorial duchies. The
fluid political conditions of the reign of Louis the Child made
possible the emergence of the four national duchies, Saxony,
Franconia, Suabia and Bavaria, and shortly afterwards, the duchy
of Lorraine, which was not an old, pre-Carolingian entity, a
'tribal duchy', but the remains of the old corridor kingdom of
Lotharingia. The emergence of ruling families of the national
duchies had indeed preceded the reign of Louis the Child: in
Saxony, the Liudolfing Bruno had headed the wars against the
Danes and Wends and gained for his family such a position as
early as 880: count Liutpold of Bavaria attained the local rule and
defence of his 'duchy' by about 900: duke Henry, afterwards
king Henry the Fowler, was ruling Saxony by 906. These old
tribal duchies were the easier to rule in that they had their own
laws and customs, and were old entities submerged for some generations in the Carolingian empire, often with their own sharply
defined frontiers. Their new local rulers, charged with the duty
of defence, found it the easier to command their local counts and
margraves, to usurp revenues and powers properly belonging to
the monarchy, and to hand on their own position, estates and
privileges from father to son. The great opponents of the centri-
fugal drift were the bishops, so long attached to the old concept
of unitary rule: but the urgent necessities of the times overbore
their resistance to the new ducal usurpations.

As to the five great duchies: the ducal house of the Liudolfings
in Saxony was descended from a duke Liudolf of the east Saxons,

who, in the days of Louis the Pious defended Germany from the Danes and Swedes; his son Bruno was killed fighting the Danes, and his second son, Otto, added to Saxony the march of Thuringia. This Otto succeeded in appropriating many regalian rights, and at the same time in keeping the goodwill of the church; his predecessors had given great endowments to local churches and abbeys. The Liudolfings became unquestioned masters of Saxony without civil war.

The duchy of Bavaria was also a frontier march of Germany, in this case against the Slavs, and it too emerged as an independent duchy without violence. The margraves of Bavaria often bore the title of duke, and were closely attached to the Carolingians. For a short time, under Carloman, son of Louis the German, Bavaria even became a kingdom. When Arnulf, son of Carloman, became king of the Germans, he gave Bavaria to his friend, count Liutpold, and treated it as a march against the Slav Moravians. Liutpold prospered, gained Pannonia, Carinthia and other fiefs, and married Kunigund, sister of the Suabian counts Erchanger and Berthold. When he was killed fighting the Magyars, his son Arnulf proclaimed himself duke 'by the grace of God' and ruled Bavaria as an independent state.

The duchy of Franconia, centring in the valley of the Main, the old motherland of the Franks, proved naturally less easy to weld into an entity. It was strongly attached to Frankish tradition and therefore to Carolingian rule: it was not a march, and its defence needs were therefore slightly less pressing. The formation of a duchy was hindered by the contesting claims to power of two great families, the Conradins of western Franconia and the Babenbergers, whose interests lay round Bamberg and eastern Franconia. The representatives of the Babenbergers at the turn of the century were three sons of the count Henry who had been killed at the siege of Paris by the northmen in 886: that of the rival family, Conrad the Old, father of the future king of the Germans, Conrad I. King Arnulf had long favoured the Conradins, and after battles between the two factions in 902, when one of the Bamberg brothers was killed and another taken prisoner and beheaded, royal sentence was pronounced (903) condemning the Bambergs and confiscating their lands. The remaining Bamberg brother, Adalbert, refused to submit, and raised rebellions in 903, 904 and 905, finally defeating Conrad the Old and killing him in battle. The regency council was, however, strong enough to deal with him: he was accused of treason and executed in September 909. The Conradins were left in power in Franconia: when Louis the Child died at the age of

eighteen in 911, the German magnates elected Conrad, duke of
Franconia, king of the Germans. The situation in Germany was
so desperate that the Carolingian tradition went by the board, and
Conrad was elected on his merits. He had been chosen in the
secular interest, and saw no reason to strengthen his position by
receiving anointing and coronation from the church.

Suabia also became a duchy in the reign of Louis the Child,
though precariously. Burchard, count of Rhaetia, with his brother
Adalbert were the great magnates in the region, once the old
territory of the Alemanni; but their position (and especially
Burchard's use of the ducal title) was opposed by Solomon III,
bishop of Constance. In the resultant civil strife, Burchard was
killed in 911, and the enmity of Solomon was able to procure
the exile of his son, which was followed by the assassination of
Adalbert. The newly-founded duchy of Suabia was, however,
to recover its independence later.

The duchy of Lorraine had been merged in the German kingdom from the beginning of the reign of Louis the Child. The
regency council appointed as duke, not a local Frankish magnate,
but the Conradin Gebhard, who ruled Lorraine till he was killed
in battle with the Magyars in 910. Subjection to a Franconian
duke was, however, resented in Lorraine, and two counts of
Lorraine, Gebhard and Matfrid, raised rebellions; they were
finally beaten by Conrad the Young, and exiled. The magnate
Renier then rebelled, witnessing to Lotharingian discontent; and
when Louis the Child died in 911, and there was no longer a
German Carolingian, Lorraine offered its allegiance to the last
Carolingian ruler, Charles the Simple. Lorraine had been the
Carolingian homeland, and Charles the Simple was not only
received willingly as ruler and defender against Conrad, king of
the Germans, but thereafter showed a preference for residing in
Lorraine. Only in 925, after conquest by Henry the Fowler, king
of the Germans, did Lorraine reappear as a duchy.

The new German duchies were an outward sign of the weakness
of the new German kingdom: they menaced also the spiritual
power, the Carolingian church in Germany. The German bishops,
supported by great demesnes and rich revenues, had been in the
Carolingian period great personages in the state: but the new
dukes, with their usurped regalian rights, could not tolerate a
position of mere equality in the counsels of the king. They feared
the episcopate, not only as richly endowed but as well organized
under a metropolitan, obeying, that is, a power often outside the
boundaries of their own duchies. The bishops could not readily be

submerged in the local duchies, for they met in the synods of the ecclesiastical province, or in even wider synods summoned by the metropolitan: they issued canons binding on all Germany. In Suabia it was the bishop of Constance who had opposed the setting up of the duchy, and episcopal influence was hostile elsewhere. The bishops needed supra-ducal protection, and could only find a protector in the person of a strong king: they were the natural supporters of the monarchy, poor substitute as it was for the Carolingian empire. The desired *entente* between the bishops and the ruler was finally achieved in the reign of Otto the Great.

Meanwhile, among the west Franks, Carolingian rule survived only intermittently between 888 and the beginning of permanent Capetian rule with Hugh Capet in 987. France did not disintegrate into tribal duchies under a single weak monarchy, as in Germany: but the fiefs of the magnates were semi-independent under a king elected now by one territorial interest, now another.

Military valour in fighting the northmen had influenced the election of Odo, count of Paris, as king, in 888: he was strong in Neustria, being not only count of Paris, but of Anjou, Blois and Tours; he was moreover lay abbot of Saint-Martin of Tours and Marmoutier, as well as other Neustrian abbeys. He was crowned at Compiègne by the archbishop of Sens: but he was unacceptable to Fulk, archbishop of Reims and a considerable party of Franks who objected to being ruled by one not of the royal race, and by Neustrians. Opposition to Odo, however, gradually gave way: Baldwin, count of Flanders, submitted, until Odo's fresh defeats by the northmen encouraged him to revolt in 892. Fulk, meanwhile, had been working in the Carolingian interest: in January 893 while Odo was absent in Aquitaine, he had the thirteen-year-old Carolingian Charles the Simple crowned at Reims. In spite of requests for recognition to the pope and king Arnulf, Fulk could not establish Charles as king; but when Odo was dying he begged the Frankish lords to accept the Carolingian as his successor. He died in January, 898.

Charles was therefore acclaimed king in 898, even Odo's brother, Robert, count of Paris, greatest of the Neustrian magnates, supporting him. But Charles lacked the ability to restore Carolingian rule in his own line: he was rash and presumptuous, and the most important act of his reign (898–922) was his concession of a Danelaw to the northmen in Normandy. They had already settled in some numbers on the lower Seine and he could not eject them: but their leader Rollo tried and failed to take, successively, Paris and Chartres, and both sides were willing to negotiate. At a meeting in 911 between Charles and Rollo at St Claire-sur-Epte, Rollo agreed to accept Christianity and vassalage to Charles, together with the fiefs of Rouen, Lisieux and Evreux and the country lying between them and the sea. The treaty was realistic and seemed to interpose a coastal barrier between the northern raiders and Neustria. Charles's other achievement was his acknowledgment by the Lorrainers; but he never obtained the loyalty of all the west Frankish magnates, and had always to contend with an opposition led by the church of Reims. He was captured by his enemies and Raoul (Radulf), duke of Burgundy, was crowned king at Soissons in 923: Charles died in prison in 929. His son, Louis IV, called d'Outremer because he was long in exile in England, reigned from 936–954, his grandson Lothair from 954 to 986, and his great-grandson Louis V from 986 to 987: Carolingian power had long been shadowy, and supported by lands and revenues insufficient to give the king a more than titular authority over the great magnates.

Meanwhile, in the high noon, the twilight and the sunset of Carolingian power, two other foundations were being laid in south-west Europe: that of an Islamic civilization within Europe itself, in Spain (and Sicily) and that of medieval Christian Spain which grew out of the resistance groups of the Asturias and the western slopes of the Pyrenees. In the Iberian peninsula and Sicily the Arabs and the Berbers were bringing an eastern culture and an Arabian religion over to the west: the finest period of the schools of Cordoba and the court of Palermo were to fall in the tenth and eleventh centuries, but Islamic power prevailed in the Iberian peninsula from 711, and in Sicily from the capture of Palermo in 831, and the whole island in 917. By the end of the Carolingian period Islam held both ends of the Mediterranean, and Sicily in the centre. Eventually, the heirs of the Christian Roman empire, in east and west, were to drive her back, but not before the schools of Cordoba had transmitted their version of the old Greek learning, and the science of Baghdad, to the west.

In Spain, the Visigothic king Roderick had been defeated in 711 (see p. 106), and the Saracens passed northward, in pursuit of Visigothic nobles still resisting: by 718 they held nearly the whole peninsula. The rivers of Spain and her mountain ranges run east and west, forming natural boundaries: and the invaders, used to a warmer climate, had no wish to settle north of the region where at least the olive would grow. But apart from small groups of rebels in the Asturias mountains of the north, and large numbers of Basques, still unconquered, at the western end of the Pyrenees, the Muslim tribal chiefs now ruled Spain. They were not, however, themselves united: the more numerous Berbers from north Africa settled in separate groups from the Arabs and Syrians, who, however, received the best of the conquered territories. The whole of Moorish Spain, called by the invaders Andalusia, ranked as a province of the Umayyad caliphate of Baghdad: the caliph, however, had small enough control over it. About a fifth of the conquered land was retained for the state and allotted to the conquered Visigothic peasantry, who paid a heavy food rent. The rest of the land went to the Muslim conquerors and was also cultivated by Christian peasants; they paid a capitation tax as well as the food rent.

Islam in north Africa had worked out a manner of living with and using a conquered Christian population, and the same method was used in Spain. The Christians, the Mozarabs, were allowed their own religion and laws, and conversion to Islam was not encouraged, for that involved the loss of the capitation tax on the new convert. Nevertheless, in the ninth century religious troubles provoked persecution, and some Christians, called by their fellows *renegados*, embraced the religion of the Prophet: others fled to the Christians in the north. The Jews, on the other hand, profited from the Muslim invasion: they had earlier been persecuted, but were now tolerated. From the days of Muhammad they had always been nearer than the Christians to Islam and had indeed once been her teachers; like the Arabs and Syrians they traded in the Mediterranean, and their trade now increased.

The economic prosperity of Spain was affected both by the continuous civil war with the Christians in the north, and by the improved methods of agriculture, new industries and enlarged export trade brought about by the invaders. There was always, in fact, a wide band of ravaged country between Andalusia and the Christians of the Asturias, and, later, Asturias-Leon; for it was the practice of the Moors, when forced to retreat southwards, to lay waste the countryside they evacuated. The practice bred as much bitterness as the long frontier war itself, and apparently more than the rapid original conquest.

In Moorish Spain, however, a brilliant civilization developed, partly conditioned by economic prosperity. The great estates of the Visigothic nobles were broken up: there was more irrigation, and new crops were introduced, such as rice, the sugar cane, the pomegranate and many more fruit trees. The black plums of

Damascus were now grown in Spain, together with new cereals, the olive and, in much greater areas than before, the vine. Both gold and silver were worked in the mines.

Industry again flourished under the double stimulus of sale to a rich home market, for the tribal chiefs, their officers and above all the court of the amir of Cordoba lived with a splendour and comfort then known only in Constantinople and the east: and to an export trade borne in Arab shipping to a relatively backward Europe. Woollen cloths were woven from the fine Merino sheep on the hills of central Spain, silks from the silkworms and mulberries of the south, while metal work, glass ware and paper were all produced. Arab pottery had always been of peculiar beauty, with its borders of Arabic lettering, fine bold ornament and beautiful glaze: the skill of finer artists than elsewhere found an outlet in the decoration of this relatively cheap and coarse material (see p. 206). Toledo became famous for its sword-blades and weapons, Cordoba for its leather goods (cf. the English term *cordwainer*), and Moors, Syrians and Jews grew rich on an overseas trade handled chiefly through Seville and Malaga. Arab shipping took out cargoes of raw silk, wine, sugar, olives, dried plums and figs and the weapons, textiles and pottery made in Moorish workshops. They took also Christian slaves to the markets of the east: they sailed to Africa, Constantinople, Italy and the east Mediterranean, and brought back oriental silks and purple textiles. With a relatively large merchant class, Andalusia attained a more extended literacy than the rest of western Europe.

Even after the Muslims had reached the limit of their conquest in 718, they suffered long from tribal rivalries, such as that between the Quais and the Kalb. Better leadership and a measure of unity were, however, afforded to Moorish Spain when in 755 'Abd ar-Rahman, a member of the Umayyad family who had been driven from Damascus by the Abbasids, arrived in Spain. In 758 he set himself up as an independent amir in Cordoba, a city largely inhabited by Christian renegades who had no tribal loyalties to render his rule unacceptable; his descendants ruled there till 1031. But while Cordoba was, for a time, a semi-independent republic, its hold on the other Moorish provinces was slight: Saragossa, on the river Ebro, not far from the Pyrenees, tended to break away, and the amirate seemed likely to lapse. 'Abd ar-Rahman I's son, Hisham I, however, ruling from 788 to 796 with military skill, ruthless cruelty and eastern craftiness, maintained his power: his *faqihs*, theologians, thronged Cordoba, and drove the Christian renegades to discontent and sedition. The turbulent *faqihs* and other rebels were dealt with in the reign following, and the rebels of Cordoba and Toledo subdued by massacres and exile: but it was not till the reign of ʿAbd ar-Rahman III (912–962) that Moorish Spain attained a peak of security and prosperity. ʿAbd ar-Rahman III beat back attacks from the Christian provinces of the north, largely by substituting a single mercenary army for the earlier, tribal army, which had been fighting under its own Arab or Berber chiefs. The provincial rulers themselves were subdued, among them Umar ibn Hafsun who had made himself independent for some years in southern Andalusia: by 930 all the independent Arab and Berber chieftains were subdued. Not only internal disunion and civil war had been dangerous: but the establishment of the Fatimite caliphate in Egypt in 909 had led to religious disunion in Spain. The Fatimite caliphate was heretical and Shi'ite, and Shi'ite propaganda spread to Spain among the Berbers.

ʿAbd ar-Rahman III, however, coped with all these dangers, and asserted his supremacy in Andalusia and his equality both with the Abbasids of Baghdad and the Fatimites of Africa. In 929 he assumed the title of caliph and commander of the faithful. The caliphate of Cordoba, his capital, was to last from 929 to 1061 and to see the flowering of Muslim civilization in Spain, a civilization which had grown up under the amirate. The amirs and caliphs of Cordoba were hereditary and absolute rulers, using viziers (ministers) and a council of state. The *wali's* governed the cities, the *cadi* judged offences against Muslim law; Arabic was so widely used that nearly all the inhabitants of Spain were bilingual and the Romance tongue of the conquered adopted a very large number of Arabic terms.

Though the rulers of Spain were Umayyad, their attitude to learning was liberal and Abbasid rather than narrowly Meccan: the schools of Cordoba, like those of Abbasid Baghdad, became famous. Cordoba in the tenth century became the most cultured city in Europe: later, it was to reintroduce Aristotelian logic and Aristotelian science to western scholars. Arab astronomy had been transported by the Muslims into Spain and was studied at Cordoba and Toledo; in 1081 the Toledan Tables, mainly based on Ptolemy and al-Khwarizmi (see p. 209) were drawn by al-Zarqali, to be translated into Latin by Gerard of Cremona (d. 1187). Arab medicine was studied in Spain, though the first beginnings of the famous school of Arabic medicine at Salerno sprang from contact with Arab Africa rather than Spain; Constantine the African who had long wandered in the east, fled from his recent home in Tunis to Salerno just before the coming of Robert Guiscard. The Englishman, Adelard of Bath, visited both Cordoba and Salerno and wrote his treatise, *De Sphaero*, on Arabic cosmology (built upon that of Ptolemy): he was wandering in Arabic Spain in the early years of the twelfth century.

The small Christian states, meanwhile, maintained themselves with difficulty: compared with Moorish Spain they were very poor. They fell into two groups: those based upon the hills that border the southern shore of the Bay of Biscay, and those based upon the Pyrenees. Between the Roman Asturica Augusta and the Bay, the Asturian mountains sheltered the Visigothic nobles and their followers who retreated from the Moors: the Cantabrian mountains, the eastern end of the range, had also their bands of refugees: the whole range was to form the earliest kingdom of Christian resistance, that of the Asturias. The Pyrenean Christian states were to become kingdoms later.

The history of the kingdom of the Asturias is associated with the victory of a fugitive Visigothic noble, Pelayo, at Covadonga (718) over his pursuers: the battle is reckoned the beginning of the long Spanish *reconquista*. Alfonzo I (739–757) erected the small Christian province into the kingdom of the Asturias, and for a century its existence was precarious and its southern frontier fluid. The confusion and decline of the amirate of Cordoba, however, gave opportunity for Asturian advance: the frontier reached the Douro valley and a line of towns, including Oporto and Burgos, were fortified. The splendid reigns of 'Abd ar-Rahman III and his successors, the unity and military strength of the new caliphate, checked Christian advance for a time, but the capital was moved from Oviedo to Leon, and the kingdom of the Asturias became the wider kingdom of Leon, covering all north-western Spain. The union of the small Christian states of the Iberian peninsula was long ahead: but the eventual winning of the Atlantic coast of southern Europe, and eventually the New World, for the old Greco-Roman-Christian civilization was opened.

BIBLIOGRAPHICAL NOTE

See A. Fliche, *L'Europe occidentale de 888 à 1125*, 1930: G. Barraclough. 'The Problem of the Duchies', in *Medieval Germany, 911–1250*, 1938. For the rise of a feudal society, see F. L. Ganshof, *Qu'est-ce que la féodalité?*, 1947 ed., translated by P. Grierson as *Feudalism*, 1952: M. Bloch, *La société féodale: la formation des liens de dépendance*, 1939: J. Calmette, *Le monde féodale*, ed. 1951: F. L. Ganshof, 'Charlemagne et le serment', in *Mélanges d'hist. du moyen âge dédiés à la mém. de Louis Halphen*, p. 259 ff. See also J. Calmette, *L'effondrement d'un empire*; E. Lévi-Provencal, *Histoire de l'Espagne musulmane*, tom. i, 1950; Sanchez-Albornoz y Meduina, *En torno a los origenes del feudalismo*, 3 tomes, 1942, and *La España musulmana ségun los autores islamitas y cristianos médievales*, 2 vols., 1946. Marc Bloch's great book on feudalism is now available as *Feudal Society*, trans. by L. A. Manyon, 1961, and for the Carolingian fisc, see W. Metz, *Das Karolingische Reichsgut*, 1960. See also, R. Boutruche, *Seigneurie et Féodalité*, Paris, 1959; for good illustrations specially, D. Talbot Rice, *The Dark Ages*, London, 1965.

GENERAL REFERENCE BOOKS

Chambers Encyclopedia, published the most recently of the general encyclopedias, in 1950, is most useful, both as regards articles and bibliographies. The last ed. of the *Encyclopedia Britannica* was published in 1929: its articles are sometimes longer. The *Catholic Encyclopedia*, though published in 1907, etc., is still useful as including ecclesiastical personages and subjects not found in the general encyclopedias, as does the Herzog-Hauck *Realencyclopaedie*, and its English version, the Schaff-Herzog.

There are two great collections of medieval Latin texts, of importance to historical study: the most recent and best edited is the *Monumenta Germaniae Historiae*, comprising series of ancient authors, early medieval writers, letters, laws, verse writers, annals, diplomas and Merovingian and Carolingian capitularies (royal edicts). The other great collection is Migne's *Patrologia Latina* and *Graeca*: there is also, for Byzantine history, the *Corpus scriptorum historiae byzantinae*, ed. B. G. Niebuhr, 50 vols., 1828–97. For lists of rulers, bishops and other officials, with dates of their office-holding and much useful information, see J. M. J. L. de Mas Latrie, *Trésor de Chronologie*, 1889, and in a forthcoming ed.; for bibliographies: L. J. Paetow, *A Guide to the Study of Medieval History*, ed. 1931: A. Molinier, *Les sources de l'histoire de France*, part i, 1901: Wattenbach-Levison, *Deutschlands geschichtsquellen im Mittelalter*, part i. The following, not mentioned in earlier notes, are useful in connexion with special aspects of European history: H. Breslau, *Handbuch der Urkundenlehre fur Deutschland und Italien*, vol. i (for lists of referendaries and other officers): F. Cabrol and H. Leclercq, *Dictionnaire d'archéologie chrétienne*, 1903 etc.: R. Naz, *Dictionnaire de droit canonique*, 1924, and in progress: L. Thomassin, *Vetus et nova ecclesiae disciplina* (useful for ecclesiastical officers in this early period): C. Eubel, *Hierarchia catholica medii aevi*, 1913: the *Encyclopaedia of Islam*, 1908–1938: C. H. Philips, 1951, *Handbook of Oriental History: The European Inheritance*, ed. E. Barker, G. Clark and P. Vaucher, 1954.

CHRONOLOGICAL LISTS

Last emperors of east and west:
Zeno, at Constantinople, 474–491
Romulus Augustulus, at Rome, 475–476

BYZANTINE EMPERORS, FROM 491–959

Anastasius I	491–518	Anastasius II	713–15
Justin I	518–27	Theodosius III	715–17
Justinian	527–65	Leo III; the Isaurian	717–41
Justin II	565–78	Constantine V	741–75
Tiberius	578–82	Leo IV: the Khazar	775–80
Maurice	582–602	Constantine VI	780–97
Phokas	602–10	Irene	797–802
Heraclius I	610–41	Nicephoras I	802–11
Constantine III	641	Michael I	811–13
Heracleonas	641	Leo V	813–20
Constans II	641–68	Michael II	820–29
Constantine IV	668–85	Theophilus	829–42
(Pogonatus)		Michael III	842–67
Justinian II	685–95	Basil I; the Macedonian	867–86
	and 705–11	Leo VI	886–912
Leontius	695–98	(Alexander	912–13)
Tiberius III	698–705	Constantine VII	912–59
Justinian II (restored)	705–11	(Porphyrogenitus)	
Philippicus	711–13		

RESTORED ROMAN EMPIRE IN THE WEST (800–899)

Charles the Great	800–14	Charles III: the Fat	881–87
Louis the Pious	814–40	Guy of Spoleto	891–94
Lothar I	840–55	Lambert of Spoleto	894–98
Louis II	855–75	Arnulf of Carinthia	896–99
Charles II: the Bald	875–77		

POPES (440–911)

Leo I: the Great	440	(Laurentius	498–505)
Hilary	461	Hormisdas	514
Simplicius	468	John I	523
Felix III (II)	483	Felix IV (III)	526
Gelasius I	492	Boniface II	530
Anastasius II	496	(Dioscurus	530)
Symmachus	498	John II	532

POPES—*continued*

Agapitus I	535	Gregory III	731
Silverius	536	Zacharias	741
Vigilius	538	Stephen II	752
Pelagius I	555	Stephen III (II)	752
John III	561	Paul I	757
Benedict I	575	(Constantine II	767)
Pelagius II	579	Stephen IV (III)	768
Gregory I: the Great	590	Hadrian I	772
Sabinian	604	Leo III	795
Boniface III	607	Stephen V (IV)	816
Boniface IV	608	Pascal I	817
Deusdedit I	615	Eugenius II	824
Boniface V	619	Valentine	827
Honorius I	625	Gregory IV	827
Severinus	640	Sergius II	844
John IV	640	Leo IV	847
Theodore I	642	Benedict III	855
Martin I	649	(Anastasius	855)
Eugenius I	655	Nicholas I	858
Vitalian	657	Hadrian II	867
Deusdedit II	672	John VIII	872
Donus	676	Marinus I	882
Agatho	678	Hadrian III	884
Leo II	682	Stephen VI (V)	885
Benedict II	684	Formosus	891
John V	685	Boniface VI	896
Conon	686	Stephen VII (VI)	896
(Theodore	686)	Romanus	897
Sergius I	687	Theodore II	897
(Pascal	687)	John IX	898
John VI	701	Benedict IV	900
John VII	705	Leo V	903
Sisinnius	708	(Christopher	903)
Constantine	708	Sergius III	904
Gregory II	715		to 911

OSTROGOTHIC KINGS (493–553)

Theoderic	493–526	Hildibad	540–41
Athalaric	526–34	Eraric	541
Theodahad	534–36	Totila	541–53
Witigis	536–40	Teia	553

VANDAL KINGS IN AFRICA (439–534)

Gaiseric	439–77	Thrasamund	496–523
Hunneric	477–84	Hilderic	523–31
Gunthamund	484–96	Gelimer	531–34

VISIGOTHIC KINGS IN SPAIN (446–711

Euric	466–84	Gundemar	610–12
Alaric II	484–507	Sisebut	612–21
Theoderic and		Recared II	621
Amalaric	506–26	Swinthila	621–31
Amalaric alone	526–31	Sisenand	631–36
Theudis	531–48	Chintila	636–40
Theudegesil	548–49	Tulga	640–42
Agila	549–54	Chindaswinth	642–52
Athanagild	554–67	Receswinth	653–72
Leova I	568–72	Wamba	672–80
Leovigild	568–86	Erwig	680–87
Recared I	586–601	Egica	687–701
Leova II	601–03	Witiza	701–09
Witterich	603–10	Roderick	709–11

LOMBARD KINGS IN ITALY (568–774)

Alboin	568–72	Grimoald	662–71
Cleph	572–74	Perctarit (again)	671–88
Authari	584–90	Cunipert	688–700
Agilulf	590–616	Luitpert	700
Adaloald	616–26	Aribert II	700–12
Arioald	626–36	Ansprand	712
Rothari	636–52	Liutprand	713–44
Rodoald	652	Hildebrand	744
Aribert I	652–61	Ratchis	744–49
Godepert ⎱	661–62	Aistulf	749–56
Perctarit ⎰		Desiderius	756–74

CALIPHS (632–932)

Abu Bakr	632–34	Yazid II	720–24
ʿUmar	634–44	Hisham	724–43
ʿUthman	644–56	Marwan II	744–50
ʿAli	656–61		

UMAYYADS

Muʿawiya I	661–79		
Yazid	679–83		
Muʿawiya II	683		
Marwan I	684–85		
ʿAbd al-Malik	685–705		
Walid	705–15		
Suleiman	715–17		
ʿUmar II	717–20		

UMAYYAD AMIRS OF CORDOBA

ʿAbd ar-Rahman I	756–88
Hisham I	788–96
Al-Hakam I	796–822
ʿAbd ar-Rahman II	822–52
Muhammad I	852–86
Al-Mundhir	886–88
ʿAbdullah	888–912
ʿAbd ar-Rahman III	912–29:
	caliph, 929–62

CALIPHS—*continued*

ABBASIDS		Al-Wathiq	842–47
		Al-Mutawakhil	847–61
Abu'l-Abbas	750–54	Al-Muntasir	861–62
Mansur	754–75	Al-Musta'in	862–66
Al-Mahdi	775–85	Al-Mu'tazz	866–69
Al-Hadi	785–86	Al-Muhtadi	869–70
Harun ar-Rashid	786–809	Al-Mu'tamid	870–92
Al-Amin	809–13	Al-Mu'tadid	892–902
Ma'mun	813–33	Al-Muktafi	902–08
Al-Mu'tasim	833–42	Al-Muqtadir	908–32

INDEX